The Telegraph

BOOK OF

THE FIRST WORLD WAR

Born in Surrey in 1966, Michael Wright was educated at Windlesham House and Sherborne and graduated with a first in English Literature from Edinburgh University. He spent several years working as a theatre critic, arts columnist and literary diarist in London before moving to rural France, where for ten years he wrote the much-loved *C'est La Folie* column in the *Daily Telegraph*. He has since published two bestselling books about his life-changing experiences in the French countryside, *C'est La Folie* and *Je t'aime à La Folie*, and is the co-author with Stephen Grady of the bestselling memoir, *Gardens of Stone*, about an English boy in the French Resistance. A passionate cyclist, he still lives and races in France with his wife, two daughters, two dogs, one cat, one long-suffering fish and six very small sheep.

Gavin Fuller is head of the *Telegraph* library, responsible for maintaining that newspaper's archive. He is also a former mastermind champion and the editor of *The Telegraph book of Readers' Letters from the Great War*, *Leaves on the Line*, and *Lovely Bits of Old England: John Betjeman at The Telegraph*.

The Telegraph

BOOK OF

THE FIRST WORLD WAR

AN ANTHOLOGY OF The Telegraph'S WRITING FROM THE GREAT WAR

→← EDITED BY →→

GAVIN FULLER

→← INTRODUCTION BY →→

MICHAEL WRIGHT

Aurum
Press

First published in Great Britain
2014 by Aurum Press Ltd
74–77 White Lion Street
Islington
London N1 9PF
www.aurumpress.co.uk

A catalogue record for this book is available from the British Library.

ISBN 978 1 78131 375 6
eBook ISBN 978 1 78131 382 4

1 3 5 7 9 10 8 6 4 2
2014 2016 2018 2017 2015

Typeset in Dante by Saxon Graphics Ltd, Derby
Printed and bound by CPI Group (UK) Ltd, Croydon, CR0 4YY

Contents

Introduction

Michael Wright

A hundred years on, the First World War has still not lost its power to clutch at the heart. I was born fifty years after the Battle of the Somme, yet its effects have resonated throughout my life. How can any of us not feel a pang of fear and pity when we begin to reflect, with all the benefits of tragic hindsight, upon the war's chaos of causes; its untold suffering; its lastingly toxic effects? So much is known about this 'war to end all wars' which merely served to usher in, two decades later, an even bloodier and more devastating conflict. But how much do we *really* know, beyond what we have absorbed by osmosis, and from our unseeing familiarity with the rain-lashed war memorials which dot every town and village in the country? And, even if we do know, how on earth do we make sense of so much senseless slaughter?

The more I have read, while preparing this introduction, the more I have become aware of my own ignorance about the First World War and how it was fought, let alone reported. I had a picture of hundreds of thousands of men, living for months in flooded, rat-infested trenches; a nightmare only relieved by the deathly wake-up call of being sent over the top. I imagined an almost constant artillery bombardment; the impossibility of sleep; the inevitability of death.

I had swallowed whole the view popularised in *Oh! What a Lovely War* and Alan Clark's book, *The Donkeys*, that most of the fighting in the war amounted to the pointless slaughter of the common man, ordered by out-of-touch Generals (Sir John French and Sir Douglas Haig, especially) living in safety and grandeur, miles behind the lines.

I had no idea that British soldiers during the conflict were sent to the front, not until they perished, but for four days at a time, where often they would see no action at all, before being rotated back to safety and lighter duties behind the lines, spending four days in support, and four at rest. I do not mean to suggest that they therefore had it easy, because of course they did not. But I have been forced to recognise that a typical soldier's life in the First World War was often very different to the one that haunted my imagination for so long.

Even the relative terms 'Western Front' and 'Eastern Front' struck me as confusing, because they describe the fighting from a German-centric perspective:

France to Germany's west, where most of its armies were engaged; Russia to Germany's east, where a smaller force was bent on subjugating France's dangerous ally. And why Gallipoli and the Dardanelles? Why Salonika? Why Africa, if the war was really being fought in France? This takes us back to the stalemate in the trenches, which led to such wild throws of the dice as the Battle of the Somme in 1916, and the struggle to find solutions or distractions elsewhere. As John Keegan, in his seminal study, *The First World War* puts it: 'By the end of 1915, none of the original combatants was fighting the war that had been wanted or expected.'

I mention these various aspects of my own former ignorance, not out of a masochistic desire to make myself look stupid, but to emphasise how difficult it is to read the dispatches in this book with an open mind. Yet it is only by doing so that we may transport ourselves back to the breakfast tables of 1916; to the knife-board of the omnibus, or to the smoky compartments of the GWR steam train, where the people of Britain were anxiously scanning the pages of their daily newspaper, with no shadow of a doubt that what they were reading was the truth, and nothing but the truth.

Historians still disagree about the war's inevitability; still argue about the culpability of the diplomats who might have prevented it, and of the generals who prosecuted it; still squabble over factual questions such as the number of soldiers wounded or killed. We will never know for sure. Yet there remains a gripped fascination with the mysteries of this cataclysm – a great crack across the table of history, as Virginia Woolf described it – and with what life must have been like for those who lived through it.

It is especially difficult, a century after the event, to imagine the fog in which the war was fought. Keegan even goes so far as to suggest that the conflict might have been avoided, had modern communications – and specifically the telephone – been available. Much slaughter might have been prevented, too, had radio communications allowed generals to issue orders with some immediacy, rather than their being subjected to the sluggish transmission of written messages carried by runners, as soon as fragile field-telephone wires had been cut by the latest bombardment.

Today, someone fires a shot on the other side of the world, and we read about it online a few seconds later. Our access to information is instant, usually with eye-witness footage attached. People panic when the internet goes down for a few minutes. Back in 1914, with storm clouds gathering over Europe and a cataclysm erupting in France and beyond, the lack of even days-old information must have been terrifying. 'War came out of a cloudless sky,' as Keegan puts it, 'to populations which knew almost nothing of it and had been raised to doubt that it could ever again trouble their continent.' Radio was in its infancy. The television was still decades away. So the daily newspapers became an important lifeline; the one source of factual information about how the war was going in the midst of a churning soup of rumour, falsehood and fear.

Newspapers such as the *Daily Telegraph* were, for the British public, their only access to official news about the progress of the war. Yes, Pathé's *Animated Gazette* offered four-minute, silent vignettes for cinema-goers, but there were as yet no radio bulletins from BBC announcers with reassuringly plummy accents, nor had *British Movietone News* yet come into being.

As a result of this and the continuing freedom of the press, the broadsheet newspapers were one of the pillars of British democracy. In a world where a man's word was his bond, the integrity of their newsgathering and reporting was not in doubt, and their ability to publish editorials challenging government policy without fear of censure was a sign of freedom of speech in action. So the man and woman on the street relied upon them and were, indeed, entirely dependent upon them for the little they might glean about the progress of the war.

In this simple truth lies the terrifying fascination of this book. You might imagine that such a compilation of newspaper articles from 1914–18, reported from the depths of a muddy trench, written to the accompaniment of artillery fire and published in the very week that a battle took place, was about as close to the truth of the soldiers' lived experience as one could get. Journalism has been described as being 'the rough first draft of history' and, indeed, what could be more immediate that these horse's-mouth dispatches from the scenes of the bloodiest fighting?

Unfortunately, war is more complicated than that. We human beings have, after all, a dread fear of the truth and its imagined impact, not upon ourselves – for we are tough and realistic and able to face anything, are we not? – but upon everybody else; people more weak-minded and easily influenced than ourselves.

So I feel obliged to come clean at the start, and observe that what these reports reveal is not what happened in the First World War at all. No, reality is far more poignant than that. This book is a time-machine. Its contents take us back into the very eye of the storm; back into people's living rooms and to their breakfast tables where, sick with worry and doubt, they compared these reports from France or Jutland or the Dardanelles with local gossip, and with the casualty lists from the same battles. Millions of mothers and fathers, wives, sons, sisters, cousins and friends could do little but sit staring out of the window at a cold grey sky, reading and re-reading these dispatches over and over again, wondering what was really going on in France or Russia or the Dardanelles, as their forgotten toast grew cold.

Herein lies, I think, the special fascination of this book. There is an almost excruciating sense of dramatic irony as we contemplate the gap between our modern mental picture of the war, true or false as it may be, with this map of what people were assured was happening at the time.

As *The Globe* newspaper – published in Australia, and therefore more outspoken than the patrician UK newspapers of the time – demanded to know in 1915: 'The public has been buoyed up by exaggeration, and the disappointment and reaction are today proportionately great. Why should the Press Bureau pass falsehoods when they are agreeable, and suppress the truth when it is not?'

Sometimes the gap between the news report as published, and the truth of the event that has subsequently emerged, is nothing less than sickening – as any attempt to pull the wool over the eyes of the public must always be, no matter how much our leaders may claim (as leaders will) that they have the public's best interests at heart in doing so.

'It was a long time before the grisly facts about 1 July penetrated the British consciousness,' writes John Terraine of the Battle of the Somme, in his 1984 history of the First World War. 'But when at last the British public learned what the loss of life had been in that short span of time, the paroxysm was tremendous.'

During the war, these reports would have appeared in the newspaper alongside casualty lists whose length was often bizarrely out-of-kilter with the upbeat reports of the battles in which they had been sustained. We have not reprinted such casualty lists here. But the names upon them lie invisibly in the spaces between the words of every page in this book. Indeed, to give a sense of scale, roughly two British soldiers died for every single one of the 350,000 words printed here. And four Frenchmen. And five Germans.

The 'Daily Telegraph Affair' of 1908

Amongst the myriad causes of the First World War, fingers are often pointed at an extraordinary interview with Kaiser Wilhelm II, published by the *Daily Telegraph* on 28 October 1908.

Six years before war broke out, there was already considerable unease at the way Germany was building up its navy. And when Kaiser Wilhelm did his best to allay British fears by allowing his private political views to be published in the *Daily Telegraph*, his gaffe-strewn and hopelessly ill-judged comments only made things a whole lot worse.

How the interview found its way into print was a comedy of errors, at least from a German point of view. Wilhelm made a state visit to Britain in the summer of 1908, and enjoyed himself so much that he opted to stay on, renting Highcliffe Castle, near Bournemouth, for the purpose and inviting its owner – Colonel Edward Stuart-Wortley, formerly the British military attaché in Paris – to join him as his guest. The Kaiser seems to have been having a lovely time, and talked at length to Stuart-Wortley about his love of all things British; about his frustration, too, at how the British public misunderstood his best intentions. Stuart-Wortley took careful notes, and then requested permission to distil his jottings into an article for the *Daily Telegraph*, explaining that if the British people only knew the full extent of the Kaiser's Anglophilia, then relations between Britain and Germany might be greatly improved.

The Kaiser could have no grounds for claiming to have been quoted out of context. On the contrary, he received a copy of the manuscript and – in line with the dictates of the German constitution – submitted it to his Chancellor, Prince Bernhard von Bülow, for comment and approval. Claiming to be too busy to deal with this task, Bülow passed the piece to the Foreign Office with a note: 'Please read the enclosed article carefully, transcribe it in clear, official script …

duplicate it, and enter in the margin such corrections, additions or deletions as may seem suitable.'

The State Secretary was away at the time, so the article was passed on to the Under State Secretary, who forwarded it to one Reinhold Klehmet, a counsellor in the Political Division. Klehmet interpreted Bülow's instructions literally, merely making a couple of factual and stylistic corrections, and sending back a fair copy of the piece to the Chancellor. Later, Bülow always claimed that he never actually read the interview, and merely sent it back to the Kaiser, saying that he saw no reason not to publish. Delighted, the Kaiser returned it to Stuart-Wortley, who passed it – surely anticipating its likely impact – to the *Daily Telegraph*.

The article appeared in the *Telegraph* on 28 October 1908. This extract captures its inflammatory tone and content:

> *'You English,' he said, 'are mad, mad, mad as March hares. What has come over you that you are so completely given over to suspicions quite unworthy of a great nation? What more can I do than I have done? I declared with all the emphasis at my command, in my speech at Guildhall, that my heart is set upon peace, and that it is one of my dearest wishes to live on the best of terms with England. Have I ever been false to my word? Falsehood and prevarication are alien to my nature. My actions ought to speak for themselves, but you listen not to them but to those who misinterpret and distort them. That is a personal insult which I feel and resent. To be forever misjudged, to have my repeated offers of friendship weighed and scrutinised with jealous, mistrustful eyes, taxes my patience severely. I have said time after time that I am a friend of England, and your Press – at least, a considerable section of it – bids the people of England refuse my proffered hand and insinuates that the other holds a dagger. How can I convince a nation against its will? I repeat,' continued His Majesty, 'that I am a friend of England, but you make things difficult for me. My task is not of the easiest. The prevailing sentiment among large sections of the middle and lower classes of my own people is not friendly to England. I am, therefore so to speak, in a minority in my own land, but it is a minority of the best elements as it is in England with respect to Germany. That is another reason why I resent your refusal to accept my pledged word that I am the friend of England. I strive without ceasing to improve relations, and you retort that I am your archenemy. You make it hard for me. Why is it?'*
>
> *… His Majesty then reverted to the subject uppermost in his mind – his proved friendship for England. 'I have referred,' he said, 'to the speeches in which I have done all that a sovereign can do to proclaim my good-will. But, as actions speak louder than words, let me also refer to my acts. It is commonly believed in England that throughout the South African War Germany was hostile to her. German opinion undoubtedly was hostile – bitterly hostile. But what of official Germany? Let my critics ask themselves what brought to a sudden stop, and, indeed, to absolute collapse, the European tour of the Boer delegates, who were striving to obtain European intervention? They were feted*

in Holland, France gave them a rapturous welcome. They wished to come to Berlin, where the German people would have crowned them with flowers. But when they asked me to receive them – I refused. The agitation immediately died away, and the delegation returned empty-handed. Was that, I ask, the action of a secret enemy?

'Again, when the struggle was at its height, the German government was invited by the governments of France and Russia to join with them in calling upon England to put an end to the war. The moment had come, they said, not only to save the Boer Republics, but also to humiliate England to the dust. What was my reply? I said that so far from Germany joining in any concerted European action to put pressure upon England and bring about her downfall, Germany would always keep aloof from politics that could bring her into complications with a sea-power like England. Posterity will one day read the exact terms of the telegram – now in the archives of Windsor Castle – in which I informed the sovereign of England of the answer I had returned to the Powers which then sought to compass her fall. Englishmen who now insult me by doubting my word should know what were my actions in the hour of their adversity.

'Nor was that all. Just at the time of your Black Week, in the December of 1899, when disasters followed one another in rapid succession, I received a letter from Queen Victoria, my revered grandmother, written in sorrow and affliction, and bearing manifest traces of the anxieties which were preying upon her mind and health. I at once returned a sympathetic reply. Nay, I did more. I bade one of my officers procure for me as exact an account as he could obtain of the number of combatants in South Africa on both sides and of the actual position of the opposing forces. With the figures before me, I worked out what I considered the best plan of campaign under the circumstances, and submitted it to my General Staff for their criticism. Then, I dispatched it to England, and that document, likewise, is among the state papers at Windsor Castle, awaiting the severely impartial verdict of history. And, as a matter of curious coincidence, let me add that the plan which I formulated ran very much on the same lines as that which was actually adopted by Lord Roberts, and carried by him into successful operation. Was that, I repeat, an act of one who wished England ill? Let Englishmen be just and say!

'But, you will say, what of the German navy? Surely, that is a menace to England! Against whom but England are my squadrons being prepared? If England is not in the minds of those Germans who are bent on creating a powerful fleet, why is Germany asked to consent to such new and heavy burdens of taxation? My answer is clear. Germany is a young and growing empire. She has a worldwide commerce which is rapidly expanding, and to which the legitimate ambition of patriotic Germans refuses to assign any bounds. Germany must have a powerful fleet to protect that commerce and her manifold interests in even the most distant seas. She expects those interests to go on growing, and she must be able to champion them manfully in any quarter of the globe. Her horizons stretch far away.'

Pandemonium resulted, as far afield as France, Russia and Japan. It is tempting to say that the Kaiser must have meant well, and was not well-served by his underlings and advisers. But Wilhelm appears to have been such an arrogant, misguided and generally dislikeable character that it probably served him right when this unvarnished version of what he actually thought somehow found its way into print in one of the most important newspapers in Europe.

Puerile as it would be to suggest that this single newspaper article was somehow responsible for starting the bloodiest war in history, the so-called 'Daily Telegraph Affair' did little to clear already turbid waters, and certainly put paid to any hopes of an alliance between Britain and Germany. Bülow resigned from office in June 1909, and the Kaiser himself kept a very low profile for months after the affair.

The *Daily Telegraph* in 1914

The Victorian author and journalist Edmund Yates once described the *Daily Telegraph* as 'the organ of the knife-board of the omnibus', referring to the cheaper seats on the upper deck from which passengers might enjoy, as James Payn puts it in his *Lights and Shadows of London Life* (1867), 'the advantages of surveying English life from a slow-moving, unexpected, and exalted point of view'.

Harry Lawson, chairman of the Newspaper Proprietors' Association, was the newspaper's proprietor at the time. But the key figure in the *Daily Telegraph*'s coverage of the First World War was its managing editor, John Le Sage.

As a reporter, Le Sage had been the first British journalist to provide an account of the entry of the German Army into Paris in January 1871, and was sent to report on the coronation at St Petersburg of Alexander III, as well as being received in audience by Pope Leo XIII and by Sultan Abdul Hamid. But it was when he took over the management of the newspaper that Le Sage appears to have come into his own, even if some of the conservative views he espoused – he was firmly opposed both to women's suffrage and to the idea of giving the vote to working-class men – seem almost shocking to modern sensibilities. Indeed, as his biographer, J. B. Firth, has noted, 'Le Sage's gifts were better suited to the last two decades of the nineteenth century than to the first two of the twentieth … For many years he had rooms in Clement's Inn and, punctual to the minute, twice a day, he trod the Fleet Street pavement – an erect, imposing and well-groomed figure.'

Le Sage ran the paper for almost forty years, and was known as 'the autocrat of Peterborough Court'. Already seventy-seven in 1914, he gave full support to the government during the war and was rewarded in kind when David Lloyd George arranged for him to receive a knighthood in 1918.

Le Sage fiercely upheld the traditions upon which the *Daily Telegraph* had established its special position. According to J. B. Firth: 'Le Sage regarded the middle class as the backbone of the country, and had little sympathy with democratic reform and reformers: "To let well alone" was one of his working principles. News interested him more deeply than politics, and the minutiae of any political controversy bored him. He liked it presented, as he said, "in six lines". Le Sage made up his mind quickly – a sovereign editorial virtue. As a judge of men he reposed great faith in what he called his "journalistic instinct", which worked "in flashes". The criticism of outsiders he met with imperturbability: it was a fixed article of his creed that enemies of the *Daily Telegraph* always came to a bad end, sooner or later.'

One of Le Sage's favourite sayings perhaps reveals, more than anything, his high-Victorian temperament: 'If in doubt,' he would declare, imperiously, 'don't.' Yet the challenge and pressure of managing the newspaper's coverage of the First World War appears to have filled him with new energy, despite his advancing years, and the patriotic fervour and moral certitude of some of the leader-writing in these pages, especially in the early months of the war, undoubtedly owes much to his influence. On the other hand, the *Telegraph*'s heavily poetic, evocative and almost imagistic description of the Palace of Westminster on the eve of war – 'Last Night in London' (4 August 1914) – probably doesn't.

The Race to Report the War

The Boer War had given British journalists a vision, and in some cases a taste, of the excitement and fame that work as a war correspondent could bring. So when war broke out in 1914, there was no lack of volunteers eager to take on the assignment of reporting from the front line of the war zone, wherever that might be. In his 1915 book, *The Soul of War*, Philip Gibbs of the *Daily Telegraph* and *Daily Chronicle* described the scene thus:

'In Fleet Street, which is connected with the wires of the world, there was a feverish activity. Walls and tables were placarded with maps. Photographs, gazetteers, time tables, cablegrams littered the rooms of editors and news editors. There was a procession of literary adventurers up the steps of those buildings in the Street of Adventure – all those men who get lost somewhere between one war and another and come out with claims of ancient service on the battlefields of Europe when the smell of blood is scented from afar; and scores of new men of sporting instincts and jaunty confidence, eager to be "in the middle of things"; willing to go out on any terms so long as they could see "a bit of fun"; ready to take all risks. Special correspondents, press photographers, the youngest reporters on the staff, sub-editors emerging from little dark rooms with a new excitement in eyes that had grown tired with proof correcting, passed each other on the stairs and asked for their chance. It was a chance of seeing the greatest drama in life with real properties, real corpses, real blood, real horrors with a devilish thrill in them. It was not to be missed by any self-respecting journalist to whom all life is a stage play which he describes and criticises from a free seat in the front of the house.'

In the event, however, it was an American explorer living in Belgium, with the Mills-and-Boonishly romantic name of Granville Fortescue, who supplied the *Daily Telegraph* with one of the very first scoops of the war. On 2 August 1914,

Fortescue sent a report to the paper about how German motorcycle troops had already been spotted in Belgium, not far from Liège. At a time when nobody was quite sure whose armies were where, and how seriously to take Germany's attempts to play down its own bellicosity, this was very big news. That evening's editorial conference at the *Daily Telegraph* must have been a fraught affair: to publish, and risk the accusation of fomenting anti-German hostility with an erroneous report; or not to publish, and fail to announce one of the most dramatic developments in the escalating crisis? In the event, the paper went ahead and published the story ('from our own correspondent, Brussels, Monday') beneath the banner headline: 'Country Invaded by German Troops'.

Now the excrement really hit the ventilation system. According to Phillip Knightley in his book, *The First Casualty*, 'Within hours the *Daily Telegraph* was on to Fortescue at his Brussels hotel with furious reproaches. No other newspaper had the story, and the Foreign Office had denounced it as untrue.' These days, one might imagine that any newspaper would be delighted with such a result. But not in the respectful, hierarchical world of Britain of 1914. Challenged by his editor, Fortescue insisted he was right, feeling aggrieved that the *Telegraph* did not believe him. 'Twenty-four hours later,' notes Knightley, 'the *Telegraph* phoned Fortescue again, with fulsome apologies, and offered him a contract as a roving war correspondent. Britain had just declared war on Germany on the grounds of its violation of Belgian neutrality. Fortescue's story had given the *Telegraph* a twenty-four-hour world scoop, and the other British papers were rushing men to Europe to try to catch up.'

Unfortunately, this rush to Europe ended in frustration for almost all the journalists bidding for a role in France, including the *Telegraph*'s own correspondents. All would-be correspondents had to be extensively vetted before a licence was granted and, even then, they were still forced to kick their heels in London, many of them having already shelled out on horses and servants to accompany them on their travels. Compared with the relative freedom afforded today's war correspondents, the regulations governing their predecessors in 1914 were draconian, as Martin Farrar describes in *News from the Front*, his intriguing book about war correspondents on the Western Front:

'Each correspondent was only allowed to take one servant and one horse with him. His personal baggage was not to exceed more than 110 lb and they could draw the ordinary army rations, which was all at their paper's expense. Correspondents were not allowed runners or dispatch riders and were banned from bringing motor vehicles. Any communications would have to be submitted in duplicate to the Press Officer who would accompany the correspondents, and he in turn submitted them to the Chief Field Censor for authorisation. There were strict rules about what could and could not be included in a correspondent's dispatch. No reference could be made to the morale of troops, casualties, troop movements, their strength, location or composition, and criticism or praise of a personal nature was also forbidden. Once on the register and licensed, the correspondent had to wait in London, horse and servant at the ready for his call-up by the War Office.'

If it had been up to Winston Churchill, himself a former war correspondent who had covered the Boer War for the *Morning Post* and contributed to the *Daily Telegraph* at £5 a column while serving in the Malakand expedition, all of the war correspondents would have stayed put in London. 'A colleague of mine about this time met Mr Winston Churchill,' recalled the *Daily Mail*'s war correspondent, William Beach Thomas, after the war, 'who told him for his information that the war was going to be "fought in a fog" and the best place for correspondence about the war was London.' When Kitchener was made Secretary of State for War on 5 August 1914, the sticky wicket on which the prospective war correspondents found themselves soon became an unplayable one.

Nowadays, we would probably call Kitchener a control freak. But his attitude was, according to Farrar, a direct result of his personal experience of the press during the Boer War. For the first time, the human-interest side of the war had been reported with the sort of fervour usually reserved for the tactical details of battles, as editors discovered that this helped to sell their newspapers. Correspondents such as Edgar Wallace (*Daily Mail*) and a certain Winston Churchill (*Morning Post*) became household names as a result.

It must have come as a bit of a blow to the British generals when news of their victory during the Zulu War of 1879 at the Battle of Ulundi was written up in *The Times*, thanks to the quick work of the newspaper's war correspondent, Archibald Forbes, before they had had a chance to announce it to the world themselves. At a stroke, the Thunderer had stolen their thunder. Kitchener, in the Sudan, took censorship into his own hands, and by his own methods, as Knightley describes in *The First Casualty*: 'Kitchener's tactics were to make the twenty-six correspondents with him run exactly the same risks as his soldiers, to limit their telegraphic facilities to 200 words a day, and to give them no help, no briefings, no guidance, and little courtesy. It was not surprising that they hated him, and his disdain for them was behind what was to happen over war news at the outbreak of the First World War.'

The Press Bureau

In 1914, Kitchener immediately informed the prospective war correspondents that they would not be joining the British Army in France until the French General Staff had called up its own war correspondents. And this was merely the first salvo in a barrage of time-wasting and obstructiveness which would last for the next two years. While the war correspondents kicked their heels and fed their expensive horses in London, Kitchener's War Office set up an organisation called the Press Bureau under F. E. Smith (later Lord Birkenhead), to censor such news and telegraphed reports as they came through from the British Army, and to disseminate these via the British press and abroad. The Press Bureau's first newsflash, released on 11 August 1914, gives a taste of the less-than-gripping tone and content of its bland, factual communiqués, which read almost like parodies of news reports, from which any trace of actual information has been wilfully excised:

Noon – About two German Cavalry divisions are reported in the neighbourhood of Tongres; three German corps are still opposite Liège: other German troops are reported to be entrenching the line of the river Aisne … Several individuals from German patrols have been captured both in France and Belgium. In all cases they are reported to be short of food for both men and horses, and to have made no resistance.

What is noticeable, between 11–18 August, when the Press Bureau's F. E. Smith finally released a communiqué announcing that British forces were in position in France, is the depth of the news vacuum, as revealed in the reports published by the *Daily Telegraph*. Although Granville Fortescue scores another hit by observing, with extraordinary prescience, that 'wire entanglements will be the special feature of defence during this war', there is nothing about the British Army, by then in France in large numbers, and on 13 August the news editor, for want of a weightier source, has to rely upon printing at length a letter from a 'highly educated' Belgian soldier to his brother in Wales, to give a flavour of events.

There is a telling addendum, too, following the Press Bureau's 18 August statement about the British Expeditionary Force having landed in France, when the *Daily Telegraph* points out, with more than a hint of frustration: 'As early as 8 August, the French Government issued an official notification which appeared in the paper called the *Moniteur de la Flotte*, dated 15 August.'

In other words, 'this information has been in the public domain in France for ten days, and in print for the last three, yet we have still restrained ourselves from publishing it.'

Filling the News Vacuum

And so it begins. 'No news is communicated,' laments the *Telegraph*'s special correspondent in Boulogne. 'What the eyes can see may be believed, but, an individual must see all he knows, for confirmation of anything he has heard is impossible. It was no surprise to me to be told I was mistaken when I mentioned that I had witnessed Sir John French's arrival. The officer I spoke to knew I was wrong – "because he had heard nothing of it".' This is a pattern of things to come for, as J. E. Edmonds would put it, after the war, in the *Official History of the Great War*: 'Complete secrecy and the denial of all information to the enemy are of such importance at the opening of hostilities, and it is so difficult to give any information to the newspapers without it reaching the enemy, that absence of news must be regarded as part of the price that the public pay for success in the field.'

Yet Philip Gibbs for one felt strongly that the news vacuum created by Kitchener's draconian diktats, forbidding the presence of official correspondents in the war zone, merely led to the spread of negative, despairing and often wildly far-fetched stories in the press, as the newspapers struggled to feed the appetites of a public ravenous for news. 'Reading the English newspapers in those early days of the war, with their stories of starving Germany, their atrocity-mongering, their wild perversions of truth, a journalist proud of his profession must blush for shame at its degradation and insanity.' The *Daily Telegraph* was not immune to printing such atrocity stories, as witnessed in the story of the Belgian refugee reported on 29 August 1914, and of German outrages in France reported on 8 January 1915.

'In long hours of danger nothing is more nerve-wracking than silence,' declares William Maxwell, another *Telegraph* correspondent, in a report from Ghent in 1914. 'I have seen its devastating effect in war, and those who would maintain an impenetrable silence will surely learn this lesson before the greatest of all wars is ended. Armies may manœuvre and fight in the darkness, but nations cannot live and struggle and hope.'

By 26 August 1914, as the news from Mons begins to emerge, the *Daily Telegraph* is passionately advocating the need for conscription. Presumably, the newspaper's editorial staff already had a clearer sense of how badly the war was going than they felt able to share in print. This was a trying time for the public, for the first French statement admitting to heavy casualties had just appeared in the press, and Mons was the first action in which British troops were reported to be engaged. It is uncomfortable, even now, to trace the optimistic, almost triumphant, tone of the early reports in these pages slowly beginning to darken towards something closer to realism.

Now it was the turn of the *Sunday Times* to have a scoop that was almost uncomfortably close to the bone. While the *Daily Telegraph* was writing about a 'dastardly' Zeppelin raid on Antwerp, on 30 August, the newspaper published what is now known as the famous Amiens Dispatch, in which Arthur Moore told, for the first time, the unvarnished truth about the fighting to date. Extraordinarily, this was a report which had been passed and even beefed-up by the Press Bureau's official censor, F. E. Smith:

> *Regiments were grievously injured, and the broken army fought its way desperately with many stands, forced backwards and ever backwards by the sheer unconquerable mass of numbers … Some divisions have lost nearly all their officers. The regiments were broken to bits … To sum up, the first great German effort has succeeded. We have to face the fact that the British Expeditionary Force, which bore the great weight of the blow, has suffered terrible losses and required immediate and immense reinforcement. The British Expeditionary Force has won indeed imperishable glory, but it needs men, men, and yet more men.*

The resulting outcry explains the shrill communiqués (i.e. hasty official statements), including that of Sir John French, the commander-in-chief, which swiftly followed, as published in the *Daily Telegraph* and elsewhere (see 31 August 1914). But one senses that this was too little; too late. The cat was out of the bag. It must have been all-too-clear to the benighted British public that the War Office was either completely in the dark about how the war was progressing, or else was deliberately withholding unfavourable news for its own ends.

A House of Commons debate about the roles of the war correspondent and the Press Bureau swiftly followed, and the *Telegraph*'s report ('Paris in Wartime') on 1 September already seems to strike a new and more sombre note, as well as emphasising the difficulties faced by war correspondents in France:

'It is difficult now for a journalist to get anywhere. They are being watched and spied upon with energetic zeal by everyone. It is a wonder that we are even allowed to leave our homes or hotels, and to have our drinks at the cafés like any other inhabitants not under such grave disabilities.

'In vain we ask for a permit to go to places fifty or a hundred miles from Paris. We are told at once, *"Pas de journalistes"*. A journalist, therefore, is everywhere tabooed, an outlaw and an outcast in the eyes of the strict public official.'

The Battle to Strike the Right Note

In an attempt to reassure the public (and Parliament) that they were receiving a true picture of events from France, Kitchener then came up with a new strategy. On 7 September 1914, he appointed Colonel Ernest Swinton, an army railway official, to GHQ in France, with a brief to write articles on the progress of the army there. These dry communiqués, written under the byline 'Eyewitness', were personally vetted by Kitchener himself, before being sent out to the press. This was a heavy-handed attempt to gain control of the reporting of a war which was itself spiralling way, way out of control. But few were duped, and Swinton's bland 'Eyewitness' reports soon became universally known as 'Eyewash'.

It is tempting to see in the *Telegraph*'s evocative report of 3 October 1914 ('A Train of Wounded', from 'our special correspondent' in Paris) the hand of Philip Gibbs, who would later become one of the five officially sanctioned war correspondents, reporting almost daily for both the *Daily Chronicle* and the *Daily Telegraph*. Certainly, the finely honed prose and plangent tone are typical of Gibbs, and it is striking how the piece goes far more deeply into the physical suffering of the wounded than anything published to date, albeit creating a sense of distance by focusing upon foreign troops. Here, again, one senses a reflection not just of the progress of the war, but of the public's desire for it to be reported in a different way: in familiar terms of flesh-and-blood frailty, rather than distant military strategy.

I would put my money on the writer being Gibbs, too, for the way 'our special correspondent' somehow manages to capture the pure essence of the conflict in just a couple of paragraphs, only two months after the start of a war which still had four whole years left to run:

It is doubtful whether anyone is seriously to blame. The number of wounded is so enormous that no organisation can cope with it. Warfare under modern conditions is simply slaughter by machinery. Many of the wounded to whom I talked had never seen a German. One man epitomised modern warfare as follows:

'For four weeks I had been marching. I was hungry, dirty, and worn out. Then one day we were ordered to run across a field, and I received two bullets in the chest. For hours I lay there listening to the sound of the cannon. Then at last someone picked me up. Voilà ce que c'est que la guerre, monsieur.'

The end of 1914 sees the arrival in these pages, too, of another star war correspondent, Ellis Ashmead-Bartlett, whose report entitled 'The Situation at the Front' (3 November 1914) opens with characteristic humour: 'The German Army possesses one remarkable quality which stands out above all others, namely, its power of continuing a useless offensive.' But it is Ashmead-Bartlett's stark observation, aimed at the Germans, about what can be learned from the Russo–Japanese War which now seems so chillingly prophetic, and which makes one wish that the likes of Sir John French, Joseph Joffre and Haig might only have heeded his words:

The Russo–Japanese War taught one great lesson – namely, that modern armies of more or less equal strength may go on fighting indefinitely without either being able to gain the crushing victories which decided campaigns up to the period of the Franco–German War. That war also taught the lesson that the losses of the attackers are out of all proportion to those of the defenders, and that, even if ground is gained, the result is immediately neutralised by the extreme exhaustion of the victors, which precludes all hope of following up a temporary or local success.

For different reasons, the heart somewhat sinks at the hollow description by 'our military correspondent' of the 1st Battle of Ypres ('Our Greatest Battle', 20 November 1914), with its uncomfortable use of weather imagery to describe, in jaunty fashion, a few British regiments holding out against 'the type of attacks with which we have learnt to be familiar': 'Storms of big projectiles, showers of shrapnel, a constant sleet of bullets, punctuated occasionally by rushes with the bayonet at dusk or dawn ...'

In other words, never mind the bombardment, chaps: just put up an umbrella. Such writing exposes, with uncomfortable clarity, how easy it is for war correspondents to strike false notes when they try too hard with their prose, especially when attempting to mitigate the horrors of war. The latter is far better done, if it must be done at all, with the kind of laconic bravado evinced by the aristocratic Patrick de Bathe, a diplomat-turned-soldier, whose report headlined 'The Gallant Seventh' (1 December 1914) ends with the dry observation: 'At one time their trenches were so close to those of the enemy that during an occasional lull in the fighting they threw beetroot into the German lines, into which they stuck messages announcing the name of their regiment and their intentions towards their antagonists, which, I am told, were anything but reassuring.'

Individual Flair vs Official Hogwash

One of the finest pieces of writing in these early months of the war is the long eye-witness account by Luigi Barzini of a medal ceremony in which the heroes of an Italian battalion known as the Garibaldian Legion are to receive decorations from the French Republic ('Garibaldian Legion's Fight For France', 13 February 1915). Barzini brilliantly uses this sombre ceremony as a framing device to describe, with hair-raising detail and panache, the stirring exploits for which the Italians are being thus honoured. Yes, his Garibaldians do bear uncanny similarities to the heroic Gascons of Edmond de Rostand's *Cyrano de Bergerac* ('When the Garibaldians desert it is at any rate towards the enemy'). Yet there are also vivid details – of the sound of sapping, or the contortedness of human bodies in death – that zing with personal experience. Barzini's account must have caused quite a stir at the time. Not only did it remind the British public that the Italians were worthy allies, but it also fed their appetite for the kind of hero-myths which, amid the bleak shelling of northern France, were in such short supply.

At this distance of history, and reading, say, Granville Fortescue's response to the arrival of the first batch of permanently disabled British prisoners on 18 February 1915 ('The sight of these broken men stirs one first with a sense of the tragedy of war, and then to a swift realisation of the glory of England'), or the observation of 'our special correspondent' in the same week that 'Their regret was their inability to return to the fighting line', it is easy to imagine that Britain was so brainwashed with patriotic fervour that it was impossible to see the war for what it was. Yet Ashmead-Bartlett is able to refer bluntly to 'the awful realities of war' in his dutiful report from GHQ on 6 March 1915, and questions were again being asked in the House of Commons about the suppression of news in early 1915. Mr Joynson-Hicks MP is quoted in Hansard as saying that 'the people did not in the least mind knowing the truth if there was bad news'. A sentiment emphasised by Mr Hume-Williams MP, who declared: 'The only thing that could create a panic in this country is for the public to get the idea that they are not being told the whole truth.'

The situation only grew worse when the official (victorious) reporting of the Battle of Neuve Chapelle by the Press Bureau, Eyewitness and Sir John French in March 1915 was suddenly overturned by Sir John French's darker assessment, a month later, of what had actually transpired. 'That awful disaster was no victory!' noted Vera Brittain in her war diary, in response to this latest dispatch. 'It was the result of a terrible blunder – they were being fired upon by our own guns ... It is too terrible – this reckless waste of life, the only thing worth having in the universe. Naturally this horrible truth does not come out in the dispatch – it would undoubtedly stop recruiting if men thought they were to enlist only to be shot down by their own guns.'

Since the *Daily Telegraph* had, in common with all the newspapers, followed this official line, we have not reprinted the reports here. Yet the impact of Neuve Chapelle on the public was considerable. As Phillip Knightley observes in *The*

First Casualty: 'The average Englishman had been accepting it all his life that if something was printed in the newspapers, then it was true. Now, in the biggest event of his life, he was able to check what the press said against what he knew to be the truth. He felt he had found the press out, and as a result he lost confidence in his newspapers, a confidence to this day never entirely recovered.' Once again the rug had been pulled out from under the public's feet, leaving them wondering whom or what they could trust, apart from the lengthening casualty lists still being printed in the daily papers. The need for a group of war correspondents – rather than simply an official spokesman in army uniform – at the front was fast becoming a hot potato.

The Official War Correspondents

The *Daily Telegraph*'s Philip Gibbs, in his post-war memoir, *Now It Can Be Told*, describes the frustration and clamour for news of progress of the war, especially on the Western Front, which led to Kitchener finally giving permission in May 1915 for five official war correspondents to report on the Western Front:

> *In 1915 the War Office at last moved in the matter of war correspondents. Lord Kitchener, prejudiced against them, was being broken down a little by the pressure of public opinion (mentioned from time to time by members of the government), which demanded more news of their men in the field than was given by bald communiqués from General Headquarters and by an 'eye-witness' who, as one paper had the audacity to say, wrote nothing but 'eye-wash'. Even the enormous, impregnable stupidity of our High Command on all matters of psychology was penetrated by a vague notion that a few 'writing fellows' might be sent out with permission to follow the armies in the field, under the strictest censorship, in order to silence the popular clamour for more news. Dimly and nervously they apprehended that in order to stimulate the recruiting of the New Army now being called to the colours by vulgar appeals to sentiment and passion, it might be well to 'write up' the glorious side of war as it could be seen at the base and in the organisation of transport, without, of course, any allusion to dead or dying men, to the ghastly failures of distinguished generals, or to the filth and horror of the battlefields. They could not understand, nor did they ever understand (these soldiers of the old school) that a nation which was sending all its sons to the field of honour desired with a deep and poignant craving to know how those boys of theirs were living and how they were dying, and what suffering was theirs, and what chances they had against their enemy, and how it was going with the war which was absorbing all the energy and wealth of the people at home.*
>
> *'Why don't they trust their leaders?' asked the army chiefs. 'Why don't they leave it to us?'*
>
> *'We do trust you – with some misgivings,' thought the people, 'and we do leave it to you – though you seem to be making a mess of things – but we want to know what we have a right to know, and that is the life and progress of this*

war in which our men are engaged. We want to know more about their heroism,
so that it shall be remembered by their people and known by the world; about
their agony, so that we may share it in our hearts; and about the way of their
death, so that our grief may be softened by the thought of their courage. We will
not stand for this anonymous war; and you are wasting time by keeping it
secret, because the imagination of those who have not joined cannot be fired by
cold lines which say, "There is nothing to report on the western front."'

Already, in this acerbic 1920 summary, one detects more than a hint of Gibbs'
post-war remorse for the sanitised version of events he felt he had been obliged
to present to the public. 'The ideal situation for GHQ would have been a war
correspondent who would write what he was told was the truth and not ask
questions,' writes Martin Farrar, in *News from the Front*, before adding, with
scathing bluntness: 'This is exactly what the military got with Philip Gibbs (*Daily
Chronicle*, *Daily Telegraph*), Herbert Russell (*Reuters*), William Beach Thomas
(*Daily Mail*, *Daily Mirror*), Perry Robinson (*Daily News*, *The Times*) and Percival
Phillips (*Daily Express*, *Morning Post*).'

The five newspapermen were all given an officer's uniform and the right to
wear the green armband of the intelligence services. 'It was a brilliant move,'
writes Lyn Macdonald in *Somme*. 'From now on, the war correspondents, attired
in the King's uniform, were, to all intents and purposes, officers of the Army,
conscious of their debt to it and conscious, too, of their duty to keep up morale
and to reinforce that continuing loyalty of the people at home.' So the very move
aimed at increasing the public's knowledge and understanding of the war in fact
had the opposite effect. As Philip Gibbs would write in *Adventures in Journalism* in
1923:

We identified ourselves absolutely with the armies in the field, and we wiped
out of our minds all thought of personal 'scoops', and all temptation to write
one word which would make the task of officers and men more difficult and
dangerous. There was no need of censorship of our dispatches. We were our
own censors.

Both Farrar and Knightley, in their scholarly analyses of the official war
correspondents' work, are harsh in their assessment of just how craven and
biddable all five of them were. Yet as Colin Lovelace has identified in his essay on
'British Press Censorship During the First World War', the press was too
powerful an institution to be stifled, and what comes through in this collection of
Daily Telegraph reports and dispatches, several of the best of them by Philip Gibbs,
is a variety of unique voices, few of which have the hollow twang of being merely
a tool of government.

The difficulty, for the reader, in separating the truth from the spin, is that
there are precious few instances where any war correspondent consciously lied.
On the contrary, they were a band of honourable, upstanding men, whose
characters had been forged in an era when a man's word was his bond. It isn't

what they wrote that is the problem. It is what they *didn't* write. In reporting a war, after all, what I do not tell you – what I withhold – can be a form of propaganda every bit as powerful as the tissue of lies and falsehoods I peddle to convince you that I am, every day, coming closer to that victory which I have already persuaded you is just and righteous and necessary, no matter what the cost (although I'll do my best to hide that from you, too).

This said, there were one or two journalistic nadirs for which there can be little excuse. One of the paradoxes of this book is the fact that the *Telegraph*'s correspondents tend to show all the more flair and ingenuity when there is a desperate paucity of material. Yet as the war progresses, and the relationship between the press and the military becomes more established and symbiotic, they clearly have access to more raw news, yet their ability to distance themselves from it and question what they are being fed begins to seem somewhat blunted. As Phillip Knightley writes in *The First Casualty*:

> They were in a position to know more than most of the nature of the war of attrition on the Western Front, yet they identified themselves absolutely with the armies in the field; they protected the high command from criticism, wrote jauntily about life in the trenches, kept an inspired silence about the slaughter, and allowed themselves to be absorbed by the propaganda machine.

At the Battle of the Somme, British Army casualties on 1 July 1916 amounted to 57,470 men; more in a single day than the total number of casualties from the Crimean War, the Boer War and the Korean War combined. Yet the war correspondents, aided by the army, were quick to send back their reports of this 'splendid' day's fighting; of a triumphant conquest which would live in history. 'They were all grinning as though they had come from a "jolly" in which they had been bumped a little,' writes Philip Gibbs, in these pages, of a lorry-load of soldiers wounded at the Somme. 'There was a look of pride in their eyes as they came driving down like wounded knights from a tourney … The men who were going up to the battle grinned back at those who were coming out.'

The Somme has, of course, gone down in history as a battle never to be forgotten. Yet as the truth dawned of the terrible gap between appearance and reality – between the gurgling euphoria of the news reports and the steady spatter of blood being spilled in France – the effect upon morale on the Home Front must have been devastating. Whom could anyone trust any more? The plangent report entitled 'Soldiers' Stoicism', published in the *Daily Telegraph* on 18 August 1916, may well have been an attempt to redress this balance.

As William Beach Thomas, the *Daily Mail*'s correspondent, wrote in his memoir *A Traveller in News* after the Somme:

> For myself, on the next day and yet more on the day after that, I was thoroughly and deeply ashamed of what I had written, for the very good reason that it was untrue, so far as I had transgressed the limits of description. Almost all the

official information was wrong. The vulgarity of enormous headlines and the
enormity of one's own name did not lessen the shame.

Gibbs himself, after the war, had misgivings about accepting the knighthood he
was offered. 'I was not covetous of that knighthood,' he confessed in *Adventures
in Journalism,* 'and indeed shrank from it so much that I entered into a compact
with Beach Thomas to refuse it. But things had gone too far, and we could not
reject the title with any decency.'

At Passchendaele in October 1917, fearful of a repeat of the disastrous
reporting of the Somme, the war correspondents adopted a more realistic
approach. At the same time, however, the publication of casualty lists in the
leading newspapers was slowly dropped. The *Daily Telegraph* had printed full
casualty lists of all ranks up to 1916; now that practice ceased – perhaps as it
became apparent how devastating an impact an exposure to too much truth can
have upon public morale.

Gibbs appears to have been haunted by the gulf between the things he had
seen in the war, and the way he had chosen to report them. The several books he
wrote after the war about his experiences appear to be an attempt to redress this
balance. In *The Realities of War* (1920), for example, he responds with outrage to
General Haig's suggestion that, during the Flanders campaign, some of the war
correspondents' dispatches tended to exaggerate the horror of battle:

> *As a man who knows something of the value of words, and who saw many of*
> *those battle scenes in Flanders ... where his dead lay in the swamps, and round*
> *the pill-boxes ... and where our guns were being flung up by the harassing fire*
> *of heavy shells, I say now that nothing that has been written is more than the*
> *pale image of the abomination of those battle-fields, and that no pen or brush*
> *has yet achieved the picture of that Armageddon in which so many of our men*
> *perished.*

This may well be true. And, if so, one can but wish that a man of Gibbs' skill at
painting pictures with words had, along with his contemporaries, devoted more
of his energies to painting a true portrait, rather than a varnished caricature, of
their infinitely painful subject.

Steering the War: Ashmead-Bartlett at Gallipoli

Ellis Ashmead-Bartlett, the *Daily Telegraph*'s official correspondent in the
Dardanelles, clearly knew how to enjoy himself. 'He appeared to have an
unlimited expense account and used a large portion of it to purchase liquor from
the navy,' notes Phillip Knightley in *The First Casualty*. 'One of the sights of
Imbros was the regular line of Greek porters staggering up the hill to the press
camp loaded with supplies for Ashmead-Bartlett.'

His fellow journalist, Henry Nevinson, captured his style perfectly when he wrote:

> *About him hung an atmosphere of magnificence that often astonished me, as when, among the rocks of that savage island, among the pigs and sheep that infested our camp searching for the last leaves and grapes of summer in a vineyard hard by, he would issue from his elaborately furnished tent dressed in a flowing robe of yellow silk shot with crimson, and call for breakfast as though the Carlton were still his corporeal home.*

Brilliant, charismatic, arrogant and unpopular, Ashmead-Bartlett was one of the newspaper's finest correspondents of the First World War, not least in his own estimation. The opening of his first report (supposedly sent on 24 April, but not published until 7 May) reveals an inkling of his skill at boosting the excitement of a story, and his own self-importance, at one and the same time. The dispatch is written to give the impression that the attack on Gallipoli has not yet begun, yet somehow the *Daily Telegraph* correspondent already knows the entire Allied mission plan. Clearly Ashmead-Bartlett could not possibly have written or sent such a cable without the risk of passing operational secrets to the enemy. So it must be with the benefit of hindsight that he writes, with knowing irony: 'It is generally considered that the critical period of the operations will be the first twenty-four hours, and the success or failure of the whole enterprise will depend on whether these covering parties are able to obtain a firm foothold and seize the positions which have been assigned to them.' So, too, his dark reference to the Australians receiving 'a last hot meal', with its prophetic resonance of a death sentence about to be carried out.

Shameless as Ashmead-Bartlett may have been, on occasion, even his chief rival, Charles Bean, the official Australian war correspondent at Gallipoli, secretly admired him, as a diary entry from September 1915 makes plain: 'His written dispatches are full of life and colour, hit hard, and give a brilliant idea which is remarkably true. He exaggerates a bit to make his points … and yet he's a lover of the truth.'

All these qualities are to the fore in Ashmead-Bartlett's celebrated report of the landing at Gallipoli on 25 April: an account whose hair-raising description of the intense fighting and the heavy losses of the Anzacs must have come as a jaw-dropping shock to newspaper readers that day. Not because the bloodshed at Gallipoli was worse than at Mons or Neuve Chapelle on the Western Front, but because a different censor, Captain William Maxwell, a former *Daily Mail* correspondent, appears to have allowed Ashmead-Bartlett a little more leeway to write what he has actually seen, rather than what he might have seen if the invasion had for the Allies been going swimmingly.

As Charles Bean later wrote of Ashmead-Bartlett's 25 April report:

> *The despatch describing the Anzac landing electrified the world … it displayed the first terrible struggle on Gallipoli, and the qualities of the Australian and*

New Zealand soldiers, in one brilliant flash before the eyes of every nation and the world has never forgotten. Even today the tradition of the Anzac landing is probably more influenced by that story than by all the other accounts that have since been written ... He was the first to impress on the world the main facts of the landing and the impression is still there.

Indeed, the impact of Ashmead-Bartlett's description of the Anzacs' struggle has made it difficult – and unpopular – for any subsequent account of the landing to attempt to deviate from its heroic-romantic tone, let alone for people to recall that Britain lost four or five times as many men at Gallipoli than Australia and New Zealand combined.

Journalists were made unusually welcome during the Gallipoli campaign, partly because it was first conceived as a naval operation, and therefore came under the auspices of the Admiralty (i.e. Churchill) rather than of the Army (in the shape of Kitchener). It helped that the man leading the operation, General Sir Ian Hamilton, held the thoroughly modern conviction that the public had a right to be kept informed about the progress of the war. Even so, Ashmead-Bartlett bitterly resented the way his copy was butchered by GHQ, with Captain Maxwell apparently under instructions not to allow a word criticising Hamilton's leadership or strategy, no mention of setbacks, and certainly no totting-up of the mounting casualty figures.

According to N. P. Hiley in his essay 'Making War: The British News Media and Governmental Control', the trouble was that Hamilton had his own personal interpretation of what 'freedom of the press' really meant: 'Hamilton carefully separated freedom of information from freedom of opinion, believing that the correspondents had no right to disagree with his optimistic interpretation of events.'

On 18 July 1915, Ashmead-Bartlett recorded his frustration in his diary:

I thought there were limits to human stupidity but now I know there are none. The censorship has now passed beyond all reason. They won't let you give expression to the mildest opinions on any subjects ... There are now at least four censors all of whom cut up your stuff ... All hold different views and feel it is their duty to take out scraps. Thus only a few dry crumbs are left for the wretched public. The articles resemble chicken out of which a thick nutritious broth has been extracted.

Many journalists are precious about having their deathless prose butchered by censors or sub-editors, but Ashmead-Bartlett perhaps had more reason than most. He seems to have taken the growing disaster of the Gallipoli campaign very personally, to the extent that he wanted to do whatever he could to fix it. If he could not give Hamilton tips on strategy, then he could at least begin to work to have him removed. In this way, of all the official war correspondents in France and beyond, he was the one who completely broke the mould. N. P. Hiley notes:

What Ashmead-Bartlett did which was of great importance, and which was unique among the official war correspondents, sprang from his conviction that he remained free to record his own impressions. Whatever his motives, he attempted to describe exactly what he saw and to report precisely what he felt, holding that this was not inconsistent with his official status, and the significance lies not in the influence that this may have had with politicians at home, but in the reactions of his fellow journalists. Remarkably they all agreed with the military that in performing this simple function he had gone beyond his rightful duties.

Mind you, even Ashmead-Bartlett is not immune to the chin-up litotes of the time, as when he describes a midshipman just sixteen years old, 'shot through the stomach, but regarding his injury more as a fitting consummation to a glorious holiday ashore than a wound', or Australian soldiers who have been 'shot to bits and without hope of recovery' feeling happy simply because 'they knew they had been tried for the first time in the war and had not been found wanting'.

A-B loves a bit of old-fashioned pugilistic swagger as much as the next man, too: 'Their magazines were not even charged, so they just went in with cold steel, and I believe I am right in saying that the first Ottoman Turk since the last crusade received an Anglo-Saxon bayonet in him at five minutes after 5 a.m. on 25 April.'

Soon after the landings, Ashmead-Bartlett's dismay at the futile sacrifice of so many men begins to become apparent. On 10 May, his *Daily Telegraph* dispatch warns readers of the strength of the Turkish troops; a very different message to that in the upbeat official communiqués from GHQ. A couple of weeks later, he survived the sinking of HMS *Majestic* when it was torpedoed by a German U-boat and – after a return to Britain to buy a new wardrobe and equipment – headed back to Gallipoli, much to Hamilton's disappointment. Here, Ashmead-Bartlett became more and more pessimistic about the overall progress of the campaign, being likened to Jeremiah, Jonah and Cassandra by his fellow journalists at the press camp. Staff officers at Helles are even said once to have hidden behind rocks so as to avoid lunching in his disagreeable company. And when a young Australian journalist called Keith Murdoch – the father of Rupert Murdoch, the media tycoon – turned up in Gallipoli, looking for a story, Ashmead-Bartlett gave it to him.

According to Phillip Knightley in *The First Casualty*:

Ashmead-Bartlett poured out to Murdoch's sympathetic ear all the frustration he had accumulated over his difficulties in filing stories, spun a gloomy description of the way the campaign was being conducted, and convinced Murdoch that a major disaster would occur during the winter unless the British government and the British people could be told the truth.

So Ashmead-Bartlett wrote his bombshell letter, and Murdoch agreed to smuggle it back to Britain. Unfortunately, however, an insider at the press camp appears to have tipped off the authorities, and Murdoch was arrested in Marseilles, where the letter was confiscated. Undaunted, Murdoch wrote his own letter, based on as much as he could remember of what Ashmead-Bartlett had written and told him, and sent it to the Australian Prime Minister, Andrew Fisher. Within days, Lloyd George had read the letter, and urged Murdoch to send a copy to the British Prime Minister, Asquith, who then circulated it to the Dardanelles Committee. General Hamilton's active service career was brought to an end a month later, and the evacuation of Gallipoli began on 12 December 1915.

Ashmead-Bartlett's account of being torpedoed aboard HMS *Majestic* in 1915 – bizarrely, the ship sank on 27 May, yet his dispatch was not published until six months later, on 4 November – is one of the more hair-raising first-person accounts in this book. But it was his exposure of the sheer folly of the Dardanelles campaign which was his finest hour, and which undoubtedly saved many soldiers from a futile death. 'If the war correspondents in France had only been as enterprising,' notes Phillip Knightley, witheringly, 'the war might not have continued on its ghastly course.'

Daily Telegraph Correspondents of the First World War

Sir Philip Gibbs (1877–1962) The home-educated son of Henry James Gibbs, a civil servant at the Board of Education, and the fifth of seven children, Gibbs settled early on a career as a writer. He had his first article published in the *Daily Chronicle* when he was just seventeen, began working for the publisher Cassell in 1899, earning £2 10s a week, and published his first book in the same year. By 1902, he was working in Fleet Street, first as the literary editor of the *Daily Mail*, and then writing for the *Daily Express* and, in 1908, moving to the *Daily Chronicle*. In 1913 and early 1914, Gibbs visited Germany for the *Chronicle*, returning much alarmed by what he found there, yet convinced that war could yet be avoided. But in August 1914, he began his wartime adventure. As *The Times* would later put it: 'In early August of that year – clad, so it was said, in a lounge suit and carrying a walking stick – he started off for France.' As one of the five officially accredited war correspondents, Gibbs distinguished himself with his elegant and often highly evocative writing for the *Daily Chronicle* and *Daily Telegraph*. Later, haunted by the way he had felt obliged to censor his own reports, he made a name for himself with a series of books about what he had witnessed, including *The Soul of the War* (1915), *The Battle of the Somme* (1917), *From Bapaume to Passchendaele* (1918), *The Realities of War* (1920), *Now It Can Be Told* (1920) and *Adventures in Journalism* (1923).

Dr E. J. (Emile Joseph) Dillon (1854–1933) Dillon was the newspaper's Russian correspondent from 1887 to 1914. Born in Dublin and having begun to train for the priesthood, he later studied Oriental languages in Paris and became a brilliant linguist with doctorates from universities in Germany and Belgium as well as a professorship in Sanskrit, classical Armenian and comparative philology at the University of Kharkiv in the Ukraine. As a journalist, Dillon was not above disguising himself in order to be able to get closer to the action, as he did when sent by the *Daily Telegraph* to cover the Turkish massacres of Armenians in 1894.

Granville Roland Fortescue (1875–1952) Fortescue was a dashing US soldier and presidential aide, who also worked as a war reporter for the *Daily Telegraph* and London *Standard*. A cousin of US President Theodore Roosevelt, and extremely wealthy thanks to his marriage to a niece of the inventor Alexander Graham Bell, Fortescue was a charming and talented character of considerable panache, who wrote several books about his First World War experiences, and was highly decorated for his service as an artillery officer.

William Maxwell (d. 1928) A professional war correspondent, Maxwell had already covered the Anglo–Egyptian victory at Omdurman, the Second Boer War and Siege of Ladysmith for the London *Standard*, before resigning to become a foreign correspondent on the *Daily Mail* during the Russo–Japanese War and Balkan War of 1912. He reported on the 1st Battle of the Marne (September 1914) for the *Daily Telegraph*, before enlisting as a captain and joining the general staff of the British Army. Unfortunately, he is now best known as the official censor during the Gallipoli campaign, doing his best to hide the truth of the disaster in the Dardanelles, rather than to illuminate it. For his efforts, he was knighted by the King in 1919.

A. Beaumont Little is known of Beaumont, a naturalised US citizen born in Alsace, although – given the inside knowledge he occasionally shows of what French airmen are up to during the war – it is tempting fancifully to wonder if he may have been the André Beaumont who beat Roland Garros to win the European Air-Racing Circuit of 1911 and won the first round-Britain air race, the Circuit of Britain, in the same year. Sometimes designated as a 'special correspondent' of the *Daily Telegraph*, Beaumont appears to have reported in an unofficial capacity from all over the Western Front and beyond (Bale, Béthune, the Vosges, Milan, Rome, Trieste, Smyrna), after very nearly being shot as a spy. At the end of the war, Beaumont's 'Heroic Story of the Czecho-Slovak Legions' was published by the Czechoslovakian Foreigners' Office in 1919 in a slim volume reprinted from the *Daily Telegraph*.

Luigi Barzini (1874–1947) Aged twenty-six, Barzini was sent as an Italian war correspondent to Qing dynasty China, where he distinguished himself with his first-hand reports of the Boxer Rebellion, before being embedded with the Imperial Japanese Army during the Russo–Japanese War of 1904–05. He then achieved fame when he accompanied Prince Scipione Borghese in winning the two-month-long Peking-to-Paris motor race, and his dazzling memoir of the exploit was published in eleven languages. During the First World War, Barzini was the official correspondent with the Italian Army; after the war, his pro-Fascist sentiments led him to become a senator under Mussolini. He died destitute in Milan in 1947.

Rudyard Kipling (1865–1936) The celebrated short-story writer, poet and novelist was one of the most popular writers of his day, so it must have been a coup for the *Daily Telegraph* to be able to print reports such as his long essay on the Army Service Corps, 'Territorials in a Park', on 9 December 1914, or 'Our Destroyers in the Battle of Jutland' on All Souls' Day in 1916.

Arthur Conan Doyle (1859–1930) The creator of Sherlock Holmes did not write a great deal for the *Daily Telegraph* during the war. Nevertheless, his wonderful report, on 28 October 1916, on the mysteries of the manufacture of high explosives in a former peat bog remains a masterpiece of evocative reportage, as uncomfortably beautiful as it is bizarre.

Archibald Hurd (1869–1959) The editor of the *Naval and Military Record* between 1896 and 1899, Hurd was the *Daily Telegraph*'s first full-time naval correspondent, appointed at the time of the Russo–Japanese War. 'In recognition of his provenance,' writes Lord Burnham in *Peterborough Court: The Story of the Daily Telegraph* (1955), 'Le Sage [the newspaper's autocratic managing editor] always referred to him in the office as Togo, and persisted in so doing for many years when the Japanese admiral's name was only remembered in the reference library.' Besides being the newspaper's resident expert on all things nautical, Hurd also edited several editions of Brassey's *Naval and Shipping Annual*, and was knighted for his efforts in 1928. He was the great, great uncle of the Tory politician, Douglas Hurd.

Leonard Spray (1887–) Born in Penzance, Cornwall, Spray was the *Telegraph*'s Rotterdam correspondent, with a particular focus upon naval stories which was perhaps inevitable given his surname. Later, he travelled to Russia to cover the Revolution before returning to England to compile verse and stories about his beloved Cornwall.

G. J. Stevens (–1917) The newspaper's Athens correspondent, often reporting from the Allied base in Salonika, also contributed to the *Daily Chronicle* and supplied syndicated reports for the Press Association. Ironically, it was Stevens's return to the relative safety of London in 1917 that did for him; Stevens was killed shortly afterwards in an air raid. *Flight* magazine reported at the time: 'Probably no journalistic work during this war has carried more weight with it than the remarkably vivid articles to the *Daily Telegraph* from the pen of the late Mr G. J. Stevens, who during a brief visit recently to this country from Greece was one of the victims of the Gotha night-raiders during the harvest moon. There will be a very great many therefore who will applaud the graceful act of the Greek Government, who are passing a Bill allowing a pension to be granted to the daughter of Mr Stevens, for services rendered to Greece by the English journalist.'

Perceval Gibbon (1879–1926) Born in Wales, and educated in Baden, Germany, Gibbon was a merchant sailor who travelled widely in Europe, Africa and the

Americas, before becoming a war correspondent with the Italian Army from 1917–18. Towards the end of the war, he himself became a Major in the British Royal Marines. Now best known for his short stories, he was a friend of the author Joseph Conrad, and dedicated his book *Flower o' the Peach* to Joseph and Jessie Conrad.

William Thomas Massey An unofficial correspondent in France in 1914 and subsequently a special correspondent with Allenby's Egyptian Expeditionary Force in Palestine, Massey became one of the most famous First World War correspondents, despite being based in the Middle East. He went on to become news editor of the *Daily Telegraph* from 1923–25. A tall, austere man, with a shock of white hair and an almost-cockney accent, Massey is described by Sidney Dark in the 1932 anthology *Fleet Street: An Anthology of Modern Journalism* as 'working Fleet Street at its best: conscientious, reliable, efficient'. He received a CBE in 1920.

Ellis Ashmead-Bartlett (1881–1931) One of the best journalists and also one of the most colourful characters in these pages. Tall (5ft 10in) and slim, with grey eyes and fair hair, Ashmead-Bartlett had his first taste of war at the age of sixteen, when he accompanied his father, the former civil lord of the Admiralty, as a guest of the Sultan during the Greco–Turkish War. He then served as a Lieutenant in the Bedfordshire Regiment during the Boer War before cutting his teeth as a correspondent reporting on the Russo–Japanese War. But it was at Gallipoli that he made his name, first with his dazzling eye-witness reports and, later, with his bitter criticism of the way the campaign was being waged.

Čedomilj Mijatović (later **Cheddo Miyatovich**) (1842–1932) Mijatović was a giant of the Serbian academic and political establishment. A university professor at the age of twenty-three, and Minister of Finance by the time he was thirty-one, he spearheaded the creation of a Serbian railway network, did his best to reform the Serbian Orthodox church, and worked valiantly to bring Serbia into the twentieth century. A committed Anglophile, he spent much of his later life in exile in Britain, and acted as a cultural bridge between Britain and Serbia, not least in the various reports he contributed to British newspapers such as the *Daily Telegraph*.

G. Ward Price (1886–1961) A star correspondent for the *Daily Mail* whose work occasionally appeared elsewhere, Ward Price is now mostly remembered for the soft interviews he conducted with Hitler and Goebbels in the early days of Nazism, when Rothermere's old *Daily Mail* espoused Mosley's Blackshirts for a time. He was, nevertheless, an experienced journalist, who had served as a war correspondent with the Turkish army in the Balkan War in 1912, before being sent to the Dardanelles as an official correspondent in 1915 and subsequently transferring to Salonika. Ward Price was still plying his trade in the Second World War, doing pieces to camera for *British Movietone News*, and working as an official war correspondent in France with the British Expeditionary Force in 1939, followed by a stint in Tunisia in 1943 and a return to France in 1944.

Major M. H. Donohoe (1869–1927) Born in County Galway, Ireland, Martin Henry Donohoe began his career in Sydney, where he was known as an 'undistinguished but most painstaking, hard-working and deservedly liked reporter', before joining the crack New South Wales Lancers regiment and fighting with them in the Boer War. When the *Daily Chronicle*'s Boer War correspondent was killed, Donohoe started sending off his own dispatches, and acquitted himself so well that he was at once offered a job and detached from his troop. After being captured and released during the fall of Pretoria, he followed the Japanese army during the Russo–Japanese War, and covered the Turkish and Portuguese revolutions as well as the Italian–Turkish War in Tripoli. Best known for his 1919 book, *With the Persian Expedition,* about his adventures with General Dunsterville's 'Hush-Hush' Brigade, Donohoe appears to have been a model war correspondent, of whom the *Daily Chronicle* wrote in his obituary that modern censorship made him 'almost the last great survivor of his class'.

Laurence Jerrold (1872–1918) Based in Paris, Jerrold was a journalist, essayist and drama critic who co-edited an art magazine and wrote a number of books about France for a British readership, such as *The Real France* (1911), *The French and the English* (1913), *France, her People and her Spirit* (1916) and *France, To-day* (1916). In 1906 he had covered the Courrières mining disaster in Lens for the *Daily Telegraph,* and subsequently served as the newspaper's Paris correspondent during the First World War.

Perceval Landon (1868–1927) An Oxford-educated barrister with a lifelong interest in heraldry, Landon is now best-known for his classic ghost story, *Thurnley Abbey.* A close friend of Rudyard Kipling, he became a war correspondent for *The Times* during the Boer War and afterwards travelled almost constantly, working for the *Daily Mail* in India, China, Japan and Siberia, and for *The Times* in Tibet, Mesopotamia, Syria and Nepal. During the First World War, he reported from France, Italy and the Vatican, often travelling with Kipling, in the grounds of whose house, Bateman's, he had a cottage for a time.

Herman Whitaker (1867–1919) Born in Huddersfield, Whitaker joined the British Army's West Riding Regiment when he was sixteen, and subsequently became its fencing master. After emigrating to Canada and then to California in 1902, he scraped together a living digging ditches and building barns to supplement his income as a struggling writer, on the periphery of a Bohemian set which included Jack London et al. When the US entered the First World War, Whitaker became the *Oakland Tribune*'s war correspondent in Europe, and – already fifty-one – he gamely followed the troops wherever he was allowed, including the trenches, a seaplane, a destroyer, a minesweeper and a submarine.

Whitaker's 1916 novel, *Over the Border*, was later adapted for the John Ford western, *3 Bad Men*.

Patrick de Bathe (1876–1939) The youngest son of General Sir Henry de Bathe, 4th baronet, and the brother-in-law of Lillie Langtry, de Bathe was a dashing former diplomat who had been attached to the British embassies at St Petersburg and Berlin before joining the British Army. He married Violet Wood, 'a bride of altogether exceptional beauty', according to the *Washington Post* in 1920, which then bluntly announced: 'The war was responsible for the shipwreck of their union, for on its outbreak Patrick joined the army, received a commission, and from that time on spent most of his time in France and in Belgium. There he became infatuated with other women and wound up last summer by announcing that he had made up his mind not to resume married life with his wife.' Divorce followed, and the couple's only son, Sir Christopher de Bathe, 6th and last baronet, was killed in action in 1941.

Frederick Calvert History is full of Frederick Calverts, but this one – who wrote little for the *Daily Telegraph* – proves difficult to trace. He could perhaps have been been the author, traveller and mining engineer Albert Frederick Calvert who was born in Kentish Town in 1872, and died in Islington in 1946. In between, Calvert travelled and wrote widely, discovering the rare Spinifex Parakeet in Australia and becoming something of an expert on mining and minerals, Spanish art, Nigeria, German Africa and Freemasonry. It is not impossible that a sojourn in Salonika in 1916 was also on his itinerary.

John N. Raphael (1868–1917) On 18 May 1917, *The Mercury* (Tasmania) reported: 'Numerous scrap-books were left behind by John N. Raphael, the English journalist, novelist, and dramatist, who died in Paris recently. Raphael was a famous and always entertaining correspondent in the once gay city of various London journals … It was he who did the stage adaptation of Du Maurier's novel, *Peter Ibbetson,* which made such a furore when produced in London, and he also translated *Madame X* into English, and *Potash and Perlmutter* into French.' In *Who's Who* Raphael gave his recreations as 'other people's motor-cars and a lazy life', but few writers worked harder. 'What made him perhaps unique among newspaper writers was the fact that he could produce for inspection practically every line that he had written … At the finish he had more than fifty huge albums, carefully indexed, at his charming old house in the Boulevard de Clichy.'

Sir John Hare (1844–1921) Born John Fairs, Hare was an English actor and manager of the Garrick Theatre in the late nineteenth century. Hare had established his popularity on the London stage of the 1880s as a character actor in 'man of the world' roles, and went on to have a long and successful career as both an actor and producer. Knighted in 1907, Hare retired from the stage in 1912, but appeared in two films a few years later, including *The Vicar of Wakefield*

(1916). He appears in these pages as a result of being in the wrong place at the wrong time, as a tourist stuck in France in 1914.

A Woman/An English Lady In 1848, Margaret Fuller had become the first accredited female foreign correspondent when the *New York Tribune* sent her to cover the Roman revolution, and Jessie White, the daughter of a Hampshire builder, had served as an accredited war correspondent for *The Scotsman*, *The Tribune* and *The Nation* during the Franco–Prussian War. Yet these pioneering women (not featured here) were very much the exceptions to the rule. Journalism, in pre-emancipation Britain, was viewed as no game for a woman. The writer Arnold Bennett summed up the state of affairs with typical priggishness in his 1898 handbook, *Journalism for Women*: 'Of the dwellers in Fleet Street,' he opined, 'there are not two sexes, but two species – journalists and women-journalists – and the one is about as far removed organically from the other as a dog from a cat.' Hence the regrettable fact that the female voices represented here are merely credited as 'A Woman' and 'An English Lady', when one cannot help but feel that the entire reporting of the First World War might have been considerably more truthful, heartfelt and revealing, if only more of it had been entrusted to the cats, rather than the dogs.

Envoi

Time has not been kind to these reports from a century ago. 'There was no more discreditable period in the history of journalism,' thunders Arthur Ponsonby in his 1928 book *Falsehood in War-time*, 'than the four years of the Great War.' Yet, as a journalist myself, I can see how impossible the job of the war correspondents and their editors must have been. It must have been a unique kind of nightmare and taken a special kind of courage, to be obliged to describe the indescribable without giving any hint as to its true horror; attempting to distil some hint of clarity from the morass of rumour and allegation in the midst of the fog of war – 'the most depressing and terrifying atmosphere man can breathe', according to the *Daily Telegraph*'s William Maxwell, reporting from Ghent on 22 August 1914; struggling to find tales of heroism amid the piles of mangled corpses blown apart by the latest bombardment. 'The truth was that the military mind was obsessed with the necessity of fighting this war – "our war", as the regulars called it – in the dark,' writes Philip Gibbs in *Adventures in Journalism* (1923), 'while the non-military mind knew that such a policy was impossible, and might be disastrous.' The advantage of doing anything in the dark is, of course, that you cannot be caught or blamed or recognised as a failure, as the post-war Gibbs knew only too well. 'Again, it seemed to us that the guiding idea behind the censorship was not to conceal the truth from the enemy, but from the nation, in defence of the British high command and its tragic blundering.'

Above all, in the gulf between what these reports do and do not reveal is laid bare an aspect of our humanity that we would do well to face. I mean our readiness as human beings to lie to ourselves and to each other, when we are convinced of our own righteousness. And our blind willingness to believe such lies, when our judgment is clouded by a noxious cocktail of herd instinct, trust and fear. As the war poet Siegfried Sassoon puts it in his *Memoirs of an Infantry Officer*: 'I wonder why it was necessary for the Western Front to be "attractively advertised" by such intolerable twaddle. What was this camouflage war which was manufactured by the press to aid the imaginations of people who had never seen the real thing?'

That is what makes this book so terrifying. Between the vagueness and blandness of the official reports, and the wild claims of progress often made by 'our special correspondent', one senses the tireless energies of many outstanding journalists doing their utmost to report the war as powerfully and truthfully as possible. Yet what I think the book mostly reveals, in the end, is how little the ordinary British people were told about the carnage and abominations and well-meaning blunders being committed daily upon land and sea over a four-year period in their name and at their expense; the expense, above all, of their most precious flesh and blood.

It is easy for us now. We know, as we read these same reports, 100 years on, that our ancestors' war would be over by November 1918. They, our poor, innocent forebears, could only wring their hands, and turn their eyes to heaven, and hope that tomorrow's paper would bring some better news, or at least some news in which they might believe.

La Folie, France
2014

Chapter 1

Europe Goes to War

29 June 1914

ASSASSINATION OF THE HEIR-PRESUMPTIVE TO THE AUSTRIAN THRONE
Archduke and Wife Murdered

Another ghastly chapter was added yesterday to the tragedy of the Royal house of Austria–Hungary.

We deeply regret to announce that the Archduke Franz Ferdinand, Heir-Presumptive to the Imperial Crown, and his wife, the Duchess of Hohenberg, were assassinated at Sarajevo, the Bosnian capital.

The Archducal pair had been attending the manœuvres in Bosnia, which concluded on Saturday. Yesterday they paid a visit to the Town Hall in Sarajevo, and near the building a bomb was thrown at their automobile. The Archduke warded off the missile with his arm, and it exploded near the car following, in which two persons were injured. The thrower, a Serb, was arrested.

The Archduke and his wife attended the reception in the Town Hall as arranged. They were continuing their progress through the town, when shots were fired at them by a man in the crowd armed with a magazine pistol. Both were fatally injured, and died soon afterwards.

The second assassin, a Serb student of nineteen, was with difficulty saved from the fury of the crowd, and arrested.

It was known that the Archduke's life was threatened by a conspiracy of Serb political desperadoes, who resent the annexation of Bosnia to the Empire as a blow to the cause of 'Greater Servia'. The Archduke was warned, but decided not to change his plans.

At noon the terrible news was conveyed to the aged Emperor at Ischl.

The horror felt throughout Europe at the crime must be mingled with deep anxiety as to the effect of this last shock upon a monarch weighed down with years and broken by so many tragic sorrows. 'I am spared nothing,' he is said to have murmured when the news was broken to him.

In any event the political consequences of the assassination are likely to be grave.

The next in succession to the throne of the Dual Monarchy is the young Archduke Karl Franz Josef, a nephew of the deceased Archduke.

The King and Queen, who were informed of what had happened by a telegram from the British Embassy in Vienna, were deeply distressed at the news, and caused inquiries to be made at the Austrian Embassy in London, while a telegram expressing their deep sympathy was despatched to the Austrian capital.

It was announced last night that the English Court goes into mourning for one week, dating from yesterday. Tonight's State Ball has been postponed.

GRAPHIC STORY OF THE DOUBLE MURDER
Archduke and Mayor, *Sarajevo, Sunday Afternoon*

The following details of the assassination of the Archduke Franz Ferdinand and his wife are now available.

At ten o'clock this morning the Archduke and the Duchess left the military camp in their automobile for the Town Hall. The car halted for some minutes while a number of young girls, who were drawn up in festive attire, greeted the Royal pair, who accepted some flowers from them and spoke a few kindly words.

The car moved on, but scarcely had it moved more than a few yards when a man, who has since been identified as a printer named Čabrinović, sprang out from the crowd and hurled a bomb full at the Royal couple. The infernal machine fell at the back of the car, just where the Archduke was sitting, and, rebounding on to the road, exploded.

The Royal car had by this time moved several yards, and the full force of the explosion fell on the following automobile, which contained four members of the suite. They were Count Boos-Waldeck, Baron Rummerskirch, Countess von Lanjus, lady-in-waiting, and Lieutenant-Colonel von Merizzi, aide-de-camp to the Archduke. The last-named received a splinter in the neck and was badly hurt.

Meantime the would-be assassin had been seized by the police, who had the greatest difficulty in saving him from the fury of the crowd.

The Archduke, after ascertaining the extent of the injuries to the aide-de-camp, and seeing that he was medically attended to, gave the order to proceed, and the Royal car soon afterwards arrived at the Town Hall.

At the entrance to the building were the members of the Town Council, with the Burgomaster at their head. The Burgomaster was about to read an address to the Royal visitors when the Archduke raised his hand, and spoke as follows in a voice in which resentment was blended with emotion: 'Mr Mayor – We come to Sarajevo to make a friendly visit, and are greeted by a bomb. This is outrageous.'

Then, after a pause, the Archduke said, 'You may now speak.'

The city fathers stood thunderstruck, and could not conceal their chagrin. The Burgomaster, however, recovered himself, and delivered the speech he had prepared. The Archduke made a suitable reply, and, with his wife, spent half an hour inspecting the Town Hall.

The Archduke then stated that he was going on to the garrison hospital to see how Lieutenant-Colonel Merizzi was progressing. The Royal couple, escorted by the town councillors, descended the steps leading to the entrance to the building, re-entered their automobile, and drove off.

The car had reached the corner of the Franz-Josef and Rudolf streets, when two shots, in close succession, rang out. The first struck the Archduke in the right cheek, inflicting a mortal wound, while the second penetrated the body of the Duchess, severing a main artery. The unfortunate lady sank unconscious into the arms of her spouse, who a few seconds afterwards also fainted.

With all speed the car was driven by the chauffeur to the Konak, but almost before a doctor could reach their side the Royal couple had expired.

The assassin, who was a Servian student named Gavrilo Princip, was seized and disarmed. The crowd made a desperate attempt to drag the murderer from the protecting police, but they succeeded in rescuing him and conveying him to the police-station.

ASSASSINS QUESTIONED
A Second Bomb, *Sarajevo, Sunday (6 p.m.)*

The assassin of the Archduke and his wife is a student named Gavrilo Princip. He is nineteen years of age, and was born at Grahavo, in the district of Livno. He studied for some time in Belgrade.

On being interrogated, Princip declared that he had intended for a long time to kill some eminent personage from Nationalist motives. He was waiting today on the Appel Quay for the Archduke to pass by, and made his attempt at the point where the Archduke's motor-car had to slacken speed when turning into the Franz Josef Gasse. As the Duchess was also in the car, he hesitated for a moment, but afterwards quickly fired two shots. Princip denies having any accomplices.

A few yards from the scene of the second and fatal attempt, an unexploded bomb was found, which is thought to have been thrown away by a third assassin, after he had seen the success of Princip's attack.

30 June 1914

HORROR IN AUSTRIA
Vienna, Monday

A cry of horror echoes throughout the whole Monarchy at the iniquitous deed done at Sarajevo. All the political parties agree in condemning the terrible assassination of the Heir to the Throne, even those who had not sympathised with him heretofore. The entire Press discusses at length the causes of the outrage, and agrees unanimously that it was the result of a plot which had been long prepared. This may be seen from the fact that the first unsuccessful bomb attempt of the printer Čabrinović was followed by the second and more successful outrage, perpetrated by Princip, a pupil at the commercial school.

It appears also that there was still another assassin ready in case the second attempt failed, for shortly after the catastrophe a bomb was found which a third intended assassin had held ready in his hand, but which he threw away when he saw that the shots fired by Princip had taken effect.

All the papers point out that the Heir to the Throne had always shown the warmest sympathy for the satisfaction of the national aspirations of the Southern Slavs, from whose ranks his murderer sprang.

In the confusion that ensued immediately after the outrage in Sarajevo yesterday it may be understood that none of the spectators were able to give any connected narrative of events. Today many details have been learnt which give a complete picture of the affair. The bomb which the printer Čabrinović threw at the automobile in which the Archduke Franz Ferdinand and the Duchess of Hohenberg were driving to the Town Hall struck the back of the car, glanced off, and exploded and split up into hundreds of pieces. Many persons were injured, among them Adjutant First Lieutenant von Merizzi, who was badly cut about the throat. Čabrinović, who is twenty-one years of age, and is the son of an innkeeper in Sarajevo, tapped the bomb on the quay wall where he stood until it caught fire, and then he threw it at the Archduke's automobile. The Archduke had the presence of mind to ward off the missile with his left hand so that it fell backwards.

The would-be assassin sprang into the Miljacka river after the attempt, while a hairdresser named Marossy jumped after him, and a detective followed both. They struggled with the criminal in the water, caught him, and brought him to the police-station.

Great excitement and confusion ensued. The Archduke and his wife were full of consternation in the first moment, but regained their calm very quickly. Nevertheless, the Archduke, when he entered the Town Hall, expressed his feeling of displeasure by saying to the Burgomaster: 'This is a shameful affair. We come on a visit to your city and we are received with bombs. It is very distressing.' After a pause the Archduke continued: 'Burgomaster, you may speak now.'

When the Burgomaster had delivered the address of welcome and the Archduke had answered him, the Archduke and the Duchess started to return to the Konak. The chauffeur drove on the right side of the road instead of on the left by accident when passing the corner of Franz Josef Gasse, where the assassin Princip stood and fired two shots at the automobile from a distance of five paces. The first shot struck the Archduke in the vein which runs down the temple. The Duchess immediately rose and tried to shield her husband with her body. Then a second shot rang out, which struck the Duchess in the right inguinal gland, and she sank into her husband's arms. While the Archduke expired after hardly three minutes, the Duchess of Hohenberg was still alive when she was conveyed to the Konak. She was, however, unconscious, and did not come to her senses again before drawing her last breath.

The public had meanwhile half beaten the murderer to death, and the police had some trouble in saving his life.

Sad to say, the Archduke fell a victim to the strong self-will which he had shown so frequently in life. After the unsuccessful bomb-throwing, every effort was made to persuade him to return direct to the Konak, and to abandon all other visits. He, however, insisted on going to the hospital, whither the wounded First Lieutenant Merizzi had been transported, as he wished to see him. The chief of police begged the Archduke not to make the visit, and the Governor, General Potiorek, joined in the appeal. Before the Archduke quitted the Town Hall with this wife, the chief of police entreated him once again in the most pressing manner to take the shortest way back to the Konak. The Duchess of Hohenberg joined in the entreaties, begging him to take the shortest route to the Konak, but all in vain, as the Archduke was determined to visit First Lieutenant Merizzi in the garrison hospital. The Duchess of Hohenberg declared that she would also go with him, whereupon the car was set in motion and went on to the quay.

At the corner of the quay and Franz Josef Gasse, Princip suddenly sprang forward and fixed the fateful shots. Spectators say that Princip was accompanied by two other youths. They all wore the Servian tricolour in their buttonholes. Three young girls approached them just before the attempt. Unfortunately, the news is confirmed that the police took hardly any special precautions. This is accounted for in Sarajevo by the fact that the Archduke forbade any attempt to watch him, as well as all measures for his safety, as he always considered that a soldier ought not to allow himself to be guarded by police.

The Governor of Bosnia, General Potiorek, who was seated on the back seat of the motor-car when the Archduke and the Duchess were murdered, says that neither the Archduke nor his wife knew that they were wounded, for everything occurred with such lightning rapidity. The Duchess sank suddenly into her husband's arms, while blood streamed from his throat. The Archduke exclaimed to his wife, 'Sophie, you must live for the sake of our children.' Immediately afterwards he sank into unconsciousness, and died while still in the car. The Duchess died some minutes after she was brought into the Konak.

Before he started on the fatal journey from Ilidža to Sarajevo the Archduke wrote a telegram for his children, in which he described the events of Saturday. The message closed with the words, 'Greetings and kisses from Papa.'

The murderer Princip told the examining judge today that his deed was an act of revenge for the oppression of Servia.

This morning the corpses were embalmed, when it was seen that the veins in the right temple and throat of the Archduke were completely torn open. Death took place very quickly as the result of hæmorrhage. The projectile was discovered intact inside the Duchess's abdomen, and was given to the State Attorney. No bullet was found in the Archduke's body, and it probably remained fast in the neck-bone.

The *Reichspost* in special editions which appeared this evening, gives the narrative of a military personage in the entourage of the Archduke. He says: 'The first bullet struck the Duchess, who thereupon sank into the Archduke's arms.

He rose, saying, "What has happened to you?" Immediately afterwards the Archduke himself sank to the bottom of the car, his hands outstretched. His neck was bleeding profusely, and the coat of his uniform was quickly soaked with blood. General Potiorek tore the Archduke's coat open, and then the Duchess got up and tried to staunch the fearful wound in her husband's neck too. With a scream of "My God! My God!" she sank helplessly to the floor. When the automobile went through the open palace gates some minutes later the Archduke and his wife lay gasping in the bottom of the car. They had both lost consciousness. We carried the two expiring bodies into the Turkish salon on the right hand of the ground floor. The Archduke opened his eyes several times as we went into the Konak and beat the air with his arms. A Franciscan monk named Mihacevic, who was fetched from the monastery near by, gave both the dying victims the last absolution. Six doctors who arrived on the spot were unable to do anything.'

Martial law has just been proclaimed in Sarajevo and its environs. This afternoon there were great anti-Servian demonstrations in Sarajevo. The populace demolished a Servian school and the Servian Club and some houses belonging to Serbs. Servian flags were burnt and thrown from the windows. The military were forced to intervene.

Shortly after the attempt there were violent anti-Servian demonstrations in Sarajevo by the Croatian and Moslem youths. Students progressed through the streets singing the national hymn, and shouting, 'Hurrah for the Emperor!' They yelled, 'Down with the Serbs!' 'Away with them!' 'We don't want murderers!' 'Down with the enemies of the Monarchy!' The demonstrations became more and more violent. The Croats and Moslems commenced a bombardment of the Hotel Europe, the property of the Serb leader, Gligorije Jeftanović, father-in-law of the Servian Minister in St Petersburg, and broke all the windows. The police were unable to disperse the demonstrators, whereupon the military intervened to restore peace.

Gavrilo Princip, the murderer of the Archduke and his wife, went through four classes of the middle school. He then proceeded to Belgrade, and returned after a stay of four weeks, having, it is reported, already arranged the attempt. The murderer behaved with great cynicism. In reply to a question of the examining judge as to why he had come to Sarajevo, he answered: 'You can see for yourself.' Another question was: 'Why did you kill the Heir to the Throne?' He replied: 'Because I looked upon him as the representative of Imperialism.'

In Princip's lodgings a large sum of money was found – it is reported 2,000 kronen. The bombs used were bottle-shaped, filled with nails and lead. Princip's Browning pistol still held four bullets.

Today a number of arrests were made, including several women and girls. All the prisoners were taken to the military gaol, where twenty cells were in readiness for them. Yesterday at midnight three Montenegrins were arrested.

It must be remembered that in Bosnia and in Servia yesterday a great national fête day was celebrated in commemoration of the battle of Amselfeld, and, as usual, the national feelings of the Serbs were rendered more intense by the chauvinistic journals. This day is the anniversary of the liberation of the Serbs, and on this occasion the journal of the Servian Opposition, *Narod*, printed jingo articles, encircled in the Servian tricolour. A copy of this paper was found in the flat of the printer, Čabrinović. The *Novosti* in its Thursday's number published a remarkable article on the visit of the Archduke, in which it said: 'The Austro–Hungarian Heir to the Throne should look well at Bosnia and Herzegovina, for this is the last time that he will see them.'

Some of the Vienna papers reproduced a report that investigation has already established the fact that the bomb with which the first attempt was carried out was manufactured in Belgrade, and that both the assassins came from there. This is not confirmed so far.

I have received the following declaration from a Minister: 'There is no doubt that the attempt was prepared a long time beforehand, and that it was excellently organised. The Heir to the Throne was surrounded like a wild beast, and no escape was possible. Even had the Archduke returned to the Konak immediately after the bomb attempt, the bullet would have reached him, perhaps on his leaving Sarajevo, for these young people were determined to commit the deed and carry it out at any price.'

In 'big Servian' circles there was a great agitation against the Archduke's journey as soon as it was known that he intended going. Warnings were also not wanting, which came to the notice of the authorities, and were communicated to the Archduke. He declared, however, that he would not retreat before threats, but he only decided with great difficulty to take his wife to Bosnia. The Duchess, however, allowed nothing to prevent her travelling with her husband. It is related in her entourage that she was filled with misgivings, and repeatedly expressed doubt whether her husband would ever wear the Imperial crown.

As regards the political effects of the outrage, it is to be feared that Bosnia will be more difficult to govern than ever. The murders are the consequence of the continued agitation against Austria–Hungary. It was not directed against the Archduke personally, but against the State. Now that the Emperor has arrived it will be decided what measures are to be taken. Martial law has not yet been declared in Sarajevo.

The Emperor Francis Joseph, who left Vienna the day before yesterday to go to Ischl for the summer, returned here today. The streets from the railway to Schönbrunn were closed by large numbers of police, but many thousands of people waited behind the ranks of the policemen. They greeted the Emperor at first in silent and deep sympathy. At the railway station the Archduke Karl Franz Josef, now Heir to the Throne, awaited the Emperor, who walked along the platform alone and went towards the Archduke, who bent over his Majesty's right hand and kissed it. The Emperor and the young Archduke both had tears in their eyes as they stood together. They exchanged some words, and then the Emperor took the Archduke's arm and they left the station. The public burst into a storm of cheers at the sight of the aged monarch who, in spite of all the fatigue and mourning of the last few hours, looked healthy and fresh.

In the streets near Schönbrunn more than 100,000 persons awaited the Emperor and shouted along the whole route, 'Long live the Emperor!'

The burial of the Archduke and his wife can hardly take place before next week. The corpse of the Archduke will not be laid in the Capuchin vault, where all the Habsburgs lie, but in the mausoleum which he had built in his Castle of Artstetten, in Lower Austria, some time ago. It is reported that the Archduke has left testamentary dispositions that he wishes to be buried in Artstetten. He probably took this course because he knew that the Duchess of Hohenberg, who did not belong to the Imperial family, could not be laid in the Capuchin vault. The lying-in-state and the benediction will not take place in the Hofburg Parish Church, because it is intended to have a joint funeral.

ASSASSINS' CONFESSIONS
Sarajevo, Monday (2.30 p.m.)

Besides the two actual perpetrators of yesterday's outrages, several persons suspected of complicity were at once arrested. It results from the investigations made that both the assassins are natives of the province, and belong to the Servian Orthodox Church. Čabrinović admitted having been a short time ago in Belgrade, where he obtained bombs for the special purpose of committing an outrage on the Archduke.

The second prisoner has confessed that since his return from Belgrade he had been determined to shoot a highly-placed personage out of revenge for the supposed oppression of the Servian nation. In carrying out the assassination he had purposely taken up a position between two well-known students whom he knew to be not under suspicion. He knew nothing of the Čabrinović bomb outrage, and when it actually occurred he was so bewildered that when the Archduke drove by for the first time he did not feel able to fire.

Well-informed quarters are convinced that the perpetration of such acts by Bosnians would have been impossible had not, as is well known, an agitation from abroad been carried on among the loyal Servian Orthodox population. This agitation is believed to have gained particular influence among the secondary school boys and Socialists belonging to the Servian Orthodox faith.

2 July 1914

MURDERED ARCHDUKE
Dramatic Confession of the Assassin, Vienna, Wednesday

The following account has been received from Sarajevo of the examination of the murderer Princip by the *Juge d'Instruction*. The assassin is a small dark man, with sunken eyes, and it is evident that he is suffering from tuberculosis. His head is bandaged. The expression of his face is quiet, but his eyes gleam. He said to the examining judge: 'I am guilty. I came here with the object of perpetrating the attempt. I was not under foreign influence. When I attended the fourth class of the Sarajevo Gymnasium I had already read Anarchistical books and Anarchism was my passion. This passion I have now been able to satisfy at last. I have read various books about Anarchists and the news given by the papers about all kinds of attempts, and I am convinced that there is nothing better in the world than to be an assassin. I made up my mind to kill one of the heads of the Austro–Hungarian Monarchy. I have succeeded at last.

'At the end of May of this year I heard in Belgrade that the Heir to the Throne was coming to Sarajevo in the month of July. I determined to utilise the occasion for the perpetration of my plans. I took lodgings with my friend and companion, Danilo Illić, a former board school teacher. A Komitadji in Belgrade presented me with the revolver and the cartridges, but I did not tell him my intentions. On the day of the attempt I did not think much, but I was quite determined to abide by my intention. I wanted to make the attempt as the automobile drove to the Town Hall, but as meanwhile another man flung a bomb I changed my plan, and I decided to await the return. As the automobile returned from the Town Hall I caught sight of the Heir to the Throne. By him sat a lady, and at the first moment I wanted to desist on account of her presence. Immediately afterwards, however, I changed my mind, and my intention was reinforced by the idea of killing the lady too. I began to shoot as the automobile turned the corner, and could not see whether I had attained my object or not. I could not see, as I was immediately seized and hit by everybody.

'I do not repent my deed. I am content that I have carried out my original intention. With the attempt which was made just before mine I have nothing in common. As I heard the explosion of the bomb I thought to myself, "Really there are people who feel and think just like me." That strengthened me in my decision.'

A council was held at the Foreign Office yesterday, at which, besides Count Berchtold, the War Minister, General Krobatin, the Chief of the General Staff, and Baron Conrad were present. Count Berchtold intends to address a request to the Servian Government calling on it to institute an inquiry with regard to the persons who may be responsible for the outrage of Sunday, as all the indications point to a conspiracy hatched in Servia. The excitement felt in Austria–Hungary against the Servians, in whose capital, as is known quite certainly, the instigators of the crime are to be found, has been increased still more throughout the Monarchy by the language employed by the Belgrade Press.

Servian journals spread the infamous story that the Archduke Karl Stefan, who is supposed to have been at variance with the Heir to the Throne, was responsible for the attempt being made. The building of the Servian Legation here has been surrounded by a strong police cordon. During last night noisy demonstrations were made by a number of German students. They broke into stormy shouts of 'Down with the Serbs! Down with the murder band!' After this the Servian tricolour was burnt.

Some remarkable utterances were delivered today by Archbishop Stadler of Sarajevo, who said: 'The outrage is the consequence of historic development. It is no simple accident that it was committed on the anniversary of the battle of Amselfeld, for all the Servian movements on Austro–Hungarian soil always occur on this day or thereabouts. It is quite certain that if the Archduke and his wife had not been murdered on the spot where the catastrophe happened, they would have been the objects of another attempt on the same day, for the conspirators would have found another opportunity of carrying out their dreadful plan. All Sarajevo was full of plotters, who were ready to remove the Heir to the Throne from their way.'

The Archbishop also says that bombs were found even in the trees along the route over which the Archduke passed. This information was confirmed by the President of the Bosnian Diet, who adds the following: 'The Heir to the Throne was surrounded by more than ten conspirators, who were waiting for him, some with revolvers and some with bombs. If Princip's shots had failed, some seconds later a second conspirator would have fired again. Moreover, a bomb was found among the branches of a tree on the road over which the Archducal pair drove. The murderers had spun a net from which the Archduke could not escape. In case, however, he managed to evade all the conspirators on the streets, a bomb attempt was planned to take place in the Palace. There was to be a banquet there on Sunday at noon. Under the table two bombs, activated by clockwork, were hidden. In the chimney of the dining-room there was also a bomb with clockwork.

ANTI-SERVIAN FEELING

Vienna, Wednesday (10 p.m.)

More than 1,000 people are making a demonstration again tonight in the vicinity of the Servian Legation. The police have prevented them reaching the Legation itself, but they are continuing the uproar in the neighbouring streets, screaming 'Down with Servia!'

3 July 1914

CONFESSIONS OF THE ARCHDUKE'S ASSASSINS

Story of the Plot, Vienna, Thursday

One of the Hungarian journals publishes some very interesting information which it has received from Advocate Persicin, of Sarajevo, who had taken over the defence of Princip. When this lawyer had his first conversation with his client yesterday, in prison, the murderer said: 'I do not fear death. I reckoned with the possibility of being hanged. I got the bombs from a rich merchant in Belgrade, named Miko Ohkanovic. He also gave me money. Already during the manœuvres I wished to carry out the attempt at Tarc, where the operations took place, but I was not able to get near the Archduke because of the *gendarmerie*. I have been following the Archduke about ever since he set foot on Bosnian soil.

'I confess honestly that we had been preparing the attempt for weeks in Servia. We wished to murder the Archduke Franz Ferdinand, because we knew that his ascent of the throne would be a misfortune for Servia, for he would wish to occupy that country as the monarchy occupied Bosnia and Herzegovina long ago. When I started out to commit the murder I carried poison with me. This was given me by a man who directed me to commit suicide after I had made the attempt and was about to be arrested. I lost the poison, however.'

The lawyer for the defence further says that Čabrinović and Princip would not take anything to eat. It seems that they have decided to carry out a hunger-strike. A letter has been addressed to Princip from Belgrade, bearing an illegible signature, in which he is congratulated on his deed. Naturally he did not get the letter.

Today two detectives arrived in Sarajevo from Belgrade. They came with an offer to lend their assistance for the inquiry into the crime, but their help was refused.

The examining judge, Dr Pfeifer, makes some very remarkable utterances. Among other things he says: 'The result of the inquiry shows plainly enough, and without a shadow of doubt, that there was a conspiracy. Princip and Čabrinović denied this at first, but now both acknowledge it. We cannot now divulge the names of the eleven conspirators, as some of them are not yet arrested. This is neither a socialistic nor a terroristic attempt. Both the assassins committed deeds for national ideals, and in the interests of the Servian National party. Whether the deed was originated in Servia or whether the men acted on their own account cannot be determined. It is very remarkable that a sum of 2,000 kronen (£80) was found in Princip's dwelling, most of it in gold. It is only with gold that quite special services are paid for in the Balkans. The investigation has today further shown that not only Čabrinović, but also Princip, has passed his twentieth year, and that both can be punished with death.'

According to statements made by the State Attorney, Dr Svara, Čabrinović, who threw the bomb, confessed: 'I had made preparations for the attempt for a long time beforehand. With the bomb that I threw at the Heir to the Throne and his wife I wished to destroy the present regime. I knew that the Archduke Franz Ferdinand was one of the greatest supporters of the old regime. I wished to annihilate him.'

Here, Dr Svara added, the assassin declared expressly that he did not mean by those phrases the reform of the monarchical State under the present regime, but that he meant destruction of the rule of the House of Hapsburg, and he hoped that the murder of the Heir to the Throne would assist the design.

The State Attorney then said that Princip had confessed that: 'Although I was born in Bosnia, the big Servian idea has always existed in me since my earliest childhood. I considered it unjust that a foreign power should be established in Bosnia, where the Serbs, on account of their numbers and their commercial and economic position, should take part in the government. It pained me that Austria should oppress us, for she is the old and eternal enemy of Servia. I also knew, though, that the first place among those who were hated by Serbs was occupied by the Archduke, Franz Ferdinand.

'I knew that he is the sworn enemy of all Servian aspirations, and that he had sworn to destroy Servia and the Servian dynasty. I hope that the fatal revolver shots will open the way to the Servian army to march here to occupy Bosnia, for this land is destined by its inclinations and traditions to belong to Big Servia.'

Finally, the State Attorney says that the conspiracy was concocted in a Belgrade café, where they knew days ago what was planned against the Heir to the Throne. In Belgrade it was openly said that Archduke Franz Ferdinand would not leave Bosnia alive.

'Although,' said Princip, in this connection, 'I received no command from anyone in Belgrade. I knew what my duty was as a Serb.'

The fresh examination of Čabrinović this morning brought out some sensational revelations. He said that he got the bomb from Major Milan Pribićević, who is in the Servian military service, and who is also secretary of the 'Narodna Obrana', an anti-Austrian society. Pribićević, it is stated, was acting as representative of the chief of the Servian General Staff. He is the brother of the Croatian deputy, Swetozar Pribićević, and of Valerian Pribićević, who played a role in the 'Big Servian' treason case in Agram in 1908. Pribićević told Čabrinović and Princip to apply to a well-known Komitaji, Cyganievic, whom he commissioned to get the bombs from the arsenal of Kragujevac. Čabrinović and Princip got six bombs and six Browning pistols, but had to promise to find four more conspirators for the plot.

Further, each of them was told to hold the bomb in the right hand as the Archduke passed, and a bottle of cyanide in the other, which he was to swallow immediately after throwing the bomb. Cyganievic gave Princip enough cyanide to kill six persons. Čabrinović and Princip were able to find a third conspirator in the person of a Belgrade student, Trifke Grabes. The conspirators went to Sarajevo separately. The bombs were handed out on the day of the attempt, in the morning. At ten the three conspirators met in a confectioner's shop kept by one Wleinic. Princip brought the bombs and pistols with him. He gave one of them each to Čabrinović and Grabes, and also gave them the poison.

Čabrinović declares that there were three more conspirators, whom he will not name. After they had remained some minutes in the shop they went away again. Čabrinović took up his position near the Comaris Bridge, Princip on the Appel Quai, and Grabes some paces further on. Čabrinović does not know where the other assassins stood.

After the examination of Čabrinović and Princip, detectives went at once to the confectioner's they had mentioned in their confession, and arrested the proprietor. In the afternoon Grabes was arrested in Pracan, and was immediately handed over to the Governmental commissioner, Gerde, who examined him during the night. Grabes confessed that he received the bomb, revolver, and cyanide in the confectioner's. He did not let the bomb go off because he saw that the Archduke and his wife were already fatally wounded.

Princip also made a full confession to the examining judge today, and promised that he would divulge the names of the other conspirators tomorrow. To a question of the judge as to why he would not at once confess everything, he answered: 'I must first order my thoughts. Do not be afraid. I repent my deed completely. If I could be let free I would run through the streets of Sarajevo and scream until I was hoarse, "Let the Serbs be burnt on a scaffold."'

Extraordinary precautions have been taken for the conveyance of the corpses from the Vienna Southern Railway Station to the Hofburg Chapel tonight. For tomorrow's service in the Hofburg and the removal of the bodies to Artstetten similar precautions have been adopted. The Archduke Karl Franz Josef, the new Heir to the Austrian Throne, said his wife will attend these ceremonies.

This evening it is reported with great certainty that the German Emperor's decision not to come to Vienna was not due to illness, but that he was persuaded by the Berlin police to abandon his intention of travelling to Vienna. The brother of the German Emperor, Prince Henry, who had already come from Kiel to Berlin, is also not coming to Vienna. From a good source I hear that two arrests were made in Vienna today of two known Servian Anarchists.

The tremendous excitement reigning among the population of Bosnia and Herzegovina as a consequence of the outrages in Sarajevo has resulted in martial law being proclaimed throughout the two provinces, as I reported late last night. The official announcement of this measure explains its necessity by the disturbances which are taking place among the Catholic and Moslem peasants of Tuzla and Maglaj and the sacking of a Servian church. The authorities define the object of martial law in Bosnia as necessary to prevent the innocent Servian population being made responsible for the acts of foreign agitators. Since the proclamation of martial law there has been quiet in Sarajevo. Three persons accused of sedition have been arrested. They are all Serbs, who said that they are enemies of Austria and of the Emperor. One of them, a merchant, named Nikolić, made a speech to the people in which he said that King Peter and the Crown Prince Alexander would march into Sarajevo tomorrow to avenge the plundering of the Serbs. The police are making fresh arrests in connection with the outrages.

The Belgrade Press continues its attacks and threats against Austria, although the Servian Government has declared spontaneously that it has taken the strictest measures to prevent this. The Servian Minister here has also informed the Vienna Cabinet that these steps have been taken. These official declarations from Belgrade are not considered a sufficient guarantee in competent quarters for the stoppage of Servian intrigue and the treasonable manœuvres of Serbs on Austrian territory.

Late this evening the bodies of the Archduke Franz Ferdinand and his wife were brought from Trieste. Many thousands of persons congregated in front of the Southern railway station, and an immense number, which it was impossible to compute with any certainty, stood in the streets awaiting the passage of the bodies from the railway to the Burgkapelle. Long mourning flags hung from the houses, while the balconies of many were decorated with rich mourning draperies.

When the special train, with both coffins, arrived, the funeral coach was flanked by a bodyguard of the Imperial Trabant guard in their picturesque uniforms, with their panther skins hanging from their shoulders. Non-commissioned officers lifted the coffins and carried them to the waiting-room, which was arranged as a chapel ardente, and in which the Court clergy gave the last benediction in the presence of all the members of the Imperial family, the Lord Steward of the Court of the Emperor, and many dignitaries.

The coffins were then carried to the mourning coaches, which were both drawn by six black horses, and the procession set out. At its head were two postilions in magnificent red and gold Court uniform, with lanterns in their right hands. Upon this followed a division of Hussars, then the Court functionaries on horseback, and a number of Court carriages with two horses, in which were members of the Archduke's household.

Close in front of both the funeral coaches there were again two outriders with lanterns. Non-commissioned officers flanked the funeral coaches, which went at a slow pace through the streets, where the crowd stood with uncovered heads in silent greeting.

Twelve members of the bodyguard attended each funeral coach, and by their sides rode bodyguards with drawn swords. The rearguard was formed by a cavalry regiment.

This last journey of the Heir to the Throne, along the finest streets and handsomest squares of the city, and past the Belvedere, where he dwelt, made the deepest impression on all the spectators in its dark magnificence. As the procession passed the Burg Gate the watch presented arms and gave a salute with trumpets and muffled drums in sign of military mourning for the dead.

In the Schweizerhof of the burg where the Emperor's master of ceremonies awaited the bodies, the coffins were lifted from the funeral coaches and were transported to the Hofburg Chapel with the same ceremonies as at the railway station. Singers of the Hofburg Choir chanted the 'Miserere'.

Pages with torches accompanied the coffin to the catafalque, upon which it was raised. German and Hungarian guards in their magnificent uniforms ranged themselves beside the coffin, with swords stretched out, and thus kept watch. After the Imperial Master of Ceremonies had taken charge of the key of the coffin, the chapel was closed. Tomorrow morning the public will be admitted to view the lying-in-state.

6 July 1914

FUNERAL OF THE MURDERED ARCHDUKE
Burial in a Storm, *Vienna, Sunday*

The Emperor Francis Joseph issued an autograph letter today, in which he thanked his people for their sympathy in connection with the tragedy of Sarajevo. His Majesty first refers to the loss of the Archduke and the Duchess, and then continues: 'A murderous band has robbed me of my relative and true helper; has inflicted indescribable sorrow on children of the tenderest age, who need the care and protection of all that was dear to them in the world; and has heaped woe on their innocent heads. The madness of a small band of misguided men will, however, not shake those bonds which bind me to my peoples. It does not touch the feelings of innermost love, which has again been manifested in such a touching manner to me and all the members of the Ruling House from all parts of the Monarchy. For six and a half decades I have shared sorrows and joys with my people, and even in my heaviest hours I have always thought of my duty, that I was answerable for the fate of millions to the Almighty. The fresh, painful trial that God, in His inscrutable Providence, has sent to me and mine, will strengthen my determination to continue on my recognised path, acting for the welfare of my peoples until my last breath.'

This autograph letter is very moving, and the last phrase is very much remarked, as it distinctly contradicts all reports spread during the last few days that the Emperor intends to abdicate.

The Emperor has also issued an order to the army and the fleet. The Monarch expresses his feeling that the death of the Archduke will be a great loss to the army, but concludes with the words: 'I do not, however, give up hope of a worthy future, for I am convinced that in all the trouble that may visit us, Austria–Hungary may firmly trust in the capacity of sacrifice until death shown by her army and navy, which are unshakeable in devotion to duty.'

The arrangements for the funeral of the Archduke and his wife led to a severe conflict between the Austrian and Hungarian nobility and the Master of the Ceremonies, Prince Montenuovo, and brought about a remarkable demonstration on the part of the aristocracy. The plans for the mourning ceremonies were extremely simple, the reason given being that the full burial honours due to the Heir to the Throne could not be accorded to him because he was buried with his wife, the Duchess of Hohenberg, who was not of Royal birth. The members of the high aristocracy who had received no invitations to the funeral were most indignant, as the Duchess of Hohenberg, as Countess Chotek, belonged to the very old nobility, and on Friday evening, when the funeral procession left the Vienna Hofburg for the Western Railway to proceed to Artstetten, over a hundred members of the Austrian and Hungarian aristocracy awaited its passage in the streets and joined it in a body. The gentlemen were in military uniform or in official Privy Councillors' costumes, and they followed the coffins as far as the railway station. This deputation was naturally much noticed by the public.

In military circles also the arrangements made by the Master of the Ceremonies were much objected to, as they had no possibility of paying their last respects to the Archduke. The Emperor, however, decided at the last moment that the entire Vienna garrison should turn out and accompany the funeral cortège to the Western Railway. The position of Prince Montenuovo, who bases his action on the strict Spanish ceremonial which is observed at the Austrian Court, is shaken, as the new Heir to the Throne, the Archduke Karl Franz Josef, also showed his displeasure, and was present at the arrival of the corpses in Vienna, although this was not provided for in the plan drawn up by the Master of the Ceremonies.

The termination of the disastrous week which has passed over Austria–Hungary was marked by the funeral of the Archduke Franz Ferdinand and his wife at the castle of Artstetten, on the Danube, which the Archduke in his lifetime had chosen as the last resting place for himself and the members of his family. The Imperial Master of the Ceremonies had arranged that the bodies should be taken over the ferry at Poechlarn immediately on their arrival there, but this programme was not carried out on account of a storm, and the conveyance of the corpses was attended by scenes of great confusion.

It was long after midnight when the small procession accompanying the hearses with both coffins arrived at Poechlarn Station. In the carriages were the Master of the Ceremonies of the late Archduke, Baron Rummerskirch, and his adjutant, the members of the household of the Archduke, and a number of officers of both regiments to which the Archduke belonged. At the railway station itself a number of gendarmes and the veterans and reservists' union of Poechlarn, with some civil functionaries, awaited the cortège. It was arranged that both corpses should receive the Benediction before being conveyed to the Castle of Artstetten, but, just as the priests were commencing the service, a terrible storm commenced. Rain fell in torrents, while the lightning was dazzling. The order set for the procession was not regarded, all the rules and regulations were forgotten, and everyone fled to the station, which was much too small for the crowd. High officers, gendarmes, veterans, and peasants ran this way and that, while outside on the railway line water streamed on the hearses in elemental force. As it was not possible to continue the route in this weather, the coffins were finally brought into the railway station waiting-room.

At last the heavy and richly gilded metal coffins were lifted from the hearses and carried through the noisy crowd into the waiting-room. The people thronged here and there, and all Court ceremonial was forgotten. The late Archduke's Master of the Ceremonies, Baron Rummerskirch, stood as pale as death beside his master's coffin, and he was immediately afterwards overcome by the strain and excitement of the scene. Veterans and gendarmes were mingled with railway officials and employees; while many cavalry officers and the Archducal servants were among the crowd.

Amid this scene of confusion the Benediction was proceeded with. Just as the ceremony was at an end the thunder and lightning recommenced with increased violence, and the rain again descended in torrents. It was impossible even to think of conveying the coffins across the Danube under these conditions and there was nothing left but to leave them on the dais until the weather had become finer. People pressed around the coffins, quite forgetting that they were in the same room as the corpses of the Archduke Franz Ferdinand and his wife. It was only after the expiry of an hour that the removal of the caskets across the Danube became possible and they were again lifted on to the hearses, and the procession moved painfully through the morass of the village streets to the banks of the river. The line of veterans had long been dispersed, but mounted officers who were present rode right and left of the hearses to keep up an appearance of ceremony. Some few torches lighted up the sad picture, a black-draped ferry-boat awaited the procession. It had great difficulty in making the crossing, but at last it succeeded in bringing its sad burden to the other side of the river.

Many mourners arrived by special trains in the early morning to attend the funeral. The Archduke Karl Franz Josef, Heir to the Throne, and his Consort, the Archduchess Zita, the stepmother of the deceased Archduke, the Archduchess Maria Theresa, and his sister, the Archduchess Maria Annunziata, his sister-in-law, the Archduchess Marie Josefa, the three children, and the nearest relatives of the Archduke and Duchess were among them. The only brother of the Archduke, Herr Ferdinand Burg, formerly the Archduke Ferdinand Karl, who, as is known, renounced all his titles and honours on marrying a commoner, and changed his name to that of Burg, was also there, having come alone by an ordinary train. A large number of the aristocrats who made the demonstration here also attended.

The funeral took place in pouring rain. At twelve noon exactly both bodies were laid in the mausoleum of Artstetten. After the Requiem Mass in the church a procession was formed behind the coffins, which were guarded by cavalry officers and soldiers, the Archduke Karl Franz Josef, and by many members of the aristocracy. Just behind the coffins the three children of the murdered couple walked, silent and with dry eyes. Prince Ernst carried a small parcel in his hand, a portrait of the three children, that he wished to place between the coffins of his parents. The Archduke Karl Franz was carrying a candle in his hand. He was at the head of the procession of male members of the House of Habsburg, among whom Ferdinand Burg was also seen, while the Archduchesses also moved in procession.

Slowly the cortège moved through the castle park, and arrived at the pillared hall of the mausoleum. Black carpets had been laid down, on which two low biers were placed. Here the coffins, containing the mortal remains of the Archduke and his wife, were deposited. Between is a small silver coffin, with the body of a stillborn daughter born to the Archducal pair three years ago. Numerous crosses and wreaths, including those of the children, were laid on the coffins. The religious ceremony was short, and immediately afterwards the guests left the palace.

20 July 1914

AUSTRIA AND SERVIA

Opinion in Berlin, *Berlin, Sunday Night*

According to information which has reached the *Börsen Courier* from 'a well-informed and very trustworthy source', Austria has decided to 'demand from Servia a straightforward, plain, and unambiguous declaration that she will, to the full extent of her power, prevent the "Greater Servian" agitation from encroaching on the territory of the Dual Monarchy'. This step was originally planned for last Thursday, but was postponed for a week 'to allow careful reconsideration of all the pertinent factors'. Should Servia refuse the assurance required 'an appeal to the armed forces of the State would decide'.

The paper adds that 'much, if not all, will depend upon Russia', but that the Government of that country has the intention of adopting under all circumstances an attitude of reserve.

In the semi-official Press an increase of nervousness on this question is noticeable. The organ of the Foreign Office expresses the hope that the 'prompt acquiescence of Servia will prevent the arising of a grave crisis', and that 'the settlement of accounts that may take place between Austria–Hungary and Servia will remain isolated'.

22 July 1914

AUSTRIA'S DEMANDS ON THE SERVIAN GOVERNMENT
Strong Note Impending, *Vienna, Tuesday Night*

The Foreign Minister, Count Berchtold, left Vienna last night for the Imperial Court, which is resident at Ischl just now, and was received by the Emperor in a very long audience today. Count Berchtold placed the results of the investigation in Sarajevo before the Emperor, and reported on the step which is to be adopted in Belgrade.

I learn that this step will be taken this week in Belgrade. The Austro–Hungarian Government will couch its wishes in a very polite form, but will insist on their fulfilment with much emphasis and within a certain time.

The demands made by the Austro–Hungarian Government in Belgrade will embrace several points, and include the following: An immediate investigation into the guilt of Servian subjects and organisations in regard to the Sarajevo outrage, guarantees being given that the inquiry shall be truly and thoroughly made so as to complete the Sarajevo inquiry.

That the Servian Government shall proceed against those organisations and societies of youths which carry on the agitation against the Austro–Hungarian frontiers, and shall put an end to the fostering of those sentiments from which the outrage sprung, by not allowing such associations to exist any longer.

The Austro–Hungarian Government is also to express the wish that the frontiers should be more carefully watched.

These demands signify that the Monarchy not only desires that certain abuses shall cease, but that the Servian Government shall altogether change its policy into one of enduring and continued peace.

In circles in close touch with the Foreign Office here the situation is regarded as serious. The Government has resolved not to abandon any point of its demands in the Note, which will probably be handed in at Belgrade tomorrow with a forty-eight hours' limit. The sudden breaking off of the leave of the Chief of the General Staff, Baron Conrad, who travelled from the Tyrol to Vienna the day before yesterday and left the city again immediately, is also connected with the situation.

The Bourse was very disturbed today. There also it was considered that serious decisions in the Servian question might be expected.

25 July 1914

SERVIA AND AUSTRIA
The Sarajevo Tragedy

By Cheddo Miyatovich

The Sarajevo tragedy is more tragical than the first impressions led the public opinion of Europe to believe it to be. If we attempt to analyse it with philosophical coolness, free from all partisanship and political prejudice, desiring only to bring to light its true nature, motives, meanings, and consequences, desiring to do justice as much as humanly possible to all the actors, we cannot fail to discover speedily that this tragedy is not a common tragedy of the assassination of Royal persons by the Anarchists who hate and detest the modern State and society. It is indeed quite a special tragedy, grander and sadder than most tragedies of modern times. It is a tragedy in the sense of the classic conceptions of what a tragedy is.

Besides the *dramatis personae* whom the world could see, the world could not see, but distinctly felt, the presence of a third, horrible, superhuman, and I should say divine person – fate. The victims have been withdrawn for ever from the world's stage, the perpetrators of the crime will soon disappear from that stage, but fate still remains, and will be in the occupation of the stage of Providence. Look at these two young men, the conspirators, who are already buried under an avalanche of opprobrious appellations and curses, even of their own countrymen. They were, no doubt, patriotic in their own way, but ignorant and blind, unable to foresee that the deed by which they thought to prove their love for their country would recoil against their own nation. They have murdered the Heir-Presumptive of Austria–Hungary intentionally and his wife unintentionally; yet they have contributed nothing to the liberation of their country but have rather created a pretext to strengthening the chains which bind Bosnia and Herzegovina to Austria.

They did not understand that the cause of the Servian nation being a holy cause cannot possibly be forwarded by unholy methods. Every act of violence damages the cause in the name of which it is committed. The assassination of the Archduke could not weaken the Monarchy, nor could it strengthen the position of the Servian nation in Europe and in the world. Its effect could only be – and actually has been – rather the other way. No sensible Servian could for a moment approve of the deed. We can only deeply and sincerely deplore it. But no sensible Austrian, and no chivalrous Hungarian, could find fault with me when I claim pity with the misunderstood and misguided patriotism of those poor ignorant young men.

Let us now glance at the tragedy of the Archduke Francis Ferdinand. As a man he was not hateful and was not hated. On the contrary, personally he had qualities of heart and character and possessed abilities which drew to him, if not love, then certainly respect and admiration, even of his political opponents. He was one of those superior men who bravely do their duty – or what they honestly believe to be their duty – in all circumstances and in all dangers. He did not go to Bosnia to spite and intentionally, as some Servians believe, to irritate the Servians, but he went there to do what he considered to be his public duty. He died in the fulfilment of that duty. There is no honourable Servian who would refuse to pay his respect to a man who fell in the fulfilment of his duty.

We regretted the want of tact which resulted in the Archduke receiving the homage of the capital of Bosnia on the very day on which all the Servians were rejoicing because the fatal Battle of Kosovo was at last avenged by the Servian victories in 1912 and 1913. But when the news of the assassination reached Belgrade, the population of the capital of Servia spontaneously stopped all further festivities and rejoicings. It was, indeed, the capital of Servia which was the first to pay a voluntary tribute of regret and respect to the murdered archducal couple. With sincere sorrow we only reflected on the tragic fact that the Archduke should die a violent death in the capital of the provinces, the annexation of which was practically his work.

Of course, the annexation of Bosnia and Herzegovina caused the average Servian to believe that the Archduke was an enemy of the Servian nation. But in reality Francis Ferdinand was not an enemy of the Servians. He had much more sympathy with them than he had with the Magyars. His only mistake was that he thought that all the Servian countries could, and ought, to be united into a self-governing national body, under the crown of the Emperor of Austria. There is an additional tragedy in the fact that Francis Ferdinand should be murdered by a schoolboy belonging to the Servian nation, the very nation the union of which he was planning, in his own way.

The Archduke's mistake lay in his not being aware that Austria long ago missed her true opportunity of uniting all the Servian provinces into one autonomous national State under her double-headed Black Eagle. He refused to believe that the Servians had now advanced towards the unification of all their territories by their own efforts into an absolutely independent national State.

I think it hardly necessary to mention that the murder was not specially meant for Francis Ferdinand as such. He was murdered not because he was Francis Ferdinand, but because he was one of the representatives of Austria–Hungary. If any other Archduke, a less pronounced and defined personality, had been sent to the manœuvres of the Bosnian army, his life would have been equally endangered by the conspirators. The attempt was a political protest, written in blood, addressed to Austria–Hungary. Even as such it ought to be deplored; the more so as it was absolutely superfluous.

Austro–Hungarian statesmen know perfectly well what are the true sentiments of the Servian people in the annexed provinces, and they know, too, what are the sentiments of the Servians outside the Dual Monarchy. Russia knows them as well, and no doubt has acquainted her ally, France, and her friend, England, with them. I repeat: that horrible bloody protest was in no way necessary, and from the Servian point of view was in every way most deplorable.

Now I come to the still greater tragedy lurking permanently in the relations between the Servian nation and Austria–Hungary. I must speak with perfect frankness, which probably will hurt more my own people than Austria–Hungary, but I know that in telling the truth I am serving the best interests of my country. If we look closer into those relations we cannot help observing that they are ruled by a strange fatality.

A part of the Servian Press never ceases to decry Austria as the personification of diabolical wickedness and of deep hatred of the Servian nation. That is not true. The truth is that Austro–Hungarian statesmen are not guided by hatred of the Servians, but by the consciousness of their duty towards their own country. To keep their position in the Adriatic is absolutely a vital interest of Austria–Hungary. To preserve and strengthen that position they must keep and develop Dalmatia. They cannot develop Dalmatia and make it prosperous without obtaining a hinterland for her.

Looking at it from an impartial point of view, I do not see how the Austrian statesmen could have worked otherwise than they did. They, of course – doing only their patriotic duty – came into conflict with the vital interests of the Servian nation. The inevitable duty of the Servian statesmen was, and is, and for ever shall be, to work at the unification of all the Servian territories into one independent self-governing national State.

We Servians cannot possibly reconcile ourselves with the prospect that Bosnia, Herzegovina, and Dalmatia should for ever remain the provinces of the Austrian Empire. Part of the Servian Press likes to represent the Austro–Hungarian regime in Bosnia and Herzegovina as most autocratic and oppressive, impoverishing and demoralising the Servian people of these provinces. I think that Press policy is quite wrong, because it is not based on the real facts. In truth, Austria has done very much to elevate the moral and cultural level of these countries and to increase the prosperity of the people.

The truth lies in this fact: the Austrian regime may be ten times more humane, wise, and successful than it has been up to now, and yet the Servians will not be satisfied with that regime, simply because it is foreign, and they naturally desire to be their own masters. There is no doubt a serious and deep divergence between the vital interests of the Austro–Hungarian Monarchy and the Servian nation. It is a fatality, but it is a fact, and inevitably we must come one day to the supreme struggle for the great problem: to be or not to be.

That struggle would involve indeed such stupendous risks that it is clearly in the interest of both the Dual Monarchy and the Servian nation to delay that struggle as long as possible. I have just returned from Servia, where I had interviews with political men of all parties, the members of the Government, and the Crown Prince Alexander. Honestly, nobody there dreams of provoking a war with Austria. Everybody is deeply anxious that the Servian nation should have peace, a long lasting peace, which would enable it to heal the wounds inflicted by the last two wars and to progress in prosperity and culture.

Of course, in Servia as well as in other countries, there are irresponsible newspapers which trade in violent and bitter words and sensational outpourings. But in these critical moments Servia has for her leader a statesman of undoubted patriotism and great abilities, who has repeatedly during the past years given proofs of cool judgment, great moderation, and conciliatory disposition. I have no doubt that Count Berchtold and M. Pashitch will speedily arrive at a *modus vivendi* which will enable Servia and the Dual Monarchy to live as good neighbours and secure to those countries a long peace.

But to attain that happy result it is most to be desired that the Press of Vienna, as well as that of Belgrade, should earnestly try to restrain its exaggerations and its bitterness. Still more is it to be desired that Count Berchtold should not demand from the Servian Government what the patriotic leaders of a high-spirited and somewhat excitable nation could not honourably perform.

27 July 1914

WAR OR PEACE?

Servia's Reply to the Ultimatum

Although the outlook yesterday was exceedingly black, some slight hope was still entertained in diplomatic quarters that a conflict between Austria and Servia might be averted at the eleventh hour. But it must be admitted that this view was only held by the most optimistic.

At a late hour last night the following were the salient features of the situation which has arisen out of the Austro–Servian dispute: The Vienna Foreign Office on Saturday politely, but firmly, rejected the Russian request for an extension of the time limit.

On the same evening the Servian Government replied to the Austrian Note in terms which the Minister, Baron Giesl, declared unsatisfactory, hut which, as we state elsewhere, contained very important concessions.

Thereupon Baron Giesl left Belgrade with his Legation staff, and proceeded across the Danube to Semlin.

The Servian Minister in Vienna, M. Jovanovitch, has also been handed his passports, and diplomatic relations are thus broken off.

Yesterday's assertion that 'war had been declared' is inaccurate. It is possible that Austria may make no formal declaration of hostilities.

But it was expected that the Austrian army would be in occupation of Belgrade by yesterday (Sunday) evening. News of this step had not reached us when we went to press, and we learn that down to six o'clock, Vienna time, no overt act of the sort had been committed.

What is undoubtedly an 'act of war' was, however, committed on Saturday night, when the Servian Chief of the Staff, General Putnik, was arrested at Buda-Pesth, while en route from Styria to Belgrade.

He was released speedily on the direct personal orders of the Emperor Francis Joseph. But the arrest was an 'extremely grave measure', only 'to be interpreted as meaning that in the view of the Hungarian authorities a state of war already existed'.

The Servian Government has transferred itself en bloc to Kragujevac, a strongly fortified town almost in the centre of Servia. The King, the Crown Prince, and the Court have also gone there.

On Saturday afternoon orders were issued for the mobilisation of the entire Servian army.

In Austria–Hungary also a partial mobilisation has been commanded by the Emperor, who has, in addition, decreed universal martial law and the suspension of all Parliamentary and judicial institutions.

Various reports of Russia's intentions were current after the councils which were held by the Tsar on Saturday and Sunday. It was stated that orders had been issued for the mobilisation of several army corps or even that a general mobilisation was about to take place.

The truth really seems to be that down to the present Russia has not made clear her intentions, though she has let it be known clearly that she cannot watch with equanimity the crushing of Servia.

Feeling in Russia is extremely strong on this question, and it is held to be impossible for the Tsar's Government to hold aloof if once Austria commences military action against Servia in earnest.

It is in the attitude of Russia, indeed, that the danger of the present crisis centres.

The rumours of mobilisation in France are untrue. But the French Government is taking all necessary precautions, and will not allow itself to be surprised.

Kaiser Wilhelm has cut short his Norwegian tour and is returning rapidly to Berlin, where he is expected today. The German Chancellor and General von Moltke, Chief of the General Staff, have also gone back to Berlin.

'GRAVEST CRISIS' SINCE THE WAR OF 1870
'All Europe Involved', *Paris, Sunday Night*

All Europe today is involved in the gravest crisis known in this generation. I speak with full knowledge and some authority. I cannot say all that I know, or specify from whom my knowledge is derived. But I repeat that this is the gravest situation known by the present French generation – that is to say, since the Franco–Prussian War of 1870. I have consulted today in French official quarters and in foreign diplomatic circles in Paris. All views tally only too well. 'There are chances left for peace,' I was told in a French quarter. This I am bound to say was the most optimistic opinion I heard.

I do not want, and I should not consent, to be an alarmist. But even when one measures one's words as carefully as possible, one has to say that the present European crisis is much more dangerous than, for instance, that which followed the coup d'Agadir or – to go much further back – that which concerned France and Germany over the Schnaebelé incident. One hesitates to write the word war; for this would be a war such as has never been known before; but one has to do it.

There is no sort of pugnacity in the French people; there is no cry of 'La Revanche', and on this Sunday Paris is as peaceful as it could be. But it would be hiding the truth not to say that the most serious and tragic thoughts are in the air. I noted today how curious and, as it were, telepathic a communication there seems to be between those who know in Paris Government offices, the Foreign Office, and the War Office, and the man in the street.

I came from some of these offices, where despatches were being received, and where orders were being sent on every moment of this crucial Sunday, down to the boulevards, and found every little 'bourgeois', every waiter, every taxi-driver even, talking quietly and good-humouredly of what may happen by Tuesday next or thereabouts. One said: 'I have twenty-three days to serve in the reserves in September. Possibly I may serve them quite soon; perhaps tomorrow.' And the man laughed quite cheerfully.

I do not want at all to give the impression that this people wants war. The few demonstrations last night recorded below are very natural, and anyhow much milder than those which are reported from Berlin and Vienna. But I want quite earnestly to point out, first, with what perfect good humour this people envisages the most tragic possibilities, and secondly the extraordinary quickness with which they have guessed at a situation that can be understood really only by those who are more or less behind the scenes of diplomacy.

It is difficult to make the real significance of impressions felt. All I can say is that I have never before obtained from certain French official quarters so complete an impression of a critical situation in Europe and of resolution in France. The perusal of the French Press gives no idea of the real gravity of the situation. I have known many occasions on which the French Press and the Press of other countries also was Cassandra-like, and French diplomacy was cool and cheerful. French diplomacy is cool; but I am bound to say that it is not cheerful.

The following are the main points in the situation in French official opinion. Two chances of peace have gone, to begin with. Servia might have submitted entirely. Alternatively, Austria–Hungary might have accepted Servia's qualified surrender. Neither thing happened. The rupture between Austria–Hungary and Servia is an accomplished fact. In about a couple of days, let us say by Tuesday or

Wednesday, the question of peace or general war in Europe will be decided. Until Austria–Hungary invades Servian territory the path of negotiation will be open. If Austria–Hungary invades Servian territory by Tuesday it is 'inconceivable that Russia will not intervene'.

I had this opinion not only from French but from foreign diplomatic quarters in Paris. 'When Russia intervenes against Austria, then *la parole sera à l'Allemagne*' – which means of course that France and England will have their say also.

The whole point of the situation, and the whole danger of the situation, is this. Throughout the crisis of the Balkan war it was believed, and I think rightly believed, that European peace was preserved largely by the fact that a war arising out of Austrian plans of conquest upon the Southern Slavs was not at all the war that the German Empire wanted. Up till a day or two ago competent observers held the same opinion. Today that opinion has changed. It is impossible to avoid, and the French Government does not avoid, drawing the conclusion that the present crisis is the result of a deliberately planned scheme.

The assassination of the Archduke Francis Ferdinand and his wife was committed some four weeks ago. The Austrian move now is made at the precise moment that the President of the French Republic and the French Prime Minister and Minister of Foreign Affairs are cruising in Scandinavian waters, and at the precise moment that the Conference summoned by the King about Ulster fails.

Austria–Hungary combined the move with Germany. All authorities whom I saw considered it unthinkable that she should have acted as she has unless definitely and completely backed by the German Empire. If that be so, then the move is a German move, and the alternative prospect is a general European war or a humiliation of the Triple Entente. This theory was put to me today by a foreign diplomatist in Paris: 'The German Emperor thinks that the moment has come to strike a decisive blow. Russia is making strenuous efforts, but is not ready. France is not quite ready; but is making equally strenuous efforts. The allied Balkan States are still worn out by their war. In a few years, say three or four, their combination will amount to a formidable Power, dangerous to Austria–Hungary.'

28 July 1914

THE WAR CLOUD IN EUROPE
More Hopeful Outlook

The outstanding feature of yesterday was the announcement by Sir Edward Grey in the House of Commons of his proposal for a conference of the Ambassadors of France, Germany, and Italy with himself, whose object it would be to find some means of mediating effectually in the Austro–Hungarian–Servian dispute.

There is no doubt that during the past twenty-four hours the feeling of black pessimism which characterised Saturday and Sunday has given way to a more hopeful view of the situation.

Especially important is the statement of Sir Edward Grey that the German Emperor – who arrived at Potsdam yesterday afternoon on his return from Norway – had agreed to 'mediation in principle', because it is fully realised that, so far as Austria's attitude is concerned, she is unlikely to press matters to extremities if the predominant partner in the Triple Alliance expresses a definite wish for a pacific settlement.

So far as can be judged the feeling in St Petersburg is considerably calmer. This seems to have been in a large measure due to the interview which M. Sazonoff had on Sunday with the German Ambassador, to certain assurances given by Austria, and also to the less minatory tone adopted towards the French Government by Baron von Schoen, who obviously was acting on fresh instructions from Berlin.

While, as we have stated, the general outlook was last night regarded as less gloomy, the semi-official communiqué issued in Vienna accusing the Servian Government of bad faith and 'a spirit of dishonesty' in its official reply to the Austrian Note, has created an unfavourable impression, as signifying that the Dual Monarchy's attitude is one of unbending rigidity.

'Moreover,' says Our Berlin Correspondent, 'in German official circles it is still insisted that no action likely to hamper Austria in any way in the execution of her plans has the least chance of success, and that the next developments depend on Russia, as to whose attitude nothing definite is yet known.'

Significant in this connection is the view taken in certain Austrian quarters that the proposed Conference will have to deal not with the Austro–Servian conflict, but only with the question of preventing complications between the Great Powers.

According to what are described as 'authoritative and uncensored' telegrams received in Washington, orders have been given to mobilise the whole of the Russian army. There are good reasons to believe that this report is unfounded. In any case, Washington is unlikely to possess information that is denied to the rest of the world.

Military precautions of one sort and another are, of course, being taken by all the Great Powers concerned in the present trouble, but down to the present they are quiet and unostentatious; not more extensive, in fact, than might be expected under the circumstances.

The report of fighting on the Danube between Austrians and Servians is unconfirmed. The temptations to the Austrians to portray Servia in the guise of aggressor are obvious.

From Servia itself there is no news of importance, as communication through Austria–Hungary is cut off, and news can come but slowly by the indirect route through Roumania.

Great nervousness continues to characterise the financial world. The Vienna and Buda-Pesth Bourses have been closed for three days, an almost unprecedented occurrence.

The report that President Poincaré met the Kaiser on his way back to Paris is, of course, baseless.

THE CONFERENCE
Attitude of the Powers

The three important events of the moment are:

1. The publication of the Servian Note.
2. The delay of the Austrian declaration of war.
3. The announcement made in the House of Commons by Sir Edward Grey that the four Powers which are not directly interested in the present crisis – Germany, Italy, France, and Great Britain, are to participate in an Ambassadors' Conference, which will meet in London, in order to evolve, if possible, a middle solution between the opposite points of view held by Austria and Russia as to the Servian question.

The impression caused by the Servian Note in diplomatic circles here is very favourable. It is admitted on nearly all hands that Servia has practically conceded all that the Dual Monarchy required. But she has met with a blunt refusal of further negotiations. In less than forty-five minutes the Austrian Minister in Belgrade, Baron Giesl, had time to read the Servian document – a very long one – to decide that it did not afford a suitable basis for further pourparlers, to write a reply to M. Pasitch, and to embark in the train! These facts would suggest that on the Austrian side exists the wish to push things to extremes. On the other hand, no act of war has taken place so far, while it would be an easy matter for Austrian troops to cross the Danube. In some quarters it is concluded from this fact that perhaps the time is ripe for the mediation of the Powers, which, as indicated yesterday in these columns, has been maturing since Saturday.

As Sir E. Grey admitted very openly, the proposal for an Ambassadors' Conference of the four Powers is still in the initial stage of its progress. France has accepted it, and while expressing some reserve as to the procedure to be followed, Italy is inclined to sanction it. But, so far, the assent of Germany has been given to the 'principle' of mediation only, irrespective of the actual shape it would take.

At the present moment discussions are taking place between the Governments of the Triple Alliance. In the light of the latest developments they are reconsidering the decision arrived at between them in the course of the last few weeks. It is to be hoped that they will agree to alter them for the sake of general peace.

The main hopes of a peaceful settlement centre on Germany, and specially on the German Emperor. So far it is not known whether Germany has begun to exert her friendly pressure on her ally in Vienna. But yesterday she appeared to be distinctly more inclined to do it than she was on Saturday.

The order to the Fleet issued on Sunday night by Mr Churchill, and the tone of the declarations of Sir E. Grey yesterday afternoon, have caused great satisfaction in France and in Russia.

29 July 1914

CALM ATTITUDE OF FRANCE
Views on the Crisis, *Paris, Tuesday Night*

In spite of alarming or alarmist telegrams from Vienna, which have been showered over Paris all day, the French Government does not take the view that the situation is more serious than yesterday. The hopes of preserving general peace are still slender, but they are not less than yesterday. That hostilities between Austria and Servia are inevitable is a foregone conclusion, if by hostilities be meant the occupation of Belgrade by Austria, Austria having just officially declared war on Servia. Fortunately, the almost unthinkable consequence, a general European war, is still not inevitable. The following are the reasons entertained by the French Government, and in other competent quarters, for this modest amount of optimism.

First, it is not certain that Russia, though undoubtedly mobilising, will retaliate upon Austria if the latter occupies Belgrade. Russia may allow Austria to take that step. What Russia never will allow will be the crushing of the Southern Slavs by Austria. The mere occupation of Belgrade, which is defenceless, will hurt no one, and may be a satisfaction to Austria. After that Russia may step in and say, 'You have had your satisfaction. You have humbled Servia. That is enough. We can allow no more.' And Austria then may agree, without loss of self-respect, to negotiate.

The one certain thing is that if Austria goes beyond a certain point in her attack upon Servia, Russia must and will intervene. That means an invasion of Galicia by Russia, with Roumania most probably attacking next door. That means Germany compelled, not only by Treaty, but in self-defence, to take up arms for Austria. The first stroke in the defence of Austria by Germany must, of course, be an attack upon France. The German plan is a violent and sudden attack upon France, after which, it being assumed that the attack is overwhelmingly successful, Germany will just be in time to turn round upon Russia, always slow in her mobilisation.

Finally, all this means the British Fleet making a swift dash to annihilate the German. In short, the conflagration once lit, no one knows where it will stop.

The first reason for hoping that this inconceivable calamity will be averted is the fact, as explained above, that Russia seems inclined to forbear yet a little. The second reason is Sir Edward Grey's proposal for negotiations in the form of a quadruple conference, or in some other form. This proposal has not been rejected by those concerned so far. The French Government, which, of course, is entirely favourable to the proposal, has not lost hope that something will come of it.

Baron von Schoen called once more this morning at the Quai d'Orsay. The report got about that he had made a communication of a threatening nature. Six Socialist members of Parliament, with M. Vaillant and M. Jaurès at their head, called on M. Bienvenu-Martin, Foreign Secretary *ad interim*, to make inquiries. The Minister replied that the report was quite unfounded, and was the reverse of the truth. Baron von Schoen had, on the contrary, assured the French Government that the German Imperial Government had every wish to be conciliatory, and accepted in principle the British proposal with certain reservations. This statement tallies obviously with that made in other capitals, and with the announcement made by Sir Edward Grey.

There, is a third reason for believing that the peace of Europe, except between Austria and Servia, will be preserved. That is the firm attitude of the Triple Entente. The latter has made an ever firmer stand at each successive aggression – the annexation of Bosnia–Herzegovina, in which the Triple Entente made a very poor show; the coup d'Agadir, in which it possibly averted war by its display of energy; and thirdly the present crisis, in which the best argument for peace precisely is the obvious determination of the Triple Entente.

Sir Edward Grey's speech in the House of Commons is considered in political quarters here to be an admirable exposé of the situation. It is frank and fearless, and those are the qualities most wanted at the present moment. The final passage has produced the greatest sensation here: 'It must be obvious to any person who reflects upon the situation that the moment the dispute ceases to be one between Austria–Hungary and Servia, and becomes one in which another Great Power is involved, it can but end in the greatest catastrophe that has ever befallen the Continent of Europe at one blow. No one can say what would be the limit of the issues that might be raised by such a conflict; the consequences of it, direct and indirect, would be incalculable.'

Sir Edward Grey's intention is well understood here. The passage, first, implies the absolute 'solidarity' of the Triple Entente, and has thus given the greatest satisfaction to France. Secondly, it puts pithily and clearly the crux of the situation, which it was feared here the man in the street in England did not grasp.

A European war about Servia? The idea seems ridiculous. If the calamity does come, it will not be a war about Servia at all, but a war for the defence of the life interests of at least two of the Powers in the Triple Entente, England and France. It will be a serious matter for Russia also, but not a matter of life and death, as Russia, in the long run, must be impervious even to the worst military defeat.

I have already pointed out the astonishing quickness with which the man in the street in Paris grasped the real issues at stake, and understood that the quarrel between Austria and Servia was only a detail.

The President of the Republic and M. Viviani will arrive at Dunkirk early tomorrow morning in the battleship *France*, which I am told is making twenty-six knots or so on her homeward voyage. The President and the Prime Minister, on landing, will travel instantly by special train to Paris, and on their arrival M. Poincaré will at once preside at a Cabinet Council at the Elysée. All due military and naval preparations are being steadily made day and night by the War Office and the Admiralty. No details may be given, save such general particulars as that the railways, the bridges, &c., are guarded; the orders for, and material preparations for, the railway despatch of troops are ready, special trains are taking back all the men on leave to their respective corps, and military and civil authorities all over the country have their mobilisation orders ready to be sent out at a moment's notice.

It is significant that the French Press now publishes no particulars whatever of military preparations. Two Cabinet Councils were held today, M. Delcassé being asked to attend as Extraordinary Adviser, owing to his long experience of foreign affairs.

The Foreign Secretary *ad interim* received several Ambassadors, among them being M. Iswolsky, Russian Ambassador; Count Szecsen de Temerin, Austro–Hungarian Ambassador; and, as said, Baron von Schoen. The Parliamentary Commission of Inquiry of delegates from the Finance Committee and the Army Committee has adjourned *sine die*, after reporting that all the information received from competent quarters in particular on the subject of the state of the artillery and stores proved that recent alarms were not justified. This, of course, is an allusion to the recent debate in the Senate.

A large number of deputies are back in town, and Parliament could be summoned in a few hours if necessary. There is no idea of summoning it at present.

The French people is perfectly quiet and resolute, without of course wanting war. In contrast to the runs upon the savings banks reported from several German towns, including Berlin, is the absence of panic here. Small holders withdrew a considerable amount of deposits today in the Post Office Savings Bank, but the total is estimated at only twice the average figure. There has been no run on the banks at all. However, all payments are made now only in notes or silver, and gold is scarcely to be seen at all.

French police precautions are being taken this evening to prevent any demonstrations for or against war, as last night. In any case, the anti-militarist demonstrations mean nothing at all. It is significant, indeed, to read the Anarchist Gustave Hervé today, who comes out with 'Alas! our beautiful dream of an international general strike against war! Where is it now? We had dreamt of popular risings against Governments to compel them to settle their conflicts by arbitration. But here we are face to face with hard facts, and now every one of us has only one care for the moment, that of defending his native land against invasion, as his forefathers did before him.'

A non-Parliamentary Socialist group issues the manifesto, 'Down with war! By all means. But if our Austrian and German comrades are unable to stop the crimes of their Government, the duty of a French citizen is plain sailing. Like his forefathers of 1793, he must take arms to defend his country.'

30 July 1914

THE WAR CLOUD IN EUROPE
Increasing Gloom

The gravity of the international situation was certainly not diminished yesterday by the news which reached London of a partial mobilisation in Russia. Information to the same effect appears to have been received in official quarters in Berlin.

A private telegram received in London late last night indicates that Russia has definitely made up her mind to support the Servian cause at all hazards.

It is true that the mobilisation ordered is only a partial one, extending to four military districts out of twelve, and mainly threatening the Austrian border, but it is felt that Russia has taken a very serious step calculated to complicate the position.

Dr Dillon, in a message sent from Vienna on Tuesday night, but delayed in transmission, informs us that the Russian mobilisation will certainly be followed by similar measures on the part of Germany. This, of course, will necessitate France also putting her army on a war footing, but down to the present neither of these countries has moved, although it is clear that each has taken all the necessary precautions.

In Germany the Russian military measures are creating great uneasiness, and if the Government there receives official confirmation of the report it is not doubted that orders will be given to correspond with the Russian steps.

An ominous symptom is the virtual breakdown of the direct negotiations between Russia and Austria, which were looked upon with optimism in many quarters.

It is understood that England will now put forward a fresh suggestion for a settlement, but under the circumstances no very strong hopes are entertained of its success, in view of the Austro–German rejection of the earlier proposal.

So far as is known, the Austrian army has not yet occupied Belgrade, but we have received from our Athens Correspondent confirmation of a report, sent earlier in the evening from St Petersburg, to the effect that the Servian capital has been bombarded.

The town is stated to have been considerably damaged, and a banker, Andrevitch, was killed. The bridge over the River Save having been damaged, communications are cut off.

There seems no reason to doubt the accuracy of this intelligence, which has been received by the Servian Legation in Athens from Nish.

The venerable Emperor Francis Joseph has addressed a strikingly eloquent manifesto to his people on the occasion of the outbreak of war. Our Vienna Correspondent states that the octogenarian monarch is working fourteen hours a day with only brief pauses for meals.

In a significant address to naval cadets just promoted to the rank of officers, the Tsar made pointed allusions to the existing crisis.

Yesterday the Stock Exchanges, or rather such as were open, again bore witness to the gravity of the position. In London there were seven failures, and in all directions stocks showed the effects of the present international tension.

Food prices are also beginning to be affected, and in Vienna food riots have occurred.

31 July 1914

PEACE OR WAR?
Mobilising the Nation

'We are ready.' In these words one of his Majesty's Ministers referred last night to the present condition of the forces of the Crown, and the various services on which their efficiency would depend in the event of war.

'We are united.' This statement was made by another statesman. The party leaders have sunk their differences over domestic affairs, and it can be said with complete assurance that the whole nation – and indeed the Empire – presents a united front.

It is of the utmost importance that the bearing of these two facts should be appreciated, because they may have an important bearing on the issue of the present crisis.

It has been assumed in some quarters abroad that a Liberal Administration, which has reiterated its social aims, would not in any circumstances proceed to the arbitrament of war. Any conclusion based on such a hypothesis is – as the events of the past few days have shown – entirely unfounded.

Sir Edward Grey in his negotiations and the Prime Minister and Mr Churchill, responsible for the Army and Navy respectively, must, by their departmental actions, have dispelled the last doubts which may have existed as to the sincerity of the Government.

Similarly, yesterday's incident in the political field will convey to the world at large a sounder view of the Irish crisis than has been hitherto formed. By an almost involuntary movement all parties have closed their ranks. Politicians of all shades of opinion stand behind his Majesty's Government.

There was no break in foreign policy when the Liberals came into office in 1905, and today the Foreign Office is acting, not as the instrument of a Government of a particular political caste, but on behalf of the whole of the United Kingdom, and of the Empire, with its immense – indeed, almost incalculable resources.

During the present week both the Admiralty and the War Office have been working at high pressure. No act has been committed which need occasion alarm. All that has occurred is that a number of precautionary measures have been taken.

Thanks to Mr Balfour's foresight the machinery has been created in the past ten years which enables this country to pass almost automatically from a state of profound peace to one of complete readiness for any eventuality.

In accordance with plans prepared in advance, large numbers of orders, affecting every branch of our communal activity, have been issued by the Admiralty, the War Office, the Home Office, and the other departments of the State.

So well has the groundwork been laid that the process of mobilising, not the fighting forces, but the other services of the State on which, in time of war, those forces would have to rely for the defence of these islands and the Dominions overseas, had been brought last night, without commotion or excitement, to the culminating point when it could be said that we are ready for whatever may occur.

At a moment when the issue of peace and war in Europe is in a balance as delicately adjusted as at any moment for a hundred years, so that the slightest inclination in one direction may have the direst consequences, any Administration responsible for the safety of 440,000,000 people of the world which failed to place its 'house in order' would commit a crime against humanity.

It may not be out of place in this hour of grave anxiety to state that the organisation which has been so patiently created has been found to work even more smoothly and efficiently than had been hoped. This can be declared on high authority. Over confidence would be folly, but there is ground for satisfaction in such an assurance.

At the same time no minatory action has been taken. We are not at war, and cannot be at war until certain well-defined formalities have been gone through. Two facts may be borne in mind:

1. The army cannot be mobilised without a Royal Proclamation calling out Reservists. In spite of the measures taken this week, it is still on a peace footing.
2. The Navy, though it is its claim that it is always on active service, cannot be fully mobilised without a Royal Proclamation, which would bring to the depots for drafting afloat Royal Fleet, Royal Naval, and Royal Naval Volunteer Reservists. Without a proportion of these men the Navy cannot be placed on a war footing – that is, the older ships which constitute the Third Fleet cannot be supplied with full crews.

The First and Second Fleets are manned by active service ratings, and at this moment they are prepared, with coal and stores on board, to respond instantly to any order which the Admiralty may issue.

It is advisable that these considerations should be borne in mind.

The present position is that everything of a preliminary nature suggested by prudence and foresight has been done by the departments concerned – short of the issue of the Royal Proclamation. That final act, necessary for the mobilisation of the naval and military forces, rests with the King, acting on the advice of his Ministers.

If the terrible arbitrament of war is forced upon the nation, the usual formalities follow, including a message from the Throne to Parliament asking that supplies be voted.

Though we are confronted with 'conditions of gravity almost unparalleled in the experience of everyone' – to quote the Prime Minister's solemn words – we are still at peace, and no warlike movement of any description has yet been made by this country.

The nation stands united, and ready to face any emergency. The British people are on guard. That and nothing more.

1 August 1914

THE WAR CLOUD IN EUROPE
Waning Hopes

Although no official announcement of mobilisation has yet been issued in Germany, little doubt is felt in well-informed quarters that in reality the German Government is proceeding with that operation as far as possible without declaring it publicly.

France watches the situation calmly, but vigilantly. She, too, is making all preparations possible, short of actual mobilisation, and last night it was expected that the order would go forth as soon as definite knowledge of the German movements reached the French Government.

The suspension of telephonic communication between France and Germany on the one hand and Belgium and Germany on the other, and the stoppage of all international trains through Belgium at the German border are significant facts, pointing to what is going on in the Kaiser's empire.

The censorship over both telephones and telegraphs being exceedingly strict, it is, of course, impossible to obtain any really authentic information, but indications are sufficient in themselves.

It was stated yesterday that conversations had been resumed between Russia, Austria, and Germany, but our Paris Correspondent says he is informed in an authoritative quarter there that these conversations are but 'whisperings round a death bed'.

No doubt during the next few days many wild rumours will be current, but these must be accepted with the utmost caution in the absence of official confirmation.

The statements that either the Grand Duke of Hesse or Prince Henry of Prussia, brother of the Kaiser, was to go to St Petersburg to negotiate with the Tsar's Government are declared to be devoid of foundation.

The closing of the London Stock Exchange was followed by remarkable scenes in the City. The increase of the bank rate from 4 to 8 per cent in one day caused an enormous sensation.

At Liverpool, Manchester, and several other provincial centres, the exchanges were also closed.

Reports from all parts of the country indicate that the cost of food is steadily increasing. At a meeting of the London Flour Millers' Association yesterday the prices for certain qualities of flour were again advanced, taking an increase for the week of five shillings per sack.

FINAL CHANCES OF A SETTLEMENT
Austria's Conditions, *Vienna, Thursday (5.30 p.m.)*
By Dr E. J. Dillon

For the urgent humanitarian task which now lies before the non-belligerent Powers of Europe no coherent scheme has yet been worked out, or even suggested. The all-sufficient reason is that a concrete basis for common or individual action is still wholly lacking. The sole object of the Powers is to keep the hostilities within their present limits. This implied limitation of their functions entails abstinence from mediation between them. Mediation would not be attempted unless the mediating Governments had first obtained the assent of both Powers, and, as I announced from the outset, Austria's resolve to deal with Servia directly, without the intermediary of any foreign State, is immutable.

That being so, the momentous question arises, what attitude will Russia take up, and by what order of motives will it be governed? And as yet no adequate answer has been received, or even conjectured. To blame the Russian Foreign Minister for failing to elucidate this matter, as many Austrian journals have done, appears to be unwarranted. The Russian Ambassador here has had several conversations with Count Berchtold, during which each endeavoured to ascertain the intentions of the other in order, if possible, to strike up an agreement, not about Austria's relations to Servia, but about Russia's attitude towards Austria–Hungary.

But the Tsar's Ambassador, who had been absent in St Petersburg on leave, and only returned a couple of days ago, was unable to supply a comprehensive and precise answer. In all probability M. Sazonoff himself would find it extremely difficult to draw up a formula which would satisfy the Austro–Hungarian Government and yet leave himself adequate liberty of action in case of unforeseen contingencies.

And herein lies the crucial difficulty. By way of simplifying Russia's task Austria has announced her resolve to abstain from territorial extension at the cost of Servia or any other State. But Russia, on her side, deems this self-denying undertaking inadequate. For it leaves unsolved the question which for the St Petersburg Foreign Office is decisive – namely, in what plight will Servia be left at the close of the campaign? Will she be so crushed, so exhausted, so diminished in territorial extent, or so weakened financially, that, although independent in name, she will be crippled and helpless politically?

Now this query opens up ground which Austria–Hungary considers reserved to herself. Servia, for her, is an independent State and a belligerent, and, if defeated, will fare as defeated belligerents usually do fare. So long as Austria herself does not annex any portion of Servian territory no third Power can, she contends, meetly claim to have a voice in arranging the peace terms; consequently, Russia cannot expect further information on the subject. Beyond this point, which has not carried the two States very far, they have not yet advanced, but the conversations are still being carried on in a perfectly amicable tone between their representatives in Vienna and St Petersburg, and there is no reason to suppose either that they will not continue, or that they will necessarily prove unsuccessful. Indeed, there is more likelihood of their leading to a mutual understanding than there is of achieving this end by the combined efforts of the other Powers at this particular conjuncture. Later on the mediating States may find a larger and less compromising opening for beneficent action. But the indispensable condition is that meanwhile no military measures shall be adopted by Russia which would necessitate the mobilisation by Austria of the remaining eight army corps.

And although no mobilisation order has yet been announced in Russia, private advices affirm that certain partial military measures are being quietly adopted there which are the recognised forerunners of mobilisation. I am unable to verify these statements, and consequently I suspend judgment, but if Russia should mobilise, Austria and Germany will follow suit, and then only the most heroic faith could anticipate favourable results of mediation by disinterested States. It is, doubtless, in the light of these considerations, abstract and concrete, that the Hungarian Premier said in the Buda-Pesth Club, 'In spite of the best will in the world, I am unable to say today whether the localisation of the war is possible.' To my thinking this utterance on the part of a statesman who is one of the initiated, and has played an important active part throughout the crisis, is extremely grave.

Localisation of the conflict is still undoubtedly possible, but whether it will be achieved is open to question.

2 August 1914

WAR

German Kaiser and Tsar of Russia

Germany has drawn the sword. Last night she formally declared war on Russia.

The Kaiser's Ambassador has left St Petersburg with the staff of his Embassy.

Yesterday both the French and German Governments gave the order to mobilise the whole of their forces.

France's mobilisation began at midnight last night. Germany, it is believed, has been secretly mobilising for several days.

But it is clear that in each case the Administrations have been taking the fullest measures short of actual mobilisation in the full military sense of the word.

So far no rupture has taken place between France and Germany. The latter probably will await the decision of France, who will certainly go to the aid of her attacked ally.

Meanwhile, the German Ambassador was still in Paris last night, despite reports to the contrary.

But it is evident that his departure can only be a matter of hours.

As was announced exclusively in yesterday's issue by the Rome Correspondent of the *Daily Telegraph*, the news that Germany had sent ultimatums to Russia and France was reported from diplomatic quarters on Friday night, and the extreme gravity of the situation was therefore palpable even to the most optimistic.

It was also stated that the time allowed by Germany for replies was very short, and it was fully expected that unless these answers were satisfactory the German army would be mobilised.

That step was adopted by the Kaiser during the afternoon. At 5.15 p.m. he issued an order for the mobilisation of the entire German army.

Almost simultaneously the corresponding measure was sanctioned by the French Cabinet, and both armies are therefore now in the process of being brought up to their full war strength.

Exactly how long will elapse before this elaborate though highly systematised process can be completed is the secret of the military authorities concerned.

But it is generally supposed that it will take a fortnight.

Nevertheless, it must be remembered that on the Franco–German frontier each Power keeps several army corps always on what amounts to a war footing, and that in the event of hostilities being declared they could be in contact with very little loss of time.

In the case of Russia, the time required for mobilisation is understood to be considerably longer. That is to the advantage of Germany, who may strike at France in the hope of crushing her before her powerful ally in the north is ready.

The Austro–Hungarian army is also now in course of complete mobilisation.

The report current on Friday that Russian troops had already crossed into Austria is not confirmed from any sources.

Italy has taken a very important step in declaring her neutrality.

Throughout yesterday the diplomatic world was very busy. A meeting of the British Cabinet was held, and another meeting will take place today.

The King himself, it is understood, made a final effort for peace by communicating direct with the Tsar. The result of this intervention can only be deduced from the momentous event which occurred in St Petersburg yesterday.

Financial circles continue greatly perturbed by the condition of affairs in Europe.

The Bank of England rate has been raised to 10 per cent from the 8 per cent at which it had stood on Friday. The Stock Exchange remains closed.

Traffic to South Germany has ceased, and it is evident that with the mobilisation in progress travel to other parts of the Empire must also stop.

THE POSITION OF ENGLAND
Statement of the Actual Facts

The policy of Great Britain will not be affected in any way by the announcement that Italy has declined to remain neutral on the ground, as she alleges, that no *casus fœderis* has arisen for her intervention under the precise terms of the Triple Alliance.

This merely proves how brittle an instrument the treaty is, and Italy will have to settle later on with her own partners as to the justification for her action or inaction.

The French Government has never, directly or indirectly, been led to believe that Great Britain was pledged to any particular method of discharging her obligations to France, although she will remain strictly loyal to the spirit and letter of the understanding.

His Majesty's Government have not decided if they will interfere, or, if so, when they will interfere, in the European war which has now broken out. They have always reserved to themselves the right of determining how we shall play our part in the Triple Entente.

No particular course of action has been decided upon, although both at the Admiralty and the War Office various schemes of action have been worked out to the smallest detail, including the posting of officers commanding-in-chief, their staffs, and their subordinates.

The Cabinet will decide, in the light of events, what course England will pursue, but it may be taken for granted she will be absolutely loyal to her friends.

3 August 1914

WAR: THE SWORD DRAWN
German Declaration to Russia

Germany has drawn the sword. On Saturday night she formally declared war on Russia.

The Kaiser's Ambassador has left St Petersburg with the staff of his Embassy.

On Saturday both the French and German Governments gave the order to mobilise the whole of their forces.

Although France has not yet declared war on Germany, or Germany on France, the Kaiser's troops have already committed grave aggressions.

The neutral State of Luxemburg has been invaded by a German army and its railways seized.

Neutrality has been violated in the case of two other States – Switzerland and Belgium.

German troops have seized Bale Station, and a message received early this morning states that German cavalry penetrated as far as Arlon, thus entering Belgian territory.

At two points German troops have invaded French territory from Luxemburg.

German troops have also penetrated France at another point, and a telegram from the French Prime Minister states that two German cavalry officers were killed.

These acts have been perpetrated without any formal declaration of war whatever.

Russian troops in some force have invaded Germany and burnt a post office just across the frontier at Eydtkuhnen.

Towards England Germany's action is most provocative.

She has seized two British steamers in the Kiel Canal.

This, if the Government here likes to take it up, is in itself an act of war.

It is expected that the British Government will ask Parliament today for a credit vote of £50,000,000 for defence purposes.

As was announced exclusively in Saturday's issue by the Rome Correspondent of the *Daily Telegraph*, the news that Germany had sent ultimatums to Russia and France was reported from diplomatic quarters on Friday night, and the extreme gravity of the situation was therefore palpable to even the most optimistic.

Continental, and especially French, attention is now concentrated upon the probable attitude of Great Britain towards this conflict. England is vitally interested in the preservation of the neutrality of Belgium and also of Luxemburg.

Germany has already violated the neutrality of the latter despite her signature to solemn treaties. She may violate the neutrality of the former at any moment.

Questions have already been put by the British Government to Berlin on this subject. It is stated that the German Foreign Minister maintains silence.

The general attitude of the German Government towards Great Britain is sufficiently exemplified by her seizure of British steamers. This is an intolerable piece of provocation amounting in itself to an act of war. Down to a late hour last night the final decision of the British Cabinet on these grave issues had not been announced. It is expected that Mr Asquith will make an important statement in the House of Commons today.

All the naval reserves of every class have been called out. This will raise the personnel of the Fleet to upwards of 200,000, and will enable all the older ships to be placed immediately in commission. It is conjectured that the First and Second Fleets are now at their war stations and that the North Sea is for effective purposes closed.

As a result of conferences between the bankers and the Chancellor of the Exchequer it was decided yesterday to declare a moratorium or suspension of business.

Italy has taken a very important step in declaring her neutrality.

Throughout Saturday and Sunday the diplomatic world was very busy. Several meetings of the British Cabinet were held, and another meeting will take place today.

BELGIUM INVADED
Paris, Sunday Night

German troops are in possession of Arlon in Belgium.

By penetrating to Arlon the Germans have violated the neutrality of Belgium, guaranteed by the Treaty of London in August, 1839. England is a signatory of this treaty, and is therefore pledged to enforce its provisions.

At Belfort the German cavalry has penetrated a distance of 10 kilometres into French territory, and at the village of Suart, where the Mayor had requisitioned the horses for the French army. The Germans took possession of them and compelled the inhabitants to drive them themselves towards German territory. They were then checked in their advance by French outposts, 10 kilometres on the French side of the frontier.

4 August 1914

WAR: GREAT BRITAIN AND GERMANY
Strained Relations

England's attitude towards Germany, in view of the latter's threatened violation of the neutrality of Belgium, now becomes of paramount importance.

The German Government demanded from Belgium free passage for its troops through Belgian territory.

Belgium was given twelve hours in which to accept this ultimatum, but promptly rejected it.

England is bound under her treaty to defend the neutrality of Belgium.

In the House of Commons yesterday Sir Edward Grey made an extremely grave statement on this question.

He declared that the nation would stand by its pledges.

The British Navy is fully mobilised and on a war footing.

A Proclamation will be issued today calling up the Army Reserves and the Territorials.

That the relations between Great Britain and Germany are now strained to breaking point is sufficiently indicated by the speech of Sir Edward Grey.

Germany is exerting every possible influence, both overt and covert, to secure a free hand in her design of 'smashing' France.

It is in pursuance of the plan of campaign devised by her General Staff that she desires passage for her troops through Belgium in order to strike at the flank of the French defences.

She is endeavouring to secure Britain's neutrality to this scheme. But England is bound by most solemn obligations to resist, by force if necessary, such an international outrage.

And it is now evident that if Germany pursues her present policy nothing can prevent an open conflict between her and this country.

So far there is no confirmation of the report that German troops have actually entered Belgium, though they have done so in the case of Luxemburg, another neutral State guaranteed by Great Britain and other Powers.

Today the Proclamation will be issued for the mobilisation of the British Army and the embodiment of the Territorials. This step, of course, is a precautionary measure, rendered necessary by the attitude of Germany. It is clearly the intention of the Government not to be caught napping.

Further evidence of that fact may be found in the prompt and smooth mobilisation of the Navy.

German official sources deny that their troops have invaded France, but the news from French official sources leaves very little doubt that this act of aggression has really been committed.

From Berlin it is announced that German troops have entered Poland and occupied several towns after some slight fighting.

With this exception there was little or no actual war news yesterday.

The report of a naval battle between the German and Russian fleets in the Baltic is not confirmed.

Strict rules for the control of wireless telegraphy have been issued by the Admiralty. All private experimental stations must be closed at once.

It was no London that Londoners had ever known before that swarmed and swerved and roared last night all round the sombre majesty of the Houses of Parliament, clean-cut against a cloudy moonlit sky, the green and diamond curve of our own Embankment, the sudden space and splendour of the Square, and the long, lean, glittering avenue of the Strand.

The blaze of electric arcs up and along the huge stone secret-houses of Whitehall did but illuminate the throng to make its mystery more mysterious. It seemed no mere crowd. It was the massing, the almost visible massing, of power. Fearless, orderly, intent, and, above all other human attributes, at one – terribly at one – with itself, one-half of this gigantic nest of men that men call London gathered together into a most amazing and most splendid human pavement, that on it the feet of Justice and Honour might be placed.

There was neither much cheering, nor was there much of any other display. Awfully in unison, the multimyriad soul of London beat its single intention and its huge will towards and through the rooms and halls in which the directors of our fates even then were working and labouring, in the last and expiring hours of peace, for our good and for the good of that white Western civilisation which is nearly all that this turning planet has wherewith to claim mercy from God and from our own consciences.

If ever the minds and souls of men have been dominated, directed, strengthened, cheered, and set on a straight path of duty by the unanimous will of a united people it was last night. In the manner of radium, the clear certain encouragement of a restrained and determined populace pierced through the shell of carved stone within which the last great council of the proudest of all races was being held. London was speaking. She rarely speaks. Once on a cold January morning she bowed her head in grief; once she flinched before the horror of a December week; last night, beneath a clouded August sky of purple and bronze, she looked up and gave a clear command.

KING AND HIS PEOPLE

Patriotic Scenes at Buckingham Palace

Patriotic scenes were witnessed outside Buckingham Palace last night. Soon after 8 p.m. 5,000 people assembled, and loud cheers were given for the King and Queen. Just before going to dinner their Majesties appeared on the central balcony, with the Prince of Wales and Princess Mary, and acknowledged the salutations of the crowd.

Soon after they had gone to dinner a procession marched up the Mall, headed by men carrying Tricolors and Union Jacks, singing as they marched.

The procession took up a position outside the Palace, and the crowd, which had by this time increased to well over 10,000, sang 'Rule! Britannia!' and the National Anthem, while flags were waved with enthusiastic vigour.

As the King and Queen did not again come to the balcony the male portion of the crowd commenced to chant, 'We want King George' to the tune of the Westminster chimes.

In response to this demonstration the King and Queen made a second appearance, this time on the balcony outside the dining room.

The King and Queen were in evening dress, as also was the Prince of Wales, who stood on his mother's left. The demonstration continued for several minutes, and then the King and Queen, with a final bow to the crowd, retired to their apartments. The crowd sang the National Anthem and quietly dispersed.

5 August 1914

WAR: GERMAN ATTACK ON ENGLAND
Naval Vessel Sunk by Emperor's Warships

War has been declared between Great Britain and Germany.

But already, by the action of her fleet in sinking a British mine-layer and chasing a British cruiser, Germany had begun war with the British Empire, as she did in the case of France – without a formal declaration.

Before this she deliberately violated the neutrality of Belgium by sending her troops into that country.

Because the Belgian Government declined to aid and abet in this act of international brigandage she has declared war on the realm of King Albert.

His Majesty called on Great Britain to help him in his dire strait.

The British Government in its turn sent Germany an ultimatum demanding before midnight last night a definite assurance that she will refrain from attacking Belgium and will fulfil her Treaty obligations.

Germany has at last declared war on France, and her Ambassador has left Paris.

Austria–Hungary, strangely enough, has not yet declared war against either Russia or France.

A Royal Proclamation under the King's own hand was read by Mr Asquith in the House of Commons yesterday calling out the Army Reserve and embodying the Territorials.

These operations have already been begun, and the call to arms is meeting with a rapid and enthusiastic response.

The Fleet is already on a full war footing. The Army will likewise be so in the course of the next few days.

Relations have been broken off between Great Britain and the Kaiser's Government, war has been declared, and England is plunged into the greatest conflict since the Napoleonic era.

Germany's reply was awaited with the deepest suspense, but with the calmest confidence.

Inquiries in German diplomatic quarters left little doubt that the answer would be unfavourable. It was even thought possible that the German Government would not reply at all.

It is significant that Sir Edward Grey has requested the German Ambassador, Prince Lichnowsky, to call on him at the Foreign Office this morning, when, no doubt, his Excellency will be handed his passports.

In accordance with the notification given overnight, the Army is now being mobilised and the Territorials embodied.

Today all the British railways will be placed under military control, and a joint board of railway managers has been appointed to deal with the traffic arrangements.

Reports current yesterday of naval battles in the North Sea are officially denied.

The Kaiser has delivered a flamboyant speech to the Reichstag in which he repeats his amazing request for British neutrality if Germany refrains from attacking the French coast.

The censorship on the Continent remains very rigid, and no definite news arrives of what is proceeding at the front. It is, however, tolerably evident that nothing has yet happened beyond a few small patrol skirmishes. This remark applies equally to the Russo–German and the Franco–German frontiers.

Throughout the British Dominions a wave of patriotic enthusiasm has swept. In messages to the Governors-General of Canada, Australia, and New Zealand the King has expressed his 'pride and appreciation' of the offers of aid. Already Australia has come forward with the proffer of all her ships and an expedition of 20,000 men.

Germany has addressed to Italy what may be described as an almost agonised appeal to revert from her attitude of neutrality and join the other two members of the Triple Alliance in the war. The Rome Cabinet has flatly refused to do so, on the ground that Germany is not being attacked, and that a *'casus fœderis'* has not arisen.

THE KING'S MESSAGE
Royal Proclamation

Mr Asquith proceeded to the Bar, and there announced: 'A message from his Majesty, signed by his own hand.'

(Cheers.)

The right hon. gentleman then walked up the floor and handed a typewritten paper to the Clerk, who passed it on to the Speaker.

The Speaker read the document, which was as follows: 'The present state of public affairs in Europe constituting in the opinion of his Majesty a case of great emergency within the meaning of the Acts of Parliament, his Majesty deems it proper to provide additional means for the military service and, therefore, in pursuance of those Acts, his Majesty has thought it right to communicate to the House of Commons that his Majesty is, by Proclamation, about to order that the Army Reserves be called out on permanent service.

'That soldiers who would otherwise be entitled, in pursuance of the terms of their enlistment, to be transferred to the Reserves, shall continue in Army service for such period, not exceeding the period for which they might be required to serve if they were transferred to the Reserves and called out for permanent service, as to his Majesty may seem expedient.

'And that such directions as may seem necessary may be given for embodying the Territorial Force, and for making such special arrangements as may be proper with regard to units or individuals whose services may be required in other than a military capacity.'

When the Prime Minister rose to read the above fateful despatches the House of Commons became still as the grave. The only sounds heard were the calm, level voice of Mr Asquith and the rustle of the papers from which he read.

Sir Edward Grey was not present while his chief read out the text of his telegram to Berlin, courteous, restrained, but firm as steel. A loud, resolute cheer greeted the phrase 'this flagrant violation of the law of nations'. This cheer was renewed even more loudly when the request for an assurance was found to be accompanied by a request for 'an immediate reply'.

A murmur of surprise went round the Chamber at the jack-boot tone of the German reply to the Belgian Government's refusal of the 'well-intentioned' offer from Berlin. The reference to 'the French menace' caused an ironical laugh.

Then came the clumsy insolence of the despatch from the German Foreign Office to the German Embassy in London – with its cool suggestion that England entertained some mistaken distrust of German intentions, which might be 'dispelled', and its repeated accusation that Franco had planned an attack across Belgium against Germany. Solemn as was the moment, several members could not restrain an incredulous and derisive laugh.

The Prime Minister paused for a moment. 'I have to add this,' he said, in his strongest tones, and cheers broke out all round as he declared that the Government could not regard this as in any sense a satisfactory communication. And then he announced that the Government had that morning repeated their request for an assurance that the neutrality of Belgian territory should be respected, and had asked for 'a satisfactory answer before midnight'.

The House, of course, seized at once the import of the last grave words. The request was an ultimatum. As such it was loudly cheered. It meant war at midnight.

6 August 1914

LORD KITCHENER

It is with no common satisfaction that we announce this morning the appointment of Earl Kitchener as Secretary of State for War. We can imagine no decision more likely to inspire confidence both in this country and among our allies on the Continent, and we heartily congratulate the Government on a step which will add largely to the full measure of esteem and trust which has already been given them by all sections of the community. As a matter of fact, the appointment was suggested in our columns yesterday. Lord Kitchener is so clearly the man marked out for an office of this kind in such an emergency as this, that ordinary words of praise and approbation seem superfluous. His past record testifies in conspicuous fashion to his merits. The General who smashed the pretensions of the Mahdi at Omdurman, and who by his patience and thoroughgoing methods brought the lingering South African War to a brilliant close, has deserved and won the unforgetting gratitude of his countrymen. Lord Kitchener is, above all, an organiser, and we hope we may also adopt the French phrase and call him an organiser of victory. He is at his very best in carrying out all those laborious preliminary details and those minute and important arrangements and correspondences on which depends the ultimate success of an army in the field. He understands the nature of his human instruments; he knows how to choose his subordinates, in whom he can inspire unswerving obedience; he has an iron will, and is not moved from his purpose by any of those distracting accidents which often mar the resolution and spoil the judgment of weaker men. Nor is it the least of his recommendations that his name is famous abroad, and that France, in especial, in whose defence he originally drew his sword, will welcome his appointment as the best proof of our determination to see this weighty matter through.

Indeed, there is no more exhilarating feature of our present situation than the obvious absence of all party distinctions and the absolute unity of the whole Kingdom in the task set before us. We are none of us for a party; we are all for the State. Mr Redmond, with fine eloquence, shows how patriotism obliterates even deep-lying dissensions. Sir Edward Carson, echoing the spirit of his rival's words, offers us the service of his Ulster battalions. Mr Austen Chamberlain sits beside Mr Lloyd George and consults with him as to the best measures to cure financial stringency. Lord Kitchener is, of course, not a partisan in any political or other sense of the word, but he is chosen for a position of unique importance for the sole reason of his efficiency and his personal value. If the crisis has taught us nothing else, it has, at all events, graven deeply in our minds the necessity for union. We recognise with a curious sense of wonder how absolutely immaterial are the ends for which ordinary unthinking humanity strives as compared with that great end of all social and political life – the salvation of the State. The shock of a great episode in our national career has opened our eyes at last, and we now speak and move and take counsel together, not as Unionists or as Liberals, but only as Englishmen. And in the same spirit we welcome all fellow-workers – all those concerning whom we are certain that their heart is set on the same objects as ourselves. When Lord Haldane was reported on Tuesday to have visited the War Office, some peculiarly ungracious criticisms were passed as to the character of his claims on the mere assumption that he was to be War Secretary. We entirely dissociate ourselves from any such attitude, and deprecate hasty inferences and unworthy innuendoes. Lord Haldane probably offered his services, as others have offered theirs, in precisely the same spirit, and with all the more reason because of his large and valuable experience in military affairs. The State needs the help of all citizens, and rejoices in the many signs of self-sacrificing loyalty with which its claims have been recognised far and wide. The Government is England's Government, and its policy is the policy of us all. To the enforcement of that policy, to the carrying out of the stupendous tasks to which we are committed, no labour and no sacrifice, whether offered by Lord Kitchener or the humblest unit of our society, can ever be too onerous or too costly.

Chapter 2

The Western Front 1914–15

10 August 1914

GERMAN ATTACK ON BELGIUM

Spies and Treachery, *Brussels, Sunday (10.30 a.m.)*

By Dr E. J. Dillon

It is a noteworthy fact that during the fierce fighting of the past few days a disproportionately large number of officers as compared with privates were disabled owing to their distinctive uniforms, and among the officers were a disproportionately large percentage of surgeons, whose uniform is still more conspicuous. The War Minister's attention is being drawn to the advisability of rendering the outward marks of rank differences less noticeable at a distance.

The Belgian Government has decided not to proceed to the expulsion of Germans en masse, although the country is infested by spies and agents, who make desperate efforts to reveal and frustrate the plans of the military authorities. In the German Consulate and the German school wireless telegraphy apparatus were discovered. At Antwerp, where the Germans had for years wielded paramount influence, many of them repaid the hospitality shown them with perfidious hostility.

Two sons of the principal German firm in Antwerp, which has been established for over twenty years there, have been arrested on a charge of treason. Even the School of Aviation had trusted a caretaker of German nationality, who has occupied this and similar posts for eighteen years, and was discovered on Friday working the wireless telegraph apparatus. He was arrested, tried, and condemned.

Nowhere in Belgium were the Germans more at home than in Antwerp; nowhere have they proved such relentless enemies to their hosts. When quitting the city on Friday some of them exclaimed, 'We are going now, but we will return shortly escorted by troops.' The bitterness against Germany in Antwerp is intense, but there and throughout Belgium the German prisoners and wounded are treated with the utmost consideration.

The Germans, who were hospitably received in Holland, fed, and sent home, were not, as the Belgian Press believed, soldiers, but fugitive civilians. Holland has scrupulously discharged her duties as a neutral State.

The Flemish population of Belgium is making heroic sacrifices for the struggle, which has only been begun. The smiling suburbs of Antwerp, with their gardens, lawns, thickets, and luxurious villas, are being disfigured beyond recognition in order to meet the requirements of the military strategists, and the owners look on with grim approval at the destruction of their cherished property.

The narrative of how the neutrality of Luxemburg was violated is interesting. On Sunday morning while I was painfully travelling through Bavaria towards the Rhine the population of Luxemburg awakened to find all the ways of communication in German hands. Everywhere detachments of German soldiers were stationed, but what most astonished the simple-minded citizens was this – that the detachments were commanded by the employees of commercial and industrial firms established in Luxemburg who two days previously had been at their offices as usual.

Now, attired in military uniform, they were at the head of bodies of German troops leading them through the streets, directing them to places where perquisitions might be made or arrests effected, and giving them the benefit of their admirable knowledge of the town and people.

This they did with noteworthy results. Thus they denounced some 200 Alsatians who had not served in the German army, and who naturally reckoned on a safe asylum in neutral Luxemburg. These unfortunate men were roused from their sleep and spirited away, their appeal for humanitarian treatment being answered by violence or threats.

A German major who was first to cross the Adolf Bridge found his way barred by the Cabinet Minister M. Eyschen, who, having arrived in a motor, turned the car lengthwise across the bridge. Taking out a copy of the Berlin Treaty he showed it to the German officer, who remarked, 'I am acquainted with it, but have orders which I must execute.' Immediately afterwards the Grand Duchess Marie Adelaide drove up in an automobile, which she also turned lengthwise across the bridge, saying that the neutrality of Luxemburg must be respected, and that she would telegraph to the Kaiser, whereupon the major curtly answered, 'You had better go home quietly.'

The commander of the Luxemburg army, Vandyck, came up just then and remonstrated with the German officer, who retorted, 'If these are not your methods they are ours,' and, putting a revolver to his head, cried, 'Clear out!'

Soon afterwards the work of military destruction began, villas and farmhouses being demolished, and thickets cut down for strategic purposes. Terror reigns throughout Luxemburg since then. A farmer with provisions, being stopped and his wagons seized, grumbled. He was arrested, taken before a court-martial, and has not been heard of since. From Luxemburg to Rodange the fields are devastated, houses razed to the ground, trenches dug, and whoever casts a glance at these is arrested as a spy. In a word, the population of the Grand Duchy is learning the meaning of the words 'reign of terror'.

Military experts here hold that some days must elapse before important aggressive operations are resumed by the German army. They explain the miscalculation of the invaders as follows: Germany secretly moved forward about 900,000 men towards the Franco–Belgian and Russian frontiers during the week ending 2 August, with the object of being able to surprise and overpower the resisting forces at the very outset of the war.

In order to accomplish this stroke, which would have had an immense effect upon the morale of the troops, the men were despatched without adequate provisions or ammunition, on the assumption that they would find the former in the conquered districts, and could await the latter from their own trains of supplies, which would follow shortly afterwards. The reception at Liège upset this reckoning, and explains why the prisoners complained of hunger.

These unexpected reverses, which have given time for the junction of the French and Belgian forces, will now necessitate the definitive concentration of the German army, which includes the second line of another million men, and this operation is at present in full swing. It involves the mobilisation of the Landsturm, or Territorial Army, and according to trustworthy private advices received here, the officer commanding the Cologne military district has already called all the men of the Landsturm to arms.

In other words, a tremendous effort will shortly be put forth to burst through the Franco–Belgian barriers of the forts and men, and inundate France with German soldiers.

In view of this mighty tide of armed men and the relatively narrow area through which they must force a passage, it is nowise impossible that they may at the last moment choose a route northwards of Visé, and violate Dutch territory. This eventuality should be borne well in mind by those interested in preparing for it.

One of the curious methods of warfare employed by the Germans is the despatch of Uhlans in groups of six and eight, who ride for miles in advance of the army, enter undefended towns and villages, announce the arrival of the bulk of the troops, and return. It is amazing how far ahead of the army they advance.

On Friday evening they entered Arlon, and were received in silence, but when leaving they heard the report of a revolver in the principal café. Then, turning sharply, they discharged their firearms at the house, and one rushed with pointed lance against a woman sitting at a window. She was wounded mortally.

The municipal authorities, fearing further reprisals, drove out in a motor, with a white flag, found the commanding officer, and tendered their excuses, promising to punish the person guilty of firing.

General Leman was conferring with the General Staff when deafening noises were heard outside. A member of the staff exclaimed, 'This uproar is intolerable, we cannot go on working here.' He went to the door. The moment it was opened several revolvers were emptied into the group of officers. Colonel Marchand fell dead. Two German officers and six privates stood at the door.

They endeavoured to elbow aside the members of the Belgian Staff, the better to slay General Leman. General Leman cries, 'Quick, hand me a revolver.' One of his subordinates, a man of enormous size, answers, 'You have no right to risk your life, General.' 'I will, I must pass out to them,' insists General Leman, but the military Goliath, seizing General Leman, hoists him up above the foundry wall and drops him on the other side, and rejoins him.

From the windows of neighbouring houses the contents of several Brownings were sent after them, but the colossal officer pushed his general into the little workshop of the foundry, saving his life.

In certain houses in Liège many thousands of rifles, quick-firing guns, and harnesses have been discovered, which were presumably deposited there for German troops and German civilians, who had entered the city without arms, so as not to arouse suspicion.

In anticipation of the enemy's advance between Liège and Huy, which I announced as probable, the bridges of the latter town are guarded by the military.

Nobody is allowed out after eleven at night, and industrial works are closed.

11 August 1914

HEROIC DEFENCE OF THE FORTS AT LIÈGE
Germans Foiled

The following letter is of special interest, because it is the first narrative of the events of Liège sent by an English correspondent from his own personal observations. Mr Granville Fortescue was in Liège during the first two days of the German attacks, and then proceeded to Brussels, whence he transmits this narrative.

By Granville Fortescue

Liège, 6 August 1914

Last night and early this morning the Germans attacked this city in force. About 11.30 p.m., on hearing heavy cannonading, I crossed the river by the bridge Fragnée, and took position on the heights to the south of the city. It was full moon.

The German attack was directed against the forts at Fléron, Embourg, and Boncelles. The artillery practice was perfect. Shell after shell was exploded fairly on the ramparts of the forts. The return fire of the Belgians I could not judge for effectiveness, as the German gun positions were admirably concealed. The rough nature of the country and the darkness favoured the attackers. In my opinion no siege guns were in action. The Germans used a high explosive shell that burst with extraordinary vividness.

About 3 a.m. infantry fire broke out in the woods west of the River Ourthe, between Embourg and Boncelles. It was impossible to distinguish anything except the flashes of the rifles. About this time I heard infantry fire in the west. The country in the vicinity of the forts has not been cleared, and evidently only hastily fortified.

The Belgian infantry, 9th and 14th Line Regiments, held the country between the forts Fléron, Embourg, and Boncelles. The 9th Regiment bore the brunt of the attack, which was repulsed along the line.

With the first rays of daylight, about 4 a.m., I was able to make out the troops of the German line of battle.

They were fighting in close order. I could not believe I was watching the first line, as this seemed to me to be a return to old-fashioned tactics. But there could be no doubt as to their formation. The engagement attained its fiercest stage about 5 a.m. About this time the fort at Fléron was silenced. I was afterwards told that the German fire had smashed much of the machinery of the disappearing gun carriages.

Small parties of German cavalry could be seen in the intervals between the infantry battalions. But there was no attempt at a cavalry attack.

Towards 8 a.m. there was a lull in the attack. The accidental nature of the country to the south favoured the concealment of the Germans. I would not attempt to estimate closely their force at this point. It might have been a division. They were occupying the intervals between the fortresses, and had as their objective the bridges south of the city.

The attack was checked all along the line. Battalion after battalion was thrown back by the Belgians, whose 9th Regiment of the Line fought like demons.

My own adventures were many and varied. The most stirring was when I was held up by a lancer, who kept his revolver pointed at the pit of my stomach while I explained that I was not a German. Four times I was arrested and brought before the authorities. When I got back into the town the crowd that swarmed on the streets would one minute surround me and threaten me as a German, and the next loudly acclaim me as the first of the arriving English.

That was the question in every mouth. 'When would the English come?' The whereabouts of the French was another topic eagerly discussed by the mob.

Panic-stricken refugees came hurrying in during the morning, and continued throughout the day to flood the city. Wherever they could find listeners, which was easy, they would tell the story of their night's experiences. One woman with her two daughters had spent the whole night in the cellar of their home. A shell had exploded in the kitchen. Had any of her family been injured? someone asked. 'Yes, monsieur, the poor cat was dead.' A stout gentleman, with a pointed grey beard, was inconsolable because his 'collection of little birds' had been left behind at the mercy of the Germans.

This influx of frightened outsiders had a very baleful effect on the people of Liège itself. Naturally the discussion of the number of killed and wounded on both sides was the principal topic.

Motors carrying wounded soon began to arrive. These stopped before the hotels or establishments which had been turned into improvised hospitals. 'Fifteen beds ready,' 'Ten beds for wounded here,' were signs posted on the doors of many houses.

The news was soon current in the city that the fighting had ceased for the moment. There was to be a conference with the Germans.

The Palace of Liège was now the centre of attraction. 'The Germans demanded the immediate surrender of the forts and the city.' 'The Belgians had asked for twenty-four hours in which to consider this proposal.' 'The Germans refused, and threatened to bombard the city at once.' These and a dozen other rumours ran through the crowds.

Suddenly a loud explosion set every heart thumping. 'Had the bombardment commenced?' 'No, the Belgian engineers had blown up the arches of the bridge.'

But as the afternoon wore on it became known that the Belgian commanders had refused to give up the city. The bombardment was to begin at 6 p.m. That was the last word I got.

The last train out of the city was crowded with refugees fleeing with such little property as they could gather together. The scenes were pitiful in the extreme when the train pulled out. Never can one forget the expression of those left behind.

And the scenes in the train!

I carried a woman who must have been between eighty-five and ninety years old up the step of the vehicle and to a rude bench in a third-class carriage. A Sister of Mercy was her only attendant. Before we were half-way to Brussels a priest had given her extreme unction. Opposite me sits a man with four five-week-old puppies and the mother in his lap. In the next car are herded a score of German prisoners. The helmets covered with cloth. The insignia gone.

12 August 1914

IMPENDING CLASH OF THE MAIN ARMIES
First Skirmishes, *Brussels, Tuesday (5.55 p.m.)*
By Dr E. J. Dillon

It is still impossible to throw any light upon the military operations which may culminate on Thursday or Friday in a terrific collision between the forces of disruption and those of civilisation. For never before, not even during the Japanese campaign against Russia, have the movements of an army been shrouded in such impenetrable mystery.

Considering the number, audacity, and ingenuity of the German agents still in Belgium, these precautions may be indispensable. Anyhow, the War Office, which is the unique source of intelligence here, contents itself with a brief assurance that the news is satisfactory, or that there is no news of importance to communicate. Concrete facts we learn mostly from Paris or Holland.

Today it is learned for the first time that the first serious encounter between the main armies of combatants may be expected in a few days.

Another fact which is beginning to dawn upon the public is that the heroic resistance of the Belgian army was offered hitherto to covering troops only, and that the enemy's losses do not exceed 5,000, although three German army corps have been thoroughly beaten.

It is believed here that the hostile main armies may be ready any time after tomorrow night. Yesterday several detachments of their covering troops were sent forward to the Belgian advanced posts as feelers. The Belgians when possible concealed themselves in thickets or in fields, and captured a considerable number of the invaders.

One Belgian lancer, named Bogaerts, deserves especial mention. His habit is to sally forth alone, lance in poise, and dash forward against the Uhlans, one of whom he generally kills or wounds, whereupon the remainder give themselves up. In this way he has taken fourteen prisoners, wounded several Uhlans, and killed three, without suffering the slightest injury.

Even now encounters are frequent in the district stretching from Liège to Tongres, Hannut, and Tirlemont, whither two divisions have succeeded in penetrating today.

Already the airships of the different combatants float gracefully into the visual range of the Brussels population, but at such a height that one can only conjecture the nationality of each, and the authorities are warning the public neither to fear nor attack the Uhlans.

Anxiety respecting Holland's neutrality is not yet wholly dispelled. Nobody doubts the firm resolve of the Dutch Government to maintain its right to hold aloof from the war, but certain misgivings are entertained as to the adequacy of the troops stationed in the district where the violation of territory by the Germans is most probable. Suppose, for instance, the enemy should plan the invasion of Belgium from the north, after having entered Dutch Limburg. Are the means of resisting this encroachment available and efficacious?

Some months ago Dutch Limburg, possessing only a few squadrons of cavalry, was practically defenceless. Since then a number of infantry battalions have been stationed along the frontier from Maastricht to Venloo, together with several companies of the local Landwehr.

If, as many military men believe, these troops are the only obstacle to a German advance in Holland, they constitute an inducement rather than a deterrent.

German spies and secret agents are still numerous and audacious. Ten days before the declaration of war all trees near the sources of water in the forest of Soignies, outside Brussels, had notices pasted up in German, with the words, 'Potable water'.

The Mayor of Brussels had these placards removed, but today and yesterday they were found pasted up anew. This morning, when leaving the American Legation, I saw two municipal guards arresting a lady, whom they politely conducted to the police-station. My chauffeur cried, 'That's no lady. He is a German spy.' A couple of men hearing this rushed up and attempted to maltreat the prisoner, but the guards protected their charge effectually.

At the station the prisoner, who looked quite collected, was found to be a male German agent possessed of apparatus for cutting telegraph wires and also of compromising documents.

Belgian treatment of Germans, whether civilians or prisoners, errs on the side of humanitarianism if it errs at all.

13 August 1914

WHAT WAR MEANS

Terrible Scenes in a Belgian Town, *Cardiff, Wednesday*

A highly educated Belgian soldier, named Waroquiers, who has been in the thick of the fighting around Liège, sends to his brother, who represents a Belgian firm in South Wales, the following thrilling stories of the horrors of war: 'I shall never forget the sight of it. One hundred and thirty houses, and the church of Boncelles, forming one big blaze in the middle of the night, and the poor inhabitants helping the soldiers to destroy their own little homes and all their contents. I cannot see how our friends in Great Britain – I mean the people who have never been abroad to fight – can grasp the idea of war and all its horrors the same as we do. Our little country has always been the battlefield of Europe, and whether we had not to fight we had all the same to suffer the terrible consequences.

'It was about ten o'clock on Monday night when the peaceful inhabitants of Boncelles once more were abruptly reminded of the horrible significance of the word 'war'. An engineer officer, surrounded by an army of sappers, knocked at every door, and gave the message that the houses had to be burnt down to allow the fort to operate their guns without obstruction. There was no time to be lost, and those who liked could find shelter in the fort. While the officer was speaking the sappers were already bringing in wood, cotton, and petrol.

'The inhabitants round the forts are informed, at once and for all, that in time of war the necessity might arise for the fort authorities to destroy their houses, but in this case they had not been warned during the afternoon, and most of them had already gone to rest when the knock on the door came to tell them their fate in the middle of the night. I could not describe all the heart-rending scenes we had to witness that night. It needs a better pen than mine. All I remember is women in tears and children praying. Think that most of those women have husbands, brothers, or sons at the front, and now they come to burn their houses.

'And all they do is – weep. Some of them implore the soldiers to let them, at least, take some furniture away, and throw themselves at the officer's feet. But they are gently raised by the arm, and led outside in the dark. In the meantime the soldiers rushed in and threw bundles of wood under the staircase and poured petrol over them, and lit them. In an instant the house was ablaze. A woman tried to rush in and save some souvenir, a photograph, a cradle, anything, but was ordered back by the soldiers. Perhaps her own son was amongst them. It had started raining, and at some places the fire had gone out, but immediately the soldiers came on with fresh lots of cotton saturated with petrol, which they stuck through the window at the end of their bayonets.

'A man who had just been led out of a house, and who had been standing outside with his wife and children, watching with stupid look the progress of the fire, rushed away, as if mad, got hold of a mass of saturated cotton, and helped the soldiers in their work. The example had been given, and in a moment all the other peasants followed. At half-past ten the church alarm bell (tocsin) started ringing, and then at least fifty little homes were already burning.

'Then fire had to be set to the church of Boncelles, the old quaint church with the square tower, where only two hours ago the peasants whispered their prayers in solitude. Wood and cotton had to be heaped up as far as the altar, and in the tower as high as possible. A little later all that remained was a high burning torch, which soon listed over and came down in a cloud of smoke and flames. One hundred and thirty houses were destroyed in that way, and then all trees in the neighbourhood were cut.'

14 August 1914

FURIOUS FIGHT AT HAELEN
Belgian Bravery, *Brussels, Thursday*

Again the Belgian soldier has proved more than a match for the most highly trained troops of the Kaiser. The reconnaissance in force which the Germans attempted yesterday failed utterly. Two of their finest cavalry divisions and two regiments of Jaegers have suffered heavy losses in killed, wounded, and prisoners. The attack was made at two points, one to the north of Namur and the other near Diest, which is a railway junction.

About ten in the morning cavalry patrols reported the advance of the enemy towards Haelen, a village about three miles south of Diest. At the head of the force rode the famous 17th Dragoons; behind them marched a regiment of Jaegers with a battery of artillery and machine-guns. Belgian carbineers awaited them at Zelck and succeeded in checking the advance until they could retire on Haelen, which was formerly a fortress.

With reckless courage the Dragoons galloped into what was an armed cul de sac. In front of them was a battery on the mound of the fort, and the road was trenched and barricaded. The Belgians opened fire from buildings which had been loopholed to meet an attack from that quarter. Under cover of artillery fire and aided by machine-guns, the cavalry attempted to carry the position by assault. It was an enterprise that does more credit to the courage than to the judgment of the German soldier.

At manœuvres in Germany some years ago I remember the Kaiser asking Sir Ian Hamilton what he thought of the infantry formation. Sir Ian ventured to suggest that the formation was too dense. Whereupon the Emperor rebuked him with these words: 'Half of those men would be killed, but we can afford to lose them.' The cavalry seem to act on this principle. Without a pause they rode upon the barricade which they attempted to leap. I counted seven dead horses close to the barricade, while others lay writhing 100 yards off, bearing testimony to the bravery of two-score men who now lie side by side awaiting burial. So stout was the resistance of the 700 Belgians who held this position against a division of cavalry and a regiment of infantry that the enemy soon found it prudent to withdraw.

Not allowed to retire unmolested, though pursuit beyond Zelck would have been folly, they left behind about forty dead, many wounded, and 300 prisoners.

It is remarkable how readily some of these brave men surrender. One Belgian officer captured three officers. The first question they asked me was, 'What is England doing?' They were evidently ignorant that we had declared war. Their second question was, 'What of our fleet?' The wounded were treated not only with skill and kindness, but even luxury, which I have never seen among any other people.

The object of the raid was to feel the nature and strength of the opposing force, and, if possible, to capture points on the railway as well as to threaten the capital in order to strike terror – a phrase so often on the lips of their War Lord – into the heart of the people. But so confident are these brave Belgians that it will take more than a cavalry raid to disturb them.

A DESPERATE STRUGGLE
Brussels, Thursday (11.15 a.m.)

A more detailed version of the Haelen–Diest fight on the road to Louvain says that the encounter lasted all day. The Germans were supported by a battery of artillery. The Belgian field forces fought desperately, and Lieutenant Van Doren even enlisted the Diest fire brigade against the enemy, whose loss in killed, wounded, and prisoners was comparatively heavy.

Many of the prisoners were fainting, and the horses were dying from hunger. The German attacking party had probably been detached from the Liège right wing for an audacious raid on Louvain and Brussels.

Brussels, Thursday (12.12 p.m.)

The authorities here deny a rumour that King Albert while travelling yesterday in a motor-car with a constable in civilian clothes passed another car, probably containing Germans, who threw a bomb at his Majesty, who escaped uninjured, thanks to the speed of his car.

The Belgian success at Diest is confirmed. Two-thirds of the German forces there were put hors de combat.

This morning the Belgians attacked further to the southwards another big raiding party, beat them, and captured some machine-guns on motor-cars.

3,000 GERMAN CASUALTIES
Brussels, Thursday (5.33 p.m.)

Further details about the Diest–Haelen combat show that the German losses must have approached 3,000.

This morning's action, where the German *mitrailleuses* (machine-guns) were captured, took place north of Eghezée, on the road from Liège to Namur.

Of course, the main German forces continue to be arrested before Liège, but they send forth detachments in every direction to make believe that they have carried everything before them in their rear and create popular panics. Now each of these detachments is, so far, being beaten in its turn, and slowly weakening the large forces intended for the great general battle, and estimated at about seven army corps, or about 250,000 men.

18 August 1914

BRITISH EXPEDITIONARY FORCE LANDED IN FRANCE
Official Statement

The Expeditionary Force as detailed for foreign service has been safely landed on French soil.

The embarkation, transportation, and the disembarkation of men and stores were alike carried through with the greatest precision and without a single casualty.

The above statement was read to the Press representatives by the Right Hon. E. E. Smith, KC, MP, Director of the Press Bureau, at 9.45 last night. Mr Smith added: 'Lord Kitchener wishes me to add that he and the whole country are under the greatest obligation to the Press for the loyalty with which all references to the movement of the Expeditionary Force in this country and of their landing have been suppressed.

'Lord Kitchener is well aware that much anxiety must have been caused to the English Press by the knowledge that these matters were being freely described and discussed in the Continental Press, and he wishes to assure the Press in this country that nothing but his conviction of the military importance to this country of suppressing this movement would have led him to issue instructions which would have placed the Press of this country under a temporary disadvantage.'

As early as 8 August the French Government issued an official notification which appeared in the paper called the *Moniteur de la Flotte*, dated 15 August: The disembarkation of the English troops has commenced. The units which landed were greeted by the population with great enthusiasm. The disembarkation was quickly carried out, and in very good order, under the direction of French officers able to speak English fluently. The men rapidly took up their quarters. Their conversation showed that the exasperation of the English people against Germany is at its height. The British soldiers expressed themselves as delighted to come to fight on the Continent by the side of their French and Belgian comrades. The arrangements between the two staffs ensured that the programme of embarkation would be carried out in a perfectly regular fashion.

OFF TO THE FRONT
British Troops at Boulogne, *Boulogne, Friday*

Over the sides of a big transport towed and steered into the harbour by four tugs this afternoon appeared the high mast and wireless aerial of a British warship. Along the piers which flank the waterway there were ringing French cheers for the soldiers crowding the transport's sides and rigging, but the crowds dispersed before the ship of war steamed into port. And yet if the Boulonnais had known that a British warship, which had made what was probably a record passage from Dover, carried Field-Marshal Sir John French and the headquarter staff of the British Expeditionary Force, they would have turned out to the last of the old men left in the town to welcome the leader of an army in whose co-operation they place implicit faith.

Sir John French's unexpected arrival was quite in keeping with everything that has been done in Boulogne. No news is communicated. What the eyes can see may be believed, but, an individual must see all he knows, for confirmation of anything he has heard is impossible. It was no surprise to me to be told I was mistaken when I mentioned that I had witnessed Sir John French's arrival. The officer I spoke to knew I was wrong – 'because he had heard nothing of it'. Thousands of others would have laughed at me, though I had seen the gallant field-marshal on the after deck of the warship as she ran very rapidly up the fairway to the mail steamer berth. I was present, too, when General Daru, military governor of the Pas de Calais, the sous-Prefet, M. Brien, and the Mayor of Boulogne, M. Adams, greeted Sir John French on the vessel. And even when I explained that I had seen the British Army headquarter staff leave the quay courteously saluted by a people who honour a uniform, the statement was received with an incredulous smile, and it is doubtful whether one per cent of the people of Boulogne understand that the leader of the British troops is with them tonight. The Boulonnais will regret it, for the citizens were anxious to give a characteristically warm welcome to the military chief of their loyal allies.

That was why the crowd on the pier hurried round the harbour to see the disembarkation from the trooper rather than wait for the berthing of the trim, silent light cruiser. The welcoming of the warship was left, as the distinguished officers on board would have wished, to a couple of hundred frequenters of the quay, and British Tommies got the reception which a warm-hearted people would have been proud to bestow upon the chief of the army in the field.

Even the scene of the flower of British infantry paraded near the dock sheds was not as inspiring as one would have expected. There was no lack of real, genuine enthusiasm, but the popular delight at witnessing England's share in France's struggle did not find expression in cheering. The people here have sent their fathers, husbands, and brothers to the far-flung battle-line, and at this moment they may be in deadly grips with their enemies. They do not grumble at the sacrifice, but the peril of their relatives and their country's position prompt them to avoid great popular demonstrations. Thus they turned out to line the streets, to raise their hats to the troops, or to march with them to one or other of the great camps formed on the heights, hut scarcely a cheer was heard. But Tommy Atkins knew the reason, and seemed very proud of his friends.

The French soldier and his ally became good comrades in arms the instant they met. Men of the 7th Regiment of Infantry were on duty at the Bassin Loubet, where the troopships landed their freights, and so soon as the men filed down the gangways they shook hands with the guard and spoke of their pride in being able to give a supporting hand. Boys and girls clamoured for regimental badges and brass names from shoulder-straps, and many got the keepsakes. Some soldiers passed a professional eye over the French infantrymen, declared they looked hard and fit, and were of the right stamp for marching, but thought it was a pity they should have to wear long coats on a blazing hot day. The Frenchman in turn admired the physique of his British friends and closely examined their equipment, voting it well packed and carried.

I do not know when the information I am about to give will see the light of day. This letter has to lie for two days in the English military post-office here, because a forty-eight hours' censorship has been established, and it has to pass the English censor before it can be published.

No doubt on grounds of public policy it would be improper to give the number of troops already landed, or to indicate the nature and amount of stores put ashore, or the extent to which Boulogne is to be used as a base. These are secrets which the public may well be content to leave to the authorities, who, it seems to me, are working with an orderliness which could not have been surpassed if they had had six months' notice of the outbreak of war. In place of excitement and bustle, everybody seems to be doing an everyday job. The precise contents of every ship's hold seem to be indicated before the vessel arrives, and immediately troops have left the decks the cargo is taken out and carried to pre-arranged places in the sheds, where just the right amount of space is allocated to it.

Anyone who has watched the landing of the troops will understand the value of the lessons taught by the South African War. When the *Mombassa* brought two infantry regiments early this afternoon I saw three companies of each battalion march off the quay twelve minutes after the two gangways were in position. The men were drawn up on a sandy patch of ground near the docks which reminded the men of the Long Valley, and in less than an hour after the transport was made fast the two battalions were marching away to their encampment. The ship lay off the Isle of Wight, but from daylight no one on board had an idea that they had an escort until a submarine fully submerged was seen passing astern of the trooper. The incoming troops looked magnificent on parade. Most of the men were big, broad-shouldered fellows, who made light of their heavy kit, and they swung through Boulogne behind their bands as if they had been campaigning all their military lives. At the Hotel Bristol, the British military headquarters in the town, the Military Governor of Boulogne took the salute, and General Daru must have formed an excellent impression of the splendid contingents which landed today.

MODERN DEFENCES

Barbed Wire Labyrinths, *Dinant, 14 August (10.30 a.m.)*

By Granville Fortescue

Wire entanglements will be the special feature of defence during this war. You may have noticed in the accounts of captures of German scouts the captives are always reported to have wire-cutters as part of their equipment. The Belgian reports then go on to infer that these are for the sole purpose of cutting telephone and telegraph wires. While they serve this purpose yet I think that the wire-cutters are issued to the troops generally for use in the wire entanglements.

And judging from the country between here and Namur they will have plenty of opportunity for trying this distinctive article of equipment. The roads are a labyrinth of barbed wire. Every bridge over the Meuse is defended in a similar manner. The whole front is rapidly being protected by entanglements which will stretch almost without interruption from Namur to Givet.

I came in contact with a certain French line regiment shortly after leaving Namur. French outposts guard all the bridges over the Meuse. They have built the customary sandbag protection at all commanding points. The contrast between the Belgian soldier and the French is striking. The former takes his work most seriously. The latter meets every circumstance of war with a smile. The strain of picket duty at night, the travail of trench-digging under a broiling August sun in a uniform more suitable for winter than for summer campaigning, the sleepless nights of scouting are all matters to joke about.

I cannot give you any direct information on the disposition of the forces for obvious reasons. We are on the eve of the first encounter. If you look up the lines of communication on your map you will be able to make a close guess of the front where the main attack will develop. The cavalry screen which was so effective before the Königgrätz campaign and in 1870 is again being employed. But with aeroplanes everywhere circling overhead it is not easy to conceal the 600,000 Germans sweeping on towards the Meuse. Yesterday at Yvoir the French killed five Uhlans within a mile of the river. As I write the whole population rushes to view the bodies of two more German cavalrymen just brought in, and a couple of wounded French soldiers have come back from the advanced posts, all of which signals the coming of the battle.

Aeroplane reconnaissance is constant. How far it is effective it is yet too early to judge.

It is the fashion to surround the science of strategy with much mystery. Actually the whole foundation of military success has been picturesquely summarised by that remarkable example of the born soldier, the Confederate General Forrest, 'Getting the most men there first.' And it is on this principle that the Germans are at this moment operating. There is but one mistake that the Allied Armies must guard against – the mistake of allowing themselves to be attacked separately. Without doubt the enemy will attempt to employ the historic strategy of Napoleon, beating the opposing forces in detail.

I wish there were some special mark by which an Anglo–Saxon could be distinguished from a German. Instead of allies you might suppose we English were enemies from the manner in which we are treated. While I can excuse the circumstances which led to my numerous arrests in Liège, the constant surveillance to which I am subjected here seems unnecessary.

A squad of French cyclists have just come in with a report of considerable numbers of German cavalrymen in the vicinity of Ciney. It is the same story all along the front, from Namur to Givet.

21 August 1914

BEGINNING OF THE GREAT STRUGGLE
Example of Belgium

By E. Ashmead-Bartlett

The reports which are coming through from the front make it perfectly clear that the first great battle of the war has commenced. There have been encounters reported at various points, from Belfort in the south to Diest in the north. Everywhere the great armies are apparently on the move, and in the course of the next few days the first stage of the war will be definitely settled. That is to say we shall see whether the German offensive against the Allies is to come to an abrupt standstill, or whether the operations which are now commencing will enable them to commence their postponed attack on the French frontier line, Lille–Valenciennes–Maubeuge.

On Wednesday the Belgian Government issued an official communiqué setting forth in the clearest possible language the true state of affairs. This document will surely rank amongst the finest and most courageous examples ever given by a Government to its subjects in a time of grave crisis. In it is shown the determination of the Government to abandon temporarily to the enemy a large portion of the country rather than interfere with the grand strategic plan of the Allies. This quotation will surely become historic, 'To sum up one may say that what is going on at our gates is not the only thing to be thought of. A strategic movement, conceived with a well-defined object, is not necessarily a retreat.' It is the finest example ever given of taking a broad outlook at a moment when so many lesser men would have resorted to panic measures. How easy it would have been for the Belgian Government to have said to France and England: 'We have thrown in our lot with you. We have risked everything, and have made great sacrifices to resist the invader. Our people have suffered the greatest hardships and miseries without a murmur, but we can hold out no longer; you must send your armies to protect our soil, so as to prevent the enemy from occupying another inch of our territory.'

Such an appeal would have been hard to resist, but it would have meant sacrificing a preconceived plan of campaign to meet a temporary emergency, and the great result which the Allied commanders hope to obtain from the operations which are now commencing might have been lost for ever. But the Belgian Government has done none of these things. It has appealed to the people to suffer still more in order that they may obtain a lasting peace in the future. The people are responding nobly to this appeal. The Belgian Army, in the words of the communiqué, by its heroic defence of Liège, 'has caused the Germans to lose a fortnight attaining this result, which is all to the credit of our arms.' Yes, a fortnight has been lost, and fortnights can never be regained in modern warfare. These two examples, that of the army at Liège and the frank courage of the Government, should send a thrill of pride and determination to imitate through the heart of every soldier of the Allied forces.

The public are naturally alarmed because news has come through which seems to point to German successes in the north. We learn today that masses of cavalry are swarming over north Belgium, that Diest, Tirlemont, and Louvain have been occupied, and that the main Belgian army is falling back on Antwerp. We learn that further masses are pouring across the Meuse between Namur and Liège. This means that the covering armies are leaving Brussels to be defended, if it is so determined, by the 20,000 National Guards, who have been organised for this purpose. Brussels is not a fortified town, and can stand no siege. Its retention apparently plays no part in the broad strategic plan of the Allies, and only a certain moral importance will attach to its fall. On the other hand, every obstacle and delay placed in the way of the German armies may have the most important results elsewhere. It must be remembered that there are really three vast theatres of war in which armies are operating at the present time. In the north is the line of the Meuse, and the broad plains north of that river, with innumerable roads converging on Brussels. This stretch of country is ideal for the deployment of large forces. It presents but few natural obstacles, and there are no fortified towns or positions once Liège is passed. It is, in fact, the route which has long since been decided upon by the German General Staff as being the only practical one for the invasion of the northern frontier of France.

The second theatre of war may be described as that of the Ardennes. It is that vast stretch of woody forest land south of Namur extremely difficult for the deployment of large armies, and possessing but one line of advance for either the French or German armies, namely, that known as the Stenay–Longwy trouée, just south of the Franco–Belgian frontier, which enables a German army to invade the north of France or a French army to invade Luxemburg.

The third theatre of war stretches along the Franco–German frontier line of Alsace and Lorraine from Verdun in the north to Belfort in the south.

We receive but little accurate information of what is happening, but one thing is remarkable. We hear a good deal of the movements of the German and Belgian armies in the northern theatre of war. We receive General Joffre's official reports of the gradual forward movement of the French armies in Alsace and Lorraine, but the movements of the main French army which entered Belgium from Lille–Valenciennes and Maubeuge remain wrapt in profound mystery. That is to say, we are allowed to hear of what is taking place in the most northern and southern theatres of war, but what is taking place in the centre is rigorously suppressed. That there have been encounters in this district we know from the recent fighting at Dinant, and also from the report which is announced today of an encounter between the French and German cavalry at Florenville, which is on the Franco–Belgian frontier almost due east of Sedan.

If the information at our disposal is correct the Germans have not yet abandoned their attempt to turn the left wing of the Allies by a general advance en masse down the left bank of the Meuse. This seems a most dangerous move against armies of almost equal strength and with two million Russian troops concentrating on the eastern frontiers of the Empire. Already, without the intervention of any French corps, this movement has been delayed for a fortnight by the Belgian Army and the resistance of Liège. It seems impossible to obtain any decisive strategic result by occupying Brussels and north Belgium, but perhaps the General Staff hope to save their face before definitely surrendering the offensive, which they will eventually be obliged to do, and also the occupation of the capital might do something towards restoring the morale of the army which has suffered badly from the recent checks. At Liège we saw the remarkable example of a town being occupied while the forts defending it have continued for over two weeks to resist. The results from the occupation of the town were therefore nil.

Now that Brussels is occupied we shall see almost an identical state of affairs on a vast scale. Because if the German armies continue their movement south towards the French frontier, they will be leaving two fortresses on their flanks, namely, Antwerp on their right and Namur on their left. Now we see the immense significance of those words, 'The Belgian Army is falling back on Antwerp.' This means that the Germans are leaving an army powerful in numbers, and which has just proved its fighting capacity, right in their rear. This army can retire behind the fortifications of Antwerp, and either harass their lines of communication if they attempt to advance south, or tumble on their flank if they suffer a reverse and are obliged to retire across the Meuse.

Meanwhile the Allies are not remaining idly on the defensive further south of Namur. We do not know, and in any case we may not say, what role the British Army may be called upon to play, but remaining quietly on the defensive is opposed to all the principles of French strategy. Somewhere in the centre theatre of war a great counter-stroke is being prepared by General Joffre, but where the blow will fall remains a secret.

It will probably be aimed to separate the northern German armies from the armies and garrisons of Alsace and Lorraine by an invasion of Luxemburg, through the country south-east of Namur, probably by the Stenay–Longy route. Hence the significance of the engagement between the French and German cavalry at Florenville reported this morning. The armies in this quarter are already at grips.

Until the great counter-stroke makes itself felt the people of Belgium are being asked to make fresh sacrifices, and to allow their country to be overrun by the Kaiser's barbaric hordes. If we cannot employ our armies to aid them at once there is no reason why we should not assist them materially. They have suffered horribly and have had great losses. We in this country have already collected nearly one million and a half to aid our soldiers and their families. No other country has the means or the organisation to do these things. The moral effect of granting a lump sum from the Prince of Wales's Fund towards the aid of the families of the Belgian soldiers who have already fallen in our quarrel would be tremendous. We can spare it, and they need it.

A calm consideration and careful study of the map will show how little the Allies have to fear from the German advance into northern Belgium. On their right flank and rear they are leaving a powerful fortress, Antwerp, and a powerful army. On their left flank they are leaving another fortress, Namur. What troops they will encounter in their march south we do not know. But somewhere on the northern frontier of France lies the British Army, in addition to other French corps. Their left flank is threatened by the great counter-stroke south of Namur through the Ardennes into Luxemburg. Their eastern frontier is already being overrun by no less than 45,000 Cossacks, and behind this cloud of horsemen two million armed men are slowly but surely concentrating. A very big miracle will be required to make their offensive in the north effective, and only Divine intervention could make it decisive.

From the north and centre let us turn for a moment to the southern theatre of war in Alsace and Lorraine. This is the district in which General Joffre gives us such frank information about the movement of troops. Therefore it may be assumed that for the time being it is the least important, from the strategical standpoint, but highly important from the moral. No one need look for decisive results in this theatre of war for a long time to come. The great chain of fortified posts and towns, Verdun–Toul–Epinal–Belfort, along the French frontier, are faced by a similar chain of fortified posts, Neue–Brisach–Strasburg–Molesheim–Metz–Thionville–Guentrange–Illange along the German. Between the two is a highly difficult kind of Tom Tiddler's ground of mountainous and woody country, allowing little scope for the deployment of large armies, and offering every facility for the defence. The operations in this quarter must necessarily be very slow. They are rather in the nature of a series of small sieges of one strong position after another, and when the line of fortresses is reached the difficulties become almost insurmountable.

The German armies have shown no signs of taking the offensive against the fortified French frontier. There is only one route by which the French can pass in this quarter, that of Les Vosges–Metz, divided into two narrow passages by the marsh of Dieuze and the canal of Houillères, opening the roads to Sarrebourg and Sarreguemines. The Germans had intended to block the roads by constructing field works and a fort at Moncheux, but it is doubtful if they were finished before the outbreak of war. It is reported also that Moncheux has been occupied today by the French army, which seems to bear out that they were not. In any case no great forward movement having a decisive effect on the operations in the north need be expected in this quarter, because any army invading Germany by this route leaves on its left flank the fortress of Metz, which would hopelessly compromise its communications. On the other hand, the moral effect on the French people of this gradual forward movement in Alsace and Lorraine is very great, and that is why these movements fill up almost the whole of General Joffre's meagre reports.

22 August 1914

ARRIVAL OF THE ENEMY

A Calm Population, *Ghent, Friday*

By William Maxwell

Convinced that for the moment the active resistance of the Belgian troops was exhausted, and that the army must be content with taking up a strategic position that will enable it to co-operate with the Allied armies of Great Britain and France, and feeling certain that the entry of the enemy into the capital could not be delayed many hours, I left Brussels late last night.

Even then the citizens were without certain knowledge as to the military situation, though a vague uneasiness was apparent in all public places. To the eternal credit of the people it must be said that they betrayed not the slightest sign of panic, but faced their painful uncertainty with dignity and courage.

The Belgian army has won laurels that can never fade, and history will draw a moral from the glorious story of how this brave little nation kept at bay for three weeks the hordes of the Mad Mullah of Europe. The capital is proud of the army, and will do nothing to lower its prestige. Of that there can be no doubt.

The Civil Guard, of whom 20,000 were in Brussels, are uniformed men, and may be compared to our old volunteers. They had made preparations to resist the capture of the city, and had covered the approaches with trenches and barbed wire entanglements. But Brussels is not a fortified place, and armed opposition would have involved severe penalties. The Guard, therefore, withdrew from the capital soon after midnight. They retired with the honours of war, singing songs of victory.

For some days the citizens have recognised the possibility of having the Germans for their uninvited guests, and when Louvain was abandoned they accepted the inevitable. The spirit they have manifested is reflected in the dignified and courageous proclamation of their burgomaster.

At six o'clock in the morning the enemy's cavalry appeared at Tervueren, a distant suburb of the capital. From that hour every door was closed, and every window was darkened, with shutter or blind. From the outskirts people began to flock into the heart of the city, yet there was no panic-fear. At nine o'clock the capital was surrounded, but no entry was made until after two o'clock. The occupation proceeded with method. Railway stations and telegraph and telephone offices were taken over, and sentries were posted on all the main roads. The city, which was crowded twelve hours before, looked like a deserted city.

The Germans will naturally make the most of their victory, and will represent it as the defeat of the Belgian nation. But, as I said in my last despatch, Brussels is of no military importance, and its occupation will in no way affect the Allied plan of campaign. Neither the army nor the nation has been defeated. They are as determined as ever to destroy this military monster, and are as eager as ever to make every sacrifice for the common cause. Europe owes a debt of gratitude to Belgium, and will repay it one day.

HUNTING FOR AN ARMY
Well-Kept Secret, *Ghent, Friday*

By William Maxwell

'Where is the English Army?'

Nobody seems to care a bit where the German Army is – that can be found at any moment. But the English Army – where is it, and what is it about?

Hundreds of people have asked me the question – some in challenging tones, as if they suspected me of hiding the Army in my portmanteau; others in despairing tones, as if we had deserted them in their agony. But some have asked with a look and tone that make the coldest Briton hot with pride.

I, too, have been anxious to find the British Army. It was early, no doubt, but in these days, when the fate of kingdoms and of civilisation trembles in the balance, you do not measure time by the calendar. Instead of three weeks it is a year since the enemy of the world's peace invaded this dauntless little country, and though it is not twelve hours since I fled in the night from Brussels, it must be a month at the very least since the Uhlans rode into the amazed city. Like many other people, I am quite aware that an army cannot be mobilised in a day, that 60,000 or 100,000 men, with their equipment for war, cannot be transferred from one country to another in an afternoon, and that the official timetable fixes three weeks as the minimum time necessary for launching the British Expeditionary Force on the continent of Europe. But the hardest facts carry no conviction in hours like these. You look for a miracle. Who thinks of gathering the hemp and making the rope to throw to a drowning man?

So I set out on my quest, though reason told me I was pursuing a phantom of hope. And there were guides in plenty, for despair breeds rumours like maggots. Eye-witnesses affirmed that the British had landed in Antwerp, despite the neutrality of the Scheldt, which is Holland water. It had been seen at Ostend, and Calais, and Boulogne – at every possible port and every impossible seaside resort on the coast. You may imagine it impossible to hide 60,000 soldiers in a small country like Belgium, but you would not think so if you were here in the dense fog of war – in the most depressing and terrifying atmosphere man can breathe – this black, impenetrable fog, where you are conscious of mighty forces working destruction.

It is not the man in the street alone who puts that question. It is often the man who, one would think, ought to know. 'This silence is terrible!' exclaimed one in high place and authority. In long hours of danger nothing is more nerve-wracking than silence. I have seen its devastating effect in war, and those who would maintain an impenetrable silence will surely learn this lesson before the greatest of all wars is ended. Armies may manœuvre and fight in the darkness, but nations cannot live and struggle and hope.

Only one answer would satisfy these multitudes of anxious inquirers. It was this – the British Army is here, but its position must not be known to the enemy. It is a secret well kept. That satisfied as long as the heroic little army of Belgians could hold back the torrent from the East. But when the flood broke through all barriers and swept over the North once more the cry arose, 'Where are the British?'

THE DEFENCE OF DINANT
Fight for a Bridge
By Granville Fortescue

The following despatch from Mr Granville Fortescue forms the first independent account of the fighting at Dinant and the situation there from an eye-witness.

Dinant, 15 August

A considerable force of German light infantry, supported by mountain batteries, today made a determined attack on this town. The fight lasted from daylight till dark. Although the Germans had some success in the morning, the arrival of French reinforcements compelled them to evacuate the excellent positions they had taken.

The first shell just missed the clock above the railroad station, which marked ten minutes past six, and fell through the roof. It did little damage beyond shattering numerous windows. The railroad station is directly opposite my hotel. The second shell tore through the chimney of the hotel. The kitchen was filled with bits of bricks and mortar. The breakfast coffee was spoiled.

Captain X, who was here on a special mission, made his escape in a motor, accompanied by a squad of khaki-clad couriers on motor-cycles. The guests of the hotel scuttled to the cellars.

It was nearly seven o'clock before the infantry began firing in earnest. The only French troops in the town were some of a regiment of the line. The French had 110 artillery when the action opened.

The position was in a certain state of defence, which might have been improved. However, the streets were barricaded and a field of wire entanglements stretched across the bridge, which was also commanded by a mitrailleuse.

Dinant lies in a well, one might say, on both banks of the Meuse. High limestone cliffs tower above the town. On the east bank these are steep, and are crowned by an ancient fort known as the citadel. The fort dominates the whole adjacent country. On the west bank of the Meuse the town scrambles up a hillside, covered with trees.

When the engagement opened I joined Commandant A and Lieutenant B, who were in charge of the detachment defending the bridge.

At this time the Germans were making a strong effort to capture the citadel. It was held by a small French force, perhaps one company.

The cliffs resounded with the rifle and gunfire. The din and the falling shells drove the population en masse to the 'caves'.

Members of the Volunteer Hospital Corps, however, hurried along on their bicycles searching the streets for wounded.

The German mountain batteries fired with accuracy, although the small projectiles had little effect. I picked up the fuse of one shell, a Dapp, cut at 4,000 metres.

About ten o'clock the Germans held the crest of the cliffs across the river, and soon took the citadel. They sent down a veritable hail of lead on the defenders. Behind the cover of the bridge abutments the French reply gallantly. Thus the fight goes on for an hour. One hears nothing save the irregular explosions of rifles, the machine-like sputterings of the mitrailleuse, punctuated by the shock of shell-fire. It rains, but this in no way halts the firing. About thirty wounded are brought in when the French troops change position to the high ground back of the town. A sudden increase in the volume of sound tells me that the wished-for reinforcements have arrived. Soon a half-company of a regiment crowd into the hotel, expecting to find there a good field of fire. They bring with them a dozen frightened women who have been hiding in the station.

About noon the firing slackens, and the rain ceases. A few limping figures in blue coats and red trousers stagger into the hotel. A doctor stationed here gives them first-aid attention. While the lull continues a woman crosses to the pillar-box and drops in a postcard.

About one I return to my post of observation. The German flag has been hoisted over the citadel. This is a signal for renewed firing. The sight of the hated flag seems to rouse the French troops to fury. About 2 p.m. I hear for the first time the welcome sound of French field artillery. One of the first shots cuts the German flag across. Two French batteries have arrived, and they hail projectiles into the citadel with extraordinary accuracy. Another line regiment arrives to reinforce the troops here, and under a smothering fire I see the heads of the Germans that dotted the ramparts of the fort begin to disappear. At this time I also hear heavy firing in the south-east. About ten minutes before six I cannot distinguish a German on the ramparts. The only firing is some scattered shooting from the French side. A cheer greets the coming of another new regiment, and soon the French troops are back in the positions they held in the morning.

But the road back of the bridge is dotted with the dead. They lie in all sorts of contorted positions. Their blue coats are splashed with red, their red trousers are stained a deepest crimson.

And the cheers of the troops who have just arrived die down as they pass this grim testimony of what war means.

26 August 1914

BRITISH ARMY AT THE BATTLE OF MONS
Graphic Tribute of French Officers, *Paris, Monday*

Last night we received from Mr Alfred J. Rorke, Special Correspondent of the Central News, the following remarkable message, which had been passed for publication by the Press Bureau:

Graphic stories of how the British troops at Mons fought during the two days in which they bore the brunt of the main German advance reached Paris in the early hours of this morning, when officers arriving from the front reported at the War Office, and, in subsequent conversation with their closest personal friends, told of the wonderful coolness and daring of our men. The shooting of our infantry on the firing line, they said, was wonderful. Every time a German's head showed above the trenches and every time the German infantry attempted to rush a position there came a withering rifle fire from the khaki-clad forms lying in extended formation along a big battle front.

The firing was not the usual firing of nervous men, shooting without aiming and sometimes without rhyme or reason, as is so often the case in warfare. It was rather the calm, calculated riflemanship of the men one sees on the Stickledown range firing with all the artificial aids permitted to the match rifle expert whose one concern is prize money.

When quick action was necessary the firing and the action of the men was only that of prize riflemen firing at a disappearing target. There was no excitement, no nervousness; just cool, methodical efficiency. If the British lost heavily heaven only knows what the Germans must have lost, because, as one of their wounded officers (whom the British took prisoner) remarked, 'We had never expected anything like it; it was staggering.'

The British troops went to their positions silently but happily. There was no singing, because that was forbidden, but as the khaki-clad columns deployed and began to crawl to the trenches there were various sallies of humour in the different dialects of English, Irish, and Scottish counties. The Yorkshireman, for instance, would draw a comparison between the men they were going to fight and certain dogs that won't fight which the Yorkshire collier has not time to waste upon at the pit-head; the Cockney soldier was there with his sallies about 'Uncle Bill', and every Irishman who went into the firing line wished he had the money to buy a little Irish horse, so that he could have a slap at the Uhlans.

And the cavalry! Officers coming from the front declare that our cavalrymen charged the much-vaunted German horsemen as Berserks might have done. When they got into action with tunics open, and sometimes without tunics at all, they flung themselves at the German horsemen in a manner which surprised even their own officers, who had themselves expected great things of them. The Uhlans, whose name and fearful fame had spread terror among the Belgian peasants and the frontier villages of France, were just the sort of men the British troopers were waiting for. The Britishers, mostly Londoners, who, as Wellington said, make the best cavalry soldiers in the world, were dying to have a cut at them; and when they got into clinches the Uhlans had the surprise of their lives.

From the scene of battle, the point of interest in the European war drama, as far as England is concerned, shifted in the small hours of this morning to the railway station at X, where officers and men of the Army Service Corps awaited the arrival of the wounded – the British wounded from the firing line. Everything was perfectly organised; there was no theatrical display; the officers and men of the British Army waited silently and calmly for the toll of war, which they had been advised was on its way.

The station at the time was crowded with Americans coming to England from Paris after their release from Switzerland, and cheer after cheer, in which the French in the station joined, echoed under the arched roof. Britishers who were there felt very proud of their Empire and their soldiers at that moment. The men who were waiting for the wounded had not been in the first line of battle it was true – that was not their job – but their work was probably the greatest of all. It was for them to watch and wait, while every fibre of their inmost being thrilled to the note of war; and yet to restrain their desires while they practised that which the Iron Duke called the wonderful 'two o'clock in the morning' courage. So they waited in a draughty station for their comrades, thrown back temporarily from the scene of action, to fit them to return, if possible, immediately.

While the crowd waited for the wounded, train after train rolled slowly through carrying more of 'our boys' to the active front. They were sleeping in horse trucks alongside their equine friends; they were sleeping in cattle wagons; yet they stood up when the cheering reached their ears, looking fresh, fit, clean, and healthily British from their service caps to their puttee straps. All young, all full-blooded, all British; happy and eager to get at grips in what is to them a holy war. And then, at the end, as the boat-train was creeping out in the early morning, the wounded arrived.

It was my privilege to witness, on the road between Boulogne and Paris last Saturday, a scene as picturesque and deeply inspiring as a page from Froissart. The two English Cardinals, Cardinal-Archbishop Bourne and the Cardinal Abbot Gasquet, famed as an historian, had left London to journey to the Conclave at Rome. On the line the train in which they travelled was stopped, and by a curious chance a train in which a regiment including in its ranks a large number of Irish Catholics – these men, like the Plantagenets of old, wearing a sprig of green in their headdress – was drawn up for a moment alongside.

The Cardinals, who, under their cassocks, wore the red of their rank, stepped into the corridor, and, leaning out of a window, said together, 'May God bless you, my children.'

In an instant every Catholic soldier in the open trucks of the troop train dropped to his knees to receive the Cardinals' blessing. It appears, maybe, a simple affair, but in its spontaneity and sincerity, its mingling of the spiritual with the grimly material, it was eloquent and moving beyond the comprehension of those who only read what others saw.

FRENCH STATEMENTS ON THE POSITION
Heavy Casualties, *Paris, Tuesday Morning*

The Ministry of War issued the following communiqué at midnight: 'On the west of the Meuse the English Army, which was on our left, has been attacked by the Germans. Its behaviour under fire was admirable, and it resisted the enemy with its customary coolness.'

The French army, which operated in this region, attacked. Our army corps with the African troops in the first line, carried forward by their overeagerness, were received with a very murderous fire. They did not fall back, but later by a counter-attack by the Prussian Guard they were compelled to retire. They did so only after having inflicted enormous loss on the enemy. The flower of the Prussian Guard suffered very severely.

On the east of the Meuse our troops advanced across very difficult ground. They met with a vigorous attack as they left the woods, and were compelled to retire after fierce fighting on the south of the Semoy.

At the order of General Joffre our troops and the English troops have taken up their position on the covering line, which they would not have quitted had not the splendid courage of the Belgian army permitted us to enter Belgium. The covering line is intact. Our cavalry has not suffered. Our artillery has proved its superiority. Our officers and our soldiers are in splendid physical and moral condition.

As a result of the orders given the struggle will change its aspect for several days. The French army will for a time remain on the defensive. When the proper moment comes, as chosen by the Commander-in-Chief, it will resume a vigorous offensive.

Our losses are severe. It will be premature to estimate them or to estimate those of the German army, which, however, has suffered so severely as to be compelled to halt in its counter-attack and establish itself in new positions.

The communiqué then proceeds to deal with the situation in regard to Lorraine. It says: 'Yesterday we four times counter-attacked from the positions we occupy on the north of Nancy, and we inflicted very severe losses on the Germans.'

Generally speaking, we retain full liberty to use our railway system, and every sea is open for our re-provisioning. Our operations have permitted Russia to enter into action and to reach the heart of Eastern Prussia. It is, of course, regrettable that, owing to difficulties in execution which could not have been foreseen, our plan of attack has not achieved its object. Had it done so it would have shortened the war, but in any case our defence remains intact in face of an already weakened enemy.

All Frenchmen will deplore the momentary abandonment of the portions of annexed territory which we had already occupied. On the other hand, certain portions of the national territory must, unfortunately, suffer from the events of which they will be the theatre. The trial is inevitable, but will be temporary.

Thus, some detachments of German cavalry, belonging to an independent division operating on the extreme right, have penetrated into the Roubaix–Tourcoing district, which is defended only by Territorial forces. The courage of our brave people will support this trial with unshaken faith in our final success, which is beyond doubt.

In telling the country the whole truth, the Government and the military authorities afford it the strongest possible proof of their absolute confidence in a victory, which depends only on our tenacity and perseverance.

Day after day we have repeated the warning against excessive optimism in regard to the war in Western Europe, and the official news which came to hand yesterday will force home upon very many people in this country the fact that Great Britain is taking part in a struggle from which she cannot conceivably emerge without terrible bloodshed and loss. We do not make too much of the rough estimate of British casualties furnished by Sir John French to the War Office – 'rather more than 2,000 men *hors de combat*' since the beginning of active operations. As Lord Kitchener, in his first speech to the House of Lords, pointed out yesterday, European fighting causes greater casualties than the campaigns to which we are accustomed in other parts of the world; and the information from all sources is unanimously to the effect that the British troops engaged have withstood hard pounding with admirable courage, and are ready to meet whatever the fortune of war may bring with a spirit all the more resolute for what they have undergone. As to that, we publish today a despatch from the Central News Agency's correspondent which will make most Englishmen who read it flush with pride. The battle which has raged throughout the past few days in Belgium is beyond all comparison the greatest in which British troops have ever been concerned. No officer or man now with the colours has ever known warfare of the sort that is raging upon the French frontiers, or borne so tremendous a responsibility as is shouldered by the men of our people who are facing the German nation in arms. 'Our troops,' said Lord Kitchener yesterday, 'have already been for thirty-six hours in contact with a superior force of German invaders. During that time they have maintained the traditions of British soldiers, and have behaved with the utmost gallantry.' And at midnight on Sunday Sir John French had telegraphed to the War Office: 'In spite of hard marching and fighting, the British Force is in the best of spirits.' In the words in which the War Minister replied to that message, we are all proud of them. The task that they have so brilliantly begun will not be relinquished until German aggression has been trampled into the earth upon which it has recklessly and wrongfully set foot. So long as France remains upright, and so long as the British Empire stands unshattered, the fight for security and just dealing will be maintained in the Western theatre of the war, and the British soldier will renew on broader and yet bloodier fields the laurels that crowned him after Waterloo.

It is still, and it may for some time remain, uncertain what the precise nature of the fighting was in which our Expeditionary Force of today had its introduction to war on the great scale. But as regards its general features, the candid account published yesterday by the French Government makes it plain that the situation has hitherto been somewhat misunderstood. For reasons which the historian will be able to unravel, but which it would be waste of time to discuss today, the French armies of the north had never, it would seem, been pushed so far into Belgium as was assumed. They had not taken position in force upon the Meuse and the Sambre; their right did not rest upon the fortress of Namur; and the German armies were both to the north and the south of that stronghold before the great battle was joined. Namur, in short, was isolated; it was under bombardment by the German siege artillery; and it could not be succoured. Namur fell; but it did not fall as an indispensable resting point of the Allies. The French had, to put it briefly, advanced from more southerly positions in a movement of attack along several lines; a movement which was repulsed by overwhelming numbers. It was a movement which could not have been made but for the chance given by the gallant resistance of the Belgian troops to the invasion of their own soil. It has ended in a withdrawal, without serious disaster of any kind, to the defensive lines which the French leaders had originally intended to occupy; and the British on the left wing, who held the most advanced position of the whole battle front at Mons, have fallen back in conformity with the general movement of recoil. For some days now, it is stated by the French Ministry of War, the Allies will remain on the defensive. The battle has been of a wholly indecisive character. It has been obstinate and bloody, however; and every hour of it has been of fearful cost to an enemy which has every available man in the field, yet which has not even begun to reckon as yet with the Russian host now pouring steadily towards and across its eastern frontiers.

But neither we nor any other combatant of the German aggression can afford to leave this war to the slow and dragging decision of time. Every day of it is an added agony and an added danger. Germany has proved herself thus early an enemy prepared to embrace the most fearful risks of war; she is, as we declared some time ago, in a desperate position, and desperation makes brave men doubly dangerous. The supreme need of the Allies is greater numbers; and there is but one quarter from which that additional strength can be drawn. That is the population of this country. To end the war as soon as may be is the life-and-death interest of Great Britain, as it is of France. It will be a long war in any case. The longer it lasts the more fatal it will be for us. The greater military strength we can develop in the supreme emergency, the shorter it will be. We believe the time has come for resorting to the ultimate measure of national safety, and imposing compulsory service upon those of this nation who are fit to fight for its life and freedom. The ordinary process of enlistment, enormously as it has been stimulated by the country's need, and though it will probably suffice almost immediately for the pressing requirements of the Army, does not hold out any prospect of providing Great Britain with the reserves of fighting strength which may prove to be her only guarantee against destruction. We have to provide against all possibilities – all! And while the Empire stands threatened with nothing less, if things go ill with us, than incurable ruin, what proportion of our vigorous manhood is giving ear to, and acting upon, that call of necessity? Does the public realise that thousands of men with family responsibilities are volunteering for foreign service today, simply because they know that the country needs men, and that those who have none but themselves to protect and strive for are not coming forward fast enough? We urge it upon the Government that fearless measures should be taken to meet this situation. Modifications of the universal system which makes every able-bodied Frenchman a soldier may be possible in our case; we say nothing as to that or any detail. But the simple fact is that this nation is in the death-grapple with a foe which will know no mercy in the event of triumph; and if ever there was a case for the assertion of a country's right to the service of her sons, that case is Great Britain's now.

27 August 1914

BELGIAN REFUGEES IN FRANCE
Terrible Experiences, *Paris, Wednesday*

I have just seen a sight which brings home to one the horrors of war almost more really than the spectacle of the battlefield. Thousands of Belgians from Mons, Jemappes, Tournai, and Courtrai have arrived in Paris, and thousands more are expected. They have fled from their homes, starving and destitute, from villages which are now piles of ruins. One had read of the ravages made by the German troops in Belgium. The appearance of these unfortunate refugees surpassed anything that I had yet read.

The sight at the Gare du Nord was tragic. Women, small children, aged and infirm old men, some carried on stretchers, poured out of the station. They had left their villages last Sunday. They had to walk miles; to the French frontier, and they reached Paris by train three days later. Most of them had had nothing to eat for days. Not one of them had a penny piece. Many children were half-dead with hunger and thirst. The Paris population round the station received them with the kindest sympathy, and the authorities are doing all they can for them, lodging them temporarily in vacant theatres, public halls, and schools.

I saw policemen carrying crying and hungry babies in their arms. The newspaper women in the kiosks, who are not rich, gave pennies to many of the children to buy bread with. All the shops round the station gave food and drink to the Belgian refugees for nothing. One unhappy woman to whom I spoke had come through with three little girls, aged twelve, eleven, and the third a babe in arms. She had left her three sons in Belgium to look after her father, who is bedridden. By now her old father and her three sons are almost certainly dead. Her own village was razed to the ground, every house set fire to, and every farm destroyed.

Between 2,000 and 3,000 refugees who arrived from Mons by train at two o'clock this morning were quartered in the Cirque de Paris, and thither I went to see them. The Avenue Motte Picquet, on which the Cirque faces, and which runs between the École Militaire and the Esplanade des Invalides, was alive with groups of men and women, who stood round the fugitives. All listened eagerly to their tales of the ravages of the war.

The first group I come up against consists of a wretched peasant with a dazed look and haggard face, and his wife at his side with her eyes and cheeks all red from tears, and an infant in her arms. Two or three small children cling to her skirts. Two policemen and half a dozen people from the quarter stand around and question them. The man is too stunned by his misfortune to speak, and his wife alone is able to tell of some of the horrors they witnessed.

They had five children, and had fled across a river in a crowded boat with other fugitives. 'We thought we were all together,' said the poor woman, wiping the tears from her eyes, 'but when we got to the other side one of my children was missing, a girl of four. If I only knew where she was. It was impossible to go back and look for her. Just think, the shells were falling on the houses. I was in the house when a shell carried off our roof. I wonder we were not all killed.'

In another group a peasant woman from one of the villages near Mons tells a similar tale. 'It was on Sunday morning. Neighbours came running and knocked at my door and said, "Come away. The Germans are coming." I was going to take some of my things when the shells burst over our houses. I ran away with the others in terror. We did not know where we were going.' In other groups I find men who are telling what they know of the fighting. They are full of admiration for the British soldiers. Says one of them: 'You should see the English soldiers in a fight. What men! They don't care for the bullets. They would have licked the Germans had they been more numerous. They were driving the Germans back when we left.'

In other groups I hear similar tales about the English soldiers. The Belgian villagers speak of their courage and boldness with awe and admiration. As I come to the entrance of the Cirque I find a number of French ladies already busy helping the refugees. One French lady with white gloves and a veil drawn back from her face goes round speaking to the women. She asks one mother: 'Have you had something to eat?' and gives her a franc to buy bread. 'Have you enough milk for the baby?' she asks another, who is standing with a child in her arms.

As I enter the building two representatives from the Belgian Legation arrive to see what can be done for the destitute refugees. Inside the Cirque I see more than 1,500 tired and wretched people of all ages, men of fifty and sixty, women of thirty and forty, and children scarcely able as yet to walk, occupying the boxes, the orchestra stalls, which have not been removed, and filling nearly all the seats from the balcony up to the top of the amphitheatre.

Most of the adults have a look of helpless wretchedness in their faces. Never before, I believe, could a theatre have presented a sight of more real human misery. One turns away with a heart too oppressed for words. A young woman seated in a stall buries her face in her hands.

Her aunt, a peasant woman, also in tears, tries to console her. She says to me: 'We have lost everything. Our house was on fire when we left. The Germans shot her husband and her father, and she was married only a month ago.'

28 August 1914

SITUATION AT THE FRONT
The Fog of War

By E. Ashmead-Bartlett

Every day it becomes increasingly difficult to understand what is happening along the French frontier. The news which filters through is vague and contradictory in the extreme. All information as to the positions of the French main armies of the north is rigorously suppressed, and we are merely informed that the British army has again retired, and has been engaged again today with the German forces. It appears from the official communiqué published in Paris on Wednesday night that the British army retired south-west from Mons, and was holding a line from Cambrai to Le Cateau. This position was some 40 miles south-west of Mons, in rear of the French fortified line Douai–Valenciennes–Maubeuge. The French armies which fought at Charleroi are also reported to have retired.

The deduction which the official communiqué draws from this fact is that both sides were resting yesterday after their strenuous exertions. However, it is obvious that as the extreme left wing held by the British had been engaged all day, and had been obliged to fall back on the line Cambrai–Le Cateau, that the Germans are very active in this quarter, and were still engaged in trying to turn the Allies' left.

We do not know whether this wide sweeping movement is being seriously carried out by several army corps, or whether it has been confined to cavalry raids for the purpose of creating a panic in the north of France, perhaps in the hope of forcing the Allies to abandon their position in front of the German main armies. Their cavalry have been reported south of Lille, between Douai and Cambrai, ravaging the country and burning villages. These raids are reported to have been repulsed with heavy loss, probably by French Territorial Reserves. Lille, which was reported to have been occupied yesterday, is apparently still in French hands, although for the time being isolated from the main armies.

Of the fresh positions taken up by the three French armies of the north we know nothing definite. The army which was repulsed at Charleroi has fallen back. The other two armies – namely, those which entered the Ardennes from Sedan and north Woëvre – have also, apparently, fallen back, and have not been engaged since Sunday. In view of the great strength disclosed by the German right wing and the impossibility of making a successful counter-attack to the east of the Meuse, the army of Sedan has probably been moved by rail further west to join up with the army of Chimay, which has fallen back behind Maubeuge. This would seem the only practical step now that the offensive has been definitely abandoned, and the Allies' efforts are being concentrated on a defence of the French frontier. Therefore, as far as it is possible to judge anything from the meagre details which we are allowed to know, the French armies held on Tuesday the line behind Valenciennes–Maubeuge–Hirson–Mézières, with the extreme left wing held by the British thrown considerably back between Cambrai and Le Cateau to check any effort of the Germans to turn the left flank of the fortified line of the frontier and the main battle position.

Apparently, although all details are lacking, the Germans have made a great effort to break through the French line between Nancy and the Vosges, but have been repulsed everywhere except on the extreme right, where the French were obliged to retire to St Die.

But it is waste of time to attempt even to follow the fortunes of the combatants in Alsace and Lorraine. They fluctuate like a stock market during a panic. One day the French are everywhere victorious, and the next they are apologising to the unfortunate inhabitants for being obliged to withdraw temporarily. The operations in this quarter are of small importance compared to those along the northern frontier, and the result of the next battle in the north will decide the future operations on the eastern frontier. The whole situation will clear up in the course of the next few days; we cannot go on being left indefinitely in the dark.

The inner history of these operations will make interesting reading some years from now. A great many important points will have to be cleared up which are at present inexplicable. For instance, how is it the Allies have been so badly served by their aeroplane service, if it is true, as officially reported, that the unexpected strength of the German army took the French General Staff completely by surprise when they attempted the abortive forward movement last Sunday from Chimay to Charleroi? How is it that absolutely nothing was definitely known of the strength of the German right wing, which was only held back by the strenuous resistance of the British Army? Why is it the German cavalry has been allowed an absolutely free hand to overrun the whole of Belgium and the north of France, thus causing something like a panic and perhaps forcing a withdrawal of the Allies' left wing? What has become of the masses of French cavalry on which so much reliance was placed, and whose brilliant operations have been the feature of all their manœuvres of recent years? Surely no more favourable ground could be found for the employment of these independent cavalry divisions than the north of France and plains of Belgium? Yet we read of these continuous German cavalry raids and of the immense screen of horsemen which have concealed the movements of the main armies since they entered Belgium without any corresponding effort on the part of the French cavalry to check them.

29 August 1914

BRITISH WOUNDED AT SOUTHAMPTON

Soldiers' Stories of the Fighting, *Southampton, Friday Night*

The first batch of wounded soldiers arrived at Netley tonight, whither they had come from Southampton Docks by the hospital train. I chanced to be on the little covered and well-lighted platform that runs alongside the great and noble institution when the train, having sent up a whistling shriek by way of announcing its coming, hove into sight. I was one of a quiet band of people who had waited silently for many long hours for the arrival of the disabled soldiers who had fought so heroically last weekend.

Colonel Lucas and staff were all in readiness. Here were wheeling chairs, there stretchers. Not one thing likely to be of service was missing. The preparations for the reception of the broken Tommies could not have been better, more elaborate, or more human.

It was the humanity of it all – the quiet consideration that told of complete preparedness – that made not the least moving chapter of the story that I have to tell. And out of the train stern-faced men began to hobble, many with their arms in a sling.

Here was a hairless-faced, boyish-looking fellow, with his head enveloped in snowy white bandages; his cheeks were red and healthy, his eyes bright and twinkling. There was pain written across his young face, but he walked erect and puffed away at a cigarette. One man, with arms half clinging round the neck of two injured comrades, went limping to the reception room, his foot the size of three, and as he went by he smiled and joked because he could only just manage to get along.

When the last of the soldiers able to walk found his way into the hospital, there to be refreshed with tea or coffee or soup, before sending him to this or that ward, the more seriously wounded were carried from the train. How patient, how uncomplaining were these fellows! One, stretched out on a mattress, with his foot smashed, chatted and smoked until his turn came to be wheeled away. And when the last of these wounded heroes had been lifted out of the train I took myself to the reception room, and there heard many stories that, though related with the simplicity of the true soldier, were wonderful.

The wounded men were of all regiments and spoke all dialects. They were travel-stained and immensely tired. Pain had eaten deep lines into many of their faces, but there were no really doleful faces. They were faces that seemed to say: 'Here we are; what does it all matter; it is good to be alive; it might have been worse.'

I sat beside a private, named Cox. An old warrior he looked. His fine square jaw was black with wire-like whiskers. His eyes shone with the fire of the man who had suffered, so it seemed, some dreadful nightmare.

'And you would have me tell you all about it. Well, believe me, it was just hell. I have been through the Boxer campaign; I went through the Boer War, but I have never seen anything so terrible as that which happened last Sunday. It all happened so sudden. We believed that the Gentians were some 15 miles away, and all at once they opened fire upon us with their big guns.

'Let me tell you what happened to the ----. When a roll call of my company was taken, there were only three of us answered, me and two others.' Cox, when he had stilled his emotion, went on with his story. 'So unexpected and so terrible was the attack of the enemy, and so overwhelming were their numbers, that there was no withstanding it.'

Before fire was opened a German aeroplane flew over our troops, and the deduction which Private Cox and several of his comrades with whom I chatted made was that the aeroplane was used as a sort of index to the precise locality of our soldiers, and, further, that the Germans, so accurate was their gunnery, had been over this particular battlefield before they struck a blow, and so had acquired an intimate knowledge of the country. Trenches that were dug by our men served as little protection from the fire.

Said Cox: 'No man could have lived against such a murderous attack. There was a rain of lead, a deluge of lead, and, talk about being surprised, well, I can hardly realise that, and still less believe what happened.'

By the side of Cox sat a lean, fair-haired, freckle-faced private. 'That's right,' he said, by way of corroborating Cox. 'They were fair devils,' chimed in an Irishman, who later told me that he came from Connemara. 'You could do nothing with them, but I say they are no d---- good as riflemen.'

'No, they're not, Mike,' ventured a youth. 'We got within 400 yards of them, and they couldn't hit us.'

'But,' broke in the man of Connemara, 'they are devils with the big guns, and their aim was mighty good, too. If it had not been they wouldn't have damaged us as they have done.'

A few yards away was another soldier, also seated in a wheeling chair, with a crippled leg – a big fine fellow he was. He told me his corps had been ambushed, and that out of 120 only something like twenty survived.

On all hands I heard all too much to show, that the battle of Mons was a desperate affair. Two regiments suffered badly, but there was no marked disposition on the part of any of the soldiers with whom I chatted to enlarge upon the happenings of last weekend. Rather would they talk more freely of the awful atrocities perpetrated by the Germans.

'Too awful for words,' one said. 'Their treatment of women will remain as a scandal as long as the world lasts. We shall never forget; we shall never forgive. I wish I was back again at the front. Englishmen have only got to realise what devilish crimes are being committed by these Germans to want to go and take a hand in the fight. Women were shot, and so were all men, and so were young girls. In fact, it did not seem to matter to the Germans who they killed, and they seemed to take a delight in burning houses and spreading terror everywhere.

'I have got one consolation, I helped to catch four German spies.'

With rare despatch the 190 wounded men, after having been given what refreshment and food they desired, were conducted to the different wards allotted to them and quickly put to bed to enjoy rest that they had so nobly won.

TERRIBLE STORIES OF GERMAN SAVAGERY
Murder and Outrage

Appalling details of the atrocities committed by German soldiers on defenceless Belgian women and children are given in the course of the following narrative by M. Isadora Felix Cruls, a Belgian refugee, who has just arrived in London from Ostend. M. Cruls carried on a prosperous printing works at Saint Josse, a suburb of Brussels, giving employment to several men. His wife is stricken down with an internal malady, and when hostilities broke out a rumour gained currency in Brussels that the Germans had poisoned the drinking water, and her husband sent her and her three children to Ostend. Here he rejoined her, and the family were eventually able to get to London.

'When hostilities broke out,' commenced M. Cruls, 'I was called up for service in the Guard Civic, and was stationed on the Chaussée de Louvain, the road between Louvain and Brussels. This was on 29 July, but it was not until 8 August that we had anything to do. On that day the wounded began to arrive. My wife was suffering from an internal complaint, and as a rumour was spread through Brussels that the Germans had poisoned the drinking water I took her and our three children to Ostend. So disorganised was the railway system that it took seven hours to do the ordinarily two hours' journey.

'I returned to Brussels in a taxi-cab, and for sixty hours on end I had no sleep and very little to eat. That will give you some idea of what the Belgian people had to go through even in the early days of the war. At midnight on 19–20 August I was on duty on the Chaussée de Louvain watching the refugees come in from the various towns and villages. The road was blocked when I got near. I saw that a party of German Lancers were at the rear of the procession of refugees. I saw one of the Lancers prodding a woman, who had four or five children walking by her side.

'There was an old woman, evidently the mother of the young woman, walking with them. One of the Lancers was amusing himself by pricking this old woman with his lance in order to make her walk along more quickly. The young woman turned round and shouted something at the Lancer, either by way of remonstrance or insult. I was not near enough to hear what she said. The Lancer took up his lance and ran it through one of the little girls who were walking along, clutching the hand of her mother. She was a fair-haired girl of about seven or eight years of age. When the crowd saw blood spurt through her white dress, they became infuriated, and a panic ensued. The Lancers bore down upon the people, scattering them in all directions. What became of these people I do not know.

'I want to be perfectly fair to the German soldiers, so I will say here that I saw many of them behave properly. The atrocities were not in the nature of an organised series of insults.'

Referring to the case of two little children from Diest, whose parents were murdered before their eyes by the German soldiers, he said: 'The people were so filled with pity for the children that some men picked them up and pitched them into a train as it was going out of the station for Ostend. The children fell on the tender of the engine, and thus travelled to Ostend, where they arrived covered with coal dust. A stewardess of the *Marie Henriette*, a mail steamer plying between Ostend and Dover, was so filled with sympathy with the terrible sufferings which these two little mites had undergone that she herself took them on to the boat.

'Another story I have to relate was told me by the mother herself. It happened near Lens. A squadron of about 500 Uhlans marched through the town, and, alleging that somebody had shot at them as they were passing through the streets, went round to all the houses searching for firearms, smelling the rifles in order to see if they had been recently fired. At the house at which this woman lived there could be no question that a rifle had been fired, as there was not a firearm of any description in the place.

'The family circle consisted of a grandfather, the father, mother, and a girl of seventeen or eighteen, and a young boy, who, upon seeing the approach of the German soldiers, fled and hid himself. The soldiers came in, and without any questioning fired at and killed the father. They were going to shoot the grandfather, when the mother and daughter fell on their knees and begged the soldiers to spare the life of the old man. The officer, or under-officer, of the party then said, "Yes, we won't trouble about the old people," and touching the cheek of the young girl with his fingers, he added, with a significant laugh, "Pretty youth is better." He thereupon violated the girl before her mother's eyes.'

The following story was related to M. Cruls by a gentleman with whom he was closely acquainted on his arrival from Liège. This gentleman had a friend who was impressed into the service of the Germans as a motor driver for transport purposes. The man was told to go to headquarters to get further orders. He either did not hear or did not understand what the order was, and a sentry thereupon shot him dead.

A man who saw this from a window shot at the sentry, whereupon the Germans brought out twenty mitrailleuses and poured whole volleys into that quarter of the town, killing men, women, and children. This started a fire, and it was not until the flames had assumed such dimensions that the whole town was threatened that the Germans allowed anybody to come in and put them out. It is considered certain that between thirty and forty houses were burnt down, and that many men, women, and children were burnt to death.

A family who lived in the Rue de la Loi, in Brussels, went to stay at their villa at Genck, about six kilometres from Brussels. When the Germans arrived at the village they went to the villa and smashed up the whole of the place, stealing everything they could lay their hands on, and even taking away the wedding ring that the husband wore on his finger. They took away the men first, and nobody knows what has become of them. A member of the family and two servants fled from the house in terror, but returned when they saw the German soldiers going.

This is what they saw: 'The body of an old lady of seventy years of age lying on the floor with her throat cut. A governess, about thirty years of age – I cannot tell you her nationality – was found hanging from a tree, stark naked and disembowelled, and the rest of the family managed to make their way back to Brussels, where they now are.'

M. Cruls went on to say that he did not care to speak of some of the awful atrocities he had seen. He expressed his gratitude at the manner in which he had been treated by English people, and remarked that when the stories of the atrocities became known in full they would startle the world.

[The Censor does not object to the publication of the above, but does not guarantee the correctness of the statements.]

30 August 1914

BANDIT ZEPPELIN
Full Story of the Crime of Antwerp
From an Antwerp Diary

We have already published a brief announcement of the dastardly outrage committed upon the city of Antwerp against all the laws of modern warfare. We are now able to give the full story of the bandit Zeppelin's coward raid: Wednesday, 26 August. – In a few sentences yesterday I wrote all that was then public of the crime of Antwerp. I now tell the whole story so far as it can be pieced together.

The Zeppelin that flew over the sleeping city had mapped out a career of terrifying destruction. In a trail of devastation it meant to leave in ruins the Palais du Roi, the Bourse, the Palais de Justice, the Banque, the Minerva motor works, possibly the Grand Hotel. A German who knew Antwerp well – one of the many to whom the city opened its doors wide in days before the war – guided it, and indicated the position of the buildings. But in no case was the treacherous aim attained. Not one target was struck. Seven people have lost their lives, and some twenty others have been wounded; there has been some destruction of property. It is sad enough. But from the Zeppelin's point of view the cowardly attack, delivered with full force, in circumstances which will not recur, utterly failed.

The bombs which were to have killed the Queen and the little Princes and Princess Marie-José, as they slept in the quiet, grey house in the Place de Meir, and to have shattered the Bourse, fell in the Rue des Douze Mois, a street about the width of your Shoe-lane at its Fleet-street end. It runs from the Place de Meir, near the Palais du Roi, to the Bourse, and, looking down it, there is a suggestion of King-street and the Guildhall. Two floors of a house in this street were shattered, and two women injured. But neither the Palais nor the Bourse was touched by a single splinter.

The Palais de Justice is a modern structure, built about forty years ago by Baeckelmans, in the style of a Louis XIII château. Down one side of it runs the Rue de la Justice, of which the Rue du Palais is a continuation. Bombs fell in both these streets. In the former a hole was hollowed out in the roadway and the houses on both sides were struck by stones and earth. Pictures were flung to the ground, chandeliers dashed from their place, porcelain and other fragile and precious things shattered in houses in the latter. But the Palais between the two streets escaped without a scratch.

The bomb destined for the destruction of the Banque fell in the Rue des Escrimeurs, which begins on the other side of the Place Leopold, upon which the Banque on one side gives. It struck the attic of a house in the street, and killed a servant as she slept, injuring also two other domestics; and all round there was a shivering of glass. But the bank, with its round-corner turrets, still stands as Beyaert erected it thirty-five to forty years ago (for it was five years a-building), not a stone of it has been turned.

As for the bomb which was to destroy the Minerva works, it fell into the grounds of an empty house in the Rue Lozanne, scooped out a hollow in the earth, tore leaves and branches from surrounding trees, and plucked handfuls of stucco and brick from neighbouring houses – the gashed stucco with brick of rose-colour flushing through shows like a wound. But the works are untouched.

Of the other bombs, one fell in the middle of the Jardin Botanique, in a massif of shrubbery. It plunged into the earth, digging out a deep funnel-shaped hole, uprooting shrubs, blowing a bench that was there into fragments, of which none remains. And it plucked also from their frames windows of the St Elisabeth Hospital, where the wounded are, so that the beds were flung open to the street. The glass of many windows in the adjoining Rue Leopold fell smashed by flying fragments. In other streets, in the Rue Verdussen, where the Salle von Bary missed destruction by a miracle, in the Rue Karel Ooms, where a bomb fell in the garden, damage was also done. And, as the Zeppelin sailed into safety over the Plaire Falcon, it threw a bomb down upon the barracks there, to wound and slay. Again it missed its mark, but a civilian in a house near, sitting at his window, was killed on the spot, and another a few doors away was injured by a splinter on the thigh.

But it was in the little square which is called the *poids public*, where, in other days, the public weights and measures were, that the death-roll was greatest. The people heard the humming of the motor and the alarm of the guns; they rushed out to see what was happening. As the Zeppelin passed above them it dropped a bomb.

Five people were killed on the spot – a police-officer of thirty-five, who leaves a wife and seven children, two dockers of thirty-eight and thirty-two years, a young innkeeper, and a woman. A second police-officer was mortally wounded, having his leg severed, and the third had his foot carried away. The wife of a fourth police-officer lost her right eye. And again, there was the sound of smashing glass and tiles were torn from house-tops and flung out upon the night.

That is what the Zeppelin set out to do and what it achieved. Its aim was to inflict losses of millions and sow terror and dread. It has killed a handful of poor men and women, destroyed one or two floors of houses, smashed much glass, and dug great holes in the earth. Terror and dread it sowed none. I wrote to you of the city's calmness immediately after. It has given since further proof of its self-mastery.

No Zeppelin coming in the night to Antwerp henceforth will find its way lighted by the city it comes to destroy. To meet our Vandal enemy we have gone back to the Middle Ages. When the dusk falls we go to bed. It has been decreed that after eight o'clock no light shall be seen in the city save the few sentinel street lamps left at intervals, according to a plan. Until the danger passes away Antwerp, in the French saying, 'coucher avec les poules'. I sit writing this in a far corner of my room by the light of a candle, sheltered from sight by a barricade of travelling bags. Half an hour ago I watched 'Leerie' go down the street extinguishing what, it seemed, he had but newly illumined. People were moving in hundreds on the way homewards. They drifted past silently, and one could not see their faces. It was like a company of ghosts trooping in some monstrous dream. Now and then the throb of a motor was heard, and it flashed a great space of light presently into the night, and then was gone. The last car has beaten a clangorous way home. For three hours yet, I suppose, in London you will live in light. At eight o'clock we sit in darkness.

It was decreed so on the very day of the marauder's coming, and already on the second night Antwerp is taking it almost placidly. Last evening the order was not generally known, and patrols scoured the city, making people acquainted with it. Today the Press made it public, and all Antwerp is going home. The citizens have also been instructed, if they hear the sound of cannon in future, as they will in the case of any further attempt, not to rush to the windows, but to the cellars. Not an atom of damage anywhere was done in any house at a level below the roadway by any bomb that was thrown from the Zeppelin yesterday; in the cellar, then, there is safety.

The good burghers have read with satisfaction that last night an attempt was actually made by the Zeppelin to repeat its performance of the previous night, but that it turned back on discovering that its course was likely to be interrupted to more effect than on the occasion of its first visit.

The bandit Zeppelin appears to have set out from the aviation ground at Berchem–Ste–Agathe–les–Brussels, to which it probably returned. Observers say they counted four bright flashes of a 'cannon lance bombes'. That is to say, four bombs, for some reason (an unexpected deviation of route, it is suggested), were discharged obliquely; the others were dropped vertically down. The explosive was probably pierite. The bombs were cylindrical in form, and very powerful. The Matin quotes an officer as authority for the statement that they were such bombs as are intended to be dropped on the deck of a ship of war. A subscriber to the Metropole, who should have a dash of Walloon blood in him, writes that he is keeping a piece of one which he picked up as a paper-weight, and, after the war, should a German traveller call upon him, he intends to say: 'We don't want anything more to do with the scoundrels who made war by throwing on a peaceful city, which always gave them welcome, such murderous engines as that of which I hold in my hand a piece. The door is behind you.'

That is the full story of the crime of Antwerp, so far as it has been revealed to the light of day. For you in London it is perhaps told at too great length, but the night is vivid in Antwerp's souvenirs, so I have set down for you in full its history.

There is only one thing I would add – the story of a marvellous escape. The hero of it is M. Vainberg, a cigarette maker, who has now, if not before, had his romance. Had he slept in the bed he usually occupied on Monday night, he would have been a dead man. But for some reason – or for no reason – he chose another bed in another room, his wife being absent in the country, and so saved his life.

The bed which Madame Vainberg occupies when at home was crushed by the falling roof. More than that, having been aroused by the sound of the cannon, and having jumped out of bed and rushed down to the first floor, M. Vainberg found himself suddenly hanging from the window, the house having fallen about his ears. He was delivered from this position by the firemen.

As the night fell this evening hundreds of refugees came flocking in from Malines. The sight was pitiful in the extreme. Mothers with young children, whom they carried in their arms and who plucked at their skirts, fathers laden with bundles that held the family all, white-haired women and bent old men, all clearly from their aspect children of the field, drifted, drifted, drifted from the station through the town. I spoke in French to several of the refugees, but they knew Flemish alone. Their story, however, was written upon the dust of their feet and the seeking of their eyes.

They had fled from danger to safety, perhaps to shelter. The 'perhaps' was in their minds only, for the big-hearted Anversois will not leave them comfortless. Many people stopped the line of 'fuyards', and groups formed round this or that mother and her children.

Lodging is being found by the authorities, here or elsewhere, for the refugees till the hour of their distress passes; private kindness doubtless aids as well. It brings home to one more and more the agony of Belgium in this war. Of all that England can give of sympathy and admiration for her army's bravery, of money and of other help for the ruined and the broken-hearted, Belgium has need. For the war means for her the giving up of the flower of her youth. She has yielded it without a faltering, almost without a tear. But there is a pang at her heart which nothing can take away. All that can be done is to assuage it. England must see that this is done.

31 August 1914

SIR JOHN FRENCH ON THE GREAT BATTLE
Glorious Stand in Four Days' Fighting

Last night we received through the official Press Bureau the most important statement that has yet been issued concerning the tremendous conflict now raging along the French frontier, with special reference to the part taken in it by the British Army.

This communication, which has been made to the Press Bureau by Earl Kitchener, Secretary of State for War, does not, it will be seen, bear out the sensational reports circulated yesterday afternoon concerning the position and prospects of our army. On the contrary, it gives a very different account of the situation.

'THE TRUE PERSPECTIVE'
Press Bureau Warning, *Sunday Evening*

Soon after communicating the official statement the Press Bureau forwarded to us the subjoined statement: The Press Bureau is issuing an official statement this evening describing the fortunes of the Expeditionary Force during the past few days. This statement, the terms of which have been carefully considered, accurately and fully describes the present condition.

The Bureau has not thought it necessary to forbid the publication of messages sent by correspondents of newspapers dealing with the recent operations, provided that such messages neither give away military information nor disclose the organisation or position of the troops. These messages, however, should be received with extreme caution.

No correspondents are at the front, and their information, however honestly sent, is therefore derived second or third hand from persons who are often in no condition to tell coherent stories, and who are certain to be without the perspective which is necessary to construct or understand the general situation.

It is hoped that the statement issued tonight will dissipate any apprehensions caused by such reports, and restore the necessary perspective to the recent operations.

1 September 1914

PARIS IN WARTIME
First Wounded Arrive, *Paris, Sunday Night*

War signs in Paris are multiplying. The three weeks of the quiet mobilisation are now followed by the return to the Bois de Boulogne of ...

At this point the message breaks off, several hundred words having been deleted by the Censor. It continues: The first wounded are making their appearance, and impressing us with the visible effects of this terrible war. Hitherto the Red Cross trains carefully avoided the capital, and proceeded to the provincial towns. But now the Paris hospitals must take upon themselves their share of the work. I succeeded in smuggling myself into one of the stations where trains of wounded were arriving. It is difficult now for a journalist to get anywhere. They are being watched and spied upon with energetic zeal by everyone. It is a wonder that we are even allowed to leave our homes or hotels, and to have our drinks at the cafés like any other inhabitants not under such grave disabilities.

In vain we ask for a permit to go to places 50 or 100 miles from Paris. We are told at once, 'Pas de journalistes.' A journalist, therefore, is everywhere tabooed, an outlaw and an outcast in the eyes of the strict public official. We have, therefore, to make the best of it, and it is only through some exceeding act of condescension or toleration that we may venture into a railway station.

A train arrives. Some officers with arms or head bandaged step out. Red Cross attendants ask them if they will have a chair or a stretcher. 'No,' say the officers, 'reserve those things for our men, who are more seriously wounded than we are.' They all have heroic stories to tell. One says: 'We were at Stenay. A German slashed my arm with a stroke of his bayonet, ripping it open from the elbow to the shoulder. At the same instant a bullet pierced my left thigh. I fell down. The German fellow was going to finish me, but I did not let him. I dealt him a blow with the butt end of my rifle, which I held in my left hand. After this effort I fainted. When I awoke I found myself in a French ambulance.'

Another tells the following story: 'We were in a marsh near the Belgian frontier. I saw a wounded German officer, who was groaning, and seemed to be suffering great pain. I approached, intending to help him, when he struck out with his sword and cut off my ear as I was bending down to raise him up.' ... (Excision by Censor.)

A Zeppelin today reached Paris. It did not come, however, on a glorious flight, but was ignobly brought in pieces on six military trucks. It was one of the Zeppelins destroyed in the Vosges, and the trucks remained for some time at La Villette, where crowds were allowed to feast their eyes on the debris of a huge German airship.

3 October 1914

A TRAIN OF WOUNDED

Pathetic Scenes at a French Station, *Paris, Tuesday*

At four o'clock yesterday afternoon I left Paris to motor to A---- a railway station some 15 miles outside the capital. I wished to assist a party of French and American ladies in their voluntary task of feeding the sick and wounded soldiers as they pass through in the trains on their way from the front to hospitals in the remoter provinces of France.

A----, the full name of which I abstain from giving at the request of that little band of helpers, who are giving so much in wealth and personal service, is a typical French suburban station. Round the dingy railway buildings crowd the factories and dwellings of an industrial city.

The former are now all closed, and over the latter hangs that spirit of desolation which in wartime pervades a conscript country. There was no trace of architectural or natural beauty to relieve the sombre drabness of the genre. The station approaches and the platform were guarded by French reservists in the red and blue uniforms of a past generation. The officer in command told us that many had passed in the day, and that many more would pass in the night, begging us to lose no time in getting ready to receive them.

Within half an hour four large cauldrons containing coffee, milk, soup, and rum tea were simmering over charcoal fires, and upon trestle tables placed along the platform were bread, cheese, chocolate, biscuits, and other solid foods for those who might be well enough to eat them.

Night settled slowly down on the scene. From time to time great endless trains, drawn sometimes by three labouring engines, toiled slowly through the station, carrying food and other supplies towards the front. Once an express engine and one coach went shrieking through at 60 miles an hour, carrying a staff officer from the front into Paris. A group of bearded, slouching reservists, looking in their red and blue uniforms like pirates out of some impossible romance, gathered about the fires watching our preparations with hungry interest. The officer in command of the station hurried about raising difficulties with the infinite resource of the official mind. A table must be moved here, a stove there. Rum must not be given to the wounded men in their tea, none of the party must approach the infirmary, and so on.

When all our preparations were completed there followed an interval of waiting, until at about eight o'clock the 'jack in office' hurried up, crying: 'Messieurs, mesdames, un train contenant quatre cents blessés va arriver a l'instant.'

Jugs were filled with hot drinks, baskets with provisions and clothes, and then slowly there crept into the station out of the darkness a great train made up for the most part of third-class carriages and those rectangular box-shaped cattle-trucks which are specially designed in conscript countries for purposes of mobilisation. The wagons stretched far beyond the platform to where the maze of glistening, writhing rails was lost to sight in the night. Instantly at the windows of the third-class carriages appeared faces pale and bearded for the most part, and crowned with an indescribable variety of headgear. These were the slightly wounded. They held out their little tin cups begging for food and drink, which we distributed to them. Chocolate was especially popular, particularly among the Algerians, Tunisians, and the coal-black Senegalese infantry. The front part of the train was filled almost entirely with these slight cases, the men being cheerful but very tired and dirty. Many of them had not been able to change their shirts since the war began; it was weeks since most of them had had any sort of wash.

Towards the end of the train were carriages where no faces appeared at the windows, and on opening the doors one saw some ragged and helpless victim of the war lying amid straw, crying feebly for drink, and asking if here at last was the hospital where his sufferings were to end. Further back still were the great cattle-wagons, the doors of which were fastened with iron bars, and which when opened revealed six, eight, or even more men lying helpless in the straw, sometimes in total darkness, sometimes lighted by one lantern, the pale rays of which only added to the horrors of the scene. How can I describe the condition of these men? Some of them were crying like wolves: 'A boire! A boire!'

In one wagon eight of them were uniting in a ghastly chorus of suffering. We could hear them before we had slid back the great wooden doors, like voices crying from the tomb. The wagon was in darkness, so I fetched a lantern, and in its pale light saw their white faces staring up at me in various expressions of delirious agony. They were lying in the straw like animals unable to move hand or foot, their limbs swathed in bloodstained bandages, with no one to care for them or give them a drink. For nearly two days they had lain in this dark and airless cattle-wagon, burned by fever, their wounds throbbing and stabbing at every movement of the train. They had no idea of time or place, and for forty-eight hours they had heard no sound save the grinding of iron wheels and the cries of their comrades.

We did what we could for these poor wounded, giving them food, drink, and clothing, for which they expressed the most touching gratitude. In many cases I had to crawl about in the semi-darkness over the prostrate bodies in the straw, lifting up the heads of those who could not move themselves to drink. On every hand one heard the most pitiable cries and lamentations from men who a few days before had been strong and in the prime of life, now reduced to helpless wrecks, many of them for life. One man, who had received two bullets through the chest and one in the shoulder, had relieved himself of all clothing in the intensity of his fever, and was tossing about naked in the straw. I wrapped him in a blanket and gave him some hot milk, but as I left the wagon I heard him still crying, 'Mon Dieu! Que de souffrances! Qui l'aurait cru possible? Oh mon Dieu, ayez pitié de moi.'

In another wagon, a soldier, a peasant from the Morbihan, was lying on his back crying like a child. He had been wounded in the head, and the bandages were soaked in blood. I offered him some hot milk to drink, but he refused it and continued to moan and cry. Then a soldier lying beside him, and whose leg had been shattered by a shell, said to me: 'Le pauvre camarade, il a perdu sa médaille.'

I thought at first that he meant some war medal won in a previous campaign, but a Frenchman on the platform explained to me that it was the little aluminium image of the Virgin handed out to each soldier on the day of mobilisation. Another soldier in the wagon said to me, 'Tenez, monsieur, donnez-lui la mienne.'

So I placed in the hands of this poor sufferer a little round disc with the image of Christ on one side and on the other that of the Virgin and Child, surrounded by the words: 'Virgo Carmeli, ora pro me.'

The man clasped the medal, and instantly became quiet, whilst his comrade said: 'Ah! Pauvre camarade! Priez la sainte Vierge. Elle vous guerira bien vite.'

Another man with a shattered leg told me that he had lain for twenty-four hours on the battlefield before a stretcher party had picked him up. Most of the soldiers had been wounded as much as four days previously, but the number of casualties is so great that it has been impossible to deal with them before. Everywhere one heard the cry 'Sommes-nous enfin arrives?' and when one answered, 'You have only a little further to go,' the poor fellows would reply, 'Plus loin, mon Dieu! C'est toujours plus loin.'

I opened the door of a third-class carriage. It was in total darkness, but I could dimly discern a dark mass amid the straw. I climbed up the steps and crawled along the wooden bench to avoid the soldier who I knew was lying on the straw, calling to him, '*Veux-tu à boire, mon ami?*'

He did not answer. I called again, and still there was no reply. I fumbled for a box of matches and struck a light. The flame spluttered and then burned clear. An infantryman was lying on his side with his face buried in the straw. I leaned over and raised his head, but his face was white and his staring eyes lifeless. And of a sudden I was filled with nameless terror at the thought of this lonely death amid the straw on the floor of a dark railway carriage, far from family or friends, with no one to comfort his last moments, no priest to give the supreme consolation of religion.

All through the night train after train rolled in from the battlefield, and dawn breaking haggard across the silent city found us still at our task. By seven in the morning, when others relieved us, thirteen trains, containing over 3,000 wounded, had passed. Three thousand at one station in a single night. So it has been going on day and night for over fourteen days, and these are only the victims of one section of the battlefield. In the trains were some German wounded. With their mud-coloured uniforms, closely shaven heads, and simian cast of countenance, they looked grim and terrible, symbolical of the ruthless military despotism that they represent.

To one wagon-load of Germans I said: 'I hope you are pleased at the suffering in which you have involved Europe.'

They replied in unison: 'Do not blame us. We did not want to fight. We were forced to by our officers. We have had enough of it. It is awful.'

Among the wounded there were no English, for they are dealt with by their own organisations, which, according to the testimony of the French surgeon-major at A----, are admirable, and '*tout à fait différents des nôtres*'.

The sufferings of most of the wounded men were, unfortunately, not destined to end at A----. After we had fed them the trains were placed in sidings, and the most serious cases removed and sent off to hospitals in the neighbourhood, but by far the larger number, after receiving some attention, are carried to so-called sanitary trains, to be transported to Brittany, the Vendée, or the south of France.

All the men that I saw had received the most excellent dressings and first care, and in no single case had any of the dressings become loose or displaced. But it is three or four days sometimes from the time they are dressed in the field ambulances before they arrive at a hospital where they can be properly attended to.

It is doubtful whether anyone is seriously to blame. The number of wounded is so enormous that no organisation can cope with it. Warfare under modern conditions is simply slaughter by machinery. Many of the wounded to whom I talked had never seen a German. One man epitomised modern warfare as follows: 'For four weeks I had been marching. I was hungry, dirty, and worn out. Then one day we were ordered to run across a field, and I received two bullets in the chest. For hours I lay there listening to the sound of the cannon. Then at last someone picked me up. *Voilà ce que c'est que la guerre, monsieur.'*

The scenes that I witnessed at A---- have left an indelible impression on my mind, and as I write I can still see those pale, suffering faces, hear those cries of pain from fine men laid low in the prime of life, and the pitiless grinding of those endless trains bringing men from the front as fast as other trains are taking them up.

10 November 1914

INDIAN TROOPS IN THE BATTLE LINE
A Severe Trial, *Paris, Sunday*

The Indian troops have not been the least severely tried, nor have they proved the least indomitable. They were thrown into the centre of a furnace, as it were. During eight days of battle they suffered, without flinching, losses that were sometimes enormous. There was a company of engineers, too, which in the very first engagement lost all its officers and 60 per cent of its effectives. This was no doubt an exceptional case, but their trial was no less severe than that of other sections of the Army, and not for an instant did their commander fear the least flinching on their part.

If our Allies, in sending to the front these Indian troops, wished to make an experiment, that experiment has already given decisive results.

Moreover, if the English Army has suffered substantial losses, these losses seem insignificant in comparison with those of the enemy. The battle of Flanders has been, along its whole front, as in the outskirts of Lille and on the Yser, one in which the Germans have lost most heavily. The night attacks have been no less deadly than those launched by day. Several times it has happened that at dawn, after one of these night attacks, a single English battalion has been able to count 600 or 700 German dead bodies in front of its trenches. Two or three days ago an English battery surprised a German brigade in close formation and placed 4,000 men *hors de combat* in a few minutes.

The testimony afforded by German prisoners is very curious. To begin with, these men reveal an astonishing degree of ignorance. Today, as three months ago, the German soldier believes all that his chiefs tell him. He is convinced that the Emperor is a man of genius, and that the suburbs of Lille are at the very gates of Paris. He will not admit that the Allies have gained a single victory, and he thinks that Warsaw is in the hands of the Germans. Try to dispel these illusions, and he turns away in disdainful silence. One must not speak too hastily, however, of German demoralisation; that demoralisation will only occur on the day when the German army shall have been expelled from France and Belgium. On the other hand, it appears, from the same testimony, that in order to take the offensive at any price, Germany has thrown into Belgium masses of men insufficiently trained and of a quality very inferior to that of their army of the first line.

Nothing is more striking, in that regard, than the story of a Lorraine prisoner, told in the vicinity of Neuve Chapelle ten days ago. He was a very young man – almost a boy – who had been forcibly enrolled at Metz after the outbreak of hostilities, along with men of thirty-five and forty-five years of age who had never really belonged to the army. This heterogeneous regiment had been hastily drilled for a couple of months, without having been familiarised with the handling of the Mauser.

Towards the end of October the regiment was sent to Lille, and detailed to the trenches. There the training of the men was still so inadequate that the officers used to drill them at a time when they ought to have been sleeping. One morning, about one o'clock, the young Lorrainer's company were ordered to unload their rifles and to fix bayonets. The officers took up position behind their men and ordered them to attack the English trenches. Reaching the bed of a stream which separated the two lines of trenches, the men came suddenly under the English fire. From their position in the immediate rear the officers obliged their men to resume their forward march. Some minutes afterwards the entire company was annihilated by the accurate fire of the English infantrymen, and the officers, in spite of their precaution to march behind their troops, were killed to a man. The young Lorrainer was hit four times, and seized the first occasion to give himself up as a prisoner. The young man ended his story by saying that a great number of his comrades were fighting against their will.

Will the Germans continue for long to send us new troops of this sort? On that question depends, without doubt, not so much the issue of the war – which, after all, is not doubtful – but its duration. If, as one may hope, they are compelled to reserve their last reinforcements for their eastern frontier, the battle of Flanders must have a speedy denouement entirely favourable to the Allies. The struggle may last longer if the Germans still have a large number of young soldiers to send to the slaughter. But, to be fair, one must recognise that if the men of the Landwehr show very much less 'bite' than the others, these young fellows fight very well. They, no doubt, lack experience, and they shoot abominably badly, but they know how to die, and whilst their numbers remain considerable the German attacks will maintain their violence.

TALES FROM THE FRONT
Wounded Officer's Experiences

'I have been in several engagements previous to the present campaign,' my friend remarked, 'but I never imagined any feeling could be so terrible as modern artillery fire. I was one of those fortunate ones who have been only wounded, but I never expected to come out alive, and I think I must have a charmed life when I think of what I have gone through. I do not believe any other soldiers except the British could have gone through what we have gone through in the recent fighting.

'Our men are indeed remarkable. As long as they have an officer to lead them nothing will induce them to retire unless ordered to, and then it is often very difficult to get them to obey. You understand in war how difficult it is to know what is really happening to any other unit except your own. You live and die in a little world whose limits are your eye-sight, and those limits are extended only by sound, which tells you very little. In Flanders, which is a perfectly flat country, your little world is extremely small.

'On 18 October our regiment was ordered to advance and attack the enemy, who were reported to be retiring. We marched along a flat road for some distance, and then came under a fairly long-range artillery fire, which caused us to extend. We continued our advance to some crossroads, where we came under the fire of the enemy's infantry, which was fortunately high. Now that we have these double companies there are two captains. Captain B---- was my senior, and led one platoon whilst I led the other. I saw a wood in my front, which seemed to offer some cover from the shells, so I led my men towards it. We then entered the wood, and had quite a lively time driving out the German infantry.

'The enemy are no match for us in this kind of fighting, and we enjoyed thoroughly the work of hunting up the Germans, whom we shot down like rabbits. When we reached the outskirts of the wood we came under a terrible artillery fire from the enemy's guns, which were only 800 yards away. I withdrew my men under the cover of a ditch, and then moved towards the left to find out what had happened to Captain B---- and our other platoon. I met two stragglers, both wounded, who said the platoon had been completely wiped out, and Captain B---- seriously wounded.

'I took eight men and again moved to the outskirts of the wood, where I found a perfectly flat turnip field stretching away towards the enemy. About 300 yards out I saw a line of our infantry lying flat on the ground, and made my way towards them. No sooner did we leave the cover of the wood when the enemy's guns opened up on us. I shall never forget traversing those 300 yards. The enemy's guns, which were only 800 yards away, fired with extreme accuracy.

'It seemed impossible that my little party could escape. Three were almost immediately hit, but we others kept on and reached the line lying in the open. Half a platoon were extended at five paces. To my horror I found all were dead or wounded except about three men, who were keeping perfectly still. I found the Subaltern Lieutenant B---- on one knee, with one hand resting on the ground just in the attitude of a runner who is waiting the signal for the start of a race. He was stone dead. A shrapnel bullet had pierced his head.

'The man next him, who was badly wounded in the thigh, told me they were ordered to support the firing line, which was 200 yards ahead, and had only advanced 300 yards from the wood when the entire line was struck down as if by lightning. He said that Lieutenant B---- after being hit merely said, "Go on, please, I can't move; I must be wounded." This man begged me to cut off his pack, which prevented him from moving. He had three shrapnel bullets in the thigh and another in his shoulder. I cut off his pack, and found the whole base of the shell lodged between his pack and his back. This is an amazing escape, as, if it had touched him, he would have been instantly killed.

'Several other wounded cried out to me, begging me to cut off their packs, which prevented them from getting away. I ordered my four surviving companions to do this, and told the wounded not to move for the present, as the least movement caused the enemy to open fire again. I then crept forward another 200 yards, where I found our firing line, under Captain B----. They were lying, every man killed or wounded, within about 400 yards of the enemy's guns, which we could not even see. In the centre a bunch of twenty-five men lay all in a heap, having massed as they advanced for mutual protection, which, as you know, all men do in an attack.

'I have never seen such wounds. At this short range many had been blown to bits by the shrapnel. One man had twelve bullets in his legs. Another had his chest blown away. Many were dead; others dying. I found Captain B---- still alive, with his thigh shattered and another wound in his neck. He was talking incoherently, and ordered me to take the guns by assault. This, of course, was impossible, as I only had four men with me, and in any case it would have meant instant death.

'As long as we lay quiet the enemy's guns did not fire, but directly anyone moved we would get another shell right on top of us. I saw that unless Captain B---- received speedy attention he would die. I therefore collected two rifles and made a stretcher out of a great coat. Meanwhile, before moving, we cut off the packs from all the men still living so as to give them a chance of crawling away. When those who could not move saw I was leaving the firing line they begged me not to leave them. I said: "I must take Captain B---- back, but will come again, for the rest of you." We carried Captain B---- almost to the edge of the wood before the enemy's guns noticed us. Then they opened fire, but we reached cover.

'I then got some more volunteers from my platoon and four stretchers, and these brave fellows crawled right up to the dead firing line and carried others out under a heavy fire. Several wounded were again hit on the way. I went to the extreme right of the line to cut off the pack of a man who was very badly wounded and had been calling out for assistance. I heard a shell coming and instinctively put up my arm to guard my face, and tried to throw myself on the ground. But I was too late. I felt a terrific blow, just as if someone had hit me with a giant red-hot poker. I was spun round and seemed to go on spinning, and then fell to the ground. I thought I had been killed, as I felt a violent blow in the abdomen.

'Then I discovered that my right arm was broken and useless. It was bleeding freely. I looked at my stomach, where I felt the greatest pain, but, to my great relief, saw no blood. I then found that a bullet had cut the ring on my Sam Browne belt and carried away the hilt of my sword. I lay on the ground for a few minutes, and then the enemy commenced to shell us again. I got up and ran as hard as I could towards my left. I felt this would be safer, and that I might get out of the line of fire. I only went a few yards when I fell from exhaustion, and hurt my bad arm horribly.

'After a short time I again got up and went on running, only to fall every twenty or thirty yards. Shortly after I came to a road with a small bank, and, as the enemy's shells were falling freely, I lay down. A first-aid man then came up and looked at my wound. I said to him, "Help me to the wood, and then dress my wound." He replied, "The regulations prescribe that all wounded must be first dressed in the firing line." This seemed very funny to me at such a moment, when at any moment either of us might be hit by another shell. The gallant fellow then proceeded to dress my arm, under a heavy fire.

'Other wounded came up, and also wished to reach the wood, but this first-aid man would let none of them go, always prefacing his remarks with, "The regulations prescribe." Finally, after a rest, I ran as hard as I could to the wood, and went through it. On the other side it was fairly safe, but I had to walk a long way before I was put in a common country cart with several other wounded. There were no motor-cars and no ambulances.

'Finally we reached a field hospital, where I was given morphia. I was then put in a train with hundreds of other wounded, and took three days and a half to reach Boulogne. I had no splint put on my arm, and suffered horribly. I found Captain B---- in the same train. He lay for three days with his smashed thigh, also without a splint. I asked the RAMC Colonel in charge of the train to give me morphia, but he replied, "Stick it out; it is bad for you." I do not see what harm it would have done me, considering how much I was suffering.

'Our wounds were dressed every day on the journey, and we were well fed. I finally reached London, and am now in a comfortable home in X street. Twelve pieces of lead have already been taken from my arm, and the doctors have decided to leave the rest in. This is all I know of the war, and have not the least idea whether we won or were beaten on the day I was hit.'

12 November 1914

INDIAN TROOPS IN THE FIRING LINE
Stoical Bravery, *France, Saturday*

By A French Officer

It was a curious sight to all of us, French or English, the day when the Indians arrived in a dreary little town of northern France, which had been recaptured from the enemy a few days before. Large grey clouds were hanging low over the square in front of the Town Hall, the tower of which had been beheaded by a shell, while the broken windows of the café opposite bore testimony to the fierceness of the recent battle in the streets. The inhabitants were standing on their doorsteps with calm and sad faces, eager to see what troops were coming up. And there were also a number of French cavalry, mainly Moroccan Spahis, with their red coats and blue breeches, who had been enjoying a much-needed rest, and were walking leisurely on the muddy pavement as if they had been at home. And then you could see, of course, some British Tommies of the transport service corps playing football in a field near the street, where the lorries were halting, like a goods train in a railway station.

Suddenly the Indian Lancers appeared, and the pavement on both sides of the main street was at once filled by a crowd of soldiers and civilians watching the procession, as a London crowd will do in Whitehall on the day of the opening of Parliament. In fact, those Indians looked all like kings. The lancers sat proudly in their saddles, with their heads upright under the Oriental crowns; then came a regiment of Sikhs, walking at a brisk pace, all big and strong men, with curled beards and the wide 'pagri' round the ears; the Pathans followed, carrying on their heads that queer pointed bonnet, the 'kullah', which reminds one of the warriors seen on old Persian tapestries – a more slender type of men, but equally determined, and with faces at the same time smiling and resolute.

Everybody gazed with wonder at these newcomers. Of course, the inhabitants of this unhappy region had seen all sorts of men – British and French, Moroccans, Algerians and Tunisians, even black Senegalese from French West Africa. But they had no idea of those brown men from the East who were coming to the rescue of Western civilisation. After a moment their amazement turned into frank delight. The Moroccan Spahis seemed more pleased than anybody else. They laughed, made in broken French wondering remarks about that Ally which was sent to them by Allah, and I heard one of them shout out to a passing Pathan, 'Moslem!' Being all great experts in the fighting value of men, our Moroccans at once understood that the strange soldiers they saw passing by were among the finest in the world. Nothing could be more striking than the tribute they paid to their new friends from India. The queerest thing of all was that such a meeting between the hillmen of two Oriental countries should have taken place in a cold, rainy, commonplace little corner of northern France.

The Indians did not wait long to prove that that flattering impression was fully justified. On the very day they arrived here some regiments were at once sent to the trenches. The day after we heard that during the night one of the Sikhs regiment had had to recapture a trench which the Germans had taken by surprise, and that their bayonet charge was so tremendous that the enemy did not dare to counter-attack. Almost immediately after that feat an order came not to allow the Indians uselessly to expose their lives by walking out of the trenches. The fact was that in order to show their contempt for death some of the Sikhs had refused to hide themselves in the trenches and had immediately drawn a fierce fire on their regiment. Fortunately, they did not insist on playing that sort of game, otherwise the Indian Army Corps would have disappeared in one week's time out of sheer bravery.

It took them, however, a few days before they were taught how to adapt themselves to the conditions of European warfare. From what I have heard and seen, I gather that the Indian troops are in some respects like our 'Turcos'. Their natural instinct is to jump at the enemy's throat as soon as he is seen. It is very hard for them to refrain from moving too quickly forwards, the more so that they do not realise that the line of battle extends for hundreds of miles on their right and on their left. So with our French–African troops; they lost many men at the beginning, only because they could not always be prevented from charging with fixed bayonets when they ought to have waited patiently until the batteries had finished their preparatory work. Then, for the Indians, as well as for Moroccans or Algerians, any hardship would have been pleasant in comparison with lying for days and nights in a muddy ditch with rain pouring down. European warfare is a game of patience which does not appeal to Eastern imagination.

Anyhow, the Indians have made up their mind to go through the ordeal with unflinching tenacity. Each native regiment walks at night into his trenches with as much order as if he had already fought the battle of the Aisne. The Sikhs have by now corrected a mistake they made at the beginning; they used at first to lean their elbow against the trench and lift their left hand rather high above the ground, the result being that many of them were wounded in the hand and the forearm. As for the little Ghurkas, they usually found the trenches too deep for them, but they have now found a means of remedying this inconvenience by digging loopholes in front of them; every day, at nightfall, they place their rifle in the loophole, aim carefully at the enemy's trenches, and leave the rifle there so that they can fire during the night attacks without even lifting their heads.

The only thing that makes them sometimes uncomfortable is the sniping which takes place at their backs when some daring Germans manage to crawl between the trenches and fire at our men from behind. But stalking is a favourite sport with hillmen, and there are reasons to believe that the German snipers will find before long that crawling through an Indian line is a somewhat dangerous exercise.

I hope some account will be given after the war of the numerous acts of gallantry which are occurring nearly every day. I wonder whether people realise in the quiet homes of France and England that all along the huge line of battle, from Belfort to Nieuport, thousands of men are at every minute doing silently their duty in a way that would suffice, under normal circumstances, to make every one of them famous. I will quote only one instance.

A few days ago, a company of native sappers and gunners found itself in a very critical position, the main attack of the enemy being directed against them. Not only were the Indians under machine-gun fire, but there were plenty of 'Black Marias' pouring over them from all sides. At one moment one of those unpleasant shells fell quite near a sapper while he was lying on the ground and steadily firing on the advancing foe. It did not hurt him, but dug a hole 6ft deep at his side. The sapper – a Sikh, I believe – waited until the smoke had gone, and then jumped into the hole. He soon found that the position was a comfortable one, and started firing from the cover the Germans had dug for him; according to officers who were standing by, he managed to kill some fifteen or twenty Germans by himself, and would have remained there for ever if he had not been eventually ordered to retreat. He was warmly congratulated afterwards, but did not appear to think he had done anything remarkable.

The same spirit is noticeable throughout the Indian corps. A staff officer two or three days ago visited a battalion which had suffered some rather severe losses in a recent engagement. He found the men quite cheerful, and eager to return to the firing line. The officer thought it necessary to say a few kind words about their losses. 'Never mind the number of killed,' said one of the men, 'as long as the regiment's honour is safe.' Another man was almost moved to tears when the Sahib shook his hand, and said 'Shabash!' ('Well done!')

Curiously enough, the same men had refused to touch any biscuit, and break their caste vow the night before the battle, so that they had been fighting on an empty stomach. They did not complain, however, for they had taken the oath, before leaving India, not to abide by their caste regulations in cases of emergency, and knew that the British transport service could not at that special moment supply them with their ordinary food; so the responsibility rested with themselves, and they bore it in a stoical way.

It would be interesting enough to know what they think of the war and the country they are in. I have tried my best to find out from every side what they were saying. It was not always an easy matter, for they are usually a reticent sort of men, even with their own British officers. A strange but rather disappointing experience took place a fortnight ago in another French town, while the Indian corps was on its way to the front. We had heard that some German prisoners were kept in the Law Courts of the place, and three of us – two British officers and myself – went to pay them a sort of flying visit. We thought it would be rather useful to show some German uniforms to our Sikhs, so we took with us two splendid fellows, who, with their pagris and long overcoats, looked like priests. The confrontation was a silent one. The German prisoners were either shy or contemptuous, and did not even so much as lift their eyes on the Indians. As for the Indians, they gazed at the prisoners without uttering a word. One of us asked them afterwards what they thought of the men they had just seen. 'Well,' said he, 'the German uniform is less conspicuous than the French.'

They apparently never want to look as if they might be startled by anything. Our French 'Turcos' are much the same. Their main ambition is to make people believe that they fear nothing, and also that no device, however ingenious, of our Western civilisation can evoke among them the slightest astonishment. They carefully conceal, for instance, their bewilderment at seeing our flying machines. The Indians are still more proud. If a British officer asks them on a rainy day if they do not feel cold they at once assert that they do not mind, and that, they are prepared for worse. 'We will go,' they say, 'where the "Sirkhar" wants us to go.' They make a point of being not impressed by the noisy display of German artillery fire, and speak of the enemy in a scornful way: 'They came like dogs,' said a Sikh the other day; 'we received them like dogs.'

I have no doubt, after what I have already seen, that most of the Indians are quite devoted to their British officers. A pleasant instance occurred the other day, in a village where I happened to be with a British colonel who had long been in command of a regiment of Sikhs. By a fortunate coincidence, this very regiment marched through the village while we were there. The men recognised at once their former chief and quite spontaneously started cheering him, rank after rank, and asking the God of the Sikhs to give them victory. The colonel waved his hand, and it was clear that he and the Sikhs were equally pleased to see each other again. That little scene is of a kind one is not likely to forget.

17 November 1914

BATTLE OF THE NORTH
Enemy's Vain Attacks, *Calais, Sunday*

By A. Beaumont

From Ypres to Armentières, Lille, and Arras the guns are still heard rending the air from morning to night, but the violence of the attacks is no longer what it was a few days ago or during the earlier stages of this huge Battle of the North, which has already cost Germany upwards of 100,000 men. The Germans are showing signs of fatigue. Such a gigantic effort cannot be kept up indefinitely. It would perhaps be premature to conclude that the enemy is demoralised and ready to retreat. Discouragement certainly has begun to pervade the ranks, and is visible in the officers as well as in the men. They have in the past few weeks made superhuman efforts to carry certain points, and then found that all their labour was in vain.

It was of no avail to them to have taken Dixmude the other day, any more than it was of any advantage to have approached Nieuport or bombarded and destroyed Ypres. Dixmude was a little village of some 4,000 souls, and most of the inhabitants had fled. The Germans entered it when it was a heap of burning ruins, and the next day they only found that they were subjected to a cross-fire from opposite sides from a relentless defender, who made them pay dearly for their momentary advantage. For the pleasure of having spent a few hours in the midst of the ruins of Dixmude the German troops left thousands of their comrades behind. This is the story of nearly every town and village which they occupied and then evacuated with losses during the last few weeks.

The Allied armies also have their losses in each of these actions, but they are mostly far inferior to those of the enemy. The positions, moreover, which they capture from the enemy are always positions that are worth holding, and which in the ensemble of the great struggle add constantly to their advantage. This is the lesson to be gathered from the last month's fighting, when it may be remembered the German outposts had actually reached as far as Hazebrouck. They are a great distance from Hazebrouck now, and one even learns that fighting is receding along many points which it is not yet advisable to mention. People from towns and villages where the guns had been creating a furious din for three weeks or more every morning now state that the artillery is no longer heard or its reports are becoming more distant. The sound of the guns is receding with the line of battle ever farther from the coast and from that port of Calais into which the Germans a month ago had fondly hoped to enter.

People a week ago would not believe that the Germans had been driven out of the region of Warneton. This is now confirmed. The attack of the German troops, a furious one, and also one on a considerable scale, was met here by the combined forces of the French and British. The Germans had directed a heavy bombardment from one of their batteries on the French wing. Later in the day a French battery opened fire and sorely interfered with the German gunners. They moved their guns about, and when night came they seemed fairly exhausted. Two French infantry battalions made a rapid march in the dark, taking further advantage of the fog, and in the morning they captured the guns and took many of the Germans prisoners. The village where these guns and prisoners were captured is some four miles north of Warneton, and it enabled the Allies to hold a position of great importance, from which they afterwards repulsed the successive attacks of the enemy in much larger numbers.

The taking of Dixmude, and holding it for a short time, cannot compensate for the losses which the Germans constantly sustained at nearly every point in actions like this for the last three weeks. In this case alone, a sort of preliminary attack though it was, the Germans lost an entire regiment. One who was there says that the French troops had simply surrounded them during the night. The Germans, fatigued by their prolonged effort, had taken up quarters in the village, and had considered themselves safe for a while. Besides, other and more numerous troops were behind, ready to come to their support. But the French did not give them time. At eight o'clock in the morning, when the fog began to lift, the French battalion to the left, which had been hiding in a wood, came out and attacked them in the village. The Germans hastened to organise their defence, but before they could do so the French had already succeeded in occupying half the houses. Soon afterwards the other battalion made a rush into the village from an opposite quarter, and surprised the men who were hurrying to get the battery into action. Before they could do so there was a hand-to-hand fight, in which the Germans were cut down and the guns were taken. The struggle then continued for a while longer in the streets of the village, and, although the Germans had been more numerous at first, they soon lost that advantage, and were cut up so badly that not one of the regiment escaped. The French took 350 prisoners, six guns, and a number of machine-guns.

At noon it was all over, and then news came that the British troops had made a similar advance to the south, and the subsequent German attack en masse completely failed.

People from Furnes now tell me that the guns are no longer heard from that town, which nevertheless is practically deserted. But a little more than a week ago the Germans came very near taking it. This was one of the surprise attacks which they have attempted at various points. Their first move was on Ramscapelle, a big village which it was very important to hold. If they succeeded in establishing themselves strongly here, their next move would have been to bombard Furnes again and to occupy it definitely. Therefore some ten days ago the Germans made a sudden and furious attack on the village, taking the Belgian troops, who had been worn out by a prolonged campaign, completely by surprise. Many of the Belgian troops had been sent for a rest to the vanguard, and those who remained were obliged to fall back in the presence of overwhelming numbers.

The Germans, noticing it, pushed their advantage, and in one morning they succeeded in rushing the town, occupying it with infantry, cavalry, and artillery. As soon as this was known, a number of French troops received orders to go to the support of the Belgians and to drive the Germans out of their positions at any cost. The German move upon Furnes, in fact, might have had serious consequences. Ramscapelle was only one step removed, and they had to be driven out. Hardly twenty-four hours, therefore, had passed, when, after a forced march, a number of French troops, including Chasseurs and Turcos, made a dash to recover the lost position. They advanced upon the town from two sides, the Chasseurs on one side and the Turcos on the other, both making a big detour to avoid arousing the suspicion of the enemy. They took the Germans completely by surprise, and dashing into the town from opposite directions, they engaged in hand-to-hand combat and bayonet charges, which lasted for more than an hour, and after which the French were masters.

But the Germans did not give up the struggle. Finding that they were in superior numbers they continued the fight outside the village and gradually returned, getting their machine-guns into action and setting up one of these murderous instruments at every turning and street corner. The Chasseurs and the Turcos however, after a moment's hesitation, again resumed the offensive, and carried one point after another, fighting from street to street and making a stronghold of every house and barn. The struggle lasted all day, and the advantage swayed constantly to and fro. The Germans again and again entered the village, and were as often driven out. Night came on, and the commander of the French *tirailleurs* and Turcos, seeing that the result was still undecided, got together a number of his men and led them on to a final charge. They were to take the enemy's machine-guns if there was to be any rest, and after a furious charge on the enemy they succeeded. The Turcos made such a dash on the men serving the guns that those were seized with panic and fled in the presence of successive bayonet charges. The Chasseurs then started in pursuit, and for a considerable distance beyond Ramscapelle they kept firing at the fugitives until the roads from Ramscapelle to Pervyse, and from Pervyse to Dixmude were lined with the enemy's dead, and the Germans had to recross the Yser. Many of the fugitives also tried to escape by the fields and canals, and their bodies are still found in great numbers. As in many other places in the north, quite a number of these Germans are very young, apparently under eighteen, or more than fifty years of age.

King Albert of Belgium desired in person to honour the French troops who had helped to reconquer the village, and an impressive ceremony was held a few days later. The King passed in review the survivors of the gallant companies of

Turcos and Chasseurs in the little square of Ramscapelle. They were assembled at eight o'clock in the morning, and drawn up in a square in the presence of a French general. The King arrived in a motor-car and alighted at once. Three buglers, who had gone through it all, sounded the call, and the Commander of the troops moved forward to salute them. The King likewise raised his hand in a long and silent salute. Then, accompanied by the General in command he passed down the lines, after which the troops in turn defiled in his presence. The buglers did their best, but their shrill notes were not in accord; yet tears came to the eyes of many spectators of this scene, and not the least moved among them was the King himself. The General then rode forward, and in a loud voice said: 'The King desires me to transmit to you his hearty congratulations for your splendid conduct at Ramscapelle; this is an honour of which your commander is justly proud.'

These are some of the everyday events along the long line of the Battle of the North, and in which the Germans invariably, after a short and futile offensive, are beaten back with heavy losses.

Similar engagements, according to an officer who was wounded last Monday, took place farther down, between Dixmude and Ypres, where the French and British troops are fighting.

'We had,' he says, 'during three days to support the most furious attacks since the beginning of the war. My brigade extended over a front of four kilometres north of Ypres. It was on this line that the Germans finally made a desperate rush. They were met on our part by a stubborn resistance, but in spite of their heavy losses they were not discouraged. Driven back again and again, they returned each time more numerous to the charge. Our men fought against such odds till the next evening, and although they sometimes yielded ground a bit they always recovered it again. There have been places like that which during these violent attacks were lost and taken seven times or more in a single day.

'There was a short respite, but then the Germans returned to the attack with still greater violence. It seemed as if they were staking their all to break through at that point. They made the attack with infantry, cavalry, and artillery, and brought some of their heaviest guns to bear upon us. We lost heavily, but the German losses were still greater. Our 75mm field-guns and our machine-guns did fearful execution. I was witness of the following incident only, which shows the fierceness and violence of the fighting.

'A German regiment, with flag flying, approached our trenches to about 300 yards. It was met by a heavy discharge of our machine-guns and rifle fire, and fell back in disorder. It immediately, however, reassembled some distance away, and once more we saw it advance with ranks that were already thinned. It came to within 100 yards of us, when it was received as before, and again beaten back. This time the order was sent through our trenches to let them come on to twenty yards. We did so, and then the order to fire at will was given. Two-thirds of the regiment had already fallen in the first two attacks, and now the remainder was wiped out. Not one of the wretched assailants got to our trenches.'

The German waste of men and lives in their attacks around Dixmude and Ypres would be incredible were the facts not confirmed by numerous eye-witnesses who have seen the latest holocausts of the Kaiser's army in that region.

20 November 1914

YPRES AND THE YSER
Our Greatest Battle

Owing to the rigorous censorship which restricts the news of the war from reaching our people, few of us realise that the greatest battle in which the British Army has ever been engaged, however such events are measured, has just been fought almost within sight of Dover, and has not yet concluded the agony of its final convulsions. When the cunning strategy of the enemy framed the long line of battle in northern France with salient angles which invited us to go forward into the present theatre of strife, the actual emergency became more vitally serious for us than for our Allies, for the crushing of our right wing would have led to the interception of all Allied troops north of the point of German penetration, and a serious tactical disaster could hardly have been prevented. The additional fact of the battlefield being close to the Straits of Dover lent heightened interest to the collision, though as a matter of fact the capture of the localities on the French coast which were immediately threatened would not have exercised any decisive effect on the campaign. At the end of August German troops could have occupied them unopposed.

The country north of Lille first focused the interests of the combatants when German cavalry swarmed over it after the failure of the main German army to throw off the pressure of the Anglo–French forces on the Aisne in mid-October, and when their attempt to break through the French at Roye, near the Oise valley, had likewise failed. Then came the German grand attack on Antwerp, followed by the concentration of masses of fresh troops to strike at the Allied left to turn it, or alternatively to cut it off and pin it against the coast.

Our Army was successfully moved to the new battlefield partly by marching and partly by rail. Motor-buses played an important part in carrying troops, too, besides provisioning them. The German cavalry, in spite of their vaunted faith in shock tactics and long lances, cleared off when our cavalry appeared on the scene, but German infantry and guns hurried forward, and the mighty conflict began by some fights between advanced guards encountering one another north-west of Lille. Gradually the battle developed in a way which recalled the Aisne by infantry entrenching and counter-entrenching, by the deployment of long lines of field-guns on either side, and finally by the erection of long-range and heavy artillery batteries in a third echelon behind the infantry and field artillery, so as to fling huge projectiles over the heads of their friends.

As the fighting continued daily, as one sanguinary attack after another decimated our regiments of foot, and as the masses of the foe increased and extended, our line had at the same time to contract for more concentrated effort at the decisive points of which the town of Ypres in our centre was the most important, and to extend in order to face the ever-extending line of enemy, which threatened to outflank and envelop our right wing. To meet this threat the accomplished horsemen of the cavalry corps had to leave their chargers in the bivouacs or in such shelter as could be found behind the fighting line, and to take post on the flank of the sorely pressed infantry.

For such work it is true the cavalry have some advantages. They reach the field fresher, they can carry more ammunition and other necessaries along with them, and probably the men are, on the whole, of finer physique and better shots than the sister arm, but of necessity their numbers are relatively smaller. A cavalry division numbers but twenty-seven squadrons, and at this stage of the war a squadron may be thankful to have eighty horsemen in its ranks. Of these not less than one in six have to be left to look after horses. Then the work of the bivouac is more arduous because of the vulnerability to shell-fire. Very often the lines have to be changed after dark, no easy job in the profound gloom of a stormy winter's evening. A move has equally to be made before it is light. Saddling up, and the collection of all the tackle in use under such difficulties, tries the discipline and efficiency of mounted troops.

Between Messines and Armentières, roughly on the right of the British line, and linking it with the nearest French forces, our horsemen were led on 31 October, when a fresh German army corps tried to outflank us and to intercept our army from the French at Lille. For not less than seven miles the small parties of dismounted troopers stretched themselves, having dismounted at least two miles in rear of the infantry trenches. They made their way in the murky grey of the autumn morning across cultivated fields much enclosed in hedges, past farmhouses and hamlets hastily fortified up to the trenches which they had to take over from our exhausted infantry; also fresh ground which had not yet been fought over, and had to be hastily entrenched or fortified with whatever implements could be procured at the moment.

Along this imperfect battle line, hastily seized for the emergency, the little troops of Hussars, Lancers, Dragoons, and Life Guards held out for forty-eight hours against the type of attacks with which we have learnt to be familiar. Storms of big projectiles, showers of shrapnel, a constant sleet of bullets, punctuated occasionally by rushes with the bayonet at dusk or dawn from dense masses whose numbers were irresistible when once they managed to get close to the thin array of riflemen defending a trench. Thus the line held on by the eyelids during this anxious period of the great battle. Here and there it was dented by attacks which locally drove it in or perforated its continuity. To redress the balance some infantry had been despatched to support the cavalry. Some Indian riflemen, the London Scottish, and the Honourable Artillery Company in turn delivered furious counter-attacks which brought welcome succour, and cut down heaps of German officers and men.

When at length the exhausted survivors of the cavalry squadrons were relieved, and rallied in rear of the ground they had clung to with the tenacity of veteran infantry, intermingled with the brave Territorials, who had also fought so splendidly, there lay in front of them the debris of a whole German army corps, which they had compelled to abandon the attack and to give place to fresher troops from the German reserves. These attacks have been repeated and continued against the reinforced British line, but with no better success. Our squadrons are weaker by the loss of the heroes struck down, but the thin ranks of the survivors are ready as ever to ride to the aid of any portion of the line which may be temporarily in difficulties. They would yet more eagerly welcome the order to follow up a German retreat, and seek for a chance of the much-longed-for charge with the point of the sword.

1 December 1914

THE GALLANT 7TH

Famous Belgian Regiment, *Northern France, Friday*

By Patrick De Bathe

The north-east corner of the Allies' lines presents a very different aspect today from that of a week ago. Furnes has become one of the busiest towns in the whole theatre of war. Its well-built houses and orderly streets are full of the brave sons of Belgium, and of our gallant Allies the French. Furnes is the advance sentinel in whose ear the unceasing and not far distant sound of cannon is ever present. The eyes of suffering Belgium are turned in hope towards her. Furnes is the soul of the oppressed nation, of that nation that patiently awaits the hour of her deliverance from the hated and cruel yoke of an unprincipled and treacherous enemy.

Here, in the centre of the town, are many trophies of war drawn up upon the 'place', for here are some seven or eight of the heavy German mortars abandoned by the enemy in the flooded districts round Dixmude. These engines, which did serious damage amongst the Allies' trenches, are most easily described in a word, 'German' – cumbrous, unwieldy, and as thick-set as their boots, their figures, and their 'kultur'.

Suddenly one's attention is diverted from these spoils of war. A regiment marches by. It is not at first so easy to recognise it, so mud-stained are the men, so few are the distinguishing marks and numbers left amongst its ranks. Then, in a moment, no doubt is left. It is the gallant 7th of the Belgian line. This is the regiment that fought so well at Liège in the early days of August, when, in a few hours, they lost half their number, putting up a stubborn and glorious resistance against overwhelming odds between the forts of that town under the very eye of its heroic defender, General Leman. They have been in the field ever since then, and only a few days ago their colours were decorated by King Albert in recognition of the valour displayed by the regiment at Pervyse, where they defiled under a murderous fire from the enemy between two hedges to the relief of their comrades in the trenches.

The 7th are followed by their dog transport. Harnessed two by two, these wonderfully trained animals draw their lightly built carts. Perfect order prevails amongst these sagacious 'friends of man'. Without guides they keep their distance, one team from the other, following the column with never an attempt at breaking away. They know their work well and perform it with, one is inclined to believe, a sense of duty. They seem to have thoroughly entered into the important role confided to them.

In one of the teams the dog on the right attracts much attention. He has been wounded. A big bandage envelops his head, and many are the words of encouragement shouted to him as he passes sedately by, straining at his traces made of cord, his stump of a tail wagging furiously the while. In no other way does he seem in the slightest degree impressed. His attitude is energetic, but grave. The regiment passes on, the dogs follow, and again the gallant 7th has gone forward to help in the deliverance of its beloved country.

At one time their trenches were so close to those of the enemy that during an occasional lull in the fighting they threw beetroot into the German lines, into which they stuck messages announcing the name of their regiment and their intentions towards their antagonists, which, I am told, were anything but reassuring.

15 December 1914

GUNS AND AIRSHIPS

Allies' Fine Work, *Northern France, Sunday*

By A. Beaumont

Whilst there has been great satisfaction here at the news of the British naval victory in the South Seas, there is no less satisfaction at the good news constantly received from the French, British, and Belgian operations in the field. A few days ago there was suddenly a rumour that a repulse had been met with, and this was rather a shock, considering that a repulse anywhere along the Franco–British front is, according to a foregone conclusion, impossible, and it was received, therefore, with incredulity. This was entirely justified, for the so-called repulse consisted simply in the loss of one advanced trench, which had been insufficiently guarded, and which the French immediately recaptured the following day, and to the success of which they added by capturing several other trenches in the same district from the enemy. It was another instance to prove that the Franco–British ascendancy is asserting itself more and more over the enemy, who may sometimes capture a trench, but is never able to hold it long, whereas the Allies thoroughly maintain themselves in every position conquered.

A great part of this is due to the heavy artillery with which the Allies are now well provided, and which is beginning to make its presence felt to such an extent that within the last two weeks the Allies have been able to destroy eighteen German guns and to silence forty-eight more or compel them to change their positions.

The French aeroplanes have also been active, and they have replied to the German attack on Hazebrouck by dropping bombs on the stations at Lille and Douai used by the enemy, and destroying his convoys.

The French and British troops are sparing the interests of the inhabitants along the fighting line as much as possible, but for military reasons a large number of villages have had to be evacuated. The Germans have made it a practice to shell and destroy every town or village from which they are driven, especially if it is still inhabited, and the order, therefore, given by the French to their own people is a humane one. In some places it is also a preparation for a very decided operation, and may be taken as a precursor of an advance in those quarters. There are several sections along the northern lines where people have been told to leave their villages recently, and beyond which the Germans have subsequently been driven a considerable distance.

We periodically hear rumours that Lille has been retaken either by the British or French, and so far the wish has been father to the thought. But I learn that the positions of the Allies have constantly improved, and that the French and British troops are not far from that important centre. One of the considerations kept in view is not to give the Germans, once they are driven out, a pretext or an opportunity for bombarding that town. Even when driven a considerable distance from a town the Germans do not give up their hope of destroying it, and when their shells no longer reach it they send their aeroplanes to drop bombs. A few days after the French had succeeded in throwing some shells on the railway station of Freiburg-in-Brisgau, the Germans took revenge by dropping more than half a dozen bombs from an aeroplane on a small town in the north of France 20 miles from the firing line, in which they killed fourteen persons and injured about twenty-five others.

Two, however, can play at this game, and the German Press itself now mentions that two French or English aeroplanes have again been seen in the Rhine Province and have been flying over Düsseldorf. No doubt it was not for nothing they went there. We are not told what damage they did to the military structures. In another instance the Germans complain that French aviators flew over an undefended town and dropped bombs. The Germans seem to know nothing whatever of what their aviators have been doing over Paris, where their bombs have killed civilians, as well as at Troyes, and at Amiens, where I myself saw a bomb explode which killed a poor woman, and more recently at St Omer, Hazebrouck, and Dunkirk.

The German Zeppelins tried to rival their aeroplanes, and they also have been flying over towns, and killing non-combatants. Of late they have abstained, it is true, because of the danger to themselves. The French dirigibles, on the other hand, are only now coming into action. I related some time ago how one of them destroyed a railway junction used by the Germans in the Vosges. A few weeks ago a French airship proceeded at night to another railway junction used by the Germans in the north for the transportation of German troops. The station at the time was filled with trains, with German soldiers, guns, and war material. The French dirigible, after hovering over the station, descended to within a convenient distance and dropped explosives on the engine-house, destroying a number of locomotives, and, proceeding a short distance beyond the junction, it dropped other explosives on a viaduct over which German troop trains were passing east and west, and destroyed it also, so that this particular railway line was put out of service for some time. At another point a French airship discovered an important ammunition centre of the Germans, and, by dropping some melinite bombs on it, succeeded in destroying all the war material accumulated there by the enemy. Two other successful raids were carried out at night by French airships in different places, when they succeeded in destroying the stations and railway junctions utilised by the Germans for the transport of troops and ammunition.

By the way, 10 December, when the Germans were to be at Calais, has come and gone, and they are not yet there. In connection with this there is a current joke, in spite of the tragic circumstances, in the cafés. When asked what is the Kaiser's favourite dance, the reply is, 'La Pas de Calais!' He has danced it so much that he is ill!

The heaviest cannonades during the past week have been between Ypres and Lille, and Lille and Arras, where the enemy has lost his superiority. The British heavy guns now at the front have a longer range than the heavy German artillery, and numerically the British field-guns are now also equal to those of the Germans. It was here that the British mortars and the French 75mm guns compelled the Germans to evacuate several positions. The infantry of the Allied armies, in each case, strongly organised the new positions taken. The British troops are still progressing north-east of Ypres.

The Germans have tried to regain the positions they lost on the Yser without success. In revenge they bombarded all the villages within reach of their guns, including Lampernisse, Coxyde, and Oostduinkerke. The French and Belgians have taken a number of prisoners lately in this district, especially at Bixschoote, where a Würtemburg battalion surrendered after losing half its men. One of the Belgian divisions distinguished itself greatly in taking an important position at Dixmude. It attacked the Germans at night and drove them from one of the last points they hold on the left bank of the Yser, cutting off a large detachment of the enemy by destroying a temporary bridge which the Germans had built. The entire detachment was annihilated.

1 January 1915

NEW YEAR PARTY AT THE THEATRE OF WAR
Thrilling Scenes, *Rouen, Wednesday*

Of the fact that the pathway of the railway traveller in France is not exactly strewn with roses in these times of war, the New Year Party now engaged in entertaining our troops at the theatre of war had today a somewhat painful experience. In my last despatch, hurriedly dashed off as the company were rushing for the train, I mentioned that an all-night journey to a destination that could not then be specifically mentioned lay in front of us. That journey proved a great deal longer and much more tedious than any member of the party anticipated when it was undertaken, and I mention the circumstances only for the purpose of showing that the work which Mr Seymour Hicks and his artistic friends have undertaken is no joy-ride or frivolous picnic, but a serious enterprise, involving real and strenuous labour.

Let me just mention the bare facts. Fresh from a successful entertainment given at the Allied Forces' Base Hospital at Boulogne, the New Year Party set out from their hotel in the Channel port at half-past four o'clock yesterday afternoon in order to reach Rouen by a military supply train to which a comfortable corridor carriage was specially attached for their use. Exactly twenty hours elapsed before the company reached their journey's end! Nor was the duration of the run the most irksome part of it. What was rather trying to the temper of the party was the fact that their train should have been held up for so many hours at a large railway depot absolutely within sight of Rouen. Again, to mention details, the train reached Sotteville – which might almost be described as a suburb of Rouen – at ten minutes to eight this morning, and it was exactly twenty minutes past midday when the party, after journeying two more miles, found themselves on Rouen platform, with no means of transport whatever available to convey them and their luggage to their hotel. It afterwards transpired that the whole business was the result of an unfortunate misunderstanding, and the episode was speedily blotted out by the profound interest of the events which befell in the course of the day.

It is one of the most remarkable features of the present tour that each gathering before which the New Year Party appears seems distinctly more interesting than its predecessor. When the company performed in the Boulogne Fruit Market on Monday night they were absolutely thrilled by the direct appeal which that gathering made to their sympathy and their imagination. The sight of 2,000 hale and hearty soldiers singing in patriotic chorus on the fringe of the theatre of war and clothed in war's habiliments is not a thing to be easily forgotten. But there were far more thrilling sights today. It is the common observation of the members of the company that the scenes they have witnessed at the gatherings they have entertained will remain in their recollection while memory holds its seat. We Britishers are apt to regard ourselves as a stolid and unemotional people. To see the emotional scenes that we have witnessed among our gallant soldiers over in France during the last four days will dispel that notion from our minds for all time. Well might Mr Seymour Hicks speak of the furtive tear that rushes to eye, of the lump that gathers in the throat, as one contemplates the audiences that we have seen and notes the effect which these entertainments exert upon them. Only now do we realise what our gallant fellows are doing and suffering for their country's sake. I have witnessed this week all manner of episodes which I shall never forget. Let me mention just a few. I have seen brave men weeping – stealthily, it is true, but nevertheless weeping under the influence of the spell which the artistry of Mr Hicks and his friends have cast over them. Only today an officer came up to Mr Hicks – who happened to be an old friend – and frankly confessed that he had openly wept while this afternoon's entertainment was in progress. I can still picture to myself – and, indeed, I shall never forget – the pale and intellectual-looking face of a bed-ridden officer who was only prevented from swooning away yesterday afternoon by the tender ministrations of a gentle nurse. The emotions aroused by the concert were for one brief moment almost more than this stricken officer could bear. And in discussing the psychology of such scenes it is well to remember how large a part gratitude to the artists plays in them. These brave men have absolutely no words with which to express to the ladies and gentlemen who are entertaining them the debt they owe for physical suffering lightened, for monotony dispelled, for slumbering memories awakened, for ardent hopes revived. Assuredly Mr Hicks and the ladies and gentlemen who are so sympathetically supporting him in the present adventure never did a better week's work in their lives than they are doing now.

Of the pathetic instances I have beheld of sorely stricken soldiers struggling bravely to smile or to raise enfeebled arms in the effort to applaud I must not speak. The emotions they awaken are too acute. But let me mention one incident which occurred this afternoon.

In the company of one or two of the artists I was driving through a muddy camp on the conclusion of a remarkable entertainment which I have yet to describe. The car was threading its way slowly among groups of dispersing soldiers, when presently a bright little fellow in khaki stepped forward. 'Is Mr Seymour Hicks here?' he inquired, almost shyly. 'No,' I replied, for I happened to be sitting nearest to him. 'Oh,' he said, 'would you please give him this?' as he thrust into my hand an object which I was unable to recognise in the gathering darkness. 'Certainly, my lad,' I replied; 'I shall do so with the greatest pleasure.'

On hearing these words his pensive, deep-set eyes glistened. 'What name shall I mention?' I asked, as he walked beside the car. 'It is written inside,' he answered. 'And would you please mention to Mr Hicks that it has been through Mons?' he added. 'I certainly shall,' I promised. 'Please don't forget,' he said almost plaintively as the car moved off. 'It's a souvenir.' And what do you think the souvenir was? A prayer book, with the name and regimental number of the donor pencilled on the fly-leaf, and the fact mentioned that it was presented to Mr Hicks as a souvenir.

Mr Hicks, I could see, was deeply touched when I handed the little book over to him. Thoughtfully he pondered the inscription; then he thrust the booklet into his pocket without a word. It may be a satisfaction to the humble donor to know that Mr Hicks will cherish this memento as one of his most precious possessions. I know that he will try to find the man tomorrow in order to thank him personally. If he fails to find him he means to send him a letter of thanks which will warm his heart and be to him, in turn, a valued keepsake. And so the forces of patriotism and mutual sympathy act and react as this wonderful tour proceeds.

Today's gatherings, two in number, were amongst the most striking which the tour has so far brought together. The former of the two took place in what might be described in general terms as a sort of rest camp, situated some miles out of Rouen. In a huge circus tent somewhat reminding one, in its proportions, of the Umbrella Tent at Bisley, were assembled well nigh 2,000 wounded and sick soldiers. Quite a large number of them had been brought in by conveyances from a hospital in the district. The great majority of them, I was told, had only recently come down from the battle front, and the convalescences of most of them, I was also informed, had so far advanced that the men hoped very soon to be able to return to the firing line. All manner of corps were comprised in the gathering, which packed the tent to overflowing. Made up so largely of men who had but recently been in the trenches, and of men who were speedily regaining the health and fitness that would enable them to take their places there once again, the assembly was of just the sort which the New Year Party have from the outset been sighing to be brought into contact with.

It did your heart good to watch the exhilarating effect which this concert had upon the men. They instantly forgot all their troubles and gave themselves up without reserve to the enjoyment of the music and mirth that were lavishly provided for them. Not a joke did they miss; they eagerly seized upon every chorus that came along. At one moment they rocked with hilarious laughter; the next, they sang in chorus so vigorously that the canvas of the tent seemed in danger of being ripped by the sound. They followed Miss St Helier's 'rag-time' leads with the greatest alertness, and avidity; their shout of 'No!' punctuating the song 'Are We Downhearted?' might have been heard in Rouen; 'It's a Long Way to Tipperary' was balm to their cheery souls; 'Sister Susie's Sewing' Shirts for Soldiers' was an enormous success; and it was curious to observe that when Miss St Helier asked them to name yet another song which she might submit to them, their choice fell upon 'The Rosary', just as it did at Boulogne on Monday night.

Tonight's concert, presented in the Theatre des Beaux Arts, was the most imposing entertainment which the New Year Party have yet given. There was an enormous demand for admission, and the theatre, which at a rough estimate might accommodate 3,000 persons, was packed from floor to ceiling with men in khaki. Saving that a larger proportion of the men appeared to be in sound health, the temper of the gathering was very similar to that shown by the camp audience earlier in the day. The scent for a joke was even keener, the readiness to take up a popular chorus was quite as noticeable. And again it was patent to every eye and ear that the entertainment which the New Year Party are to provide is of precisely the sort that our soldiers love. No wonder the programme was carried through with such triumphant success; the mere sight of such an audience was calculated to inspire any artist.

8 January 1915

GERMAN OUTRAGES IN FRANCE
Commission's Report, *Paris, Thursday Evening*

The official report of the Commission of Inquiry into the atrocities perpetrated by the German troops in France has been published by the French Government today. No document ever drawn up equalled this one in horror; no such appalling list of hideous crimes has ever in history been proved against an army since armies have been armies and not wild hordes of savages. A universal cry of wrath and horror will go up over the whole non-German world at the perusal of this frightful indictment.

The Commission consists of MM Georges Payelle, First President of the Court of Accounts; Armand Mollard, Minister Plenipotentiary; Georges Maringer, Councillor of State; and Edmond Paillot, Councillor of the Court of Cassation. All the evidence obtained was taken down on oath, which the Commission had powers to administer. I begin with passages in the covering letter addressed to the Prime Minister: 'Entrusted by the decree of 23 September with the duty of proceeding into an inquiry respecting acts contrary to the rights of nations committed by the enemy in the French territory which he occupied, and which has been reconquered by the armies of the Republic, we submit the first report of our mission. This includes only a small part of the statements we might have set forth had we not exercised the severest control on all the information we obtained. We record only facts incontrovertibly proved, discarding all those which were insufficiently proved. We entertain, accordingly, the firm conviction that none of the incidents we give will be questioned in good faith. The proofs are not derived solely from our observations, but are moreover supported by many photographic documents and by deposition made on oath.

'Our painful duties would have seemed to be almost intolerable had we not found comfort in contact with our splendid troops, and with the admirable and brave population, from which we never heard a complaint, although the terrible sufferings we witnessed surpass the horror of anything the imagination can conceive. It may, indeed, be affirmed that no war between civilised nations ever bore a character of such savage ferocity as that shown by our implacable enemy. Pillage, outrage, arson, and murder are the common practice of our enemy; and the facts daily revealed, which are so many crimes against all laws, punished as such by all countries, prove the most astonishing regression in the German mentality since 1870.

'Assaults on women and girls have been of a frequency unknown in warfare before. The many cases we have established can be but a negligible proportion of those committed. Had the commanders troubled to prevent such outrages, fewer would have been perpetrated, but they may in the last resort be considered as isolated and individual acts of brutality. The same cannot be urged for the theft, murder, and incendiarism of the German troops. The German command, up to the most highly placed, must bear before humanity the crushing onus of these crimes.

'Wherever our inquiry has taken us we have found that the German army showed utter contempt of human life, that soldiers and even leaders despatch the wounded, slay pitilessly inoffensive inhabitants of invaded territory, and in their homicidal fury spare neither old men, women, nor children.

'The Germans have always given the same pretext, viz, that the civilians had fired upon them. This allegation is false, and those who made it could not render it plausible even by firing shots in the neighbourhood of houses, as has been their custom. Of this we have definite proofs.

'Here is one among many: One evening, when the Curé of Croismare was standing near a German officer, a shot was heard. The officer cried out, "M. le Curé, that is enough to have you shot and the Mayor as well, and to burn a farm to the ground. Look, there is one burning already."

'The priest replied, "But you are too intelligent not to recognise the sharp sound of your own rifles." The officer did not reply.

'Liberty, like life, is despised by the German military authorities. Almost everywhere citizens of all ages have been torn from their homes and taken into captivity. Many have died or were killed on the journey. Incendiarism, even more than murder, is one of the usual proceedings of our adversaries, either as a means of systematic devastation or of intimidation. The German army is fitted out with a complete incendiary apparatus, including torches, grenades, fuses, petrol-pumps, sticks of fusing matter, and pastilles composed of a very inflammable compressed powder. In our report on the incendiary fury of the German army, we have taken care not to include the villages where the devastation has been due to shells or to causes impossible to determine.

'As for looting, we do not hesitate to say that wherever the German troops have passed they have in the presence of their officers, and even with their participation, given themselves up to methodical pillaging. Cellars have been emptied to the last bottle; safes forced; silver, pictures, furniture, artistic objects, linen, women's dresses, sewing machines, even children's toys carried off, then placed on vehicles, and sent over the frontier.'

The report proceeds to give details of the outrages in the districts covered by Commissioners, namely, Seine et Marne, Marne, Meuse, Meurthe et Moselle, Oise, and Aisne. Many of the outrages are of so unthinkable a brutality it is impossible to recount them. Especially is this the case for the Seine et Marne, the department closest to the invaders' great objective, Paris. Incendiarism and murder as well as outrages on women were practised everywhere. On 6 September at Constacon, a band of soldiers belonging, it is believed, to the

Imperial Guard, after burning the majority of the houses of the village, took with them five men and a boy of thirteen, and throughout the whole of the engagement exposed them to the French fire.

In the same commune a lad belonging to the 1914 class was cruelly done to death. The Mayor of the commune, asked as to the military status of the youth, said he had passed the doctor's, but that his class was not yet called out. The Germans stripped the boy to judge his physical condition, and then shot him.

'We note, according to the statement of the municipal councillor of Rebais, that two English cavalrymen, surprised and wounded in this commune, were despatched by the Germans, though they were dismounted, and one of them held up his hands to show that he was disarmed.'

In the department of the Marne, at Sermaize, a labourer, one Brocard, was among the hostages. When the soldiers came to take him and his son, his stricken wife and daughter-in-law, terror-stricken, ran and flung themselves into the Saulx. The old man managed to free himself from his captors, and made several efforts to save them. But the Germans overtook him and dragged him back pitilessly, leaving the two wretched women to drown in the river. When, four days later, Brocard and his son were released and recovered the dead bodies, they found bullet wounds through the heads of each.

At Champguyon Madame Louvert, seeing her husband dragged away by a band of soldiers, who were bludgeoning him, ran to the railing of her house and tried to kiss him. She was brutally thrown back, and fell to the ground. Her husband was killed just outside the village. When his wife found him he was terribly disfigured. His skull was crushed, one of his eyes hung outside the socket, and one of his wrists was broken.

In the department of the Meuse the village of Dommeilles is only a heap of ruins. It was set on fire by the Germans by means of apparatus resembling bicycle pumps. When the village began to burn Madame X, whose husband is with the colours, took refuge in the cellar with her four children, aged eleven, five, four, and eighteen months. Several days after the dead bodies of the whole family were discovered in a pool of blood. The mother's right arm and right breast had been cut off. The foot of the girl of eleven had been severed, and the throat of the boy of five cut.

Clermont-en-Argonne was first pillaged and then burned by Würtemberg regiments. While the houses were burning the soldiers entered the church, which stands apart on a height, and danced to the sound of the organ before returning to the work of destruction.

At Trivaucourt, the Germans burned the village and organised a wholesale murder of the inhabitants. They began by setting fire to the house of a peaceable proprietor, whom they shot down as he ran out to escape the flames. Fearing for their lives a young woman Mlle Procés, her mother, her grandmother of seventy-one, and an old aunt of eighty-one, tried to climb over the wall of their garden. The girl succeeded and was saved. The three older women failed and were shot down. The curé of the village had the bodies carried back into the house.

During the night that followed the Germans played the piano in the room in which the bodies of their victims were lying.

In the Department of Meurthe et Moselle the most tragic of all the terrible scenes at Nomény took place in the cellar of M. Vassé, in which a number of the inhabitants had taken refuge. At four o'clock fifty German soldiers broke into the house and set fire to it. As the unhappy refugees attempted to escape they were shot down. A boy who was carrying his baby sister in his arms fell. As he was only wounded a soldier put the muzzle of his rifle next to the boy's ear and blew his brains out.

Next it was the turn of the Keiffer family. The mother was wounded in the arm and shoulder. The father, a boy of ten, and a little girl of three, were shot down. The murderers continued firing on them as they lay on the ground. The last to leave the cellar were a girl of seventeen and her sister of three. The younger child was struck by a bullet in the elbow; the elder flung herself to the ground and shammed death. A soldier kicked her as she lay.

At Gerbéviller, of 475 houses only twenty are now habitable. More than 100 persons have disappeared. Fifty at least were murdered, some in their houses, others in the fields. Thirty-six corpses have so far been identified, among them are six women and a child of fourteen.

The Germans entered the house of the Hingenheld family, seized the son, aged thirty-six, who was bearing a Red Cross armlet, dragged him into the street, and shot him. As he still moved the Germans soaked the body in petrol and set fire to it before his mother's eyes! They then returned to the house, dragged out the elder Hingenheld, and shot him in the evening.

Madame Rozier heard the cries of 'Mercy! Mercy!' coming from the lofts near her house. An individual who acted as interpreter to the Germans has stated to a Madame Thiébaut that the invaders had boasted of having burned above a father with his five children in spite of their cries for mercy. This statement receives confirmation from the fact that in one of the lofts were found charred human remains.

On 29 August the Superior of the hospice, Sister Julie, whose devotion has been admirable, having gone to the parish church, noticed that an attempt had been made to force the steel door of the sanctuary. The Germans, to gain possession of the sacred vessel, had fired shots round the lock. The door had been pierced in several spots, and the holes were symmetrical, which proved that the shots had been fired point-blank. When Sister Julie opened the door she found that the ciborium had been pierced by a bullet.

12 February 1915

FAMOUS COUP FOR THE KAISER'S BIRTHDAY
How it Failed, *Flanders, February*

The recent fights in front of La Bassée seem to have attracted a good deal of attention. Some wonderful descriptions have been published in several papers, which we have read here with delight and also with amusement. I have been, and still am, fortunate enough to be very closely associated with those who know what is going on in that part of the front; but I must confess I have never heard of a shrapnel killing a number of sparrows on a tree as was recently stated by an interpreter who happened to be interviewed after the battle. Nevertheless, I have learned enough of the fight – a fight which is still going on – to think that everything has not yet been told about it. It was, indeed, a curious affair. The main feature of it was that the Germans had apparently started a new game – that of trying to make the British hate the French, and vice-versa.

They are a cunning race. As a matter of fact, they had tried to sow mutual distrust between the Allies long before the big 'coup' which they attempted to achieve as a birthday present to their Kaiser. It is already known, I believe, that their aviators drop proclamations in the French lines in which they politely ask the French to desert England. When they were compelled to abandon Vermelles, which lies a few miles south of La Bassée canal, they left an inscription on a wall, which ran about thus: 'Frenchmen! Are you not aware that you have been led into this frightful war by England's intrigues? Do wake up, &c.'

According to what I heard quite recently, the 'Boches' do even better than that. Among the numerous spies whom they manage to keep among the Allies, some are specially entrusted with the task of stirring up bad blood between the two Allied armies. Extraordinary news is spread among the 'piou-pious'. On a fine morning they are suddenly told by nobody knows who that the English have been badly beaten somewhere, that they are afraid of the Germans, and cannot be trusted to hold their part of the line. The same process is repeated on the English side, where the 'Tommies' are informed by some benevolent civilian, whom they have never met before, that the French are retiring in disorder, and that the British Army is going to be left in the lurch.

I came personally across one of those rumours on the very morning of 25 January, after the battle in Givenchy and Cuinchy had begun. While I was talking to a French officer in a village near by, an excited soldier came and asked us if it were true that the English had just lost several miles of ground, and that the French left had been turned by the enemy. The officer smiled, and said it was just one of the 'canards' they heard almost every week. It is fortunate, indeed, that the war has not entirely deprived both English and French of their common-sense, otherwise the German agents would have had a chance of creating trouble.

Now the fighting which started on both banks of the canal on 25 January, is only the outcome of this secret and unsuccessful preparation. The whole German scheme was rather well conceived. Not only was the attack to be a sudden one, but it was to be directed at the same time on the British right, and on the French extreme left. The German idea was obviously to break through at any of these two places, and then attack the other fellow from behind, so as to make him sick with his neighbour.

I am not going to repeat here what has already been described in the official and semi-official accounts. The interesting fact, however, is that, if the understanding between the Allies had not been what it is, the Machiavellian plan of the enemy might have succeeded. The first main attack on the British trenches, had been so sudden and so overwhelming that the Tommies had to evacuate their front line for a time. The 'Boches' availed themselves of that temporary retirement to assault the French trenches from behind. The result was that the French had to give up some ground also. But then the British counter-attack succeeded in recapturing the best part of the ground, when the Tommies found that the French trench immediately to their right was some distance behind them. Both sides began wondering what their friends had been doing. It was, for a moment, an awkward feeling.

The trick was, however, too conspicuous to be very effective. As soon as it was possible to exchange some necessary explanations, both sides laughed heartily over their mutual suspicions, and set themselves to work to prevent the little German game from going on any longer. The experience of the last few days has shown that the Germans must give up any hope of making any headway at all in that particular place. Moreover, instead of creating a sort of distrust between the Allies, the Germans have only managed to draw them closer together. This last achievement is not a new one. We have seen it often since the days of Algeciras. It is, indeed, to be wondered if France and England would ever, without Germany's help, have managed to reach their present happy and lasting intimacy.

But the Germans are obstinate. Having come to the belief that the best fun to be had is around La Bassée, they do not seem to have given up in the least the new game they started at the end of last month. Some of the attacks they are delivering are so preposterous that everybody is wondering if they do not send their men to the slaughter for the mere pleasure of seeing them ascend to the Paradise of the 'old German God'. A few days ago, for instance, they launched a whole battalion on the French trench. The attack was made during the day, without any preparation by artillery fire. Of course, the French were on the watch. The first two lines of Germans were simply mown down; the third managed to reach the trench, where it was received by French bayonets. One hundred and fifty dead Germans are now lying in front of that particular trench. The French only lost ten men. One of them had been shot by a German captain, commanding the attack, after that captain had been made a prisoner. After such a deed the German hero was, of course, instantly sent to a better world. The Allies only wish that the enemy will go on sacrificing in such a way the lives of their bravest men as soon as they arrive at the front.

Meanwhile, the co-operation between the British and the French troops does not confine itself to the mere defensive, but is daily becoming more unpleasant for the enemy. I do not think one can lay too much stress upon the useful work performed by the combined fire of the British and French artillery. Their association is already an old one. On the day the Germans launched a big attack on Givenchy, north of the canal, the batteries of '75s' belonging to the neighbouring French division suddenly started firing across the canal on the German masses, which were advancing against the British trenches. Since that day, the combined artillery fire of the Allies has not given an hour's rest to the Germans. While the field artillery is firing mostly at the trenches, the heavy guns are searching day and night the villages and roads behind the German firing line, which are known to be occupied by troops.

In order to appreciate the worry this continuous firing is causing to the enemy, it is necessary to proceed to the trenches. There you hear every now and then the whistling of a shell which flies over your head and explodes a few hundred yards further over the holes where the 'Boches' are hiding, or seems to lose itself in the air until a distant and formidable explosion announces that a French or British 'Black Maria' has safely landed in the very place where the German general is enjoying his breakfast. The unpleasant nature of this bombardment is mainly due to its variety. For one hour, the '75' will remain silent, and suddenly the explosive shells will pour like hail over the enemy's trenches for a minute or two. The British howitzers are even more wicked. They allow the Germans to go to sleep, thinking that they will have at last a quiet night. Then at some impossible hour, such as 2 or 3 a.m., the loud voice of 'Teddy' or 'Mary' makes itself heard all over the country, and you know that the German night will not have been so quiet after all. The German reply is always weak. I have been informed that for every four or five German at least twenty or twenty-five have been counted coming from the Allies' side; on that day life must have been very uncomfortable in La Bassée.

Most prisoners agree to this. Some of the recent ones had that tired and anxious look which is peculiar to people constantly worried. They stated that the Allies' fire was killing men every day in some unexpected place; that they had been living themselves in a state of perpetual anxiety, which had been telling upon their nerves. One of them had been without food for two days because the supply column which was bringing up the rations had been stopped on the main road by our shells. No wonder he seemed quite relieved at the thought of being away from that hell.

There is indeed every reason to believe that such a daily process will slowly, but surely, wear out the moral resistance of the Germans. We will hear of other offensive movements against the junction of the British and French army. This is, however, only due to the fact that the Germans must keep the offensive, or at any rate pretend to keep it, until there is not one man left on their side. The Allies know it; they also know that they have nothing to fear and everything to gain from that obduracy.

13 February 1915

GARIBALDIAN LEGION'S FIGHT FOR FRANCE
An Epic of Devotion, *In the Argonne, January*

By Luigi Barzini

On the muddy meadow that stretches behind the farmhouse of Grange des Côtes the regiment is forming square – the preface of military ceremonial.

The day is sombre, mournful, chill, with a fine, cold rain that is but snow melted; steadily, evenly it falls, yet imperceptibly and without sound. Around, the forest of the Argonne darkens. Its profile is cut in the billowing line of the hills, and the dark, dense masses of its trees cover the slopes with a cloudy, greyish softness, as a monstrous fur coat.

After the calm and spreading plains of the Marne and the Aisne the land crisps, roughens, farrows; then, as it approaches the frontier line, rises with blunt menace, interposing its barrier also on the threshold of France. As it passes eastward the land loses gradually that aspect of peace which is given by the secular trace of cultivation, the tilled lands grow fewer, turn to wild, reach once more the primeval condition. Here one would say Man came only to fight. Unrolling in the winter desolation the landscape is unspeakably cruel.

The valleys are filled with a deep, echoing roar, borne from afar. It comes from the Gruerie, from the Chalade Wood, from the wood of Rechicourt, from Varenne, from Verdun – a furious arc.

One gets the impression that the battle runs in the forest like some gigantic hunting. On hill and in valley the tremendous battue is loosed. It lingers in dark frozen gorges that roar like craters, slips rustling through entangling briars as the shrapnel strips the boughs, advances as the grenades prune them under the endless colonnade of trees, over the thick soft yellow carpet of the fallen leaves. Now here, now there, the full-throated cannon resound – a baying of Titan hounds.

Towards the Grange des Côtes the forest reaches lands that know the plough. The multitude of trees opens out, advances in a straggling fashion by strips, disciplines itself, and finally draws up in array as the cleared lands begin. On the borders of the muddy pasture land are only meadows, regular as the ranks of a giant militia. At the farthest edge of the camp a wood sways; the swaying stops as it meets a marshalled rank of trees, whose leafless trunks stand out clearly in the gloomy background. Round the regiment which is forming in square a superb phalanx of ash and elm makes a greater square. Dark, silent, dominating, these trees arrayed have an indefinably majestical air.

It is the 4th Service Battalion of the First Foreign Regiment that is manœuvring there. Since it has been in action it has, even officially, another name. It is the 'Garibaldian Legion'. In fight it has won the distinction it claimed. It has shown that they were the Garibaldians who fought side by side. The historic name, like a title of nobility, had to prove legitimacy by blood.

It is making ready now, this Legion, for a solemn ceremony, which is the consecration of its work. The general commanding the division comes to convey to the regiment the honours with which the French Republic decorates it. To all who deserved, the General Staff could not give the hero's reward; there were too many. The officially rewarded are fifteen; four military medals and eleven Crosses of the Legion of Honour make up the first garland of glory which the Garibaldians gathered in the trenches of the enemy. More numerous still are the 'mentions' in Orders of the Day.

Nothing could surpass in force and efficacy the 'motive' of the honours given, as the documents of the General Staff set it down. Never was so much poetry packed in so little compass of prose. They sound with the note of a hymn, these reports in the style of a guard corporal. In two or three lines of a blunt, military, almost violent concision, there is all a wonderful episode, a whole furious fight with its changing phases. They are cold and without colour; and when you read them it is as though grains of powder were fired, and one looked on the light of undying flame. Here, counter-signed by Joffre himself, is the 'motive' why Peppino Garibaldi receives the Cross of the Legion of Honour: 'On 26 December, on foot, in the front line of the French trenches, he did not cease to expose himself and to encourage his men, during two attacks delivered against the enemy's trenches fifty yards away. On 15 January he conducted, with the same brilliant valour, his regiment, which captured the positions assigned to it.'

One seems to see it all. In the terrible morning of 26 December Peppino Garibaldi was on the extreme right of his men, in an advanced trench, a hail of bullets whistling about him. Former defenders of the trench plucked him by the sleeve. 'Get down, Colonel. You'll be killed.' He made a refusing gesture, and went forward with uplifted sword, raising his battle-cry. Around him fell the wounded. Even as he was emerging from the trench a corporal sank back in his arms. But he said: 'It is nothing. Go on.'

The company he had disposed dashed on with him, like an avalanche; not far forward they broke on barbed wire in the wood. Their commander at their head, wave after wave of men flung itself forward. 'Italy! Italy!' In another's war the sacred name of country rushed up from their throats – an evocation, a prayer. As each line passed, Garibaldi gave it stirring greeting. 'Brave souls, on!' They vanished all into the dense underwood, which filled with noise and shouting. Without waiting for the order, the reserves flung themselves into the assault, so burning with impatience were they. It was then that Peppino Garibaldi saw for the last time his brother Bruno. 'Bravo! Bruno.' 'Peppino, adieu!' And Garibaldi had a premonition of unavailing sacrifice.

By a fatal misunderstanding the first rush of Garibaldians was to fall, not on the German trenches, but the French. The plan was to drive the Germans from a wooded height of the plateau of Bolante, which dominates the surrounding region. The German trenches crowded the height. A French trench furrowed the slopes. There was need that the summit should be taken. Fifty metres only separated the trenches of the adversaries. The assault was to be directed upon the south-east of the plateau. On the 22nd Colonel Garibaldi made a reconnaissance to establish the order of attack. On the 24th the General Staff decided it would be better to make the assault from another point. Time was lacking to prepare the full details. On un-reconnoitred ground Garibaldi had to form his plan according to the information furnished by guides. There were three lines of French trenches; it was thought there were two only. The Italian Legion disposed itself behind the second, in the belief that before them were the trenches of the enemy. And they fell upon the French trench as into a trap.

The enemy, who had heard the shout of the charge and saw no troops arriving, had time to make ready, and the fire of their machine-guns swept the ground as a scythe sweeps the grass. Their defence had the maximum of efficiency. And yet the assault succeeded.

The Garibaldians, helping each his fellow, climbed out of the trench of the French like madmen, and continued their course. They were caught in the wire entanglements stretched for the protection of the trench; it was here the most fell. A few paces away sounded excited German voices. From this point the attack was individual. Separated from each other by the growth of the wood the Garibaldians yet rushed on with such irresistible impetus and such force that the enemy, imagining they were faced with a formidable offensive, abandoned their trench, first blowing part of it in the air. The fight was at an end, and the Germans had been driven from the position.

But the Garibaldians could not occupy the post. There were none but dead in their first line, and the second line lay on the ground to escape the hurricane of shells which came from the second German line, which searched the ground narrowly, and punished with death an incautious gesture.

Amongst those who had penetrated farthest under the withering fire was Bruno Garibaldi; he lay now a few feet from the enemy's trenches. And the carrying of his body to its last resting-place which was to end with the apotheosis of Rome and a multitude of people began slowly – very slowly – under fire, in the covering night, amid the eerie silence of the forest. It was two hours and a half before the little space which in the last twenty seconds of his life he had leaped was retraced.

A youth who was to die in the next fight, who was already marked down by destiny, whose hours were numbered, whose agony was already near, was among those who stumbled in the mud under the burden of the body. A glimmer of light slipped between the clouds. From the trenches men watched with beating hearts the imperceptible approach of the little band; a dark mass rustling in the leaves. The Germans, too, marked the rustling. At each louder sound they fired. The bearers heard the soft thud of bullets lodging in the body they bore. The movement of the mass ceased. Five, ten, fifteen minutes passed. 'It is over. Is he dead too? Are there two?' 'No. They are moving still.' Then the mass, confused, indistinct, shifting, resumed its march of inches. A heroic funeral.

But on 5 January 'the regiment captured the positions'. That was the revenge. The Garibaldians burned for it. The height of Bolante had still to be taken. The French threatened on a certain sector the first German trench; the Germans threatened the French. One must soon blow the other up. There was no time to lose. The galleries of the French mine had not yet reached the enemy's position; there were five to ten inches still. No matter; the charges of dynamite could be increased. The Garibaldians were to make the assault when the explosion was fired.

It was a scene of cataclysm. From sixty cannon 18,000 grenades were vomited to prepare and sustain the attack. The flashes made a continuous blue lightning, quivering, fantastic, dazzling in the darkness of early morning. The eyes of the combatants were blinded by the flame. It was in an inferno of lights, burstings, whistlings, growlings, on ground that quaked and trembled, the assault took place with everything in convulsion, under a rain of rocks and stones falling on the earth.

For the Garibaldians did not wait the signal. The trumpet was to sound the charge when all the mines were exploded. The legionaries were at their post near the bridge that crossed the French trench, crouched like hounds on a leash. At the first explosion they departed; the reserves also. They entered the earthquake. And in the devilish clamour of the forest, in the eruptions and the convulsion, there was one dominant cry, the strong shouting of voices crying 'Italy! Italy!' the war-cry of the race.

They knew that at bottom it was for Italy they fought. In the hour when the worth of nations is measured and their valour in war, this Italian phalanx put the precious metal of its blood to the touchstone of the great war. And it burned with splendour, a purple flame.

The skilfulness of manœuvres, the correctness of tactics, the objective, the fight carried against the enemy, the uniform worn, have for Italians a secondary importance. It is the manner in which those sons of hers faced death that exalts them: the scorn of it, the rush, to a man, to meet the danger, the enthusiasm, the heroism, which make of what they did a national heritage. It sufficed for Peppino Garibaldi to evoke the souvenir of country for every hesitation to disappear in any moment of ebbing.

Driven out of the first, then the second trench, the Germans delivered a strong counter-attack out of the third, from Varenne. Beneath the thrust of over-whelming masses the Garibaldians wavered. 'On for Italy!' At the word they flung themselves again into the fray. Many re-emerged with prisoners in their grip, demanding them with the pride of the hunter who claims a rare prey. 'He is mine. He is mine.' And then, with one accord, they carried them simply to Garibaldi. 'Keep them for us, Colonel.' And they went out to seek for more.

Among the Garibaldians was a boy of thirteen. They found him during the night march on the Chalade road, seated on a stone. 'What are you waiting for?' 'For the Italians.' 'We are the Italians.' 'Here am I.' He rose up and followed them. He had no one left to him – the house had been burned by the Germans. So he sought the army. He was first with a battery, afterwards with a regiment of Zouaves. Then he heard of the Garibaldians, and went to look for them. The commander of the battalion with a gruff kindliness, repulsed him. 'This is no place for a boy.' He went off, but returned again.

At the attack he was there with his new friends, a gavroche of the forest. 'May I have a rifle?' he asked a lieutenant. There were rifles to spare, for blood had been shed. 'Find one.' The boy scampered off into the wood under the burden of the enormous weapon which he took from a dead sergeant, carolling with delight. At the second counter-attack he disappeared. They found him as they came to take up the captured positions. He was lying in his own blood. The fair head rested on his rifle, the arms were open, the breast torn. They touched his cold brows. 'Poor little trampled flower; and no one even asked thy name.'

A company of Italians remained in the trenches at Bolante till yesterday. After the assault of the Garibaldians the combat took fantastic forms. Five yards separated the French and the Germans. The Germans recaptured their first trenches on the edge of the plateau, and the French occupied excavations caused by the explosions which went beyond the German trench.

There were eight deep craters, reached by the mine galleries, converted into approach trenches. As, finally, these approaches would be too exposed, they were retained in tunnel form. So narrow were they that you passed sidelong. Occupying the bottom of the craters, the French began sapping to join them together. They dug by night, throwing up shovels of earth on the German side, round little wood loopholes, prepared and adjusted to the leafed masked edge of the trench border. A machine-gun, placed in position, protected the work from surprise. Meanwhile, the Germans were occupied with pursuing the work of their trenches. The labours of both proceeded parallel, and the widest apart points were ten yards from each other.

Every now and then a shot, a cry, a blasphemy; the German 'sniper' has reached his target – the hand of a French soldier as he raised it with the shovel, and the man writhes with the pain of his smashed fingers.

Then the machine-gun would awaken with a tata-ta-ta-ta; presently there was quiet again, and in the silence of the forest you heard only the regular boring of the sap into the hard soil and dull falling of earth on the parapets. The Italians were behind, ready to sustain the position, still uncertain against the rush of a counter-attack.

Before the enemy's trenches there are two great trees whose trunks touch. Behind the giant boughs was ensconced a German observation post. A short approach leads to it, safely. Now the parapet of the new French trench came as far as the foot of these trees. And so it happened that French and German were only separated by the thickness of a tree-trunk. You heard if the enemy's sentinels, in moving, rubbed the tree.

At this distance apart it is not possible to extend, in front of the trench, defences of barbed wire. So *chevaux de frise* are made out of heavy interlacings of wood, arranged easel fashion, and bristling with points, as men used in the Middle Ages, and these are thrown out beyond the parapet to constitute an obstacle. Sometimes they are launched with such violence to worry the Germans that 'one, two, three' and a *cheval de frise* has landed on their heads. Teutonic curses, a discharge of fire, groans, and laughter. 'I say there's something coming over from the other side.' And '*Ein, zwei, drei,*' screeching and swaying, the thing comes back again.

There is always firing, and at such a distance not a shot misses. It is enough for a cap to show above the ramparts to be pierced through. Let a loophole be unmasked, and the man behind it is dead. To shelter from the cold the Germans often put glass in the loopholes, stolen from Heaven knows where, leaving only opening for a rifle barrel. At times the reflection betrays them – between the branches the French distinguish the Boche in the glass. They focus him, and then fire as at some stalked quarry. Smash goes the window with a shivering, and 'I have broken his pipe', says the man who had fired contentedly. The dead here are more numerous than the wounded, for the wounds are almost always head wounds. As with the submarines, periscopes have been made so as to observe the ground without exposing one's head. The periscope allows one to see what is not to be seen from the loopholes.

Between the two parapets of these adversaries, so near to each other, corpses lie, mud-caked, rotting, in their last tragic gesture – German corpses and Italian. The air of death is all around; a heaviness as of sepulchre pervades the life in the trench. A German lies on the parapet of the enemy's trenches. He thrusts out his hands and his head from the trench. No one pulls him in or casts him forth. You see the spikes of helmets pass and repass this horror tranquilly. It is an indifference terrifying and splendid. Death has become a familiar. He is always there; he comes and goes, tapping this or that one on the shoulder, gathers all, and for those who fall is neither shuddering nor respect. A dead body is a companion who sleeps and will not waken.

All the wounded cannot be recovered. In certain positions the gravest cases remained on the ground. The air was filled with lamentations. Then the groans sank, a few feet from the trench and one was able to do nothing. At every sound in the night there was a discharge of fire and the bursting out, lividly, of hand-grenades. The forest lighted up with the long flare of the rockets, which the Germans launched at the slightest rustling.

But the corpses help the work of reconnaissance. From time to time in the night hours, such deep silence comes as to make one think the enemy is no longer there, and there is always some daring spirit who will go and see. Without arms, capless, covered with mud, he climbs out. His companions throw out now and then a grenade, and at each explosion he makes a little movement forward. A light blazes out, three, four, five seconds pass, while the wood grows a gay splendour beneath Bengal lights. There is nothing. Only the dead. But the man is there, holding his breath, stiffened as to stone; another corpse. Some time afterwards he returns to say that in the German trenches there is a new company. Fresh troops, a little fearful, are always silent.

There is a Garibaldian, the orderly of a French lieutenant of the Legion, who is unsurpassable in this 'game of the dead man'. He played it in sheer sport. He used to go among the dead gathering German outfit, made a collection of knapsacks, belts, bayonets, and helmets, carried his excursions as far as the parapets of the enemy's trenches. They had the notion of looking at him once under Bengal lights, but, even two hand-breadths away, he was indubitably dead. He had observed that corpses lie never in a reposeful attitude, and had penetrated the secret of their bizarre and terrible mimicry, and at the slightest alarm would be with his forehead on the earth, his feet twisted, one leg drawn up, one arm in the air, perfect. He died half a dozen times over thus.

One could almost feel the enemy in those windless nights, when the forest held its breath. They were so near that you might hear coughs, the blowing of noses, whispered conversations, the click of arms. In other sectors of the immense front it seems that, this nearness improved relations, and that, between trench and trench, men granted each other a little respite, a partial armistice, had meetings even. Here the relations had no amenity. It was a ferocious intimacy. They hated each other; there was too much blood between them. They spoke to curse only, the man who showed himself was struck down. People fired quite uselessly sometimes out of madness, when the Germans sang and when they laughed.

This war at a voice-length has taken on an antique cast. Disused weapons, got out of military museums, have entered into the conflict. In the French trenches in the Argonne you may see short, squat, wheelless mortars set upon a great board, with their throats in the air. Some of them were in use in Napoleon's time; the most modern have written upon them 'Liberté, Egalité, Fraternité, République Française, 1849.'

Hand bombs with a fuse are launched, charged with powder according to the weather. There is here a question of hydrometrics. The Germans, going farther back in the history of wars, have found an apparatus insensible to variations of the temperature. They have revived the ballista.

Its missiles arrive almost without warning; you hear a rustling among the boughs of the trees, and down from the heavens comes a great metal packet that bursts with a devil's own noise. From the German communiqués we know they call it an 'aerial torpedo'. It is really a kind of stove-pipe closed at each end and filled with explosive and grape-shot. Meantime the cannon beat upon the roads, the paths of the forest. The shrapnel falls in showers on the tracks, covering them with branches struck from the trees. There is no tree that has not its wound. The wood has been torn and mangled – there are places where it would seem a cyclone had passed.

The sapping goes on underneath in the depths in all directions. The mining began again at the position the Garibaldians took, and counter-mining. New assaults were prepared to be delivered at the moment of explosion. In the trenches, their feet in mire, the soldiers, immobile, listen to the enemy's digging underneath – a dumb, far beating. Engineer officers lay, their ears to earth, with the concentrated attention of a doctor at a stethoscope while he sounds the chest of a patient. Where is the disturbance? They try to find out, to locate the direction of the regular, hollow beat. There is a threat in the mysterious sounding but, at the same time, it reassures. So long as one hears sapping it means that the mine is not ready. Falls a terrible silence, the boring ceases, there is an anguish of waiting which would be insupportable without the fatalism which the soldier gets in war, when he plumbs the depths of indifference fathoms deep, does not think, does not want to think, shrugs his shoulders and waits.

Another sector of the forest, a little further east of the tragic height of the Bolante, is evoked in the laconic reason for the cross given to battalion commander Comillo Longo. 'In the fight of 8 and 9 January he drove back the enemy with the bayonet and reconquered at the head of his battalion the ground lost.'

This was the struggle of an Italian battalion against a Bavarian brigade; and the brigade retreated.

The line had been broken – 'Forward, Garibaldians!' In a night surprise a trench had fallen, a company had been scattered. The dyke burst, the flood of the enemy poured in. A battalion of fiery Jaeger Volunteers led the German assault. The French resisted heroically at the second and third lines of defence, but the breach in the first grew broader and details were outflanked. 'Forward, Garibaldians!' Called to the front, they had been held in reserve ready.

The enemy pressed on, advanced, came like a wedge of which the point penetrated first a kilometre, and then a kilometre and a half and then two. A troop recoiling cannot stop – there is a law of inertia of fighting bodies. So a counter-attack was needed. 'Forward, Garibaldians!'

Forward where? What followed? They did not know. They saw nothing beyond the road before them, the road of the Stone Cross. They pushed into the wood, met ambulances and carriages coming back swaying, heavy vans, caravans of wondering wounded, groups of soldiers without arms, stores of food being carried to safety, bread and meat. They met cannon, caissons, baggage. The ways were full of vehicles, horses and tumult. Round a huge siege piece, deep in the mud, clusters of excited artillery men were sweating at the wheels, pushing and pulling, the horses rearing and shaking their heads in their heavy collars as the drivers lashed. They met infantry silent, weary, coming back in bands. They walked on the side of all this, the Legionaries, a little rivulet meeting a broad stream, observed with curiosity, with looks which said 'Whither go ye?' Perhaps they guessed. But they went forward, towards a clamour ever nearer. And behold a sloping glade on the right of the way.

From the height descended a confused mass of troops falling back. An old colonel, bare-headed, sought to stop the movement – pleaded, wrung his hands, raised with threatening gesture a branch he had torn from a tree. But for seventy hours the soldiers had been fighting bravely without rest. Now they were dazed and overcome, and the slope drew them fatally. The battalion spread out in order of battle, and ascended to meet them.

'Stop!' they called to them; 'there is a French trench that still holds.' It was a trick of fortune. The French line had rested on the flank, and the position was uncovered. But the Garibaldians, believing they had the French in front of them, pushed on without firing a shot, and entered swiftly into the thick forest. A hail of shot greeted them; they did not respond, believing at first it was a misunderstanding. They continued their advance resolute, with bayonets fixed. The attack disturbed the Germans. In a wood you cannot count men, you can only guess how many there are. The fire gives the measure; a silent enemy is unnumbered. What strength must not be supporting this first line pushed on so coolly and tranquilly? The advance guards of the Jaegers fell back. It was evening – in the forest, night. The Garibaldians halted, took up position, and cast themselves upon the earth.

'My flanks are uncovered,' signalled Longo; 'send me supports.' Had he advanced he would have been surrounded. A company was despatched to the left to the dead girl. Everything is mournful in the forest, even the names – Wolf's Lair, Stone Cross, Monk's Furnace. Relics of crimes, legends, superstitions, distinguish the wildest and strangest points; those places where man was most afraid. A counter-attack would be delivered on the thin Italian line when the dawn revealed it. Not to be attacked, the battalion itself attacked, maintaining thus the doubt as to its numbers.

While the Germans still prepared for action, the Italians moved on. The Germans are methodical people. They develop a movement according to rules. They do not improvise as one may. They take no step unless they know, or believe they know, where they are putting their foot, hence all their fire shells and reconnoitring. Every action they enter upon is preceded by revealing symptoms. Longo felt the attack coming, but he did not wait for it. He gave orders for an advance and individual firing. From this tree and that tree, this thicket and that, firing burst out sudden, intense, formidable, and the enemy, surprised in his preparations, yielded the ground – 200, 300 metres at a time.

At dawn the Italians were dead beat. For seven days they had marched in the night or watched. On the dawn of the eighth they had entered into action, and they fought all night from the eighth to the ninth. They had been fasting for two days, because no severity can prevent the Garibaldian from eating up his reserves of food almost as soon as he gets them. There is a scheme for varying the regime and lightening the knapsack. But the Garibaldians have only a platonic respect for regulations, and they prefer hunger to a heavy knapsack. Hunger, they argue, is a thing that may happen and may not, but the burden of the food in the knapsack is certain, so long as the food is there. A distribution of preserves was twice made to them, with the same results. At the moment of need they had nothing to appease their hunger.

'My soldiers are done up,' Longo sent word to the commander; 'they have been thirty-six hours without food or rest.' The reply came: 'Resist at all cost.' To that he sent the message: 'If you cannot give us rest or food at least send us some ammunition.' This came, and there came also reinforcements. The Germans had been driven back on their positions, the battle was at an end.

The combatants crept back into their holes and the war of moles began again. No one will ever tell the valour of episodes of this war; every man has had his own.

What boldness and what action are not described in these words: 'He has given proof in every circumstance of coolness and exceptional courage.' It is the 'motive' of the Cross conferred on Ricciotti Garibaldi. Captain Cappabianca has his Cross for 'valour, coolness, and fine conduct in the command of his company'; Captain Evangelista for superb behaviour under fire; Captain Angelozzi because, 'though wounded, he continued to lead his company until the end of the fight';

Lieutenant Bousquet because 'on 5 January he repulsed all the counter-attacks upon a trench taken from the enemy'; Lieutenant Maribini because, 'though wounded, he had himself attended to summarily and returned to the firing line'; Lieutenant Oggero because he 'took possession of a trench, captured a machine-gun, and, wounded in the head by a rifle shot, returned to the assault after placing the machine-gun into safety'; Sub-Lieutenant Zambrini because 'in three successive fights he was always amongst the first to leap into the enemy's trenches'; Sub-Lieutenant Thomas because, 'wounded on 26 December, he did not leave his section in the fighting which followed, and gave proof always of extreme valour'.

Marshal Furri wears his military medal because, 'ever ready for the most dangerous mission, he carried out fifteen reconnaissance patrols in the depths of the woods'; Quartermaster Cascarini because he 'remained continually by the side of his battalion leader in the midst of the attack, and after this superior officer was killed made every effort to carry his body to the rear, although all his comrades round him had fallen dead or were severely wounded'; Private Garda because, 'sent by his captain on patrol to assure the contact of his company with the battalion, he accomplished his mission with a bravery worthy of all praise, passing some yards distant from the German trenches, and, when his mission was over, rejoined his section and took part in the attack of a German trench'; Corporal Haddad because he arrived first at the enemy's trench, where he took possession of a machine-gun, and, wounded, returned to the firing line after having conveyed the machine-gun to his own trenches.

There is a conscious and authoritative coldness in this military laconicism. It does not describe, it engraves, 'fixes' facts, seals truths. It has the air of making an entry in the records of history.

In the midst of the Grange des Côtes meadow those who are to receive decorations wait in a group. They are not all there, for some are stretched upon a hospital bed. There is a roll of drums, and, under the cold rain, the battalion, bristling proudly their bayonets, form square, and then move again, march, counter-march, wheel in a kind of general test. The Legionaries are not invincible on the parade-square.

Parade for them is a school lesson. They do not see the need of square and compass to bayonet the Germans. But they have agreed to practise forming square, in view of exceptional circumstances. And of course they prefer marching to standing still. Ask their lives of them, but do not ask them to stand stuck in a row for an hour in the rain. If it is a fight, of course; but for parade …

Apart from the attack for which they are always burning, the Garibaldians see few things in the military life as absolutely necessary, as obligatory, and not to be disputed. Take away discussion from life, and what is left? And so they have always some objection, some remark to make, some protest. If a man is not satisfied 'I will go and see Peppino,' he says, and he goes to Peppino Garibaldi.

For Peppino, as they call him simply, is accessible to all. Anyone may enter his chamber, air his grievance, and go out again with a kind word. Soldiers often come, and have nothing to say to him. What is your business? 'Nothing; I just came to pass the time of day.' Those who come are usually without the gift of expression, the most uncouth, the humblest, who feel and cannot speak, who wish to be near their leader because they love him, and remain to look with eyes of faithfulness and devotion, ready to kill and be killed for his sake – the colonel's mastiffs. 'You want to pass the time of day? Very well, then. Go over there a minute, and keep quiet.' The mastiff lies down, satisfied.

Officers of the Regular Army are terrified and moved to horror at the sight of a faith which to them is only heresy. They behold it as an earthquake shaking the keystone of the arch, a shattering of all traditions. The temper of the soldiers becomes here an important element, which influences the nature of orders. You cannot ask the Garibaldians to do what they do not want to do. They separate the indispensable from the relative; they are obedient with a difference, they reserve to themselves, at least, the right to grumble. There are things in their view which they didn't come there for – trench-digging, troublesome fatigue duties, the 'chores' of war. They came to shoot; all the rest is a secondary business. 'We attack? No? Well, then?' they have the air of saying. They disobey orders with a smile, 'thee and thou' their officers, and go tranquilly about other business. Is rabbit hunting prohibited? Rabbit acquires for them an irresistibly delicious savour, and somehow or other finds itself at the mess-table. The legionary is an Independent. The commissariat gives him all he needs for subsistence, but he prefers a broiled cat, caught after much toil, to a beefsteak from the State. If there is a prohibition to leave the camp without permission, the camp empties, and the regiment disperses through the neighbouring villages. Any Garibaldian who is worth his salt knows how to get in and out, despite the sentinels. He goes everywhere and is joyous and *débrouillard*.

When the regiment was at Mailly, and men grew tired of being there, they simply left and went into Paris. They were missing for several days, and then came back in good humour. Threats, arrest, courts-martial seemed to these misdemeanants wholly disproportionate rigours for so small a matter. One of the more modest, who only went as far as Épernay to buy some Champagne, reappeared gravely between two gendarmes with the bottles under his arm. The state of inaction continuing, a new kind of exodus began; individuals deserted with arms and baggage for the front. When the Garibaldians desert it is at any rate towards the enemy.

One day there was a plot hatched. The Garibaldians had had enough of Mailly: they would be done with Mailly. So they resolved to leave in a body for the front, naturally taking officers with them – abducting them. As they saw the matter, all that had to be done was to present themselves at some point of the front; the rest was a matter of arrangement between Joffre and Peppino. And one night very quietly they got ready, saddled the officers' horses, and were on the point of launching the ultimatum. As it happened Peppino was not there, being indeed then at headquarters precisely to get the authorisation to advance.

Eager, impassioned, without discipline, voluble, unbalanced, tumultuous, generous, heroic – such are the Garibaldians. They are a corps of attack, the specialists of assault, a kind of human grape-shot, shell, bayonet. Other operations do not concern them. All that is to do is to fling them against the enemy at the right moment, and then support them. For they carry positions rather than hold them; their function is to fight forward; to defence they prefer counter-attack – like a sledge hammer which you strike with, swing back and strike again. They are pioneers of the offensive, piercing a way forward, but behind them must be a supporting troop to hold the forced position, and remain as a wall.

Put them in the trenches, and they become irritated, and lose strength. They have an antipathy to hole-fighting. For them battle is battle, an onward dash, with shouting. They are fashioned by the glory of a tradition. They detest the war of mines. It is the German way. Problems, calculations, the needs and methods of modern tactics are for them so many impositions of the enemy. They are out of the picture amid so much science, in which they disbelieve. It is the Phalanx, stupefied to find mathematics on the battlefield. How much simpler to do or die? You have to come to an agreement with them. 'Now, lads, shall we go?' 'Go is the word. Forward! Down with the Germans! Long live Italy!'

The farmhouse of the Grange des Côtes is in emotion. The automobiles that bring the General and his staff are in sight. But the regiment in square – where is it? The boggy meadow is empty. With one accord the soldiers have decided to suspend the useless manœuvring. People are running everywhere, sounding the call of assembly. 'Look sharp. To your places.'

Will they be ready in time? The General has already got down from his car, and is walking forward. Peppino and his aides-de-camp advance to meet him; the little group goes towards the meadow slowly, with the step of ceremony. What will they see when they turn the corner? There is a striking silence. One would say there was nobody there on the meadow. Is there anybody?

Behold the three battalions massed, rigid, a splendid wall. The trumpets shrill out, the drums roll. 'Present arms!' As one the bayonets are raised, the line, its height added to by the uplifted hedge of rifles, takes on a giant-like stature.

The General stops, salutes, turns a grave look upon them. He has before him a wild and strange company. There are young and old, boys, tall athletes, men less than the height of the weapons they carry, people of all classes and every condition, a promiscuous company united by the cry of 'Help, Italians!' Turbulent, hardened, shaggy-bearded, dishevelled, in stained and muddy uniforms (from which, indeed, you could not separate all the mud that has been gathered in, as the wearer stumbled in his rush to the assault), caps thrust on in haste, ill-assembled clothing, men more seasoned in twelve days than by a long campaign, and aflame with an indefinable expression of savage, overmastering resolution, they are the wolves of war. In the fixed rigidity of the salute only their looks flee from the discipline, are darted hither and thither eloquent, piercing, anxious, making restless inquiry, replying, proclaiming, commenting, crying aloud. You feel that the spirit cannot be still as the bodies are, and the unmoving lips. Hence the clamour of eyes.

The ranks close up, for the regiment has left many dead and much blood in the wild forest. One of the three battalions is commanded by a subaltern, a section by a corporal. The Legion has sacrificed itself with an impulsive generosity. It has proved so the Garibaldian spirit. Men, diverse, belonging to all parts of Italy, with wide gulfs of character, habits, culture, education, sensibility have burned with the same flame, like boughs stripped from a tree and cast upon one pyre. The tradition has fused them. Becoming Garibaldians, they became what they now are. The name of Garibaldi is a trumpet note. Out of the past came a living and prodigiously inspiring breath. In the instant of combat the Garibaldians were sustained irresistibly by the inspiration of an epic that is eternal.

Tall, spare, graceful, the French General unsheathes his sword and raises it to return the salute. His officers in their turn unsheathe theirs. Four paces from him, erect, the hilt to his face, the blade erect, Colonel Garibaldi waits.

His breast swells with emotion. Clean-shaven, young, alert-looking, he has the look of an English officer. But the high brows and the deep eye, the leonine nostril, bespeak the race. The long chin and the little mouth, on the other hand, betray the English mother's blood. And in his mind also there are two springs. He is sentimental and reflective, positive and broad. He has one side in peace and another in war. If the world is tranquil he seeks a livelihood, works, shows grasp of business, is active and keen. But he leaves it all when there is fighting to do. The combat calls him to Venezuela, to Mexico, and to Greece, anywhere. Then he goes back to his business again, without illusions, the mouth a little bitter at times, as not always certain of the worth of the cause he fought for, with increased experience of men. But this time be knows the cause is a good one.

'Colonel Giuseppe Garibaldi,' says the General, slowly, 'in the name of the President of the French Republic, in virtue of the powers that are conferred upon me, I decorate you Commander of the Legion of Honour.' Then he advances, and, with the point of his sword, touches him on both shoulders, with the ritual, secular gesture of investiture. He pins the order upon his breast, and embraces him, kissing him on both cheeks. In such a place, among such men, the simple consecration acquires an unspeakable solemnity. It is like a magnificent salutation to the blood of Italy.

The trumpets sound. There is a moment of statue-like fixity. Not a blade moves. But what a hurricane of acclamation in the shining eyes. Now a whispering begins. The Legionaries cannot bear it longer. They have never been in such fetters. 'Hush! Silence in the ranks, lads!' The shout that was in the throat is choked back, but everyone feels the tremendous 'Long live Italy!' that passed there.

Now it is Garibaldi's turn to invest his officers, who wait in a line. A moment of anguish for Peppino. He would much prefer to be under fire, ceremonies for him being very much like parade for his soldiers. He halts some seconds perplexed. The words of the formula have fled him. He had prepared it, written it, and now it has gone from him, frightened away by so many people. He pursues it with an effort of recollection, retrieves it, and brings it to utterance, a little abashed after the struggle and recapture. 'In the name of the President of the Republic.'

One by one the crosses and the medals are fixed upon the breasts of the heroes, and embraces and greetings are exchanged – a strange rite this, which remains with the Republic the kiss of the Apostles to Christ. There is dead silence. Only the rumble of the guns is heard. The battle continues in the twilight day under the mournful skies. The rain is still falling; from time to time a faint, cold wind cuts, the trees awaken, all round the regarding wood rises a vast, profound murmur.

The battalions move off to file before the General and the decorated heroes. As they pass in file of companies a sound of singing arrives from the distance. Some volunteers left on duty there at the Grange have been kindled by the passion of an Italian air that spreads and fills with a strange mystery the cold heart of the Argonne:

'O brothers of Italy,
Beheld she hath awaked.'
Not yet; not yet. But she stirs.

18 February 1915

FIRST EXCHANGE OF WAR PRISONERS
Home-Coming of Wounded Soldiers

By Granville Fortescue

I am coming across from Flushing to Folkestone with the first batch of permanently disabled British prisoners. The sight of these broken men stirs one first with a sense of the tragedy of war, and then to a swift realisation of the glory of England.

When I speak of them as broken men, I refer only to their bodies. Their spirits are undaunted. Here I have seen the halt, the maimed, the blind. Not old men. Strong, virile soldiers they were; now physical wrecks. But though they have lost leg, arm or eyesight, their heart has never been shaken.

Most of their stories go back to the early dark days, when the little English force was making such desperate efforts to hold back the flood of invasion that was engulfing Belgium. Of the 200 prisoners who have at last returned to England after weary months of waiting and concentration, the most date their disability to Mons and the fights of the great retirement.

Among so many stories of sacrifice it is difficult to pick out one of greater worth than another. In the cabin opposite mine lies Private Jones, of the Middlesex Regiment. He was first hit by a rifle bullet in the left leg. The bone was shattered, and he fell. He lay for hours during the heat of conflict, hoping in vain for the end of it. Suddenly his hopes die with the echo of an exploding shrapnel.

The base of the man-killing projectile crashed into his other leg, striking the knee and tearing off the knee-cap. Other bits of shell struck various parts of his body. The German line of advance passed him as one dead. Fortunately he was picked up and taken to a Belgian hospital. For six months he has lain in the care of the good Madame Bradunt. The leg with the broken knee-cap will not heal.

As Private Jones finished this story, which I worked from him with much questioning, he said: 'But when I get back home, sir, it will heal. It only needs a little touch of British soil to heal it.'

In the next cabin is Private Smith, of the King's Royal Rifles. Smith was a football player. Now his right leg has been cut off from the hip.

'Better than losin' two legs, sir,' said Private Smith, ''an lots better than losin' your 'ead. I'm satisfied if the Government is.'

No word of complaint, no self-pity. Just a soldier playing the game.

Of course we all know now that the humorous element in the English Army is absolutely irrepressible. But I candidly admit in regard to the two incidents I propose now to relate, that, if they had not come before my personal notice, I might have been tempted to say the writer was carried away by the emotional setting of the picture.

One of the men is a sergeant in the Grenadier Guards. His right leg was gone above the knee. The other – he had had the regimental marks torn from his tunic – had lost his left foot. Stepping out of my cabin I saw the first playing a sort of hopscotch along the passage way. He shouted back to his comrade, 'Come along here, Bill. They got rings to "hop in".' 'Bill', who followed on his crutches, came up just as I was taking in my boots. Pushing his good foot in front of him he said gaily, 'Cheer, oh. On'y one boot to clean.'

In a darkened cabin lies Private Brown. He has five scars on his face where the German bullets have entered. The cabin is darkened because he cannot see. As he lies stretched out on his bed it is not difficult to estimate he is over 6ft tall, and more than thirteen stone.

Out of the semi-darkness came the crude words of 'It's a Long Way to Tipperary', sung in a minor key. I could go on multiplying the stories of these sacrifices until I had gone through the roster of these wounded. The three cases I cite are typical.

They are, according to the agreement of exchange, the completely disabled; disabled they are in body, but not in mind.

In talking with the few officers who have been exchanged, they were careful to say that the Germans treated them with all the care possible. In fact, both officers and men agree that in the hospitals they could not have been treated with better care. Once away from the hospitals, however, and this fairness which is due to all enemies was forgotten.

In the concentration camps an invidious distinction was made in the treatment of French and British soldiers.

This distinction was not apparent in the treatment of the officers. But the enlisted men were always detailed to do the most degrading and difficult duties about the camp. The Germans considered the English proud and disdainful, and determined to break their spirit. If this was their hope, they have certainly not succeeded.

There was one complaint of their treatment I heard voiced by the men. I noticed a number of English soldiers grotesquely dressed in the uniform of the French. Their own uniforms had been destroyed in battle, or worn out. When these were gone there was nothing left except such as the wastage of war supplied. In this case our Allies provided. Three of the men whom I saw were wearing the uniforms of dead French soldiers.

It so happened that our English wounded met the Germans in the waiting room of the station at Flushing. There they saw these men well-dressed in mufti. They were clothed in the ragtag and bobtail of the field hospital. This seemed unfair, at least from their point of view of the exchange, for clothes were included. As to their rations while with the Germans, the men made no complaint. 'They gave us as good as they had themselves,' but one, who appropriated to himself two plates of ham and eggs for breakfast, remarked, with a sigh of satisfaction, 'This is better than turnip stew.'

It has been my fortune to see the fighting men of nearly all the armies in this war, and I have made many judgments based on what I have seen of men before they go into action. This has been the first opportunity of seeing soldiers who have been ravaged by war. It is a splendid test, and from what I have seen of these broken men the soul of the British people is as strong today as it was under the Iron Duke.

THE LANDING ON BRITISH SOIL
Maimed But Cheerful, *Folkestone, Wednesday*

One of the roughest days experienced here for some time preluded the arrival of the first batch of wounded British soldiers released by Germany. All day huge seas broke over the Harbour Station, one great wave smashing in the side of a railway guard's van, and throwing two trucks off the line. Heavy rain accompanied the gale, and it was impossible for a landsman to stand in any exposed position at the station.

Shortly before 5 p.m. the *Mecklenburgh* was signalled, and at 5.05 p.m. she came alongside the lighthouse, buffeted by breakers, clouds of spray sweeping across her decks. She displayed bands of red, white, and blue round her khaki-coloured funnels, and her name was painted on her side in huge white characters.

Within a minute of dropping the anchor a hospital train, composed of Midland Railway stock and one carriage each of the London and South-Western and London and North-Western, drew up, and with military precision and alacrity stretchers and slings were in readiness.

No one without authority was allowed in the station, and those who were to aid the military had been well organised, so that the work of transferring from ship to train was carried out in the best possible manner.

Directly after the first gangway was thrown the men, in khaki and nondescript uniforms – mostly the latter – began to appear on deck. First there was a long procession of men on crutches wearing the French red trousers, most, alas! with one trouser-leg pinned up close to the body. These men came from Lille. They were followed by others who had lost an arm, or an eye, or were otherwise incapacitated from further military service.

Then the luggage slings were got to work, the cranes swinging back to shore from ship with human freight, a melancholy spectacle. These were the 'cot cases', those of men so dreadfully injured that they had been brought across in the tempest on their beds.

They came up three and four at a time, and were carefully conveyed to the hospital train. There were sixty-five such cases in a total of 215 officers and men.

To the few non-military observers present it was a sad scene, this long procession of maimed men, some of them looking so young. It was a strange march of heroes, and bravely they bore themselves. Their regret was their inability to return to the fighting line. Just 100 of them had been in Germany, the others having been in hospitals on Belgian and French territory held by the Germans.

As they reached the train each was provided with tea, food, fruit and cigarettes, and mutilated as they were, they were soon singing a version of 'Tipperary', which condemned the Kaiser to travel a 'long, long way to St Helena'.

They had shown the spirit in which they returned upon reaching the shore end of the gangway, where they paused before taking their crutches in order to return the salute of the officers who were waiting to receive them. They scorned pity and were proud of their wounds.

Visiting the men in the train, I found their stories in perfect agreement. Those who had been in Germany were unanimous in their assertions that the British prisoner was selected for worse treatment than the Belgian and the French. They complained of lack of food and clothing. During bitter weather two were given an overcoat and were told they must take turns to wear it. They could not obtain clean linen. 'One day,' said one of them, 'a new shirt was brought in, and I had to fight a crowd to secure it. This is it.' He drew attention to what looked like a cheap flannelette garment.

'They left me on the field,' said another, 'for six days. I had only been shot in the calf, but blood-poisoning set in, and now I've only got one leg to use.'

In a compartment where there were six men not one had a complete uniform. Each was a kind of crazy collection of French, Belgian, German, and British uniforms, with a blend of civilian attire. One had a woman's cape. Three of them had lost a leg, two an arm, the other a toe. The last had 'a dead foot', the use of it having completely gone. He also had bullet-wounds in his left arm and in each leg. 'It's a great finish,' he said, 'to the German excursion, and I'm sorry I've had to come back without seeing all the sights. I wasn't far from Berlin, and it was very cold, but we could get nothing warm to put on. They wouldn't even let us smoke. My wife sent me some cigarettes, and they took them out of the parcel and threw them away.'

'That's quite right,' said another, 'and I could not get a hat, although it has been snowing so much. When we were coming home they changed, and got almost kind to us, and gave me this nice soft felt hat. German people who could speak English told us they were tired of the war. We saw the German prisoners we are being exchanged for at Flushing, and it was easy to see how much better they had been treated than we had. I must say they treated the Irish very well, and one or two American–Irish they were absolutely kind to.'

Those who had been on Belgian or French territory stated they had been well treated, and were generally under the care of French doctors and nurses, who had been taken over with the hospital by the Germans.

On the way home all were treated very kindly indeed by the Dutch, and it was during their passage through Holland that they received the rosettes of red, white, and blue ribbon which each proudly wore in his headgear.

The Earl of Onslow brought the men over from Flushing to Folkestone, and they were received by Colonel Wilson, RAMC, Captain Gibbs, ASC (Transport for the Wounded), Major Aytoun, DSO (Argyle and Sutherland Highlanders), Major Noblett (Royal Irish Rifles), and Major Anderson and Lieutenant Lucas, of the Embarkation Staff.

Mr F. Bennett-Goldney, MP, rendered valuable assistance to the officers and the wounded. Mrs Spens (wife of General Spens) was in charge of the energetic party which provided every man with refreshment. The railway and shipping arrangements were perfect.

As the hospital train started off for London, men leaned from the windows to thank Mr Goldney, the officers who received them, and the ladies who had so kindly waited upon them, and as the train slowly gathered speed there came back to those left behind the sound 'It's a Long Way to Tipperary.'

TREATMENT IN GERMANY
Rotterdam, Tuesday Night

Whilst in hospital in Germany their treatment was praised, but many of the men complained bitterly of the conditions in the prison camps. One non-commissioned officer said: 'For the slightest complaint some of our fellows were kicked, and for what Germans considered serious breaches of discipline they were tied to posts for hours. The food consisted mostly of beans, and when men complained that they were starving, they were told: "Your friends in England have cut off the food supply."'

The places from which the officers came were Crefeld, Würzburg, and Cologne. There were at Crefeld 200 Russians, 250 French, and 130 English officers. Discrimination against the English as compared with the French was very noticeable. One of the officers said that the especial hatred of the English was obvious; the superior officers seemed filled with this sentiment of hate, and the men hate to order, in a sort of instinctive obedience to commands.

'Food sent from England was very gladly handed over to us,' said one officer, 'because Germany's own supplies are getting scarcer every day. After Colonel Vandaleck escaped from Crefeld our treatment improved. We were allowed to receive eight letters a month, instead of two. We were also permitted to have musical instruments.'

Neither at the War Office throughout yesterday, nor at any of the railway stations at which our wounded arrive from the Continent, was there any certainty as to when the first batch of injured men exchanged for an equal number of German prisoners, might be expected to reach London. It was not until late in the day that it became known that officers and men would reach Charing Cross some time in the evening, and the hour was so uncertain that only a small number of people actually remained to welcome them.

As a matter of fact, the long, grey train with its huge red crosses painted on the outside of each compartment, although expected at 8.30 p.m., did not draw into the station until exactly two hours later. Every carriage was filled by wounded men, with their attendants and nurses, and at once the long process of transferring them to private motors or the string of ambulances of the Scottish branch of the Red Cross Society, which had been waiting at the bottom of Villiers-street, was proceeded with.

None but officials had been allowed on the platform, and as the inspectors of police went round the groups of watching people asking for silence out of consideration for the serious condition of many of the soldiers, the work of getting the injured into the vehicles and sending them off to various destinations was carried on in scarcely interrupted silence.

The party included seven officers and ninety-three men. The names of the officers were given as:

Major Davy, Middlesex Regiment
Captain Hyslop, Dorsetshire Regiment
Captain Wyatt, Lincolnshire Regiment
Captain Marston, Royal Horse Artillery
Lieutenant Adams, Lincolnshire Regt
Lieutenant Robertson and Lieutenant Hay, Gordon Highlanders.

So quickly was the work of removal carried out that even friends and relatives were unable to greet the returning soldiers. But the crossing from Flushing to Folkestone had been extremely rough, and in the teeth of a strong south-westerly wind and rainstorm, and it was obvious that it had greatly tried many of the enfeebled and suffering ex-prisoners. They were as cheerful as could be expected, and manifestly delighted to be 'at home again', as one of them expressed it. Their cheerfulness, subdued though it was, was all the more striking, since most of them were greatly injured, the German authorities having been careful to select only those for exchange whom no amount of nursing could by any possible means restore to effective soldiers.

Only a few were able to walk with the help of crutches or the assistance of their attendants. Some had lost one or both legs, or arms, by shell explosions, and in some cases, perhaps the most touching of all, the men had been deprived of the sight of one or both eyes. Many were bandaged about the head, partial or total paralysis having followed in a few of these instances.

Very tired and pale, they were helped or carried as speedily as possible from the train which had brought them home, and passed into the dim-lit streets beyond amid the silent sympathy of the watchers.

From some of those who came with them it was gathered that the voyage across the Channel had been particularly uncomfortable. The wounded soldiers had been collected from different centres, and had mostly received their injuries in the earlier months of the war.

From the little that was told by this pitiful party of men who have suffered so heavily in the cause of their country it appears that the general opinion was the treatment experienced in the enemy's hospitals, under all the circumstances of the moment, did not give much cause for complaint, and a good many of the sufferers had spent almost the whole period since they received their wounds in these places.

The concentration camps, on the other hand, were generally admitted to be bad and ill-managed, English prisoners in them being treated worse than either French or Russians. The food especially was described as deplorable both in quantity and quality, the men having to sell their clothing and any little trinkets they happened to have about them to procure more. Any complaints were treated with harsh punishments, German military discipline being extended with added severity to the English prisoners.

Pathetic as yesterday evening's return of men, 'broken in our wars', inevitably was, it was brightened to some extent by the unmistakable delight of one and all to be amongst their countrymen again, and by the knowledge that everything which the most tender nursing, aided by this spirit, can do will be done to make them as sound and well again as is humanly possible.

6 March 1915

AT THE FRONT WITH THE BRITISH ARMY

The Personal Factor, *General Headquarters, France, Thursday*
By E. Ashmead-Bartlett

The heart in the body of man or beast occupies a relatively small space compared to the importance of the functions it performs over all the other members which it controls. But if anything happens to the heart the whole of the rest of the body is brought to a standstill altogether, or else hopelessly disorganised. In the same manner the headquarters of a huge army, such as we now have on the Continent, occupies an equally small space in size and outward show in comparison with the immensity of the numbers it controls. Yet if anything goes wrong with headquarters the malign influence will be immediately felt by every branch and unit of the forces under the direct control and management of the General Staff. The Headquarters Staff send the life-blood of an army percolating, either strongly or feebly, as the case may be, through the innumerable veins which give animation to each unit wherever it may happen to be on the vast chessboard of war. No athlete, however sure he may be of his limbs, dares extend himself to the full in a race or in a glove fight if he knows his heart is weak, and that at the critical moment, just when the final spurt is needed, it may fail him altogether. In like manner no general in command of a division or a brigade will do himself justice on a modern battlefield, where success depends on the certain co-ordination between units and the throwing in of the necessary supports at the critical moment, unless he has absolute confidence in the small group of men sitting in offices miles away from the actual fighting, who cannot see, but who have to feel and understand the true value of certain moves on the extended battle front.

Nothing has impressed me more during my visit to the British Army than the perfect confidence which the subordinate commanders or units have in their immediate chiefs, whether he be the general of a brigade or the commander of a division, the chief of a corps or the commander of a group of armies, and all in Sir John French and the Headquarters Staff. The British Army is, in fact, an immense happy family, without petty jealousies, every member of which is engaged in a common task, the fulfilment of which alone occupies his mind and engages his attention. The goal which all have in view is the crushing of the Prussian Hydra by exerting all their energies and all their efficiencies. I have not met a single general or private who is fighting for personal fame or glory. If any ever had any such ideas in mind they have been dissipated by six months of the awful realities of war. This happy and most desirable state of affairs is principally due to the supreme confidence which the Army commanders and corps commanders and generals of divisions have in Sir John French and the members of the Headquarters Staff. We have in the field the very best brains of the Army in the positions for which they are best suited. There has been no favouritism in the selection of men for particular posts. Scattered all over the area covered by the British Army, in little towns, in small villages, and dilapidated farmhouses, are men of immense ability, whose names are absolutely unknown to the outside world – men who work for sixteen hours a day, without hope of obtaining the immense rewards which civilian industries offer to thousands who conduct business that does not require one-half of the ability and does not impose one-tenth of the responsibility.

These are the type of men who have built up the Empire in the past, and are devoting the best years of their lives to maintaining the Empire in the future. All they wish to obtain is the respect and admiration of their countrymen, and they hope that the example which they are now setting will not be forgotten by future generations. I mean by this that I have found throughout all ranks an intense and absolutely sincere desire that England shall never again be caught asleep in any great emergency which may threaten us in the future. Thousands have already given their lives, thousands more must give their lives in the future, before the great work is accomplished. Thousands of others are devoting all their energies and risking their lives to make good the errors and deficiencies of the past. Had we really been ready for war there is not the slightest doubt that at this stage we would have obtained far greater results. I have often had this question put to me, 'Can we rely on the Government and on the people to preserve for the future the splendid army we are now gradually building up?' The past six months have, in fact, been a period of education for both generals and men. The ablest minds require time and experience to handle the immense army we are gradually concentrating in northern France. Nothing is more discouraging for the men who are building this superb structure of national defence than to feel that whether the war ends tomorrow or a year from now their labours will be immediately forgotten and wasted, that the lessons of unpreparedness will be immediately forgotten, and that this the finest fighting force ever put by the Empire in the field, drawn as it is from all four quarters of the world, will immediately collapse like a pack of cards, and its elements be dissipated into the air.

I have been shown so much of the inner working of this vast military machine than I am quite appalled with the task of attempting adequately to describe what I have seen. Also any writer is faced with another great but unavoidable difficulty. The censorship is necessarily strict. I am not allowed to mention the names of towns, generals, or units when referring to particular events, or the peculiar role played by individuals. This, of course, takes away greatly from that personal interest which always attaches to the performances on the battlefield of particular individuals or units. It is like trying to paint an immense panorama of war while leaving out the towns, villages, and all human beings. But these things cannot be helped. The science of war has been brought to such a fine art that any little statement which to the eyes of the average layman may appear to have absolutely no importance, may yet give to the Intelligence Department of a watchful enemy information of the highest importance. In the ordinary course of events there would be little harm in writing of the great deeds of our Army after an interval of several months has elapsed, but in this abnormal struggle, owing to circumstances for which we were not responsible, the British Army still finds itself fighting on the very same ground it was fighting over five months ago. In fact, some of that ground in front of Ypres, where one of the most glorious pages in our military annals was written in blood, is now in the hands of the enemy. Thus, these old fights and geographical descriptions still possess a significance if too minutely described, and must remain buried in comparative obscurity until the Army moves forward to further victory. Therefore, I am compelled to restrict myself to generalities, and to avoid figures, individuals, and names of places.

To attempt to convey to the lay mind the organisation of a modern army in the field is a task which few would care to face, and no one, unless given ample time, long investigation, and a volume of several hundred pages for the publication of one's labours. Therefore I shall only attempt a short summary, confining it to the smallest possible dimensions. There have been great changes in the reorganisation and composition of the Army since the war started, because our Expeditionary Force has swollen to a size undreamt of before the war. Not only have the component units been built up, but the machinery for controlling them has also had to be created. But very few of our officers in the higher commands had had experience of handling numerous army corps in the field. They have had to learn, just as the new recruit for the New Armies has had to learn how to handle his rifle, 'form fours', and salute his superiors. In this delicate task, as in so many others, the British character has shown its ability for hasty improvisation. An Englishman can play no game without having the ball at his feet. He is no lover of make-believe. He must have the real thing if his interest is to be kept alive. Thus our lack of preparation before the war has been balanced in a large measure – although with little credit to our acumen – by the splendid manner in which all have struggled to acquire the finer points of the game directly the ball of German ambitions was thrown into the midst of the European scrum.

When armies grow over a certain strength it becomes necessary to decentralise the commands. That is to say the Headquarters Staff can no longer undertake to exercise direct control over the movements and organisation of all the numerous units. Generals of proven ability are selected to command these armies, and they in turn have staffs which play on a minor scale exactly the same role as the various members of the General Staff. Thus, for instance, it would be quite impossible for General Joffre or the Grand Duke Nicholas personally to supervise with their staffs the movements of every corps, extended as they are over fronts hundreds of miles in length. The Commander-in-Chief can only exercise a general supervision over the whole. If he wants an operation carried out in a particular section of the front he sends a general summary of his ideas to the commander of the group of armies or corps in the district. The latter, with the assistance of his staff, must work out all the details and is responsible to his chief for their punctual and satisfactory accomplishment. When a general movement of several armies takes place, such as we saw at the battle of the Marne, the Headquarters Staff exercises a general control over the co-operation of the various groups of armies so that their movements conform with the view of obtaining a decisive result.

In like manner the British Army has now grown to such dimensions that it has become necessary to divide it into two main armies, each under a responsible chief. The administration of all armies is divided under several heads. There is the Commander-in-Chief, and there is the Chief of the Staff and his department, subdivided under several heads such as intelligence, map drawing, &c. The Chief of the Staff controls all the active operations in the field. Then there is the Adjutant-General's department, which deals with appointments, the keeping of units up to strength, discipline, and casualty lists. Then there is the Quartermaster-General's Department, which is responsible for the feeding of the troops and the supply of ammunition, railway communications, and a hundred other details. These are the three great departments which control the movements of armies in the field. The Army Commanders have exactly the same organisation for the control of the various corps under their commands, and in a lesser manner the Corps Commanders and Divisional Commanders. If Sir John French wishes a particular operation carried out he communicates his plans to one of his Army Commanders, the latter works it out in greater detail and decides what units are necessary for carrying the General's wishes into effect. The Commander of the Army then communicates his views to the particular Corps Commander, who works out further details, which are then passed on to the Divisional Commander, and from him to the Brigadier. Thus everything is done to decentralise as far as possible the work which is required to carry out the simplest military operation.

The Quartermaster-General of the General Staff now controls the arrangements for the supplies of food and ammunition to the Army, and also decides what railways and railheads shall be used by the various armies. He sees that the necessary supplies arrive at these railheads, after which the Quartermaster-Generals of the armies thus served take charge of its distribution to the various units. The Headquarters Staff also has another most important duty in this war, namely, to co-operate with our Allies, and to carry out the general understandings which may be arrived at for combined operations.

These are only a few of the functions of the various departments. There are hundreds of details of which the civilian knows nothing. For instance, perhaps the most important service of a modern army is its Intelligence Department. From all parts of the front – hundreds of miles in extent – information is hourly arriving from prisoners and from spies and from aerial observation. All such information, if of any real value, must be immediately forwarded to Headquarters. There it has to be carefully investigated and sifted, and compared with other information which has been received on the same subject. This work is highly technical, and requires great experience. A summary of all the true and reliable information thus obtained must then be laid before the Chief of the Staff, who has to consider its bearing in relation to any proposed operations in a particular area. Information must also be exchanged with the French and Belgians.

Modern armies are no longer composed of a comparatively small professional class, whose absence is hardly felt by the civil population of a nation. Modern warfare consists of vast migration, of almost the entire male population of a nation to a foreign country. Even the British Army, which is relatively tiny compared to the vast hordes of Germany, France, and Russia, would, if collected together, fill one of the largest cities in England. Imagine, therefore, what consternation would be caused in the local Town Council of, say, Manchester, Sheffield, or Birmingham, if it was suddenly announced that the whole population would be transferred to a foreign soil, and that the Mayor and Corporation would be responsible for feeding, clothing, and housing them, whilst at the same time they might expect an enemy in even greater strength to do his very utmost to capture the lot. The Mayor and Corporation would probably resign right away rather than undertake such a tremendous task. Yet this is what the General Staff of an army are suddenly called upon to undertake. It is difficult enough when an army has been occupying the same ground, as has the British Army for five months past. The task becomes immeasurably greater when the army moves forward, and all the railheads and centres of communication are changed day by day. Feeding half a million men on the move when you never know where they may stop at night, and when they may move on, is one of the greatest problems of war.

The only way in which to understand in a measure the ramifications of the organisation of an army is to start from headquarters and gradually work your way forward through the headquarters of the army commanders, then to the corps commanders, and so on through the divisions, brigades, and battalion headquarters, until you crawl into the trenches, where you find the mud-stained, khaki-clad, cheerful hero who has raised British prestige on the Continent to a height it has never reached since the Peninsular War. He has also proved how even the greatest of men can be hopelessly wrong when attempting to lay down rules for the English soldier. The great Von Moltke once said, 'I consider the well-established supremacy of the British infantry over Continental troops will disappear in these days of long-range weapons, when the bayonet can no longer be used as it was of old.' Recent fighting has proved that the great Field-Marshal was for once hopelessly out in his calculations. I shall therefore, in attempting to give some inadequate description of the life of the British Army, gradually move forwards from headquarters towards the front, until I reach the trenches, where I hope to arrive within the next twenty-four hours.

Aviation has entirely changed the character of war. So much has been written on its effect on the actual operations in the field that I shall not attempt to dwell on that aspect of the question here. I am not allowed to give, and quite rightly, minute details of the British Aviation Service, but I need hardly mention that all the machines are not concentrated at headquarters. Each Army has a wing attached which can be utilised by the commander of that Army as he may think fit. In case of need a concentration of several wings can be made if some operation of peculiar importance has to be undertaken. The aviation service is also subdivided into sections, each of which has its peculiar duties to perform. For instance, some keep in touch with the enemy's movements, whilst others are engaged in observing the effect and correcting the fire of batteries. The result of the reconnaissances of all the aeroplanes attached to the different armies is communicated as soon as possible to Headquarters, and if it is of importance it is communicated throughout to other units.

Nothing has come as a greater surprise in this war than the supremacy which the British aviator has established over all his rivals in the field. His cleverness in observation, his daring and resourcefulness, have excited the admiration of both friend and foe. The British aviator is also taught to fight in the air, and never hesitates to engage an enemy. The naval aviator has shown remarkable pluck and resourcefulness in this war, and we have heard a great deal of the naval aviators, because of their great raids over German ports, which are highly spectacular. The Army aviators have no opportunity or occasion to make such raids on vast scales in great numbers at the same time. Their work is allotted to them each day, and it is carried out with a thoroughness and expedition surpassed by none. The Army aviator works quietly and unobtrusively, buried in the obscurity of the Censorship. The duty is risky, and requires great nerve. Even at a height of 6,000 yards the aviator is not safe from artillery fire. The machines have been hit innumerable times by shrapnel, and there is hardly one at the front which does not show marks of the enemy's bullets. And when you see a machine soaring overhead and see it come to earth with the grace of a seagull alighting on the water, it all seems so simple and easy. When you read of one of these great raids you think how simple it must be to collect the machines and despatch them on their daring fight.

It is only when you are permitted to see the actual working that you fully grasp the immense amount of detail, thought, and labour which have to be expended before an aeroplane can rise into the air. Every machine requires constant supervision. Every detail of its complex structure must be in perfect working order before it can be used for the dangerous work of sailing over the enemies' lines. The functions of the Chief of the Flying Corps are now one of the most important in any branch of the service. He has to collect, sift, and collate all the various reports which reach him hour after hour, and forward his summary to the head of the Intelligence Department, who must then examine their bearing on other information he has received from different sources, and then in turn forward his summary to the Chief of the General Staff.

It will be as well to deal with the system of communications of an army such as the British. Wireless is used for various purposes, but not for important messages, as it is so liable to be trapped by the enemy. For instance, an installation receives each morning the summary of news sent out from Spandau and the Eiffel Tower. It also gets the communications scattered broadcast by the German Wolff Agency. As an instance of the triumph of art over even the greatest of wars, a message came in amidst the war news from various parts of the front that 'Sarah Bernhardt is progressing most favourably after her operation.' The old field telegraph still maintains its supremacy over all other means of communication with the front. Whenever a unit moves forward, whether it be to new ground, or to a captured trench, the telegraph is carried there with a minimum of delay. It has been proven to be the surest and the safest means of direct communication with the advanced lines. The telephone takes longer to install, and if an operator is killed there may be no record of the message he was receiving at the time. As a matter of fact, all the centres of corps, divisions, brigades, and armies are now connected up with the telephone, and are frequently used. The telephone can, in fact, be fitted to the ordinary telegraph line. Another of the disabilities of the telephone in the trenches is the difficulty of hearing under heavy fire when shells are bursting and guns are being fired close by. Of course in action the lines of the telegraph are frequently broken. They are duplicated and triplicated to avoid all severance of communication, but frequently, more especially in the heavy fighting round Ypres, communication could only be maintained with the front by means of motor-cyclists.

This remarkable body of men, which is being used in warfare for the first time, have proved that they are worth their weight in gold. The majority are volunteers who joined at the start of the campaign, bringing their own machines.

They are a class all by themselves, and enjoy the respect and admiration of the entire army. The roads are execrable in this part of France and Flanders, and no sane person would take a 'joy-ride' over them for mere pleasure. These motor-cyclists, regardless of breaking their own necks or that of anyone else, rush hither and thither at speeds varying from 40 to 60 miles an hour. Clad in leather clothes, their heads bent over the handle-bars, covered with mud and oil, their faces half hidden by dust, their machines oscillating and wobbling on the cobbles or slithering about in the thick mud, they present a picture of sternness, ferocity, determination, and absolute fearlessness, which strike terror into the hearts of everyone they encounter in their path. They respect no one. They regard the road as their own peculiar right of way. Everyone, from the Commander-in-Chief downwards, has to yield precedence to them. They recognise no authority, once a message for delivery has been placed in their hands. No one dare stand in their path until it has been safely delivered. Generals, regiments on the march, civilians, children, cows, pigs, and chickens must all take their chance if they cross the right of way of one of these terrible motor-cyclists in the performance of his duty. It is the pride of the corps that never, except in the case of death, have they failed to deliver a message along the battle front. They have run terrible risks; many have fallen, but others have taken their places. In times of emergency, when the wires have failed, these human substitutes have never failed. All the units of the Army are connected with Headquarters by telegraph and telephone. Thus, messages from the trenches are sent from the Regimental Headquarters to the brigade. From the brigade it is passed on to the division, from the division to the corps, from the corps to the General Headquarters. All this, of course, if its importance warrants such a procedure.

I will imagine that we have now left the Headquarters, and are motoring to the Headquarters of one of the two main armies into which the British forces are now divided. We are traversing a perfectly flat and thoroughly uninteresting country, which no sightseer would care to visit just for pleasure. It is a vast, flat plain, only relieved by small patches of trees, numerous farms, and small country towns. Your range of vision is extremely limited. You do not see a town, except perhaps the spire of some church, until you arrive almost at the gates. The country is entirely given up to agriculture, the principal crops produced being beets. The country people differ from those you encounter elsewhere in France. They seem to be of Flemish origin, and have the Flemish cast of features. The roads are mostly bad, and have been cut up by the passage of troops, cavalry, and heavy motor-lorries. Some are paved, and these are naturally the best. At the side of the paved roads are aisles of mud, and if you get your back wheels off the stones you are liable to skid into a ditch. Where the roads are not paved the going is awful after the heavy rains. The weather in this benighted part of the world is peculiar. It rains incessantly, and after rain the heavy soil becomes almost impassable for the passage of men and guns. No one seems ever to have taken the trouble to have made a minute study of the meteorological conditions before the war. It apparently rains for about nine months out of twelve. The question you continually hear asked is when will the country become dry enough for an army to move. No one has apparently any clear answer to this question. In certain parts the ground rises a few hundred feet and there are large grass fields. These grassy districts are almost exactly like Leicestershire. On the roads leading from headquarters to the Army commanders you encounter few of the outward evidences of war. Some motor transport, a few motor-cars conveying officers, and small detachments of cavalry. Finally, after half an hour's run, you enter the headquarters of the first army. Here you see rather more bustle and movement than at headquarters. There are more soldiers in the streets, and more of the terrifying motor-cyclists dashing through. There are also great trains of motor transport waiting for orders to move to the various corps and divisions.

5 April 1915

UNDER ARREST

Exciting Adventure of a War Correspondent, *In Belgium, March*

By Luigi Barzini

When at the station of Esschen, in the midst of an intimidated and well-disciplined crowd of passengers, who had just alighted from the train, I felt myself touched on the shoulder by a mellifluous personage, who murmured, almost in Italian, '*Appiate la bontà di venire con me*' (Haf' the cootness to gome vit' me), I thought at first that I was about to enjoy some extraordinary privileges.

I had, in fact, arrived in Belgium with a special authorisation from the Governor-General, with a passport duly *visé* by the German Consulate at Rotterdam, and with a letter – the viaticum of the German Minister at The Hague – addressed to the German civil and military authorities. Evidently there was a desire to spare me the annoyances of a long and minute inspection, awaiting which the passengers were huddled together in silence, with their papers in one hand and their luggage in the other, surrounded by men of the territorials, solemn-looking under their leather kepis, with two peaks (one in front, and one – who knows for what purpose? – behind).

The crossing of a frontier is always accompanied by troublesome formalities. Even in times of peace the reception which every nation reserves for its guests is not exactly overflowing with cordiality and confidence. Crowds in squalid Custom houses, peremptory and polyglot invitations to 'declare' something, hurried laparotomies of valises on long and dirty benches, fantastic flourishes traced with chalk on innocent bags, pushings and strugglings, tips, lost umbrellas – all these rise in the memory of travellers on the recollection of frontiers crossed. With the war came the extraction of passports, safe-conducts, and permits with appropriate visas, seals, stamps, signatures and counter-signatures, and photographs, the whole forming a little pocket archive for presentation at the frontier. But nothing can compare with the ceremonial which awaits those passengers whom fate compels in these calamitous times to pass from Holland into Belgium.

There is only one train a day from Esschen for Antwerp, and any time-table for it has had to be abandoned. It waits for hours while the rites are being accomplished. A solemn and implacable order governs every act – even the act, so simple for us who are wanting in method, of alighting from the train on arrival. One waits for a signal, and at the signal the passengers in the first carriage alight. Two minutes' interval. The passengers in the second carriage alight. Two minutes' interval. The passengers in the third carriage alight, and so on.

The personage who touched me on the shoulder was perhaps calling me to join the elect who do not undergo inspection. 'Were you advised of my arrival?' I asked him. 'Yes, signor, advised.' Full of gratitude, I followed him.

He conducted me towards the elect.

We entered a bare, cold room, with no furniture except a table in the centre. On the table were being heaped the clothes of a pale and disdainful gentleman, who was slowly taking them off, despite the temperature. Already there lay on the table his overcoat, jacket, and waistcoat, and the gentleman proceeded with his spoliation, having apparently decided to continue to the end. Meanwhile a taciturn, spare individual, with a bureaucratic air, examined the articles one by one, patted them, turned the sleeves inside out, explored the pockets, and so forth. Our arrival did not seem to disturb the operation. But on coming to the trousers the examiner abandoned the rest. The pale gentleman dressed himself again, and was dismissed with a wave of the hand. Evidently he was not one of the elect.

My guide and the man with the bureaucratic air then had a sotto-voce confabulation, examined my papers, extracted documents from a drawer in the solitary table. Afterwards my guide, who spoke the Italian of the guards of Trieste, a smiling creature with the head of a German workman, said to me: 'H'm … There is some difficulty!'

'Difficulty?' I asked in surprise.

'Yes. Your name is written in a little book which we have. When a name is in the little book … '

'Well?'

'Come, now. Tell me frankly, do you know the person who gave you this letter?'

It was the letter from the German Legation.

'Certainly; he is the German Minister.'

'Do you know him?'

'Personally.'

That authoritative and official letter evidently embarrassed them. The two had another discussion. Then the strange interrogatory continued.

'Be careful now,' said the brave policeman, 'tell the truth. Why did you frequent the "Brasserie Suisse" at Rotterdam?'

'I don't even know where it is.'

'Do you know an English lady and an English gentleman, who are called … ' (and names were mentioned).

'But,' I interrupted, not without impatience, 'explain yourselves. What do you want of me? I do not enter Belgium secretly. I never go anywhere in secret. I have the authorisation of the Governor, telegraphed from Brussels to the German Legation at The Hague. My papers are in order. What do you want?'

'We have orders to place you under arrest.'

'Under arrest? And why?'

'Because the German Admiralty reports you to the military police, you and the two English people mentioned, as agents who have carried on espionage in Belgium, and the military police have issued the order.'

I laughed.

'This is a joke,' I exclaimed, 'or a stupid mistake, which you can dissipate by a telephone call.'

'Have you ever been in Belgium before now?'

'Never in the Belgium occupied by the Germans. I have always followed the Belgian army. But what does that matter? The Headquarters in Brussels must already have discovered the mistake. I have permission to visit Belgium, given only yesterday.'

'But the order for your arrest arrived this morning.'

This observation made me thoughtful. The date of the order neither increased nor decreased the ridiculousness of the accusation. Something both serious and perverse arose from this contemporaneity, but it could not affect me. The suspicion arose that the special safe-conduct and the order for arrest were associated; that the legal guarantees of personal liberty had been accorded for the purpose of capturing me; that the moment in which I became a guest had been chosen for transforming me into a prisoner; that, in fact, a disloyal trap had been laid for me.

No; it was impossible. The permission to visit Belgium, honestly asked for by me, had been as honestly granted, its exceptional nature being emphasised at the same time. It was clearly an act of confidence in me, and of homage to the impartiality of my work. There must be some inexplicable mistake.

'Telephone to the Governor-General of Brussels,' I asked, 'and the matter will be immediately cleared up.'

The bureaucratic person withdrew, carefully closing the door behind him. Five minutes later he returned, and whispered a few words to my obliging policeman-interpreter. The latter began to look at me with evident embarrassment.

'It is unpleasant,' he said, with commiseration and an air of encouragement. 'You must be patient, you know, in time of war … '

'But telephone!'

'We have telephoned.'

'And what was the reply?'

'The reply was, "Carry out the orders!"'

The orders were carried out with extreme delicacy. Half an hour later I was travelling in a separate compartment, together with the secret agent, who was instructed to hand me over to the police at Antwerp. My arrest had caused an additional delay to the train, which, ready and full, the windows crowded with compassionate passengers, only waited for me.

'I understand what has happened,' my guide confided to me in a consolatory tone.

'Oh, happy man!'

'A spy has seen you in Holland, and has telegraphed. That is all.'

'Clear as the sun.'

To distract me he explained the landscape and its changes.

'Here a great "pattle". There you see a fortress – "Pelgian", destroyed. Great "pattle" also here; therefore trees cut down, also houses.'

As we approached Antwerp the train ran through the regions of the siege – still deserted, desolate, lugubrious, full of the ruins of houses razed to the ground, shaggy with the remains of devastated woods, bristling with the stumps of fallen trees, which seemed like the stubble left after the reaping of a gigantic harvest. The ground was scored with trenches and covered here and there with thick networks of wire, grey and regular, with their rows of posts, resembling sinister metallic vineyards. All was barren, devastated, crushed by the cruel feet of the war.

Hundreds and hundreds of Belgian locomotives lined the rails of the endless station, but they were useless, shapeless, rusty, having been shattered by dynamite before the retreat. Nothing moved, nothing lived among the innumerable sheds, warehouses, docks, and quays of the great Belgian port. Entering the echoing shadows of the immense roof, the train slowed down. Grey sentries beside the rails, spiked helmets, bayonets; we had reached Antwerp.

On alighting the passengers were lined up beside the train. 'Halt! Everybody stop. Out with passports!' Another examination. I alone, by the incontestable advantage conferred by my captive condition, was conducted at once outside the military cordon. My guide had only to show a badge of the secret police. Every road was opened.

I left behind the common herd of free-footed passengers. It was a melancholy crowd of Belgians returning home. Not many, perhaps 150. They were recalled to their country by the cruel threat of a tenfold tax on the absent, equivalent to the confiscation of their property.

Then the miraculous badge of the secret police, opening every way, conducted me to an office (furnished this time) at the end of the station. Here my polite agent – who meanwhile had informed me that he had learnt Italian while working in Italy (working at what, I wonder?) – said to me with the courtesy of a tailor taking a measure:

'Kindly raise your arms.'

'Raise my arms?'

'Oh, it is inconvenient, but necessary. A little higher, please. That will do.'

And, quite tranquilly, he began a minute exploration of my person. He emptied my pockets, read the letters he found, asked for explanations of the words he could not understand, searched and rummaged patiently and perseveringly. Meanwhile the passengers coming from the train passed before the open door.

They passed and looked. Beneath those glances I felt almost proud. There was not a glance that was not one of sympathy; in those eyes there was a sad, timid, silent salutation. And I accepted it motionless, posed, arms outspread, resigned and seraphic, like the good thief.

At the same moment a soldier methodically inspected my baggage. He carefully examined every object, undid even the packets of cigarettes and looked at them one by one for fear that secret messages might be written on the thin paper. My letters were turned over by an inspector, and a dapper young officer, who seemed to be the chief of the office, watched the scene with a detached air.

Some emotion was caused by the discovery of certain strange black sheets covered with vague superimposed traces of mysterious and indecipherable writing. Messages? Love letters of the British Fleet? No; merely carbon paper for copying. I demonstrated its use in a convincing manner.

The search gave what in newspaper slang is termed a 'negative success'. After this the Esschen policeman handed me over formally to his colleague and took leave of me effusively.

'Sorry to leaf you, but my train is starting. My pest – how do you say it, – Glückwünsche – Ah, yes vishes, my pest vishes. And pon voyage!'

His large person vanished in haste towards the barrier of the departure platform, in the vast, black solitudes of the idle station. My new custodian, an inspector of the Antwerp police, the type of a commercial traveller, but very serious, a commercial traveller in a dubious line, speaking no language but German, was necessarily laconic. He knew, however, in French the professional phrase 'Venez avec moi', which every policeman of every nationality knows how to express in every idiom.

'Venez avec moi.'

Away through the echoing corridors and the great atrium, and we are outside, in the square. A military motor-car awaits us. A few groups of silent people, attracted by the arrival of the train observe us from a distance.

'Where are we going?' I ask my custodian, after the car has started.

He reflects for a moment, then explains: 'Venez avec moi.'

A few minutes later my adventure enters upon a new phase. I passed from the hands of the political police into those of the military police. I am conducted into a lordly house transformed into an office. I believe it was the English Consulate now become the prey of war. Pictures of sport decorate the walls, and elegant furniture gives the surroundings an appearance of intimate comfort. Two officers receive me with eager courtesy, like an invited guest: 'Pray be seated. Would you like anything? Coffee? No? A glass of wine? A drop of cognac? Nothing? Well, you will be taken to Brussels to the Kommandantur. Oh, a mere promenade. Ever been in Brussels? Be careful ... Then it is the first time that ... Strange! ... If you will be so kind, the car is ready. Have you a fur? Then put it on. It is very cold motoring at night. Wrap yourself up. That's right. *Au revoir!*'

My strange journey began as the day was ending. The car travelled rapidly along the plain of the Nethe as the shades of night fell. Beside me was a polite and voluminous lieutenant, well gloved, muffled in a military fur coat, his flat cap pulled down to his ears. He spoke to me. The cold wind made a turmoil of his words; but fragments of sentences reached me.

'Look there … houses destroyed by the Belgians! … Poor village, bombarded by the Belgians! … Ruins left by the Belgians! … Pillaged by the Belgians! …'

In good French, but with a strong German accent, he developed the argument – which was not without originality – that the Belgian troops were the principal authors of the devastation of Belgium. The devastation was everywhere. In the cold twilight we saw ruined villages, blackened walls, branchless trees. In the houses that remained intact lights began to glimmer; a quiet, resigned, humble, tenacious life showed its sparks here and there, like the timid remnants of cinders on an immense extinct hearth.

The poor peasant carts met on the road had the effect of exasperating my guide.

'Why don't they get out of the way? There is a regulation. They ought to have a red light behind, and keep to the right. They do it on purpose. Ach! If I was not in a hurry they should see! They pretend not to hear the horn.'

And passing beside the guilty vehicle the officer stood up shouting: '*Je vais vous apprendre!*' ('I'll teach you!')

On the cart we perceived for a moment a poor old man who, terrified by the roar, trembled, and pulled the reins, looking at us with the stupefied face of one who is suddenly awakened. We passed like the wind, and were a long distance away before the peaceful driver emerged from his dark perplexity as to the meaning of the threat that had been hurled at him. In the German pronunciation the phrase sounded, '*Scher vais fous apprentre.*'

It was the war-cry of a broken regulation. At every moment this furious didactic promise was uttered. We scattered it all over our road.

In a little village near Malines three children dressed in black (how much mourning there is in this land!) were playing at the roadside and prattling joyously. Their thoughtless cries, shrill as the trilling of a lark, silvery as the sound of bells, made my lieutenant jump to his feet. After having recognised in the words a subversive intonation he hurled at the children the imperious '*Scher fais fous apprentre à fous,*' and the children became mute – terrified.

Then, turning to me, he said affably: 'Ach! The people are still stubborn. You perceive that we are approaching Brussels. Brussels is obstinate; it does not know what war is; it has seen nothing, learned nothing.'

Soon we touched the suburbs of Brussels. Except for a few tramcars, the roads were empty. Brussels wore a midnight aspect. Throughout our journey the way had been barred by sentries, who, on seeing a car of the military government, stood back, saluting. On arriving at the capital there were more guards and more salutes. At a certain point of the straight and solitary Rue Royale sentries were at every corner; the way was closed. In the vicinity of the Kommandantur, the ancient Palace of the Ministers, all traffic is prohibited without a special permit.

But all barriers are opened for us – urgent mission. We turn the corner of the deserted, silent, sinister Rue de la Loi, with its motionless sentries in couples at every door of the Palace, at every corner, at the gates of the park; the street itself seemed to be a prisoner of war. At the principal entrance of the Ministry two guns stood threateningly in position, one on either side. We had arrived.

Passing through a great glass door I saw successively a hall as vast as a church, a guardhouse, tramping sentries, a marble staircase, and, finally, an office, on the velvet chairs of which the Lion of Brabant persevered in extending its rampant heraldic elegance. Two superior officers received me with grave correctness.

The military police invited me to sit down.

On the capacious writing-table was deposited a large bundle of typewritten papers – my dossier. After turning it over, the elder of the two officers addressed me.

Some readers may perhaps remember that, following the Belgian retirement from Ghent to Ecloo, Bruges, and Ostend, I was able to leave the latter port at the moment of the German invasion, by boarding, together with four English colleagues, the Red Cross yacht, *Grace Darling,* which was the last boat to sail. This fact seemed to have a tremendous interest for the German military police. You would like to know why? So also should I. The first duty of a secret police is to be scrupulously secret. For that reason I was not able to gain even the remotest idea of the crime of which I was accused. It is at any rate operatic that that naval excursion formed the subject of my interrogatory.

I related the story of my departure from Ostend as accurately as I had originally written it. Involuntarily my article was revived in my words with exasperating monotony. The elder officer, seated opposite me, made a sign of approval now and again with his head, then, turned over the papers, and pointed out a phrase here and there to the other officer, who, standing behind him, was reading in silence. His words seemed to have a singular importance. What were they? That is a mystery.

Suddenly he turned to me with this strange question, which I submit for the meditation of Italian readers: 'In the month of October, at Milan, a gentleman staying at a hotel inquired for you and telephoned to you. But you were absent. This gentleman is named A---- (a foreign and unknown name). Do you know him?'

I do not know him; but that does not matter. The interest lies not so much in the man as in the fact that a telephone message at Milan should come under the control of the German secret agents.

On hearing my curt 'No' the officer rose and said: 'Now you are free.'

'My arrest is at an end?' I inquired.

'Arrest?' he exclaimed. 'Arrest? Oh, but you have never been under arrest! No, no. We only wanted to ask you for a few explanations. It is done.'

Stupefaction rendered me dumb. 'Good heavens!' I thought to myself, as in the same car and with the same officer who had conducted me to Antwerp I was conveyed to an hotel indicated by the authorities, 'if I had been arrested whatever would have happened to me?'

1 May 1915

DEFENCE OF ST JULIEN
Bugler Hero

'I dropped, wounded in the leg. We were in the open. Bullets of rifles and machine-guns were whizzing around us, and shrapnel was bursting above. I did not think it was so bad when I first struck through my puttees.'

Thus spoke a young Canadian private from Montreal, now in an English hospital. 'But a gallant English bugler stopped and picked me up,' he continued. 'Like many another hero, he is now dead. We were engaged in a retiring movement. The bugler stuck to me, although I was a burden. A shell burst immediately above us. A piece of the explosive struck him in the chest. We fell. I turned and looked into the face of my brave friend. He was no more. Lead and shrapnel still rained around us. I crawled to a spot behind a turnip patch. There I was seen by a stretcher-bearer. My rescue was swift. The work of the stretcher-bearers is always swift and glorious. He lifted me on to his back, and proceeded to carry me. Only a few yards had been covered when he was hit, and we both fell to the ground. But there were more hero stretcher-bearers, and in a few moments we were rescued and taken to a dressing station. And, would you believe it? I was wheeled away in a baby carriage.'

The young Canadian could not resist a smile as, lying in bed, he thought of the mode of his conveyance from the danger zone.

'Yes, a baby carriage,' he added. 'It was strange, but there was something more ludicrous, and that was to see Germans masquerading in kilts and khaki, as some of them did in the offensive movement. Unfortunately, with their poisonous gases, followed by a withering artillery fire before St Julien, their aggressive tactics were temporarily successful, although by this time on another part of the line the Canadians, we now know, had recovered their lost guns. But we had to retire for a time, and I am afraid we lost heavily in the engagement which followed the heroic charge of our Canadian comrades on Thursday night.

'On the morning following that battle we moved to St Julien, having with us several English regiments. We took up a position on what may be described as a large open plain. There were no trenches, and we understood that the Germans were about 400 or 500 yards in front of us. We dug ourselves into a small trench, and at four o'clock the next morning (Saturday) we were the object of a tremendous fire from the Germans who were in front of us just on our left. They stormed our trenches, and what are commonly known as "coal boxes" followed in quick succession. So hot was the fire that it was impossible for us to hold the position. Then a large body of Germans were noticed coming up almost behind us on our right.

'The only means of retirement was across what was practically an open plain, consisting of three fields, one with turnips, another with hay, and the third with stubble. It was in the turnip field that I crawled before being rescued by a stretcher-bearer. I was not wounded when the retirement commenced. A slight ridge commanded the plateau over which we crossed. Upon this the Germans had placed machine-guns and we were retired amid a heavy fire. I am afraid our losses were heavy. The order to reform was afterwards given and obeyed, and subsequently, reinforcements arrived. Before then I had been wounded and had met the English bugler, whose name I do not know, but whose face will live with me for ever.'

The conversation turned again on German methods and poisonous gases.

'Let me tell you something humorous,' said another wounded Canadian soldier, two beds away from the private who had been describing his experiences.

'On Friday morning last, in the fighting around Ypres, a German soldier left his trench, which was immediately in front of ours, and walked towards that in which we were situated, at the same time holding his hands high in the air. In broken English, he shouted to us to "surrender". Walking towards us until he came quite near, he continued to shout "Surrender" until our boys were "tickled". We invited him to join us, but as he did not seem inclined to accept our invitation we shouted at him to go back. He then turned round and we gave him an opportunity of returning safely to his comrades. And then the firing began.'

These stories were told by Canadian soldiers who, with their comrades, had taken part in the fighting around Ypres towards the end of last week, where men from the outposts of the Empire, from Quebec to Saskatchewan and the Pacific Coast ranged themselves alongside gallant troops from the Mother Country. They spoke of the dastardly methods of the Germans.

'I was in the trenches,' remarked a private of the 8th Canadian Battalion, 'when the poisonous gases rolled over us. It was at a time when the Germans were commencing an attack. In our rear was a house which had been used as headquarters, and although at times there were many of us who would have liked to make for it, it was impossible, because to do so would have been to court certain death.

'The effect of the gas is that you cannot get air. The sensation is horrible. In the trenches I saw men collapsing around me. I managed to retain consciousness, but unfortunately I was wounded in the right arm and shoulder. A "chum" dressed my wound in the trench, where we remained for several hours.

'Eventually, at what seemed a favourable opportunity some of us decided to make an attempt to reach the house, and we succeeded. We found that the upper part of the building had been completely blown away by the German artillery fire, and there were some occupants in the cellar, above which had been piled potatoes to protect it from the shell-fire. After remaining there a brief period some of us who were wounded but could walk, or were suffering from the effects of the gas, decided to search for a dressing station, and, I think, eleven of us started the journey. It was about eight o'clock in the evening. We were just able to drag ourselves along.

'Star shells at this moment were more welcome than usual; they showed us the way along the road. The light fell upon a weird scene. On all sides were the signs of battle and the destruction wrought by shells, which were continuing to burst above us. The number of dead horses by the roadside was awful. We also observed a motor-cycle machine-gun evidently smashed by artillery fire. It seemed miles that we walked along that road, furrowed by shell, but this probably was fancy, because we could not walk fast. Without uttering a word to each other we made our way. Another shell, another flare, and then darkness again. Another flare, and then joy. In front of us was a Red Cross sentry. We knew we had reached a dressing station. It did not matter to us whose it was. We limped in, and received attention, and I was removed to hospital.'

All of the Canadians spoke of the terrible effects of the poisonous gases and one, condemning the methods of the Germans, stated that a hospital in which he was placed after being wounded was shelled, and the wounded had to be taken out.

30 September 1915

BRITISH ATTACK ON GERMAN LINES
Storming of Loos, British Headquarters, Tuesday

By Philip Gibbs

I am now able to write a straight, clear story, with many interesting details of the fighting which began on Saturday morning last and still continues upon the same ground.

For some time it was impossible to obtain anything like a connected narrative, as divisions, brigades, and battalions disappeared into the smoke, and could only send back brief messages to tell how the day was going, how severe was their ordeal, and great was their success.

Now, however, after the first rush is over, there is time to tell the story of one of the greatest achievements gained by British troops in this war.

There were many battalions of New Army men among those who led the attack, and amongst them were Scottish regiments, who had their full share of horrors in the first assault.

Many of them, though belonging to regiments with famous old traditions which have already won undying glory on the Western Front, were recruits to Kitchener's Army but hardly arrived in Flanders.

Older men were among them, regiments which had already been battered and scarred in many terrible days of war. But the majority were of the younger and less experienced class, and not less keen because of that.

These splendid boys listened through the night of Friday last to the intense bombardment which preceded the assault. That in itself was a tremendous test of nerve, but at 6.30 a.m. on Saturday, when the company officers gave the word, the battalions leaped out of the trenches and ran towards the enemy's lines with a wild hurrah. Their point of attack was the village of Loos, some three and a half miles away. They reached the enemy's lines of trenches without sustaining many casualties, and found that the first two lines of barbed wire had been effectively broken down by the artillery bombardment.

The third line was uncut, and was very strong wire, with great barbs. The first two trenches were carried with a rush at the point of the bayonet, a large number of Germans being killed, but the uncut wire made the first check, and was a formidable obstacle.

But our men, reckless of their lives, attacked it desperately. They stood up under the deadly fire of machine-guns, and bit by bit forced a way through the entanglement.

One of the most extraordinary incidents among the grim scenes which took place in the smoke-laden mist was when a company of kilties, advancing at the charge, came face to face with a very tall German, who, although stone dead with a bullet through his brain, and with his face blackened with the grime of battle, stood erect in the path, wedged in some strange way in a low trench.

It was so startling and uncanny that, with one accord, the wave of men parted and swept each side of him, as though some obscure spectre had barred the way.

Rank after rank streamed up, and at last a great tide of men poured through and swarmed forward to the village, and then three-quarters of a mile farther on. As they ran, shouting hoarsely, they were faced by the fire from an enormous number of machine-guns, and from every part of the village there came the steady rattle of these weapons pouring out streams of lead.

There were machine-guns in the windows of many of the houses, and on the top of the 'Tower Bridge' – the tall mine cranes which rose 300ft from the centre of the village – and in narrow trenches dug across the streets.

In the cemetery, to the south-west of the town, which our men had to pass, there were no fewer than 100 machine-guns, so that it was in itself a 'fortin' of great strength.

But once again, as many times during this war, it was proved that in personal combat, when high explosives and heavy artillery are no longer the chief agents of battle, but when the human quality counts, our men are the masters of the enemy.

These battalions were hardly checked after that first dash through the barbed wire. Over the dead and wounded bodies of their comrades other men went on, bayoneting and shooting the enemy with a fierce élan.

It was eight o'clock when those who had not fallen reached the outskirts of the village of Loos, and for nearly two hours there was street fighting of a terrible character. Many battalions were mixed up, many of their officers were killed and wounded, and the battle was made up of individual combats, or small groups fighting their way from house to house, and of separate encounters in rooms and cellars.

Although the town had been severely damaged by our shell-fire, and the church in the centre was in ruins, no fire had broken out, and the shells of the houses still stood. They were crammed with the enemy's troops, who used the cellars as trenches from which they could fire upon our men through apertures in the street. They also fired through the windows and doorways behind the shelter of the walls, and some of them had their machine-guns in the garrets.

Here and there small parties of these German troops defended themselves with the courage of despair, and would not yield until killed to the last man. Others were cunning rather than courageous in their methods of fighting. The great mass of them were undoubtedly surprised and demoralised by the rapidity and sweeping strength of our attack, and it was by their wholesale surrenders that we took the large number of prisoners whose appearance I have already described in a previous despatch.

The men of this class, after their first resistance at rifle range or with machine-guns, seemed to have no fight in them at all. In one house, entered by a little kilted signaller – a tiny fellow with a stout heart – thirty Germans, including an officer, surrendered to him, after he had shot down three who tried to kill him.

Yet, as I have said, the resistance was prolonged in some parts of the village, and there were many cellars from which a rapid fire caused heavy losses to besiegers. They were silenced by bombing parties, who flung their hand grenades into these subterranean forts from the head of the stairways. In Loos the cellars are still full of dead.

In one of these cellars an amazing incident happened which reveals the highest form of courage and self-sacrifice not to be denied to our enemy. The Colonel of a battalion which will be given a high place in history for this day's work, came into Loos after his men had already gone forward to Hill 70.

With his signallers and other men he established his quarters, according to previous arrangement, in a house practically untouched by shell-fire. At this time there was very little shelling, as the artillery officers on either side were afraid of killing their own men, and the house seemed fairly safe for the purpose of a temporary signal-station.

But the Colonel noticed with surprise that shortly after his arrival heavy shells began to fall very close, and the German guns were obviously aiming directly for this particular building. He ordered the cellars to be searched, and three Germans were found. But it was only after he had been in the house for forty minutes that, in a deeper cellar, which had not been seen before, the discovery was made of a German officer who was actually telephoning to his own batteries and directing their fire.

Suspecting that the Colonel and his companions were important officers directing general operations, he had caused the shells to fall upon the house, knowing that a lucky shot would mean his own death as well as theirs.

In any case, he was certain to die, and he died, bravely, having made this supreme sacrifice of courage. The telephone apparatus is now a trophy in our hands.

Meanwhile some of the battalions who had fought their way through Loos were now struggling ahead to gain Hill 70.

It was nearly a mile further on, eastwards and southwards, and the road was swept with shrapnel and machine-gun fire as it rose steadily up to the rising ground; which is really a slope rather than a hill.

On the further ridge is a village called the Cité St Auguste, held by the enemy, overlooking our advancing troops.

From the windows of the cottages on the highest ground, and from entrenchments in the vicinity, there was an incessant storm of fire which raked over the approach.

Nevertheless our men held on, and, finding a kind of ridge or parapet, dug themselves deeper in, so that they had useful protection.

The first men to reach Hill 70 arrived at about ten o'clock, and clung to their position at all costs and with heroic endurance until eleven o'clock that night, when they were relieved by other troops, who carried on the struggle next day.

This concludes the chronicle of the battle in and beyond Loos until Sunday, when the position was organised, and the advance continued with varying success around Hill 70.

But I must go back to the dawn of Saturday, where another attack was in progress further north towards the town of Hulluch. It was another triumph for the New Army men who formed a very good proportion of the massed troops. The struggle here was fierce and formidable, and our men had to advance under terrible fire. That, however, was after the first assault upon the enemy's trenches, which were carried swiftly.

Our machine-guns, of which we had a considerable number, were brought forward rapidly, and the Germans lost very heavily, the bayonet finishing the work of the bullets.

Then our men stormed on for three miles or more, until they reached the outskirts of Hulluch, which bristled with the enemy's machine-guns at all points.

Hand-to-hand fighting took place, and the enemy yielded ground wherever our men could come within reach of them, but they were swept back again and again by the tempest of bullets. The struggle continued in this direction for two whole days.

Later I hope to continue the story of this battle, down to the present moment, and to relate the heroism of more recent hours. Some of the men who were engaged in the first part of the operations were enjoying a rest today, and as long as life lasts to me I shall remember those villages behind the fighting lines through which I passed today, thronged by these tall, mud-caked lads who had fought through one of the hardest encounters which have ever given victory to British arms.

They had seen many of their comrades fall, they had tramped on through the shambles of the battlefields, but they looked proud and exultant because they had led a great assault and broken the German line.

During part of the day Sir John French rode about these mining villages, and whenever he met a group of these men he leaned over his horse and spoke to them, and gave them his personal thanks for the gallant work they had done.

FIGHT FOR LOOS AND HILL 70
Saxons Surrender

'It was my first real charge,' remarked a young soldier to a representative of the *Daily Telegraph* last night. The brave man, in the bloom of youth and full of enthusiasm, despite a wounded foot, was referring to the great advance by the British force in France on Saturday. 'It was terrible,' he continued, 'but nothing could stop us.

'"Come on, nothing can beat you," shouted our sergeant. Again and again I heard those encouraging words. And he was right – nothing could. We just went on, and the Germans retired and retired.

'You see, after we had taken the second trench the officer who was leading immediately in front of us was wounded, and it was then that our sergeant began to lead, and he did it well.

'For days we had known that something big was to be attempted, and although we were ignorant of the hour, it was pretty well understood that it would be on Friday night or Saturday morning. With the other regiments in close proximity to us in the front line we moved quietly into our trenches. The order was passed along that we were to keep ourselves in readiness to attack the Germans, of whom there appeared to be thousands. The warning did not come as a surprise; we were ready and perhaps a little excited at the thought of a big event about to happen.

'Our artillery in the rear was blazing away, and in the distance in front of us we could see the bursting of the shells. As the gunners did their work we anxiously awaited for our turn. The waiting was rather trying. We all endeavoured to keep calm, but really we were anxious to begin, and the hours seemed to pass slower than ever they did before.

'The fire of our artillery was answered by that of the Germans, and so the duel was kept up until the first signs of dawn broke across the dark sky. Then the intensity of the bombardment from our side increased. Our bomb-throwers began operations, and their aim was deadly. We knew now that our long watch was at an end, and we awaited the order for the first advancing move.

'It was a grey morning, but the light was sufficient to enable us to see distinctly the German trenches. I should think the first German trench was about 100 yards in front of us. Shells seemed to rain down on the German position, and as for the work of the bombers just before we advanced and afterwards it was great.

'I cannot quite explain what that moment was like when right down through the line came the order, "Prepare to mount the parapet," followed shortly afterwards by the word "Charge".

'With a tremendous shout we leaped from the trenches, and went forward at a great pace towards the first German line. I scarcely know what happened, but I remember that the noise of bursting shells and bombs was terrible. I was in the front rank, and our orders were to take the German trenches, and then still go forward. Any Germans who were left after we had gone through them were to be settled by our supports immediately in our rear. I don't think there were many who put up any fight after we had passed.

'I am certain that the Germans are fearful of the bayonet charge, and on this occasion the work of our bombers was so deadly that the Germans began to leave their first trench before we reached it. We could see them retreating, and we took possession of it without much difficulty; but in front of us German machine-guns about fifty yards apart were sending out a raking fire. One remembers that now, looking backward calmly. Then it was a frenzied rush forward.

'"On!" came the cry, and on we went. No machine-guns or rifle fire could stop us now. Again the Germans retreated – it seemed to us hastily – to the third trench.

'That fell to us, and now we had the Germans in the open, with the village of Loos in the rear. Now it was no more trench work, but fierce use of the bayonet. "Nothing can beat you!" cried our sergeant, and we were all certain that he was right.

'They were Saxons who were fighting us, and as we came among them with our bayonets they seemed to realise that they could not withstand the onslaught. They fought hard, but many a time they appeared to be only too glad to surrender.

'We forced our way across the open to Loos, where the Germans began to put up a very stiff fight. They had placed machine-guns in the houses. But our artillery had the range splendidly, and wrought great destruction. Still there was a terrible fire from the German machine-guns as we approached. With a rush we went into the village and through it, and the Germans for whom we were unable to account were accounted for by our rear lines.

'It was severe fighting, and just as we had captured the place I was wounded, I think by a machine-gun, in the foot. I could not go on, but I saw our regiments continuing the advance, and they finished by taking Hill 70.

'And now as I reflect I think our sergeant was right; "nothing could beat us". We just meant to take the German position, and I really believe that many Saxons were not sorry to surrender.

2 October 1915

GROWING ANXIETY IN THE GERMAN ARMY
Staff Lies Not Believed, *Rotterdam, Friday Afternoon*

There is ferment, uneasiness, and anxiety among the German troops behind the lines in Belgium. This atmosphere has spread to the frontier, where the guards on duty are in a mood of depression, which they make no effort to hide. Reports of huge captures of French and British prisoners, purposely disseminated from the German Headquarters, with a view to stopping the rot that has set in, are no longer believed. Appearances and recent events belie them in an unmistakable manner.

The soldiers have been told, for instance, that the bombardments of the Belgian coast by British warships resulted only in a small number of civilians being killed. And then they see hundreds of wounded marines arriving in Bruges, evidence that gives the lie direct to the 'official' news which reaches them. All is going well, they are assured. How is it, then, they ask, that Belgium has been scraped of every spare man for duty in the firing line, that the garrisons in the towns and villages are denuded, that frontier work is being forced on soldiers who, though only lightly wounded, ought still to be in hospital?

Yesterday there were men who had been on duty continuously for three days and three nights. This was the case at several points on the border. 'Where are the reliefs?' ask these soldiers, who no longer attempt to hide their dissatisfaction. They know well the reason. They are perfectly aware that the comrades assigned to take their places were rushed to the front to try to stem the Allies' advance. Practically all the frontier posts are now composed of men belonging to detachments who a few days ago had just been relieved from the trenches, but were robbed on Sunday of their expected rest, and instead made to do what some of them have openly described as forced service.

This is only one minor bit of evidence of a fact well known all over Belgium, that a state of something approaching demoralisation has set in among the German troops. Be it understood that the Allies' victories, not only in Flanders, but also in Champagne, are a matter of full knowledge among the Belgian population. The Germans may try their hardest to cut off the unhappy country from the outside world, but they have never been able to prevent good news from reaching Brussels and every other large centre, from whence it penetrates even to the remote villages.

The Belgian people today were never so hopeful and optimistic. A thrill of joy has passed through the country, and they are already looking forward to an early day of release from their bondage.

This has reacted on the army of occupation. Instead of welcoming victorious warriors come to make new conquests, they see long trains of wounded passing almost continuously towards Germany from the Western Front. They know that Ostend, Blankenberge, Ghent, and other centres have been evacuated of even the seriously hurt men to make room for the freshly wounded. Messages from the frontier today speak of this unending stream of misery still flowing over the railroads of Belgium towards the east.

A significant item in this connection comes from Cleves, just on the German side of the Gelderland front. Here there arrived within an hour two hospital trains, comprising altogether twenty-five wagons, all crammed with badly wounded men. An interesting point is that these had come north from Cologne, clear proof of how the accommodation in that part of Germany has been strained by the need of finding room for terribly large numbers of cases from the Champagne district.

But with it all it must not be disguised that the enemy is, with unflagging energy, bringing into the field all possible resources. There is as yet no question of giving up any part of Belgium or northern France without a tremendous struggle, for the prosecution of which reinforcements of every description are arriving. Already, in fact, the shortage of men and supplies that occurred during the weekend after the Allies' first overwhelming attack is being made good. The temporarily ungeared machinery is beginning to work again. True, the depots of supplies in Belgium itself were exhausted in the feverish demands made upon them during last week, but now they are being replenished.

In the meantime there is a marked state of nervous tension in the whole district in enemy occupation between the coast and the Dutch frontier.

Lieutenant 'X', writing from 'Somewhere in France' to a friend in North Wales, where he was a noted Bangor University football player, says: 'On Saturday last our battalion took part in a terrific charge. In fact, we advanced into a tornado of shot. My company and another company led our line. I found myself forty yards from the German wire entanglements with two men and a wounded officer. We dug ourselves into a shell hole, where the four of us lay twelve hours in all, under machine-gun and bomb fire from the German line. We had given up hope of ever returning, and prepared to make a last stand against anyone who came against us. The officer was after wounded in the right chest and the thigh. I dressed his wounds and gave him a bomb, which he was to throw with his left hand, but we cheated the Huns of our lives, and eventually crawled back. When I returned I found I was "reported missing, believed killed".'

'It was a big job. We made a grand bayonet charge,' is the way Private H. Worthington describes the great charge in the recent fighting to his wife. 'When we captured those three lines of trenches the Prussians ran like greyhounds. A general said that we had fought like tigers.'

12 October 1915

THE GREAT ADVANCE
Artilleryman's Vivid Story

A British artilleryman, writing to friends in reference to the recent great battle, says: 'You know now that the attack was made on several points of the line, most of which were "feints", whilst the main attack developed on a certain front, which succeeded, and which is now, of course, common property. But you must recollect that each one thought the main attack was to be pushed home on his particular front, and the man directing operations doesn't say, "You will make a feint attack here," otherwise it might turn out a half-hearted affair only.

'For a week before the 25th the heavies had knocked spots off the German trenches and redoubts during the day, and we had prevented them from repairing the damage during the night. Wonderful preparations had been made to make this attack a success. Two days before the attack we cut to ribbons all the barbed wire, which was in places up to a man's shoulder in height. This was done deliberately, as we had practically an unlimited amount of ammunition. We also shelled continuously all the trenches, communicating trenches, and observation posts, and all round must have created a little hell for the Germans, in the first two lines of trenches at any rate.

'On the evening of the 24th all was ready. All through that night we were drawing ammunition and setting the fuses ready for the preliminary bombardment which was to herald the attack; the shells being put into various heaps according to the programme, as there's no time to set fuses once the tap of hell is turned on.

'At 3 a.m. we received our orders. We laid down for a couple of hours' rest, which we badly needed. All watches down the line were corrected at 4 a.m., and punctually at 5.50 a.m. we let them have another bit of Neuve Chapelle. Then we formed a barrage, that is, a curtain of shrapnel, in rear of the German first-line trenches, to prevent supports from reaching them – and then the infantry charged. Then we lifted our fire again another 200 yards, and enabled the boys to go on again. They took the first two lines with only a couple of casualties. The order was given, "No one to fire under 8,000 yards," a slight pause, then "3,400," another pause, "3,600." We were all wildly excited, especially when a battery behind us limbered up and galloped to an advance position, and we waited for our turn.

'The rain came down, and it got dark and misty, and we swore and cursed at everybody and everything. We were ordered to fire on a certain cross roads behind the German trenches to keep their reinforcements from coming up. Meanwhile the ammunition column could only bring the wagons up to about 800 yards from our guns. We had to let two men carry on at each gun, and everybody else had to go and fetch ammunition across this 800 yards of fields shelled all the way. This was a warm job in more senses than one, and it nearly made me bow-legged, as the guns were firing as fast as we could carry the ammunition. We kept changing over at the guns, which gave everybody the same respite, but if you think it's much of a joke you try and carry 45lb in each hand (by the fingers) for 800 yards in the rain across ploughed fields.

'There followed a period of suspense, during which we practically lost communication with the infantry, and from wounded we could only get very little information, such as, "----- at foot of ridge," "----- cut off," "----- captured fourth line and waiting for supports."

'Another period of suspense, during which we were practically out of communication altogether, and the wretched weather made aerial observation impossible. Then we got the news, "Back to where you started from," and "Huge German reinforcements up."

'When the news was confirmed; not one of us spoke a word. We were splattered with grease, and covered from head to foot in mud, and utterly exhausted. The faces of the men were an object-lesson.

'Then the Germans started, and we swore by all the Gods that not one blessed inch of our ground should the Huns take whilst we were living, though fifty of the Kaiser's Army Corps were opposite us. The weather helped the Huns at Neuve Chapelle, again at Aubers, again at Festubert, and now here, and we began to wonder whether we were always going to fight against the weather as well.

'Morning came eventually, and with it a telegram from our army corps commander "congratulating us on having achieved our object in drawing off huge German reserves", which helped the boys to do the trick further along the line. This showed us the true situation, and, of course, we were mightily pleased that the main attack was such a success.'

Chapter 3

The Eastern Front 1914–16

27 August 1914

VICTORIES IN THE EASTERN THEATRE
Influence of the Serbs

By E. Ashmead-Bartlett

It has become almost an accepted axiom of war that whatever happens Austria is almost sure to suffer defeat. In the excitement and uncertainty of the great struggle almost at our gates we are apt to overlook the immense importance of the great Servian victory which has been won against apparently four Austrian Army Corps. Details of these series of engagements are lacking, but apparently the Austrian armies attempted to invade Servian territory from Bosnia along a line formed by the junction of the Drina and the Save. There have been fierce fights at Shabatz, Matsbwa, and Mount Tzer upon the River Yadar, with the result that the Austrian armies have been completely routed and driven back into Bosnia and Slavonia with the loss of 12,000 prisoners and over fifty field-guns and howitzers. Apparently the enemy retreated in such confusion that it became impossible to withdraw these guns across the river.

Now we read the amazing official announcement from Vienna that, owing to the war with Russia it is impossible to continue an active campaign against Servia, and that henceforth the struggle with that country will merely be regarded as a 'punitive expedition'. There is something distinctly humorous in this official view of a crushing defeat, which opens up the road for the Servian armies to invade Austrian territories north of the Save or to overrun Bosnia and Herzegovina. This great victory of the Servian army comes as no surprise to me. Personally, I always felt confident that the Servians would be able to more than hold their own against any force Austria could send against them, even if that little state had been left to conduct her war singlehanded. No State has earned for itself a greater military reputation than Servia in the course of the last two years. The Servians were not severely tested in the war with Turkey, although the battle of Kumanovo was a decisive success, and the divisions sent to Adrianople acquitted themselves admirably. The crushing rout of the Bulgarians at the battle of the Bregalnitza came as a surprise to many, and the latest successes over the Austrian corps will remove any lingering doubts in the minds of those who have persistently regarded the Servian armies as a negligible quantity in the present world struggle.

The news from the Russo–German frontier is even more gratifying. According to the official news from St Petersburg a great battle has been fought between Goldap and Gumbinnen, in which the Germans employed almost all their available troops in Eastern Prussia, namely, the 1st, 3rd, 5th, 17th, and 20th Corps, and three Reserve Corps. Apparently three corps, 160,000 strong, were hurled at the Russian right flank resting on Gumbinnen, and, after desperate fighting, were repulsed. Meanwhile the Russian centre and the left wing resting on Goldap took the offensive, and completely routed the enemy who fled in confusion, leaving many prisoners and guns and much material in the hands of the victors. The immediate result of this victory has been the occupation of Intersburg, and the line is now open for the advance on Königsberg–Thorn and Danzig. However, the ground is extremely difficult in this region of lakes and marshes, as Napoleon found to his cost in 1807, and some time must elapse before any of these fortresses can be masked or invested.

According to later information no time has been lost in following up these successes.

A tremendous amount of hard fighting and marching lies in front of the Russian armies before they can hope to reach the capital, and we must not be unduly optimistic. Nevertheless, satisfactory progress has been made all along the line, and the result of these operations must be causing intense anxiety to the General Staff in Belgium.

This battle of Goldap–Gumbinnen, and the Servian victory on the Drina, are the first great battles of the war. The news has doubtless been circulated throughout the Allied armies in Belgium, and must have a most inspiriting effect on the men who are now engaging in that terrible struggle, which must have decisive results on the future of the campaign. It is curious how all calculations have been upset in this campaign. The Germans always hoped to deliver a smashing blow at the French army of the north long before the Russians could make their numbers felt in Eastern Prussia. Yet the main armies in Belgium are only just coming into contact when the first big battle in the east has been fought and won. Again we have to thank the Belgians for this remarkable result.

Germany's latest opponent has lost no time in striking. A despatch states that the Japanese Fleet has already commenced the bombardment of Tsingtau. In a few days another of the Kaiser's pet schemes will have vanished for ever. Germany's colony in the Far East will have fallen into other hands. Her warships must either succumb or enter neutral ports; the remnant of her Far Eastern shipping will be swept from the seas.

In all history there has never been anything quite so remarkable as this manifestation of a common hatred against an individual and a caste. The sole effect of an exaggerated militarism which drags into its insatiable maw not only men who fight for love of adventure, but all those who hate scenes of violence and bloodshed, has been to cause almost the whole world in any way interested to rise and crush the common enemy of humanity. The policy of the 'mailed fist', which despatched Prince Henry on his famous journey to the Far East, is now being challenged by no fewer than seven different peoples. In Europe, France, Russia, Belgium, England, and Servia are in line. Portugal is willing and anxious to send a contingent to the plains of Flanders. In the Far East, Japan has taken up arms. Men are coming from Canada, Boers are fighting in South Africa, and Australia is sending her forces to our aid. Only a word of approval is required to let loose a horde of Sikhs, Ghurkas, and Pathans, who would volunteer to a man to aid the common cause.

Why is it that all the various races are willing to leave their homes and risk their lives fighting on European soil? Many have no direct influence in the quarrel. It is the revolt of the spirit of the age against the antiquated methods of the Middle Ages. Man is no longer content to be ruled by brute force and the dread of the sword. Is there any military force which can long resist this united protest of seven indignant races? Already the victory is half won. Not a colony remains to Germany; not one of her merchant vessels dares show her nose on the ocean; her fleet dare not venture from port; her eastern frontier is being overrun by three million Slavs; and her credit has almost disappeared.

Even if her cause were just, her brutal methods of conducting war have alienated the sympathy which many might otherwise have felt at the spectacle of one nation, with an unwilling ally as a tool, contending against so many enemies at one time. The conduct of the German armies, their brutal murders of civilians, their taking of hostages, their levying of war tolls on captured towns, their arrogant brutality to the temporarily vanquished, their strewing the high seas with mines, which is contrary to the laws of war, carry us back not to the methods of 100 years ago, but to the epochs of Tamerlane and Attila.

31 August 1914

THE BATTLE OF GUMBINNEN
Big German Defeat, *St Petersburg, Sunday*

Unofficial first-hand news of the operations of the Russian armies is at last commencing to come through. An account of the battle of Gumbinnen, which, apparently, resulted in breaking the back of the German resistance in East Prussia, is supplied by the correspondent of the *Novoye Vremya* at the front.

He states that on 19 August, simultaneously with a Russian cavalry attack at Liedenthal, the infantry advanced on Pilkallen and drove out the enemy, who fell back to the west, concentrating at Gumbinnen. The German corps, which had been defeated on the 17th, also retreated in the same direction, sustaining further heavy losses.

The night, which was spent in attending to the wounded and bringing up munitions, passed quietly, but it was only the calm before a storm. By the morning the preparations of the Russian force had been fully completed, and it moved forward once more. This time, however, it encountered a very stubborn resistance, the enemy having meanwhile received reinforcements. At daybreak a terrific artillery duel had commenced, hundreds of guns being in action on each side.

In face of the storm of projectiles from the German heavy artillery the Russian infantry broke into skirmishing order and moved forward to the attack. Soon they came under the fierce fire of the field and machine-guns, but nothing could withstand the determination of their advance, and the enemy was driven out of his positions one after another. Several times the German cavalry attempted to carry out counter-attacks, but in every case they were beaten back with heavy losses.

In the heat of the fight one of the Russian infantry regiments annihilated an entire brigade of the enemy with machine-gun fire. As the result of a well-directed stream of projectiles, 3,000 dead were left on this part of the field. Several positions were most fiercely contested and were won, first by one side and then by the other, but in the end they all remained in the hands of the Russians.

Great havoc was wrought by one Russian battery on a force of the enemy's infantry, which was making a particularly firm stand. To counteract the action of this battery a concentrated fire of howitzers and field-guns was brought to play upon it, and the commander was mortally wounded in the abdomen. He was carried back to the field hospital, where he shortly afterwards expired in full consciousness, after having calmly given directions for his burial and the arrangement of his affairs.

Till his last breath this gallant man continued to relate to those about him the story of the triumphant advance of the Russian army. His final words were: 'I am quite satisfied. My battery is in good hands.'

During the fighting on this day, which lasted fourteen hours and was only interrupted by the fall of night, the Russians captured thirty guns and thirty-six limbers. Apart from wounded sixteen officers and 400 men of lower grades were taken prisoner. In the evening the enemy retreated on Gumbinnen, which had already been evacuated by the civilian population.

The engagement of 21 August opened with the expulsion from Pilkallen of three German cavalry regiments and ten horse-guns which had reoccupied it on the previous day. They appear to have offered little resistance, but on perceiving that the town was surrounded on three sides by a Russian infantry regiment, to have fled in disorder, flinging away their carbines and lances as they rode. In this affair four officers and eighty men were made captive.

During the fighting round Pilkallen three Russian field hospitals were moving towards the front line, when they came under a sharp shrapnel fire. They were then noticed by the German cavalry and ordered to halt. Though the doctors vigorously protested and pointed out that they were going to render assistance to the wounded of both sides, the German cavalry commander ordered the whole equipment to be burnt and the staff to be sent as prisoners to Pilkallen. Before, however, the town was reached, the German convoy was attacked by Cossacks. The German escort then screamed out, 'Cossacks!' in terrified tones and fled precipitately.

In the confusion a nurse was wounded. The hospitals continued their way to Pilkallen, which had meanwhile been reoccupied by the Russians, and on the following day one of the doctors had the magnanimous satisfaction of supplying cigarettes to the German officer who had commanded his escort.

On the evening of the 23rd a Russian attack was made on Insterburg, but the enemy made no attempt to hold his entrenched positions. A portion of the Russian army then occupied the town. The remnant of the German force fell back in the direction of Königsberg, hotly pursued by the Russian advance guard.

During their retreat the Germans lost heavily in killed and wounded, and particularly in prisoners. The correspondent adds ironically that the capture of Insterburg took place on the twenty-first day after the opening of the German campaign against Russia, exactly a week earlier than the date fixed by the Emperor William for the occupation by his troops of the line St Petersburg–Vilna–Kieff.

The 'German war news' officially circulated through the German wireless stations and received by the Marconi Company, says:

Berlin, 30 August

A big battle has been raging in Russia since 28 August without any decisive issue so far, but the position of the Austrians in this battle is favourable. Austrian troops followed up their success near Krasnik by another victory over ten Russian divisions on 27 August, forty-five officers, including a general, and 2,000 men being captured, as well as much war material.

The latest news from Allenstein indicates that the German army is energetically pursuing the Russians, among whose ranks the carnage has been terrible.

German troops in East Prussia under the command of General von Hindenburg defeated a Russian army, consisting of three army corps and three cavalry divisions, which advanced from Narew. Fighting took place in the neighbourhood of Gilgenburg and Ortelsburg, and German troops are pursuing the enemy across the frontier. The resident magistrate of Osterode, in East Prussia, reports that the enemy has been defeated, and that fugitives may now return.

13 November 1914

RUSSIAN ARMY AND ITS LEADERS
Tremendous Forces, *Petrograd, Thursday*

By Granville Fortescue

'On this side Germany is fighting not a nation, but a continent.' A certain military attaché used these words in the course of a discussion on the situation here. This fact is the first impression made on anyone coming into the war zone, when one tries to get an understanding of the forces engaged along the Russian front. The mind at first refuses to accept the figures of this staggering total. A part are now in East Prussia and in Poland, and are advancing against Cracow. Only such numbers allowed of the grand tactics which have characterised the Russian operations.

Despite these armies already in the field, Russia has not called on the vast supplies of men in the remoter sections of her domain. The pregnant fact is that Russia is able to put a force against the Germans at any point. This preponderance must ensure victory.

The Russian Tommy, or, as he is called here, Ivan, son of Ivan, is a most impressive-looking soldier. Nearly all over 5ft 6in in height, and of splendid build, they recall certain Irish regiments in size and swagger. For as soon as the peasant has donned the long, light terracotta-coloured overcoat and learned to set his cap at a jaunty angle, he assumes the martial swagger. The Russian military overcoat is the best bit of soldier's wearing apparel I have seen in any army. Not only is it smart in cut and colour, but eminently practical. No better protection against the winter cold could be devised. I used to think that the English military overcoat was the best made, but the Russian is better. It is not necessary to emphasise the importance of having a good covering in Russia in winter.

I have been much impressed by the European Russian army. In every detail it is superior to the Russian army I saw nearly ten years ago in Manchuria. There is every indication that the standard of intelligence is higher. The reorganisation of 1910 has worked wonders in the personnel. Also there can be no doubt of the popularity of this war with the rank and file. For years hatred of Germany has been smouldering in the breasts of the Russians, and now it has burst into flame.

The Germans have always affected to despise the Russian military organisation. They could give a categorical list of its defects. That it could for one moment stand against the German 'machine' was not to be dreamed of. Such was the firm belief at Potsdam. This is one more miscalculation of the arrogant enemy, and now he pays dearly for his mistake. Not only is the rank and file of the army bettered, but already the war has developed some subtle tacticians among the Russian generals. General Russky, who commands the army moving on Kalish, has shown himself to be a field commander of high ability. As yet it is impossible to make a complete study of his tactics, but from such information as comes to hand his advance along the River Pilitza was nothing short of masterly.

Another name that will soon be known all over Europe is that of General

Ivanoff. General Ivanoff was considered the deepest military student in Russia. When Przemysl falls the name of Radko Dimitrieff will ring around the world. For a month this commander has been closing his grip on the garrison which blocks his path. For sufficient reasons he has not hurried in the task. When gaunt disease raises its menacing head in an invested city the besiegers can afford to wait and make of it an ally.

But the real head in name and in fact of all the armies of Russia is the Grand Duke Nicholas Nikolaevich. He is a Russian of the old school. Never sparing himself in the service of the Emperor and the country, he demands the same sacrifices from those who work with him. Spartan in his own standards, his example has had a splendid effect on the whole Russian army. Severe he is, but only as a great soldier must be. When one carries the responsibility of one-sixth of the world on his shoulders, one cannot listen to excuses. In the army he is the law and the word. No amount of influence can save a general who has failed. No explanation can excuse an officer who has been neglectful.

This master works only with the best weapons. If Bismarck was a man of iron, Nicholas Nikolaevich is a man of chilled steel.

23 November 1914

CAMPAIGN OF THE RUSSIAN ARMY
Fierce Battles, *Petrograd, Sunday*

For more than a week western Poland has been in the throes of a gigantic conflict, and there are still no signs of a definite decision. The statement issued last evening by the staff of the Commander-in-Chief dismisses both these operations, and the others in which the Russian troops are engaged with the utmost brevity. It says: 'The fighting in the country between the Vistula and the Wartha, and on the Czenstochova–Cracow front continues. In East Prussia only small skirmishes occurred on 20 November. Our troops continue their advance in Western Galicia.'

The last indication of the line which the battle with the Germans has now assumed was contained in the General Staff communiqué on Friday, when it was announced that the Russians had captured a battery of heavy guns and other trophies to the north-west of Lodz. At the same time, it was made known that the enemy's plans aimed at the rupture of the centre of the Russian position.

There seems no doubt that the Germans are employing enormous masses of troops in this effort. According to current report they assembled no fewer than half a million men on the railways to the south of Thorn before they commenced their counter-attack. They also apparently made a move forward from their great Vistula fortress along the right shore of the river, though no details of the results of this step have become known.

It is still a moot point whether these tactics will retard or accelerate their final defeat. Among the maxims governing German strategy the first place has long been held by that which declares that the attack is the most effective form of defence. The truth of this principle depends, however, on the success of the attack, and, for reasons which have repeatedly been stated, the Germans have much better chances of victory on their own than on Russian soil. Their first movement towards the Vistula brought them nothing but a weakening of their armies and a sense of failure, and it is highly probable that the issue of this second blow in the same direction will be very similar.

But this time their retirement would not be a simple matter, for, after their first invasion, they so radically annihilated the railways and destroyed the roads that they would no longer be able by falling back with rapidity and decision to weaken the impact of the pursuit.

On the whole the conditions of the battle may be said to favour the Russians much more than was the case during the first attempt of the Germans to establish themselves in winter quarters on the Vistula.

Though nothing more than slight skirmishes are mentioned by the official announcement as having taken place in Eastern Prussia, a message from a correspondent with the active army reports with circumstantial detail the capture of Gumbinnen by the Russians. The second big battle which has been fought for the possession of this town lasted, according to this account, four days and fifteen hours, and covered a front of about five miles.

The action on the first day was confined to an artillery duel. The Russians found a good target in the trains ranged up on the railway sidings, and with their opening volley succeeded in setting some of these on fire. Attempts by the Germans to extinguish the flames were unsuccessful.

This bombardment was kept up till late at night, and on the following morning Russian infantry advanced to attack a large force of the enemy, which held a position traversing the railway from Stallupönen to Gumbinnen.

Once more the Cossacks were the heroes of the most stirring incident of the struggle. A regiment of this cavalry charged one of the enemy's batteries, threw those who were serving it into panic and flight, destroyed the utility of several guns, and then galloped back to the Russian lines. It was found during the day that the Germans were not willing to await the issue of the bayonet attack, and towards evening the Cossacks were able to penetrate to Gumbinnen, which, however, they evacuated during the night.

But the definite occupation of the town was only briefly delayed, for the Russian troops were soon entering it in triumph. It was discovered to be half-demolished by shell-fire, and entirely abandoned by its population.

Change of seasons is now bringing about completely fresh campaigning conditions. Very cold weather has again set in here; intermittent showers of snow are gradually covering the country with its winter coat of white, and the rivers are full of drifting ice-blocks, which will presently freeze together into a solid surface. It would be difficult to exaggerate the importance of this transformation on the course of the war.

24 November 1914

GERMAN REPULSE IN POLAND
Advance Stopped, Petrograd, Monday

By Granville Fortescue

The Crown Prince is again thwarted. The army under his command, which during the last five days has threatened Warsaw, has been severely repulsed. Thus his hope of being hailed as the 'Sieger' of the Polish capital dies, as did his chance of being the 'Sieger' of Paris. His ambition to shine as a strategist seems destined never to be fulfilled. He is the 'Jonah' of the German army.

Yet his new army, consisting possibly of the Guard Reserve, the 20th, 17th, and two other corps, arrived alarmingly close to Warsaw before it was finally checked. The master military minds which surround the Crown Prince planned and carried out a remarkably daring coup that only he, with his genius for doing the wrong thing, could have muddled. His military councillors knew the great advantage they commanded in mobility. Operating on exterior lines, and served by one of the best strategic railroad systems, it was possible for them to attempt an attack at any point they chose. Obviously they chose the weakest point along the Russian front. At Plozk, five German corps were opposed by but two Russian, which, after putting up a desperate defence, were compelled to retire. This left the road to the capital open.

With remarkable celerity the German army pushed ahead, staking all on arriving at Warsaw before reinforcements could be hurried to the scene. Their lines of communications were left to take care of themselves. The Russians in this section adopted their traditional tactics and destroyed everything that might be of use to the enemy. A stand was made on the Bsura River. But the Germans were always in superior numbers, and the positions on which to offer battle were not favourable to the Russians.

A number of Russian corps were moving slowly towards the threatened area. The difficulties of marching and transportation through Poland are the limit. It was the terrier and the mastiff over again. And the mastiff was occupied with another bone, Cracow, when the more agile dog attacked him. Now he has turned. The terrier runs.

If it were not for their extraordinary skill in the retirement of their forces the present position of the Germans would be considered extremely perilous. They have come in on a long tongue of land between the Vistula and the Wartha rivers, depending entirely on these walls of water to defend their flanks. No commanding general would take such chances unless he knew that it was impossible for his opponent to smash through on his flank. This is not impossible. General Rennenkampf is operating in the north. Let this hint suffice.

In the south General Rusky, who has been on the sick list for a few days, has abandoned for a moment his attacks on the German frontier to give his attention to bigger game.

For the present no further information can be given. A careful study of the map will tell the rest of the story. Unless the god of battles is unexpectedly generous, the military star of the heir of the Hohenzollerns will suffer a sudden eclipse.

In order to give this new invasion of Poland every chance of success the German armies in the other theatres have been exceedingly active. On the Czenstochova–Cracow front the combined German and Austrian forces are unremitting in their efforts to force back the flood which threatens to engulf them. A general attack is going on, which is as yet undecided.

In East Prussia a vigorous offensive has also been under way. Near Stallupönen the whole weight of the German Northern army has been thrown against the Russian left, with the hope of turning it. For the briefest time it looked as if the manœuvre might be crowned with success. But certain reliable reserve corps were thrown into the action at its critical juncture, and the enemy was not only checked, but forced to move back to a new position 30 kilometres (19 miles) in the rear.

Meanwhile spirited contests were raging along the borders of the Mazur lakes. The terrain here is about as difficult as any commander could hope to find. It is all forest and swamp. From the descriptions which have been given me it must resemble the Wilderness country, where General Grant made his famous campaign in the Civil War. The Germans have, in spite of the enormous natural difficulties, constructed some half-dozen railways crossing the passes between the lakes. [There is apparently an excision by the Russian Censor at this point.] After they have possession of the roads leading beyond the lakes, the Russians can turn their attention to the Insterburg–Allenstein–Thorn Railway, which, if controlled by them, would be of superlative strategic importance. No one more than the German commander here realises this. From Lotzen he watches with unquiet eyes the advance of the Russian line, which extends north and south from Angerburg to Johannisberg. To the military student the campaign for these lakes will make fascinating reading.

The news coming from Przemysl is always favourable. That it can be taken at any moment is certain. Only the fact that the Russians prefer to lose a little time rather than many lives prevents their carrying Przemysl by assault within a week.

20 January 1915

AT THE FRONT WITH THE RUSSIAN ARMY
Vistula Campaign, *Warsaw, Saturday (via Petrograd, Tuesday)*
By Granville Fortescue

The German advance through north Poland is meeting a strong Russian counter-offensive. The skilful dispositions of the enemy for a time concealed his main objective, but now the indications point to a vigorous drive over the country between Warsaw and Mlava. It is just possible that the Germans hope to tempt the Tsar's troops from their present long line, figuring that the arrangements for a sustained forward movement are not yet completed on this side. But the war area here has become the scene of extraordinary activity during the last ten days, and it was clear that new dispositions were under way.

Masses of cavalry swarm over the country on the Vistula, and smother such forces of the enemy's mounted troops as they encounter. One cavalry division had considerable success in an engagement at Radzanof, while another has pushed its patrols beyond Serpez. This is ideal country for cavalry operations on a large scale, open and rolling. The Cossacks now skirmishing beyond Serpez are backed by important forces of mounted infantry and field artillery.

So successful has been the deployment of this army that the Germans are trembling for the fate of Vloclavek. The Lovicz–Thorn railway makes a bend at this town which brings it close to the Vistula, and the present Russian march threatens this link of the enemy's communication. Rumours that I have not been able to check state that Lovicz is being abandoned. Large fires are reported in the vicinity, and the inference is that the enemy is devastating the country previous to retirement. Such a collapse of the Warsaw campaign was not expected so early, and if the rumours should be verified we have another indication of the skill with which the Russian North Vistula campaign is opened.

Already the two opposing armies face each other across the mighty river. The importance of the river in the Polish campaign is obvious. If it can be definitely established as a Russian line of communication the operations in the spring will be enormously facilitated.

Warsaw now breathes more easily. Not that the citizens showed the least apprehension, even when the enemy was making his most vigorous efforts to capture the city. 'Business as usual' is the motto of the Varsovians in this time of trial. What they have done is to attempt to relieve the situation of the non-combatant population. The plight of the Polish refugee equals that of the distracted Belgian and up to the present it has been impossible to do much to help him. The Russian Government has responded splendidly to the call of these unfortunates, but with so much of the country in the enemy's hands the relief work is fraught with great difficulties.

Seeing that the Poles are so nobly taking up their share of the Russian military burden, the mother-country owes these citizens her help. The greatest need of the moment among the refugees is milk. The head of the Warsaw Relief Committee tells me that a shipload of condensed milk would be a godsend to the Polish sufferers.

But the Russians are not leaving the present line of defences before the city, although the enemy has retired 12 miles at certain points. The Russians are not to be drawn into any trap. A new plan of campaign to suit the altered situation is being worked out by the Grand Duke and his able associates. This plan varies only in detail from the first Russian strategic scheme.

The plan at present is to rid Poland of the enemy. While the operations of the different armies seem to have no general scheme of co-operation in their arrangement at this time, such is not the case. The conditions developed by the enemy have made it necessary that the Army of the North and the Army of the South should act independently. The question of mobility, which has so interfered with the previous operations, is being carefully gone over. If Lovicz is evacuated we have one answer.

But the failure of the assaults on Warsaw is of extraordinary importance alone. This is the second time Germany has thrown her might against the capital of the ancient kingdom and failed. It is a tremendous moral victory for Russia. Besides this, it has given the Russian troops confidence. They now know that the vaunted German military power breaks before their dogged resistance. More than this, they have heard the German guns and realise how exaggerated are the stories of their destructiveness. Nine-inch siege pieces have been used by the Germans against the Warsaw positions. I have witnessed how ineffective these enormous guns are against a simple trench. It was some time before I became convinced that the enemy was using cannon of such large calibre in an open country campaign, but the fact is established beyond dispute.

The Russians whom I see around here are becoming better fighting men with the passing of each day. There has never been any question of their ability to hold on, and with improvements in their transport organisation they will make a record in pushing onward.

22 January 1915

AT THE FRONT WITH THE RUSSIAN ARMY
New Offensive Imminent, *Warsaw, Monday (via Petrograd, Wednesday Evening)*

By Granville Fortescue

The first stages of the new Russian plan are unfolding, and before a month passes a new theatre of war will hold the focus of the world's attention. A new offensive will develop, and the character of the warfare will be particularly suited to the composition of the Russian army. It will not be trench fighting. The plan includes a gigantic scheme of co-operation, and, if it succeeds, it will be a remarkable demonstration of the military ability of the Russian General Staff. There is every reason to believe it will succeed.

The cavalry is in splendid condition, and the horses are extraordinarily fit. The Cossacks entrained yesterday morning, and I have never seen cavalry looking so well after prolonged campaigning. The colonel commanding told me that they have just finished sixty-three days' active field work, but, save for wear and tear of saddles and bridles, which was to be expected, the troopers and horses showed little sign of breaking down. The Turcomans are an aggressive-looking lot, and have already made a fine record.

The secret of the success of the Russian cavalry movements is their light transport. The squadrons are followed by carts that can go along almost any place where a single horseman can ride. Combine this with the fact that the horses live on the scantiest fodder, and you understand why the Russian mounted troops are still a factor to be reckoned with in this campaign, when the original cavalry of the other armies is wiped out.

The country over which the cavalry will operate in the new advance would not suit European mounted troops, but the Russian cavalry officers assure me that it is just the terrain they like best.

I can give no further hint as to where the new war area will be. Meanwhile the situation around Warsaw is almost normal. At least, so accustomed have the population become to having the enemy wasting himself in futile fighting 30 miles away, that the daily attacks hardly promote any tea-table talk. The Germans batter themselves like waves against a seawall. On Saturday another violent assault was made in the vicinity of Sochaczef, but, after nearly twenty hours' furious fighting, there had been no appreciable change in the position of either army.

The whole line had been quiet previous to this, so the attack could only have been a bluff to hold attention to the Warsaw front. Nothing better than the second defences of the city has ever been constructed in field fortification. The line runs for 80 miles from the Vistula to the Vistula, and consists of six rows of supporting trenches, superbly built. The work shows the skill of the Russian artisan, combined with good military judgment. The position is occupied by a force amply able to hold it indefinitely, and the Warsaw problem no longer holds the attention of the General Staff.

Wherever an offensive, in the opinion of the Grand Duke and his advisers, against the German lines is impracticable, the enemy will be held with a containing force. Thus, the main body of the Russian army will be free to carry on the war in a manner unaffected by the presence of the Germans on Polish territory. The policy will be to engage as many of the enemy's corps as possible, and to immobilise them, while bringing up fresh armies to operate in the selected regions. While great masses of cavalry are beginning the offensive, these fresh armies are forming behind them. The work of these armies is to hold the country invaded by the cavalry.

The new plan of campaign contemplates active operations which will continue, at the shortest, for six months, and as much longer as the resisting power of the enemy may entail. Time is of the least importance. The main point is that we have a definite, workable plan, which has not been the case since the temporary success of the enemy's Vistula campaign. Now, with the whole available German force committed to certain lines, it is reasonable to believe that a change of front will be extremely difficult.

Not that the Russians under-estimate the resourcefulness of the enemy. But every contingency appears to be provided for. The failure of the first Russian offensive was, in a measure, due to the fact that we left to the enemy certain obvious openings, which his superior mobility enabled him to seize. At present he is so strongly engaged that it is believed he dare not attempt a counter-offensive. Wherever he moves be will be counter-checked, while the might of Russia moves irresistibly onward.

6 February 1915

CAMPAIGN OF THE RUSSIAN ARMY
Fight for Warsaw, *Petrograd, Friday*

Nothing is more reassuring about the present situation on this front than the smiling complacency with which it is regarded in military circles here. Those who know most, and are best able to form correct views, seem to look upon the present tactics of the enemy as an extreme case of that madness with which the gods afflict those whom they intend to destroy. One cannot avoid feeling that by rushing at the Russian lines behind the Ravka like an infuriated bull Von Hindenburg is merely doing what the Allies want him to do, and that, if he persists, the only result he can arrive at is to dash out his own brains.

The demonstration theory has now been definitely abandoned. Nothing but a passionate determination to do or die could induce the Germans to mass, on a front of seven miles, no fewer than as many divisions, and to see their men swept down in thousands by the deadly fire of the Russian artillery and machine-guns. Appearances and probabilities have once more been deceptive, and there can no longer be the slightest doubt that the enemy is firmly resolved to get to Warsaw. Fortunately, there is just as little doubt that he will not get there. Even if our Allies should be driven from their present lines there would still be an even more formidable position to surmount. But, far from giving way, or even standing merely on the defensive, the Russians are parrying thrust with thrust, and, according to the latest official news, it is they, not the Germans, who are gaining ground.

It is evidently believed here that both the fierce battles now raging will be decisive, in the sense that their result will leave one side much greater liberty of movement, and will impose upon the other a longer or shorter period of inactivity and recuperation. At the same time, the struggle in Poland is proceeding over an area which, according to modern standards, is of exceedingly restricted dimensions. A General Staff bulletin, issued last night, indicates the main centres of the conflict by three names – Borshimoff, Gumin, and Volya-Shidlovska. A line, drawn from north to south through these places, would be almost parallel to the Ravka, but would tend slightly to the east. Thus, Borshimoff lies two miles and Volya-Shidlovska three from that river. The distance from Borshimoff to Volya-Shidlovska is about three miles, and Gumin lies almost exactly midway between them. From the railway line at Lovitsch-Sokacheff to a point somewhat to the south of Gumin, an open plain extends from the Ravka to the Russian lines. Borshimoff and Gumin are both situated on the western verge of a forest, which stretches for five miles from north to south, and varies in breadth from a quarter of a mile to two miles. Volya-Shidlovska is situated just beyond the southern extremity of this forest, but is approached from Bolimoff through the northern projection of another, which spreads out in all directions to the north of the Skierniewice–Warsaw railway. On both sides of the Ravka the banks rise somewhat, and immediately to the west of the river there is undulating ground, on which no doubt the Germans have the heavier of the hundred batteries which they have in action.

It is on this comparatively limited battleground that the Germans are making their supreme, and, as it is almost certain to prove, their final attempt to blast and hew a road through to Warsaw. Never have they been prodigal with blood and ammunition. Fighting goes on day and night, without cessation, but the enemy makes use of the hours of dusk or twilight for his most determined efforts to push his infantry forward to the Russian trenches. As is pointed out here, military science is playing no part whatever in the present tactics of Von Hindenburg. He is relying solely on the reckless expenditure of the lives of his sheep-like soldiers and a hurricane of shells to batter his way through our Allies' front. Regiments are exterminated or flung back in shaken and useless remnants, fresh units are ruthlessly driven forward to take their places; and a constant stream of reinforcements keeps pouring up from the rear.

It is too early as yet to make any estimate of the enemy's losses, but they must have been appalling. The sudden flash of Russian searchlight reveals a German regiment advancing in close order under the supposed cover of night, and in an instant it is raked by well-aimed artillery fire. Whole ranks are swept away by field and machine-guns, so that not a man remains alive and uninjured. Russian bayonet attacks often annihilate entire companies. Such carnage cannot be of long duration, and if present indications are of any guide, can only have one issue.

From one extremity to the other of the battle front the Russians, far from giving way, have won ground from the enemy by their gallant counter-attacks. At Borshimoff two lines of German trenches have been captured. Gumin is now in the hands of our Allies, and the fight has also taken a favourable course on the estate of Volya-Shidlovska. That is of excellent omen. However, the battle continues with unabated fierceness, and the trenches, which have already changed hands time after time, may not yet be in possession of their final occupants. Still, Wednesday's conflict has evidently not brought the Germans one inch nearer to the coveted goal of Warsaw.

In the Carpathians the line of battle has been extended further to the east, as we hear that the attempts of the enemy to force his way through the Tartaroff Pass have been repulsed with heavy losses. It is by this pass that the railway from Kolomea to Marmaros-Ziget crosses the ridge, and the fact that the Austrians are trying to penetrate here, shows that they hope to cut into the rear of the Russian forces operating in Bukovina. Altogether the fighting along the range seems to be developing in a very satisfactory manner.

On their extreme right wing the Russians are near Svidnik, 10 miles within the Hungarian boundary line, which they have here crossed by the Dukla Pass, and are advancing rapidly, capturing many prisoners. Similar success is attending their movements due south of Yasliska, where they are operating in the valley of the Hungarian river Laborch, by the side of which runs the railway from Sanok, and also on the line from Sambor to Uzhgorod (Ungvar). It is only on the Galician side of the next two passes, the Uzhok and Beskid, that they have fallen back before superior numbers. No evil auguries are, however, to be drawn from this retirement, as our Allies have only effected it in order to obtain the advantage of a carefully chosen and prepared position, from which they will more easily be able to repulse the enemy's attacks.

Viewed as a whole, latest developments on this front can only be regarded with gratification.

27 July 1915

THE RUSSIAN STAND
Battle of Lublin–Cholm

The information which has hitherto reached London concerning the crucial struggle now being fought out in south-eastern Poland is tantalisingly meagre. The operation in this district, however, must bear a much closer resemblance to the decisive actions of former wars than most of the fighting of the present war. The principal struggle on which the event of this campaign may be said to hinge is the attack of General von Mackensen directed against the south-eastern communications of Warsaw with the interior of Russia. Mackensen's army is moving downstream between the Vistula and the Bug, and gradually fighting its way towards the Lublin–Cholm railway on a front of about 30 miles. On Mackensen's right a group of three or four army corps are acting as a flank guard, and are fighting a Russian army in the Bug valley. On his left an Austrian army, under the Archduke Joseph, is trying to outflank the main Russian position, but these Austrians have been held up by a Russian group of corps.

The forward march of the German main army has been stubbornly disputed. Only by degrees has the German Marshal been able to force back the Russian advanced posts, which clung tenaciously to every village and every fold of the ground. The Germans are descending from an undulating plateau into the great plain of Poland, the country in their front is densely wooded, and is interspersed with meres and marshes. Local resources are slender, and the country is badly provided with roads; only one main chaussée traverses the country from north to south, and it forms the axis of Mackensen's march. The main German army consists probably of ten army corps, which may by now consist of 300,000 troops out of the 400,000 which would be their total complement. This army is already 60 miles from its railhead in Galicia, and depends upon motor lorries both for food and ammunition.

Such are the general features of the military situation as the German columns establish contact with the Russian main position. The strength of all positions depends on the time which the defenders have had to prepare and improve their natural facilities for a prolonged trial of strength, and the delays of the German advance necessitated by the difficulties of transport, as well as the stout defence of their advanced posts, have afforded the Russians the opportunity for adequate preparations. Another all-important condition is, of course, the supply of munitions, and in this respect the Russian chief command has the very important advantage of ample railway transport to within a few miles of the line of combat.

The German attacks resemble the operations at the beginning of the war and the fighting in Champagne which brought the Fourth German Army to a check. Heavy artillery fire, both from field-guns and howitzers, concentrated on the immediate objectives of the assaulting infantry, precedes all close action by the latter. Heavy artillery from the high ground dominates the landscape, and hurls the big projectiles on to tactical points where Russian batteries may be posted, or where reserves are lying ready to support their comrades in the front line. The attacking infantry entrenches and fortifies all the ground it captures, and then seeks to approach nearer and nearer to the Russian main position under cover of German artillery fire. It rushes the Russian advanced positions by night, or saps gradually up to them, if they are too well posted to be shattered by artillery fire. Where the fighting takes place in the woods themselves leadership is more difficult, hazard plays a greater part, for units break up and the lines of entanglements which bar access to the interior of the thickets are not continuous, the adversaries pass one another, meet unexpectedly in forest glades, and fight hand-to-hand with desperation. The roads and edges of woods are particularly dangerous zones, for they are swept with machine-gun fire.

The experience of a great number of battles in this war has proved that these conditions are far less favourable to German tactics than the wide, open spaces which give full effect to artillery fire, and which enable infantry attacks to be conducted according to programme. The German soldiers do not excel in hand-to-hand fighting with the bayonet, and seem to lose their impetus when the personal control of their officers is absent or impeded. The weather conditions are good, but the Russians are the better provided with food and ambulance facilities than their enemy. While the extended fronts and extensive woods afford opportunities for skulkers to slip away from the battle. Such defection frequently attenuates infantry regiments in the crisis of a long struggle.

The flanks of both armies in this great battle are very lightly connected with the masses operating on their right and left, about as much as the British at Waterloo were with the detachment at Hal on their right, so that scope for enveloping manœuvres still exists.

The heavy losses in such a battle send a continuous stream of wounded and war-weary men to the rear, while their fighting line becomes thinner and more exhausted as the fighting proceeds. For this reason alone a tremendous effort such as the German offensive against the Lublin–Cholm line stands a poor chance of success unless a continuous stream of reinforcements from the rear replace these losses and relieve the troops in the front line, for the fighting goes on continuously day and night. The Russians, operating in a district which they have held for several months have facilities for command and manœuvre which are denied to the Germans, and so long as they have enough troops and enough munitions to counter-attack when the chance offers, there remains the chance of ruining the invading army.

31 July 1915

THE GREAT BATTLE FOR WARSAW
Retreat Prepared

The prolonged defence at the Polish quadrilateral by the gallant armies of Russia offers only the barest hope that at the eleventh hour a military event may compel the enveloping German armies to relax their grip. A campaign is never quite lost while the contending armies continue fighting. Nevertheless, it is no secret that every preparation has been made by the Russian Staff to abandon Warsaw, and to withdraw the field army from the line of the Vistula before the invaders can reach points whence they might cut off the retreat, if retreat finally becomes unavoidable.

For every reason the stubborn defence of the Vistula line is a great gain to the Allies. The German armies are kept busy, and are expending their vital strength. The retreat is protected by the prolonged defence, for the enemy will be too exhausted to profit by their success until they have paused to rest and refit. Finally, the moral effect of the gallant stand on friend and foe alike is very important.

If, as now seems probable, the Russian Chief Command elect to withdraw their field forces behind the River Bug, they will continue to retain the gates of Poland, whence the offensive in the Vistula Valley can be resumed when it suits, but the first result of such a withdrawal is likely to be a concentration of forces by both adversaries in the northern area of the Eastern seat of war, where decisive fighting may be expected. The contraction of the Russian front and closer concentration of the Russian armies, as well as the prolongation of German communications, will be so many points of advantage for our Ally.

Between the rivers Naref and Bug hard fighting has taken place since 25 July, in which the Russians have attempted to overwhelm the German advanced guards which recently obtained a footing on the eastern bank of the Naref. In this war the rivers roughly mark the battlefields, because they form a natural obstacle to cover a line of defence, besides giving the necessary field of fire from one bank or the other. The progress of an invasion is marked by the forcing of one river passage after another, and the procedure of the Germans on the Naref is typical. By concentrating a superior artillery fire, preferably on a salient bend, they capture a footing on the defenders' bank, whence they strive to extend up and down stream till they have captured space enough on the defenders' bank to deploy solidly a broad line of battle. The role of attacker is then thrown upon the erstwhile defender, who makes desperate efforts to recover the lost ground, and to clear his bank of the stream before the menacing wedge of the enemy can penetrate further and extend his wings.

The battle of Lublin–Cholm is an exception to the usual type, because the mass of German troops led by Marshal von Mackensen are pressing downstream on either bank of the River Vieprz, and between the two great arteries the Vistula and the Bug. Mackensen is also trying to gain ground downhill, for his masses are emerging from the undulating country on the Galician border towards the great plain of Poland, in the centre of which stands Warsaw, with its satellite fortresses of Ivangorod and Novo Georgievek. The latest enemy report, it will be seen, claims that the Lublin–Cholm railway has been cut by the Germans.

The longer this struggle can be protracted the better is the Russian chance of saving Poland, for Mackensen's difficulties in the poor forest country into which he has penetrated with no fewer than a dozen army corps must be enormous. It has been a nice problem for the Russian Command so to distribute their troops that the line of defence north-east of Warsaw and thence up-stream to Ivangorod remains unbroken, while sufficient forces remain for the principal task of defeating Mackensen. In former campaigns, as late, indeed, as the Franco–German War of 1870, the situation would be very favourable to the army fighting within the circle of converging attack, for the reserves could have been massed for a decisive stroke at one hostile army before the other could intervene. The changed conditions of today, however, enable local defence to be protracted wherever adequate entrenchments are promptly constructed and so long as ammunition can be brought up in sufficient quantity to ward off decisive attacks.

The main conditions of the present struggle continue to be what they have already been described in these columns. Mackensen's attack on the vast circle of Russian armies in Poland is the most dangerous, but owing to the lack of convenient roads and railways connecting the fighting line with the supply base, its task is the most difficult. What appears evident from the Berlin communiqué is that Mackensen has now resumed the offensive, which was held up a few days ago. At the same time the secondary attacks by Marshal von Hindenburg's forces in the Naref Valley and by the Austrians operating on Mackensen's left are on a scale seriously to threaten the Russian host unless they are at any rate held in check.

Further afield the Austrian on the Dniester and the German armies on the Niemen also threaten the security of the Russian main army by intercepting railway communication. Of these the Germans, under General von Bulow, who are striking at the Warsaw–Vilna railway, threaten the most dangerous mischief.

The sanguinary deadlock cannot continue indefinitely, because the lines are not quite continuous, though the different attacking and defending armies are lightly linked with one another, so that prolonged lines of entrenchments with flanks secured, such as both adversaries have constructed in France, have not yet become a feature of the Eastern struggle. The next big development is, therefore, to be expected from the appearance on the scene of decisive conflict of a fresh mass of troops. The manipulation of such a reserve, called in technical language the mass of manœuvre, is usually the decisive factor in a great battle. At Waterloo it was the charge of the British cavalry after the repulse of the French Guards, at Gravelotte the encircling attacks of the Saxons at St Privet turned the scale, and at Mukden it was the adroit manœuvre of Nogi's Port Arthur army, which turned the scale. As time passes and the range of weapons increases so also do the scope and distance to be traversed by these outflanking or penetrating masses which turn the scale against armies already exhausted by a long struggle.

There is nothing yet reported which indicates whether Von Falkenhayn or the Grand Duke Nicholas can last the longest or throw the last army into this gigantic field of battle. It may be taken for granted that the Commanders-in-Chief of the other Allied Powers realise the extreme gravity of the present situation, and are doing all in their power to prevent the Germans from reinforcing their armies on the Russian frontier. Unfortunately, the degree of success which has attended the German schemes of separating the Russian Empire absolutely from contact with her Allies renders it very difficult for the British and French forces to join in the crisis of the struggle.

6 August 1915

WARSAW: RUSSIANS' POSITION
Fortress and Capital

When the German army of General von Gallwita forced the passage of the Naref at Peltosk, north of Warsaw, and the Russian counter-attack between that stream and the River Bug failed to fling the assailant back to the right bank, a critical state of things arose for the troops defending the capital of Poland.

The peril was enhanced by the menacing onward pressure of a vast group of armies deployed between the Vistula and the Bug across the valley of the Vieprz, and roughly parallel to the railway, through Lublin to Kieff. This group of armies, led by Marshal von Mackensen, linked on to another group which stood on guard at Sokal on the Bug, so that the German right flank might not be molested while the attacking army corps struggled and sapped their painful progress northwards, so as to threaten the line of retreat by which the Russians on the Vistula might retain the left bank of the Bug.

At the same time reinforced German and Austrian armies continued to ply their exhausted adversary at every point along the wide front on the Vistula and north of it, so that any subsidiary attack might become the decisive one, and the converging effect of the whole lot put the greatest imaginable strain upon the Russian forces, and never relaxed it for a day.

The climax of the situation arose when Marshal von Mackensen's right flank succeeded in overlapping the Russian left north of Cholm, while at the same time various German attacking columns gained important local advantages. Lublin was captured by the Austrians; the Lublin–Cholm railway was crossed in the valley of the Wrepens, and the German pressure on the line of Blonie, which has so long barred the road to Warsaw, began to prove successful. Two days ago the outworks of Ivangorod also fell, so that this important fortress lay at the mercy of a fresh assault, covered by the shattering fire of the German artillery.

As these columns have pointed out, the Russian decision not to stake all upon the defence of the Vistula line very seriously handicapped the defence, since material of all sorts required for the struggle had to be sent rearwards just when it was most required. The Vistula fortresses became mere pivots in the gigantic rearguard action which the Grand Duke has fought in order to cover the retreat to the River Bug. There can be no question but that his decision was correct. It would have been folly to imperil the whole army of Poland in an out-and-out defence of its capital, but the strategic situation thus brought about favoured the Germans.

The details are still lacking as to the latest scenes of the drama on the Vistula. There is every reason to hope that not only have the bulk of the Russian masses succeeded in falling back without losing their military entity, but that they have also succeeded in inflicting almost as much loss of men upon the Germans as they have suffered themselves. The most critical stage, however, of this huge operation is the retreat from the fortified lines across a country inadequately endowed with railways and roads to a fresh defensive system on the Bug. Every movement must be closely co-ordinated with the action of neighbouring units; every defensive ridge must be held just long enough and not too long. It is the problem we had to face after Mons on a greatly enhanced scale, and it would be fatuous to hope that the thing can be effected without some misfortunes and mistakes. Still, the previous record of this indomitable army and the proved skill of its leaders and staff justify the confident hope that the general execution of the retirement will be successful.

As to the more immediate consequences in the general situation in the Eastern theatre of war, it is premature to hazard opinions until we are better informed as to recent events, and as to the actual state of the contending hosts after the tremendous buffeting they have each sustained. But it may be predicted that nothing in the nature of a forward rush, such as the Germans executed at the beginning of the war in northern France, is possible for them in the East. Their progress must necessarily be slow, and their units, dislocated by heavy loss of life and wearied by the long strain, must need time to collect themselves before undertaking a renewed offensive on a grand scale. Moreover, the next Russian line will be stronger in that it will be straighter, It will not jut out like a bastion into a hostile zone of country inviting attacks to envelop both its flanks and dangerous even to its rearward communications. A prosecution of the German invasion eastward is not at present a promising enterprise, and a very considerable interval of time, not less than a month, must elapse before the German masses can be regrouped for another grand attack in a fresh direction.

It is clear from the course of events that even the Germans themselves did not know how completely heavy artillery can dominate fixed fortifications. There is no question now of leaving a garrison to defend some important political or strategical centre such as Warsaw, for as soon as the outstretching mass of fieldworks is turned or penetrated the girdle of forts become exposed to a concentrated hell of howitzer fire, by which they are quickly demolished. The type of warfare of which the long defence of Strasburg, Metz, and Paris was typical seems to have passed away. Plevna gave an inkling of the present-day type, and Manchuria enforced the lesson, but much of the fighting in the great American Civil War was of the same nature; notably the defence of Richmond by the Army of Northern Virginia against the encircling hosts of Ulysses Grant.

Even if Warsaw has fallen the loss of the place itself is not a great military disaster. In the present type of war one locality resembles another like Dr Johnson's green fields. So long as there remain convenient river valleys to occupy and entrench, and so long as these new river lines are properly fed by road and rail, the Russian armies can indefinitely renew their opposition to the invader. The Russian troops are like our own in their stubborn contempt for reverses of fortune and their refusal to admit defeat.

Although the latest reports do not preclude what in French military language is called a *retour offensif*, that is, a counter-stroke on such a scale as to change the course of events, yet the general tenor of the news shows that at present the Russian forces are not able to stop the flood of German invasion altogether, though they are checking it continually at every point and making it pay dearly for every mile of its advance on Russian soil.

The most important result which the Russians are gleaning from this harvest of death is the moral impression of their stubborn valour and unalterable resolution to fight to the end. Every fierce rearguard action, every post that is held on after the certainty of ultimate retirement is reached, costs the Russian army heavy loss in gallant lives, but with every such battle the spirit of the surviving Muscovite hosts rises and expands, so that the task of the ruthless invader becomes more difficult with every material success he wins. This is a very important military consideration. One of the shrewdest of the military spectators accredited to the Allied Army has stated that the Germans have undone themselves by their unsoldierlike conduct. Had their methods of waging war been as chivalrous as their conduct of it has been capable, they would not now be meeting the desperate resistance which characterises the defence of the Allies.

Nor must it be overlooked that every fresh offensive movement, however successful and however judiciously planned, entails great loss of German life, and that even the population of the Central Empires cannot indefinitely endure such a strain. In estimating the chances of success of the rival coalition, therefore, the moral factor is of immense importance. If the Germans fail to break the resolution of the Allies, they can hardly expect to conquer by destroying their material strength.

Before the outbreak of the war the pros and cons of encountering the shock of a German attack east of the Vistula were openly discussed in the military Press of the period, particularly in Germany, where keen interest was always manifested in the progress and development of Russian armaments from the line of the Vistula. There is one entirely new condition, however, to the existing crisis which was never popularly discussed. Before the inception of a new campaign on the Bug the opposing armies will have been engaged in the greatest European war in all history from the Baltic to the confines of Bessarabia. They are not the brand-new first-line troops which was assumed in all the technical forecasts would strive for the mastery on the banks of the Bug and Niemen. Which side has gained by the change in the problem thus introduced? Unquestionably the Russian.

During the last twelve months Russian armies have overrun great provinces of the Prussian kingdom. They have conquered Galicia, and their cavalry has raided the valley of the Oder and the great plain of Hungary. The vaunted hosts of Hindenburg and Mackensen have been held up and forced to retire by the solid Russian line of battle, and the armies of Austria were repeatedly defeated before the German General Staff took over their reconstruction. Special circumstances have doubtless given a temporary superiority to the Germanic forces, but every big encounter furnishes fresh convincing proof that the Russians as soldiers are competent to meet and defeat their formidable enemies.

Nor has the Russian military hierarchy any reason to feel ashamed. Before the war, no doubt, the Germans enjoyed a vast prestige in Russia, but the result of the prolonged anti-sanguinary struggle between the forces of the two empires has been to show that the Teuton is not invincible, and that the Slav possesses some military qualities which all armies must envy. The advance of the German army for fresh adventures after the exhausting struggle of the last ten weeks cannot lead to decisive events for a long while, during which many military events will occur, and the Russian armies will recuperate and refit.

2 September 1915

WAR IN RUSSIA: FIGHTING FOR TIME
Wings Engaged

In spite of the astonishing rapidity with which the German armies have pressed forward since their successful passage of the Vistula, the Russians have nevertheless managed to check the pursuit long enough to achieve a very important purpose. No decisive stroke against one of the three Russian military centres could now be executed before the beginning of the winter. It does not therefore follow that no such attempt will be made, for the German leaders know well that it is only the impossible, or what is deemed impossible, which wins the greatest results, but if, for example, the Germans attempt to attack Petrograd this autumn they cannot avoid committing their troops in a life and death struggle at a great distance from their base, in a sparsely inhabited country covered in forest, and traversed by a barrier of lakes, which narrows the front of attack, thus facilitating the task of defence. If this enterprise is also impeded by cold, heavy rain, impassable forest roads, and, finally, by snow storms and frost, its chances of success diminish to a remarkable degree, and its costliness in human life and war material is enormously increased, whether it succeeds or not.

Whichever of the three chief goals for an invading army the Germans eventually select – Kieff, Moscow, or Petrograd – their real target will always be the same, namely, the Russian field forces. When once the Russian armies have been sufficiently shattered to prevent their resuming offensive operations on a dangerous scale, for six months or more, the Germans can be trusted to direct their principal strokes against a more remunerative foe.

A German army which menaces the central point of Russian national life undoubtedly constitutes a danger to the State, which must be warded off as long as possible. The occupation by the enemy of Coorland, and possibly of Livonia, cannot be viewed with indifference, nor can the chief cities of old Russia be abandoned with as little loss of prestige and of national strength as was entailed by the retreat from Warsaw.

While, therefore, the Germans inflict real wounds by every considerable inroad they make good into Russian territory, and while they leave no stone unturned to derive military and political advantage by their progress, yet it is a shattering of the Russian legions by the shock of battle which they primarily seek, and which they still hope to achieve by threatening all that is most precious on Russian soil within the reach of their marching columns.

So far no such knock-out blow, no such battle without a morrow, has befallen the great Russian army as a whole, though the losses during the long retreat have torn great gaps in the compact array which overthrew the Austrians last autumn. So long as the core and framework of the Tsar's army remains intact, the losses can be replaced from the unlimited resources of Russian manhood. A greater difficulty is the need for war material, and for leaders of all ranks to replace the losses of the war.

In order to crush the life out of the Russian retreating host, the German strategy has continuously aimed at an encircling attack upon an important fraction of it. This envelopment was hoped for at Warsaw, at Siedlice, and again at Brest-Litovsk. The latest intelligence shows that both wings of the invaders are being thrown forward in energetic attack in the north, on the River Dwina, and far south in Galicia also. Though the rate of intercepting the Russians as heretofore is probably confided once again to the redoubtable Marshal Mackensen, whose central mass will be required to wheel northward when it has succeeded in overlapping the wing of the retreating army north of the Pinsk marshes, we may confidently hope that once again he will be baulked of the prize he covets, while every forced march he executes thins the ranks of regiments which have been fighting and marching hard and without respite since last May Day.

A talented German staff officer, Count Yorck von Wartenburg, who lost his life in the Boxer campaign of 1900, wrote an interesting study of the Emperor Napoleon I, in the shape of a criticism on his career as an army commander; it was called 'Napoleon als Feldheer'. The author was very scathing in his contemptuous reflections on the errors of the conqueror of Jena. In particular, he denounced the folly of sacrificing military to political considerations when once war has been let loose. When he discussed the great campaign of Russia, he sharply reproved the folly of carrying on doubtful expeditions at the opposite ends of Europe simultaneously with insufficient military resources. It will be an irony of fate if Von Falkenhayn is driven by the same stress of military and political necessities likewise to attempt the impossible and to fail. Count Yorck's book was written by a young man, it is marred by arrogance of tone, but it throws an interesting light upon the characteristic mentality of the German General Staff.

Chapter 4

Britain at War

12 August 1914

MOBILISATION OF THE TERRITORIALS
A Great Success

Last night the Press Bureau issued the following communication: 'The mobilisation of the Territorial Force is now on the point of completion. During the course of last winter Lieutenant-General E. C. Bethune, the Director-General, carried out a thorough inspection of the mobilisation arrangements in every division and mounted brigade, with the result that the machinery has now worked without the smallest hitch.'

That every detail has been considered is shown by the fact that practically no questions at all have had to be referred to the War Office, and a gratifying feature has been the entire absence of confusion or flurry at the headquarters of units.

Every single unit is believed to be now up to establishment. Since the first days of the present crisis recruits have come forward in daily increasing numbers; while the National Reserve, in particular, has stepped in and helped to fill up the gaps of peace time.

As is known, certain units of the Territorial Force have for some time accepted a liability to serve overseas if required, and further volunteers are now being asked to follow their example. A great response is anticipated, and it is probable that in many cases brigades, and even divisions as a whole, will come forward.

24 October 1914

CLEARING LONDON OF ALIEN ENEMIES
Continued Arrests

So closely have the police authorities in London and the provinces applied themselves to the carrying out of the Government order for the detention and internment of all male enemy aliens between the ages of seventeen and forty-five that some temporary slackening of their efforts was necessitated yesterday by reason of the fact that the accommodation provided for the detained people was taxed to its utmost limits.

The great clearing house at Olympia witnessed something like serious overcrowding because of the great addition made to the numbers housed there. Prisoners could not be sent out quickly enough, and consequently some of the more recently detained foreigners had to be kept in outlying police-stations and barracks. As soon as accommodation can be found in the concentration camps, the clearing house at Olympia will be relieved, and the police will be able to continue their work.

Only in special circumstances are naturalisation papers being issued to Germans or Austrians now, but even that qualification does not make the alien enemy immune from official inquiries. There are approximately 40,000 German or Austrian subjects in London, and, as these are registered, it is not a difficult task for the police to round any of them up when it is convenient to do so.

Among the crowd outside Olympia yesterday was a young Englishwoman, who waited to see her German sweetheart. She informed a neighbour that the wedding had been arranged for three weeks hence, and she was quite hopeful that everything would be all right, although she admitted there were difficulties.

There has been some reserve in official quarters regarding the order, but yesterday a Government official said to a Press representative: 'As a matter of fact, the order has been in force for many weeks, and not a day has passed without arrests being made of registered Germans and Austrians liable for military duty. On some days the number has been small; on others, such as this week, it has been large.' Asked why this week had witnessed such an outburst of police activity, he explained that it is because the authorities were not in a better position to enforce the order actively.

Had arrests been carried out on a large scale hitherto there would have been no place in which to accommodate all the prisoners. The War Office had now provided more detention camps.

'Even now,' he added, 'we have been asked to go slowly in London, because there will be pressure on the accommodation from all parts of the country. At the present moment lack of accommodation is still a hindrance. Many of those whom we have been obliged to arrest have married Englishwomen, and their entire interests are bound up in this country. They have been here for years, and are not likely to try to injure us; but for the safety of the nation it is impossible to discriminate.'

It is a singular and significant fact that all the German colonies established in and about London in the last decade or so are to be found in such places as Hampstead, where a well-known German colony has existed for years. Highgate also shelters many Germans. Then, on the south side of London, the neighbourhood of Sydenham and Gipsy-hill is one of the strongest of German strongholds. The number of Germans living there is probably thousands.

Not far away, at Forest-hill, there is another German centre, while German residents are to be largely found in some of the large boarding-houses and private hotels at Herne-hill, Champion-hill, and Denmark-hill.

During the past few days over 100 arrests of Germans living in and about the vicinity of the Crystal Palace have been quietly made by the police. Some of these aliens and potential enemies have been detained and sent to a concentration camp. The British residents of that highly important district, are even now, however, far from satisfied at the precautionary measures adopted by the police, and a strong agitation is still being conducted by a number of well-known English householders there.

Proceeding westward to Muswell-hill, Highgate, Parliament-hill, and Hampstead, one naturally looks – in view of discoveries elsewhere – for possible secret preparations, and for extra vigilance by the police with regard to enemy subjects in the districts.

Vigilance has not been lacking in any direction, but arrests have been few, the most serious being that of a man who was found to be armed with a revolver. With regard to preparations, such as bases for Zeppelins or concrete beds for big guns, there is a circumstance which renders such proceedings extremely difficult, if not impossible. These parts are almost entirely occupied by open spaces belonging to the people.

That being so, the land has not been on the market, and could not be purchased by an enemy for the purpose of secret preparations. There is literally a belt of parks. There has been no lack of diligent search, and British residents have not failed to give information as to foreigners residing near them.

In several cases it has been found that the subject of the report was a Belgian refugee, and in one case there was a more amusing side. This was that of a man who was seen to leave home in the small hours and had been heard speaking 'in a foreign tongue'. He was 'rounded up', and was found to have recently arrived from a rural part of Wales, and was employed at a dairy on the breakfast round. He spoke his native language – Welsh.

Mill-hill, which is still separated by open fields from the great neighbouring wilderness of bricks and mortar, retains, in spite of its modern villas, much of the character of a country village. It has but few alien inhabitants, and, apart from the weird story to which reference has been made, it has remained practically undisturbed during the present spy hunt.

6 November 1914

MEN WANTED FOR OUR NEW ARMY
Nation's Urgent Need

As was indicated in the *Daily Telegraph* yesterday, the response which the young men of the country are making to the call to arms is not commensurate with the urgent requirements of the authorities.

This week a subtle and powerful enemy has come to our very shores; yet men are hanging back. Bravery and enthusiasm are not lacking, but, in spite of all efforts of the authorities to disclaim it, a feeling has spread that men were enlisting as rapidly as they were required. Without any qualification this is an entirely erroneous impression.

There is a growing feeling that unless men came forward other measures may have to be taken. These, it is believed, would include a household census, showing the age, height, &c. of every male person, in order that it may be known what material there is to fall back upon should the voluntary system fail.

London has done well, but everywhere are to be seen strolling in the streets and open spaces youths well fitted to undergo the training to arms. There were over twenty strapping young fellows lolling on the railings at St James's Park yesterday afternoon watching the lazy pelicans. The recruiting tents close at hand failed to interest them. On 7 September there were 5,000 recruits. Now a fifth of that number is a good day.

'We want,' stated a leading article in the *Daily Telegraph* two months ago, 'the old soldiers, the ex-non-commissioned officers, the commissioned officers now in retirement, to help in the work of training the bodies of recruits ... The work of enlistment and training must go on together.' There was a good response, but more men are wanted.

On 4 September Mr Asquith, speaking at Guildhall, said: 'Mobilisation was ordered on 4 August. Immediately afterwards Lord Kitchener issued his call for 100,000 recruits for the Regular Army, which has been followed by a second call for another 100,000. The response up to today gives us between 250,000 and 500,000. I am glad to say that London has done its share. The total number of Londoners accepted is not less than 42,000 ... We want more men, men of the best fighting quality.'

Old public school and university men, sportsmen, professional men of all sorts, and numbers of artisans responded, but the proportion of the last-named has never been comparable, it is stated, with their percentage of the population. Need for patriotism was never greater than today. The way to show it is by attending at the recruiting offices, lists of which are freely advertised on hoardings and public buildings throughout the country.

There should be no difficulty in supplying the men for whom Lord Kitchener has appealed since the requests referred to by Mr Asquith. We are better able to do so than Germany or France. There is no lack of material. This country contains a larger proportion of young adults than Germany or France. The age distribution of England and Wales and Scotland shows that. Ireland is not quite so much favoured.

Take only the unmarried men between the ages of eighteen and thirty-five in England and Wales, and we find there are over 3,000,000. The figures are:

Age	Age
18–322,721	27–141,143
19–313,992	28–123,545
20–301,181	29–104,342
21–284,322	30–95,846
22–262,209	31–78,027
23–237,988	32–74,414
24–211,637	33–64,981
25–186,031	34–60,172
26–161,144	35–56,464

Large numbers of married men are fighting for King and country, for hearth and home, for humanity and peace, and not one-fourth of the single men have answered the call. They are leaving their protection to those who have wives and families.

In the northern counties it is hoped to have a revival of recruiting. In Cumberland, Durham, Lancashire, Westmorland, Northumberland, and Yorkshire there is a very large percentage of single men. In Yorkshire, including the males of all ages, the proportion is: married, 742,427; unmarried, 1,129,909.

The arresting of the advance of the enemy in France and Belgium has had the effect of stemming enlistment. It has created a feeling of more security, the fact being quite ignored that the fighting will be more difficult and the need for men greater as the Germans are pushed back to the places they have so strongly fortified. This applies especially to strongholds on German territory. With more men they can be hurled back and victory assured. Without more men the task appears to be almost superhuman.

TERRITORIAL FORCES
Successful Recruiting in the London District

As distinct from recruiting for the Regular Army, the enrolment of men for the Territorial Forces, as far, at any rate, as London is concerned, proceeds satisfactorily. The whole of the units administered by the City of London Territorial Force Association have recruited both a 1st and a 2nd Battalion to full strength, and, with the exception of three 2nd Battalion units, the same is the case with the County of London Territorial Force Association. When, therefore, the question is asked as to 'What steps are the Territorial Associations taking to raise fresh men for the front?' the reply can be the very encouraging one that all the units have been recruited up to their full strength, except in three instances, and in these there will be no difficulty.

Within a very few days of the outbreak of war the few men required to bring the Imperial Service battalions of the City Territorial units up to their full strength were secured, and directly the Headquarters Committee was ordered to form reserve battalions it proceeded to recruit steadily. The committee aimed at securing a steady stream of recruits, and not a rush, as the latter simply meant the crowding of the drill halls with men and the upsetting of the whole machinery of enlistment. The result of this policy was that at the specified period the whole of the men wanted had been obtained, both mounted and foot. It is true that a few score are wanted to complete the 4th Battalion of the Royal Fusiliers, but this is only a small detail.

The aggregate number of these reserve units is about 11,000 men, and they are complete in both officers and men. Furthermore, every man has been given his uniform, and is now awaiting the issue of arms. The association has also succeeded in scouring for their force a nucleus of horses for all the mounted units. It is encouraging to note that all the mounted sections have long waiting lists, and the same remark applies to a number of the infantry battalions, so that should an order go out at any time for the formation of third battalions to the City units, the work of recruiting would be greatly assisted by the fact that in a number of instances hundreds of men had already got their names down for enlistment. The association is 'waiting the word' to proceed with the formation of these third battalions.

Arrangements have been made for the various battalions to occupy winter quarters in the vicinity of suitable training grounds, so that the men will be able to be quickly trained in conditions similar to those they will have to face at the front. It is recognised that it is of the utmost importance that the drilling of the men should be facilitated in every possible way, and most encouraging reports have come to hand from the various training centres of the excellent progress already made. In a number of instances large houses surrounded by parks have been secured. It is expected that at the end of this week all the City reserve units will be in the occupation of their winter quarters.

For the benefit of the uninitiated, it may be stated that the purpose of the reserve units is to take the place of the Imperial Service units when they are moved abroad or elsewhere, and to supply drafts to replace casualties. The Territorial Force carries on its recruiting independently, of course, of the War Office recruiting for the Regular Army.

Practically all that has been already said in connection with the City Force applies to the County of London units. The establishment of these is over 27,000. A very large number joined within the first week of the commencement of the war, and both the 1st and 2nd Battalions throughout the force have been brought up to their aggregate strength, except the three given below:

10th (County of London) Battalion, London Regiment, 49, Grove-road, Hackney.

23rd (County of London) Battalion, 27, St John's-hill, Clapham Junction.

24th (County of London) Battalion (The Queen's), 71, New-street, Kennington.

The first-named of these is in training at Hackney, and the other two at the White City. Men are wanted to make up the full complement, and applicants should call at once at the headquarters in each instance.

A number of the battalions have gone abroad and to the front, and behind each of these reserve units have been formed. A number of these have waiting lists. Nine battalions are in training at the White City. Recruiting to get the reserve battalions up to full strength was not pushed, as it was not desired to compete with Earl Kitchener's Army. It has been thought desirable that in addition to the 1st and Reserve Battalions, 25 per cent should be raised in order to make good any wastage from the war. This in many cases has been a very easy matter, owing to the waiting lists, which were, and will be, drawn upon. In the case of the Queen's Westminster Rifles, whose 1st Battalion is at the front, the four companies wanted – roughly speaking, 500 men – will probably all have been secured by tomorrow. When it was proposed to form the 2nd Battalion over 6,000 men applied.

It is very gratifying to note that nearly all the men in these reserve battalions have taken the Imperial service obligation, and are prepared to go to the front. This means that in every double unit in the County of London Territorial Force there are nearly 2,000 men ready to go abroad.

Whereas the County of London Association provides normally 16,000 infantry, there are now 32,000, in addition to the cavalry, artillery, engineers, and other sections, who have also joined 'for the front'. All the battalions are in training, and, as in the case of the City units, very rapid progress is being made in getting the men into shape.

For a 3rd Battalion of the London Scottish which it is hoped may be formed already 335 men have offered themselves.

23 November 1914

ENEMY ALIENS' RIOT

Fatal Affray at Douglas, *Douglas, Isle of Man, Saturday*

There was a tragic occurrence at the aliens' detention camp at Douglas, on Thursday. The camp was established about three months ago, and was gradually increased until nearly 4,000 Austrian and German civilian prisoners were interned, guarded by about 300 men of the National Reserve and Manx Territorials. Colonel H. W. Madoc was in chief command.

The prisoners were confined in two separate camps connected by a subterranean passage under the high road, but they dined together in a large hall, with spacious galleries. For some weeks the greatest quietude prevailed. The captain chosen by the aliens themselves exercised disciplinary powers, and a corporal was appointed for each tent, with a view of promoting good order and cleanliness. The prisoners belonged to various social grades, but the majority were of the working-classes – waiters, sailors, stewards, and mechanics.

Since the arrival of the latest batches of prisoners disaffection and insubordination began to make their appearance. Occasionally complaints were made by sentries that they were being insulted by prisoners. The first overt incident was the refusal of a large body of prisoners to leave the hall on a wet, stormy night about a fortnight ago. They were allowed to remain withindoors instead of being sent to their tents, and directly afterwards a commencement was made with the building of huts to provide more comfortable accommodation.

The next ebullition of disorder occurred on Wednesday last, at dinner, when a number of men, in a contemptuous and violent manner, expressed their discontent with the food supplied to them. The authorities of the camp maintain that the rations were sufficient in quantity and good in quality.

On Thursday afternoon, at two o'clock, a disturbance occurred, which resulted in the death of five prisoners and the wounding of fifteen others, who are now lying in a more or less serious condition at Noble's (Isle of Man) Hospital.

The dead men are:

Richard Fohs, formerly waiter at the Grand Hotel, Brighton.
Richard Matthias, from Blumenthal, Hanover, sailor on a German ship sunk in the North Sea.
Bernhard Warning, engineer, lately employed on the London Dock extension.
Christian Brochl, waiter, London.
Ludwig Bauer, of Wurtemburg.

Two of the men were killed outright by bullet wounds, and two died shortly afterwards. Fohs seems to have fallen or been pushed through the gallery windows falling on the floor and fracturing his skull.

At the inquest, which was opened yesterday, evidence of identification only was given, and the inquiry was adjourned for a week.

What transpired is only gleaned from unofficial sources. It appears that, after dinner violent scenes occurred. Plates, knives, and forks were thrown about, and chairs smashed. A party of prisoners then made a determined dash from the dining hall towards the kitchens. The passage was barred by a few soldiers, who at first threatened the men with the bayonet, and then fired in the air.

This did not deter the more determined aliens, who stealthily approached the guards, whereupon the latter began shooting in earnest. A fearful scene ensued amongst the terrified prisoners, most of whom held up their hands in token of submission, or sought to escape from the pavilion.

The tragic affair has caused profound dismay in the island.

5 December 1914

FOOTBALL AND THE WAR
League Clubs and Cup Ties

A correspondent writes: The decision to abandon international Association football matches will not make a vast difference to the game. It will not affect the clubs to an appreciable extent; it will entail little hardship upon the players; and so far as the majority of the spectators are concerned the loss of inter-country fixtures will not be felt. It is a decision, however, that is important and significant. It means that those officially responsible for the conduct and government of the game recognise that there is a genuine and deep-rooted objection to the playing of football so long as the nations are at war and so long as the need for recruits remains.

On Monday next the English Football Association will decide whether they shall carry on their Cup competition. The clubs connected with one or other of the various Leagues are, it is said, opposed to this tournament being abandoned, and it is unlikely that a decision will be come to readily. This is a circumstance which, to those who are out of touch with modern football, may seem strange and illogical, for we have it as the considered judgment of the authorities that the international programme, for which, like the Cup ties, they are directly and wholly responsible, had better be dropped.

The fact is the Football Association are in a most difficult and unthankful position. For their own part they would, I am sure, drop the Cup ties as they have dropped the international fixtures; they could well afford to lose some thousands of pounds by so doing. It may be that they will result to put their Cup up for competition. If they so decide they will offend the League clubs, who are in sore need of money to carry on to the end of the season, and it may be that there will be a serious quarrel, which might result in the League clubs setting up house on their own account. At all events, they are prepared to arrange and run a Cup competition of their own.

It has already been explained in the *Daily Telegraph* that the Football Association, were they so disposed, have not complete control of the League clubs, whose matches very largely make up the game. For practical purposes the League clubs are their own masters; they represent a tremendously strong body, and it will be interesting to see whether the Football Association, knowing and realising this as they must do, will hold up the Cup competition which, in conjunction with the League tournament, has for many years been the life and soul of the game, and helped to make it the great business that it is.

PATRIOTIC RUGBY PLAYERS

At the annual meeting of the London Society of Rugby Football Union Referees, last night, an interesting statement in regard to the response which Rugbeians have made to the country's call was delivered by the chairman (Mr G. H. Harnett). No organisation had, he said, given so many of its members to the Colours as the Rugby Union had. He had ascertained that 98 per cent of the men who played for the Wasps last year had joined. Three other clubs, including the Saracens, had contributed about 90 per cent of their members, while the whole of the first and second fifteen players of some of the big clubs had enlisted. 'I think our organisation shows a splendid example to every other sporting organisation in the world,' said the chairman.

Mr H. A. Taylor said that the Ealing Club last year had ninety players. With the exception of two, the whole of those players were now with the Colours. (Cheers.)

9 December 1914

THE NEW ARMY IN TRAINING
Territorials in a Park

By Rudyard Kipling

One had known the place for years as a picturesque old house, standing in a peaceful park; had watched the growth of certain young oaks along a new-laid avenue, and applauded the owner's enterprise in turning a stretch of pasture to plough. There are scores of such estates in England which the motorist, through passing so often, comes to look upon almost as his own. In a single day the brackened turf between the oaks and the iron road-fence blossomed into tents, and the drives were all cut up with hoofs and wheels. A little later, one's car sweeping home of warm September nights was stopped by sentries, who asked her name and business; for the owner of that retired house and discreetly wooded park had gone elsewhere in haste, and his estate was taken over by the military.

Later still; one met men and horses arguing with each other for miles about that country-side; or the car would be flung on her brakes by artillery issuing from cross-lanes – clean batteries jingling off to their work on the downs, and hungry ones coming back to meals. Every day brought the men and the horses and the weights behind them to a better understanding, till in a little while the car could pass a quarter of a mile of them without having to hoot more than once.

'Why are you so virtuous?' she asked of a section encountered at a blind and brambly corner. 'Why do you obtrude your personality less than an average tax-cart?'

'Because,' said a driver, his arm flung up to keep the untrimmed hedge from sweeping his cap off, 'because those are our blessed orders. We don't do it for love.'

No one accuses the gunner of maudlin affection for anything except his beasts and his weapons. He hasn't the time. He serves at least three jealous gods – his horse and all its saddlery and harness; his gun, whose least detail of efficiency is more important than men's lives; and when these have been attended to, the never-ending mystery of his art commands him.

It was a wettish, windy day when I visited the so long-known house and park. Cock pheasants ducked in and out of trim rhododendron clumps, neat gates opened into sacredly preserved vegetable gardens, the many-coloured leaves of specimen trees pasted themselves stickily against sodden tent-walls, and there was a mixture of circus smells from the horse-lines and the faint, civilised breath of chrysanthemums in the potting sheds. The main drive was being relaid with a foot of flint; the other approaches were churned and pitted under the gun wheels and heavy supply wagons. Great breadths of what had been well-kept turf between unbrowsed trees were blanks of slippery brown wetness, dotted with picketed horses and field-kitchens. It was a crazy mixture of stark necessity and manicured luxury, all cheek by jowl, in the undiscriminating rain.

The cook houses, store rooms, forges, and workshops were collections of tilts, poles, rick-cloths, and odd lumber, beavered together as on service. The officers' mess was a thin, soaked marquee.

Less than a hundred yards away were dozens of vacant, well-furnished rooms in the big brick house, of which the Staff furtively occupied one corner. There was accommodation for very many men in its stables and out-houses alone, or the whole building might have been gutted and rearranged for barracks twice over in the last three months.

Scattered among the tents were rows of half-built tin sheds, the ready-prepared lumber and the corrugated iron lying beside them, ready to be pieced together like children's toys. But there were no workmen. I was told that they came that morning, but had knocked off because it was wet.

'I see. And where are the batteries?' I demanded.

'Out at work, of course. They've been out since seven.'

'How shocking! In this dreadful weather, too!'

'They took some bread and cheese with them. They'll be back about dinner-time if you care to wait. Here's one of our field-kitchens.'

Batteries look after their own stomachs, and are not catered for by contractors. The cook house was a wagon-tilt. The wood, being damp, smoked a good deal. One thought of the wide, adequate kitchen ranges and the concrete passages of the service quarters in the big house just behind. One even dared to think Teutonically of the perfectly good panelling and the thick hard-wood floors that could—

'Service conditions, you see,' said my guide, as the cook inspected the baked meats and the men inside the wagon-tilt grated the carrots and prepared the onions. It was old work to them after all these months – done swiftly, with the clean economy of effort that camp life teaches.

'What are these lads when they're at home?' I inquired.

'Londoners chiefly – all sorts and conditions.'

The cook in shirt sleeves made another investigation, and sniffed judiciously. He might have been cooking since the Peninsular. He looked at his watch and across towards the park gates. He was responsible for one hundred and sixty rations, and a battery has the habit of saying quite all that it thinks of its food.

'How often do the batteries go out?' I continued.

''Bout five days a week. You see, we're being worked up a little.'

'And have they got plenty of ground to work over?'

'Oh – yes-s.'

'What's the difficulty this time? Birds?'

'No; but we got orders the other day not to go over a golf-course. That rather knocks the bottom out of tactical schemes.'

Perfect shamelessness, like perfect virtue, is impregnable; and, after all, the lightnings of this war, which have brought out so much resolve and self-sacrifice, must show up equally certain souls and institutions that are irredeemable.

The weather took off a little before noon. The carpenters could have put in a good half-day's work on the sheds, and even if they had been rained upon they had roofs with fires awaiting their return. The batteries had none of these things.

They came in at last far down the park, heralded by that unmistakable half-grumble, half-grunt of guns on the move. The picketed horses heard it first, and one of them neighed long and loud, which proved that he had abandoned civilian habits. Horses in stables and mews seldom do more than snicker, even when they are halves of separated pairs. But these gentlemen had a corporate life of their own now, and knew what 'pulling together' means.

When a battery comes into camp it 'parks' all six guns at the appointed place, side by side in one mathematically straight line, and the accuracy of the alignment is, like ceremonial drill with the Foot, a fair test of its attainments. The ground was no treat for parking. Specimen trees and draining ditches had to be avoided and circumvented. The gunners, their reins, the guns, the ground, were equally wet, and the slob dropped away like gruel from the brake shoes. And they were Londoners – clerks, mechanics, shop assistants, and delivery men – anything and everything that you please. But they were all home and at home in their saddles and seats. They said nothing; their officers said little enough to them. They came in across what had once been turf; wheeled with tight traces; halted; unhooked, the wise teams stumped off to their pickets, and behold, the six guns were left precisely where they should have been left to the fraction of an inch. You could see the wind blowing the last few drops of wet from each leather muzzle-cover at exactly the same angle. It was all old known evolutions, taken unconsciously in the course of the day's work by men well abreast of it.

'Our men have one advantage,' said a voice. 'As Territorials they were introduced to unmade horses once a year at training, so they've never been accustomed to made horses.'

'And what do the horses say about it all?' I asked, remembering what I had seen on the road in the early days.

'They said a good deal at first, but our chaps could make allowances for 'em. They know now.'

Allah never intended the gunner to talk. His own arm does that for him. The batteries off-saddled in silence, though one noticed on all sides little quiet caresses between man and beast – affectionate nuzzlings and nose-slappings. Surely the gunner's relation to his horse is more intimate even than the cavalryman's; for a lost horse only turns cavalry into infantry, but trouble in a gun-team may mean death all round. And this is a gunner's war. The young wet officers said so joyously as they passed to and fro picking up scandal about breast-straps and breechings, examining the collars of ammunition wagon teams, and listening to remarks on shoes. Local blacksmiths, assisted by the battery itself, do the shoeing. There are master smiths and important farriers, who have cheerfully thrown up good wages to help the game, and their horses reward them by keeping fit. A fair proportion of the horses are aged – there was never a gunner yet satisfied with his team or its rations till he had left the battery – but they do their work as steadfastly and wholeheartedly as the men. I am persuaded the horses like being in society and working out their daily problems of draught and direction. The English, and Londoners particularly, are the kindest and most reasonable of folk with animals. If it were not our business strictly to underrate ourselves for the next few years, one would say that the Territorial batteries had already done wonders. But perhaps it is better to let it all go with the grudging admission wrung out of a wringing wet bombardier, 'Well, it isn't so dam' bad – considerin'.'

I left them taking their dinner in mess tins to their tents, with a strenuous afternoon's cleaning-up ahead of them. The big park held some thousands of men. I had seen no more than a few hundreds, and missed the howitzers after all.

A cock pheasant chaperoned me down the drive, complaining loudly that where he was used to walk with his ladies under the beech trees, softie unsporting people had built a miniature landscape with tiny villages, churches, and factories, and came there daily to point cannon at it.

'Keep away from that place,' said I, 'or you'll find yourself in a field-kitchen.'

'Not me!' he crowed. 'I'm as sacred as golf-courses.'

There was a little town a couple of miles down the road where one used to lunch in the old days and have the hotel to oneself. Now there are six ever changing officers in billet there, and the astonished houses quiver all day to traction engines and high-piled lorries. A unit of the Army Service Corps and some mechanical transport lived near the station, and fed the troops for 20 miles around.

'Are your people easy to find?' I asked of a wandering private, with the hands of a sweep, the head of a Christian among lions, and suicide in his eye.

'Well, the ASC are in the Territorial Drill Hall for one thing; and for another you're likely to hear us. There's some motors come in from Bulford.' He snorted and passed on, smelling of petrol.

The drill-shed was peace and comfort. The ASC were getting ready there for pay-day and for a concert that evening. Outside in the wind and the occasional rain-spurts, life was different. The Bulford motors and some other crocks sat on a side road between what had been the local garage and a newly erected workshop of creaking scaffold-poles and bellying slatting rick-cloths, where a forge glowed and general repairs were being effected. Beneath the motors men lay on their backs and called their friends to pass them spanners, or, for pity's sake, to shove another sack under their mud-wreathed heads.

A corporal, who had been nine years a fitter and seven in a city garage, briefly and briskly outlined the more virulent diseases that develop in Government rolling-stock. (I heard quite a lot about Bulford.) Hollow voices from beneath eviscerated gear-boxes confirmed him. We withdrew to the shelter of the rick-cloth workshop – the corporal; the sergeant who had been a carpenter, with a business of his own, and, incidentally, had served through the Boer War; another sergeant who was a member of the Master Builders' Association; and a private who had also been fitter, chauffeur, and a few other things. The third sergeant who kept a poultry farm in Surrey, had some duty elsewhere.

A man at a carpenter's bench was finishing a spoke for a newly painted cart. He squinted along it.

'That's funny,' said the master builder. 'Of course in his own business he'd chuck his job sooner than do woodwork. But it's all funny.'

'What I grudge,' a sergeant struck in, 'is havin' to put mechanics to loading and unloading beef. That's where modified conscription for the beauties that won't roll up'd be useful to us. We want hewers of wood, we do. And I'd hew 'em!'

'I want that file.' This was a private in a hurry, come from beneath an unspeakable Bulford. Someone asked him musically if he 'would tell his wife in the morning who he was with tonight'.

'You'll find it in the tool-chest,' said the sergeant. It was his own sacred tool-chest which he had contributed to the common stock.

'And what sort of men have you got in this unit?' I asked.

'Every sort you can think of. There isn't a thing you couldn't have made here if you wanted to. But' – the corporal, who had been a fitter, spoke with fervour – 'you can't expect us to make big-ends, can you? That five-ton Bulford lorry out there in the wet—'

'And she isn't the worst,' said the master builder. 'But it's all part of the game. And so funny when you come to think of it. Me painting carts, and certificated plumbers loading frozen beef!'

'What about the discipline?' I asked.

The corporal turned a fitter's eye on me. 'The mechanism is the discipline,' said he, with most profound truth. 'Jockeyin' a sick car on the road is discipline, too. What about the discipline?' He turned to the sergeant with the carpenter's chest. There was one sergeant of Regulars, with twenty years' service behind him and a knowledge of human nature. He struck in.

'You ought to know. You've just been made corporal,' said that sergeant of Regulars.

'Well, there's so much which everybody knows has got to be done that – that – why, we all turn in and do it,' quoth the corporal. 'I don't have any trouble with my lot.'

'Yes; that's how the case stands,' said the sergeant of Regulars. 'Come and see our stores.'

They were beautifully arranged in a shed which felt like a monastery after the windy, clashing world without; and the young private who acted as checker – he came from some railway office – had the thin, keen face of the cleric.

'We're in billets in the town,' said the sergeant who had been a carpenter. 'But I'm a married man. I shouldn't care to have men billeted on us at home, an' I don't want to inconvenience other people. So I've knocked up a bunk for myself on the premises. It's handier to the stores, too.'

We entered what had been the local garage. The mechanical transport were in full possession, tinkering the gizzards of more cars. We discussed chewed-up gears (samples to hand), and the civil population's old-time views of the military. The corporal told a tale of a clergyman in a Midland town who, only a year ago, on the occasion of some manœuvres, preached a sermon warning his flock to guard their womenfolk against the soldiers.

'And when you think – when you know,' said the corporal, 'what life in those little towns really is!' He whistled.

'See that old landaulette,' said he, opening the door of an ancient wreck jammed against a wall. 'That's two of our chaps' dressing-room. They don't care to be billeted, so they sleep 'tween the landau and the wall. It is handier for their work, too. Work comes in at all hours. I wish I was cavalry. There's some use in cursing a horse.'

Truly it's an awful thing: to belong to a service where speech brings no alleviation.

'You!' A private with callipers turned from the bench by the window.

'You'd die outside of a garage. But what you said about civilians and soldiers is all out of date now.'

The sergeant of Regulars permitted himself a small hidden smile. The private with the callipers had been some twelve weeks a soldier.

'I don't say it isn't,' said the corporal. 'I'm saying what it used to be.'

'We-ell,' the private screwed up the callipers, 'didn't you feel a little bit that way yourself – when you were a civilian?'

'I – I don't think I did.' The corporal was taken aback. 'I don't think I ever thought about it.'

'Ah! There you are!' said the private, very drily.

Someone laughed in the shadow of the landaulette dressing-room. 'Anyhow, we're all in it now, Private Percy,' said a voice.

There must be a good many thousand conversations of this kind being held all over England nowadays. Our breed does not warble much about patriotism or Fatherland, but it has a wonderful sense of justice, even when its own shortcomings are concerned.

We went over to the drill-shed to see the men paid.

The first man I ran across there was a sergeant who had served in the Mounted Infantry in the South African picnic that we used to call a war. He had been a private chauffeur for some years – long enough to catch the professional look, but was joyously reverting to service type again.

The men lined up, were called out, saluted emphatically at the pay table, and fell back with their emoluments. They smiled at each other.

'An' it's all so funny,' murmured the master builder in my ear. 'About a quarter – no, less than a quarter – of what one'd be making on one's own!'

'Fifty bob a week, cottage, and all found, I was. An' only two cars to look after,' said a voice behind. 'An' if I'd been asked – simply asked – to lie down in the mud all the afternoon!'

The speaker looked at his wages with awe. Someone wanted to know, sotto voce, if 'that was union rates', and the grin spread among the uniformed experts. The joke, you will observe, lay in situations thrown up, businesses abandoned, and pleasant prospects cut short at the nod of duty.

'Thank heaven!' said one of them at last, 'it's too dark to work on those blessed Bulfords any more today. We'll get ready for the concert.'

But it was not too dark, half an hour later, for my car to meet a big lorry storming back in the wind and the wet from the northern camp. She gave me London allowance – half one inch between hub and hub – swung her corner like a Brooklands professional, changed gear for the uphill with a sweet click, and charged away. For aught I knew, she was driven by an ex-'fifty-bob-a-week-a-cottage-and-all-found'-er, who next month might be dodging shells with her and thinking it 'all so funny'.

Horse, foot, even the guns may sometimes get a little rest, but so long as men eat thrice a day there is no rest for the Army Service Corps. They carry the campaign on their all-sustaining backs.

15 January 1915

GREAT WAR RALLY
Mr H. Bottomley at the Albert Hall

In an individual effort to enlighten and stimulate the public on the subject of the war an active and continuous part has been played by Mr Horatio Bottomley, editor of *John Bull*. Last night he was the principal speaker at a great Albert Hall meeting organised by Mr H. J. Houston, secretary of the Business Government League, of which Mr Bottomley is president. The Rev. A. J. Waldron occupied the chair.

The meeting, besides being of such enormous proportions that every inch of accommodation was occupied, while many thousands of people were unable to gain admission, had remarkable and unusually picturesque features. The platform was 'patriotic' in the most complete sense. Occupying its wide space, with the brilliant uniform of the bandsmen of the Irish Guards in their midst, was a great body of soldiers representing the Legion of Frontiersmen, the RAMC, the Civilian Force Ambulance, and about 100 men of the newly formed Sportsman's and Footballers' Battalions. There were besides sailors, special constables, Chelsea pensioners, and Boy Scouts – a very considerable and representative gathering, in fact, of the military, naval, and civilian forces of the Crown.

Prior to the meeting commencing, the gathering audience were entertained with patriotic selections by the band, and songs by Mr Charles Coburn. They also had the pleasure of hearing Miss Constance Collier recite 'Why is the red blood flowing?', a poem written by Mr Horatio Bottomley and 'Kitchener's Army'.

Amongst those present were: Mr Alfred Butt, Mr C. B. Cochran, Mr Eric O. Ohlson (Sheriff of Hull), Mr Holbrook Jackson, Mr C. Arthur Pearson, Mr G. H. Ross Clyne (Manchester), Mr Ben Tillett, Colonel R. W. L. Dunlop, Sir Henry Dalziel, MP, Mr J. S. Wood, Madame Le Roy, Mr H. A. Ashton (of the Voluntary Recruiting League), Mrs Cunliffe Owen, Mons. E. Pollett, Mr Victor Grayson, Mr A. Birch Crisp, Lieutenant-Colonel McDonnell, Mr W. Howard Gritten, Mr Henry T. Burton, Rev. Cecil Legard, the Hon. Quetta Maude, the Rev. G. Isaacs, Mr A. G. Hales, Sir Robert and Lady Fulton, Captain W. J. Clarke (Civilian Force), Captain Wells Holland (Footballers' Battalion), Colonel Grantham (17th Middlesex Regiment), Mr E. A. Goulding, MP, Mr Frank Allen, Lady Coleridge, and Captain Percy W. Harris (Chief Recruiting Officer, Eastern Command, Hounslow).

The Chairman said there might have been wars to the initiation of which they had been opposed, but every Britisher worthy of the name believed that we had entered upon the present war with clean hands and pure consciences. (Cheers.) It was not a war in the ordinary sense, but a holy crusade against the devilries of militarism that had been the canker of Germany for forty years. We were going through with it right to the end, whatever the sacrifice called for. (Cheers.) But we scarcely yet realised its meaning. The aristocracy had done splendidly. (Cheers.) He wished the middle classes and the lower middle classes would do as well. And no better example had been shown than that his Majesty the King had shown. (Cheers.)

Mr Bottomley, having acknowledged the enormous attendance as a great personal compliment, said: I begin to wonder whether the nation has not been asleep for the last six years. I marvel how it comes about that with all the evidence of mischief and menace we then had before us, and which, as I then said, constituted a peremptory declaration of war against the peace of the world, we have waited for the convenience of our enemy. We have waited while she has equipped and completed the navy, into the possession of which she ought never to have been permitted to enter, and equipped a colossal army of such a character that there was no legitimate justification for it; until she deepened and widened that sinister waterway which today affords such welcome refuge to her much-vaunted fleet; has exploited and explored the innermost secrets of our defences, appropriated our best forces, misappropriated many of our best inventions, and filled her arsenals with material of war, with the result that, although the end must be the same, we have to fight our way to victory through seas of blood and tears, which might have been averted if we had not closed our eyes to the signs and portents that were written on the sky for everyone to read. (Hear, hear.)

But I am not here to blame anybody. This is not the time for internal dissension or domestic discord; and the man who by word or deed, tongue or pen does aught to stir it up ought to be carted off without trial as a traitor to the Tower, or better still, put in front of the firing line to have a practical demonstration of the humanity and culture of his German friends. (Laughter and cheers.) Until the last shot has been fired I appeal to you to stand shoulder to shoulder as part of a great and mighty Empire, united and indivisible.

Mr Bottomley continued that he supposed no one had been the recipient of more information and complaints on those subjects than himself, and he wished to assure those soldiers and sailors and their wives and families and dependants who had confided to him their troubles at least of this, that when the time came he would not hesitate to enlighten the nation upon many matters which it ought to know, and he would not hesitate, regardless of the persons or of the powers that be, to insist upon the trial by court-martial of every man who had taken advantage of his country's hour of trouble to line his filthy pockets with gold at the expense of the State. (Cheers.)

The other assurance he wished to give was that in the meantime every resource which he could control was being placed at the disposal of those who were doing our country's work, for the purpose of investigating alleged grievances and bringing them to notice of the Government and the various authorities, with a view to getting them recognised and, to some extent, remedied. They did not want to talk in detail of these things today, but when the war was over they were going to have a searching audit, and if he lived, whether he sat in the House of Commons or not, he intended to be one of the auditors. (Cheers.)

In any case, proceeded Mr Bottomley, vast changes are occurring around us, There is a new spirit abroad in the social, the political, the religious life of the nation. Things are happening under our eyes every day of so far-reaching a character that we scarcely realise that they are occurring.

In a thousand ways there is a quiet change taking place in the habits of the people which lead the student sometimes to reflect how much better, perhaps, the World might have been if it had taken place a little earlier in the days of peace, and not been left to the last moment under the stress of a great war. (Cheers.)

How far those changes may affect the permanent life of the community when the war is over is a matter we need not speculate upon. Personally I hope we shall some day return to the robust self-independence and reliance which has always been a characteristic of the British race, and which has been, in my opinion, the secret of its strength in past times. (Cheers.)

It is our splendid tradition of the past, the old martial spirit of our race, which explains why our 'contemptible little Army' has such a contempt for its enemies. But there is a good deal to be done before this dragon of militarism is to be finally slain, before the great nations of the earth are to cease crouching like wild beasts of the field, ever ready to fly at each other's throats.

What I want to ask is, have we fully grasped the meaning of the great, titanic struggle in which we are engaged? If we have not, is it not time that the scales fell from our eyes, and that we set about in grim earnest to tackle the great problem before us? We are not going to come triumphant out of the struggle without a mighty and stupendous effort.

Perhaps if we had listened to that voice, now still, of the great soldier who recently laid down his arms we should have been better prepared. (Cheers.) When you reflect that we have had in the past few years eight heads of the two great services, and four of them lawyers, can you wonder we are not quite prepared? Why, I almost wonder we are alive. It is a wonderful tribute to the inherent strength and vitality of the British Empire that we can withstand a test of such a character.

One of the objects of this gathering is to face the recruiting problem. I say deliberately that in this respect we are not doing as well as we ought to be. I do not blame the men altogether, because I do not believe we have yet made an adequate and concerted effort to bring home to their minds the exact gravity of the problem. I do not forget that in the early days there were all sorts of difficulties which led many a man to hesitate. Their treatment and terms of pay in the past have been scandalously, radically, and meanly inadequate. (Cheers.) I wonder that a nation which at a moment's notice can raise four or five hundred millions of money should haggle and falter over a paltry few shillings a week; to the only men who matter in a time of national crisis. (Cheers.)

Do you realise that three-quarters of Kitchener's Army at present consists of married men – men who have assumed the responsibilities of citizenship and whose proper place is to defend our shores at home while the younger men are at the front?

I do not profess to know Cabinet secrets, but I pledge myself to this – that this state of things is not going to be permitted to continue many weeks longer. (Cheers.) If the single men of the country do not come forward in larger numbers than they are doing, it will not be very many weeks before either by Act of Parliament or the operation of the common law of the land – they are compelled to go and do that which it ought to be their proudest privilege to rush and do of their own accord. (Cheers.)

I suggest that Lord Kitchener should at once announce the exact number of further men he requires; that he should state a time-limit, at the expiration of which, if the whole New Army is not ready, then, by the operation of the law, every man capable of bearing arms – and the single ones in preference – should be compelled to do their duty to their country. (Cheers.) We want to make it clear to the manhood of the country that this is a life and death struggle between the Anglo–Saxon race and the Teutonic race, which is still as brutal, as barbarous, and as base as it has been throughout the whole of its history. (Cheers.)

In my own opinion, the civilisation of Germany today, despite all its literature and spiritual attractions, belongs to a period of 1,000 years ago. When I find eminent statesmen telling us that their spiritual home is in Germany, I say, first of all, that there is no accounting for tastes – (laughter) – and, secondly, it is a dangerous thing to divorce your astral body from your physical frame, and the man whose spiritual home is in Berlin should either call back his spirit as quickly as possible, or transfer its physical encasement to its spiritual home. (Laughter and cheers.) There is a call to every Briton who values the freedom of his country and the blessings of civilisation to help to put such a barbarous foe out of existence for all time. (Cheers.)

There is no question that we are dealing with a man in the Kaiser – (a voice: 'A what?' and laughter) – who is just on the borderland between humanity and barbarism. He inherits all the madness of his ancestors. Nobody knew better than the late King Edward VII how mad his nephew was. So long as he lived he was able to keep the fellow in order. (Laughter and 'hear, hear'.)

But from the time we lost that great King, that great ambassador of peace, who did more for the peace of Europe than all the statesmen who ever lived, this man has been irresponsible and mad with ambition, only waiting for an opportunity, as he thought, by all sorts of subterfuge and hypocrisy, to catch us unawares, and give full vent to that ambition, which undoubtedly will 'o'erleap itself'. (Cheers.)

I ask young men whether they would not like to be in at the death. It is not an exaggeration to say that the claws of the lion are already getting well into the neck of the vulture, and I wish the manhood of England, and of London especially, to come forward and be able to say, 'I was one of those who gave him the finishing touch.' (Cheers.) If we do that and increase the pressure on the enemy in the field, Jack Tar will have a chance of having a go at the enemy, instead of waiting as he is doing today.

The great fleet is always looking for fog and smooth water. (Laughter.) Its new principle is this – if you cannot beat your enemy in fair fight somehow or other, contrive to trip him up. So the new culture of the fighting world is to be this. At the next championship boxing match we have, whichever of the two is fearful of his opponent, will take steps to mine the centre of the ring. (Laughter.) The Oxford and Cambridge boatrace will be decided by a mine at Mortlake. (Laughter.) The Derby will be fatal to the favourite when he steps on the mine immediately in front of the winning-post. (Laughter.) That is the new culture of the Teutonic race.

Did a fleet ever maintain the traditions of a great race better than our sailors are doing today? ('No' and cheers.) I do not know whether you recall that little tragedy of a few days ago, when the *Formidable* was going down to the depth of the sea. What was a survivor's story? 'The last thing we saw was a line of sailors saluting the old flag and singing "Tipperary" as they went down to the bottom of the ocean.' (Cheers.) These are the men that you fellows who do not recruit are allowing to be murdered by these Huns. Then if you would only answer your country's call and strengthen Lord Kitchener's forces, out of sheer desperation and necessity the German fleet will have to sail forth and give battle according to the recognised rules of the game.

It is a heavy reckoning which this enemy has to look to, and it is for us – the people – to consider what the reckoning should be. It may be, after all, for the best that this fleet is remaining intact, because it may facilitate the settlement when the time comes. That settlement is not to be a hole-and-corner affair by any party politicians. (Cheers.) I suggest that when it comes to discussing the terms of peace we should say to Lord Kitchener and to Lord Fisher or Admiral Sir J. Jellicoe, 'You have finished the job; now go over for us and reap the fruit.' (Cheers.)

We can easily all agree upon the main points of the settlement. One of the first things we want to do is to get rid finally of Turkey out of Europe. (Cheers.) German and Austrian Poland must be added to the new kingdom of Poland; Hungary and Bohemia must again be separate States; Germany and Prussia must go back to the position they were in in 1870 – a collection of little and harmless States, infinitely happier than they are today. Italy, if she will only do the right thing, and I think she will – (cheers) – must have Trieste back. Alsace and Lorraine will naturally go back to France.

The fleet of Germany, if still intact, I once thought might conveniently be added to our own, but lest that should cause any jealousy amongst the Allies, would not it be a good idea to make it the nucleus of an international fleet, manned and commanded by international officers for the purpose of policing the seas of the world and helping to keep the ports and commerce of the world free from molestation? There will, of course, be the indemnity, which will have to recoup the Allies not only their expenses of the war, but all the cost of compensation and pensions. We shall say to Germany when all other matters are settled, 'How much money have you got, and how much can you raise within the next twenty or thirty years?' and we shall divide that fairly amongst the Allies.

The Kaiser and his promising son must be dealt with. They must not be allowed to remain a day in Germany after peace is declared. (Cheers.) They can be put up to auction and knocked down to the lowest bidder. (Laughter.)

What are you going to do with Belgium? Politicians tell us we have to restore her independence and renew her shattered treasures and cathedrals; but that is only the beginning. There are two respects at least in which we can pay her something towards the debt we owe. First of all there is a little place in the occupation of Germany which she ought never to have possessed, and if I were Prime Minister I should write to King Albert, 'Would you care to be Prince of Schleswig–Holstein as well as King of Belgium?' (Cheers.)

There is that little waterway called the Kiel Canal. That has got to be denationalised, put in the hands of somebody for the trust of Europe, and the natural custodian and trustee of it is King Albert of Belgium. (Cheers.) Let the canal be put in the custody of Belgium, let Belgium take the tolls, and let there be a notice put up on the road to Heligoland for all the merchant seamen to read, 'Shortcut to the Baltic – first to the right.' (Cheers.) You may think it a little premature to talk about the terms of settlement. I do not. I am one of those who say that this is not going to be the long war that some people anticipate. You cannot have 10,000,000 or 15,000,000 of men in the field for an indefinite period without a large number of natural laws coming into play to upset your calculations.

I know that when Earl Kitchener announced in the House of Lords that he had an army of one and a quarter million men in training, that statement gave Germany a shock, and the moment she knows that that army is now 2,000,000 you will soon be hearing of those mysterious overtures the origin of which nobody can ever trace, but the purpose of which is plain to all the world.

This is a mighty struggle, a Marathon of the gods of battle, and if I were a young man I would yearn to be in the fight. Those who cannot join are at a terrible disadvantage, because when it is all over I cannot think of any prouder boast that anyone can make than that he took an active part in ridding the world of a great, barbarous menace which, but for his intervention, might have wiped out the civilisation of the past ages. I ask all young men, if they do not really feel that there is a call to them, can they not hear their comrades calling to them from the trenches, from the hospital, from the decks of those sea-dogs that are guarding our shores? If they do not hear that call they are unworthy to claim the name of Englishman. (Cheers.)

After all, we are the greatest martial race which the world has ever known. We have had a good time in the past, because we have led in the van of commerce and of trade, and perhaps the rising generation has never been sufficiently taught what is the meaning of the words 'the British Empire'. Still, I believe that the day is rapidly coming when the manhood of the nation will realise the call which is made today. (Cheers.)

The meeting concluded with the singing of the National Anthem.

20 January 1915

RAID ON EAST COAST

Bomb Dropped Near Sandringham, *King's Lynn, Wednesday (12.45 a.m.)*

At about 11.15 last night one or more Zeppelins passed over this town, and dropped five bombs in their passage.

I live about half a mile outside the town, and aroused by a terrific explosion I rushed out. I saw flashes, and heard a series of terrific explosions, five altogether, I think, although amid the excitement I could not be sure.

Shortly afterwards the special constables rushed this way, shouting the order, 'Lights out', and immediately followed the fire brigade, but so far as can be gathered the services of the latter were not required.

I am sure they were Zeppelins, and not aeroplanes, because of the noise they made. They must have passed the coast at Dersingham, near Sandringham, and then made for King's Lynn, having possibly caught a glimpse of lights in the town.

The airship which visited King's Lynn apparently approached from the north. A minute or two before eleven o'clock a distant explosion was heard in all parts of the town, but most people failed to perceive its significance, it being generally mistaken for an occurrence nearer home.

A few minutes later, however, the whirring of a propeller brought people to their doors. Then came a sudden flash, like lightning, followed by a detonation, and there was subsequently several other flashes and explosions.

In the meantime, the noise of the engine had become so loud as to leave no doubt that it originated from a powerful airship. The current was immediately switched off at the electricity works, plunging the town in almost total darkness. Police went hurriedly through the streets, directing all lights in the houses to be extinguished.

A few people claim to have seen the airship, but to most it seemed to be hidden by the clouds and darkness. It approached from the direction of Sandringham, and reports so far to hand show that a bomb was dropped at Snettisham, four miles from the King's Norfolk home.

The first missile to fall in Lynn absolutely destroyed the hydraulic-engine-house at the docks, but, fortunately, no one was injured. The next fell on a house near the docks, and went through it from floor to basement, but no serious personal injury resulted.

The worst damage occurred in the central portion of the town, in close proximity to the fine old Gothic Grey-friars Tower. Here one bomb totally destroyed three cottages in Bentinck-street, killing a lad named Percy Goat, and badly injuring his little sister Ethel Goat, aged four, Mr and Mrs Fayers, and Dan Skipper. The latter's wife and daughter had miraculous escapes. The family were in bed, and Mrs Skipper was somewhat cut about the legs, and her husband so badly injured as to necessitate removal to hospital.

Many of the houses in the street had their doors wrenched from their hinges, windows shattered, and furniture thrown about in confusion. In a parallel street in the rear, Melbourne-street, another bomb appears to have been dropped, for every window in the street was broken. In two other quarters of the town bombs seem to have fallen with no other results than broken windows.

Bentinck-street presents a scene of desolation. Fragments, either of shell or masonry, were carried long distances, some passing over the post-office and alighting on the cattle market, several hundred yards away. Many persons suffered slight injuries.

The airship was plainly seen at Sandringham, but no bombs were dropped nearer to it than Heacham, six miles away. No death or serious injury is reported from that place. The amount of damage to property is not known. Only one bomb fell.

1 April 1915

MILITARY LAW FOR LIVERPOOL DOCKS
Lord Derby's Scheme, *Liverpool, Wednesday Night*

The Earl of Derby has formulated a novel scheme with the approval of Lord Kitchener, to deal with the congestion at Liverpool Docks, in connection with which there have been numerous complaints since the war began. His lordship's proposal is to form a battalion of dock labourers on military lines.

In outlining his project today, Lord Derby wished it to be widely known that his proposals were conceived long before the weekend dock strikes at Birkenhead commenced. The scheme has the heartiest approval of the leading shipowners of the port, and also of the principal officials of the Dock Labourers' Union, both of whom were prominently represented at today's gathering. Lord Derby presented his scheme in the following, interesting statement: 'I have always had it in my mind that there were many men working in the docks who, unable to enlist owing to age, would still be glad to put on his Majesty's uniform and be employed as soldiers, but in a civil capacity. I have obtained Lord Kitchener's permission to raise a battalion, or as desirable, battalions, on somewhat novel lines, and I intend to try and get the men within a very short time.'

The following are the conditions: The men will be regularly attested, and will be in all respects under military law, but will only be employed for home service.

The constitution of the force will be by companies as on the National Reserve system. Each company will consist of a sergeant, ten corporals and about 114 rank and file. The latter figure, however, is liable to variation.

Men will be served out with khaki overall uniforms to work in.

Pay – Men will earn their civil pay plus the Army pay of their rank, but will have no claim for any allowances, such as lodging, separation, bounty, &c. They will receive their civil pay at white book rates, but every man will be guaranteed a minimum of 35s which, together with his military pay of 1s a day, will, in the case of a private, bring it to a minimum of 42s a week.

In the event of a man working more hours than will entitle him at white-book rate to receive his 35s a week, any money he so earns will be in addition to the 42s above specified.

Corporals will receive 1s 8d a day over and above their civil pay.

Sergeants will receive a flat rate over and above their military pay of 2s 4d a day.

No man will be taken unless he belongs to the Dockers' Union, and any man after enlisting who shall cease to be a member of the union will be discharged.

The force will adhere strictly to trade union rules, and under no circumstances will it be used as a strike-breaking battalion.

'I am,' continued Lord Derby, 'asking Mr Sexton (the general secretary of the Dock Labourers' Union) to become a consultative member of the staff, in order that I may be prevented from breaking any of the trade union rules.

'Three companies will be formed as a first instalment, and their sergeants will be: No. 1, Mr Keefe, president of the Dockers' Union, and himself an old soldier; No. 2. Mr M'Kibben, vice-president of the Dockers' Union, now in the Scots Guards, but home: on sick furlough, having been wounded at Ypres (he has been lent to me by the War Office); No. 3. Sergeant O'Hare, also an official of the Dockers' Union, but who is now serving with the 8th King's. He has also been lent to me by the War Office.

'Shipowners and Government departments employing the men of the battalion will be charged a fee in order to prevent any expenses falling on the Government other than the expenses for headquarter staff and the cost of uniforms, which will be defrayed out of public funds. The Cunard, White Star, and Holts have guaranteed the expense in the first instance. Work will be allotted from the headquarter office and care will be taken only to give men reasonable hours. Mr Williams, of the Labour Exchange, will be adjutant.'

Lord Derby added that as there was no drill required, or only a very small amount, to enable men to go in military formation to their work, he proposed himself to undertake the duties of commanding officer. The Town Hall had been placed at their disposal, and he proposed to enlist the men on 8 April, and commence work with them on the following day.

Colonel Henry Concannon, manager of the White Star Line, in congratulating Lord Derby upon his scheme, said some people might say that in White Book agreement there was certain freedom for non-union men, and while he had always been one to maintain that regulation, he was entirely in accord with the union, and to employ only union men. It was a definite agreement arranged by his lordship between the Government, the shipowning members of the Employers' Association, and not those outside of it, and the Union of Dock Labourers. This combination was for the prosecution of Government work in connection with meat, sugar, and other consignments. When the battalion was not needed for Government work it would be put on to other work in the national interests. The corps was in no sense a strike-breaking corps.

Mr James Sexton, speaking from the men's point of view, remarked that words almost failed him to say how much he appreciated the inspiration of Lord Derby in the matter. He (Mr Sexton) did not see how any rules of a union could prevent an individual member joining a service of that character. As a matter of fact, their members in the Firth of Clyde had already enlisted under similar conditions, with the full knowledge and consent of their union, and were doing the same kind of work at Havre now. He would tell his executive quite frankly that if they refused to accept this offer there was a possibility of men being introduced into the port to form the battalion who were not members of the union.

Lord Derby intimated that those joining the force would, at the end of the war, receive a medal of home service similar to that which was to be given to workers in armament factories.

10 July 1915

MUNITIONS DEPARTMENT
Voluntary War Workers

After over a fortnight of strenuous effort the Munitions Work Bureaux close tonight, but the work of enrolling voluntary war workers is to be continued by the Labour Exchanges.

A great many of the men enrolled will find that no call will be made upon them for some time. This is due to the fact that the Munitions Department is paying much attention to individual cases, the object being to cause the least possible dislocation of trade in allocating labour to new work. Delay in calling upon the war workers already enrolled may be regarded, therefore, as an additional guarantee that no movement of labour will take place except under circumstances of actual necessity and after thorough inquiry, and the policy thus adopted affords a further reason why all who are qualified should place their names forthwith on the roll of enlisted volunteers.

No doubt is entertained by those who are cognisant of the facts that there will be a very great demand for additional labour in the new munition works, and when the time comes the men must be available. The policy of those administering the scheme appears to be the securing of that adequate supply with the utmost possible avoidance of waste.

Mr H. E. Morgan, in an interview last night, said: 'We expect with tonight's enrolment to be well on the way to 90,000. There are, however, so many indications that there are more men willing to assist that it has been decided to continue the enrolment of war munition volunteers through the Labour Exchanges.

'More men are wanted, and we shall have to search every village and hamlet before we can get enough. Some unrest has been caused by the fact that all men enrolled have not been at once placed on war work. We fully recognise the necessity for haste, but the organisation and, in a large measure, the rearrangement of the skilled labour of the country, takes time, and has to be handled with the greatest discrimination and care if an undue disturbance of industry is not to be caused. We must know broadly the number of volunteers and the resources at our disposal before we can adjust many of the problems with which we are faced.

'Our plan is to offer men, with their credentials, to the various employers, with the terms and conditions of service, leaving the selection to the future employers. The demands are rising enormously as the various factories come under the control of the Government, and are included in the list of establishments to which volunteers can be supplied, and the mechanical facilities for producing munitions are increasing day by day. Thus, the men available are being rapidly absorbed, and more are needed.

'I may add that as the result of an interview with a deputation representing a large body of employers, I know of an instance in which 1,000 men are going to enrol en masse. Our record day brought us in over 10,000 names, and we hope that tomorrow results will even beat that. We have a staff of over 300 engaged night and day marking the necessary inquiries, notifying the large contractors who so urgently want men, and carrying out the whole of the details in connection with the transport of workers from one place to another. Let me end as I begin by again emphasising the paramount duty of all eligible men to enrol.'

KITCHENER'S CALL TO THE NATION
Stirring Appeal for Men

There was one feature of yesterday's great meeting at the Guildhall, whose significance it was impossible to overlook. It lay altogether apart from the earnestness – nay, the seriousness – of Earl Kitchener's appeal for more men, and his not too thinly disguised rebuke of the shirker. And that conspicuous feature was whole-hearted denunciation of the criticism which in certain quarters has been, and is still, being directed against certain personages in high places.

Sir Edward Carson put the matter pointedly when he declared, 'I do not know a poorer service that any man could give to his country than to attempt, even to the smallest degree, to shake the confidence of the nation in Lord Kitchener.' And the cheers that greeted the remark were amongst the loudest of the afternoon. Lord Derby was not less emphatic when he declared that 'one of the worst deterrents to recruiting consists of the innuendoes by speech, or question, or by article, which are trying to inspire want of confidence in our leaders'.

But, after all, the dominant feature of the gathering was that it stood out as a spontaneous personal ovation to Lord Kitchener. Within the hall, as in the streets outside, the Secretary for War was greeted as a great popular idol. Hardly can a public man have been received with greater enthusiasm in the venerable Guildhall than was the War Secretary when he made his appearance on the platform in blue undress uniform. His speech was earnest and purpose-like, with just an occasional touch of gravity in it. If, however, the speaker was grave at times, he was certainly not pessimistic.

He had little bits of good news to dispense as he went on. From the first, he said, there has been a steady and constant flow of recruits, and the recent falling off is due in his opinion to temporary causes. That, indeed, is why he is making a fresh demand on the manhood of the country. The larger the armies we raise, the larger the reserves that are necessary to maintain them, and make good the wastage of war; that, roughly, was the reason and justification of his fresh appeal. Another encouraging announcement of the Secretary for War was that the original drawback of lack of arms has been surmounted, and that our troops in training can be supplied with sufficient arms and material to turn them out as efficient soldiers. The difficulty of finding accommodation for the new armies has also now been got over, and we are now able to clothe and equip all recruits as they come in.

But the most striking part of the speech was yet to come. More than once Lord Kitchener dropped a hint that in future the ways of the shirker may not be quite so easy; and in particular his reference to the National Register was highly significant. 'When this registration is completed,' he said, 'we shall anyhow be able to note the men between the ages of nineteen and forty not required for munition or other necessary industrial work, and therefore available, if physically fit, for the fighting line.' Yet, on the other hand, he uttered a word of caution, upon the danger of overstatement when talking of 'slackers'. On the whole the speech was a stirring yet temperately phrased appeal for 'more men', and as such it was obviously regarded by the audience, who cheered it to the echo.

As to the other speeches, Sir Edward Carson spoke of the success of voluntary recruiting 'so far', and hinted at possibilities of conscription if the voluntary system should fail. Lord Derby also touched on the possibility of compulsion, and declared that Lord Kitchener's speech was 'as much a warning as an appeal'. Finally, Mr Churchill showed how fully verified had been the prophecy he made in that very hall ten months ago, that the navy would be found fit for its task. Likewise did he repudiate 'the dangerous and libellous suggestion', as he called it, 'that it is in some degree due to our shortcomings that the war is not going to reach a speedy conclusion this year'.

The following are a few of the striking passages in the speech: 'All the reasons which led me to think in August, 1914, that this war would be a prolonged one hold good at the present time.

'We have now, happily, reached a period when it can be said that the troops in training can be supplied with sufficient arms and material to turn them out as efficient soldiers.

'We have throughout the country provided accommodation calculated to be sufficient and suitable for the requirements of our troops.

'When the National Register is completed we will anyhow be able to note the men between the ages of nineteen and forty not required for munition or other necessary industrial work, and therefore available, if physically fit, for the fighting line.

'Steps will be taken to approach, with a view to enlistment, all possible candidates for the Army – unmarried men to be preferred before married men, as far as may be.'

16 July 1915

SUPPLIES FOR THE ARMY
Mountains of Tea

In its large warehouse in Cutler-street, EC, the Port of London Authority is quietly playing a useful part in assuring the comfort of his Majesty's Forces. From the enormous stocks of tea, totalling at the present time about 18,500,000 lb, which are under Customs' control at these bonded warehouses, large supplies are being regularly despatched, to meet the requirements of the Government. Quite recently, for example, the Port Authority's staff at Cutler-street was called upon to blend and pack no less than 57,000 lb of tea in connection with the execution of a single demand of the War Office.

In the ordinary course, the War Office will order a supply according to an approved sample. The officials at Cutler-street at once get their instructions as to the particular classes of tea which are to be put together to produce in the bulk the equivalent to the sample. Chests containing the required quantities are opened by the hundred, and their contents are heaped together until the observer sees before him a veritable mountain of tea. While some men known as 'feeders' add the contents of still more chests to the heap, others with wooden shovels are actively at work in blending the tea. As many as from fifteen to twenty men will be engaged in the task of so mixing the various qualities that, at the close of the operation, the bulk shall be equal to the sample originally submitted to the authorities by the tea brokers.

It might be thought that where as much as 50,000 lb or 60,000 lb of tea is required to be blended it would be preferable to use machinery. As a matter of fact, nothing seems so satisfactory for the purpose as hand labour, because of the skill which the men employed in the process have attained as the result of long experience of the work. The thoroughness with which the mixing has been done is ascertained by drawing samples from the blend when the task is completed.

The packing of the tea follows closely upon a consideration of campaigning needs. These necessitate the use of strong tins of handy size, packed in cases of reasonable dimension. The standard tin for war use contains 15 lb of tea, and two of these tins fill a case, giving a total weight per package of not much over 80 lb. Thus the packing of a blend of 57,000 lb of tea for military purposes means the separate weighing out of 8,800 quantities of 15 lb, the filling and soldering of the same number of tins, and the sealing of 1,900 cases. The work of the Port Authority's men is done under Customs supervision, for account has necessarily to be rendered for the weights of all tea coming into and going out of these bonded warehouses,

Altogether the Cutler-street warehouses can store 20,000,000 lb of tea, which is equivalent to something like one-fourth of the stock in all the bonded warehouses of the United Kingdom at a recent date. The bulk of it comes from India and Ceylon, with Java qualities more in evidence than usual, owing to the difficulties in the way of re-exportation from Holland, and China growths still show a steadily diminishing proportion. Not much of the brick tea of the kind specially produced in China for the Russian market reaches Cutler-street in the ordinary way, although the banking facilities of the metropolis have their influence in this matter. This brick tea is much esteemed in Russia by reason of its convenience of carriage in a country of long distance.

Not only is Cutler-street the premier tea warehouse in the Port of London, but it is the great depot for cigars and cigarettes, and carries an average stock of 100,000,000 cigars and 80,000,000 cigarettes. In these circumstances the Port Authority's staff have also been called upon to pack vast quantities of cigarettes for the use of the troops at the front, interned prisoners, and the men of the Navy.

The work is done at the instance of the various organisations which have undertaken to supply this particular form of comfort to those in the fighting line or in captivity. In many cases the packages are made up to contain tobacco and pipes, as well as cigarettes. From these Cutler-street warehouses, in deference to the war demand, cigarettes continue to go out, not in thousands, but in millions.

28 July 1915

NATION AND LUXURIES
A Comfortable Theory

A great fallacy which persists today, as it has for countless years, despite the teachings of economists and philosophers, is, it is urged, the belief that indulgence in luxury on the part of individuals, or groups of individuals, is not altogether to be condemned, 'because it provides employment for the poor'.

The phrase, in some form or other, is frequently heard, particularly at the present juncture. From time to time various great thinkers have demolished the argument. But, in spite of all analysis and criticism, the fallacy exists. A few of those who deny themselves nothing in the way of luxury and extravagance, probably know they are wrong. But there can be no doubt that a very large proportion of those who are fortunate enough to be able to gratify any whim or taste, however expensive, honestly believe that, in so doing, they are giving employment to certain trades and certain individuals.

The great fallacy never threatened more harm than at the present time. Never was there such a need for its complete exposure. There is an old Roman proverb that luxury is more cruel than war. People who persist in the indulgence of luxuries at the present time are acting unpatriotically and doing their country injury.

That is the considered judgment, based upon expert advice, and promulgated with official sanction, of the Parliamentary War Savings Committee.

Mr H. E. Morgan, who is assisting the Committee in its national thrift campaign, pointed out in an interview with a representative of the *Daily Telegraph* yesterday that people employed in what may be called, the 'luxury trades' could be far better and more usefully serving a national purpose by enlisting, by working in a munition factory (women as well as men), by going on the land, by helping to make Army equipment, or in a hundred and one practical and serviceable directions.

The Committee recognises that this is a matter which is almost entirely in the hands of women. It is women, and particularly well-to-do women, who mostly keep the 'luxury trades' going. It is open to them to give a lead and set an example by practising economy. Opinions may differ with regard to the directions in which the great denial may be made. But, said Mr Morgan, there can be no doubt about the following:

1. No one should build a house to reside in himself, or herself.
2. No costly presents should be given, except in the form of war scrip.
3. No motor-cars should be used, unless for essential or charitable purposes.
4. No entertaining in restaurants should take place.
5. Changes in fashion should be ignored or discouraged.
6. Expenditure upon funerals and mourning should be kept down.
7. Servants should be dispensed with except those necessary for the simplest requirements.
8. 'Treating' should be given up until the war is over, and until, in fact, we are able to toast the final victory.

It may be added that these conclusions have been arrived at by a council of experts and practical men, who consider that self-abnegation in all, or some, of these directions is vitally necessary in the public interest. The only way in which the war can be paid for is by every individual saving money, and also by avoiding waste. Apart from the saving of money, which is often not possible with the very poorest persons in the community, the waste that goes on is very heavy, and obtains in all spheres of society.

5 August 1915

KING AND QUEEN AT ST PAUL'S

'A Service of humble prayer on behalf of the Nation and Empire' so ran the official description of the ceremony which filled with reverent worshippers the vast spaces of St Paul's Cathedral long before the appointed hour of noon.

> Under the cross of gold,
> That shines over city and river.

St Paul's has never seen quite such a service before. Services of Thanksgiving for victories by land and sea, for Peace restored, for the recovery of kings and princes from sickness, and for long and happy reigns, have often filled the great dome with the ordered tumult of joyful sound. There have been services, too, of special Intercession, and of national mourning, when England has proudly brought her best and bravest and laid them to rest amid their mighty compeers. And kings and queens have often been to St Paul's to pray, as King George and Queen Mary and Queen Alexandra went yesterday, and the Lords and Commons have assembled there with the Judges and the Captains of the land, and the people have filled the nave and the sounding aisles and strained to hear the wandering echoes of the distant prayers and the sweet songs of the singers in the choir. St Paul's has long memories, and Britain has been a fruitful mother of heroes.

The service yesterday marked an anniversary merely, but an anniversary of the outbreak of a war which will change the face of nations. The Great Day of Thanksgiving is not yet, though it will come – never fear – in due time, as soon, maybe, as we and our noble Allies are ready to make a right and just use of complete victory. But, meanwhile, is there not cause for Thanksgiving that our statesmen drew the sword for Freedom, that our soldiers and sailors have fought so valiantly, that our people have proved that 'we are a people yet', that the British race throughout the wide world is faithful to its high tradition, and that despite all our shortcomings, and foolish self-confidences, and vain imaginings, and grievous losses, Great Britain is eager to dedicate herself anew to the Cause by a 'service of humble prayer'.

How truly national a temple is St Paul's was realised best when the earlier stir caused by the constant stream of incomers had subsided, and the places underneath the dome and in the transepts were all filled. Then one could listen in quiet to the Royal Artillery Band, as they played piece after piece of solemn music, the strains of which suggested most poignantly the struggles, the heroisms, and the painful glories of war. The air throbbed and hearts throbbed with it, and 'the shaping spirit of imagination' was palpably at work drawing vivid pictures of well-loved forms against the lurid background of the Great War.

St Paul's is a very Pantheon of warriors. The walls are consecrate to their honour. Faded and tattered colours, bearing glorious names, droop listlessly from their standards. Marble tablets struggle to preserve from oblivion the names of scores of gallant officers who counted not their lives dear unto themselves, but gladly gave them for England. The sculptured monuments tell their tale of heroes stricken down in the hour of triumph – captains who, if fate had spared them but a little longer, might have ranked with the greatest. And there, too, are the effigies of the greatest – the Mighty Seaman, with Howe and Rodney not far away, and the faithful Collingwood near by, and the Duke, in his princely monument.

It is impossible to think that these illustrious shades are not aware that their England is at war again, and engaged in such a grapple as their times ever knew. Abercrombie, who refused the soldier's blanket as a pillow in his dying hour, lest its owner should need it more sorely than he; Picton, the Paladin of fighting brigadiers; the noble Napiers; the stainless Lawrences; those splendid veterans of late Victorian days, Lord Strathnairn and Lord Napier of Magdala; the saintly Gordon and the gallant Sir Herbert Stewart, who strove in vain to reach him; and the two late-comers to their glorious company, Viscount Wolseley and Earl Roberts. Whether or not their dust lies in St Paul's or only their sculptured effigy, we may be sure that they know their native land is in peril, and that they watch, serene and confident as in life, the swaying fortunes of the fight.

By a very early hour the space left open for the public was all filled, and the nave and its aisles could hold no more. The broad expanse beneath the dome had been arranged as a square, in the centre of which were the seats set apart for the King and Queen and Queen Alexandra, with large red velvet cushions on the foot stools in front of them. Two other rows of tall chairs just behind were for the rest of the Royal party. At right angles to these, and to the left of the King, were the places reserved for Ministers of the Crown.

The Speaker was an early comer, and next to him, in a place of honour, sat Sir Robert Borden. The Prime Minister and Mrs Asquith sat at the further end of the row close to the band, which was spread out across the whole width of the entrance to the choir. Lord Kitchener was there, and Sir Edward Grey, Lord and Lady Lansdowne, Lord Selborne, Mr and Mrs J. Harcourt, Mr Birrell, Mr and Mrs Churchill, the Lord Chancellor and Lady Buckmaster, Sir John Simon, Mr Walter Long, and Mr and Mrs Austen Chamberlain. Mr Lloyd George was unable to attend, but Mrs Lloyd George was present, and there, too, were Sir George Read, Lord Halsbury, Lord Bryce, the Ambassadors of France, Russia, Japan, and Italy, and a host of other notabilities.

Little colour was seen beneath the dome. Dark was the prevailing hue, and there was no splendour of uniform to act as relief. A row of foreign attachés broke the monotony in one part, but the brightest colours were the blue uniforms and red ties of the wounded soldiers, the black and red of one band of nurses, and the white caps and aprons of another cluster at the head of the nave. The wounded were the objects of much sympathetic attention as they came streaming in, a few on crutches, others with empty sleeves, some with bandaged heads, and one or two, alas! sightless. But on their faces happiness and content. And everywhere were officers in khaki.

The porch of the southern transept was banked high, and those who saw for the first time the choir of St Paul's on an extraordinary occasion may well have wondered at its lustrous appearance when the long line of singers and clergy entered and took their places in the beautiful framework of the fretted stalls. The cathedral choir had been reinforced by choristers from the Chapel Royal, whose red and gold showed up well against the snowy white of the surrounding surplices.

There was but little sunshine. A few shafts of light came piercing through the windows of the dome, like pale searchlights, but they were rare visitors and not until near the end of the service was there a momentary blaze of hot sunlight. A few minutes before noon the band ceased playing, a sudden hush fell upon the waiting throng, and there came the muffled sound of cheering. A brief pause, and the Royal party entered by the north transept, through the Wren porch, where they were received by the Bishop of London and the Dean of St Paul's, and ceremoniously escorted to their places. King George walked between the Bishop and the Dean; Queen Mary and Queen Alexandra followed and Princess Victoria walked with the Princess Royal. Other members of the Royal family were already in their seats, including Princess Christian and Princess Henry of Battenberg, Princess Alexander of Teck and Princess Arthur of Connaught.

And then the service began with the hymn of which no one ever tires in times of trouble. 'Rock of ages' – the familiar cadences, played and sung with great feeling, slowly rolled in great waves of sound from arch to arch of the mighty fabric till they lost themselves in the far-off galleries and the deepest recesses of dome and roof.

Then the Archbishop of Canterbury mounted the pulpit and delivered a short address, the text 1st Corinthians, chap.16, v. 13, 'Watch ye; Stand fast in the faith; Quit you like men; Be strong.' It was a plain, direct address from a plain, direct text, vigorously phrased, clearly enunciated, and well heard, at any rate by those in the transepts and below the dome. The Archbishop said that this war was being waged on the simplest issues of right and wrong; that, to each man there came a decisive hour; that the call to each was a call to resolute self-surrender, not through others, but through oneself; and reviewing the past year, with all its losses and fearful cost, he boldly proclaimed, 'It is worth while.' It was a courageous, a militant, and a heartening address, containing an eloquent tribute to the womanhood of Britain, a true word in season, and appropriate to the hour.

After the address, the Archbishop and the Bishop of London moved up to the high altar, and then the choir sang, kneeling, Stainer's setting of Psalm 51, unaccompanied by any music. It was sung very slowly, with a wonderfully clear enunciation of the words by the Vicar Choral, and in one or two antiphonal passages the clear, pure notes of the trebles thrilled the listening ear. Then followed a few prayers, beautifully read, a fine rendering of the hymn 'Praise, my soul, the King of Heaven,' and a special prayer by the Bishop of London, which ran as follows: 'Look, we beseech Thee, O Lord, upon the people of this land, who are called after Thy Holy Name; and grant that in this time of anxiety and distress they may walk worthy of their Christian profession. Grant unto us all that, laying aside our divisions, we may be united in one heart and mind to hear the burdens which this war has laid upon us. Help us to respond to the call of our country according to our several powers; put far from us selfish indifference to the needs of others; and give us grace to fulfil our daily duties with a sober diligence. Keep us from all uncharitableness in word or deed; and enable us by patient continuance in well-doing to glorify Thy Name; through Jesus Christ our Lord. Amen.'

The Blessing was pronounced, and then came the hymn, 'Through the night of doubt and sorrow.' The whole congregation joined heartily in singing it, and it lifted those who sang.

> 'Clear before us, through the darkness
> Gleams and burns the guiding Light;
> Brother clasps the hand of brother,
> Stepping fearless through the night.'

Surely, that is the true human sort of hymn for wartime. The voice of the choir was whelmed and lost in the sound of all the people singing.

Once more brief silence fell. Then the drums rolled like the sound of a mighty rushing wind, and there came the crashing opening chords of the National Anthem, which was heartily, reverently, and loyally sung. The King and Queen and the whole Royal party rose and passed out in dignified procession to the strains of Elgar's Imperial March, and a little later the great cathedral was empty again and still.

Another notable page has been added to its records, and the people have been comforted and strengthened.

2 October 1915

LONDON BY NIGHT
Darkening Devices by Householders

Very little more would appear to be possible, or even necessary, in the way of measures for reducing the night illumination of London, in view of possible air raids. The new police regulations came into operation last night, and there was evidence, in whichever direction one turned, of general compliance with them. Moreover, the police were active in locating and instructing the dilatory and negligent.

Coupled with more widespread reflection, this active persuasion is gradually reducing the number of those who have hitherto been disposed to regard these precautions as matter for individual discretion. There is now greater readiness to realise that they are designed for the general good, and that it is a point of honour to comply with them. Thus it is possible to speak of the wish of the authorities as having in a very great measure been attained.

Obviously, the particular object of these later light-reducing arrangements has been to secure greater uniformity throughout the metropolis as a whole. That was the effect observable last night. Nowhere was there Cimmerian darkness, but it was less easy to discover spots of exceptional brightness. In many places, notable as great junctions, where the reduction of lighting has been conspicuous, inquiry discovered that the populace had taken to the change very well. In fact, there was something in the demeanour of the public very suggestive of the curiosity aroused by sight-seeing – though the simile ends there, for there was less than usual to see.

Undoubtedly the more stringent regulations have increased the difficulties and dangers of vehicular traffic, and thrown greater responsibilities upon drivers, as well as necessitated greater care than ever on the part of foot passengers at crossings. In order to lessen the risk of accident the police have insisted in some localities upon small handcarts carrying some kind of illuminant. Complaint is beginning to be made that the strain upon drivers troubled with defective sight is being seriously felt, insomuch that some have had to adopt glasses.

The devices adopted by tradesmen to comply with the requirements are diverse, and in some cases novel. In one district a sudden fillip was seen to have been given to the spirit of patriotism, for a number of publicans have combined to dim their lights with Union Jacks. Very many shopkeepers think it sufficient to keep their outside awnings spread. Whether that suffices is a question for the police to decide. Often it is completely effective. In other cases it still permits a considerable diffusion of light. Again, it is a common practice to draw the shop blinds half-way down – a plan which in most cases cuts off direct light to the street while keeping the goods in the windows in effective illumination.

Mostly the practice is to dim the electric lights with shades of more or less primitive character, the readiest form being plain brown paper, and the neatest a dull-coloured lamp shade, recalling the old night watchman's lantern, and capable, by means of perforations, of bearing an advertising inscription. A few tradesmen in the drapery business have combined cheapness with effectiveness by simply arranging their goods as screens. In humorous plagiarism a fruiterer in a nameless street had enshrouded his lights in a shade composed of clustering bananas.

Elsewhere an individual in the blind business saw profit in the situation, for his window displayed a boldly printed offer on terms to 'take down, clean, and refix blinds'. Whether the circumstances would be best met by clean or soiled blinds is debateable. Yet, despite this commendable and general effort to comply with the regulations, there was still to be found here and there a wilful individual who took advice badly. One such, on being invited outside his shop by a constable to be educated, made answer only by pointing over the way to a rival with even less patriotism – the true British spirit of justice.

In the street markets and side streets where booths usually stand there was little to complain of. No flares were to be seen, and such light as was indulged in appeared as a rule behind dim screens of paper or sacking.

But it may be taken that these new regulations were very largely conceived as necessary on the score of householders, and it is in the residential districts, perhaps, that their effect is greatest. There has unquestionably within the last few days been considerable inquiry for such drapers' materials as can be used for blinds, and the result is seen in a wholesale darkening of windows, both at the front and rear of dwelling-houses, that have hitherto sent out offending shafts of light. Where new or additional curtains have not been fixed the plan had been widely adopted of darkening lights on the side facing windows; provided that is done properly the result is excellent.

Where large improvement could still be effected is in those localities where the houses are of the old Victorian order, having fanlights. The rays of light in such cases come from a point very close to the glass and throw strong gleams on the pavement. In many great blocks of workmen's dwellings the regulations were most loyally followed, except for the open staircases, which alone displayed strong illumination. While it is impossible to say exactly what degree of darkening has been effected generally by means of the various regulations, it is said in some parts to represent but 20 per cent of the normal lighting at night.

BUS RIDE IN THE DARK: FROM EAST TO WEST
Variations in Lighting

After a year's experience of it, we are becoming quite accustomed to the darkness into which London is plunged each night. Personally, we may not greatly like it, but we submit to it loyally, knowing that it is for our good – knowing that disregard of the lighting regulations which the authorities have imposed on us may be fraught with extremely awkward consequences to ourselves. That, after all, is the sensible – indeed, the only – way to look at the matter. At this time of crisis our duty as citizens is not to ourselves only, or primarily, but to the community at large. Yet that is an aspect of affairs which, in regard to this very question of lighting, does not yet seem to have occurred to a great many people.

Many of us, no doubt, think that our own particular districts are the most indifferently – that is to say, inconveniently – lit of all. We miss well-known landmarks. Gone now, owing to the darkness, are our chances of picking up a bus or a tramcar at the old familiar spots. We must now make for some general stopping place, where there is a glimmer of light to assist us. Still, we bear it, as it is our duty to do. But the thought may occur to us, 'Are other districts observing the spirit of the lighting regulations in the same loyal way?'

It was in this mood of intelligent curiosity that the writer set out the other night to ascertain at first-hand how London at large is hiding its lights for its own safety from the perils of the air. The outside seat of a motor-bus seemed a handy and practical view-point for the observation of darkened London, and such a seat he accordingly sought, at no great distance from one of our chief railway termini.

Seven or eight miles he travelled from east to west by one route; and the same distance he returned by an altogether different route, so that from first to last he covered some 15 miles of metropolitan thoroughfares. A 15-mile ride in London in the dark! Eighteen months ago we should have smiled incredulously at the bare idea. Yet the darkness was very real, though in the course of the journey it varied in intensity. It was so dark, in fact, that the outside passengers could barely distinguish one another – when the bus was traversing the long distances between shaded street lamps.

On the rearmost seat was a smart little office boy, chatting intelligently with the companion who sat beside him. 'It's dark enough for an overcoat,' said the boy. He obviously meant 'cold enough', for the night was bitterly cold. The words had barely escaped him, when there loomed out of the darkness, at the head of the stairs, a big, burly man, who, not observing the little chap, proceeded to pop into the nearest seat, which was that occupied by the boy. Naturally, the boy had something to say, and the passenger, full of apologies, and muttering some high-explosive utterance about the darkness, groped his way to a seat further forward. This, however, was but an episode, trivial in itself, but welcome as serving to lighten the gloom of the night.

Two main impressions were derivable from this 15-mile bus ride in the dark. One related to the marvellous skill and nerve of the drivers; the other had to do with what seemed to be the open disregard of the regulations which was to be observed in certain of the localities traversed.

First, as to the skill and the coolness of the two drivers. How they accomplished the double journey without accident is to the writer a sheer marvel. Their unerring judgment in picking out their course whilst threading thoroughfares that were often narrow, and nearly always shrouded in inky darkness, was almost uncanny. Once, to tell the truth, we nearly ran down a man in one of the straightest, busiest, and best-known streets in all London; but the fault certainly lay with the foot-passenger, rather than with the driver, who sounded his hooter, slowed down, and finally pulled up dead, within a few inches of the man who had been deaf to all these warnings.

Nor was the care exhibited by these drivers less conspicuous than their skill. They were playing for safety all the while. Had it been otherwise there certainly must have been some mischance. When the driver on the outward run was complimented by the writer on his achievement in the darkness, he replied quite simply, 'Oh! One gets used to anything. But we have to be careful.' And careful he certainly was.

Second of the impressions suggested by the night-ride was that on this particular evening there was a glaring inequality in the standard of illumination adopted by different districts. At one time it seemed that the further the bus went on its way, the brighter was the lighting. Then suddenly the conditions would be reversed, and the bus would penetrate into deeper and ever deeper gloom. There were important avenues of traffic which, under their disguise of darkness, looked like so many model 'galleries' of a model coal-mine. In these cases one gazed into a mysterious vista of dense darkness, whose length seemed to be picked out by tiny points of light that appeared to shed no radiance whatever, but to be intended to serve the purposes of guides rather than of illuminants. These lights appeared to be even scarcer than good deeds in a naughty world, to vary Portia's famous phrase.

Elsewhere, on the contrary, one encountered fairly long stretches of roadway, in which it was pretty evident that extremely little attention was being paid to even the earlier regulations of the authorities concerning lighting – places where brilliant lights, absolutely unshaded, were casting their rays defiantly into the roadway, and, in some cases, as far as the walls of the houses opposite. Granted that instances of gross carelessness of this kind were comparatively rare. Yet they were not so few as to be quite isolated, and one was puzzled to know how they were allowed to exist at all, and how no attempt had been made to dim these lights, so as to reduce them to the average illuminating power, so to speak, of their surroundings.

In the vast majority of cases, however, it was satisfactory to observe that shopkeepers had loyally tried to conform to the regulations by invoking the aid of awnings, and the like. Yet even here one could not but notice that many of them, despite their manifestly good intentions, had failed to adjust the angle of illumination so as to prevent beams of bright light from falling on the footway.

Generally speaking, roadways which ordinarily derive their illumination from electric lights depending from lofty standards were much more brightly lit than roadways that were served by gas lamps. Despite the employment of opaque encircling bands and the use on the lamps of obscuring material, these electric lamps seemed to shed on the road below much more light than was strictly necessary – much more light, certainly, than was cast by the lamps that were often adjacent to them. Again and again, in the course of the drive, one seemed to plunge from comparative light into dense darkness, or to emerge from darkness into light, which reveals a state of things absolutely at variance with the intention of the authorities.

It comes to this, then – and this bus drive proved it up to the hilt – that in the public interest there is real need for the fresh lighting regulations promulgated by the Home Secretary, the object of which is to secure uniformity, no less than restriction of illumination.

12 October 1915

WORK FOR TROOPS
Voluntary Aid

A year ago there were superior persons who scoffed somewhat at the shirt-making and the knitting that women were doing with whole-hearted zeal on behalf of the troops. Today it is these kindly workers, who, if spiteful enough to do so, could turn round with an air of triumph at the completeness of the victory they have won. For while loudly trumpeted projects of women managing Army Remount depots or running the London motor-omnibus service have faded into nothingness, the Army Council has found the needlecraft and the surgical supplies due to the skill and generosity of ladies so valuable that it is constituting a new department under the Director-General of Voluntary Organisations. This will be the central authority between the workers on the one hand and the clamant calls of the military hospitals for the extra comforts that a winter in the trenches will demand, and will deal probably with the very difficult problem of the clothing of British prisoners of war.

There are various points in the interesting circular letter that Colonel Sir Edward Ward, the Director, has just issued, that claim attention. One of these is the system it foreshadows of the establishment of local and city centres with depots. The collaboration of Lord-Lieutenants, Lord Mayors, Mayors, and Provosts is requested in this connection, and it is in regard to the small centres in the counties, the little towns and villages, that perhaps the first need exists for fuller information and expert guidance. Speaking broadly, there was last winter not a parish, scarcely a hamlet, up and down the land that was not doing something very praiseworthy, very self-denying, through its working party or guild.

The pity of it all, however, was that each of these small organisations was a law to itself. If it was thought that lined waistcoats or socks were the primary requirements at the front, these were made on the pattern that was considered most suitable. If the presiding genius was convinced that quilts or holdalls were the essentials of the moment, these were produced quite regardless as to whether other working parties were turning them out, and in the aggregate providing far more than were required. Under the new scheme there will be co-ordination of effort, and the guild or working party which has manifested special skill in supplying particular items can be invited to concentrate its efforts in that direction.

Every worker knows, of course, that there are four great organisations which have absorbed the greater part – though far from all – of women's voluntary labour. The War Office will regard Queen Mary's Needlework Guild as a separate organisation, and it is her Majesty's wish, which has, of course, been unreservedly accepted, that this recognition should be extended to the Surgical Supply Branch, with its depot at 2, Cavendish-square. Out of this latter has sprung a network of surgical supply branches all over the country, receiving the standardised patterns and general instructions from it; and the central committee that has been formed is to be recognised officially under the new department. The St John Ambulance Committee is also recognised as a source of supply for patterns of hospital wants.

The British Red Cross Society is on the eve of big developments in the direction of central work rooms. Invitations had, indeed, been issued for a private view of the arrangements for the London centre at Hyde Park Corner, but at the last moment plans were altered, and something on a yet greater scale will claim attention on Saturday next. The attitude of the new department towards these four organisations is best summed up in the words of the circular letter, which is careful to point out 'that it is hoped through the central office to supplement and extend the great work already accomplished by these societies in connection with hospital services. They have volunteered to co-operate with the central organisation in order to secure the best results with a minimum of expenditure both in money and labour, which is so essential in existing circumstances.'

'Official Recognition' carries with it very tangible advantages. It will be conferred through county or city associations, and those possessing it will be permitted to state the fact on their notepaper and printed slips. Opportunities will also be offered of purchasing materials at the lowest cost possible, and facilities of transport will also be accorded.

By thousands of women workers the privilege of wearing a badge will be welcomed. The British Red Cross Society estimates that last winter fully 100,000 women were engaged upon some form of useful handicraft for them alone, and the other societies were also supported by vast numbers. Badges will only be given to those who are regular workers and who are registered as such at a county or city association or local branch, and the same pains and penalties will attend their unlawful adoption as in the case of workers in other spheres of war labour. They will not be bestowed for less than three months' service.

Various details are now engaging the attention of Sir Edward Ward, and fuller information will be issued as time goes on. There are critics, of course, who fear that over centralisation may check the generous impulses of some women, but it has been found at the Surgical Supply depots that ladies welcome guidance, and take a greater interest in turning out good work when they know it is what is really needed. When a hospital sends out a requisition for 1,000, say, of night shirts, and 10,000 bandages, it will certainly make for expedition in response to be able to distribute a call for them over a number of working parties or branches. Negotiations are pending between the department and the Prisoners of War Help Committee, and it is probable that a big appeal may be made to women to supply warm clothing for these unfortunate men, who are often in sore need of good garments. Meantime those women who are working for individual regiments or corps in which they are personally interested need not suspend such endeavours, and, indeed, the Army Council hopes there will be no disturbance of such useful and kindly efforts. When these, however, are fulfilled, it is hoped that the workers will collaborate with their own local movement under the Director-General of Voluntary Organisations.

'NO TREATING'
Incidents in London

Though some grumbling was heard in London yesterday against the 'No Treating' Order, there was very little evidence of any serious attempts to evade it.

At the headquarters of the Licensed Victuallers' Central Protection Society of London it was stated that the chief difficulty, which relates to the definition of a 'meal', was not so grave as had been assumed in many quarters. Publicans, it was stated, would have to consider each case on its merits. Though it had been decided that bread and cheese did constitute a meal for one man, it did not necessarily follow that a biscuit and a piece of cheese would be a meal for anybody. A suggested solution of the problem was that the publican should consider whether what was ordered was sufficient for one of the real meals of the day of the person for whom it was intended.

Naturally, there was variation of practice in places of refreshment yesterday. A substantial meal had to be consumed in some cases before the customer was considered to be entitled to pay for the drinks consumed by his friend as well as himself. In other licensed places something more in the nature of a 'snack' seemed to be considered as a legal 'meal'. It was evident, however, that from their own official quarters licence-holders will be encouraged to keep well over the dividing line between a 'snack' and a 'meal'.

Though the solution of the problems relating to 'meals' was not a serious worry until luncheon-time, licence-holders and their assistants had minor troubles earlier in the day. Many customers considered that the occasion called for a display of humour. Sometimes their wit took the form of repaying trifling debts in a bar, the money which had just been handed over to the ostensible creditor being immediately offered in payment of drinks. To this worrying of barmen intent on strictly carrying out the law was added shuffling of coins on the counter whenever the attendants turned their backs.

One little advantage which the publicans can set against their diminished receipts is the freeing of their premises from the various types of loungers who are willing to aid in spending anybody's money but their own.

In many clubs the order enjoys a certain amount, at least, of popularity. One clubman stated that it would allow the slow drinker to come into his own. As he would never more be called upon to keep pace with the 'rounds', he would be free to 'develop his meritorious inclination to the utmost'.

In the City the 'no-treating' innovation was quietly received, but even one day's experience showed that on many public-houses and hotels situated in certain special areas the new order will have a serious effect. In the neighbourhood of St Paul's-churchyard, Wood-street, and adjacent thoroughfares, which constitute the centre of the soft goods trade, business of considerable magnitude is discussed and deals made in the cosy cubicle of a wine house. It is this class of the licensed trade that will probably suffer more than any other by the new regulation.

Mr T. J. Twamley, Hon. Secretary of the City of London Licensed Victuallers' and Restaurant Proprietors' Trade Protection Society, informed a representative of the *Daily Telegraph* that he had visited eighty licensed houses during the morning distributing the Government 'No Treating' bills, for pasting in the windows. In every area he found that the introduction of the new restriction was being quietly received. There was a good spirit prevailing throughout, and no suggestion of artful evasions of any description.

20 October 1915

LORD DERBY ON HIS NEW SCHEME
Classifying Recruits

In an important speech delivered at the Mansion House yesterday afternoon, the Earl of Derby, Director-General of Recruiting, explained the details of his comprehensive scheme for providing the men whom the military authorities consider necessary for maintaining the strength of our armies in the field and for bringing the war to a successful conclusion. The occasion was a conference, called by the Lord Mayor, of Mayors, Chairmen of Urban District Councils, and Parliamentary agents in the metropolitan area. Following are the principal points of Lord Derby's speech: 'I am perfectly certain the end will come right; but the end will come sooner and the end will be more satisfactory if every man in this country recognises that a portion of the Empire's duty rests upon his own shoulders.

'The secret of the success of the scheme is not to get an unmanageable number of recruits in the first instance, but to get so many that the country may look forward with confidence to being able to supply Lord Kitchener with what he wants, not only for immediate requirements, but for many months to come.

'It is proposed to divide the men into forty-six groups; the unmarried men being put into the first twenty-three groups according to ages, and the married men also into twenty-three groups, and beginning only when the unmarried groups are exhausted.

'These men will be called out in successive groups as required, a fortnight's notice being given to every man before he need actually join.

'On appeal, men in special circumstances may be called up in a later class than that to which they actually belong.

'Men thus allowed to go on leave will draw no military pay. They will be given the opportunity of voluntarily undertaking military drill.

'Although every endeavour will be made to allot them, when called up, to whatever unit in the service they wish to join, no pledge can be given that their request will be gratified, and they will have to be allotted to whatever branch is most in need of their services.

'If every man on whom the country has a right to call will join under these conditions it will, I hope, be very many months before the older married are called on. The war may even be decided without their being called upon.

'I have endeavoured to make the scheme as elastic as possible. We are not bound in any way by red-tape to our proposals.

'In the event of more men joining immediately than the military authorities can in the first instance house, clothe, and train, men will be allowed to go to their homes until they are called up, and will draw pay and allowances at the rate of 3s per diem. Such men can be called up on twenty-four hours' notice.

'Discretion is to be given to recruiting officers in regard to men who, though unstarred, are indispensable in their employments. A supplementary list of trades in which such exemptions may be held valid, is to be prepared.

'All men will be enlisted for general service, but only a limited number of men will be taken for branches other than the infantry of the line, although individual wishes will be respected as far as possible.

'Preference for the Army Service Corps and the Royal Army Medical Corps will be given to married men.'

6 January 1916

THE SOLDIER'S VIEW
Earl Kitchener on the Necessity for Change

Earl Kitchener made a brief but important statement in the House of Lords yesterday afternoon, in which he set forth his concurrence in the proposal for a new method of recruitment for the Army, and his reasons for arriving at that conclusion.

His lordship said: 'With your lordships' permission, I should like to add a few remarks from the military point of view to what has been said by my noble friend (the Marquis of Crewe). Seventeen months ago I stated to your lordships the broad principles of the military steps which I considered necessary to meet the emergency of the war. The scheme for augmenting our forces then set on foot was based on a definite plan to secure, in successive increases to our military strength, an army commensurate with our power and responsibilities, with the proper complement of reserves and reinforcements necessary to keep up its effective strength in the field during the war. Further, we had to produce for the Army thus created the guns, ammunition, and military material requisite to maintain its fighting value.

'This scheme had to be developed under the system of voluntary military service existing in the country, and I must say that this system has given us results far greater than most of us would have dared to predict, and certainly beyond anything that our enemies contemplated. In the early stages of the war men responded to the call in almost embarrassing thousands, and until a few months ago maintained, by a steady flow of recruits, the supply of men we required in as large numbers as we could train and equip.

'The cadres of the large Army we now possess having been formed, it is necessary to keep it up to strength in the field by a constant supply of reserves replenishing the wastage of war. Recently, however, the numbers of voluntary recruits have ceased to ensure the full provision of necessary trained reserves.

'Every effort was made by Lord Derby's canvass to repair this deficiency, and at the inception of the scheme the Prime Minister, on behalf of the Government, gave a pledge in the House of Commons regarding the military service of unmarried men. It is now necessary to redeem that pledge in order to maintain the voluntary principle as regards the service of married men in the future.

'So far we have been able to provide for the large increase of the Army and its maintenance on a purely voluntary system, and I, personally, had always hoped that we should be able to finish the war successfully without changing that system which has done so well, and which has given us such splendid material in the field as the soldiers now fighting in the different theatres of war.

'I do not consider that the change proposed should be regarded in the light of any derogation of the principle of voluntary service in this country.

'It only affects, during the period of the war, one class of men, amongst whom there are undoubtedly a certain number who have but a poor idea of their duties as citizens, and require some persuasion greater than appeal to bring them to the colours.

'Whilst there are in the class affected some such shirkers, there are no doubt many whose reasons for not joining will be found valid, and I am very far from wishing it to be thought that all those to whom the new proposals will apply can be described by the term I have used for some of them. Many of these men probably have conflicting calls upon them, and will be only too happy that the Government should resolve the doubts which they have been unable to decide for themselves.

'In making these remarks to your lordships, I speak only as a soldier, with a single eye to the successful conduct of the war.

'I feel sure everyone will agree when I say that the fullest and fairest trial has been given to the system which I found in existence, and of which I felt it my duty to make the best use.

'We are now asking Parliament to sanction a change, as it has been proved that, in the special circumstances of this utterly unprecedented struggle, the existing system without modification is not equal to maintaining the Army which is needed to secure victory.'

RAISING WAR FUNDS
State Lottery Suggested

In the House of Commons yesterday, Mr Hogge (R., Edinburgh, E.) asked the Chancellor of the Exchequer, whether he contemplated using any form of State lottery in order to raise further funds for the purposes of the war.

Mr McKenna: As my hon. friend is aware a Committee is now examining the whole question of war loans designed to attract the savings of the small investor. I should prefer not to anticipate in any way the recommendations of that committee except so far as they have already been made and acted upon.

Mr Hogge: Can the right hon. gentleman say whether the Committee has actually had before it or means to have before it any proposal for a State lottery?

Mr McKenna: I believe the suggestions as to a State lottery have been made, but I do not think any report on the subject is being issued.

Mr Hogge: Will the prizes be political or financial? (Laughter.)

Mr McKenna: I do not think the proposal has so far been accepted.

8 January 1916

YMCA WORK FOR MUNITION TOILERS

Below the Pool the grey, ochreous mists that had veiled the central streets of London began to thicken; beyond the flat, sordid levels of Plumstead Marsh the line of the river could scarcely be seen. A curious extension of London this always was, with its walled factories and myriads of straightly drilled little houses, each with a garden that blossomed never so smartly as with the strange lingerie of its occupants; with its unexpected cliffs of soft, yellow sandstone standing kneedeep in the squashy marshland; with its sudden centres of population cut into by ancient stone quays; and between them its long strung-out lines of houses beside the road; its occasional churches, and its general air of 'here today and gone tomorrow', from Greenwich to Gravesend. Today the life of Woolwich and its neighbourhood has been stirred to its depth without a greatly marked change externally. More factories heave up their glossy sides of pink brick, more sea-beaten tramps patched with red lead lie in the reaches, more trains grunt slowly up and down these tangled lines, and keep the passenger trains waiting with the sour delight of a long-postponed revenge. It is not necessary to explain more than that the life of Woolwich now beats faster and in many more hearts. The knowledge that the surrounding country had no greater accommodation than the normal working population of the Arsenal required – for no man or woman ever went to live in Woolwich by choice – was enough for the YMCA to break through yet another tradition and offer to look after the feeding of the new daily population. The offer, with the careful grudgingness that sits with less ungracefulness upon the War Office because nothing more is expected of it, was accepted. The YMCA flung its prejudices and limitations to the winds, got together a fair sum of money as a start, and at once plunged into as serious a responsibility as any indirect war employment could well entail, with a clear purpose and resourceful strength.

Comparison with the regime at Aldershot or purely military centres is impossible. In an article of a day or two ago I referred to the instant willingness of the YMCA to cast away any technical or conventional limitation of their work in the past as soon as a demand for a wider sphere of usefulness was made clear to it. Still, in the Aldershot area something at least of the old life remains, and though, like Luther, they have taken all the world as their parish, something of their routine before the war subsists. In the Woolwich district it would be difficult for an old habitué of the association to trace any connection at all. Yet it is all most logically within the proclaimed ambition of the body. The Red Triangle – signifying the equal union of body, mind, and soul – here and in twenty-four other centres is ministering fully and with entire competence to the body, of which to some extent it had hitherto relied upon external sources for the more material sustenance.

In Woolwich the association has taken up a new role. The huts, libraries, and reading-rooms – though they are to be found – have yielded precedence to the needs of the multitude of munition workers. Most of these come in from London or the neighbourhood. Few of the newcomers have lodging in or near Woolwich, and at once the practical necessity arose of finding proper meals for this sudden and regular crowd. The association never had a moment's uncertainty. At the Drill Hall in Beresford-street and at the building of the Baptist community opposite arrangements were at once made for the needs of the workers. At one o'clock and at midnight a plain but simple dinner, well cooked on the latest ranges and ovens, is provided, and the voluntary helpers act as organisers, waitresses, and scullery-maids.

There is something in this instant willingness of ladies to devote their time and labour to a charity which, however important, has not either a graceful or a grateful aspect at first sight. Yet there are more volunteers than can be received. The munition workers are working to the utmost. They have but little time for their meals, and for anything else they have none. For them good and properly prepared food is essential, and the neatness and attractiveness of the tables adds to the keenness with which men who have been working for hours in the shops wait for their turn at the YMCA halls. While they dine there is always someone to play or sing to them. At the end of their thirty or forty minutes they go back to their work or works with renewed strength and heart, while their places are taken by a second shift whose dinner hour has been arranged for a later period. All through the day men who need food can obtain it. There is another full dinner served at midnight for the evening gang, and at 3.30 in the morning the Khaki-clad Women's Volunteer Reserve will be there still to help the helpers in this hour of test and trial.

There is little or nothing attempted in the way of social entertainment or evangelisation. The needs of the hard-worked body are those which claim attention, and the Government are gradually entrusting to the YMCA the catering for the ever-increasing crowd of munition workers. The movement began with the appointment of Mr Lloyd George as Minister of Munitions, and it will scarcely end before every non-resident munition worker throughout England, whether at Woolwich, Sheffield, Liverpool, Barrow, Cardiff, or a score of other places, has come to rely upon the association for his sound and sufficient daily food. But along with this need there is a growing need for lodging, and the YMCA, with a generous elasticity for which no recognition can be too grateful, have agreed to administer the hostels of cubicles required by the workers. They have ever been ready to depart from their traditions – and, indeed, their very name – in providing accommodation for women workers in this respect. They have permitted the use of their 'hut' at Crayford not merely for a Christmas party given by the workers to the children of the place, but as a parish hall – with which Crayford is not at present provided.

Into the future it is not possible to pry. There is no time. The absolute and certain needs of the moment occupy all the care and labour that can be invited and organised. Day by day and hour by hour the work of helping the munitioners goes forward, and there is no shibboleth or denominationalism demanded of those for whom this willing service is offered save that which is symbolised by the workers' badge. It is for them, and through them for the country, that this gigantic work is being done. Both workers and helpers are learning much by their daily acquaintance; and when the war is over the new problems and the vastly widened responsibilities of the association will be faced in a different and a greater spirit. It is no small thing for a great institution to strip itself of denominational limitations, and place its huge resources at the disposal of a country in her time of need. It is a greater blessing still for it to have within itself the power of indefinite expansion – a power which of all others is probably the quality that Great Britain has needed and has shown during this war. She has shown it in a manner that silenced her detractors, discomfited her enemies, and encouraged those who dare believe in her worthiness to carry on the mission she has shouldered for a hundred years, and in it the YMCA must be given its share of recognition.

The fog deepened as we crept home through tunnels and cuttings. The rigging of the ships had vanished, and an occasional moan from a fog-horn took its place. The street-openings ended in brown mist, and London itself moved carefully through the atmosphere which, of all creations of man, she alone has in turn created. Yet through the darkness the sense of those thousands of men and women one had left behind one carefully and eternally attending to the moving lathe, or the grinding tool, the uncanny certain recurrence of the chuck, or carrier, the underslung va-et-vient of the eccentric, in radiant workshops all day and all night, week in and week out, remained permanent. The effort has been vast, and it has, thank God, been adequate. But in our gratitude for those who are directly working we must not forget those thousands, organised by the YMCA in an emergency, of whom with especial truth it may be said today that they also serve those who only stand and wait.

21 March 1916

PREMIUM BONDS
Government Decision

It was announced by the Chancellor of the Exchequer last week that the Government had decided not to issue premium bonds as a form of war loan, since the existing law does not allow of the issue of Government securities having an element of chance among the inducements to be held out to the investor. It might have been thought that this difficulty could be overcome by the passing of an enabling Act, or even by incorporating a provision in the Budget that would cover such a transaction as the issue of a loan offering, in addition to modest interest, a possibility of an additional prize to be awarded by a periodical drawing. On the face of it there could be no objection in principle, it has been urged, since premium bonds have been a feature of more than one kind of local loan stock issued from time to time in France and Germany, so that the question of legality or regularity of such an issue might have been disposed of by an Act of the Legislature, in one form or another.

Other causes, therefore, must be sought for, and we believe they will be found in quite another direction. The idea of premium bonds, it is understood, was not received with hostility by the Government, and it was not discarded without very full and anxious consideration of the suggestion in all its bearings. It was a most tempting expedient for inducing the artisan in the receipt of wages he had never before realised to invest some of his excess earnings in a form that would be both secure and attractive, and the matter was carefully thought out and full inquiries were made before the proposal was turned down.

It is not certain how far afield the Government directed their inquiries, but the result of them, apparently, was to induce the conviction in the minds of Ministers that the issue of premium bonds would be regarded with extreme disfavour by a large part of the community: that there was, in fact, a strong prejudice against the introduction of the element of chance into such a serious business as the raising of a great loan for war purposes. How far this hostility to the element of chance is well-founded could only be proved by experiment, but this experiment the Government could not be brought to undertake. On the question whether the issue of bonds in this form was worthwhile, the Government came to the conclusion that the amount that might be raised from the working-class investor was an exceedingly doubtful quantity.

In accepting the evidence afforded by these inquiries, we are informed, the Government were influenced by the fact that, as it seemed to them, the issue of premium bonds by foreign countries was not of such a character as to form a suitable precedent. They could not find that such issues had been undertaken for the purposes of a State loan, the examples coming chiefly from south Germany and the French cities, where the issues of premium bonds were purely municipal. The Chancellor of the Exchequer has been criticised for having stated that foreign Governments have not resorted to the issue of premium bonds in order to raise war loans, and the example of Germany has been quoted against him, in the issue of bonds at a discount and determinable at varying dates according to the results of periodical drawings. The reply to these criticisms is that these are not premium bonds at all, but are part of a general issue, the average interest of which is calculated on a basis that differs very little from the latest irredeemable 5 per cent loan which is being offered to the German investor at the same time.

It is credible that an important factor in deciding the Government to shelve the proposal to issue premium bonds – apart from the technical reason described by the Chancellor of the Exchequer – was one of expediency. There is reason to believe that the view was arrived at that, even if such an issue were approved in this country, it was by no means certain that high financial opinion in neutral countries would endorse such a departure from the traditions of the British

Treasury. This consideration was regarded as of immense importance in the present juncture. British credit was never in a stronger relative position than it is at this moment, and the utmost care is being observed that no step shall be taken that would do even a passing injury to this precious national asset. It is understood that this all-sufficient motive overrode all other considerations; and jealousy for the credit of the country would have operated to prevent the adoption of a premium bond issue, even if the law had permitted it.

There is one form of loan issue that may be entertained by the Treasury, and one that forms a closer parallel to the latest German Treasury bond issue, and that is to offer the stock at a considerable discount, the principal to be repaid at a fixed period at par. There is no gamble in this, as the interest would be calculated on a basis that would bring the average yield within the limits of previous Treasury bond issues; but the prospect of getting an immediate margin added to the amount of his investment may tempt many a hitherto unwilling investor. This seems to be the nearest approach to a premium bond that the Government has in contemplation.

18 August 1916

MR LLOYD GEORGE ON SONG IN WARTIME
Britain's Blinds Not Down

Mr Lloyd George was present yesterday afternoon at the Welsh National Eisteddfod, which is being held at Aberystwyth, and, in the course of an eloquent address, defended the holding of the festival during the war.

The Secretary of State for War was accompanied by Mrs Lloyd George, and there were at the assembly a considerable number of Welsh members of Parliament and many other prominent people of the Principality. The large marquee in which the singing, playing, and other competitions take place was thronged when Mr Lloyd George presided at the ceremony of the chairing of the bard. On reaching the platform he was cheered with the greatest enthusiasm, and the audience, which numbered roughly about 7,000, rose and sang 'For He's a Jolly Good Fellow'.

Why, asked Mr Lloyd George, should they not sing during the war? The blinds of Britain were not down yet, nor were they likely to be. The honour of Britain was not dead. Her might was not broken. Her destiny was not fulfilled. Her ideals were not shattered by her enemies. She was greater than she ever was.

Mr Lloyd George remained at the festival for some time after making his speech. He then left, along with Mrs Lloyd George, amidst scenes of tremendous enthusiasm. As the right hon. gentleman drove through Aberystwyth he was greeted everywhere with vociferous cheers. He visited a military hospital, and then left the town. Today he again attends a gathering of the National Festival at Aberystwyth.

Mr Lloyd George, who was received with great cheering when he rose to speak, said: 'I have come here at some inconvenience to attend, and, if necessary, to defend, this Eisteddfod. I have been a strong advocate of its being held. (Hear, hear.) I was anxious there should be no interruption on account of the war in the continuity of the Welsh National Eisteddfod.

'There are a few people who know nothing about the Eisteddfod, who treat it as if it were merely an annual jollification which eccentric people indulge in. (Laughter.) There was a letter appearing in *The Times* this week, written by a person who seems to hold that opinion. He signs himself "A Welshman". He evidently thinks that the publication of his name would add nothing to the weight of his appeal, so he has – wisely, no doubt – withheld it (Hear, hear.)

'His notion of the Eisteddfod is a peculiar one, and as there might be a few people outside Wales who hold the same views, I think I must refer to this estimate of its purport and significance. He places it in the same category as a football match or horse race, and a good deal beneath a cinema or music-hall performance. The bards are to him so many racehorses – (laughter) – started round the course by Mr L. D. Jones, the chairing day being, I suppose, the bardic Oaks. (Laughter.) Sir Vincent Evans would be the grand bookmaker who arranges the stakes, and, of course, we all have something, on one or other of the starters. (More laughter.) The meetings of the Cymmrodorion, the Gorsedd of the bards, the Arts section, the Folk Song Society, the Union of the Welsh Societies, and the Bibliographical Society are the side-shows which amuse the Eisteddfodic larrikin whilst the race is not on. (Cheers and laughter.) That is where the thimble rigging and the cocoanut shies and games of the sort are carried on.

'No wonder this intelligent gentleman is ashamed to show his name. I challenge him to give it. It will be useful as a warning to readers of English papers of the class which anonymously insults Welsh institutions. (Hear, hear.) Let any man look through this programme and see for himself what the Eisteddfod means – prizes for odes, sonnets, translations from Latin and Greek, literature, essays on subjects philosophical, historical, sociological. Art is encouraged, even agriculture is not forgotten. Forsooth, all this effort should be dropped on account of the war.

'To encourage idle persons to compose poetry during war is unpatriotic; promoting culture amongst the people – a futile endeavour at all times – during the war is something every Welsh member of Parliament ought to snub. To give a prize for a study of the social and industrial conditions of a Welsh village is dangerous at any time, and during a war it is specially so. To excite the interests of the people in literature during the war is a criminal waste of public money. Above all, to sing during a war, and especially to sing national songs during a war, is positively indecent, and the powers of the Defence of the Realm Act ought at once to be invoked to suppress it. (Laughter.) "Hush! no music please. There is a war on."

'Why should we not sing during war? Why, especially, should we not sing at this stage of the war? The blinds of Britain are not down yet, nor are they likely to be. (Loud cheers.) The honour of Britain is not dead. Her might is not broken. Her destiny is not fulfilled. Her ideals are not shattered by her enemies. She is more than alive. She is more potent, she is greater than she ever was. Her dominions are wider, her influence is deeper, her purpose is more exalted than ever. (Cheers.) Why should her children not sing?

'I know war means suffering. War means sorrow. Darkness has fallen on many a devoted household. But it has been ordained that the best singer amongst the birds of Britain should give its song in the night, and, according to legend, that sweet song is a song of triumph over pain. There are no nightingales this side of the Severn. Providence rarely wastes its gifts. We do not need this exquisite songster in Wales. We can provide better. There is a bird in our villages which can beat the best of them. He is called Y Cymro. He sings in joy. He sings also in sorrow. He sings in prosperity. He sings also in adversity. He sings at play. He sings at work. He sings in the sunshine. He sings in the storm. He sings in peace. Why should he not sing in war? He sings in the daytime. He sings also in the night. Hundreds of wars have swept over these hills, but the harp of Wales has never yet been silenced by one of them, and I should be proud if I contributed something to keep it in tune during the war by the holding of the Eisteddfod today. (Cheers.)

'Our soldiers sing the songs of Wales in the trenches, and they hold the little Eisteddfod behind them. Here is a telegram which has been received by the secretary of the Eisteddfod from them. The telegram says: "Greetings and best wishes for success to the Eisteddfod and Cymanfa Ganu from Welshmen in the field. (Cheers.) Next Eisteddfod we shall be with you." (Renewed cheers.) Please God, they will,' remarked Mr Lloyd George amidst further cheers. 'That telegram is from the 38th Welsh Division. They do not ask us to stop singing. (Cheers.)

'But I have another and even more urgent reason why this Eisteddfod should be kept alive during the war.

'When this terrible conflict is over a wave of materialism will sweep over the land. Nothing will count but machinery and output.

'Well, I am all for output, and I have done my best to improve machinery and increase output. (Hear, hear.) But that is not all.

'We shall need at the end of the war better workshops, but we shall also need more than ever every institution. It will exalt the vision of the people above and beyond the workshop and the counting-house. We shall need every national tradition that will remind them that men cannot live by bread alone. (Cheers.)

'I make no apology for advocating the holding of this Eisteddfod in the middle of this great conflict.

'The storm is raging as fiercely as ever, hut now there is a shimmer of sunshine over the waves. There is a rainbow on the tumult of the surging waters. The struggle is more terrible than it has ever been, but the legions of the oppressor are being driven back, and the banner of right is pressing forward. (Cheers.)

'Why should we not sing? It is true there are thousands of gallant men falling in the fight; but let us sing of their heroism. (Cheers.) There are myriads more standing in the battle-line facing the foe, and myriads more behind ready to support them when their turn comes. Let us sing to the land that gave birth to so many heroes. (Cheers.)

'I am glad that I came down from the cares and labour of the War Office of the British Empire to listen to and to join with you in singing the old songs which our brave countrymen on the battlefield are singing as a defiance to the enemies of human right.' (Loud and long-continued cheering.)

It was then announced that the following reply had been forwarded to the soldiers of the 38th Welsh Division who had sent the message read by the Secretary of State for War: 'The National Eisteddfod, assembled at Aberystwyth, and presided over by Mr Lloyd George, much touched by the hearty greetings from Welsh soldiers in the field, wishes them a safe and speedy return, and promises them a great welcome when the time comes. Welsh soldiers will be glad to know Aberystwyth Eisteddfod is a great success.'

NEW LIMBS FOR MAIMED HEROES
Visit to Roehampton

At Queen Mary's Convalescent Auxiliary Hospitals at Roehampton, where our soldiers and sailors who have lost their limbs in the war are refitted, they challenge the visitor to guess which of a man's two legs is artificial, and duly disclose to him that both are. Youth can adapt itself to almost anything, and most of our wounded fighting men are very young. 'I have been on the top of a motor-bus already, and I have only had this leg four days,' exclaimed an eager lad, slapping the imitative mechanism, which it had been necessary to attach to his body at the abdomen, as not even a stump of his old limb had been left. He walked well with the aid of a stick, and soon he will be able to walk without any stick at all. Another cycled a few hundred yards to show – as he did – that the action of the mechanical joints is indistinguishable from that of the joints which Nature gives. A third ran across a lawn with considerable speed, though he had but one of his own legs, and the spectator could not tell at a glance which of them it was that he had lost. A young soldier who has had both his arms amputated above the elbows writes with either of the hands with which he has been fitted, and for the satisfaction of his visitors will lift a match from the floor with his artificial fingers. They will shake hands with you with their imitation hands, and you are surprised at the grip they can give.

These results are in a great measure due to practice, and the proper exercises are enforced with the rigidity of military drill – happily for the maimed soldiers, for man is so indolent by nature that they would never acquire perfection in the use of their mechanical limbs if they were not compelled to make the daily and hourly effort. But even more is due to the amazing skill with which the limbs themselves are made. At Roehampton there are a number of workshops for the manufacture of arms and legs, and each workshop is the enterprise of a separate firm, so that the hospitals have the benefit of competitive ingenuity and workmanship – British, French and American. Most of them employ men who themselves have lost a leg or an arm, and these men have made many valuable suggestions or invented devices for the further perfection of artificial limbs. One of them, for example, has designed a hand which will enable a one-armed man to play golf or cricket. Ball bearings give the joints their swivel action, and springs and rubber are used to reproduce the resilience of nature. The limb-maker does not discriminate between officers and men, but officers pay to have an extra coat or two of flesh-coloured paint added to the American red willow and calf-skin. If a patient has but a shoulder joint or hip joint left the mechanic, with the economy of art, will utilise it in the operation of the false limb, which will be bent or propelled by some little acquired shrug or twist of the surviving natural joint. One unfortunate officer at Roehampton had to have both his arms amputated so completely that there was no stump left in either case, and it was impracticable to fit him with a mechanical arm. The ingenious surgeons, however, created a stump on one of the shoulders by gathering up and twisting a piece of skin from his side and incorporating in it a piece of tibia from his leg, and upon this contrived stump an artificial arm has been fixed.

Roehampton is not content with giving the maimed soldiers and sailors arms and legs; it also fits them to earn their own livelihood under their new conditions. In well-equipped workshops it gives instruction in light leather work, office routine, electricity, motor-car repairing and driving, hair dressing, tailoring, chemistry, designing, and many other occupations. Over fifty qualified chauffeurs have been turned out by the hospital employment bureau, and over 600 other maimed soldiers have been found employment through the same agency. Employment has been found for men who have lost an arm in the following capacities: Commissionaire, gateman, gymnasium instructor, labour master in workhouse, liftman, lodge-keeper, messenger, porter, railway work (sundry duties), telephone switchboard attendant, timekeeper, traveller, ward master, watchman, weighman. Men who have lost a leg have been procured the following kinds of work: bootmaking, motor driving, domestic service, electrical work, engineering, light duties at pithead (for miners), munition work, milking, printing telegraphy.

The country owes a debt of gratitude to a great many people associated with Roehampton, and not least to those who have made this employment bureau their special care, and to the heads of firms who have themselves in many cases come to instruct the all too eager learners. The abounding cheerfulness and optimism which one finds here prove that the men are fully conscious and appreciative of the efforts which are being made to assure them of happy and useful careers in spite of the disadvantages with which they must restart life.

23 October 1916

VOLUNTEER CORPS AND HOME DEFENCE
Lord French's Tour

A flying tour through three far-stretching counties undertaken yesterday by Viscount French enabled the gallant Field-Marshal, as Commander-in-Chief of the Home Forces, to inspect some 13,000 Volunteers in the Eastern Command. Naturally it was a strenuous day, but, thanks to the facilities for travel afforded by a special train, and the occasional employment of motor-cars, a programme embracing a wide area of country was carried out with admirable thoroughness. Lord French has on various occasions – in fact, whenever opportunity has served – made known the great importance he attaches to the movement, and Volunteers welcome with real enthusiasm the knowledge that he is devoting a series of Sundays to the task of inspecting many of the excellent regiments which, in all parts of the country, constitute such a striking proof of the patriotism of our race.

Now that the days of neglect are over, and the Volunteers deservedly enjoy an official status, a spirit of added keenness has entered into the corps. Anyone who saw the men of Essex, Suffolk, and Norfolk parade before Lord French yesterday must have been profoundly impressed by the earnestness with which they performed their part in the proceedings. Whether in the suburbs of London or amid the pleasant surroundings of the Norfolk countryside, they showed that one desire only animated them – to do credit to the training they have voluntarily entered upon, and favourably to impress the distinguished soldier who viewed their ranks with critical, though friendly, eyes. Not a trace of carelessness could be detected in their bearing. They have a definite place now among the defensive forces of the country, and the soldier-like discipline displayed was evidence enough of the seriousness with which they regard the obligations they have so unselfishly assumed.

How important that place is was revealed in the words Lord French addressed to the various corps. In the course of the day the Field-Marshal, who on such occasions appears to scorn the idea of fatigue, travelled some 250 miles, covered quite a respectable number of miles on foot while inspecting the ranks of the Volunteers, and, in addition, delivered four speeches – a programme which might well have daunted a man not possessed of his untiring energy. His speeches – they were the speeches of a soldier, in that they were brief, vigorous, and very much to the point – should do much to clear away any lingering doubts as to the intention of the military authorities to utilise to the fullest possible extent the services of the Volunteers. 'The War Office,' he declared, 'regards the Volunteers as a most necessary element in the scheme of national defence.'

Lord French stated that the meeting in London last week at which the Under-Secretary for War met the leaders of the Volunteer Corps had laid the foundation for thoroughly good understanding between the Government and the Volunteers.

On the subject of arms and equipment – those great desiderata of the Volunteers – he made the definite statement that the Government was prepared to furnish the corps with all they require. There is a condition, of course, and it is that members of the force shall undertake to serve for the period of the war. That such a guarantee will be readily given by the vast majority, if not the whole, of the men who have enrolled themselves need not be doubted for a moment.

Recruiting should receive a rare fillip in all three counties after a day like yesterday. And it should be realised that there is still room in the ranks for men who are prepared to imitate the patriotic example already set by so many thousands of their fellow-countrymen.

Lord French, who was accompanied by two members of his staff, made an early departure from Liverpool-street Station. Amongst those who also travelled by the special train were Lieutenant-Colonel H. W. Thornton (general manager, Great Eastern Railway), Mr W. O. May (chief traffic manager), and Major H. Wilmer (chief engineer).

On the platform Lord French inspected a guard of honour provided by the Royal Defence Corps, and conversed with some of the beribboned veterans who have donned uniform again in the time of their country's need. The duties undertaken by the corps include the provision of permanent guards for viaducts, bridges, and other structures. There is nothing showy about their work, which may even be suspected of being not a little tedious; but these men – many of whom threw up good situations when war broke out in order to 'do their bit' – carry out their duties as if it was the pleasantest occupation in the world to remain attached to one post, perhaps a lonely one at that, year in and year out. The Royal Defence Corps then is doing good work and doing it with a cheerfulness which laughs at monotony.

Amongst the duties which would fall to the Volunteers in an emergency would be the protecting of lines of communication, and as part of their training they receive instruction in the system of patrolling railways. A portion of the route traversed by Lord French yesterday was guarded by Volunteers, and the 'rehearsal' supplied yet another proof that any duties tackled by the Volunteers are performed with a conscientiousness which merits the warmest approval.

The first break in the journey after leaving Liverpool-street came quickly. Lord French alighted at Stratford Station and proceeded to West Ham Public Park, where he inspected three battalions of the Essex Volunteer Regiment, commanded by Colonel R. Beale Colvin. The battalions were the 1st (West Ham), the 3rd (Leyton), and the 5th (Snaresbrook). In their ranks they have great numbers of men of admirable physique, and their soldier-like appearance on parade impressed most favourably the many thousands of spectators, who, despite the early hour, had assembled in the park. After inspecting the ranks, Lord French addressed the officers, and expressed the satisfaction he felt at seeing such a fine body of men.

I want the officers (he continued) to realise the fact – which I have no doubt they do – that not only are they the leaders and instructors, but that they must also endeavour to bring their men up to the highest morale by guiding their thought, by instilling the best ideas into them, and by correcting any misapprehensions which exist in their minds. The fact that such a fine body of men are assembled together, drawn from all classes of the population, and amongst whom there is evidently a vast amount of superior and cultured intelligence, seems to me to speak volumes for the innate military strength of the country to which we belong. This is especially the case when we remember that for two years we have been engaged in a devastating war, the greatest the world has ever seen, and when we remember also the great strain that has been put on the manhood of this country.

I referred just now to the necessity you are under of keeping your men's ideas correct on all points. There are two points about which many of them have a misapprehension. In fact, a wrong idea on these two points seems to have permeated the whole Volunteer Force, though I think it is getting better now. One is that you are not wanted. Do drive that idea out of the minds of your men once and for all. I can assure you that it is not the case. His Majesty the King values and appreciates his Volunteer Force quite as much as any other, and the War Office and the Government want their services. You can take that from me.

Misapprehension also exists with regard to the supply of arms, uniforms, and equipment generally. You know, of course, what a tremendous strain has been put upon the resources of the Empire to find arms and ammunition in a war such as this. War has become quite a different thing from what any of us anticipated. No country which is fighting now ever thought – Germany never thought – that war would have developed as it has done, with long lines of the heaviest artillery facing each other close to the trenches on either side. Imagine what a frightful strain that is on every country, and how great are the losses it entails. Things are better now than they were. Ammunition, equipment, and everything else that is necessary is forthcoming in greater abundance, and I think it is possible now to provide the Volunteers with nearly all they require.

Then you must explain other things to your men. You know perfectly well that any man in your ranks can leave within fourteen days. I am quite sure if you were to ask any man in the ranks today whether he contemplated doing that he would indignantly repudiate the suggestion. He would say that whatever stress was put upon him he meant to serve till the end of the war. But you must remember war is a very hard school indeed. It is difficult to fathom the depths of any man's patriotism until he has been tried in the fire of that iron discipline without which no armed body can hope for success, or, indeed, exist as an armed body at all. We are all human. Some are stronger than others. Some will give way under the stress and strain where others will not. It is reasonable to expect that under the strain of war there are men who would avail themselves of the opportunity of which I have spoken.

On the other hand you have a Government who are spending enormous sums of money, and they are bound to expend it with the utmost economy, considering the financial strain on the Empire. Therefore before they spend money on arms and ammunition they must be quite sure that they are going to get a quid pro quo from the Volunteers in the shape of a distinct understanding that they will undertake service till the end of the war. I am quite sure that if this is put properly to your men they will see it in the right light, and I ask you to prepare them for it. We had a most satisfactory meeting in London last week with the heads of the Volunteers – the Lords-Lieutenant of counties and the county commandants. The Under-Secretary for War, Lord Derby, placed the situation carefully before them. The proceedings were private, but I can tell you that they were very satisfactory, and in time you will hear something. In the meantime, prepare your men for what must be done if they are to be furnished with what they require for war, and endeavour to get them to see everything in the right light. I am quite sure they will do so.

In conclusion Lord French said he was quite sure that if and when the Volunteers were called upon they would give the very best account of themselves, and keep up the splendid record their predecessors had left them.

The next halt was at Chelmsford, where Lord French inspected the 2nd (Ongar) and 4th (Prittlewell) battalions of the Essex Regiment. The Lord Lieutenant of the county, Colonel the Earl of Warwick, and the Deputy-Lieutenant, Mr Edward North Buxton, were amongst the numerous spectators of the proceedings. In all there were on parade at West Ham and Chelmsford 181 officers and 4,912 other ranks – a total which speaks well for the patriotism of the men of Essex. The strength of the Volunteer Motor Transport section in the county was also well displayed, at both West Ham and Chelmsford.

Earl Cadogan, County Commandant of the Suffolk Volunteer Regiment, joined the special train at Colchester and accompanied Lord French to Ipswich, where the Volunteers of the county were inspected in Gippeswyk Public Park. With a parade strength of 186 officers and 4,938 other ranks the regiment made an excellent display. Here, as indeed at all the inspections, the public showed great interest in the spectacle, and Lord French was warmly cheered. After spending nearly an hour with the regiment he addressed the officers.

If he had not seen it himself, (he said) he would never have believed that after all the strain that had been put on the manhood of the country such a residue of strength and power would still remain. It was due very largely to the splendid patriotism shown everywhere by the Volunteers and their leaders. He urged the officers above all to raise the morale of their men by impressing on them the duties they were called upon to perform. They should remind them of the terrible cost in men which modern war entailed, and of the necessity of constantly sending reinforcements to the front. The defence of their native shore was a very great role, and it was well that should be impressed upon the Volunteers.

The final event of the day was the inspection at Crown Point Hall, Trowse, the Residence of Mr Russell Colman, of the six battalions comprising the Norfolk Regiment, which were under the command of the Earl of Leicester, the county commandant. The units had come from as far afield as King's Lynn and other distant parts of a county whose battalions are manned – as might be expected in an agricultural area – by men of stalwart appearance. The strength on parade was 107 officers and 2,888 other ranks.

In his address to the regiment Lord French said: 'You are now the sole representatives of that wonderful organisation, the British Volunteers, which, after sixty years' existence has become great and historic. The same patriotism and love of country which has induced you to come forward yourselves has made the Volunteers what they have become. In the sixties and seventies they had to struggle against adversity of all kinds – against want of official recognition and every kind of drawback. But their splendid leaders of those days carried them through, and in the first Egyptian War they were represented in the field. Afterwards, in South Africa, they furnished very valuable contingents. In the present war they have covered themselves with glory, and their deeds will fill some of the most brilliant pages of military history. Whenever any sacrifice is demanded of you remember that you represent that great organisation, and cast your eyes over the Channel to France, to India, to Mesopotamia, to the Dardanelles – in fact, to all those blood-stained fields where they have gained that glory.'

After referring to the willingness of the Government to provide arms and equipment for the Volunteers, on condition that they serve till the end of the war, Lord French remarked, 'Invasion is no impossibility. Do not imagine that it is. It may not be probable, but it is perfectly possible; sad it is what we do not expect that always happens in war.'

'FLIGHTY' LONDON GIRLS
Failure as Farm Workers

The Wiltshire War Agricultural Committee have decided to close down the training school for girl farm workers at Shaw for the present, the results having been wholly disappointing. Mr Stratton, at a meeting of the committee, said very few pupils stuck to the work. Women could be taught to drive milk carts or horses quite easily, but the monotony of actual milking became dreadful. London girls could not stand it. When these girls came from London to the country, he observed, their imagination was of lovely green fields, shady trees, and, in the near future, a colonial farm life with their soldier correspondent. But it all ended when they got to the actual life of the farm, with its mud, filth, and clouds.

Mr Rogers, the Board of Agriculture representative, said that most of the girls were of a 'flighty' disposition. Country girls turned out well, but town girls had not been able to face the loneliness and monotony of country life.

Miss Oliver declared that London girls were their best pupils at the training school, but they did not like the work when they went on to the farms.

ONLY MODERATELY SUCCESSFUL
Bristol, Sunday

In spite of the efforts of the Duchess of Beaufort, Lady Strachey, Lady Sybil Codrington, and others in Gloucestershire and Somersetshire, schemes to induce women to work on the land have only been moderately successful. Town girls from Bristol have not been available, because they have found remunerative employment in munition works, banks, and commercial offices. Two difficulties have militated against the schemes – poor wages offered compared with other employment available and the general belief that women cannot do men's work on farms. Some women successfully essayed haymaking, hoeing, fruit-picking, and other light duties, but fought shy of milking cows, driving horses, and other heavy work, especially in bad weather. At the same time it must be admitted that in many places farmers and labourers' daughters and some others have done excellent work in practically all departments of farming, but so far as other women are concerned experiments have been more or less disappointing.

28 November 1916

MUNITIONS MIRACLES
The Town on the Bog

By Sir Arthur Conan Doyle

One of the miracles of present-day Britain is a place which we will call Moorside. Perhaps it is the most remarkable place in the world. Only a little more than a year ago, say, September, 1915, it was a lonely peat bog fringing the sea, with a hinterland of desolate plain, over which the gulls swooped and screamed. Then the great hand of the Minister of Munitions was stretched out to this lonely and inhospitable waste, for it chanced to lie with good rail and water connections, and not too far from centres of coal and of iron. No money and no energy was spared, and half a dozen master hustlers took charge of the whole great scheme. It is a story which is more characteristic of Western America than of our sober British methods. The work went forward by day and by night. The place grew and grew, and still is growing. Already it measures nine good miles one way, with an average of one and a half the other. In the daytime there are at least 25,000 busy inhabitants. The greater part are the builders, who still extend the township. The smaller are the munition workers, who will occupy it all when it is finished. But even now, in its partially finished state, its products are essential to the war, and its output has entirely changed all the supply of the present and the expectations of the future. It is not yet fully manned – or should I say girled? – but when it is not less than 12,000 munition workers will be running the miles of factories which overlie the peat bog of last summer.

And it is not jerry-built – that is the wonder of it. In the centre of the colony is a considerable nucleus of solid brick houses, which should be good for a century or more. Here are the main offices, the telephone stations, the club for the staff (club sprinters would describe the inmates better than club loungers in these strenuous parts), the hospital, the cinema theatre, a row of shops, and a cluster of residential houses. Radiating out from this centre are long lines of wooden erections to hold the workers, cottages for married couples, bungalows for groups of girls, and hostels which hold as many as seventy in each. This central settlement is where the people live – north and south of it where they work. The one end may be called the raw material end, for all raw material needed is manufactured upon the spot. Here is a huge nitric acid plant. There further to the right is an even larger sulphuric acid installation. Some one – he must have been a chemist, and probably a German – has said that the civilisation of a nation can be measured by the amount of sulphuric acid which they use. Greece or Rome would come badly out of such a test, and I fear that for 'civilisation' 'prosperity', which may be its exact opposite, is to be read. But this place, the town on the peat bog, has, as a fact, about doubled the British output of this basic substance. Hard by are the wide buildings where the raw cotton is stored, where the crude glycerine is refined, where the ether and alcohol are distilled, and where finally the perfect gun cotton is completed.

Thence by little trams it is conveyed over yonder to that rising ground, which is called Nitro-Glycerine Hill. You probably don't know it – certainly I did not – but glycerine cannot be pumped, and so to move it along the good old primitive force of gravity is summoned. Hence the Nitro-Glycerine Hill. There the nitro-glycerine on the one side and the gun cotton on the other are kneaded together into a sort of devil's porridge, which is the next stage of manufacture. This, by the way, is where the danger comes in. The least generation of heat may cause an explosion. Those smiling khaki-clad girls, who are swirling the stuff round in their hands, would be blown to atoms in an instant if certain very small changes occurred. The changes will not occur, and the girls will still smile and stir their devil's porridge, but it is a narrow margin here between life and death. It is only constant order and care which keep the frontier intact. Look at these great leaden basins and pipes in which the stuff is handled. How is the leaden basin joined to the leaden pipe? Here is one of those queer little romances with which the history of industry abounds. Solder is impossible. The acids would dissolve it. Lead must be welded to lead. It is a rare and difficult trade, one that is handed down from father to son, and held close in a narrow circle. A lead-burner is a man of power, a man to be approached with offerings and prayers when a job is to be done. His rarity and his exclusiveness were one of the difficulties which had to be met. He had to be induced to part with his mystery, and teach it to others. But he proved to be a patriot like his fellows. Anyhow, the thing was done, as these great leaden tanks with their welded pipes will show. The lead must be as smooth as silk, too, upon the inner side. You are dealing with touchy, ill-tempered stuff. The least friction, and you will know it – you or your executors.

When I saw these enormous works and the evidences of lavish expenditure I ventured to ask those in authority how the State was to get its money back when, in the dim and distant future, the new world would become ruined and disorganised by the war coming to an end. Was that old patient peat bog waiting so silently below to finally engulf the millions of the tax-payer? The reply was reassuring. All that I had seen up to that point was a good asset and of permanent value. It was all concerned with stuff which the arts of peace could readily absorb. But now we went to the further end, where this devil's porridge, which we have traced, is finally seasoned into the fit food for our hungry guns. How hungry those guns are our minds can hardly conceive. We can never beat Hindenburg until we have beaten Krupp, and that is what these laughing khaki girls of Moorside and elsewhere are going to do. Hats off to the women of Britain! Even all the exertions of the militants shall not in the future prevent me from being an advocate for their vote, for those who have helped to save the State should be allowed to help to guide it. To the further end did we go then, passing great power houses and central controls upon the way (please don't forget as you read, the year-old peat bog quivering underneath), and there we saw pressing and kneading and stuff like brown sugar being squeezed into brown macaroni, and finally dried into black liquorice sticks, which are cut up and blended so as to get a standard strength. Here supervision is needed for a quaint cause. Girls nave been known out of love for Tommy to put an extra pinch in the brew, with the result of course of entirely upsetting its ballistic qualities. We take it for granted that a gunner shooting at three miles can speedily range off a mere slit in the ground. I saw with my own eyes a house at 6,000 yards lifted off the face of the earth at the fourth round. When you see the girls blending the stuff, with the finest care, to get the absolute standard, you begin to understand what lies behind it.

So much for the actual manufacture. I have said nothing of a military guard of over 1,000 men, factory police, workmanlike women police, central bakeries, with 400 dozen loaves at a baking, central laundries, central kitchens with 8,000 rations going out at every meal, cashiers who pay away £800 an hour in wages. And all this with the primeval ooze lying in stagnant pools around, the remains of the wilderness of September twelve months. Have I made out a case for my assertion that Moorside is one of the wonder spots of the earth, as showing what man's brains and man's energy can effect? It is but one out of nearly forty which are working on similar tasks, but it is the newest, the largest, and the most remarkable. And who did all this? The soldier gets his mention, why not these picked generals of industry behind the lines? Those in authority we know; to them be all credit.

But what about the men on the spot, the men who dug into the peat bog, who sank the foundations, who raised the town, who ran the works, who organised the plant, which in one item alone, that of ether, produces more in a month than all pre-war Britain in a year. Alas that their names may not be mentioned. They come from all parts of the British Empire, but especially from overseas. The magic builder who guides the army of 15,000 workers is Mr P., an Englishman. Beside him are a little band of enthusiasts upon explosives, drawn from all ends of the Empire. At one meeting at Nitro-Glycerine Hill it chanced that every man present was a South African. There is 'Q.', an American by nationality, a South African in experience, a man with a drive like a steam piston. There is 'G.', also of South Africa; there is 'B.', of India; there is 'L.', of Australia; and there is Major

C. on the military and Mr H. on the financial side. These are some of the miracle workers of Moorside.

There are two hampering difficulties which will no doubt be overcome like all else, but which have held matters back. They are drink and labour. As to the latter, the labour unions have acted in a way which calls for the acknowledgment and gratitude of the nation. What they had won during a long and weary fight they renounced for the sake of their country. It is among the great sacrifices of the war, and full faith should be kept with them afterwards. But the faulty national teaching of all these years cannot be eradicated in individuals. There is still a lurking feeling that patriotism is an affair of politics, and a tendency to think of one's own ease and advantage rather than the country's need. 'There are splendid fellows among them, but on the whole the girls are more patriotic than the men.' That was the conclusion of one who knew. Perhaps it is that a man's patriotism is a more silent emotion. Let us hope so. And, lastly, there is the perennial question of the drink. There the girls have an enormous advantage. There is not much drinking among the munition workers here. Their conditions are regular and comfortable. The drinking is rather among the great mass of outside workers, who are less under discipline, and who live under less comfortable conditions, so that there is some excuse for their turning to the light and warmth and temporary exhilaration of the public-houses. It is true that the Board of Control stops the sale in the immediate district, but there are considerable towns a few miles away. I have always thought, and I still think, that if light wines and beers were permitted as a safety valve, the sale and even the manufacture of spirits could and should be forbidden. Such a change would be full payment for all that the war has cost us.

But there is no need to end this description on a critical note. After all, the work is done, this wonderful work, and it is not a drink-sodden or degenerate community which does such things. We have our difficulties. Drink is among them. But they affect a minority, and in very different degrees. Does anyone suppose that Germany has not her own difficulties, very much heavier than ours? One comes away from Moorside marvelling at the adaptability of the nation, at its power of improvisation, at its reserve of brain and energy, and at the promise which all these qualities give for our future place among mankind.

9 February 1917

FAMINE IN COAL
Sacks by Motor and Taxi

'While women and children are shivering for lack of coal, it is being supplied in large quantities to warm Egyptian mummies and relics of past centuries.' This was the outburst of a prominent London coal merchant, who was seen by a representative of the *Daily Telegraph* yesterday at his wharf. 'Look on this picture,' he proceeded, pointing to heaps of coal, 'and on that,' directing attention to a crowd of women waiting with perambulators, sacks, baskets, bags, and pails to obtain all they could take away of the precious material. 'Now,' he went on to say, 'think of what happened on Sunday. An urgent order for the delivery of about forty-five tons of coal to the order of the Government was completed. The coal went to a museum, where it will be used to supply warmth where no one wants to go just now. People are too much concerned with the pressing circumstances of today to go to see what has been dug up in Syria.

'We have plenty of coal, but the Government has taken our men, and those we have are so independent that they only take on what jobs they like. A carman yesterday said it was too late at one o'clock in the afternoon to take a load just over two miles. The van was loaded and the horse harnessed, but the man would not do the work.'

Several leading merchants agreed that the cause of all the trouble was the excessive call made upon the trade for men for the Army. The Board of Trade had been appealed to, one ground being that serious results were likely to arise. In one instance a dealer was advised by the police to remove his samples of coal from his window, as women in the district were becoming threatening. At one merchant's office our representative was informed that hospitals, nursing homes, and similar institutions were given preference, and then the dealers who supplied the poor.

'Look at these orders,' he said, 'that we cannot attend to. There are about 500 that we are dealing with in rotation, and we have nearly reached those sent just before Christmas. We have the coal, but not the men. Here is a pile of letters praying for coal ordered weeks ago. Now look at this order book, and see some of our customers today.' The entries included the following:

> Lady ----, 3cwt
> The Marquis of ----, 4cwt
> The Countess of ----, 6cwt
> Lady ----, 1cwt.

'The Marquis,' said the merchant, 'obtained his 4cwt by sending his motor-car for it, and the other orders went away on taxis. Yesterday one of the largest colliery owners in the world sent his motor-car here and obtained a few hundredweight. Rich and poor are all suffering, and the so-called "substitution" scheme is an utter failure. If it is carried much further the trade will be brought to a standstill, with results which need not be dwelt on.'

28 March 1917

POTATOLESS DAYS
London Clubs' Example

It is becoming increasingly evident that potatoes should be regarded as essentially the poor man's food, and, accordingly, should be consumed very sparingly, if at all, by the more well-to-do classes. Though the reasons for this are obvious to all but the selfish minority, which does not wish to be convinced, it is not easy under existing conditions to secure general observance of the golden rule that all but the really poor should do without the popular vegetable as far as possible.

Clubland has taken a lead in various directions in meeting the Food Controller's wishes and there are signs that the admirable example of Arthur's, Brooks's, White's, the Marlborough, the St James's, the Travellers', and the Turf, which have resolved that after 1 April no potatoes shall be served to members, will be followed by other clubs. The Portland Club, St James's-square, has also decided that in future potatoes shall not be served at any meals. On inquiry at the Junior Constitutional Club – one of the largest in London – a representative of the *Daily Telegraph* was informed that in all probability potatoes will shortly vanish altogether from the menu. As over 2,000 meals a week are served at the institution a great saving in potatoes would thus be effected, though already, as at many other clubs, there are two potatoless days and one meatless day weekly.

Ladies clubs have also been prominent in the crusade for food economy. Though two potatoless days and a meatless day on Friday are the general rule, the Ladies' Army and Navy prefers a whole week of abstention from potatoes once a month, in addition to the meatless day. Here, as elsewhere, many members, from conscientious motives, only eat meat once a day. At the Ladies' Empire hardly any potatoes are being consumed.

Restaurants, however patriotic their proprietors, are naturally in a far more difficult position, though there again, partly by reason of necessity and partly by culinary art, palatable substitutes figure more and more on the menus, and the homely vegetable the place of which they take is missed less and less. Competition, in a highly competitive trade makes action in the direction of potatoless days very difficult, if not impossible, under present conditions, and it is a question of the conscience of customers. The statement made a week ago, on the authority of Mr Dennis, that the visible supplies would provide no more than 1 lb per head per week for the civilian population in Great Britain until the end of May should add to the number of people who realise that by abstention themselves they can supplement this meagre allowance for the necessitous.

If present hopes are realised, this country ought shortly to rejoice in a greatly increased fish supply, and by the old law of supply and demand, a cheaper one. The importance of deep-sea fishing has been recognised by the Government for a long time past. A few days ago the Fisheries Department had a conference with a number of trawler-owners, so a representative of the *Daily Telegraph* was informed by an influential salesman at Billingsgate yesterday. The whole effect of the Government's contemplated plan, however, may be nullified if care is not taken to deal with the labour question at Billingsgate. Already this matter is acute, as more than 60 per cent of the porters and a large number of the proprietors of one-man businesses have been taken for the Army.

6 September 1917

U-BOAT ATTACK ON SCARBOROUGH
Thirty Shells Fired, *Scarborough, Wednesday*

Scarborough's long immunity from attacks by the enemy was unhappily broken on Tuesday evening, when a submarine shelled the town in broad daylight. The day had been delightfully fine, and there were many merry picnic parties on the coast and moors, while thousands of holiday-makers thronged the north and south beaches and promenades. At a few minutes to seven, when many people were on their way to the spa, there was a loud explosion, followed by others in quick succession. Away in the direction of Filey, about three miles out to sea, could plainly be seen the outline of a German submarine. People rushed in all directions for shelter, but there was no time to go far. The shelling continued for about ten minutes. Two guns were being used, and whilst some of the shells exploded on the foreshore road, others travelled over the town and burst from four to five miles from the submarine.

The shooting was very erratic, and the guns were turned in various directions. One shell struck an empty house in Pavilion-square, the concussion breaking the glass at the adjacent railway station. Another exploded as far away as Hoxton-road, mortally wounded the wife of Police Constable Scott, and broke the left arm and leg of Alice Appleby, aged seventeen, of Whitehead-hill.

In about ten minutes all was over, the submarine fearing to continue the attack longer on account of the British mine-sweepers which had hastened to the scene and turned their guns on the boat, which submerged quickly. About a dozen shells were fired. In addition to Mrs Scott a soldier, Mr Pickup, aged sixty-four, was killed near his residence in Queen's-terrace, on the north side, and Annie Bestwick was injured. Some people never knew until all was over that there had been a raid. The workpeople at the Yorks Laundry never heard a shell fired, and worked throughout the attack. The sound of the firing was altogether different from that of the 1914 bombardment, being much smaller in volume. In fact, it resembled the firing of mortars on the occasion of a lifeboat launch. Two of the properties struck in the town were unoccupied, one being a large house which in the normal season would have been full of visitors. The fire brigade prevented a conflagration.

At Mr Coles', a confectioner in Eastborough, the occupants had marvellous escapes, a shell entering the side of the window and passing downwards to the cellar. There were several similar fortunate escapes. Many people were out boating, fishing, and bathing when the submarine opened fire. The bathers made a dash for shelter, but the boating parties had to remain afloat, and, as it turned out, they were in perfect safety. A stranded ship on the rocks opposite the spa was fired upon. In his excitement, a boy fell over the pier and broke his collar-bone.

An hour after the submarine had submerged to escape the mine-sweepers, like a rat before a terrier, the town resumed its normal appearance, and the places of entertainment were full.

The shell which struck a house occupied by Mr William Jackson, at 107, Hoxton-road, literally smashed the building. Bricks and mortar were strewn all over the sitting-room. Not a single article of furniture remained whole. They were twisted and broken beyond recognition, and ladies' jackets and hats were torn to shreds. Interviewed, Mr Jackson said as he was coming downstairs at seven o'clock he heard a terrific bang at the front of the house, and almost instantly the whole place was filled with showers of lime and dust. There were five people in the house, but not one suffered any injury. In the back bed-room were five canaries, but although the window was shattered they continued to sing merrily. Exactly opposite the house Mrs Scott, the police constable's wife, was killed. She was standing at the door, which is pierced with shell fragments.

26 September 1917

THEATRES AND THE RAID
Calm Audiences

Perhaps one of the most noteworthy features of Monday night's raid was the coolness shown by playgoers, and the perfect sangfroid with which the artists accepted the situation. With the exception of two theatres, performances went steadily on, save for a temporary break while the firing was at its height. At the Savoy, Mr H. B. Irving decided that the most prudent step was not to raise the curtain at all, visitors who had previously booked seats being informed on their arrival that they could either have their money back or have seats for some other evening. At the Royalty a start was made as usual, but towards the end of the first act of *Billeted* Mr Dennis Eadie addressed the audience, stating that it was considered wiser to suspend operations, but that everyone would be welcome to remain under shelter until the conclusion of the raid. Of this offer practically all present were only too glad to take advantage.

Both at the Haymarket and the London Hippodrome the audience assembled at the customary hour. The curtain in each case remained down until twenty minutes past nine, however, after which things followed their normal course. Mr George Robey and Mr Albert de Courville, together with certain adventurous members of the Hippodrome company, profited by the delay in commencing to ascend to the roof, from which they enjoyed an unexpected view of a spectacle far surpassing in intensity anything they had themselves ever taken part in. Mr Robey, indeed, was so fascinated by the display that he allowed himself no time to change for his first entrance on the stage, appearing in his ordinary clothes with a shrapnel helmet on his head.

The Criterion, of course, being entirely underground, offers unique attractions to all seeking a refuge. As a matter of fact, very few in the auditorium on Monday night even knew that a raid was in progress, while the hospitality of the corridors was offered by the management to any who cared to make use of them. At His Majesty's it was deemed advisable to suspend the performance of *Chu Chin Chow* for three-quarters of an hour, from 8.30 to 9.15, and practically no one left until the curtain fell shortly after 11.30. Very much the same thing happened at the Queen's, where some of the occupants of the upper circles acted upon the management's invitation to descend to the pit.

At the Lyceum an amusing little episode occurred. First there was a brief speech from the stage of a reassuring character, which was received with much applause, the audience remaining quietly seated until the sound of firing had died away. In the last act of *Seven Days' Leave* a gun is supposed to be fired at an enemy submarine by a British destroyer, an effect produced by a resounding whack on the big drum in the orchestra. On Monday the result appeared to tickle the audience's sense of humour immensely, being received with a burst of derisive laughter, amid which could be heard the voice of one of the spectators loudly declaring, 'Not a bit like the real thing.' At the Lyric there was the usual pause during hostilities, those in front being invited to take sanctuary beneath the stage, where they fraternised with members of the company in the friendliest fashion, the performance being resumed exactly at the point where it had been broken off.

Mr Leslie Henson acted as speech-maker at the Gaiety, seizing the occasion to compliment his hearers on the calm manner in which they had taken matters. 'Never in my life,' he remarked yesterday, 'have I, when proceedings were resumed, played to a more light-hearted audience or to one which entered more thoroughly into the fun of the piece.' Of the demeanour of those present at his various houses, Mr Charles B. Cochran speaks in the highest terms. 'During the course of the evening I made a tour of my theatres to see what was going on, and in every case the artists proceeded with their work entirely unmoved, while not one single individual left his place,' was his significant criticism yesterday.

Save that a few visitors to the gallery were accommodated with seats in the pit at Drury Lane, everything went on there as if nothing of an unwonted nature were happening outside, an exactly similar state of affairs prevailing at the Comedy, where late arrivals were actually buying seats at the moment bombs were being dropped, and the aircraft guns were shouting their loudest. From Wyndham's, the Playhouse, the Empire, the Palladium, and elsewhere come equally reassuring accounts testifying to the unruffled behaviour of theatre-goers generally.

A correspondent present at the Ambassadors Theatre writes: 'Men, women, and young girls, taking courage from the actors on the stage, remained to enjoy the play, and laughed at the bursting shells! What a people! Which other country could show men and women on the stage proceeding with their parts, though at times their words were punctuated by the sound of dropping bombs? The audience, appreciating the courage of the artists, were more than usually enthusiastic in their applause, which in turn almost drowned the noise of the guns. The women, above all, were splendid. They did not scream or faint. They were just British women.'

1 January 1918

LORD RHONDDA AND A NEW RATION SCHEME
Prevention of Queues

Lord Rhondda has approved a new rationing scheme, and copies have been forwarded to Food Control Committees. These bodies have power to adopt the scheme, and if they do so it will become compulsory in their district. It is particularly desired that London as a whole will favour the scheme, and to that end a meeting of metropolitan food committees will be held to discuss it. The scheme gives the quantities suggested for rationing of butter, margarine, and tea, as follows:

> Per head per week
> Margarine and/or butter – 4oz
> Tea – 1½oz

Measures for the prevention of queues are first dealt with. Queues being the outcome of difficulty in obtaining a particular item of food, it is recommended that: Every customer should be registered with one shop for the purchase of that foodstuff, and not allowed to buy it elsewhere.

The shopkeeper should be required to divide his weekly supplies in fair proportion among all the customers registered with him.

No shopkeeper should be allowed to register more customers than he can conveniently serve.

On the question of registration of customers Food Committees must adopt one or other of the following schemes:

a. They may arrange for the issue of a card direct from the food office to every household or individual in their district, leaving the customer to take the card to a retailer and deposit a portion of it with him in token of his registration. This system can only be used effectively where the register of sugar application forms is, or can be brought.

b. They may provide the retailers in their district with cards or slips on which to register customers applying to them for registration. In such a case it will probably be necessary to have a card in three sections, viz., one for issue to the customer, one to be kept by the retailer, and one to be sent to the food office for the checking of duplicate applications.

If the latter system, which saves the Food Office and the Post Office heavy work, but imposes greater strain on the retailer, precautions will be necessary. It is suggested that assistance should be given to retailers who require it for the issue of cards.

There is no objection to marking sugar cards to prevent duplicate applications, but it must be the household sugar cards originally issued, not the new sugar cards or ration papers.

Customers should have a free choice as to the retailer, and to make a choice, if desired, of different retailers for their various requirements.

Measures are under consideration for removing the effects of the different prices of margarine. A specimen card suggested for use in connection with these articles is given. The front provides for particulars of the customer's and shopkeeper's name and address, and the back gives instructions that the card must be produced at every purchase, and any misuse of it renders the offender liable to a fine of £100, and six months' imprisonment. There are spaces to be marked up weekly by the retailer showing what supplies the customer has had.

Retailers should be registered. It is probable that the Food Controller will make an Order requiring general registration, and committees, in framing schemes for the distribution of butter and tea, should: Include the registration of butter and tea retailers as part of their scheme, but use the simplest forms of application only pending the introduction of a general system of registration by the Food Controller.

Registration of a retailer may be refused if the committee is satisfied that he is unable to made adequate arrangements to keep his register of customers satisfactorily, but the committee may help a retailer requiring assistance in the clerical work involved. The retailer's registration may be revoked if he fails to comply with any direction or reasonable instruction given by the committee under the scheme. He should in every case be required in due course to report the total number of persons covered by cards deposited with him, and the quantities due to be sold by him to any caterer, manufacturer, or institution.

Directions may be given by the committee as to the number of customers that each retailer may register, and may direct a retailer to adopt a scheme for serving customers at fixed hours and on different days.

4 January 1918

BRITISH MUSEUM
Growing Opposition

Up to last night the decision to take over the British Museum as offices for the Air Council had not been altered. It is understood that the suggestion was first made by Lord Rothermere to the Accommodation Committee, There was some difference of opinion, and finally the matter was submitted to the War Cabinet, who decided that the Museum should be taken over. Lord Rothermere was accompanied on his visit of inspection to the Museum by an official of his Majesty's Office of Works, and not by Sir Alfred Mond, as has been stated.

Opposition grows each day to the ill-advised scheme, and comes from all classes of people, though, rightly, the objection is most strongly expressed by the men and public bodies whose opinions carry most weight. It is to be hoped that the Government will make an early announcement giving official assurance that the plan is to be dropped, especially as it is now abundantly evident that the building in Bloomsbury, or even part of it, could not be cleared before many months have passed; that is, if even reasonable care is to be taken to avoid damage to the priceless treasures housed there. And speed is ostensibly imperative. The British Academy has represented to the Government 'the irreparable injury that would be done to the interests of learning and humane studies by any serious damage to the priceless collections in the British Museum, and the slur which would be cast on the good name of the country by action which will be taken as implying indifference to those collections and to the civilisation they represent.' The British Archaeological Society has also joined in the protest.

Most of the objections to the proposal have already been forcibly stated, but there is one aspect which has not yet been put forward. The collections in the Museum are, to a very large extent – perhaps half of the whole number – the result of private benefactions, made because the Museum was believed to be a place of absolute security, and the faith that the nation would take the utmost care of them. Any failure in such care is at once a breach of faith with former benefactors and a discouragement of future ones. This journal is, perhaps, specially interested in this phase of the subject, for it has itself taken pride in adding to the treasures of the Museum. It was the *Daily Telegraph* which sent out George Smith on two journeys of exploration in Mesopotamia, which resulted in the discovery of the Babylonian tablets of the Creation and the Deluge, and many other valuable records. All these were presented to the Museum, and are still registered as the *Daily Telegraph* gift.

Many anxious inquiries were made yesterday as to developments on the subject. It was noted with pleasure that no start had as yet been made in packing up the treasures of the closed galleries with a view to their removal elsewhere, but the Office of Works stated that, so far as that department is concerned, there has been no change of arrangements, the decision, as it stands, being a Cabinet one. The public, however, look with confidence to the Cabinet for a speedy reversal of that decision.

Our Parliamentary Correspondent states that Lord Sudely will on Wednesday next call the attention of the House of Lords to the proposed appropriation of the British Museum to the purposes of the Air Ministry, and move: 'That this House is of opinion that the use of the British Museum for the purpose of a public office, especially of a combatant character, is undesirable in the national interest.'

18 January 1918

'DEMONSTRATION' AT BRIGHTON

Notwithstanding the disapproval of the inhabitants generally, another 'demonstration', organised by certain trade union elements in the town, took place yesterday afternoon as a protest against the alleged difficulties of the working classes in obtaining meat and other food. The proceedings consisted of a mass meeting on the Level. A considerable number of the men employed in the locomotive works of the railway company, without the slightest regard for the work in hand, 'took an afternoon off' to take part in the gathering. It is also understood that the local branches of various trade organisations intimated to their members that they were expected to put in an appearance in the show, and some amusement was caused among the crowd by the presence of members of the orchestras at places of amusement, who had been 'called upon' by the Musician Union. Not a few of the men openly expressed their repugnance to the demonstration, but confessed that they felt compelled to attend in order to avoid unpleasantness from the extreme section. Rain and gloom added a depressing element to the proceedings, which seemed to excite far more contemptuous derision than sympathy among the crowds in the streets. It is no secret in the town that these agitations are being promoted by Socialist and pacifist groups with ulterior objects.

The demonstration resulted in a fiasco. When the crowd had assembled it transpired that a difference of opinion had arisen among the organisers as to the arrangements, and after much wrangling a procession round the town was abandoned and the meeting adjourned until tomorrow.

23 January 1918

TWO MEATLESS DAYS
Drastic Order for Hotels and Restaurants

Lord Rhondda issued last night a résumé of his revised order with reference to meals in restaurants, hotels, clubs, and other places where food can be obtained. It is of a drastic character, and applies for the first time to boarding-houses and unlicensed hotels with more than five bed-rooms. The principal features are:

Two meatless days per week:
London – Tuesday and Friday
Country – Wednesday and Friday
No meat at breakfast or tea
Diners at restaurants, clubs, &c., to provide their own sugar
Limit of 3oz of meat at lunch and dinner
Rationing of butter, margarine, &c.
No meatless day has been ordered for the home.

The Ministry of Food have issued the following statement explanatory of the new Order: The Public Meals Order, just signed by the Food Controller, supersedes the previous Order dealing with the subject, and introduces a number of important modifications. Fats are rationed for the first time, and the Order is now applicable to boarding houses and unlicensed hotels in which the number of bedrooms available for letting, whether in or outside the house, exceeds five, whereas previously such establishments with not more than ten public bed-rooms were excluded.

Beginning with Friday next two meatless days a week are instituted, on which no meat, poultry, or game may be served or consumed in any public eating place. The meatless days for the City of London and the Metropolitan Police district are Tuesdays and Fridays, and elsewhere in the United Kingdom Wednesdays and Fridays.

Between the hours of 5 a.m. and 10.30 a.m. no meat, poultry, or game may be served or consumed on any day. No milk may be served or consumed as a beverage, or as part of a beverage, except with tea, coffee, cocoa, or chocolate as usually served, but it may be given to children under two years of age. Exemption from the above provisions may be obtained by a resident in a public eating place on the certificate of a duly qualified medical practitioner, showing that it is in the interests of his health.

As sugar is only permitted for cooking purposes, guests will have to provide their own means of sweetening beverages. Hotels, clubs, or boarding houses may supply sugar to persons residing therein for the major portion of any week not exceeding one ounce for every complete day, provided that the total amount for any one resident does not exceed 6oz in any week; and that the person in charge of the establishment is reasonably satisfied that no sugar ration has been obtained in respect of such resident.

Regarding teas taken in public places, no person may be served with or consume between the hours of 3 p.m. and 5.30 p.m. more than 1½oz in the whole of bread, cake, bun, scone, and biscuit.

The permitted quantities of meat, flour, bread, and sugar (except sugar supplied as above mentioned), butter, margarine, and other fats, must not exceed the gross quantities allowed for the meals served during a week, ascertained in accordance with the following scale of average quantities per meal:

	Meat	Sugar	Bread	Flour	Butter, Margarine, &c.
BREAKFAST	Nil	Nil	8oz	Nil	1–3oz
LUNCH (or midday dinner)	3oz	1–7oz	2oz	1oz	1–3oz
DINNER (including supper and meat tea)	3oz	1–7oz	3oz	1oz	1–3oz
TEA	Nil	Nil	1½oz	Nil	1–4oz

This does not apply to food served over the counter of a buffet at a railway station.

Instructions are given as to the weighing of meat, poultry, and game. Two and a half ounces of poultry or game are reckoned as 1oz of meat. Meat is to be weighed uncooked, with bone, as usually delivered by the butcher. The uncooked weight of poultry and game is to be taken without feathers or skin, but including offal. Four ounces of bread are to be reckoned as 3oz of flour. Of authorised fats not more than one-half may consist of butter and margarine.

Powers are given to Food Committees to reduce the total quantities of any of the rationed articles in any public eating-houses within their areas, or to limit the quantity of any foodstuffs which may be supplied or used. 'Meat' is defined as including butchers' meat, sausages, ham, pork, bacon, venison, preserved and potted meats, offals, and other meats of all kinds; and fats bought as part of the meat, but does not include soup which does not contain meat, poultry, or game in a solid form. Poultry and game includes rabbits, hares, and any kind of bird killed for food. Fats include all animal or vegetable fats, natural or prepared, which are not bought as part of meat. Salad oil may be served at table at any meal, but separate records must be kept of all oil so used.

Public eating places which do not serve meals exceeding 1s 2d in price, exclusive of beverages, are excluded from certain provisions of the Order, including those as to meatless days; and other public eating places which do not charge more than 5d (including beverages) in respect of meals begun between 3 p.m. and 5.30 p.m., not including meat, fish, or eggs, are also excluded from certain provisions. The Order comes into force on 3 February, except as regards meatless days.

'I expected something like this,' said the manager of one restaurant; 'I don't suppose it will make a great difference to us. People who go to the City must have luncheon of some sort, whether it contains meat or not. As for the sugar, those people who cannot do without it will bring their own, I suppose. Many people are going without sugar in tea now, but there are relatively only a few who do not use it in coffee or cocoa. These people probably will now drink tea, and that will accentuate the tea difficulty.'

The manager of a well-known West-end café said: 'To the big dining hotels and restaurants it may make some difference, because if people cannot get dishes out, then they will not dine out. I am not referring to the people who from business reasons must get meals out, but to those who dine at a restaurant as the beginning of an evening's amusement.'

6 April 1918

NATIONAL WAR MUSEUM
An Ambitious Scheme

Widespread interest has been aroused by the announcement which appeared in yesterday's *Daily Telegraph* of the Government's decision to erect a great National War Museum. In the words of Sir Alfred Mond (First Commissioner of Works), 'The scheme is of a magnificent character, and the museum will be one of the most remarkable buildings in Europe.' In conversation yesterday with one of our representatives, an official closely in touch with the project stated that the National War Museum, which is going to be permanent, and not temporary, in character, will rank alongside the British Museum and the Victoria and Albert Museum. Such a statement is in itself evidence of the great importance of the scheme now in contemplation, and assured of being carried out. The hope entertained, and the purpose in view, is that the project will develop into the creation of a National Naval and Military Museum, at which soldiers and sailors and prospective soldiers and sailors may learn the story of their country's wonderful achievements in the Great War. It is not intended to be a museum of enemy trophies. These will be exhibited, but they are not to be the main feature. The object is to demonstrate how we, a non-military people, when faced with the defence of our very existence as a nation, developed our resources, produced ships, guns, and ammunition never dreamt of, and by our national and patriotic effort, saved civilisation from the rule of the Hun.

The work of the humblest munition worker up to that of the most skilled artisan, illustrating the gradual development of the nation's efforts in the war, will be shown, and will prove to future generations an object-lesson as to the great part their predecessors played when everything was at stake. For instance, the guns of the famous *Queen Elizabeth* will be there. The complete turret of the same famous vessel will be exhibited. There will be a series illustrating every type of gun we have used during the war, and likewise a model of every ship which has protected these shores – from the greatest Dreadnought down to the most modest but pluckiest drifter which has helped to clear the highways and byways of the seas of mines. In a word it will be an exhibition of how we 'did it' out of nothing by developing our resources – moral and material.

The question of a site is exercising much attention. A committee, presided over by the Earl of Crawford (a former First Commissioner of Works), has had the matter in hand for some time, and has now placed its recommendations before the War Cabinet, with which the final decision as to site rests. The museum buildings promise to be of huge dimensions. It is stated that two sites have been definitely recommended – one in Hyde Park on a piece of ground lying above the Serpentine on the Bayswater side, and the other on the south side of the Thames, adjoining the new County Council Hall. So far as the former is concerned the site could be obtained free, while in connection with the latter there would be a cost of half a million sterling, and it would take two years to clear out the existing buildings and prepare it for the necessary work. There are, however, many who strongly object to the Hyde Park proposal, the opinion being that if the project is of such great national importance it is well worth paying for without sacrificing any portion of London's open spaces. On the other hand, there are those who consider that the site south of the new County Council Hall is most inconvenient and out of the way, while the Hyde Park position is admirable from the point of view of the thousands of people who daily visit the park, especially children, and who would be readily attracted to such a museum. For the present, however, nothing has been decided. The matter has to come before the War Cabinet and will be settled one way or another in the course of a very short time. The decision as to site will be awaited with keen interest.

It is interesting to learn that since Sir Alfred Mond, in his position as First Commissioner of Works, accepted the proposal to establish a museum in London commemorative of the war, the Germans have followed our example, and are now setting up a national war museum recording the life of Germany during the war.

16 April 1918

WAR ON THE RAT
A National Offensive

Viscount Chaplin and Lord Lambourne have issued the following appeal to farmers throughout the country: 'In your buildings, stackyards, and granaries you have an underground enemy who destroys our food supplies almost as much as the submarine. That enemy is the brown rat. In 1908 Sir James Crichton

Browne estimated the yearly damage done to food by rats in England alone at £15,000,000. The value of that quantity of food today would be close on £40,000,000. If you could afford to keep rats in 1908 you certainly cannot do so in 1918. Still less can the nation afford to keep them at a moment when every sack of corn is urgently needed. In the rush of work on the farm, which has to be done with diminished labour, rats have multiplied. They breed faster than any other vermin. The rat will breed when four months old, and has from three to five litters in a year. Her average litter is ten, but as many as twenty-three have been found in a nest. At that rate of increase, you cannot go on feeding them. But unless you are prepared to do so, it is an unneighbourly act to keep them at all. The moment you stint them of food, they will swarm over your neighbour's farm. On the other hand, if your neighbour keeps rats, and you have a harbour for them, they will soon overrun your premises, unless they are absolutely rat-proof. Therefore you must act all together and at the same time.

'At this crisis in the nation's history no farmer would care to plead guilty to the charge of sacrificing grain to vermin. But the facts remain that, on a moderate estimate, the English countryside is feeding one rat per head of the total population of these islands; and that ten rats will, apart from what they spoil, eat a quarter of corn every year. That means ten rats will consume the yearly bread ration, according to Lord Davenport's scale, of your wife and yourself. Which do you wish to feed? Save the English harvest of 1918 for yourselves, and do not waste it on rats. What are you to do? Get the Board of Agriculture's leaflet (No. 244), read it, and put the advice into practice. You should inspect your barns, granaries, and dairies. Keep your sacks and bags protected, and make the fullest use of traps, snares, ferrets, and dogs. Barn owls are among your best friends. They will help you much. When the weather is too bad for work on the land organise your staff to destroy rats. Close rat-holes with concrete and glass, and see that nothing in the shape of food is left unprotected. You will save money by doing this, and the country will save food. Protect your ricks as far as possible. Straddles – if they are high enough and your stacks are well apart – are invaluable. Careless feeding will make your premises a centre of vermin production. Take care to feed your stock and your poultry so that the food is not left about to attract the rats.

'We ask you to encourage rat-catching on your farms and in your districts to the fullest possible extent. Enlist all the help you can. Get the local Scoutmaster to train and employ his troop in rat-catching. Your rats cost you collectively millions of pounds every year. It is worth your while to give some small reward for every one destroyed. Rats will soon be leaving your premises for the fields and hedgerows. Take care that they do not return by way of your stacks, and that every point of ingress is barred. Hunt your hedgerows, whenever opportunity offers, with dogs or ferrets. Get your neighbours to do the same. Let us remind you once more that you will do no good unless you all act together, district by district. If you all do your best at the same time, the saving of grain will be the same thing as growing thousands of additional quarters of corn. We cannot afford to feed the rats. We cannot raise too much grain, and we can hardly hope to have enough for ourselves. For all these reasons we appeal to you with confidence to do your utmost to reduce the number of rats, and we would ask you to cut out this letter and place it where all who work for you may read it.'

25 April 1918

GERMAN PRISONERS ON THE LAND

The farming community has been vividly impressed with the excellent work that has been done, and is still being accomplished, by German prisoners; whose services have been utilised on the land. The almost unanimous verdict of the farmer able to judge is that the German prisoner is 'thorough' in his agricultural work. As for clearing land, and getting it into goodly appearance, many farmers testify quite openly that the German (and Austrian) prisoner has done excellent work. The almost unanimous cry is for still more men to be used in the countless odd jobs necessary in agriculture. There seems to be a desire on the part of some officials to prevent the farmer having prisoner labour. In a southern county, a very notable agriculturist, after much trouble with two or three departments, secured a gang of German labourers, but the chief constable of the county finally prevented them taking up their duties. Now the farmer and his neighbours are asking if the official notices issued early in the spring as to the employment of Germans as agricultural labourers are going to be withdrawn.

Not so long ago farmers desirous of employing prisoners of war as agriculture labourers in the shape of whole-time workers, boarding and lodging them on the farm under certain conditions, had only to apply to the County Executive Committee, who, if they approved of the application, would forward it 'to the General Officer Commanding-in-Chief of the Command'. The latter, before giving consent, would have to consult with the chief constable of the county as to the advisability of sanctioning such applications.

There is existing the machinery for putting far more prisoners of war on the land than there are at the moment. Some niggardly farmers have actually complained that the wages paid to Germans are too high – they are ruled by the current local rate, subject to a deduction of 15s per week for board and lodging – but with British labourers growing fewer and the older generation left behind proving but reeds instead of sticks to lead on, it would be better for agriculture if even more men were liberated from the German camps or agricultural depots already instituted. Clearing ditches, laying drains, carting roots, cutting logs, threshing, and, of course, ploughing, have proved farm jobs in which the German prisoner excels. It is those English farmers who have had the assistance of prisoners formerly used to agricultural duties who have loudly proclaimed that their land was never so clean as it is at the moment.

Chapter 5

The War at Sea

30 August 1914

SAILORS' STORY OF THE NAVAL VICTORY
Daring Exploit, *Harwich, Saturday Night*

Magnificent – indeed, worthy of all our great traditions as a naval Power – is the story which I have gathered here piecemeal today of yesterday's stirring fight in sight of Heligoland. From what I have seen and from what I have heard first hand concerning the fighting, I am able to say that the victory was even more splendid than the official report published this morning indicates.

Let me describe first – making the narrative as connected as possible in view of the scrappy nature of the information – how the engagement came to be fought. Two or three days ago a couple of destroyer flotillas left harbour, provisioned and oiled for four days. It was known here, but not whispered abroad, that they were going farther north than usual. They glided out of port during the night, and the fog of war descended on their movements. We now know that their task was to take part in an important concerted movement against a section of the German fleet, whose whereabouts was no secret and whose light cruisers had made occasional excursions into the North Sea. Shortly after dawn yesterday, before the night mist had vanished off the face of the waters, the flotillas of British destroyers and submarines approached the place where the enemy lurked, sheltered by the great guns in the forts of Heligoland.

Accounts differ as to the precise manner in which the attack was delivered, but all agree in stating that it was marked by splendid dash and the boldest daring. One story I have heard from a good source is that a number of our destroyers got fairly close to the German ships before they were discovered and fire was opened upon them. The forts joined in the cannonade, and our destroyers were soon hotly engaged. They gradually drew the enemy out towards the open sea, fighting furiously all the time, and before long German cruisers appeared on the scene, to reinforce the smaller craft of the Kaiser's navy. It was hot work. One of my informants says, 'It was like Hell. The noise was something terrific, and seeing the way they pounded at us I can't think how it was that more of our ships were not hit. But, to tell you the truth, the German gunners don't shoot well. They made better practice from the forts than from the ships, and I think it was the shells from land that did most damage to our ships, although to begin with they fired too high.'

I give this story as it was told to me, but I am bound to add that in another quarter it is said that the forts played little part in the engagement. Until an official account of the action is available there must be some confusion regarding details.

When the German cruisers appeared on the scene and opened their guns on our destroyers the enemy were for a time in a position which gave them a great advantage. As I gather, our battle-cruisers and light cruisers had not then come on the scene. They were steaming fast to the assistance of the 'mosquito' craft, but for some time the destroyers had to bear the whole brunt of the fighting, aided by two scout leaders. It is only necessary to see the damage sustained by the destroyers to realise how grim the struggle must have been. The little vessels attacked the enemy's ships incessantly, until the arrival of the heavy warships brought them welcome aid.

Various incidents of the fight are recounted here as showing the magnificent pluck displayed by our seamen. During one of the hottest phases of the action two of our destroyers are stated to have run in between two German cruisers. The latter were afraid to fire, or, at any rate, did so very hesitatingly, at their gallant little foes for fear of hitting each other, and meanwhile they were greatly harassed by the attack of the destroyers. Again, it is related how four of our destroyers engaged a German cruiser and battered her so much – whether she was torpedoed or not I cannot say – that she was practically in a sinking condition when a battleship came up and 'finished her off'.

These are two examples of the spirit displayed by our destroyers. They did great work. Indeed, it was remarked to me by a friend who has been on board some of the boats since they came in: 'These fellows rather feel that, judging from the newspapers they have seen, the battle squadron has got credit for some of the work they did.' Be that as it may, there is no real jealousy in the Navy; only a keen rivalry to get there first when there is work to be done.

I hear magnificent accounts, too, of the part that one of the most powerful of our flotilla cruisers played in the encounter. She was stiffly engaged with German cruisers for a long while, and the peppering she got is proved by the fact that she is reported to have been hit nineteen times. I myself have seen some holes in her sides just above the water-line which have been plugged with wood; but, wonderful to say, she has sustained no serious damage. Her four funnels are untouched, and her wireless apparently is intact. In fact, to look at her, as she lies in harbour, one might suppose that she had never been under fire, so spick-and-span is she.

This is what happened when one of the shells struck her. It caught her aft, just above the water-line, pierced her armour, and passed through the ship. It went within a couple of yards, it is said, of a steward and another man, who had tumbled out of their berths when 'half-action' sounded at about a quarter-past four. The shock threw the men down violently, but beyond some bruises they were quite unhurt. A piece torn off the shell as it pierced the armour was exhibited in Harwich tonight. It is a jagged lump of steel, about the size of a large walnut – a splinter that would have caused a bad wound had it struck anyone. The British vessel, however, was lucky all round. Both the ship and the crew escaped lightly, though some of the men had minor injuries.

It is difficult at present to form any estimate of the duration of the fight. Some say it lasted seven or eight hours; others put it at five hours. Perhaps a mean should be struck between the two.

The sinking of the *Mainz* seems to have been the beginning of the end for the enemy. An eye-witness says she was in flames shortly before she went down. She began to sink by the stem, and a moment before she disappeared her bow was raised high out of the water. Then she was suddenly lost to view.

No doubt an official version of the fight will be issued; I have merely described it from such details as I have been able to collect.

I will now recount the home-coming of the destroyers. After a night of fog, the weather this morning was brilliantly sunny. Into this peaceful harbour about nine o'clock glided two of the ships from the North Sea. As the first of them passed a warship anchored here, a great cheer went up from the sailors on board. Shouts of 'Bravo!' floated across the water to the quayside, and were taken up enthusiastically by the people congregated there. Red Cross nurses joined in the cheer, and soldiers swelled the chorus. Then the second destroyer came into view. Her appearance told instantly of the stern work in which she had been engaged. How everybody cheered her! It was a glorious demonstration.

Later I had an opportunity of examining at a little distance the damage she has sustained. Her mast was shot away, leaving a jagged stump not more than 12ft high; her wireless had totally disappeared; and her bridge was partially wrecked. I counted some fourteen holes, all in her bow. They had been roughly plugged with oakum. Some were near the water-line, but she floated on an even keel, and her crew went as calmly about their duties as if they had just returned from an ordinary cruise. On her bridge was the chief engineer, who, I understand, had brought the vessel into port.

Of another vessel, the Press Bureau informed us this morning that she was damaged. A sailor told me she was quite done for life. These are not quite his words, but rather a polite translation. However, things are not nearly so bad as that. She was hit four times. The first shot tore a hole in her midship funnel, the second plumbed among her dynamos, the third hit her forward gun, damaging it at the muzzle, and the fourth went aft. She will be repaired forthwith, and all that her crew fear is that they may be out of the 'fun' for a time.

Now comes the saddest part of my duty. In the bright sunshine this morning there were removed from one of the British ships seven of our gallant dead, including one officer. The official list of casualties should soon be published. It is better that I should not venture on an estimate of our losses. They are known not to be severe. The bodies of the men who had so bravely died were taken to the Shotley Naval Hospital, and there they await the last funeral honours.

In the fog of the early morning a destroyer brought in many of our enemies who had been stricken in the fight and humanely saved. Twelve had died on the way to port, and were buried last night at sea. Two more succumbed to their wounds as the vessel was nearing land. Nineteen were carried ashore at Shotley. They were borne carefully on stretchers to the naval hospital by the sturdy lads from the naval training establishment. They are grateful for the kindness and attention bestowed on them. One of them feebly waved his hand to a group of watchers, but most lay silent and motionless on the stretchers.

15 December 1914

DARING RAID INTO THE DARDANELLES
Turkish Battleship Torpedoed

What without any disparagement of the work of other officers engaged in the same difficult and dangerous service may be fairly described as the most remarkable and daring submarine exploit of the war, so far as it has gone, is reported in an official communiqué issued yesterday afternoon by the Press Bureau.

Lieutenant-Commander Holbrook, with submarine *B11*, actually penetrated into the Dardanelles, despite the minefields, sank the old Turkish battleship *Messudiyeh*, which was on guard duty there, and succeeded in taking his little vessel out again without damage.

This piece of intelligence is contained in the following announcement, made by the Secretary of the Admiralty: Yesterday (i.e., 13 December) submarine *B11*, Lieutenant-Commander Norman D. Holbrook, RN, entered the Dardanelles, and, in spite of the difficult current, dived under five rows of mines, and torpedoed the Turkish battleship *Messudiyeh*, which was guarding the minefield.

Although pursued by gunfire and torpedo boats, *B11* returned safely, after being submerged on one occasion for nine hours.

When last seen the *Messudiyeh* was sinking by the stern.

12 February 1915

SUBMARINE ATTACK ON A BRITISH LINER
Torpedo Avoided, *Rotterdam, Thursday*

British pluck and skilful seamanship enabled the steamship *Laertes*, of Liverpool, to escape from a German submarine in the North Sea yesterday afternoon. The adventure, which was the most exciting that has yet befallen any mercantile vessel, was reported this morning, when the *Laertes* arrived at Ymuiden, whence she proceeded up the canal to Amsterdam. She was chased for three-quarters of an hour, and was not only attacked by a torpedo but fired at from a light gun on the enemy's craft. The former missed its aim, but the shots from the latter hit the vessel, which, when she reached Ymuiden, bore visible marks of the ordeal in the shape of large holes through the funnel, ventilating shaft, and one of the ship's small boats.

It was at four o'clock in the afternoon when the *Laertes*, homeward bound from Japan with a very valuable cargo, sighted the German submarine *U2* at a point 40 miles south-south-west of the Maas Lightship, between the latter and the Schouwen Bank. The enemy immediately hoisted a signal for the *Laertes* to stop, but it was not in the mind of her commander, Captain Propert, a typical British mariner, to do anything of the sort. Instead he gave the order 'full speed' to the engine-room, and proceeded to direct his vessel on a zig-zag course, so as to make a more difficult target for the submarine if she fired torpedoes.

At the same time he hoisted the Dutch colours. The ship was not flying any flag at the moment when the submarine was sighted, and her commander decided to make use of the Netherlands blue, white, and red, because his ship's crew included men belonging to neutral nations, mostly Chinese and Norwegians.

It was evident at once, however, that no neutral flag would serve as protection, and that the Germans were prepared to sink the *Laertes* whatever her port of registry or the nationalities of the ship's company. Travelling on the surface, so as to move at her maximum speed, the *U2* made every effort to draw abeam of the steamship, and so find a favourable opportunity for launching a torpedo at her. But it was in vain.

By this time the *Laertes* had worked up to a speed of 16 knots. Though all on board realised the danger every member of the crew remained cool, collected, and obedient to the commands of the captain. Below the stokers responded magnificently to the chief's appeals to them to get all they could out of the engines, and on deck the most skilful steersmanship was shown in varying the vessel's course. Gradually but steadily the *Laertes* was increasing the distance from her pursuer.

Suddenly there was a puff of smoke from the submarine and then a small shell passed through one of the *Laertes* air shafts. Seeing himself baulked of his prey the German commander had given the order for the light gun which his craft carried, its muzzle pointing along the lines of the bows, to be brought into action. Although the first shot found its mark in the vessel Captain Propert and his brave crew were not the least perturbed. They continued on their course, even when a second shot pierced the funnel and another hit one of the ship's boats.

So far as I have learned up to the moment of telegraphing no one was injured, although, of course, their lives, those neutrals as well as others, and all non-combatants, were endangered by the fire to which they could make no reply.

The submarine continued firing from her light gun, and, although some more shots fell on the upper deck and one smashed the ship's compass, the Germans' aim was getting uncertain as the distance between them and their target drew out. The chase, however, was not given up, and meanwhile, as the *Laertes* was making one of her swift changes of direction the submarine fired a torpedo. This passed across the stern of the vessel, plainly visible to those on her decks.

Soon afterwards the submarine realised that the *Laertes* had the greater turn of speed. She fired a parting shot, and then disappeared beneath the grey waters. Captain Propert decided to make for the nearest Dutch port, and reached Ymuiden, at eleven o'clock this morning.

SUBMARINE REPORTED SUNK

Amsterdam, Thursday

From inquiries made in Ymuiden I have every reason to believe that the submarine which was the cause of the anxiety suffered a mishap, and is now probably at the bottom of the North Sea. She gave up the chase when gaining, and was last seen in a cloud of steam.

When the submarine hoisted the challenge to stop the *Laertes* put on her best speed, but hard as the stokers worked, and their efforts increased the speed of the ship to just 15 knots, the submarine gained, and then opened fire on those on board the *Laertes* with a machine-gun, some of the bullets from which are now in the possession of the captain and crew.

When the submarine got within 500 yards she launched her torpedo. It was very near the *Laertes* when the crew saw the line of white bubbles, and, with utmost speed, put the helm over. The ship answered splendidly, the torpedo just missing the rudder. A few feet more and she and her whole crew of fifty would have been lost.

Then occurred the remarkable incident of the chase. The submarine had steadily gained on the ship, and was within easy striking distance. Yet she suddenly abandoned the pursuit, and was last seen in a cloud of steam and apparently in difficulties.

The *Laertes* made the most of her opportunity, and steered straight for Ymuiden.

8 May 1915

DESTRUCTION OF THE *LUSITANIA*

Sunk off Irish Coast by German Pirates

Yesterday afternoon the German submarine pirates committed the most infamous outrage of which they have yet been guilty by torpedoing and sinking the famous Cunard liner *Lusitania*, at a point eight miles south by west of the Old Head of Kinsale, near Queenstown.

This fresh crime was perpetrated without the least warning of the submarine's intentions, and without any opportunity being given to remove the 2,000 persons aboard the steamer, who included upwards of 1,300 passengers, among them many women and children.

It was not until one o'clock this morning that the first news was received of the landing of any survivors. From the two messages which were sent out by the Press Bureau, within a few minutes of one another at that hour, it seems apparent that this latest outrage has involved a terrible loss of life, which may prove to be over two-thirds of the total number on board the doomed liner.

AMERICAN INDIGNATION
Serious View Taken, *New York, Friday Evening*

German agents here were jubilant when the news of the torpedoing of the *Lusitania* came through, and circulated reports that not only was the *Cunarder* torpedoed but the vast majority of her 2,000 passengers were drowned. It was recalled by special editions of the German Press in New York that Count Bernstorff, through the newspapers, had warned all Americans from sailing last Saturday, and that German agents in the dock personally warned many travellers against embarking.

So far as is known, everybody who booked sailed, as explained in a special despatch to the *Daily Telegraph* last Sunday.

Half an hour after the first sinister report was circulated here, New York and every city in the country was in a state of turmoil and anxiety, which recalled the days of the *Titanic* disaster.

America's note of protest to Germany regarding any loss of life of American citizens in the war zone under circumstances similar to those reported in connection with the *Lusitania* was reprinted here in full just twenty minutes after the first hint of the disaster was received. It would not be possible to describe in adequate terms the sensation created and the furious indignation provoked. 'What will President Wilson do now?' was the question asked on every side. The answer soon came from Washington to the effect that the State Department was asking for information, and meantime 'viewed the situation most seriously'.

Some of the most notable citizens of the United States were among the *Lusitania*'s passengers, several with close personal relations with the President and members of the Cabinet. The torpedoing, if confirmed, it was argued, would mean well-nigh irreparable insults to a neutral country, and, coming in quick succession to the sinking of the *Gulflight* and the attack on the *Cushing*, would precipitate a crisis, which no mere note to Berlin, no matter how severe in its terms, could adequately answer.

Friends of the Government who have laboured from the first to prevent an entanglement of America with Germany, and to that end have been inclined to turn a deaf ear and a blind eye to many acts calculated to provoke irritation, if not hostility, are frankly in despair. The torpedoing of the *Lusitania* with so many Americans on board, they argued, would be the last straw to break the camel's back. Others, less condemnatory, quote the words of Count Bernstorff's warning as a sufficient reason why the relationship with Germany should not be impaired beyond repair.

SURVIVOR'S STORY OF THE DISASTER
Two Torpedoes, *Queenstown, Saturday Morning*

His Majesty's steam tug *Storm Cock* reached Queenstown last night at 8.30 p.m., with 150 survivors of the *Lusitania*. Amongst them were numerous passengers suffering seriously from shock and from immersion. Ambulances were there and doctors to look after those who were driven to hotels and other places of comfort. There were many of the crew also amongst them, who were hatless and bootless, but they thanked Providence their lives had been saved.

The library steward of the *Lusitania*, during an interview, in relating his sad story, said the *Cunarder* had between 1,300 and 1,400 passengers, and a crew of 750 men on board. Amongst them were crowds of Americans, including Mr Vanderbilt and a host of prominent people belonging to the United States.

When 10 miles south-west of Kinsale, he continued, the passengers were at luncheon and were in the best of spirits, chatting merrily, when an awful explosion rudely shocked them. They did not know what had happened, and quickly rushed from their seats. They soon learned, however, that a German submarine had sent two torpedoes into them. One of them had entered the stokehold, and the other had burst into the hull in the forward part of the vessel.

Captain Turner and all the officers tried to pacify the frightened passengers, but their efforts failed, and water rushed into the fleet *Cunarder*, and she sank within fifteen minutes. There were five babies in their mothers' arms – a most pitiful sight to behold. The torpedoes struck the *Lusitania* on the starboard side, over to which she listed. The passengers were frantic to save their lives. The order to launch the boats was given, but in lowering them the ropes caught, and the fastenings of others broke. One of the boats fell into the water. Ten boats in all were lowered. Many of the passengers had got into the boats, but others had placed lifebelts around their waists, and fell into the sea, and were subsequently picked up by the floating boats.

Upwards of 100 of the passengers were in the water, kept afloat by life-preservers. The ten boats saved about 500 altogether. The interviewed, continuing, said the *Storm Cock* approached several of the boats and took off them 160 persons, after being on the water six hours, which were spent in anguish and great misery. There was an awful loss of life, but how many he was unable to say.

Mr Ernest Cowper, a Toronto journalist, who was coming across with his editor on business, stated that a sharp look-out had been kept for enemy craft when Ireland was being approached.

He was chatting with a friend at about two o'clock, and, though he just got a glimpse of the conning-tower of a submarine about 1,000 yards distant, he only remarked the circumstance to his friend when he noticed the track of a torpedo.

The *Lusitania* was struck forward. There was a loud explosion, and portions of the splintered hull were sent flying into the air. Shortly afterwards the liner was struck by another torpedo, and she began to list to starboard.

The crew immediately proceeded to get the passengers into the boats, and everything was done in an orderly manner.

A little girl, named Helen Smith, aged six, appealed to Mr Cowper to save her, and he put her on a boat. It is feared that her parents are lost. Her grandparents belong to Liverpool. Mr Cowper got into the last boat. Some of the boats could not be launched and had to be cut away as the vessel was sinking.

There was a large number of women in the second class and about forty children under one year old.

19 July 1915

CUNARD LINER AND GERMAN SUBMARINE
Another Outrage, *New York, Sunday*

The British verdict in reference to the responsibility for the *Lusitania* disaster, coupled with the report yesterday by Captain Taylor, of the Cunard liner *Orduna*, that a German submarine attempted to torpedo the *Orduna* without warning, are regarded as two important factors which will strengthen the hands of the Cabinet on Tuesday, when President Wilson will submit the draft reply to Berlin's latest Note. No surprise is felt here regarding the *Lusitania* verdict, because we felt that no other was possible, but the attack upon the *Orduna*, westward bound, on the morning of 9 July, came as a shock to Washington, where the impression prevailed that Germany, since America's latest protest, has been inclined to observe international law relating to warning and provision for the safety of the persons aboard before making an attack.

Captain McComb Taylor and his officers have proved to our satisfaction that they failed to see the submarine before she fired a torpedo. 'Not the least warning was given, and most or nearly all of the passengers were asleep at the time; it was almost another case of brutal murder.'

The attack was made only a few miles from where the *Lusitania* herself sank, and the 492 persons, including twenty-one Americans, on board the *Orduna* probably owe their lives to the fact that the commander of the submarine miscalculated the speed of the liner, which was making 16 instead of her ordinary 14 knots at the time of the attack, as well as to the admirable seamanship of Captain Taylor, who, with the aid of the chief engineer, Thomas Gowans, manœuvred the ship so as to confuse the aim of the submarine in its subsequent attempts to destroy the steamer by torpedo and gun fire. Seven shots were fired at the *Orduna* after the torpedo missed, and though the last few fell short, most were pretty close calls. Eighty women and forty children amongst the passengers were in their cabins at the time of the encounter.

Had the steamer gone down, the officers said, the submarine would not have appeared on the surface, and the disaster would have been attributed to the striking of a mine, as was asserted at first in the case of the *Nebraskan*. In this way responsibility for complying with international law as regards warning would have been averted.

In commenting upon the case American newspaper writers emphasise that the war on piracy and murder has not been modified, and the specious German fiction that has been spread in the United States last week or so is exploded by the attempt to destroy a steamship which bore no munitions of war, but had neutral passengers on board.

2 August 1915

THE BRITISH NAVY AND ITS WORK
Is Its Defeat in Sight?

By *Archibald Hurd*

Years ago it was certain that the submarine would arrive to influence powerfully naval warfare. We are now witnessing the realisation of an easy prophecy, for no great difficulties were involved in submarine navigation. But is there not a tendency just now to go to extremes, and to imagine that the submarine will supersede in a short time all other types of warships?

This consideration deserves attention. In the first place, under legitimate conditions of warfare, the submarine has not done any considerable military injury to our Fleet, though we have had to expose it in commanding the seas. Many naval officers hold that the losses sustained in the early days of the war – the three cruisers *Cressy*, *Hogue* and *Aboukir*, and the *Formidable* – if not the battleships destroyed by underwater craft off the Gallipolli Peninsula, were preventable. However it may be, and much as we must deplore the destruction of life, it is apparent that by some means the Grand Fleet has been preserved, without robbing it of its effective use as 'the sure shield of the Empire'. In view of all that has been thought and said of the submarine, that is surely a rather remarkable fact. It is one highly creditable to Sir John Jellicoe and the officers associated with him. Anxious as the past twelve months must have been, during which the men-of-war of the main force have stood instantly ready, by night as well as day, to meet and defeat the enemy, it must be some satisfaction to them in glancing back to realise the Grand Fleet has not been robbed of a single armoured unit. It is our surplus Fleet of older ships which has suffered, and for reasons which need not be discussed.

It was only when the legitimate operations of the German submarine had proved unfruitful and all the marauding cruisers had been sunk, that the German naval authorities conceived the idea of using underwater craft for attacking our commerce. The will of the central authority was imposed on the submarine officers and men; some of them, as they have confessed, would have given much to evade a duty which was repulsive to them, while others welcomed, as they also have confessed, the opportunity for murder and brigandage. As a whole navy glories in the splendour of its deeds of skill, courage, and endurance, so a whole navy must stand condemned by acts contrary to the laws of God and man, whatever individuals in the service may think.

And as to the character of the enemy's campaign against our merchant ships, there can be no question. In his Note on the *Lusitania*, Dr Wilson, the head of a great neutral nation, declared: 'The Government of the United States is contending for something much greater than the rights of property and the privileges of commerce; it is contending for nothing less high and sacred than the rights of humanity.'

That statement is of wide application. The submarine activity is opposed to every rule hitherto observed by civilised nations.

A national sin is rather like a boomerang; it hits the sinner eventually. Germany has already been injured by her submarine policy, apart from the losses she may have incurred, and she will be injured still worse. What is the position? When the failure of her navy to achieve any of the ends for which it was created was apparent even to the Germans, Grand Admiral von Tirpitz sent forth submarines, not only to torpedo all laws and conventions, but to sink every enemy merchant ship, and thus 'starve England'.

To the deluded population of the Empire this policy was, from the very first, represented as a great and extraordinary success, whereas from the very first it was a failure, so far as our growing strength to fight Germany was concerned. In the Naval Museum in Berlin was hung a huge map, on which the 'victories' of the submarines have been methodically marked – every passenger vessel, merchant ship, and trawler being represented. Space does not permit mention on it of the spots at which a German battleship, a dozen and a half of German cruisers, and a number of destroyers and submarines have disappeared from view.

Success has been acclaimed, it being claimed that '229 English ships' have been sunk and, therefore, further success cannot be abandoned, even though it means war with the United States. For a shadow any risk must be run.

But, in fact, the policy has been a failure which, I am convinced, will become more and more apparent in the course of time, as counted by weeks and not months, and which will exercise its influence on the general appreciation of the value of these craft. The counter measures of the British Navy will continue and improve in efficiency. That is certain.

Let it not be forgotten that no offensive weapon has yet failed to produce its appropriate defensive reply. The gun defeated the wooden ship; then armour defeated the gun; the contest has gone on, year after year passing, and at present victory lies with the gun. It has been much the same with the torpedo. At first it was held as almost invincible; then came the protective net like a crinoline round our ships; then a cutter was fixed to the nose of the torpedo, and at present, as the loss of the *Triumph* and the *Majestic* illustrates, victory lies apparently with the torpedo and its cutter. And so it has been in all developments of physical science as applied to naval warfare. Success has gone first in one direction and then in another; but always a new offensive weapon has evolved some effective defence.

Now it hardly seems likely that the submarine is an exception to the rule which has hitherto been of universal application. The frailty of submarines was the enemy's excuse for setting aside all accepted rules of warfare when they came to the conclusion that in the submarine resided their only hope of satisfying German public opinion.

In a letter I have just received, an experienced naval officer writes: 'The submarine is the most vulnerable craft that ever took the sea, as is the Zeppelin in the air; there is not a ship that goes to sea but could sink a submarine by ramming her, and that without seriously injuring herself.'

It is improbable that the submarine is about to be driven, once and for all, from the seas. It may be that the next stage in the contest between surface and underwater craft will be the defeat of the latter, with heavy loss of life – for that is inevitable. The outlook is consoling; but let there be no mistake – when the submarine has fallen in value, its sponsors will work to raise it up again. The later process will probably not be completed during the duration of the present war. It is more likely that the present struggle will conclude with the eclipse of the submarine as an agent for use in the narrow waters, and that that eclipse will be followed in due course by the apotheosis of underwater craft in some other war – and may it be delayed beyond our time.

3 January 1916

TORPEDOING OF A P. AND O. LINER
No Warning Given

The Teutonic submarine pirates have added yet another crime to the many dastardly outrages on humanity and civilisation of which they have been guilty during the present war.

On Thursday afternoon the Peninsular and Oriental Line steamer *Persia*, of nearly 8,000 tons, was torpedoed while off the island of Crete on her way from Marseilles to Port Said, and sank almost immediately.

The first news of this latest exhibition of 'frightfulness' was communicated by the Admiralty on Saturday, but it was not until seven o'clock last evening when even brief details of the affair reached us in the shape of the following telegram from Reuters Agency:

Sunk in Five Minutes, *Cairo, Sunday (3.35 p.m.)*

The survivors of the *Persia* include fifteen ladies, ten military officers, and eight foreigners.

The *Persia* was struck amidships on the port side at 1.10 p.m., and five minutes later she had completely disappeared.

It was, in fact, a miracle that anyone was saved at all.

There was no panic, and the four boats that were launched were lowered with the greatest promptitude.

It is understood that 160 have been saved out of about 550 on board, but hitherto it has been impossible to obtain exact figures.

The captain was drowned. He was last seen swimming in the water after the liner had taken her final plunge.

At 7.40 p.m. we received the following further Reuters telegram, which, however, was handed in at Cairo an hour before the first to arrive: Cairo, Sunday, 2.35 p.m.

The survivors of the *Persia*, who arrived at Alexandria last night, were the chief officer, the second officer, seven engineers, twenty-seven seamen, sixty-three Lascars, and fifty-nine passengers, the last including Colonel Bingham and Mr Grant, an American acting as agent of the Calcutta Vacuum Oil Company. Mr McNeely, the American Consul at Aden, was drowned. Another American, named Rose, landed at Gibraltar.

59 PASSENGERS SAFE

The figures given by Reuters and also received by the P. and O. Company show that the total saved is 158. Of these, fifty-nine only are passengers, of whom, according to information at Lloyd's, seventeen are women. It is therefore certain that a large number of ladies have perished.

There is no mention of any children being rescued, and it must therefore be presumed that all, or nearly all, of those aboard the *Persia* shared the same fate.

According to the telegrams from Egypt, the roll of the survivors and drowned stand approximately as follows:

Total on board	(about) 550
Passengers saved	59
Officers and crew saved	99
Total	158
Approximate number lost	390

Among the passengers who joined the ship at Marseilles was Colonel Lord Montagu of Beaulieu, who was accompanied by his private secretary, Miss Thornton. Lord Montagu, who was commandant of the 27th Hampshire Regiment, was recently appointed Inspector of Mechanical Transport Vehicles for India, and was going out to Bombay to take up his new duties. Nothing had been heard of him down to a late hour last night.

The American Consul at Alexandria confirms the death of Mr McNeely, the United States Consul at Aden, who was on his way to his post.

A list of passengers, giving those who were going beyond Marseilles, issued by the company, contains 164 names, including over sixty ladies and nearly a score of children, some of them infants.

In a short earlier telegram Reuters' Correspondent at Cairo states definitely that the *Persia* was 'torpedoed without warning'.

Thus, in spite of the German pledge to President Wilson, the crimes of the *Lusitania*, the *Arabic*, the *Faluba*, the *Ancona*, and the *Yasaka Maru*, have been repeated in the Mediterranean.

Only last week the Austrian Government, in an hypocritical Note to the United States, partially repudiated the *Ancona* outrage, and alleged that the commander of the submarine which sank the Italian liner without warning had been 'punished'.

Whether the submarine which perpetrated this fresh atrocity was a German or an Austrian one is not yet known.

3 June 1916

NAVAL BATTLE IN THE NORTH SEA
Many Vessels Sunk

By Admiral Jellicoe

At seven o'clock last evening the Secretary of the Admiralty made the following announcement: 'On the afternoon of Wednesday, May 31, a naval engagement took place off the coast of Jutland.

'The British ships on which the brunt of the fighting fell were the battle-cruiser fleet and some cruisers and light cruisers, supported by four fast battleships. Among these the losses were heavy.

'The German battle fleet, aided by low visibility, avoided prolonged action with our main forces, and soon after these appeared on the scene the enemy returned to port, though not before receiving severe damage from our battleships.

'The battle-cruisers *Queen Mary*, *Indefatigable*, *Invincible*, and the cruisers *Defence* and *Black Prince* were sunk.

'The *Warrior* was disabled, and after being towed for some time had to be abandoned by her crew.

'It is also known that the destroyers *Tipperary, Turbulent, Fortune, Sparrowhawk,* and *Ardent* were lost, and six others are not yet accounted for.

'No British battleships or light cruisers were sunk. The enemy's losses were serious. At least one battle-cruiser was destroyed and one severely damaged. One battleship was reported sunk by our destroyers during a night attack. Two light cruisers were disabled, and probably sunk. The exact number of enemy destroyers disposed of during the action cannot be ascertained with any certainty, but it must have been large.'

At 1.15 this morning the Secretary of the Admiralty issued the following announcement through the Press Bureau: 'Since the foregoing communiqué was issued a further report has been received from the Commander-in-Chief, Grand Fleet, stating that it is now ascertained that our total losses in destroyers amount to eight boats in all.

'The Commander-in-Chief also reports that it is now possible to form a closer estimate of the losses and damage sustained by the enemy fleet. One Dreadnought battleship of the Kaiser class was blown up in an attack by British destroyers, and another Dreadnought battleship of the Kaiser class is believed to have been sunk by gunfire. Of three German battle-cruisers, two of which it is believed were the *Derflinger* and the *Lutzow*, one was blown up, another was heavily engaged by our Battle Fleet and was seen to be disabled and stopping, and the third was observed to be seriously damaged.

'One German light cruiser and six German destroyers were sunk, and at least two more German light cruisers were seen to be disabled. Further repeated hits were observed on three other German battleships that were engaged. Finally, a German submarine was rammed and sunk.'

5 June 1916

RUSSIAN PRESS ON THE GERMAN DEFEAT
A Complete Failure, *Petrograd, Sunday*

Russia received the first news of the battle of the Skagerrak from the German side. She is receiving the first details and explanations of the engagement from the same quarter. This morning's papers contain three columns of telegrams based on the announcement by the Admiralty at Berlin, the speeches in the Reichstag, articles from the Chancellor's daily Press organ, and communiqués issued by the Wolff Agency, but not one single supplementary line from British official or semi-official sources. All that there has been from our side so far has been less than half a column of Admiralty bulletins, which appeared in last night's evening papers here. This morning the enemy's perversions and equivocations would have the field to themselves were it not for the benevolent commentaries on them by the Russian newspaper correspondents at Copenhagen, Stockholm, and Basel.

This is greatly to be regretted. First impressions count for much, especially at a time when overpowering events follow one another in such rapid succession. If we fail to do our reporting as promptly as the enemy there is always a danger that his version will sink in, and that ours will be swept aside by some fresh news of startling significance.

Fortunately both official Russia and the chief writers of the Press are quite able to draw a just inference for themselves, but a considerable body of Russian society is apt to obtain its conclusions from a balancing against one another of the claims put forward by the two belligerents immediately concerned. To such people a frank acknowledgment of our losses – which it should be remarked is the subject of eulogies of exceptional warmth by the Russian papers – may prove very misleading unless it is accompanied by a full statement of the strategic and other gains that go to counterbalance them.

The comment of the Press may be summed up as follows: That the German High Sea Fleet, or the great bulk of it, put to sea for the fulfilment of some specific task; that it was foiled in its purpose and compelled to take refuge in its ports; that the issue of the battle was therefore a victory for the British, in spite of our heavy casualties; and that our greater loss of ships leaves the balance of naval power substantially unchanged.

A statement, probably inspired by the Naval Staff here, says that the losses of both fleets were so considerable that it is impossible to speak of victory on one side or the other, but that the main result of the battle is to be found in the inability of the Germans to carry out the operation for which they left their own waters.

The writer in the daily organ of the sister service, the *Russki Invalid*, thinks it very probable that the entire German High Sea Fleet was engaged, and that the British 'with great skill succeeded in preventing it from carrying out any kind of serious operations', inflicting upon it a 'cruel defeat'. The Germans 'not only lost some of their best vessels', but convinced themselves of the complete 'impossibility of appearing in the North Sea for serious naval operations, and of the brilliant services of the English guardships'. The article sums up its conclusions as follows: 'What has been stated shows that our Ally's fleet, at the cost of some of its splendid vessels and of some thousands of gallant sailors, has won a very decisive victory on the sea, inflicting exceedingly heavy losses on the enemy, and, what is the principal thing, upheld in its full scope the old English principle that the naval frontiers of England are the coasts of her enemy. True to this principle the glorious English Fleet has always emerged with honour from the most difficult positions, and has consistently fulfilled the basic task of its policy, domination of the seas, to contest which the Germans have so vainly tried during the present war. Nothing but defeat has resulted from all these attempts, and the most serious defeat and most galling for German conceit was suffered on 31 May and 1 June.'

The *Novoye Vremya*, which dwells at some length and in very complimentary terms on the prompt veracity with which the British Admiralty admits the full measure of its losses, sees as the immediate result of the battle that 'the German fleet was compelled to return to harbour without carrying out the operation mentioned by the Naval Staff at Berlin'. The Germans, it adds, have clearly realised that 'all departures from a state of inactivity will be met by the opposition of the English Fleet', and that Mr Balfour was describing actualities when, in his letter to the Mayor of Yarmouth, he said that the appearance of the German ships in the open sea would be associated for the enemy with inevitable risks.

Also full of enthusiasm for the 'proud consciousness of invulnerability' which inspires the admission of the British, the *Bourse Gazette* characterises the situation left by the battle as follows: 'As before, the British Fleet rules the seas, and the German ships have been driven back to the secure tranquillity of the Kiel Canal, where they will again tarry for long months hiding from British pressure. For heavy as are the British losses they have no serious significance for the continuation of the war.'

Colonel Shumsky adopts the theory that what the Germans aimed at was the destruction by a surprise attack in superior force of the British blockading cruiser squadron. He thinks that the battle has 'not in the slightest degree altered the balance of naval power', but he foresees future operations of the Germans on a big scale, as they 'have not yet abandoned the idea of bringing maritime predominance on to their side by some means or other'.

THRILLING STORIES OF EYE-WITNESSES
Flight of the Germans, *Rotterdam, Saturday Night*

From the stories told by the crew of the Dutch trawlers who witnessed phases of the naval battle, one fact stands out clearly. All the witnesses agree that the German fleet broke off the fight and fled at great speed towards Heligoland, closely pursued by the British. In its concluding stages, at any rate, it was a running fight.

The best description of this is given by Captain Thomas Punt, of the Dutch trawler *John Brown*, who saw nearly the whole of the fighting. Towards midnight one of the German ships sent up an extraordinarily powerful light rocket, which, in the opinion of Captain Punt, was a prearranged signal to the German fleet to break off the battle. Certainly, the sending up of this rocket was followed immediately by a turning movement by the German fleet, which came south at a terrific speed, with the Englishmen, in the words of the skipper, 'on their heels'. The latter kept their searchlights on their fleeing enemies, and rained shells upon them, the Germans replying with their after-guns.

Another significant fact disclosed here is the certain loss of the German cruiser *Elbing*, of which no mention has been made in the enemy's official report. Twenty-one members of the crew of this ship, including three officers and three petty officers, were picked up by the Dutch trawler *Bertha*, which landed them last night at Ymuiden. According to the statement of these men, the cruiser was in collision with a German torpedo-boat and was so badly damaged that the crew abandoned her. Twenty-one remained behind to blow up the vessel, and after arranging the explosives took to a boat, from which they were afterwards rescued. If their story is correct, and the *Elbing* was not sunk by the English shells, it makes a case against the German Admiralty for the deliberate suppression of a loss which is absolutely clear, for the men landed state that the remainder of the crew, numbering nearly 400, were taken on board German torpedo-boats after their ship had been in collision. The *Elbing* is described as a new small fast cruiser, originally built for Russia, of between 4,000 and 5,000 tons.

The *Bertha* also landed at Ymuiden, with the Germans, an English officer, Surgeon Blurton, a survivor of the lost destroyer *Tipperary*. He states that the *Tipperary* was struck by a shell during the night and sank immediately. Dr Blurton, who had been hit in the leg by a shell splinter, swam about for an hour, when he was taken out of the water by the boat in which were the men of the *Elbing*. He says the Germans treated him very kindly, and wrapped him in blankets. After the *Tipperary* sank he saw one of her boats, in which were some of the crew, drifting away. This he reported on board the *Bertha*, whose skipper, Captain Stam, made an unavailing search for the boat.

Interviewed at Ymuiden, Captain Stam, who was fighting on Wednesday 60 miles from the coast at 56.22 N. lat., 5.45 E. long., said that in the afternoon he heard gunfire, and later saw German cruisers steaming at full speed in a westerly direction. The ships disappeared in the distance. On the following morning, after picking up the survivors of the *Elbing*, they told him that they had seen another boat with Englishmen drifting. He searched for the boat without success. During the search the *Bertha* passed a tremendous amount of wreckage and five or six bodies. He also saw a disabled German torpedo-boat, which received a final shot from an English ship and sank in a few minutes. In the same neighbourhood a big battleship, whose nationality he could not tell, was floating keel upwards.

The skipper added that on Thursday afternoon the English Fleet remained cruising about, but the Germans had drawn off. He estimated the forces engaged at sixty ships on each side. The Germans whom he picked up were very sceptical as to the result of the battle, and said nobody had won.

The story of Captain Punt, of the trawler *John Brown*, who was practically in the midst of the battle, is 'I was fishing in the neighbourhood of Monkey Rock, about 80 miles from the Danish coast, in 56.31 N. lat., 6.15 E. long., on Wednesday. At two o'clock I saw a great fleet of all types of vessels coming from the south-east and going north-west. I guessed at once it was the German fleet leaving Heligoland. They were about fifty in number, including very many great cruisers, with three or four funnels. At 4.30 there was a short heavy fight. In the evening at seven o'clock the battle recommenced, and continued uninterruptedly in my neighbourhood until eleven o'clock.

'Judging by the direction in which the German fleet was moving and also of the gunfire, I believe the English Fleet came from a north-westerly direction. The battle moved westwards, and it seemed to me as if the English Fleet had got inside the German fleet. Both fleets then moved towards the Skagerack, but the Germans were being driven in a westerly direction, and the battle moved from 6.25 E. long. to 6.40. During the fighting I saw two tremendous columns of water caused by the blowing up and sinking of two ships. Although the gunfire was terrific, it was completely drowned by these two explosions.

'At eleven o'clock one of the German ships sent up a very powerful light rocket, which dropped only five yards from my ship. This was evidently the signal for retreat, for suddenly the German fleet turned and steamed southwards in the direction of Heligoland. A quarter of an hour later several great German vessels passed us at a speed of about 30 knots. They made such a wash that the water came over our decks. The English Fleet was following them at a great speed. In fact, the English were on their heels, searchlights on the retreating enemy and firing ceaselessly. The Germans returned the fire from their stern guns. It was a deafening and indescribable noise. For some moments I was between the fleeing German fleet and the pursuing Englishmen. Some shots flew over my ship. Tremendous columns of water spurted up around the ships. Great clouds of black smoke hung about, but as the ships disappeared I could see the leading English were scarcely 200 yards behind the Germans. The warships had all their lights out, but in the beams of the searchlights I could distinctly see the German flag on the ships which were being chased. Later in the night I saw two ships catch fire, but could not tell their nationality.

'At two o'clock the flickering of the last gunshots was the last I saw of the fight. At six in the morning we met two English destroyers and three English submarines going in the direction of Heligoland.'

Captain Punt believed from what he saw that originally the English were in the minority. Very early in the fight a fast English ship went away towards the west, and later in the night many more English ships arrived and participated in the battle.

The Dutch steamer *Texel* reports having seen floating in the North Sea nearly 500 bodies.

GREATEST NAVAL BATTLE IN HISTORY
Enemy's Flight

By Archibald Hurd

Last Wednesday's naval battle was the greatest conflict which has ever taken place at sea, judged both by the number and character of the ships engaged. The men-of-war were seven or eight times as numerous as those which took part in the Battle of Trafalgar, and, unhappily, although exact figures are not yet available, it is to be feared the British casualties were three or four times as great as those which occurred on 21 October 1805, when the losses numbered only 1,587 officers and men.

Owing in the main, although perhaps not entirely, to atmospheric conditions, the second strongest navy in the world managed to evade decisive action; it cannot be doubted, in the light of the mass of information which is accumulating, that by evasion it escaped, if not annihilation, at least overwhelming defeat. Had the action taken place in the Atlantic – for instance, off the Falkland Islands, where visibility is usually good – instead of in the North Sea, where, on two out of three days on the average mist or fog is experienced, Germany would probably by this time be without a fleet. As it is, when the history of the war comes to be written, in the perspective of years, the battle will be regarded as a British victory.

In the circumstances the result of this nine or ten hours' action is disappointing, judged by the Nelsonian principle – 'Not victory, but annihilation'. But this was not the only aphorism of the great admiral. On one occasion he remarked, 'Time is everything; five minutes makes the difference between a victory and a defeat.' At another time he declared, 'There is no certainty in winds and waves.' And yet again Nelson reminded a correspondent that 'Nothing is sure in a sea fight beyond all others.' The progress of naval science has accentuated the truth of these three sayings. The Germans on Wednesday last had by chance the advantage of time; they were aided by a fog – a patchy fog; and in the final stage of the running fight they also had the benefit of the light.

But the German fleet, nevertheless, suffered heavy losses and incurred serious injuries. It is not going too far to say that for all practical purposes the German High Seas Fleet – next to our own Grand Fleet the most powerful naval machine in existence – has been rendered innocuous for many weeks, if not months, to come. While it must be disappointing to Admiral Sir John Jellicoe and the officers and men of the Grand Fleet to have been robbed of the full fruits of their action, time will show that they achieved much. We are confronted with a new naval situation, the character of which may be summed up in a few words.

1. GENERAL SITUATION – Whatever hopes the Germans may have entertained of interfering with the Allied control of the maritime communications of the world must, probably for the whole of this summer, be abandoned. The movement by sea of troops and their equipment will proceed in greater safety even than in the past. Thus this action will directly contribute to the strength of the Allied armies in the various theatres.

2. NORTH SEA – The conditions in the North Sea have in particular been improved.

    a. COAST BOMBARDMENT – There is an almost complete assurance that during the holiday season the East Coast will receive no flying visits from German battle-cruisers. The fast squadron of the German fleet, after Wednesday's experience, will be in no condition to make even a 'tip-and-run' excursion to our side of the North Sea.

    b. OUR BLOCKADE – Although British naval forces will certainly not relax their vigilant guard, the possibility of the enemy endeavouring to interfere, at least so far as surface ships are concerned, with our blockade, may for the present be dismissed.

    c. THE INVASION RISK – The possibility of these islands being invaded has been of the very slightest. For the time being the menace now has no existence, and it may even be said, with complete assurance, that a raiding policy is definitely placed for the present out of the question.

3. THE BALTIC – Wednesday's battle will react on conditions in the Baltic. The German naval forces can be in no condition to undertake for some weeks to come offensive operations in the Baltic, and thus the action in the North Sea has contributed to the further safety of the right wing of the Russian armies which rests on the Gulf of Riga.

In the light of these conclusions – which will be amply confirmed, I am convinced – although it is matter for regret that the German High Seas Fleet still exists, we have solid satisfaction in the assurance that it no longer counts for as much as it did – if, indeed, it counts at all at this moment – in the balance of power at sea. In other words, the supremacy and prestige of the British Fleet have been reinforced to the advantage not only of this country, but of all the Allies. It need hardly be added that the results achieved will in no way tempt the British Fleet to adopt a policy of complacency and ease. Eternal vigilance is the price of safety.

The encounter of Wednesday last was not sought by the Germans; the offensive was taken by the British forces. The Grand Fleet, in all its strength, was carrying out one of its periodic sweeps of the North Sea. Vice-Admiral Sir David Beatty, with battle-cruisers, armoured cruisers, light cruisers, and four fast battleships, which, it may be hazarded, were of the *Queen Elizabeth* type, was well in advance of the main body under the supreme command of Admiral Sir John Jellicoe. He was attended by torpedo craft, in accordance with the invariable custom observed during the war. When in the vicinity and to the north of Heligoland, using that phrase broadly, this advanced guard was observed by the Germans. They appear to have assumed that Admiral Beatty was unsupported, and that an opportunity offered for action, with heavy odds, in their favour.

It is admitted by the Germans that the whole of their High Seas Fleet was thrown into the action. In pursuit of some object, the character of which the Germans have not revealed, but which is officially described as 'an enterprise directed northward', the German ships had full steam up, and were in every way prepared for an encounter, though they did not expect one. They assumed that in these waters, adjacent to their own coast, their minefields, and their submarine flotillas they would meet no considerable British forces. Even when Sir David Beatty's command came into view they had no suspicion that anything lay behind. The British Admiral apparently realised that his purpose was to act with dash and courage, and, by tactical adroitness, to draw the enemy towards the main body of the Grand Fleet. Shortly after three o'clock the action opened. Sir David Beatty had under his orders the swiftest and best-armed squadron to be found anywhere. The four *Queen Elizabeths* mount thirty-two 15in guns, throwing a shell of one ton in weight. The *Lion*, *Princess Royal*, *Queen Mary*, and *Tiger* were each provided by their designers with eight 13.5in guns. Among the ships under the German ensign there is at most only one ship at present which carries 15in guns, and for the rest the most powerful weapon is the 12in gun. Unfortunately, the atmospheric conditions were not favourable so far as range of vision was concerned for the British ships. There were patches of fog, and the outlook generally was misty. Consequently, a long-range action, such as occurred off the

Falkland Islands, when the firing opened at a range of 12,000 yards, was out of the question. Though at the shorter range the bigger gun, owing to its bigger shell, is the better gun, at close range the smaller gun can be fired as accurately, or almost as accurately, as the 15in or 13.5in weapon.

In these conditions the action opened. Sir David Beatty appears to have maintained the high reputation he made in earlier actions. But he had opposed to him, and, owing to the fog at comparatively close range, the whole of the German High Seas Fleet, including nearly a score of Dreadnoughts, besides other vessels. As the action developed the Germans were drawn steadily closer to the main ships, under the supreme command of Admiral Jellicoe. This denouement suggests a reflection bearing on the scouting operations of the Germans. In the course of the war the enemy had, prior to Wednesday, lost at least thirteen light cruisers, and consequently was experiencing the weakness due to the absence of an adequate number of scouting ships. Reliance was, therefore, placed in Zeppelins. The airships were employed to supplement the operations of the light cruisers, but one is driven to the conclusion that they failed to convey to Vice-Admiral von Scheer, the German Commander-in-Chief, knowledge of the character and composition of the British Fleet. In other words, there is reason to believe that the Zeppelins failed to realise the high hopes which the Germans confided in them. The enemy, unconscious of the risk he was running, continued to advance, until suddenly he was confronted with indications on the horizon which pointed to the fact that Sir David Beatty was not without powerful support.

Down to this moment the Germans had been in overwhelming power. Admiral Jellicoe's despatch, which was published on Saturday morning, shows that the Germans did not realise the position until almost, but not quite, too late. It is stated that 'The German battle fleet, aided by low visibility, avoided prolonged action with our main forces, and soon after these appeared on the scene the enemy returned to port.' Atmospheric conditions and German engines and engineers evidently saved the German High Seas Fleet from a fate which might have amounted to practical extinction.

What happened was this. The German Commander-in-Chief, realising that owing to the failure of the scouting by his light cruisers and Zeppelins, he had been drawn into a general action with the Grand Fleet, determined to break away and return to port. This is the course which he pursued as the daylight began to fail. Even at this period luck favoured him. Visibility, the weatherwise who have studied Wednesday's conditions state, was good to the eastward and bad to the westward. The Germans thus gained no mean advantage even during this rearguard action when they were flying to their home ports. The impedance of light can hardly be exaggerated. The British ships in these conditions can have had little guide in firing except the flashes of the German guns, while the enemy had in view the silhouettes of the British ships. There is no room for any suggestion that these conditions so far as they placed the British at a disadvantage were other than inevitable. The incident, however, reminds one of the battle off Coronel. In his log describing that occasion Captain John Luce, of the cruiser *Glasgow*, recorded that while the sun remained above the horizon Admiral

Cradock had the advantage in light, but the range was too great to enable him to take advantage of it even with his 9.2in guns. Forty minutes later, when the two squadrons had closed in, the sun had set, and the visibility conditions were changed, 'our ships being silhouetted against afterglow, and fading light made enemy difficult to see'.

What a scene must have been presented in the North Sea on Wednesday as the main body of the Grand Fleet, firing hotly, chased the enemy, desperately anxious to get within his mine-protected area, and under the security of his shore guns. For the first time Dreadnought battleships were engaged in deadly conflict. All the theories of a century's peace were being put to the final test amid the roar of battle and the flashes of more powerful guns than hitherto had ever been fired in anger in a sea action. One can picture the German ships cutting their furrows through the darkening waters while here and there German light cruisers and destroyers were busy pursuing the tactics of delay and embarrassment. This chase of an enemy fleet, which makes a practice of dropping mines when in retreat and of utilising to the fullest advantage the surprise element appertaining to destroyer and submarine, must have constituted the most supreme test of natural instinct, trained skill, and courage and resource to which any men of our race were ever submitted.

A hundred years ago a battle action was fought under sail power. Men-of-war moved slowly and majestically through the water. The average speed of an individual vessel was not much greater than that of a man walking at his fastest. There was ample time for thought and preparation. After the Allied Fleets were sighted on 21 October 1805, Nelson, if I remember rightly, sent the men of the British Fleet to dinner. In these days flotillas of destroyers or squadrons of battle-cruisers entering action at full speed approach each other at a rate exceeding 60 miles an hour. Think what that entails in rapid thought and quick action – a mistake probably irretrievable! Mechanical science as applied to naval warfare – swift-running engines, the great gun, with its range of 20 miles or so in favourable conditions, and the torpedo, with its deadly burden of explosives – has made demands on the mental and physical strength of naval officers and men which even twenty years ago it would have been confidently asserted they could not stand. All the wonderful forces invented during the last half-century have now been in action on a grand scale, and men who have passed through the ordeal survive to tell the tale. The trial to which men looked forward with wonder has now come. The British Fleet has emerged from it triumphantly. The discipline and morale of the men throughout the action was beyond praise.

Under favourable conditions, the Germans, flying at their highest speed, homeward, managed to keep ahead of Admiral Jellicoe, directing the operations of the main body of the Grand Fleet. The enemy had a start. The course was a short one. He was near his own port, and thus, and only thus, the German Fleet managed to escape by flight. Until the Admiralty lift the veil nothing can be said of the circumstances in which British ships were lost. The story will be told some day in all its detail. Until then praise or blame must be withheld, with this one remark: armoured cruisers are not well suited to battle conditions in the North Sea in these days. It is sufficient for the moment to pause to emphasise the considerations which emerge from a general survey of a battle which, beginning shortly after three o'clock in the afternoon, did not terminate until late in the night.

The British Fleet was left in supreme command not merely of the North Sea, but of all the seas and oceans of the world. This battle has reaffirmed the British control of sea communications which enable us and our Allies to continue to draw that strength – military, economic, and industrial – which will enable us to complete the defeat of the enemy by land and by sea. One other point. The British Fleet issued the challenge to action, and, in accordance with its traditions, the engagement was fought on the enemy's ground, near their bases and far from our bases. The British Fleet's frontier is the enemy's coast. In that fact lies the pride, and at the same time the risk of British seamen. Off the German frontier Sir John Jellicoe, unchallenged, remained after the enemy disappeared!

No battle can be fought without loss. What was the balance of loss in last week's engagement? The Admiralty has not concealed the injury, fatal and deplorable, which ships under the White Ensign sustained. On the other hand, the Germans, before they could have collected reports from their squadrons and ships, sent throughout the world what purported to be a complete revelation of the damage they had sustained. It is apparent that the German reports were a carefully fabricated misrepresentation. Those reports were intended to encourage the German population suffering from the effects of the iron dominion enforced by the British Fleet, and it was also hoped that thereby an impression would be produced in neutral countries favourable to the Teutonic Powers. It is now revealed on the authority of Admiral Sir John Jellicoe, the last man to put forward a boastful claim, that the enemy lost two battle-cruisers of the latest type; that one Dreadnought battleship was blown up by British destroyers, while another was almost certainly sunk by gunfire; and that the enemy was robbed of four light cruisers and ten torpedo craft, destroyers, and submarines. On our side we have to deplore the sinking of three battle-cruisers, one of them, the *Queen Mary*, as fine a ship as the Fleet contained, while the other vessels were designed about ten years ago. We have also lost three armoured cruisers.

It is the capital ships which count, and so far as can be judged from the conservative statements made on the authority of Sir John Jellicoe as to the loss suffered by the Germans, the balance is approximately as under:

	Great Britain	Germany
Battleships	nil	2
Battle-cruisers	3	2

The fundamental factor which it is well always to bear in mind when an action occurs at sea is that, roughly, the British and German navies were in the proportion of two to one when the war opened. Consequently, while it may seem disquieting to read that three British battle-cruisers and three armoured cruisers have been sunk, together with a number of destroyers, it should not be forgotten that losses half as considerable as ours represent the same relative reduction of German strength. If the above estimate of the German losses be correct, the German fleet emerges from the action considerably weakened, bearing in mind that its fighting strength was only about half that of the British Fleet. The exact standing of the two navies is, of course, not accurately known, as no official information has appeared on either side of the North Sea since hostilities began in August, 1914. It is, however, certain that since the war has only been in progress a matter of twenty-two months the Germans cannot have completed any large ships beyond those included in the 1914 programme, a battleship taking at least two years to build. We may accept the Admiralty statement that as a result of Wednesday's battle, the strength of the British Fleet is now greater, not relatively, but absolutely, than it was.

Another consideration arises. Our lapses, apart from destroyers, have occurred in the battle-cruiser and armoured cruiser classes. On the outbreak of war we possessed, built or building, ten battle-cruisers – two of them the gift of the Dominions – to Germany's eight. The *Goeben* has since disappeared in the Sea of Marmora, from which she will certainly never emerge. Therefore Germany, allowing for the losses on Wednesday – almost certainly two vessels of this class – now presumably possesses only five battle-cruisers to the seven of the original ten under the British flag. But it may be assumed that our shipyards have not been inactive.

Turning to armoured cruisers, when the war opened the Germans possessed nine. They have since lost the *Blücher* – which might almost be described as a battle-cruiser – the *Scharnhorst, Yorck, Friedrich Karl*, and *Prince Adalbert*. Therefore, the High Sea Fleet has associated with it today the three remaining vessels, of which the *Roon* is the only one which can be regarded as really effective. On the other hand, the British Fleet entered the war with thirty-four armoured cruisers. It has since lost ten of these. Reviewing the situation which now exists, purely from a material point of view, and bearing in mind these facts, it is evident that the action, far from invalidating our command of the sea, must have strengthened it. The losses of ships which we have sustained are in no way vital, or even serious. Our battle fleet has not lost a single unit.

The German fleet, on the other hand, is considerably weakened. The Germans admit that they have lost one battleship, the *Pommern*. That ship was sunk in the Baltic by a British submarine; it is now used as a decoy to distract attention from their actual losses. This would be just the occasion when the enemy would admit a slight loss, in the hope thereby of lending an air of verisimilitude to the story they have issued. The German losses are far more considerable, and may be put at two Dreadnought battleships and one, if not two, battle-cruisers, besides four other cruisers.

The main fact is that our battle strength remains unimpaired. As to battle-cruisers, we still possess, owing to the splendid patriotism of Australia and New Zealand, a valuable margin over the enemy, while our resources in armoured cruisers represents a superiority actually greater than it was at the beginning of the war. In light cruisers we are better off than at any time since the war opened.

In war we must take a long view of the current of events. In studying today's story we may recall other splendid exploits of our battle-cruisers in the North Sea, and may well turn our thoughts back to the spirited action of 24 January of last year, when the Germans were robbed of the *Blücher* and had two of their battle-cruisers injured. That action enforced over a year's inactivity on the Germans. Nor can we forget the victorious issue of the battle of the Falkland Islands, which avenged the destruction of Admiral Cradock's squadron. War consists of a series of gains and losses, and its issue depends, not on isolated incidents, but on the final balance which assures the command of the sea. So far not only have we experienced nothing which need affect our abounding confidence in the Fleet's prestige, but events have increased the relative strength by which we are able to use the sea ourselves and deny its use to the enemy, and have raised yet higher the prestige of British sea-power.

But there is another aspect from which the engagement must be viewed. Sea-power consists, not only of ships, but of trained officers and men. After such an action some delay must necessarily occur before full particulars can be obtained of the casualties sustained. The British public, in view of the examination of the position as to material which has been made, will feel the most poignant regret for the heavy loss of life which has occurred. We have many ships and we have great establishments which can produce other ships, but the men who have gone can never be replaced. The Admiralty's description of the sinking of the *Warrior* happily suggests that most of the crew were able to effect their escape before she disappeared; but, on the other hand, though the Germans state that they rescued a number of survivors of other ships, of those on board the *Indefatigable* only 'two sole survivors' remain.

No words can express the sorrow which for many days to come will weigh upon the nation when it reflects that probably not fewer than 5,000 or 6,000 men of our blood, in the course of a few short hours, were called upon to pay the price of Admiralty, and, hazarding their all, sacrificed their all in the cause in which the whole Empire is willing to spend and be spent. But though the battle in the North Sea did not enable us to annihilate the German fleet, these officers and men did not die in vain. They made a contribution to final victory, the value of which we may be unable to appreciate at its real worth till time has confirmed the impressions which a cursory examination of the course of events powerfully supports.

29 July 1916

AN ACT OF MURDER

By Archibald Hurd

Another act of cold-blooded murder has been committed by the Germans, which will shock the conscience of the world: a fine sailor, and a conspicuously brave man, who did his duty by his employers and his country, has been shot in circumstances peculiarly revolting.

Captain Charles Fryatt's vessel, the *Brussels*, was captured by enemy destroyers on 23 June, and taken into Zeebrugge. It appears that he was wearing at time of the seizure of his ship a gold watch which was presented to him by the Admiralty, together with an appreciation on vellum of the splendid seamanship which he displayed when attacked by a German submarine. That award for gallantry has been seized upon by the enemy as evidence on which an audacious charge has been founded, and on which, after trial by court-martial, which was a mere mockery, this British sailor has been shot.

This terrible incident furnishes another illustration of the lengths to which the enemy is prepared to go in contempt both of international law and the dictates of humanity. The Germans presumably urged at the trial that Captain Fryatt, a non-combatant, engaged in an act of war, and therefore became subject to the severest punishment. That contention is a cruel travesty of law and tradition. This master, in new and embarrassing conditions, owing to the use of submarines for the destruction of commerce and life, acted strictly in accordance with a precedent recognised by all nations.

During all naval wars it has been admitted that a merchant captain has the right to defend himself when attacked. In the old sailing days not only might commercial ships of this and other countries carry guns in order to protect themselves, but at one time British vessels were compelled by law to do so, and were required to defend themselves by every possible means. The right, if not the duty, is still recognised by this and other countries, and the American Senate has under consideration at this moment a measure providing for the armament, at the expense of the State, of all the most serviceable ships of the American marine in order that in time of war they may not fall the unresisting prey of enemy ships.

The charge against Captain Fryatt was apparently not that he fired on a submarine, but that he endeavoured to ram her. Viscount Grey of Falloden has pointed out that that act, if it was committed, was a defensive act, precisely on the same footing as the use of defensive armament. By law and humanity there can be no question as to the validity of that claim.

But the terrible incident can, in fact, be justified in no way. The murder has been perpetrated in order to terrorise merchant sailors. The semi-official newspapers of Germany have admitted that one of the anticipated results of the submarine piracy was that British and Allied sailors, in view of the threat of inhumanity on the part of the Germans, would be afraid to put to sea. In that event, ships would neither reach nor leave this country, and the purpose of the enemy would be achieved. That expectation was not fulfilled. British sailors regarded the acts of the Germans with loathing and contempt, and refused to be terrorised. The shooting of Captain Fryatt is an act of revenge.

The British people will remember in this connection that though Lord Grey of Falloden described the policy of the submarines as piracy, and at one time the Admiralty segregated the officers and men of such vessels as were taken, it was afterwards decided that they should be treated in all respects like other combatants who had fallen into our hands. The murderous act of the Germans is the sequel to this clemency.

22 August 1916

GERMAN FLEET

Hurried Retreat to Mined Waters, *Rotterdam, Monday*
By Leonard Spray

The German High Sea Fleet has won another 'great victory'. It has appeared in the North Sea in full strength, it has cruised westwards – and it has returned to its harbours. This triumph is even more wonderful than that of 1 June, for on Saturday, except for an incidental submarine exploit, the German armada completely succeeded in avoiding encounter with British forces. According to the standard of the Kaiser's Admiralty staff, what is lacking to prevent them announcing to the world another proof that it is Germany not Britain, which holds the dominion of the seas?

Perhaps one thing among others. They realise, for instance, that scores of Dutch skippers know exactly what happened. These trained sailors witnessed all the movements of the German squadrons and destroyer flotillas. And their reports prove conclusively the only fact of importance in the day's events, namely, that on the first news of the appearance of the British Fleet the Germans turned tail and headed westwards at full speed.

At nine o'clock in the morning the Great German Fleet, at least sixty vessels of all descriptions, was sighted.

It was carefully guided by three Zeppelins. At six o'clock in the evening the same fleet was viewed further north, and this time, with its attendant airships, was steaming furiously eastwards. What had happened in the meantime? This, too, is equally clear from reports of other Dutch captains. At five o'clock in the afternoon they saw one or more British squadrons much further south than the six o'clock position of the German fleet heading almost due north in the direction of the enemy. Something else they noted. From the northwards appeared three Zeppelins. The airships, immediately on spotting the British vessels, went about in the direction of the main German fleet. Then came a swift dash. Half an hour afterwards the High Canal Fleet was in mad retreat to its home bases.

That was the last seen of any German warship in the North Sea. But for many hours after that British squadrons were sighted scouring the seas for the vanished enemy. It is no matter for surprise, therefore, that up to the moment of sending this despatch the German Admiralty has not announced the latest 'victory' of its High Seas forces. The testimony to the real course of events is both conclusive and ample, for a large number of Dutch trawlers in the North Sea on Saturday have returned to Ymuiden.

Individually and collectively their evidence comes to this: At six o'clock the German fleet disappeared, whilst for hours afterwards the British squadrons were sighted, searching for the battle which the German admirals were so careful to avoid. Into the hours of darkness the British pursued hope of contest. No possible chance to bring the enemy to that contest was missed, but, alas! in vain, for equally – and even to a superior extent – no chance that the contest should take place was risked, by the Kaiser's admirals. After their Zeppelins had reported the presence of great British forces they devoted all their abilities to escape meeting with the Fleet which they were boasting a few weeks ago they had smashed.

31 October 1916

OUR DESTROYERS IN THE BATTLE OF JUTLAND
'Carrying On'

By Rudyard Kipling

What mystery is there like the mystery of the other man's job – or what world so cut off as that which he enters when he goes to it? The eminent surgeon is altogether such a one as ourselves, even till his hand falls on the knob of the theatre door. After that, in the silence, among the ether fumes, no man except his acolytes, and they won't tell, has ever seen his face. So with the unconsidered curate. Yet, before the war, he had more experience of the business and detail of death than any of the people who contemned him. His face also, as he stands his bedside-watches – that countenance with which he shall justify himself to his Maker – none have ever looked upon. Even the ditcher is a priest of mysteries at the high moment when he lays out in his mind his levels and the fall of the water that he alone can draw off clearly. But catch any of these men five minutes after they have left their altars, and you will find the doors are shut.

Chance sent me almost immediately after the Jutland fight a lieutenant of one of the destroyers engaged. Among other matters, I asked him if there was any particular noise. 'Well, I haven't been in the trenches, of course,' he replied, 'but I don't think there could have been much more noise than there was.' This bears out a report of a destroyer who could not be certain whether an enemy battleship had blown up or not, saying that in that particular corner it would have been impossible to identify anything less than the explosion of a whole magazine. 'It wasn't exactly noise,' he reflected. 'Noise is what you take in from outside. This was inside you. It seemed to lift you right out of everything.' 'And how did the light affect one?' I asked, trying to work out a theory that noise and light produced beyond known endurance form an unknown anæsthetic and stimulant, comparable to, but infinitely more potent than the soothing effect of the smoke-pall of ancient battles. 'The lights were rather curious,' was the answer. 'I don't know that one noticed searchlights particularly, unless they meant business; but when a lot of big guns loosed off together, the whole sea was lit up, and you could see our destroyers running about like cockroaches on a tin soup plate.'

'Then is black the best colour for our destroyers? Some commanders seem to think we ought to use grey.' 'Blessed if I know,' said young Dante. 'Everything shows black in that light. Then it all goes out again with a bang. Trying for the eyes if you are spotting.' 'And how did the dogs take it?' I pursued. There are several destroyers more or less owned by pet dogs, who start life as the chance-found property of a stoker, and end in supreme command of the bridge. 'Most of 'em didn't like it a bit. They went below one time, and wanted to be loved. They knew it wasn't ordinary practice.' 'What did Arabella do?' I had heard a good deal of Arabella. 'Oh, Arabella's quite different. Her job has always been to look after her master's pyjamas – folded up at the head of the bunk, you know. She found out pretty soon the bridge was no place for a lady, so she hopped downstairs and got in. You know how she makes three little jumps to it – first on to the chair, then on the flap-table, and then up on the pillow. When the show was over there she was, as usual.' 'Was she glad to see her master?' 'Ra-ather. Arabella was the bold, gay lady-dog then!' Now Arabella is between nine and eleven and a half inches long. 'Does the Hun run to pets at all?' 'I shouldn't say so. He's an unsympathetic felon – the Hun. But he might cherish a dachshund or so. We never picked up any ships' pets off him, and I'm sure we should if there had been.'

That I believed as implicitly as the tale of a destroyer attack some months ago, the object of which was to flush Zeppelins. It succeeded, for the flotilla was attacked by several. Right in the middle of the flurry a destroyer asked permission to stop and lower a dinghy to pick up the ship's dog, which had fallen overboard. Permission was granted, and the dog was duly rescued. 'Lord knows what the Hun made of it,' said my informant. 'He was rumbling round, dropping bombs, and the dinghy was digging out for all she was worth, and the Dog-Fiend was swimming for Dunkirk. It must have looked rather mad from above. But they saved the Dog-Fiend, and then everybody swore he was a German spy in disguise.'

'And – about this Jutland fight?' I hinted not for the first time. 'Oh, that was just a fight. There was more of it than any other fight, I suppose, but I expect all modern naval actions must be pretty much the same.' 'But what does one do – how does one feel?' I insisted, though I knew it was hopeless. 'One does one's job. Things are happening all the time. A man may be right under your nose one minute – serving a gun or something, and the next minute he isn't there.' 'And one notices that at the time?' 'Yes. But there's no time to keep on noticing it. You've got to carry on somehow or other, or your show stops. I tell you what one does notice, though. If one goes below for anything, or has to pass through a flap somewhere, and one sees the old wardroom clock ticking, or a photograph pinned up, or anything of that sort, one notices that. Oh, yes, and there was another thing – the way a ship seemed to blow up if you were far off her. You'd see a glare, then a blaze, and then the smoke – miles high lifting quite slowly. Then you'd get the row and the jar of it – just like bumping over submarines. Then, a long while after, p'raps you run through a regular rain of bits of burnt paper coming down on the decks – like showers of volcanic ash, you know.' The door of the operating-room seemed just about to open, but it shut again. 'And the Hun's gunnery?' 'That was various. Sometimes they began quite well, and went to pieces after they'd been strafed a little; but sometimes they picked up again. There was one Hun-boat that got no end of a hammering, and it seemed to do her gunnery good. She improved tremendously till we sank her. I expect we'd knocked out some scientific Hun in the controls, and he'd been succeeded by a man who knew how.' It used to be 'Fritz' last year when they spoke of the enemy. Now it is Hun, or, as I have heard, 'Yahun', being a superlative of Yahoo. In the Napoleonic wars we called the Frenchmen too many names for any one of them to endure; but this is the age of standardisation. 'And what about our Lower Deck?' I continued. 'They? Oh, they carried on as usual. It takes a lot to impress the Lower Deck when they're busy.' And he mentioned several little things that confirmed this. They had a great deal to do, and they did it serenely because they had been trained to carry on under all conditions without panicking. What they did in the way of running repairs was even more wonderful, if that be possible, than their normal routine. The Lower Deck nowadays is full of strange fish with unlooked for accomplishments, as in the recorded case of two simple seamen of a destroyer who, when need was sorest, came to the front as trained experts in first-aid.

'And now – what about the actual Hun losses at Jutland?' I ventured. 'You've seen the list haven't you?' 'Yes, but it occurred to me – that they might have been a shade underestimated, and I thought perhaps—' A perfectly plain asbestos fire-curtain descended in front of the already locked door. It was none of his business to dispute the drive. If there were any discrepancies between estimate and results, one might be sure that the enemy knew about them, which was the chief thing that matters.

It was, said he, Joss that the light was so bad at the hour of the last round-up when our main fleet had come down from the north and shovelled the Hun round on his tracks. Per contra, had it been any other kind of weather the odds were the Hun would not have ventured so far. As it was, the Hun's fleet had come out and gone back again, none the better for air and exercise. We must be thankful for what we had managed to pick up. But, talking of picking up, there was an instance of almost unparalleled Joss which had stuck in his memory. A soldier-man, related to one of the officers in one of our ships that was put down, had got five days' leave from the trenches, which he spent with his relative aboard, and thus dropped in for the whole performance. He had been employed in helping to spot and had lived up a mast till the ship sank when he stepped off into the water and swam about till he was fished out and put ashore. By that time, the tale goes, his engine-room-dried khaki had shrunk halfway up his legs and arms, in which costume he reported himself to the War Office and pleaded for one little day's extension of leave to make himself decent. 'Not a bit of it,' said the War Office. 'If you chose to spend your leave playing with sailormen and getting wet all over, that's your concern. You will return to duty by tonight's boat.' (This may be a libel on the W.O., but it sounds very like them.) 'And he had to,' said the boy, 'but I expect he spent the next week at Headquarters telling generals all about the fight.'

'And, of course, the Admiralty gave you all lots of leave?' 'Us? Yes, heaps. We had nothing to do except clean down and oil up and be ready to go to sea again in a few hours.' That little fact was brought out at the end of almost every destroyer's report. 'Having returned to base at such and such a time, I took in oil, &c., and reported ready for sea at – o'clock.' When you think of the amount of work a ship needs even after peace manœuvres, you can realise what has to be done on the heels of an action. And, as there is nothing like house-work for the troubled soul of a woman, so a general clean-up is good for sailors. I had this from a petty officer who had also passed through deep waters. 'If you've seen your best friend go from alongside you, and your own officer, and your own boat's crew with him, and things of that kind, a man's best comfort is small variegated jobs which he is damned for continuous.' Presently my friend of the destroyer went back to his stark, desolate life, where feelings do not count, and the fact of his being cold, wet, sea-sick, sleepless, or dog-tired had no bearing whatever on his business, which was to turn out at any hour in any weather, and do or endure, decently, according to ritual, what that hour and weather demanded. It is hard to reach the kernel of Navy minds. The unbribable seas and mechanisms they work on and through have given them the simplicity of elements and machines. The habit of dealing with swift accident; a life of closest and strictest association with their own caste as well as contact with all kinds of men all earth over have added an immense cunning to those qualities; and that they are from early youth cut out of all feelings that may come between them and their ends makes them more incomprehensible than Jesuits, even to their own people. What, then, must they be to the enemy?

Here is a service, which prowls forth, and achieves, at the lowest, something of a victory. How far-reaching a one only the war's end will reveal. It returns in gloomy silence, broken by occasional hoot of the long-shore loafer, after issuing a bulletin, which, though it may enlighten the professional mind, does not exhilarate the layman. Meantime, the enemy triumphs, wirelessly, far and wide. A few frigid and perfunctory seeming contradictions are put forward against his resounding claims; a naval expert or two is heard talking 'off'; the rest is silence. Anon, the enemy, after a prodigious amount of explanation, which not even the neutrals seem to take any interest in, revises his claims, and, very modestly, enlarges his losses. Still no sign. After weeks there appears a document giving our version of the affair, which is as colourless, detached, and scrupulously impartial as the findings of a prize-court. It opines that the list of enemy losses which it submits 'give the minimum in regard to numbers, though it is possibly not entirely accurate in regard to the particular class of vessels, especially those that were sunk during the night attacks.' Here the matter rests and remains – just like our blockade. There is an insolence about it all that makes one gasp.

Yet that insolence springs naturally and unconsciously as an oath out of the same spirit that caused the destroyer to pick up the dog. The reports themselves, and tenfold more the stories not in the reports, are charged with it, but no words by any outsider can reproduce just that professional tone and touch. A man writing home after the fight points out that the great consolation for not having cleaned up the enemy altogether was that 'anyhow those east coast devils' – a fellow-squadron, if you please, which up till Jutland had had most of the fighting – 'were not there. They missed that show. We were as cock-a-hoop as a girl who had been to a dance that her sister has missed.'

This was one of the figures in that dance: 'A little British destroyer, her midships rent by a great shell meant for a battle-cruiser, exuding steam from every pore, able to go ahead but not to steer, unable to get out of anybody's way, likely to be rammed by any one of a dozen ships, her siren whimpering, "Let me through! Make way!" her crew fallen in aft dressed in lifebelts ready for her final plunge, and cheering as wildly as it might have been an enthusiastic crowd when the King passes.'

Let us close on that note. We have been compassed about so long and so blindingly by wonders and miracles; so overwhelmed by revelations of the spirit or men in the basest and most high, that we have neither time to keep tally of these furious days, nor mind to discern upon which hour of them the world's fate turned.

Not in the thick of the fight,
Not in the press of the odds,
Do the heroes come to their height
Or we know the demi-gods.
That stands over till peace.
We can only perceive
Men returned from the seas,
Very grateful for leave.
They grant us sudden days,
Snatched from their business of war,
We are too close to appraise
What manner of men they are.
And whether their names go down
With age-kept victories,
Or whether they battle and drown
Unreckoned is hid from our eyes.
They are too near to be great,
But our children shall understand
When and how our fate
Was changed, and by whose hand.
Our children shall measure their worth.
We are content to be blind,
For we know that we walk on a new-born earth
With the saviours of mankind.

24 November 1916

SINKING OF THE *BRITANNIC*
Scenes of Rescue

Yesterday the Secretary of the Admiralty issued the following: Referring to communiqué yesterday, there were no wounded on board the hospital ship *Britannic*. The numbers consisted solely of ship's crew and hospital staff.

A DASTARDLY CRIME
Athens, Tuesday (Midnight)

By G. J. Stevens

About 150 survivors of the hospital steamer *Britannic* were landed at Piræus this evening, of which forty were nurses. The vessel carried 700 (? 1,100)[sic] persons in all, of which 120 are nurses and officers and men of the RAMC. She was torpedoed at eight o'clock this morning, four miles off the island of Zea, while the nurses and RAMC staff were at breakfast, and sank in fifty-five minutes. Perfect order and discipline were kept, all the RAMC men lining up on deck.

Her boats were swung out by degrees, but after twenty minutes her remaining boats could no longer be swung on account of the ship's heavy list. Three of the first boats launched were caught by the screws and cut to pieces, most of those on board perishing. Some of the crew were caught by the explosion, and their egress from the forward part of the vessel cut off. The exact number of those who perished is not yet known.

All the survivors were landed by the ship's own boats at the island of Zea, whence they were picked up by vessels sent to their help from the fleet at Keratsini Bay. Some were brought to Piræus, and the remainder were taken on board the fleet.

A statement was made to me by survivors that two of the navigating officers who were on deck stated that they saw the wake of two torpedoes which struck the ship. The captain of the vessel says he is convinced that she was sunk by torpedoes launched by an enemy submarine.

But, apart from these statements, there is a fact which the commanding officer of a destroyer sent to the help of the ship from Keratsini gives which not only establishes the guilt of the Huns, but brings them out in the execrable light of cold-blooded murderers revelling over the agony of their victims. The wireless of the *Britannic* was kept going, giving out 'SOS' signals. The signals were returned from the destroyer that she was hastening to her rescue, and then the destroyer received the countermanding distress signal, evidently given out by the German submarine in a dastardly attempt to stop help reaching its victims. The destroyer, on receiving the countermanding signal, turned back, and only found out the enemy's cowardly trick when further urgent calls were received from the *Britannic*. This accounts for the delay in reaching her.

15 September 1917

THE CAMPAIGN AGAINST SUBMARINE PIRATES
Some Recent Fights

We have received from the Admiralty the following highly interesting details concerning recent engagements fought between British vessels (and in one case a seaplane) and enemy submarines. It will be seen that in several of these instances the pirates paid for their crimes by destruction.

From one of our auxiliary naval forces a torpedo was seen approaching the starboard beam. It jumped out of the water when 100 yards off, and struck the engine-room near the water-line, making a large rent and flooding several compartments. The starboard lifeboat was blown into the air, pieces of it landing on the wireless aerial. Soon afterwards a periscope was observed just before the port beam. It turned and made for the ship, but quickly disappeared as the enemy further submerged. Again it appeared to be followed this time by a conning tower. Fire was opened, and the first shot hit the base of the conning tower and removed the two periscopes. Many hits were obtained, and the submarine quickly assumed a list to port, and several men came out of the hatch abaft the conning tower. The enemy wallowed along for a space, with his stern almost submerged and with oil squirting from his side, and the crew came on deck and waved their hands. At this sign of surrender 'cease fire' was ordered, whereat the U-boat started to make off at a fair speed, evidently hoping to disappear in the misty weather. Fire was again opened. A loud explosion took place forward, and, falling over on his side, the enemy sank, the last thing seen being the sharp bow, end up, slowly disappearing beneath the water. Two survivors were picked up. Our ship arrived safely in harbour.

A British submarine sighted an enemy submarine 11/9 points on the starboard bow, so dived but after seeing him through the periscope for a few minutes lost sight of him. Our boat came to the surface again, and about three hours later saw the enemy on the starboard beam from two to three miles away. Our boat dived to attack, but the enemy altered course, and was again lost to view. His apparent objective being conjectured, course was altered in the hope of cutting him off, and eventually he was again detected on the port bow, steering as had been surmised. Course was altered as necessary, and when as favourable a position as was thought possible was obtained, a torpedo was fired. A splash was observed in line with and close to his stern, and a few seconds after the enemy was seen with his stern out of water, smoke hanging round it, and the conning tower half-submerged. A minute or two later he disappeared.

One of our small craft sighted an enemy submarine at a distance of 10,000 yards. She maintained her course, and five minutes later the enemy stopped and then proceeded towards her. Suddenly he submerged, and shortly afterwards his periscope appeared close by on the starboard bow for a few seconds, and then disappeared. Helm was ported, and when over the position where the periscope had been seen, an explosive charge was dropped. The ship then circled round, and when in position once more dropped another charge. The explosion of this was followed after two or three seconds by another and much more violent explosion, which shook the vessel from stem to stern. The water became black over a very large area, and a considerable quantity of thick oil and flotsam came to the surface.

A seaplane proceeded to attack an enemy submarine which she had observed manœuvring, apparently, into position to fire a torpedo at a passing merchant ship. Before the seaplane arrived over the submarine the latter submerged, but three bombs were dropped on the position where he had disappeared from sight. In five minutes' time a large upheaval was noticed where the bombs had been dropped. This could best be compared to a huge bubble, rising some distance above the level of the sea and distinctly visible for a minute or more. There was no further sign of the submarine.

A patrol vessel noticed a wake with a considerable amount of foam travelling almost parallel to her course on the bow a short distance away. She crossed this wake and dropped an explosive over it. Almost immediately a second charge was dropped, and after it had exploded another explosion took place. Oil and bubbles were coming to the surface, and on this spot a further charge was exploded. Two more patrol craft arrived on the scene and discharged their charges. The oil, which was still rising after an interval of twelve hours, was of a heavy brown nature with a smell like petrol.

One of our naval forces, hearing gunfire, steered for the position and soon sighted an enemy submarine on the bow. Fire was opened, and a hit obtained. A large explosion resulted but the effects quickly dispersed to reveal no sign of the enemy, whose hull and conning tower were distinctly visible before.

Two submarines attacked a defensively armed merchant vessel. The first submarine fired a torpedo at close range, which missed, and the ship sank her by gunfire. The second submarine then attacked the ship by gunfire, but was damaged and driven off.

A defensively armed merchant vessel encountered a submarine, which endeavoured to attack at close range. The ship opened fire, hitting the submarine twice, and causing her to disappear vertically, the sea appearing to boil for a considerable time after.

29 October 1917

BRITISH NAVY AND ITS WORK
What is Wrong?

By Archibald Hurd

We all have our war maps, which are studied from time to time in order to judge the importance of movements on the various fronts. How many persons ever refer to a chart, or even an atlas, when some incident occurs at sea in the effort to understand its significance? The sea is regarded as a flat expanse without features, and thus great injustice is done to the British Fleet. In point of fact, the strategic features of the oceans and seas are more vital than those of any land front; while in the latter case an army can, and does, maintain an unbroken line of trenches, at sea a navy cannot do so. Our seamen – about one-twentieth the number of our soldiers – have to patrol on a front of about 900 miles in the North Sea, always conscious that darkness invites a surprise attack by the enemy at an unknown point. Darkness and surprise are the allies of a fleet acting on interior lines and placed on the defensive. He can always make a thrust, like an adept swordsman, and he can do so with every possibility of success on a moonless night, choosing as his objective a point off the Shetland islands, or bombarding a spot on the coast between Yorkshire and Essex, or perhaps endeavouring to cut our essential communications across the Channel; in any event he has a 900-mile front open to him, and he has the enormous advantage which surprise, darkness, and speed give him.

The Navy is fighting five enemies at sea, which may be set out thus:

NATURAL FORCES – Storms and fogs and currents are conspicuous among them. This country loses many hundred lives a year at sea – what are described as marine casualties. We are at war, but nature indulges in just as fierce outbreaks, and just as baffling moods of fog and mist as at other times. Nature has to be defeated.

THE HIGH SEAS FLEET – We cannot see the German ships, but they exist. We are apt to forget that the High Seas Fleet offers a continual menace to us. No force has ever been 'contained' as the enemy of today is being 'contained'; month after month passes, and, rather than fight, he remains behind his minefields, shore guns, and submarines, with Heligoland as his impregnable advanced base, provided with destroyers, submarines, and air craft. But the Grand Fleet, with its attendant cruisers, destroyers, and auxiliaries, must be kept concentrated and at the fullest possible strength, so that if the Germans suddenly break out their defeat is certain. The Grand Fleet must always be ready for battle.

THE MINE – All the time the Germans are laying mines off our shores, in the entrances to our harbours, and in the highways of commerce. They have many mine-laying submarines always at work, creeping along unseen, and placing their 'eggs' where they are likely to do the most harm.

THE RAIDER – Since the war began, the peril of the raider has existed, and it still exists. The Germans have not got many through the net, even in the darkness and by using neutral flags and disguises, but they are continually trying to do so. Their ill-success is a tribute to the efficiency of our patrols, and to the vigilance of the Grand Fleet. In the last Great War the only trouble after Trafalgar was due to raiders which were always at sea, getting in and out of their ports in spite of the watchfulness of our blockading forces, and capturing thousands of our merchantmen. We thus lost half our mercantile marine, and the captures were more numerous after Trafalgar than before.

THE SUBMARINE – The Germans have pressed into their service the submarine, armed with powerful quick-firing guns and the torpedo, carrying an explosive charge which can sink almost any ship. The submarine has a great radius of action, and is no longer confined to the waters in proximity to its base; it can travel on the surface twice as fast as an ordinary tramp steamer, and under the water about as fast; it can operate by night as by day; it can fire its torpedo when submerged, with only a periscope showing above the surface, and the periscope, a very small object, is often undistinguishable even at fairly close quarters. The effect of arming merchantmen has been to drive the U-boats under water when attacking, and that, while decreasing our shipping losses, increases our Fleet's difficulties.

Those five paragraphs perhaps convey some idea of the tasks which the British Fleet is doing at a time when, ignoring the charts, some persons are suggesting that the work is being badly done. I have always held that this country will never appreciate the debt which it owes to its seamen until it is invaded or reduced to a condition of starvation – brought face to face with some such situation as that of Italy today. All the fighting is taking place outside this country. Why? Our armies would stand defeated if the British Fleet failed to achieve complete success at sea.

But recently the Germans sent out two swift raiders. The non-charters at once declared in indignation that someone ought to be punished. If you have an ordinary map by you, turn to the North Sea! You will notice that the incident, a very unfortunate but unavoidable incident, as the First Lord, like Mr Balfour on a former occasion, has said, occurred somewhere between Bergen and the Shetland Islands. The enemy warships, with a speed of over 30 knots and heavy guns, rushed northward in the darkness with all lights screened, keeping close in to Danish and Norwegian territorial waters; in half an hour they had completed the outrage and murder; and then they had to cover a course of 200 miles – notice the distance – until they reached the Naze and could decide whether to return to Germany by way of the North Sea or to strike home through the Sound; for the Germans, with their mines and patrols, can use the Baltic entrance for cruisers as we cannot. Two hundred miles only! The Naze is about 350 miles from the Firth of Forth, and even farther from any naval base on the English coast. Study a chart of the North Sea, draw a line from the scene of the engagement to the Naze, and the character of the incident is revealed.

One more point. The Fleet is grappling with two insidious war diseases – the raider and the submarine; the cure for the former is the cruiser, which must be more powerful than the raider, or it will be defeated; and the cure for the submarine is the destroyer. British seamen, whether 'in the Northern mists' or at the Admiralty, never know which form the trouble will take. They may provide a cruiser escort, which means that the cruiser, whose defence against the U-boat is her speed, has to keep pace with the merchantmen, going at six or eight knots an hour; and thus a big target may be presented for a U-boat, as instance the fate of a score of cruisers. Or they may decide that the submarine is the immediate danger, and use destroyers for escort, and then an enemy cruiser of great gun-power and speed may appear out of the darkness. Sometimes the enemy is bound to score. But how often does he do so? If we look at our meal tables, we get an answer: if we turn to a paper and see that about 5,000 'targets' for submarines and raiders enter or leave our ports every week, we get further evidence of the way the Fleet is doing its work; if we study the output of our munition works, largely dependent on oversea supplies of raw material, further light is thrown on the matter; if we glance at the morning communiqués describing what our sea-supported soldiers are doing, we must be reminded that folly and muddle reign neither at the Admiralty, nor in the Grand Fleet, nor in the patrols.

With limited resources the Navy is performing miracles every day, and yet we are told that there is widespread public dissatisfaction. Perhaps an invasion would cure that trouble, if it exists, of which I am not convinced, or at least such a threat as our forefathers lived under for years, when Napoleon trained the Grand Army at Boulogne and for month after month continued his preparations for overrunning this country, The great British sailors, knowing that he had no long-range guns, mines, submarines, or destroyers to support his scheme, nevertheless admitted that they could not interfere with him, and could only hope to defeat him when he put to sea. Science has come to the aid of the second greatest sea-power of the world, and some of us, after a hearty sea-borne meal, sit in our easy chairs in comfort, perhaps, smoking tobacco from Cuba, or India, or the United States, and wonder what our sailors are doing.

17 December 1917

TORPEDOING OF THE BATTLESHIP *WIEN*

Dash into Trieste, *Venice, Thursday*

By Perceval Gibbon

We have received from Mr Perceval Gibbon the following detailed account of the Italian dash into Trieste harbour and the torpedoing of the Austrian battleship *Wien*. A brief announcement of this, one of the most daring naval feats of the war, has already appeared in the *Daily Telegraph*.

There are men and deeds which shine athwart the fog of war, across its dreary routine and staleness, like a sunbeam through clouds. Such a man, such a deed, came to light when two little ships and their crews gnawed their way through the booms and nets which guard the inner harbour of Trieste, and sank the battleship *Wien*, where she lay moored to her buoy, with her sister the *Monarch* slumbering alongside of her. A guarded harbour, steel nets fringed with mines, sentries yawning by their guns on the mole and the breakwater, and the Italian sailors, under Lieutenant Rizzo, of the navy, working at the cables of the nets within earshot of the forts and the ships till they sawed them apart and could run in and do their work! It was more than a great feat of arms; it was a lark.

The *Wien* was one of three ships launched in 1895. Her sisters were the *Monarch* and the *Budapest*. She carried four 10in and six 6in guns, and a crew of 441 officers and men. She has owed Italy a death any time these two years. The Italians nearly got her a month ago when she was shelling the Lower Piave, and the motor-boats went for her with their torpedoes. She has, too, had other narrow the escapes, Now she lies on the bottom of the Vallone di Muggia in Trieste Harbour, on a clean sandy bottom in about eleven fathoms of turquoise-blue water. Lieutenant Rizzo and the crews of his two launches – craft not much bigger than a ship's lifeboat – are the men who put her there. Lieutenant Rizzo is one of those men in the Italian navy who make a weird speciality of 'tickling the Austrian in his bed'. He is thirty years of age, a Sicilian with the strong masculine good looks of his race. In charge of his second boat was a tough fire-eater of sixty-two years.

The thing had been well prepared after careful study of the mined area. It seemed that the Austrians had devised a system of combined nets and mines, so that Rizzo's chances were great, at the best, of being blown to pieces. One of his chief problems was that of the huge steel cables attached to the nets. But he cut these handily asunder. On the night of the 9th, when the two little boats set out, there was mist on the sea. It was past midnight when they crawled in towards the coast where lies the white city of Trieste, cascading in snowy terraces down its radiant hillside to the piers and docks of its port. The two boats crawled in towards the harbour mouth.

Trieste Harbour is an affair of three piers, jutting seaward, making thus two channels, one to either hand of the central pier, which is also a breakwater. These channels were closed by booms and nets with their mines, all linked to the piers by the great steel hawsers. The boats glided alongside the pier, and Rizzo climbed up its concrete side and reconnoitred the situation. There was nobody on that pier. On the middle pier, however, was the guardroom. There could be heard a confusion of voices and the barking of a dog, and from the railway station ashore the noise of an engine screaming vociferously, and between-while the slap-slap of the feet of a sentry patrolling the middle pier. Lieutenant Rizzo crawled back and gave the order, and up came his men, crawling hands and knees over the concrete, passing big cutting tools from hand to hand. Groping their way to the cables, some set to work to cut them, while two men scouted inshore lest some sentry should arrive. I shouldn't have liked to be that sentry, with those big, wet sailors lying armed behind the mooring bollards and waiting to silence him!

The cutting instruments worked well. It only needed a strong jar to set the mines exploding, but the cutters bit their way through strand after strand of the twisted steel wire. Three cables above water were severed without trouble, then five more below water were grappled and hauled to the surface and cut in their turn. At last came the moment when the weight of the net and its attachments tore the last remaining steel strands asunder. The whole great cobweb of metal and explosives sank. The harbour lay open!

Rizzo and his men crawled back to their boats, and those boats moved like shadows into the Vallone of Muggia, where the *Wien* and the *Monarch* lay nosing their buoys. Nearest lay the *Wien*; the *Monarch* slumbered 200 yards beyond her. Rizzo edged in to investigate, and then backed off till he had his enemy at 150 yards. His second boat, under the old petty officer, shifted out upon his beam to get a line which cleared the *Wien*'s bow and commanded the *Monarch*'s great steel flank. Rizzo raised his arm in that gloom, and saw the answering gesture of the old petty officer. It was the moment. 'Let her go!' In a second four long steel devils were sliding through the water for the enemy. A roar – a blast of flame – a waterspout raining on to them – and a second roar, as the *Monarch*, too, got her dose! In the motor-boats the men yelled involuntarily as the torpedoes landed on their targets.

A searchlight flashed out from the *Wien* and sawed at the darkness. An agitated scream sounded over the water, 'Wer da?' ('Who goes there?') There were shoutings and stampings along the deck of the wounded ship; searchlights waking along the shore and on the breakwaters; and anti-aircraft guns rousing everywhere. None in Trieste knew whence the attack had come – whether from air or sea. The sky was festooned with bursting shrapnel, while ships in the harbour opened with their guns towards the harbour mouth; shelling the misty Adriatic at random. By the light of that furious illumination the Italian sailors saw the great bulk of the *Wien* listing towards them. By this time they were making for the harbour month. Shells spouted around them, but none hit them; and both boats saw, ere they left, that last subsidence, that wriggle and resignation with which a dead ship goes under.

The *Monarch* still floated, but the *Wien* lay at the bottom. The conquerors breakfasted at home. Every man of them was very hungry.

4 January 1918

BRITISH NAVY AND ITS WORK
Fighting the Submarine

By Archibald Hurd

Week by week we are reminded that the Germans still place their reliance in the unrestricted submarine war. The Admiralty returns indicate that the menace continues and, if not checked, will exert its influence on all our war activities. In these circumstances we shall do well to understand the problem.

When the war opened it was recognised by all the Powers that a merchant ship must be stopped, visited, and searched, and that only in exceptional circumstances could it be destroyed even if sailing under an enemy flag, while in no condition could a neutral vessel be sunk. The practice was for vessels to be captured, taken into port, and there placed in the Prize Court. Even when destruction was permissible an obligation was laid on the man-of-war to place in safety crews and passengers if any were on board. All those regulations Germany abrogated from the time when she determined to use submarines for destroying commerce; at first she devoted her attention only to enemy shipping, but she has since treated neutral vessels in the same way, pursuing, without regard for law or humanity, her sink-at-sight policy. She has ignored all the recognised rules of war on commerce because otherwise she could not employ submarines for the purpose. But it is not perhaps understood that in doing so she handicapped the work of the British Navy. A moment's consideration supports that view. It is difficult to deal with a foe who discharges a torpedo at sight and then disappears beneath the surface, having the capacity either of remaining *perdu* for a matter of forty-eight hours or of travelling under water in an unknown direction for a distance of 100 miles or so.

Then another point deserves consideration. The Germans are using four types of submarines. There is first the cruiser class, big ships with a high speed, a great radius of action, a heavy armament, including 5.9in guns (firing a shell of 90 lb), as well as a large number of torpedoes which can be discharged while the vessel is still under the water. The torpedo – a marvellous invention – travels at a speed of 30 to 40 knots an hour for a distance ranging up to 10,000 yards, and has an explosive charge sufficient to tear away the whole stem of a ship or rip open her boiler-room. Secondly come the U-boats proper, smaller craft, of about 900 tons, also armed with gun and torpedo, and capable of operating in the Atlantic or Channel; thirdly, the mine-laying submarines are of smaller displacement, nippy little vessels; and fourthly, there are the submarines which are equipped for cutting cables. When those facts are considered it will be understood that the Navy is up against a problem of great difficulty, if only because these submersible vessels, when travelling on the surface, are about twice as swift as the average tramp steamer, and that in anything from thirty to eighty seconds, according to the type, they can disappear beneath the surface of the sea.

It is said that since the United States entered the war about 40,000 suggestions for combating the submarine have been received by the Navy Department, and nearly all of them have been impracticable. The 'Scientific American', which is in close touch with American naval opinion, recently referred to some of them. When the U-boat campaign was at the height of its success, and immediate and urgent measures were needed, it was believed that the most effective plan would be to blockade the submarines within their individual bases, or failing that, restrict their operations to a certain well-defined area. Hence the proposal to build nets of greater or less magnitude, ranging from those stretched across the separate U-boat exits to the audacious proposal to build a net 250 miles in length across the North Sea. Strategically considered, these netting propositions were perfectly sound; the objections to them were purely of a mechanical and practical character. Great Britain, both in the English Channel and at the northerly entrance to the Irish Sea, had found that the mass of seaweed carried in the swiftly running tides loaded up the nets until they bellied out like the close-reefed topsails of a frigate driving before a gale of wind; and the consensus of opinion among practical seamen ranged all the way from the belief that, if the tackle were made heavy enough, a net could be built and held in place even in the North Sea, down to the conviction that no net whatsoever could be permanently held in place in the location and on the scale proposed.

And this reputable American journal has also pointed out the weakness of other proposals – the towing of nets, steel plates, and similar protective devices, with the object of intercepting and detonating the torpedo before it reaches the ship. The objections to these devices are, first, the difficulty of holding such systems in place in heavy weather; and secondly, the fact that they cut down the speed by one-half. As regards those forms of protection which are interior to the ship itself – such as longitudinal bulkheads and the provision of wide cellular spaces between the outside skin and the interior cargo-carrying hull, the protective value of such construction is fully realised, but torpedo-proof ships would take very much longer to build. The aim of the American Emergency Fleet Corporation is to get afloat at once a large tonnage. The same considerations of urgency have led to the adoption of the moderate speed of 10 to 12 knots. It would take probably twice as long to build torpedo-proof ships having, say, 16 knots speed as it will to build the 11-knot, standard-type freight ships, which constitute the bulk of the construction that is being rushed through at the yards of the United States. Such statements are of interest only as showing that on both sides of the Atlantic every suggestion has been considered.

An examination of a German submarine shows with what ingenuity the enemy has devised double-hulled submarines. There is a light exterior hull, which is open to the sea, and an interior hull to resist the immense pressure of the water. The outer skin may be injured by a depth charge from a destroyer, or by a shell from a gun, or by impact with a merchant ship, but the vessel is not necessarily destroyed in consequence. This sketch, in association with the other considerations which have been advanced, shows how embarrassing is the problem with which the Navy is dealing. I have claimed on more than one occasion that the success achieved by our seamen is greater than there was reason to anticipate in view of the limitation of the resources available – destroyers in particular. Is that conclusion well based, in the knowledge that scores of submarines have been sunk, and that the rate of sinking is still rising? At the same time, I am convinced that science has not yet been given its proper opportunity of dealing with the submarine. So far only about £4,000 – not £4,000,000 – has been spent on purely scientific research into the various problems which the enemy has raised. The officers and men of the Navy have done wonders, but the nation cannot afford to be satisfied until the assurance is given that the scientist, as distinct from the seaman and the engineer, has been given a free hand and provided with ample funds, as at present is not the case. A change of policy in that respect is necessary – and at once, for our sea-power is shrinking week by week, and we must not let it fall so low that we cannot continue the war.

11 April 1918

FAILURE OF PIRACY
Hindenburg's Admission

By Archibald Hurd

Field-Marshal von Hindenburg, I learn on indisputable authority, has tacitly admitted that the intensified submarine campaign has failed, and that no hope can any longer be entertained that it will either starve this country or seriously interfere with our military effort in time to save Germany from fatal constriction. He was in Berlin several weeks ago, when he was moved to make a statement on war policy to a delegation of Socialists, oppressed by the economic condition – almost amounting to starvation – to which Germany has been reduced by the blockade. Over a year ago – on 1 February 1917 – in an Army Order, for which the Field-Marshal was responsible, directly or indirectly, it was announced that the submarine 'offers the best and only means of a speedy victorious ending of the war'. In the circumstances, it was not unreasonable that the Socialists should desire some explanation in the spring of 1918 as to when that 'speedy' peace would really come. Hindenburg, confronted with their threats that they would vote no further supplies if the war did not end this summer, gave the assurance that his offensive on the West was certain of success; that it would cost the lives of 400,000 Germans; and that peace would come in August next. So the Germans are living on a new promise, since the one associated with piracy has not been fulfilled, and, as is confessed now, cannot be fulfilled. We have just achieved a triumph in spite of all Germany's efforts. The Admiralty put across the Channel, in order to strengthen our line in France, about 200,000 troops in ten days – a wonderful, and indeed unparalleled, performance, which will convince the enemy more than anything else could do of the failure of his naval policy, for sea-power thus once more supported land-power, piracy notwithstanding.

What happened when preparations were begun for the Western offensive, which was to partake of the character of a 'drive' rather than a battle – for the maximum power was mobilised in artillery, cavalry, infantry, and aircraft – is revealed by the latest Admiralty returns of sinkings of merchantmen. The basis of strength in submarines, as in aircraft, is engines, and, in view of the 'stake all' policy by land, labour and material which was engaged in supporting the sea offensive, has for some time been diverted to the land offensive. The enemy, regarding piracy as complementary to the offensive, determined to send out every possible submersible vessel, so as to support the operations on land, this special effort being timed to precede the opening of the army's attack. He met with increased success for the time as the tonnage returns showed. But the maximum effort could be supported only for a matter of weeks, and then the submarines – or rather such as survived – had to return to port for fresh stores and to rest the crews. The anticipated coup failed, though more submarines were employed even than in April last – just twelve months ago – when 154 ships were sunk in four weeks, and eighty-four unsuccessfully attacked. Only 142 ships were destroyed in twice the number of weeks in the period ending on 23 March last, eighty-three being attacked unsuccessfully.

Now the reaction, owing to a shortage of submarines due to the diversion of labour and material, has set in, as it was bound to do. The Germans have been able to maintain lately far fewer vessels on the trade routes, and last week's consolatory drop to only nine ships sunk, as contrasted with an average of eighteen in the preceding eight weeks, is followed today by another good return – only six ships having been destroyed against fifteen attacked. That is one side of the picture. On the other, we have the increasingly successful efforts of our patrols, assisted by those under the American ensign. The destruction of submarines is proceeding at about twice the rate attained a year ago.

The outlook is more encouraging than it was but we may have set-backs. Once more the Germans may, as a last hope, concentrate on submarine construction. But, in any event, the crews are deteriorating. Of that there is ample evidence, the proportion of trained men showing a steady decline. While hoping for the best, we must prepare, if not for the worst, at least for the recurrence of black weeks, though they will never be as black as those of a year ago. So, as we have arrears of shipping of about 3½ million tons to make good, labour and material must be set free for the shipyards and engine shops. Our sea front is of all our fronts of first importance, and whatever success we may have elsewhere can offer no compensation for weakness by sea.

Chapter 6

The Balkans, Turkey, Italy and the Mediterranean

15 August 1914

ROUND EUROPE IN WARTIME
Mobilisation Scenes

By E. Ashmead-Bartlett

On Sunday, 26 July, I left London with instructions to join the Austrian army, which was about to invade Servia. I spent the whole of the next day passing down the valley of the Rhine and reached Frankfurt at two o'clock. From outward observation Germany seemed absolutely calm; I could discover no movement of an extraordinary nature on the line; and the railway service was running in a normal manner. All the Germans with whom I spoke laughed at the idea of a European war and took but little interest in the Austrian quarrel with Servia.

On entering Austrian territory the situation underwent a quick change. I found the railway service completely disorganised and but few civilian trains running. However, we arrived on time at 7 a.m. Tuesday morning. I immediately made inquiries as to whether war correspondents would be allowed to accompany the Austrian forces, and it took me but a short time to learn that my mission with the Austrian army would be wasted. No date had been fixed for the departure of correspondents, and I was officially informed that they would be kept at least five days behind the advancing army. I saw looming up before me a repetition of the sad day which blasted the hopes of so many at the Mustafa Pasha Pass.

I decided to quit Vienna the same day, and to try to join the Servian army at Nish, where I knew I would be welcome, having made the campaign against Bulgaria with the Servians the previous year. I was assured on all sides that no trains were running and it would be quite impossible to get through to Roumania. However, I found a train leaving Vienna at 4.50 for Buda-Pesth, and I decided to take my chance of getting on from there. The train was crowded, and it was only with difficulty that I obtained a seat. The passengers consisted of Roumanians,

Servians, Bulgarians, Russians, and a conglomeration of Levantines, all seeking to regain their own homes before communication entirely broke down. There were also a number of Austrian officers hastening to join their regiments at the front. Large crowds assembled to bid these warriors farewell, and bitter tears were shed by the ladies of Vienna when parting with their brothers, husbands, and friends.

I learnt in Vienna that it was the intention of the Austrians to employ eight army corps against Servia. Six were to invade that country by Semlin and were the 3rd corps from Graz; 4th corps, Buda-Pesth; the 8th, Prague; 9th, Leilmentz; 13th, Agram, and the 7th Temesvar. At the same time the 12th corps, Hemamtadt, was to be mobilised to watch the Roumanian frontier. The two special corps, the 14th and 15th, which during the last four years have been raised in Bosnia and Herzegovina, were to invade Servian territory from Forca, under the command of General Potovick. The troops at Semlin were placed under the orders of General von Bohm Eomolli, the whole being under the supreme direction of Baron Conrad, the chief of the general staff.

How far this mobilisation was ever carried out it is impossible to say. Personally, I do not believe the Austrians ever intended to invade Servia, and this opinion is almost universally shared, not only by the Servians themselves, but also by the headquarter staffs of Roumania and Bulgaria. The ultimatum which Austria handed to the Servian Government left no alternative to the latter except to declare war, and Austria would certainly never have taken this step without the knowledge and consent of Germany, as it was perfectly certain to bring Russia into the conflict.

In official quarters in Paris there is now a fixed contention that Germany intended to bring on a European war towards the latter end of September, but that events marched too quickly for her, and she was in a sense caught unprepared. The German manœuvres this year were to have been on an unprecedented scale. Four army corps were to take part, and four more were to be fully mobilised in their own centres, which would have meant that eight complete corps would have been ready to strike at any moment the Kaiser chose to bring on hostilities.

It is also an undisputed fact that immense quantities of grain have been caught in German ships since the outbreak of war, and that even larger quantities were waiting orders for shipment at the outbreak of hostilities. It was the intention of the German Government to get this immense supply safely into Germany, and the mass of their merchant marine in their own ports before hostilities commenced. This scheme was defeated in two ways. It was thought there would be longer negotiations with Servia, and that Russia would hesitate, and also negotiate, before definitely ranging herself with the Balkan Slavs. It is a little difficult to see why the Triple Alliance should have embroiled itself with Servia merely to seek an excuse to bring on a European war, and this bad bit of diplomacy is likely to cost them dearly in the present struggle.

The Kaiser, according to the official French standpoint, finally made up his mind to attempt to crush France after the absolute failure of the German War Loan both at home and abroad. For Germany could no longer support this burden of armaments, and rather than surrender any portion of their naval and military prowess, the war party preferred to adopt the reckless course of a general conflagration, hoping against hope that England would stand aloof and that Belgium would look quietly on while her territories were being invaded.

The train in which I found myself seemed to be the only civilian one running on the line. I carefully examined the line, and found it blocked with troop trains and war material, including several batteries of heavy howitzers. At ten o'clock we reached Buda-Pesth, and I found that a train was leaving almost immediately for Brasso, on the Roumanian frontier. This was the last train which passed through, and it was with the utmost difficulty that I managed to reach it and to collect my baggage. To enter it was quite another proposition. The only time I have ever seen a train so packed was during the flight of the entire population of Thrace after the rout of Lule Burgas. The scene and noise reminded one of the last days of the Tower of Babel. A mass of men, women, and children was struggling to obtain admittance.

All the languages of Europe seemed to rise in one despondent wave of despair as the occupants searched for seats or watched their baggage disappear amidst the crowds struggling on the platform. By brute force I made my way into a carriage, but could get no further than the corridor, which resembled one of those sombre pictures of the passage of the Beresina by the Grand Army. Every compartment was full and when no more livestock could be forced into the train the guard blew his whistle, and we moved slowly out, whilst a despairing scream arose from hundreds left behind.

We passed a miserable, hot, uncomfortable night, sleeping at fitful intervals, only to awake if anyone stirred in his sleep. From the corridor came groans of discomfort, intermingled with curses. The following day, Wednesday, we made but slow progress, stopping at every station in Hungary. It was interesting, sad, but instructive to watch that terrible machine, a general mobilisation, dragging its victims to the mill of slaughter. The raw material had been so hastily called upon that the majority had to leave for the centres of their regiments in the garments they happened to be wearing at the time the fateful slip of paper was handed to them. There were peasants with the mud of the fields still wet upon their blue, shapeless smocks; small proprietors in riding-breeches and bowler hats; clerks with pens sticking in their ears; the small tradesman with his account book in his hand.

All the various elements which make up civilian life were there; all taken from their homes and their occupations without warning to fight for a cause which not one in ten understood and in which not one in a hundred was really interested. At the stations they were being hastily marshalled by non-commissioned officers, and then packed like sardines in the waiting trucks – the proprietor with his farm hand, the country gentleman with his butcher and baker, and bank managers with their clerks. They had ceased to be human beings in the eyes of the Government; they were now so many living creatures capable of bearing arms; mere numbers to be counted and killed like sheep, so that Austrian statesmen could 'boast that their country could put 1,600,000 men in the field'.

Yet these victims of ambition seemed far from unhappy. On the faces of the majority was no look of anguish, but of extreme surprise. Such is human nature – nothing appeals to the mass of mankind so much as excitement and a change. But I could not help thinking how different would be their outlook on life before many days had passed, when the long marches commenced, when food came at uncertain intervals, when the heat of the day would be followed by the cold of the night, when the shrapnel commenced to burst over the heads of this mass of leaderless sheep, when the bullets began their mournful whistle, and when the sun would shine on thousands of hostile bayonets.

The preliminary stages of a great war are the saddest of all. It is the snatching from the home which affects one most, the last farewells, the weeping women and hard-thinking children unable to account for the sudden change in their lives. There are many who cannot bear to see a flock of sheep being driven along a country road to a market town and the slaughterhouse, yet the same housewives who will turn away their heads and comment on the cruelty of their husbands' appetites will be the first to enter a butcher's shop to select the choicest joint for their table. It is the same in war – when the conscripts are being driven to the front they command far more sympathy than when arrayed in martial attire; their natural occupation seems to be to become cold meat at any hour of the day or night.

This dreary journey continued until 4 p.m., when we reached Brasso, the frontier town before one enters Roumania. We had been told that the train would go no further, and that we would have to get out and motor to Predal, the first Roumanian station, a distance of 20 kilometres, but fortunately we were spared this crowning inconvenience, and the train carried us on to Predal, where we changed and entered the connection for Bucharest. I reached the Roumanian capital at midnight and eagerly inquired for news, but could learn nothing except that the Austrians had commenced to bombard Belgrade.

I passed one day (Thursday, 29 July) in Bucharest to find out what attitude Roumania would adopt, and also to buy some necessary articles for the campaign in Servia, as I had left London without any kit. There I found the Roumanian army anxious to march against Austria, but the Government anxious to preserve a strict neutrality. Whenever soldiers marched through the streets they were received with tremendous enthusiasm; at night-time, in the cafés, the officers, who always wear full uniform, stuck large bouquets in their buttonholes, and sang patriotic songs. The Roumanians are anxious for war to redeem their honour, and to prove that they can fight. Their bloodless intervention in the Servo–Bulgarian campaign caused them to lose caste among the other Balkan nations, and they feel their position keenly.

At 7 a.m. on Friday, 30 July, I took the train for Sofia, the line being still open. Passing through Bulgarian territory, I could discover no trace of any military movement. The population seemed perfectly peaceful and happy. They are a strange race, these Bulgarians. Less than a year ago they lost in their two wars no fewer than 140,000 of their male population dead. Yet they seem to have completely recovered from the shock, and to have entirely forgotten their losses and the enormous sacrifices made by the whole nation during the war. I reached Sofia at midnight. There was no news of any sort.

On the following day, Saturday, 1 August, I went to see our Minister, Sir Henry Bax Ironside, who also could add nothing to my knowledge of what was happening in Europe. He told me the new British Minister to Belgrade, Mr Des Graz, had gone through the day before, having to motor from the frontier, as the line was not yet open. Sir Henry very kindly accompanied me to the house of the Servian Minister, who gave me a permit to cross the frontier and to go to Nish. I dined at the Legation, and stayed there until 2 a.m. No news came through of a declaration of war by Germany on Russia. We merely heard by a telegram that the Emperor had decreed that a menace of war existed, but none of us knew what this meant.

On the following morning, Sunday, 2 August, I left at 7 a.m. by train for Nish, accompanied by a German newspaper correspondent whom I had known in the Turkish War. We were the best of friends, sharing our frugal repast together, talking of the past, and of our plans for the future. We did not reach Nish until 3.30 p.m., and, on arriving, were met by the news that Germany had declared war on Russia.

I must now describe the strange state of affairs at Nish. Nish is a country town of some twenty thousand inhabitants, about the size of Evesham. Its normal life is purely agricultural. Its houses are poor in structure and straggle over a large expanse. Some are of brick, others of wood and straw. In the centre is a large, ill-paved market place, to which the inhabitants of the surrounding districts are wont to send their cattle and their market produce. There are a few evil-looking cafés, which pass as hotels; a few Government buildings, and some unimportant private residences.

Into this miserable, squalid refuge the whole of the upper classes of Belgrade, the Court, and the Government officials retired after the declaration of war, to escape from the Austrian guns. In addition, large numbers of troops were passing through the town on their way to the front; hundreds of officers had also come there, and reservists were trooping in from the surrounding villages. The Servian Parliament was also in session there. Therefore, this market town of a normal population of some 20,000 suddenly found itself flooded by some 30,000 strangers taxing its holding capacity to the extreme limit.

I soon found it was impossible to obtain any accommodation, and, after depositing my baggage in a café, I sallied forth to find our new Minister and our first Secretary, Mr Crackenthorpe, whom I had previously known in Belgrade. It was at the Ministry of Foreign Affairs that I learnt for the first time of the declaration of war, and it was also stated that England and France had followed suit. Thus I and my German friend, with whom I had been on terms of perfect amity half an hour before, suddenly found our respective countries engaged in hostilities. We had no quarrel, and were only too anxious to live on terms of perfect amity. I could hardly believe for some time that the news was true, but it was confirmed half-an-hour later when I met Crackenthorpe at the Hotel Oriental.

On my way up in the train I was much struck by the attitude of the Servian troops. They were clamouring to be led again at the Austrians, and, although they were being mobilised for the third time in two years, there was no grumbling and no air of sadness at the hardness of their lot. The recruits and reservists turned up at the station, accompanied by their wives and families in the best of spirits. Each man had a bunch of flowers stuck in the muzzle of his rifle, and all were singing their national songs. As a matter of fact, these hardy, patriotic peasants have become so used to war that they now regard a call to arms in much the same spirit as the average man regards an invitation to a hunt.

These men were leaving their homes and their ripening crops on which the Servian nation depends for its existence at the most critical period of the year, and yet they took the field without a murmur, rejoicing at again having to defend their homes against the invader and leaving their women folk to do the field work for the third time in three years. I was told that when war was first declared there was a good deal of depression and misgiving, but this quickly passed away, and all the old confidence returned.

Nevertheless, when it became known that Germany had declared war, the enthusiasm of the army and the nation knew no limits. An enormous load of anxiety was at once lifted from their minds. No longer was it a question of defending their firesides against the invader, it now became a war of aggression and revenge. The scene in Nish on this eventful Sunday afternoon will not quickly be forgotten. The whole of the population of Nish and the emigrés from Belgrade and the innumerable soldiers and officers turned out and paraded the streets as if celebrating some great national fête. The River Save passes through the town, and there is a shady promenade along its banks. Here this mass of delighted Slavs concentrated in that same light-hearted atmosphere which one associates with Hampstead-heath on a Bank Holiday.

On all sides one heard of the war of revenge and of the anticipated march into Bosnia and Herzegovina to reclaim these provinces for the Slav family.

It may be that the Servian army will play a decisive role in bringing about the defeat and downfall of the Triple Alliance. The Servian army will certainly prove to be the decisive factor in the Balkans. Germany will never allow Austria to dissipate her forces south of the Danube when the double menace of France and Russia has to be met in Europe proper. Against the Servians, the Austrians will now be obliged to act on the defensive, and they will be obliged to keep a large number of army corps out of the European conflict to protect their Slav provinces of Bosnia and Herzegovina.

The concentration of the Servian army is now almost complete. Some 300,000 excellent troops, under the command of General Misich, are now concentrated in the Morava Valley, and a forward movement may be expected at any moment. This army should be capable of paralysing the movements of at least five Austrian corps, who will have long lines of communication passing through hostile country to keep open. The object of the Servians will be to stir up a general rebellion amongst these Slavs, which will add endless difficulties to the already shaky position of the Triple Alliance.

I need hardly say that an Englishman was made more than welcome on this historic Sunday. I met many old friends whom I had known in the late war, and received a right Royal welcome. I dined that night with one of the managers of the National Bank. He told me that when war became certain, and it was decided to clear out of Belgrade, the whole of the staff worked incessantly, packing the seventy-seven millions of gold in Napoleons which was stored in its vaults. In three days the whole of this sum was safely on its way to Nish. By way of irony they left one franc fifty in the gold safe and a 5d stamp in the silver safe, both these items duly appearing in the books.

The news of the declaration of war led me to reconsider my position with the Servian army. I felt tolerably sure that this must be followed by a declaration of war by France and England against the Triple Alliance. This view was confirmed by all with whom I consulted, including our Minister, Mr Des Graz. Therefore it became evident that no Austrian soldier would ever cross the Danube, and that the war in Servia would become of mere local importance with graver events occurring so much nearer home. I therefore decided to leave at once, and to make my way to France.

The question I had to consider was how to get there. I could not return by Sofia and Bucharest, because all the European lines would have ceased running, and I would have to pass through two hostile countries. After long consultations I decided the only practical route would be via the Mediterranean, and I determined to leave that same night at 1 a.m. in the train for Salonika. I was not sure I could get back by this route, for all depended on the attitude of Italy. If Italy declared war, the Mediterranean would be entirely closed to all shipping until the Austrian and Italian fleets were disposed of, and my only chance would be to cross over to Port Said and catch a P. and O. or some other vessel there.

My difficulties were rendered greater by the complete absence of all genuine news. Telegrams only reached Nish at uncertain intervals and generally from the most unreliable sources. But I decided to make my way to Salonika and make a fresh start from there. At 1 a.m. on Monday, 3 August, I entered the train for Uskub. I had made this same journey a year before on my way to Uskub to join the headquarters of the Servian army in the war against Bulgaria. Then the tide of war was rolling southwards into Macedonia; now the mighty engine was reversed all the tide was rolling northwards to meet a fresh invasion. Servian Macedonia has been almost denuded of troops. Only the third band of old reservists have been left to watch the railway and to hold essential posts.

The train took an interminable time, stopping at every station waiting for troop trains, and it seemed as if we would never arrive. The heat was terrific, and travelling four in a compartment meant for three represented the height of misery and discomfort. At two o'clock on Monday afternoon I reached Uskub and eagerly inquired for news. The stationmaster was full of it. This is what he told me. 'Both France and England have declared war against Germany. There has been a battle between the German and Russian fleets. The English fleet has blockaded all the German ports, and the English Army, 180,000 strong, under Sir John French, had already crossed into France. The French Army has invaded

Germany through Belgium. There have been terrible battles on the French and Russian frontiers.'

Now I knew from a mere calculation of time that most of this information was false, but it only served to whet the appetite and to strengthen the longing to reach one's native land. At four o'clock I left for Salonika in another train, rolling slowly, passed Stip and Krivolack and the banks of the Varda, which a year before were wet with the blood of countless Serbs and Bulgars. At 1 a.m. on Tuesday, 4 August, I reached the Greek frontier and again changed trains. At 4 a.m. we arrived at Salonika. I made my way to the local hotel and learnt more news from the porter, who contradicted nearly all that given by the stationmaster of Uskub, but added some interesting details of his own. Namely, that Italy had declared war against Germany and Austria; that Spain had followed suit, and also that Sir Ernest Shackleton had abandoned his expedition to the South Pole. He rejoiced me with the information that an Italian steamer was leaving at 10 a.m. that morning for the Piræus, where she would arrive at 10 a.m. the following day, Wednesday, and that I would catch a large steamer leaving at 2 p.m. for Brindisi.

7 November 1914

TURKEY'S WAR WITH THE TRIPLE ENTENTE
Invasion of Armenia, *Petrograd, Friday*
By Granville Fortescue

Russia welcomes Turkey to the world war. The hatred existing between the two nations is centuries deep. Since the reign of Peter the Great each Tsar in turn has had the ambition to push his dominions to the Dardanelles. Twice when this ambition was on the eve of fulfilment it was baulked. The Crimean War killed one chance. In 1877 Russia was again deprived of her fruits of victory. Each time a Concert of the European Powers cheated this country of its quarry.

But now the road to the coveted strait lies open. Russia will follow that road. It is well that the ghost which has haunted the Chancelleries of Europe for decades should at last be laid. It is well that the Sick Man of Europe should receive his coup de grâce. Let the diplomats who have used the Sultan as the 'Joker' in every shuffle of the European pack devise a new game. This conflict must force some mighty readjustments in geography.

Such in brief are the ideas of high-caste Russians on the new phase of the war. With the masses the reasons for fighting Turkey are rooted in even firmer soil. They go down to the strengthening strata of religion. To the moujik a war with Turkey is a holy war. The dream that is ever in the heart of the religious Russian – and he is mediæval in his religion – is the conquest of Constantinople.

The campaign against Turkey will divide into two plans of attack. The first will be from the Black Sea. The second will be across the mountains into Asiatic

Turkey. This plan is already under way. Columns of the Caucasian army are skirting the slopes of Mount Ararat. The Cossacks have slipped through the passes, and taken the Turks in reverse. The Kurds cannot hold the frontier. Diyadin is in Russian hands.

The Caucasian army has been mobilised along this Russian frontier to await just such an eventuality as that which has arisen. It must be remembered that this army is a distinct organisation, separate in staff, rank, and purpose from the other Russian armies. Since the war began it has been chafing in inactivity. It takes the field like hounds that have slipped the leash.

Russia has beaten Turkey three times, and she can do it again. This thought raises the moral of the troops in the Caucasus to the highest level. This will be a war different from that which is being carried on in Europe. Waged among towering mountains and across boundless steppes, it will have the character of a dash between primitive peoples. In this sort of irregular warfare the Cossacks will be at their best. Living on the country, they can ravage the enemy's villages, spreading terror before the advance of the main columns.

It will be difficult to move large bodies of troops because of the lack of roads. Yet this will not impede the corps of the Caucasian army as much as it might a European force. Travelling with the lightest transport, the Russians of this country can cover extraordinary distances. Eighty versts, or about 50 miles, in thirty hours was the record yesterday.

Such a record could never be approached by a European corps with its straggling column of impedimenta. The war in the Caucasus will be a game the Russian thoroughly understands. It will be carried through on the simplest principles. The mountains which dam the frontier of Turkey will be tapped and the flood of the forces of the Tsar turned loose into the land of the enemy.

Already this flood is in motion. It has swept through the pass of Karaderbent. It has inundated Ardos. As irresistible as the rising tide, it sweeps the land of the Sultan.

In the Black Sea Russia is confronted by a peculiar problem. It is essentially naval warfare. Yet it is not impossible that the invasion of Turkey in Europe occupies the attention of the Russian General Staff. It is too early to go further into this subject.

Confined, as the two naval forces are, to the waters of the Black Sea, it will be war à outrance. The Russian ships will not cease their activity while a vessel of the enemy floats. In naval circles here there is the greatest confidence. The rumour that the Germans hold high commands on all the Turkish ships has intensified Russian enthusiasm for the coming conflict. There would be little honour in overwhelming the Turk alone. But when he is backed by the German the victory is doubled.

1 April 1915

OPERATIONS IN THE DARDANELLES
Attack on the Narrows, *Tenedos, 20 March*

The description of the attack on the Narrows by the Allied Fleet on Thursday, 18 March, contained in the telegram I despatched to the *Daily Telegraph* that same evening, was necessarily incomplete, as the total results of the action were not known at the time. Until they became known and were confirmed I naturally avoided referring to the losses which the Allied Fleet sustained.

I propose now to give you in this letter an account of this memorable engagement as it appeared to me from Mount Elias, amplified and enlarged by subsequent information.

The one height in this island is the mountain called Mount Elias, which is 658 metres above sea level. It juts out towards the Straits, and commands an unobstructed view of the approaches to the mouth of the Straits and of four-fifths of the basin of water reaching from the mouth of the Straits up to Kilid Bahr, on the European, and to Chanak, on the Asiatic shores. Both places are clearly visible through field-glasses in good weather and in a clear atmosphere, and on the 18th both these climatic conditions were available.

The general lines of the plan followed by the Allied Fleet were these: The sixteen large units of the Fleet which took part in the attack were divided into three sections. Two were to advance, one hugging the Asiatic shore of the basin, and the other the European; whilst the third was to enter into action later and to advance in extended line in the middle of the basin. Finally, the *Queen Elizabeth* was to remain stationary under Kum-Kale, attacking, by indirect fire, the enemy's batteries at Kilid Bahr and Chanak. The idea of the plan was that by the time the three divisions had worked their way abreast of Point Kephez Burnu the batteries of the enemy would have been silenced. Then the Fleet, forming in line ahead, would force its way through the minefields in the Narrows, even although they lost three, four, or even five of the leading ships. The miscarriage of the plan was mainly due to the fact that when the ships got near Kephez Burnu the enemy's batteries had not been silenced. Further perseverance with the plan would have entailed the forcing of a passage over a minefield, with live batteries on both sides firing at very close range.

The first thing I noticed on rising on Thursday morning was a long string of boats being towed to the shore by steam pinnaces. These were boats from the battleships going into action, and the decks of the ships were being cleared of all unnecessary wood which might have caught fire. At 10.20 a.m. the first division, of six British battleships, with the *Inflexible* leading, and the *Queen Elizabeth* bringing up the rear, passed Seddul Bahr and Kum-Kale, at the mouth of the Straits. The *Queen Elizabeth* stayed under Kum-Kale and remained there throughout the action, in accordance with the prearranged plan of the admiral. The other five turned to the right and hugged the Asiatic shore.

The first flashes of the guns were seen at 10.40 a.m. At 11 the second division, formed by the French battleships *Suffren*, *Gaulois*, *Bouvet*, and *Charlemagne*, passed the mouth of the entrance, keeping close to the European shore of the basin. The cannonade increased, and the enemy began to reply. At 11.15 a Turkish vessel appeared round the point of Kilid Bahr. The fire from the British division was directed against it. Spouts of water were seen to rise over its sides; it turned; and disappeared quickly round the bend from which it came, emitting huge volumes of smoke from its funnels.

The following are extracts from my notebook, jotted down while watching the engagement from Mount Elias:

11.20 a.m. – Several shots drop at Kilid Bahr. Volumes of smoke are seen to rise. Two huge spouts of water are seen to rise on each side of the *Inflexible*.

11.25 a.m. – A mine explosion takes place at sea near Kilid Bahr; the spout of water seems at least 100ft high.

11.30 a.m. – The ships fire at the rate of three shots per minute.

11.40 a.m. – A seaplane rises from Tenedos Roads, flies over the ships in the basin, and disappears in the distance.

11.42 a.m. – Immense flames, and sky-high volumes of smoke, are seen rising from Chanak. The flames continue for several minutes; it looks as if a powder magazine has exploded.

12.00 p.m. – Turks are firing rapidly. Six shots drop in quick succession round one of our ships; the spouts of water they raised hid the ships for a few moments from our view.

12.02 p.m. – Two of the British ships are hit. Smoke arises from their decks; fires break out, but they are extinguished in a few minutes.

12.05 p.m. – The third division of six British battleships leaves its anchorage in Tenedos Roads and heads for the entrance of the Straits. Three ships of the first division in the basin hug the coast in the Erenkeui Basin and disappear from view.

12.10 p.m. – Flames and smoke are seen to rise from the bows of one of the French ships; the flames disappear, the smoke remains. The British ships seem to have retired in Erenkeui Bay. The Frenchmen are engaging.

12.20 p.m. – Another seaplane leaves Tenedos and flies towards the ships in the Straits.

12.30 p.m. – Bombardment is now intense; the sound of guns rings in atmosphere. One of our ships is on fire. A Turkish shrapnel bursts over our ships; it is the first shrapnel fired by enemy.

12.45 p.m. – The greatest intensity of the firing is now on. The ships are firing in salvoes; fifty and sixty flashes are seen at the same moment. The Turks are replying with equal vigour; more than twenty spouts of water are seen to rise at one time, from their dropping shells. The atmosphere reverberates sound of guns.

12.48 p.m. – Another hit one of our ships. Fire has broken out on board; she, however, keeps on firing.

12.55 p.m. – New flames break out on her.

1.00 p.m. – Ship must be in trouble; she appears to lean to one side.

1.05 p.m.–Two ships advance from round Erenkeui Bay, and cover the ship in trouble. They all presently return, and disappear behind Erenkeui Bay.

1.10 p.m. – Enemy continues firing; ships ceased firing.

1.15 p.m. – The third division of six battleships enters the Straits. They take up positions in middle of basin and engage in action.

1.45 p.m. – A lull has set in, desultory fire only is proceeding. The enemy fires occasional shots. A division of destroyers enter the Straits.

2.45 p.m. – Two ships appear to have advanced considerably towards the Narrows. The Chanak batteries are firing furiously at them.

2.46 p.m. – A terrible explosion takes place in the waters of basin; a huge volume of vapour, succeeded by volumes of dense black smoke. One of the French ships has been blown up.

2.50 p.m. – The ship that appears more advanced received two hits in succession. A huge fire is on at Kilid Bahr. The firing again becomes intense.

3.00 p.m. – Turks replying very rapidly again. The map of water in view in the basin is dotted with spouts from the dropping of Turkish shells.

3.30 p.m. – Four ships only are now visible on the map of water open to the view; the others have gone out of sight in Erenkeui Bay. The enemy is concentrating a rapid and sustained fire on these four.

4.00 p.m. – The intensity of the firing has abated.

5.00 p.m. – A French battleship is seen to come out in trouble from the Straits; it is attended by two others. It advances very slowly, and is run ashore at one of the Rabbit Islands.

This is the end of my notes made at Mount Elias. The last note refers to the French battleship *Gaulois*, which had to be beached at the Rabbit Island.

The full extent of the losses sustained by the Allied Fleet was made known today, as follows:

Total loss of the French battleship *Bouvet*, with 740 men on board.

Loss of the *Irresistible* and the *Ocean*.

Loss of a British destroyer.

Damage sustained by the *Inflexible*.

Serious damage sustained by the French battleships *Suffren* and *Gaulois*. Out of the French squadron of four battleships only the *Charlemagne* is left uninjured.

The damage done to the enemy's batteries is confidently held to be great. When night fell on Thursday Chanak was burning furiously.

Shut out from all outside news in this island, and served only by a postal service once a week, I am ignorant as to what exaggerated accounts the Turks and their German friends have given out to the world with regard to Thursday's engagement. What I can say, however, is that the above account reflects the facts I have seen as an eye-witness, supplemented by the facts since known, which I am able, from my presence in this island, to verify.

7 May 1915

GRAPHIC STORY FROM THE DARDANELLES

Historic Scenes, *Dardanelles, 24 April (via Mudros, Wednesday)*

By E. Ashmead-Bartlett

The great venture has at last been launched, and the entire fleet of warships and transports is now steaming slowly towards the shores of Gallipoli. Yesterday the weather showed signs of moderating, and at about five o'clock in the afternoon the first of the transports slowly made its way through the maze of shipping towards the entrance of Mudros Bay.

Immediately the patent apathy which has gradually overwhelmed everyone changed to the utmost enthusiasm, and, as the huge liners steamed through the fleet, their decks yellow with khaki, the crews of the warships cheered them on to victory whilst the bands played them out with an unending variety of popular airs. The soldiers on the transports answered this last salutation from the Navy with deafening cheers, and no more inspiring spectacle has ever been seen than this of the last great crusade setting forth for better or for worse.

It required splendid organisation and skilled leadership to get this huge fleet clear of the bay without confusion or accidents, but not one has occurred, and the majority are now safely on the high seas steaming towards their respective destinations.

The whole of the fleet and the transports have been divided up into five divisions, and there will be three main landings. The 29th Division will disembark off the point of the Gallipoli Peninsula, near Seddul Bahr, where its operations can be protected both from the Gulf of Saros and from the Dardanelles by the ire of the covering warships. The Australian and New Zealand contingent will disembark north of Gaba Tepe. Further north the Naval Division will make a demonstration.

The difficulties and dangers of the enterprise are enormous, and are recognised by all. Never before has the attempt been made to land so large a force in the face of an enemy who has innumerable guns, many thousands of trained infantry, and who has had months of warning in which to prepare his positions. Nevertheless, there is a great feeling of confidence throughout all ranks, and the men are delighted that at length the delays are over and the real work is about to begin.

Last night the transports were merely taking up their positions, and the real exit of the Armada from Mudros Bay commenced this afternoon at about two o'clock. The weather, which was threatening at an early hour, has now become perfectly calm, and if it only lasts the conditions will be ideal for a rapid disembarkation. Throughout the morning transports steamed out to take up their respective divisions in the open sea, and the same enthusiastic scenes were witnessed as of yesterday. The covering forces will be put ashore from certain battleships, whilst others will sweep the enemy's positions with their guns and endeavour to prevent them from shelling the troops whilst disembarking.

It is generally considered that the critical period of the operations will be the first twenty-four hours, and the success or failure of the whole enterprise will depend on whether these covering parties are able to obtain a firm foothold and seize the positions which have been assigned to them. Every detail has been worked out and rehearsed, and every officer and man should now know the peculiar role which has been assigned to him.

The Navy will have entire charge of the landing of these thousands of men. Beach parties will go ashore with the first of the troops, and officers from the ships will direct the movements of all the boats as they bring the troops ashore.

This battleship belongs to the division which will consist of the Australians, who are to land near Gaba Tepe. We are one of the landing ships, and this afternoon received on board 500 officers and men of the Australian contingent who are to form part of the covering force. They are a magnificent body of men and full of enthusiasm for the honourable and dangerous role given them.

At two o'clock the flagship of this division took up her position at the head of the line. We passed down through the long line of slowly moving transports, amidst tremendous cheering, and were played out of the bay by the French warships. No sight could have been finer than this spectacle of long lines of warships and transports; each making for a special rendezvous, without any delay or confusion. At four o'clock this afternoon the ship's company und the troops were assembled on the quarterdeck to hear the captain read out Admiral De Roebeck's proclamation to the combined forces. This was followed by a last service before battle, in which the chaplain uttered a prayer for victory, and called for the Divine blessing on the expedition, whilst the whole of the ship's company and troops on board stood with uncovered and bowed heads.

We are steaming slowly through this momentous night towards the coast and are due at our rendezvous at 3 a.m. tomorrow (Sunday), a day which has so often brought victory to the British flag.

THE COVERING FORCE

Dardanelles, 26 April (via Mudros, Wednesday)

Slowly through the night of 24 April our squadron, which was to land the covering force of the Australian contingent just north of Gaba Tepe, steamed towards its destination. The troops on board were the guests of the crews, and our generous sailors entertained them royally.

At dusk all lights were extinguished, and very shortly afterwards the troops retired for a last rest before their ordeal at dawn.

It was a beautiful night, lit up by a very bright half-moon, and the sea was absolutely calm. At 1 a.m. the ships arrived off their appointed rendezvous, five miles from the landing-place, and stopped. The soldiers were aroused from their slumbers, and were served with a last hot meal.

A visit to the mess decks showed these Australians, the majority of whom were about to go into action for the first time under the most trying circumstances, which require that four-o'clock-in-the-morning courage, to be cheerful, quiet, and confident. There was no sign of nerves or undue excitement, such as one might very reasonably have expected.

At 1.20 a.m. the signal was given from the flagship to lower the boats, which had been left swinging from the davits throughout the night. Our steam pinnaces were also lowered to take them in tow. The troops fell in in their assigned places on the quarterdeck, and the last rays of the waning moon lit up a scene which will ever be memorable in our history. On the quarterdeck, backed by the great 12in guns, this splendid body of Colonial troops were drawn up in serried ranks, fully equipped, and receiving their last instructions from their officers, who, six months ago, like their men, were leading a peaceful civilian life in Australia and New Zealand, thousands of miles away. Now, at the call of the Empire, they were about to disembark on a strange, unknown shore in a strange land, and attack an enemy of a different race.

By the side of the soldiers the beach parties of our splendid bluejackets and marines were marshalled, arrayed in old white uniforms dyed khaki-colour, and carrying the old rifle and old equipment. These men were to take charge of the boats, steer them ashore, and row them to the beach, when they were finally cast off by the towing pinnaces. Each boat was in charge of a young midshipman, many of whom have come straight from Dartmouth, after a couple of terms and now found themselves called upon to play a most difficult and dangerous role like men.

Of the splendid conduct and courage of these youths I shall have much to say later, but it was a strange contrast to see these youthful figures, clad in every kind of garment which could be scraped together for shore work, and carrying revolvers, which appeared as big as themselves, standing side by side in the dim light with these giants from Australia.

Commanders, lieutenants, and special beach officers had charge of the whole of the towing parties, and went ashore with the troops.

At 2.05 a.m. the signal was given for the troops to embark in the boats, which were lying alongside, and this was carried out with great rapidity, in absolute silence, and without a hitch or an accident of any kind.

Each one of the three ships which had embarked troops transferred them to four tows apiece, consisting of thirty boats, each towed by a steam pinnace, and in this manner men of the covering force were conveyed to the shore.

More of the Australian brigade were carried in destroyers, which were to go close in shore and land them from boats as soon as those towed by the pinnaces had reached the beach. At 3 a.m. it was quite dark, and all was ready for the start.

The tows were cast off by the battleships, the ladders taken in, and the decks cleared for action, the crews going to general quarters. Then we steamed slowly towards the shore, each of the battleships being closely followed by her tows, which looked exactly like huge snakes gliding relentlessly after their prey.

I do not suppose the suppressed excitement of this last half-hour will ever be forgotten by those who were present. No one could tell at the last minute what would happen. Would the enemy be surprised, or would he be ready, on the alert to pour a terrible fire on the boats as they approached the beach?

The whole operation had been timed to allow the pinnaces and boats to reach the beach just before daybreak, so that the Turks, if they had been forewarned, would not be able to see to fire before the Australians had obtained a firm footing, and, it was hoped, good cover, on the foreshore.

Exactly at 4.10 a.m. the three battleships, in line abreast, four cables apart, arrived about 2,500 yards from the shore, which was just discernible in the gloom. The engines were stopped, guns were manned, and the powerful searchlights made ready for use if required.

The tows, which up to this time had followed astern, were ordered to advance to the shore. The battleships took up positions somewhat further out on either flank, for to them was assigned the duty of supporting the attack with their guns as soon as the light allowed.

Very slowly the twelve snakes of boats steamed past the battleships, the gunwales almost flush with the water, so crowded were they with khaki figures. Then each lot edged in towards another so as to reach the beach four cables apart. So anxious were we on board the battleships that it seemed as if the loads were too heavy for the pinnaces, or that some mysterious power was holding them back, and that they would never reach the shore before daybreak, and thus lose the chance of a surprise. The distance between the battleships and the boats did not seem to diminish, but only for the reason that we steamed very slowly in after them, until the water gradually shallowed.

Every eye and every glass was fixed on that grim-looking line of hills in our front, so shapeless, yet so menacing in the gloom, the mysteries of which those in the boats, which looked so tiny and helpless, were about to solve. Yet for some time, not a sound and not a light was heard or seen; it appeared as if the enemy had been completely surprised, and that we would get ashore without opposition. The stars, showing above the dark outline of the hills, were frequently mistaken for lights in our nervy state. On the bridge a sharp-eyed signalman would suddenly call out, 'There's a light on shore, sir,' but then, after a brief examination it would be pronounced a star, and the discoverer would retire in confusion.

The progress of the boats was, indeed, slow, and dawn was rapidly breaking, so that at one time it did appear as if they would never land covered by the darkness. Something definite did happen. Exactly at 4.50 a.m., when the enemy suddenly showed an alarm light, which flashed for ten minutes, and then disappeared. The next three minutes after its first appearance passed in breathless anxiety; we could just discern the dull outline of the boats, which appeared to be almost on the beach.

Just previously to this, seven destroyers, conveying the other men of the brigade, glided noiselessly through the intervals between the battleships, and followed the boats in shore.

At 4.53 a.m. there suddenly came a very sharp burst of rifle-fire from the beach, and we knew our men were at last at grips with the enemy. I believe the sound came as a relief to the majority, as the suspense of this prolonged waiting had become intolerable. This fire lasted only for a few minutes, and then was drowned by a faint British cheer, wafted to us over the waters. How comforting and inspiring was the sound at such a moment! It seemed like a message sent to tell us that the first position had been won, and a firm hold obtained on the beach.

At 5.03 a.m. the fire intensified, and we could tell, from the sound that our men were firing. It lasted until 5.28 a.m., and then died down somewhat. No one on board knew what was happening, although the dawn was gradually breaking, because we were looking due east, into the sun, slowing rising behind the hills, which are almost flush with the foreshore, and there was also a haze.

Astern at 5.26 a.m. we saw the outline of some of the transports, gradually growing bigger and bigger as they approached the coast. They were bringing up the remainder of the Australians and New Zealand division during the day.

The first authentic news we received came with the return of our boats. A steam pinnace came alongside with two recumbent forms on her deck, and a small figure, pale but cheerful, and waving his hand, astern.

They were one of our midshipmen just sixteen years of age, shot through the stomach, but regarding his injury more as a fitting consummation to a glorious holiday ashore than a wound, and a chief stoker and petty officer, all three wounded by that first burst of musketry, which caused many casualties in the boats just as they reached the beach.

From them we learnt what had happened in those first wild moments. All the tows had almost reached the beach, when a party of Turks, entrenched almost on the shore, opened up a terrible fusillade from rifles, and also from a maxim. Fortunately, most of the bullets went high, but, nevertheless, many men were hit as they sat huddled together, forty or fifty in a boat.

It was a trying moment, but the Australian volunteers rose as a man to the occasion. They waited neither for orders or for the boats to reach the beach, but, springing out into the sea, they waded ashore, and, forming some sort of a rough line, rushed straight on the flashes of the enemy's rifles.

Their magazines were not even charged, so they just went in with cold steel, and I believe I am right in saying that the first Ottoman Turk since the last crusade received an Anglo–Saxon bayonet in him at five minutes after 5 a.m. on 25 April.

It was over in a minute. The Turks in this first trench were bayoneted or ran away, and a maxim gun was captured. Then the Australians found themselves facing an almost perpendicular cliff of loose sandstone, covered with thick shrubbery, and somewhere half-way up the enemy had a second trench, strongly held, from which they poured a terrible fire on the troops below and the boats pulling back to the destroyers for the second landing party.

Here was a tough proposition to tackle in the darkness, but these Colonials are practical above all else, and they went about it in a practical way. They stopped a few moments to pull themselves together and to get rid of their packs, which no troops should carry in an attack, and then charged their magazines. Then this race of athletes proceeded to scale the cliffs without responding to the enemy's fire. They lost some men, but did not worry, and in less than a quarter of an hour the Turks were out of their second position, either bayoneted or in full flight.

After the events I have previously described the light gradually became better, and we could see from the *London* what was happening on the beach. The shore in front gradually opened up as the sun rose, although, shining as it did directly in the eyes of the ship's gunners, they were not in a position to support the attack in the early hours of the morning.

It was then discovered that the boats had landed rather further north of Gaba Tepe than was originally intended, at a point where the sandstone cliffs rise very sheer from the water's edge. As a matter of fact this error probably turned out a blessing in disguise, because there was no glacis down which the enemy's infantry could fire, and the numerous bluffs, ridges, and broken ground afford good cover to troops once they have passed the 40 or 50 yards of flat sandy beach.

This ridge, under which the landing was made, stretches due north from Gaba Tepe and culminates in the height of Coja Chemen Dagh, which rises 950ft above the sea level. The whole forms part of a confused triangle of hills, valleys, ridges, bluffs and dales, which stretches right across the Gallipoli Peninsula to the Bay of Bassi Liman, above the Narrows.

The triangle is cut in two by the valley through which flows the stream known as Bokali Deresj. It is indeed a formidable and forbidding land. To the sea it presents a steep front, broken up into innumerable ridges, bluffs, valleys, and sandpits, which rise to a height of several hundred feet. The surface is either a kind of hard yellow sandstone, very soft, which crumbles when you tread on it, or else it is covered with very thick shrubbery about 6ft in height.

It is, in fact, an ideal country for irregular warfare, such as the Australians and New Zealanders were soon to find, to their cost. You cannot see a yard in front of you, and so broken is the ground that the enemy's snipers were able to lie concealed within a few yards of the lines of infantry without it being possible to locate them. On the other hand, the Australians and New Zealanders have proved themselves adepts at this form of warfare, which requires the display of great endurance in climbing over the cliffs, and offers scope for a display of that individuality which you find highly developed in these Colonial volunteers.

To organise anything like a regular attack on such ground is almost impossible, as the officers cannot see their men, who, the moment they move forward in open order, are lost amongst the thick scrub.

In the early part of the day very heavy casualties were suffered in the boats which conveyed the troops from the destroyers, tugs, and transports to the beach.

As soon as it became light the enemy's sharpshooters hidden everywhere simply concentrated their fire on the boats when they got close in. At least three boats, having broken away from their tows, drifted down the coast under no control, sniped at the whole way, and steadily losing men.

All praise is due to the splendid conduct of the officers, midshipmen, and men who formed the beach parties, and whose duty it was to pass backwards and forwards under this terrible fusillade, which it was impossible to check in the early part of the day. The work of disembarking went on mechanically under this fire at almost point-blank range.

You saw the crowded boats cast off from the pinnaces, tugs, and destroyers, and laboriously pulled ashore by six or eight seamen. The moment it reached the beach the troops jumped out and doubled for cover to the foot of the bluffs over some 40 yards of beach, but the gallant crews of the boats had then to pull them out under a dropping fire from a hundred points where the enemy's marksmen lay hidden amidst the sand and shrubs.

Throughout the whole of 25 April the landing of troops, stores, and munitions had to be carried out under these conditions, but the gallant sailors never failed their equally gallant comrades ashore. Everyone, from the youngest midshipman straight from Dartmouth and under fire for the first time to the senior officers in charge, did their duty nobly.

When it became light the covering warships endeavoured to support the troops on shore by a heavy fire from their secondary armament, but at this time, the positions of the enemy being unknown, the support was necessarily more moral than real. When the sun was fully risen, and the haze had disappeared we could see that the Australians had actually established themselves on the top of the ridge, and were evidently trying to work their way northwards along it.

At 8.45 a.m. the fire from the hills became intense, and lasted for about half an hour, when it gradually died down, but only for a short time; then it reopened and lasted without cessation throughout the remainder of the day.

The fighting was so confused and took place amongst such broken ground that it is extremely difficult to follow exactly what did happen throughout the morning and afternoon of 25 April.

The role assigned to the covering force was splendidly carried out up to a certain point, and a firm footing obtained on the crest of the ridge, which allowed the disembarkation of the remainder of the force to go on uninterruptedly except for the never-ceasing sniping; but then the Australians, whose blood was up, instead of entrenching themselves and waiting developments, rushed northward and eastward inland in search of fresh enemies to tackle with the bayonet.

The ground is so broken and ill-defined that it was very difficult to select a position to entrench, especially as, after the troops imagined they had cleared a section, they were continually being sniped from all sides. Therefore they preferred to continue the advance.

It is impossible for any army to defend a long beach in any force, especially when you do not know exactly where an attack will be made, and when your troops will come under the fire of the guns of warships.

The Turks therefore only had a comparatively weak force actually holding the beach, and they seemed to have relied on the difficult nature of the ground and their scattered snipers to delay the advance until they brought up reinforcements from the interior. Some of the Australians, who had pushed inland, were counter-attacked and almost outflanked by these oncoming reserves, and had to fall back, after suffering very heavy casualties. It was then the turn of the Turks to counter-attack, and this they continued to do throughout the afternoon.

But the Australians never yielded a foot of ground on the main ridge, and reinforcements were continually poured up from the beach, as fresh troops were disembarked from the transports; but the enemy's artillery fire presented a very difficult problem.

As soon the light became good the Turks enfiladed the beach with two field-guns from Gaba Tepe, and with two others from the north. This shrapnel fire was incessant and deadly. In vain did the warships endeavour to put them out of action with their secondary armament. For some hours they could not be accurately located, or else were so well protected that our shells failed to do them any harm.

The majority of the heavy casualties suffered during the day were from shrapnel, which swept the beach and the ridge on which Australians and New Zealanders had established themselves. Later in the day the two guns to the north were silenced or forced to withdraw to a fresh position from which they could no longer enfilade the beach, and a cruiser moving in close to the shore, so plastered Gaba Tepe with a hail of shell that the guns there were also silenced, and have not attempted to reply since. As the enemy brought up reinforcements towards dusk his attacks became more and more vigorous, and he was supported by a powerful artillery inland, which the ships' guns were powerless to deal with.

The pressure on the Australians and New Zealanders became heavier and heavier, and the line they were occupying had to be contracted for the night.

General Birdwood and his staff went ashore in the afternoon, and devoted all their energies to securing the position, so as to hold firmly to it until the following morning, when it was hoped to get some field-guns in position to deal with the enemy's artillery.

Some idea of the difficulty to be faced may be gathered when it is remembered that every round of ammunition, all water, and all supplies had to be landed on a narrow beach and then carried up pathless hills, valleys, and bluffs several hundred feet high to the firing line. The whole of this mass of troops, concentrated on a very small area, and unable to reply, were exposed to a relentless and incessant shrapnel fire, which swept every yard of the ground, although, fortunately, a great deal of it was badly aimed or burst too high.

The reserves were engaged in road-making and carrying supplies to the crests, and in answering the calls for more ammunition.

A serious problem was getting away the wounded from the shore, where it was impossible to keep them. All those who were unable to hobble to the beach had to be carried down from the hills on stretchers, then hastily dressed and carried to the boats. The boat and beach parties never stopped working throughout the entire day and night. The courage displayed by these wounded Australians will never be forgotten. Hastily dressed and placed in trawlers, lighters, and ships' boats, they were towed to the ships. I saw some lighters full of bad cases as they passed the battleship. Some of those on board recognised her as the ship they had left that morning, whereupon, in spite of their sufferings and discomforts, they set up a cheer, which was answered by a deafening shout of encouragement from our crew.

I have, in fact, never seen the like of these wounded Australians in war before, for as they were towed amongst the ships whilst accommodation was being found for them, although many were shot to bits and without hope of recovery, their cheers resounded through the night, and you could just see, amidst a mass of suffering humanity, arms being waved in greeting to the crews of the warships. They were happy because they knew they had been tried for the first time in the war and had not been found wanting.

They had been told to occupy the heights and hold on, and this they had done for fifteen mortal hours, under an incessant shell-fire, without the moral and material support of a single gun ashore, and subjected the whole time to the violent counter-attack of a brave enemy, led by skilled leaders, whilst his snipers, hidden in caves and thickets and amongst the dense shrub, made a deliberate practice of picking off every officer who endeavoured to give a word of command or to lead his men forward.

No finer feat of arms has been performed during the war than this sudden landing in the dark, this storming of the heights, and, above all, the holding on to the position thus won whilst reinforcements were being poured from the transports. These raw Colonial troops in those desperate hours proved themselves worthy to fight side by side with the heroes of Mons and the Aisne, Ypres, and Neuve Chapelle.

REPEATED ATTACKS

Dardanelles, 27 April (via Mudros, Wednesday)

Throughout the night of the 25th and the early morning of the 26th there was continual fighting, as the Turks made repeated attacks to endeavour to drive the Australians and New Zealanders from their positions.

On several occasions parties of the Colonials made local counter-attacks, and drove the enemy off with the bayonet, which the Turks will never face.

On the morning of the 26th it became known that the enemy had been very largely reinforced during the night, and was preparing for a big assault from the north-east. This movement began about half-past nine a.m. From the ships we could see large numbers of the enemy creeping along the top of the hills, endeavouring to approach our positions under cover; and then annoy our troops with their continual sniping.

He had also brought up more guns during the night, and plastered the whole position once again with shrapnel. The rifle and machine-gun fire became heavy and unceasing. But the enemy were not going to be allowed to have matters all their own way with their artillery.

Seven warships had moved in close to the shore, whilst the *Queen Elizabeth*, farther out, acted as a kind of chaperone to the lot. Each covered a section of the line, and when the signal was given, opened up a bombardment of the heights and valleys beyond which can only be described as terrific. As the Turkish infantry moved forward to the attack, they were met by every kind of shell which our warships carry, from 15in shrapnel from the *Queen Elizabeth*, each one of which contains 20,000 bullets, to 12in, 6in, and 12-pounders.

The noise, smoke, and concussion produced was unlike anything you can even imagine until you have heard and seen it. The hills in front looked as if they had been transformed into smoking volcanoes, the common shell throwing up great chunks of ground and masses of black smoke, whilst the shrapnel formed a white canopy above. Sections of ground were covered by each ship all around our front trenches, and, the ranges being known, the shooting was excellent.

Nevertheless, a great deal of the fire was of necessity indirect, and the ground affords such splendid cover that the Turks continued their advance in a most gallant manner, whilst their artillery not only plastered our positions on shore with shrapnel, but actually tried to drive the ships off the coast by firing at them, whilst their desperate snipers, in place of a better target, tried to pick off officers and men on the decks and bridges. We picked up many bullets on the deck afterwards.

Some warships started to fire over the peninsula. The *Triumph* dropped two 10in shells within a few yards of her, whereupon she retired up the straits to a safer position, from which she occasionally drops a few shells into the brown, but so far has done no damage.

The scene at the height of this engagement was sombre, magnificent, and unique. The day was perfectly clear, and you could see right down the coast as far as Seddul Bahr. There the warships of the First Division were blazing away at Aki Baba, and the hills around it, covering their summits with a great white cloud of bursting shells.

Farther out the giant forms of the transports which accompanied that division loomed up through the slight mist.

Almost opposite Gaba Tepe a battleship and a cruiser close in shore were covering the low ground with their guns, and occasionally dropping shells right over into the straits on the far side. Opposite the hills in possession of the Australian and New Zealand troops other ships kept up an incessant fire, the ships themselves being enveloped in great rolling clouds of cordite. Beyond lay our transports, which had moved farther out to avoid the Turkish warships' shells and those of some battery which fires persistently; beyond all, the splendid silhouette of the *Queen Elizabeth*, with her eight huge, monstrous 15in guns, all pointed shorewards, seemed to threaten immediate annihilation to any enemy who dared even aim at the squadron under her charge.

On shore the rifle and machine-gun fire was incessant, and at times rose into a perfect storm as the Turks pressed forward their attack. The hills were ablaze with shells from the ships and the enemy's shrapnel, whilst on the beach masses of troops were waiting to take their places in the trenches, and the beach parties worked incessantly at landing stores, material, and ammunition.

This great attack lasted some two hours, and during this time we received encouraging messages from the beach: 'Thanks for your assistance; your guns are inflicting awful losses on the enemy.'

The Turks must, in fact, have suffered terribly from this concentrated fire from so many guns, and from the infantry in the trenches. The end came with a flash of bayonets and a sudden charge of the Colonials, before which the Turks broke and fled, amidst a perfect tornado of shells from the ships.

They fell back, sullen and checked, but not yet defeated, but for the remainder of the day no big attack was pressed home, and the Colonials gained some ground by local counter-attacks, which enlarged and consolidated the position they were holding.

The Turks kept up their incessant shrapnel fire throughout the day, but the Colonials were now dug in, and could not be shaken by it in their trenches, whilst the reserves had also prepared shelter trenches and dug-outs on the slopes.

Some prisoners were captured, including an officer, who said the Turks were becoming demoralised by the fire of the guns, and the Germans now had difficulty in getting them forward to the attacks. We are well entrenched, and they will probably do likewise, and we shall see a repetition of the siege warfare out here.

4 November 1915

AT THE DARDANELLES
The Sinking of HMS Majestic

By E. Ashmead-Bartlett

The sinking of the Triumph caused a fresh and very serious problem for the Admiral Commanding in Chief. As long as a submarine or submarines remained in the neighbourhood he could not leave his battleships exposed off the coast to their attacks, whilst, at the same time, he had to consider the needs of the Army and the amount of artillery which the General might require to keep down the fire of the Turkish batteries on the European and Asiatic shores. Immediately after the crew of the Triumph had been picked up and transferred to trawlers, the whole of the available destroyer craft started a tremendous hunt after the enemy. Throughout the early part of the afternoon reports kept coming in of her movements.

First, she was said to be making her way south from Gaba Tepe towards Cape Helles, and everyone on the Swiftsure remained on the alert, as we were still at anchor, and had no nets, even if these old nets offer any protection, which is extremely doubtful. At 3.30 it was decided to send the Swiftsure back to the protected harbour, Mudros, and for the Admiral to transfer his flag to the twenty-year-old Majestic, which was now the only battleship left off Cape Helles. She lay at anchor a few hundred yards from us, with her nets down. It took a very short time to transfer the Admiral's baggage to his new quarters, and after bidding farewell to the officers of the Swiftsure he was rowed across to the Majestic, and the Swiftsure shortly afterwards disappeared at top speed, reaching her new destination without mishap. The Admiral took me with him to his new flagship. The Majestic was the oldest British man-of-war at the Dardanelles, having been launched just over twenty years ago. Then she was the pride of the British Fleet, the envy of all foreign nations, and at once became flagship of the Channel Squadron. For years she remained a flagship until superseded by vessels of superior power.

But her glory had long since departed, and for several years before the present war she had been practically on the scrap-heap, and actually waiting to be sold out of the service at the commencement of the present struggle. Necessity, however, knows no age limit. When the expedition to the Dardanelles was decided upon, she was refitted and a crew, consisting chiefly of old reservists, was placed on board her, while most of her officers were also drawn from the Royal Naval Reserve. For the last forty-eight hours of her existence, owing to the immense influence of hostile submarines on naval operations, the old *Majestic*, the veteran of the Fleet, after twenty years of laborious and honourable service all over the world, found herself once more a flagship, flying the Rear-Admiral's flag, and the only battleship left off Cape Helles to protect our Army ashore, and to brave the terrors of the enemy's submarines.

That afternoon the Vice-Admiral came down to Cape Helles to hold a consultation with the Rear-Admiral, and the two commanders met, the one on the *Majestic* and the other on a small yacht bought from a resident of Constantinople earlier in the war. Such is the malign influence exercised by submarines. Throughout the afternoon of 25 May our destroyers kept up their unceasing chase of the hostile craft or crafts. They were sighted more than once beneath the surface, but at too great a depth to ram, and after 4.40 p.m. were seen no more. Throughout the day the old *Majestic* remained defiantly at her post, with the Admiral's flag proudly flying from her foremast. At eight o'clock that evening we were told we were not to remain at anchor off Cape Helles, but to run to shelter to a certain destination which must be nameless. Escorted by four destroyers, we dashed at top speed across the moonlit ocean, the old vessel doing wonderful time considering her age and the wear on her engines. In fact, it was remarked that she never did as well on her original trials. That night, at midnight, there was another scare that the enemy's submarines were trying to get through the boom. The crew were called to their stations, but the alarm came to nothing, and probably only belonged to the vivid and harassed imaginations of those on the destroyers guarding the entrance.

On the following day, the last of her existence, the *Majestic* returned to her old anchorage off Cape Helles, to resume her chaperoning of the troops on shore. I do not think we had any submarine scares that day, and towards evening there seemed to be a general feeling that, at any rate, for the time being, the enemy had been driven off or forced to retire to some base for oil and stores. But everyone on board felt our security was only temporary, and that very shortly the submarines would again show their periscopes in our neighbourhood. That evening, 26 May, we did not go back to a sheltered port, but moved in closer to the shore in front of W. beach, so that instead of being outside the lines of transports, we were actually anchored inside the outer line, in a position where it would be extremely difficult for a submarine to get a clear shot.

Now that I come to describe the last hours of the old *Majestic*, I can only tell the story of what my own experiences were, and of what I saw of the vessel and crew when she finally plunged to her doom. Personally, although we had moved so close in shore, and inside the outer line of transports, I felt no great sense of security, and was perfectly certain that the end might come at any moment. For that reason I had not slept in my cabin for several nights, but had my mattress carried up on deck, having long since made up my mind to get off the ship the moment she was struck and swim as far away as possible before she turned over and made her final plunge. As I do not profess to be a great swimmer, I was determined not to get mixed up on her decks or dragged down by the suction. That night we sat up rather later than usual in the wardroom, and I was just retiring to rest when I met the principal medical officer, who asked me if I had a lifebelt. I was the possessor of one of those which resemble bicycle tyres, and kept it blown up in my cabin, but it was inclined to leak, so I told the principal medical officer I could do with another. He presented me with a familiar one, only quite new. In fact, it had never been blown out.

I then retired to my cabin, undressed, put some paper money in my pocket, carefully wrapped up all my invaluable notes I had made on the campaign in a waterproof coat, and placed them in a small leather bag, which, unfortunately, I left below, and did not take with me on deck. It was a beautiful night, clear and bright, with the sea as calm as a lake. I went up on the after shelter-deck, which is just above the after-turret, where my bed had been placed, lay down, and was soon soundly asleep. I do not think I woke up once during the night, and I slept soundly until a quarter-past six. When I called out to the sentry, 'What's the time?' he replied, 'Six-fifteen, sir.' I turned over and went to sleep again. The subsequent times I learned after the catastrophe. as they were all taken from the shore.

It was at 6.40 that I was aroused by men rushing by me. Someone trod on or stumbled against my chest. This awoke me, and I called out, 'What's the matter?' A voice replied from somewhere, 'There's a torpedo coming.' I had just time to scramble to my feet when there came a dull, heavy explosion about 15ft forward of the shelter-deck, on the port side. The explosion must have been very low down, as there was no shock from it to be felt on deck. The old *Majestic* immediately gave a jerk over towards port, and remained with a heavy list. Then there came a sound as if the contents of every pantry in the world had fallen at the same moment. I never before heard such a clattering, as everything loose in the vessel tumbled about. You could tell at once she had been mortally wounded, and you felt instinctively she would not long stay afloat. Although I had been prepared for days for just such an emergency, the actual realisation came as a great shock. However, having mapped out my programme in advance, I proceeded to carry it through.

I stooped down to pick up my lifebelt, and then, to my intense disgust, discovered it was not blown out. When the principal medical officer presented it to me on the previous evening I had intended to do this, but must have forgotten all about it. Thus, the first part of my plans, namely, not to take the water unless encircled by a good belt, was at once knocked on the head. I decided to not lose any time over it now, but to get off the ship at once as she was listing more over, and seemed likely to turn turtle at any moment.

I was swept down the ladder to the main deck by the crowd rushing by me, and from there made my way aft to the quarterdeck. The quarterdeck was crowded with men nearly all dressed, and many wearing lifebelts, who were climbing over the side and jumping into the sea, all determined to get clear before she went down. Just after the explosion a cloud of black smoke came up and got down my throat and in my eyes, so that all this time I seemed to be in semi-darkness. I looked over the side and saw that I was clear of the torpedo nets, and then climbed over, intending to slide down a stanchion into the water and then swim clear.

But again my programme was upset by unforeseen events, for just as I had both legs over the rail there came a rush from behind, and I was pushed over the side, falling with considerable force on to the net shelf, which is where the nets are stowed when not out. I made no long stay on the net shelf, but at once rebounded into the sea and went under. I came up at once, still holding my useless belt, and, having got some of the water out of my eyes, took a look round. The sea was crowded with men swimming about and calling for assistance. I think that many of these old reservists, who formed the majority of the crew, had forgotten how to swim, or else had lost all faith in their own powers. A few yards from me I saw a boat, towards which everyone in the water seemed to be making. She was already packed with men, whilst others were hanging on to her gunwale. I swam towards her, mixed up with a struggling crowd, and managed to get both hands firmly on the gunwale, but found it quite impossible to drag myself on board. I looked round at the *Majestic*, which was lying only a few yards away at an acute angle, and I remember thinking that if she turned right over our boat would probably be dragged under with her.

It is very tiring work hanging on by both hands with your feet trailing in the water, and I was beginning to wonder whether I would be wiser to let go and swim away, when my right foot caught in what is known as the bilge keel. This is a small slit in the keel which enables you to hang on in the event of the boat being overturned. This gave me a lot of additional support, and I felt much more comfortable. A minute later, or perhaps less, a sailor leaned over the side, seized me by the shoulders, and dragged me inside, scraping the little remaining skin I had saved from the fall on the net shelf off my legs and arms. However, at the time, I was too delighted to find myself on board to notice such minor trials. I then had time to look round. The boat was absolutely packed with men. She was a small cutter, intended to carry, at the most, thirty, and eventually ninety-four were taken off her. We were sitting on one another, others were standing up, and many were still clinging on to the gunwale, begging to be taken on board, which was, of course, out of the question.

The *Majestic* now presented an extraordinary spectacle. She was lying over on her side, having such a list that it was no longer possible to stand on her deck. About one-third of the crew still seemed to be hanging on to the rails or standing on her side, as if hesitating to jump into the sea. All around the sea was full of men, some swimming towards neighbouring ships, others apparently having their work cut out to keep themselves afloat. All the vessels in the neighbourhood were lowering boats, and many steam launches were hastening to pick up survivors, but they did not dare stand in too close for fear of being dragged under in the final plunge. I was just thinking what a magnificent photograph the scene would make when someone called out: 'If you don't loose that rope you will be dragged under.' I am told it was Captain Talbot, who was still hanging on to the quarterdeck, who saw the danger we were in, and who gave the warning just in time; for, in the general confusion, we had not noticed that our rope was attached by a rope to the end of the torpedo boom. In fact she belonged to the *Majestic*, and had been lying out all night.

This discovery caused great excitement on board, and many, to escape imminent disaster, preferred to entrust themselves once more to the sea, jumping overboard with oars in their hands. I was hesitating whether to follow suit when someone in the bows managed to clear or cut the rope, and we were free. A very few seconds later the *Majestic* rolled right over to port and sank, bottom upwards, like a great stone, without any further warning. There came a dull rumbling sound, a swirl of water and steam, for a moment her green bottom was exposed to view, and then the old flagship disappeared for ever, except for a small piece of her ram, which remained above water, as her bows were lying on a shallow sandbank. As she turned over and sank, a sailor ran the whole length of her keel, and finally sat astride the ram, where he was subsequently taken off without even getting a wetting. The final plunge was so melancholy, yet so grand, that for some seconds one forgot about the large number of officers and men who were still clinging to her when she went down. Some were dragged down by the fatal nets before they could get clear, others were probably killed inside by the explosion. Nevertheless the loss of life was small, numbering only fifty. This was due to the fact that most of the men had lifebelts. The majority had time to clear the ship before she turned over; we were anchored in shallow water, so that the suction was small and, above all, assistance was promptly forthcoming from the numerous ships, boats, and launches which hastened to pick up those struggling in the water.

The final plunge was watched by thousands of troops on shore and by thousands of men afloat. It was a sight that will not easily be forgotten. Captain Talbot, the moment the ship was struck, rushed forward with his Yeoman of Signals to seize and destroy the Confidential Signal-book. This was accomplished, and then when the ship went down he was thrown into the water, but was picked up by a launch. Then, seeing two of his men in danger of drowning, he plunged into the sea again and saved them both. Of course, it was impossible to tell until late in the day who had been saved and who had been drowned, as the survivors were picked up by various boats and taken to different ships or on shore, and subsequently transferred to Mudros Bay. But, happily, every officer got clear, including Admiral Sir Stewart Nicholson. I was taken on board a French ship, together with the ninety survivors from this crowded cutter, where we were received with every kindness and attention. Dry clothes were served out to us, and we were given coffee and brandy by our kind Allies.

By a merciful dispensation of Providence in the case of neither the *Triumph* nor the *Majestic* did the magazines blow up, otherwise there would have been hardly any survivors. As it was, owing to the prompt assistance forthcoming, the loss of life on both vessels was small, and was chiefly due to the causes I have already named, namely, men being dragged down in the nets in the final plunge.

6 November 1915

SERBIA'S PLIGHT
Position and Prospects

By Cheddo Miyatovich

The situation of Serbia is very critical indeed. But it is not yet hopeless. Her two armies are still intact. I say two armies, because on the eve of the combined Bulgarian and Austro–German attack one (and the stronger) army was concentrated in Shumadiya, with the strenuous task to defend the Sava and Danube line, the north against the Austrians and Germans, the Drina front on the west against the Austrians, and the Timok front on the east against the Bulgarians. The other army, somewhat numerically weaker, was concentrated in Macedonia, with the object of defending the Nish–Salonika railway line against the Bulgarians. By occupation of the narrow pass of Kachanik the contact between the Shumadiya army and the Macedonia army of the Serbs has been cut, and the two forces are operating independently, but according to the plans fixed some time ago.

Those armies have fought during the last three weeks with a determination, fierceness, and bravery which have won the admiration and public acknowledgment even of the enemy. They had to lose positions and retreat, but they inflicted on the antagonists severe losses for every inch of Serbian territory lost, and they are retreating always in good order and with hardly any loss in prisoners and material. Both these armies are aiming at keeping themselves intact until the arrival of the Franco–British armies enables them to undertake a vigorous offensive in combination with the operations of the Allies. The knowledge that French and British troops are already fighting the Bulgarians in the Krivolak–Strumitza sector has produced a remarkable moral effect among the Serbian soldiers of both armies. They are going cheerfully into the battles, and they say to each other: 'We must show to our British and French friends that we know how to die for our country. Let us die to the last man, knowing that our allies will not let Serbia die!' The reports which I receive on the ésprit or the morale of the simple soldiers in the retreat of the Serbian armies would make every generous Briton and Frenchman proud to have such allies.

From other sources I am informed that the political leaders of the nation, as well as the leaders of the armies, have considered the possibility of the Allied armies not arriving in time to prevent further progress on the part of the enemy: In that case the whole of Serbia may be in hostile occupation, the Serbian Government, and at least part of the Serbian forces (from the Shumadiya army) withdrawing to Montenegro. Even with such a possibility in view, no one in Serbia thinks that Serbia ought to ask for a separate peace. A few socialists, it is true, have been advising the Government six weeks ago to save the integrity and independence of the country by making a separate peace at once. But both the Government and the Skupshtina rejected the proposal with the greatest emphasis. Serbia has linked her destiny unhesitatingly and cheerfully with the destiny of her Allies. She believes in their ultimate victory and triumph. But even in the case of misfortune and disaster Serbia will not separate herself from her Allies. Of that I am absolutely certain. This is not only because the Serbians are by their national character rather a chivalrous people, having always in their heads and hearts the models of their old national heroes, who considered faithfulness to a given word as the first duty of every man, but also because the Serbians are an intelligent people, and they know very well that a separate peace, even if morally permissible, would prove itself practically useless.

We know well that Austria and Germany have engaged themselves by written and signed treaty of alliance to allot to Bulgaria (after their victory), not only Serbian Macedonia, but also all the Serbian territory eastwards of Morava. Even if both our armies were utterly crushed, even if our Allies should appear too late, no Serbian statesman could be found who would dare sign a treaty of peace involving a surgical operation which would leave Serbia an invalid, incapable of a normal and vigorous national life. Our chivalrous and gallant army, our political idealists, and our 'real politicians' all are unanimous in holding that our duty as an honourable nation, and our best political interests, advise us to stick faithfully to our noble Allies, and no disaster can shake us in that determination.

I think I ought to mention a strange thing, which may explain the mentality of the people of Serbia. Having lived for five centuries under the rule of the Turks, the Serbs are in some degree fatalists, besides, as Slavs, being highly psychic. They have suffered unspeakable agonies since this newest and most terrible invasion by Austrians, Germans, and Bulgarians. Yet our civilian population, our men and women, bear all the suffering with quiet dignity and philosophical resignation. They say: 'We knew it was coming, and it was to come, but, by God's help, it will pass!'

Many of the intelligent classes in Serbia, and almost every peasant, man or woman, knows about the famous prediction of the Serbian prophet, called Matha of Kremna. In the year 1868 that peasant dictated to the Prefect of Ujitsa and the President of the Court of Justice of the same time his visions of coming events in Serbia. Among other prophesied events, which on the whole came to pass, he said that during the reign of King Peter a foreign army would occupy the country, causing the people to suffer terribly.

Just as most Serbian peasants know the ballads about the Royal Prince Marco and the Kossovo heroes, so most of them know the predictions of Matha of Kremna. That knowledge did not adversely affect the Serbian soldier. On the contrary, it intensified his bravery, as the only means to frustrate the prophecy was to defeat the enemy. Besides, the prophet of Kremna said also that the Serbians would in the end succeed in driving away the foreign army and delivering the country, making it greater than ever. Suffering greatly at present, all the Serbians are confident that the last part of the prophecy is in the process of fulfilment now. The Serbians believe firmly in the ultimate victory of the Allies, and in the great destiny of their nation.

21 December 1915

HEROIC CONDUCT OF BRITISH NURSES
Work at Battle Front, *Milan, Monday*

By A. Beaumont

About thirty nurses and lady doctors of the Third Serbian Relief Fund Unit sent out last Spring from England have returned by way of Albania and passed through Milan on their way home, after hardships similar to those I described two weeks ago as having been experienced by the members of the Berry Mission. There was this aggravation, that having left two weeks later they found much less food on their way, and, the weather having become very bad, they had to make their way across mountains and over roads covered with ice and snow. Furthermore, most of the party being women, the journey of ten weeks accomplished by them on foot was particularly trying. One must admire the extraordinary courage and heroism of these British women, who, to come through safely, had to wear men's boots, share all the hardships of the Serbian soldiers, and make their way through parts of Albania with only a few men as escort.

One of these nurses had some Austrian cartridges; another carried a Serbian rifle part of the way; a third had had a fine revolver, which she regretted having lost; and a fourth said that for one day she had an Albanian rifle, but also left it behind. In fact, nearly everything they could not carry in the hand was left somewhere in the mountains. They belonged to field hospitals and had seen some of the hardest phases of the Serbian campaign. They had nursed the gravely wounded immediately behind the fighting line near Pirot, then moved up to points near the Danube where the battle was raging, and in one place aided in the transfer of a hospital to the rear, with numerous wounded helping to push and drag the carts and gun carriages used as ambulance wagons.

Looking at these fine British nurses, with their cheerful faces, as they were enjoying their first good meal last night, one could not help wondering how they had passed through it all. For weeks they had to live on small rations of a few ounces of dry black bread. 'We had just only what the soldiers had,' they told me, 'and when you are told that the Serbian soldiers are starving it is true. We cannot describe the hunger suffered by those men. Some have not even had bread for weeks; more are in rags. The time came when we were just longing for the taste of marmalade or one piece of sugar, and a bed to sleep on, for night after night we slept out in the cold. We found houses at different places we came to, but did not dare sleep inside. The only thing that warmed us up was hot coffee, which we were able to make, but as for milk or butter, we saw it sometimes in dreams.'

'How many men of the Serbian army do you really think are saved?' I asked their leader. 'Certainly some 140,000,' he said, 'just what was reported two weeks ago. We marched the greater part of the time with the First Army, and they held well together. The retreat was conducted in fair order, and even a large part of the artillery has been saved. But what the men want now is food. Had you seen them you would understand they are dying of hunger. Never mind sending them arms or ammunition; first send them food, and let it be done quickly. Thousands of these men are starving as they reach the Albanian coast. They will make a fine army still, once they are fed and refitted.'

23 December 1915

ALLIED ARMIES IN MACEDONIA

Life at Salonika, *General Headquarters, Salonika, November*
By G. Ward Price

Before you have been in Salonika half an hour you will have learnt the equivalent of 'Get out of the way' in half a dozen languages. 'At-tention!' 'Bros!' 'Destour!' 'Varda!' 'Hey-Oop!' Unless you can interpret the warning in French, Greek, Turkish, Jew-Spanish (a peculiar local tongue), and every British dialect from Western Irish to East Yorkshire, you will not go long without a collision.

It may be a great French or English motor-lorry, bumping fiercely over the uneven flagstones; it may be a string of wizened little horses, with untidy Greek soldiers perched sideways on their heavy wooden pack-saddles; or a motor-cycle, pitching like a Channel steamer on the uneven roadway; or a party of officers, who have ridden in from the camps; or a local cab, with two such pitiable wrecks of horses in the shafts that it would be worth a month's imprisonment to their owner to work them in London; or a Jewish hawker, with a bunch of turkeys hanging head downwards in each hand; or a patchwork patrol of French, English, and Greek soldiers, looking very self-conscious and awkward in each other's company – the streets of this Levantine Donnybrook Fair are not the place for a quiet stroll.

Salonika resembles most ports of the Eastern Mediterranean in being a picture of beauty from a distance and a sty of squalor near at hand. The sailors on board the warships in the Gulf look at it through the morning mists and envy the soldiers who are quartered there. The soldiers stumble through its muddy, rough-paved, ill-smelling streets, and wonder why a sailor with a comfortable ward-room to live in should ever want to come ashore. It is, in fact, a slatternly Levantine town, in a beautiful, mediæval setting, comely in the mass, unpleasant in detail.

As you survey Salonika from the water she has a dignified air that accords well with her historical renown, being set in stately isolation upon the steep slopes of her bare hills and girdled by ruined but still massive walls that rise to a great Venetian citadel on the landward side. Graceful white minarets that the Turks built are sprinkled about among the houses, and the quay that is the chief street of the town, lined with picturesque Greek sailing craft, stretches for a full mile along the water's edge. But ashore, shut in by the narrow streets of the 'Frank quarter', your vivid impressions of squalor and slovenliness soon make you forget the graceful picture from the sea.

The officers of that part of our Balkan Expeditionary Force that is encamped near Salonika lead curiously twofold lives. They endure a good share of the hardships of war all night and the greater part of the morning out at their camps on the Monastir road, and in the afternoon they come into Salonika to enjoy such luxuries as the town affords. The hardships are a good deal more real than the luxuries. During the snap of cold and snow at the beginning of this week the morning temperature in those tents on the bleak, wind-swept positions towards the Vardar was commonly about 15 degrees below freezing-point. By day the men had to be sent on route-marches to keep them warm, and by night it happened several times that the greater part of a battalion would have to turn out and put up tents blown down by the gale in a bitter, driving cold that made your bones ache within you.

On the other hand, the delights of Salonika are limited to one tea-shop where there are three times as many customers as seats, three kinematographs showing interminable films of a quality that would ruin an English provincial picture-house in a fortnight, a variety theatre of the kind you only visit once, having your boots cleaned, and the 'Healthy Bath Botton'. This last is, indeed, the most popular institution in the town. The last word of its title, placarded as above over the door, is the name of the proprietor, who is reaping a well-deserved harvest out of the enthusiasm displayed, to his own astonishment, by British officers for baths.

Boot-cleaning, one of the milder recreations that Salonika offers, ranks among the national industries of Greece. To sit drinking little cups of thick Turkish coffee and having his boots cleaned at the same time is the Greek's ideal of a pleasant afternoon. The 'lustros', as Greek shoeblacks are musically called, though usually of tender age, is a true artist, and is by no means content with the dull burnish that satisfies the English boot-boy. He first meticulously scrapes your boot clean of the smallest fragment of mud, then wipes it carefully, so as to have a perfectly clean background to work on. After that he applies the blacking, not by dabbing the blacking-brush into the tin, but with a variety of little metal implements and sponges. When he has brushed this to a bright polish you imagine that your shine is over, but he has really only begun, for the 'lustros' now goes on to bring out the highlights by smearing your boot over with a colourless cream, which he brushes again to great brilliance, and finishes off by two or three minutes' friction with a velvet cloth. He completes his work by painting the edge of sole and heel with a sort of varnish.

If you attempt during all this time to withdraw your foot before he is satisfied with the effect produced the lustros knocks imperiously with the back of his brush. Successful 'lustroi' even have a little nickel-plated bell which they ring to call your attention when they are ready for the other foot, as it is the etiquette of the profession never to speak to a client after first attracting his attention by hammering upon their little wooden boxes. For all this you pay the lustros ten leptas, or one penny, and walk away with a self-conscious feeling that your feet are glittering.

A fresh occupation for leisure moments of the afternoon that has been suggested by the cold of the last few days is that of buying fur coats. Our Army in the Balkans seems likely to be as shaggy a force as ever took the field. Salonika is a great place for furs. Up to the end of Turkish rule here the Jews, who are about half the population, used to wear long fur-lined gaberdines such as they brought with them from Spain in the Middle Ages. Fur being a material that soon wears out, and the Jews wearing it both summer and winter with complete disregard for the temperature, a considerable trade in skins grew up here, which gives full scope to individual tastes in the choice of fur coverings for the present campaign.

Some officers are content to have a fur lining put into their British warms: others are attracted by a deep fur collar, which gives an opulent and picturesque effect. French officers seem to have specialised in immense wolfskin coats of great bulk, while active subalterns with a lot of walking to do order short, jacket-shaped garments made of the skins of various beasts and tied on with tapes. There is great licence as to colour, and on a cold afternoon, you will find in Floca's – the tea-shop – officers both piebald and skew, some in fleeces of spotless white, others in shaggy hides of grey and sable. It only needs that the steel morions served out as headgear in France should be sent out here for the British officer to rival a Viking chieftain in barbaric splendour of appearance.

Officer's recreations being thus limited, those of the men are naturally few. Route-marches, parades, cutting drains, building roads, fill up most of the day, and for amusement in their short leisure they are thrown upon their own resources in the way of football, sing-songs, and the never-failing mouth-organ. Transport difficulties hinder the arrival of big recreation tents such as would be put up nearer home by caterers and private funds, and bell-tents do not lend themselves to the purposes of entertainment like the large pitched-felt sheds which the French use for housing their men. But though camp life at Salonika may be dull, the time of rest that the men are having cannot but be of great value to our troops, and the opportunities it gives for drill and manœuvres will enable them to tune themselves up to fighting pitch after the slackness that invariably sets in during a voyage which frequently lasts more than a fortnight.

There will be hard work enough before our Balkan Expeditionary Force, if this campaign goes on as it may be expected to do. The country is difficult to an unusual degree; the enemy is well equipped and holds strong positions. Whether Germans and Bulgars come down and attack us in the attempt to drive us out of the Balkans altogether, as travellers arriving lately from Nish say that the Germans there boast is their intention, or whether it is we who take the offensive and advance northwards towards the Danube or Sofia, is uncertain, but meanwhile the time of rest is being well used.

To those men who have come to the Balkans from the continual peril and endless discomforts of Suvla Bay – like General Mahon's Irish Division – Salonika and even our present trenches at the front may seem a welcome change. Why, indeed, they are here some of them may hardly understand.

When a man has spent the whole summer at Gallipoli, with his life hourly in his hands, and is then moved to another country where English newspapers arrive at intervals of about ten days and then only in small quantities, it is quite understandable that he should be so out of touch with the events that have brought him face to face with a new enemy that he may ask, as one did the other day, 'Can you tell me, sir, how it was that these here Bulgarians came into it at all?'

1 January 1916

EVACUATION OF SUVLA AND ANZAC

Closing Scenes of a Great Episode, *One of HM Ships, off Suvla, 20 December*

By G. Ward Price

The following is the concluding portion of Mr Ward Price's long cabled description of the evacuation of Anzac and Suvla Bay, the earlier sections of which appeared in yesterday's *Daily Telegraph*: When the whole thing was over, the last job of the work that remained to do ashore was to set light to the abandoned stores. Volunteers did this by means of time-fuses, which were only lit when the news was received by telephone 'Anzac all clear', for it was expected that the sight of the conflagration would at once open the Turks' eyes as to what was going on, and that a furious, if futile, bombardment would immediately begin. Things went off that last night just as quietly as the schedule, for the realisation of the scheme proved for once to be a perfect working out of a business-like and smoothly running programme. Yet it will be easily believed that to the people actually engaged the operation had a thrill which an account of it can hardly convey. The silence seemed intense.

An infantry attack was hardly thought likely. Normally there were only about 20,000 Turks in the first trenches in front of us at Suvla and Anzac, with 60,000 close up in reserve; and they were thoroughly anxious to avoid a fight if it were possible. One deserter came in last week who seemed to have surrendered in disgust at the apathy of his countrymen. 'Attack?' he said, in reply to a question whether his side were likely to take the offensive, 'it is as much as the officers can do to get the men into the trenches.'

In fact, our generals would rather have welcomed an infantry attack at the end. Our lines were so strong that we could have done great execution with the machine-guns, and the ships would have had a great opportunity for using heavy shrapnel, while the surprises that were in store for the Turks were many and ingenious.

All the preparations which the Turks will find made for their entry are not, however, of an explosive nature. The Australians have left many letters of the kindliest farewell, assuring 'Johnnie Turk', in colloquial English, that he is a good fellow and a clean fighter, and that the Australians hope to meet him again some day. The crowning testimony of good feeling is the gramophone, which was put in a conspicuous place in the trench on Walker's Ridge, with its disc on and the needle at ready to play 'The Turkish Patrol'.

Last night, Sunday, 19 December, was an evening of brilliant moonlight. I had spent the day at Kala Baba, where nothing was doing out of the ordinary. Which was a Turkish 3in gun dropped a few shells on to the hill, a bigger one carried out a desultory bombardment of the beach beyond, all of which resulted in one man being wounded in the arm, while some of our ships' guns replied. Farther along the coast, to the south, however, a vigorous action was going on at Helles in the afternoon.

This was an attack made at the top of the Kristhia Ravine.

Helped by the fire of the ships' guns, they captured two Turkish trenches, about 2 p.m., and in the evening, about eight, held on to them against two counter-attacks. Our casualties were not heavy.

Then, along the sandy beach, where so many men at the landing in August suffered torments of thirst, I went back to Suvla Point. And equipment! There was a most fantastic variety of headgear, pith-helmets (relics of summer), knitted woollen helmets that were to have served during the winter; field service caps, and Australian wideawake hats.

With steady, slouching gait, they came down the hillside, each man no doubt feeling lucky enough to be alive to leave a place where so many thousands of his comrades lie in the little barbed-wire enclosed cemeteries that were the hardest things of all to abandon. A milk-blue mist swam over the lower ground and the mountains stood out black and stern against the sky. Everything else was dark, except the points of golden light that were the fires burning, as one knew, by the empty dug-outs and in the deserted camps. Down the coast off Anzac the hospital ship blazed green like a brilliant emerald liner, the guns thumped out a final round, and along at Anzac the Turks were peppering away with rifles, and even now and again spluttering into machine-gun fire, but there was no note of unusual energy in the sound.

From the shore one had a splendid view of five great fires springing up, one after another, about four o'clock, as the store dumps leapt into flames, and soon into one mighty bonfire a couple of hundred yards long. Farther along the coast the Anzac's forsaken bully-beef was burning fiercely too. At 3.30 there had been a violent explosion from Anzac, with a sudden spurt of flame on the crest of the ridge. This was a giant mine, exploded by the Australians, 45ft deep, under the Turkish trenches, as a final act of hostility when the last Australian was about to leave the beach. It was fired by electric contact, from a distance, and must have killed 100 Turks it is thought.

When the sun rose the Turks began their strangely erratic bombardment, first dropping shells into the heart of the bonfire at Suvla; then at a battleship which had been pounding the piers, and then, in an irrational way, all round.

It was the greatest thing of its kind that the British Army has ever attempted, and it was exceedingly well done by both the Army and the Navy. At Suvla, on the last day, one officer and two men were wounded; at Anzac, four were wounded.

Two of the six guns left (which are, needless to say, destroyed) were howitzers twenty years old that served in the Boer War. To General Birdwood, commanding the Dardanelles Army, congratulations have already come by wire from the King. He was constantly visiting Suvla and Anzac directing the preparations, and during the last day and night he was on the spot the whole time in the Staff Ship.

Though Suvla and Anzac have cost us much in blood, it would be a mistake to regard this withdrawal as a confession of entire failure there. Both are names that will take a proud place in the list of the battle honours of our Imperial Army, for British troops from the farthest separated parts of the Empire there met and fought, not the Turk and the German alone, but disease and thirst, the heat of summer, and the deadly bitter blizzard of winter. It is not a defeat, though a German flag is flying at the top of Kala Baba this morning, for we were not driven off. Indeed, at every point along our whole front we have consistently dominated the Turk, and we could certainly still fight our way through to the narrows if the necessary reinforcements were available. Nor had the arrival of the new German guns and ammunition begun to bother us to any degree. The evacuation is rather a pulling of ourselves together – a step towards that concentration of strength upon sure ground, which is of such importance to our fortunes here at the cross-roads of the Empire. If there is one kind of strategy that would be dangerous in the Dardanelles and in the Balkans, where the great stakes of India and Egypt are almost directly concerned, it is a policy of opportunism, of small detachments, and of leaving the initiative to the enemy. By cutting our losses here we do something towards acting with greater deliberation and in better organised strength elsewhere.

4 January 1916

GERMAN SCHEMES IN ALBANIA
Threatened Invasion, *Milan, Sunday*

By A. Beaumont

News has been received from various sources that Bulgarian troops on the one hand are pushing forward from Ochrida towards Albania in the centre and the south, whilst other considerable Austro–German columns are seeking to penetrate into Albania from the north. The reports further state that owing to the impossibility of conveying heavy artillery, the Austrians are sending all their available mountain guns to the new scene of operations.

The Bulgarian objective is the Adriatic coast, in the direction of Valona, whereas the Austrians are aiming in the direction of Durazzo.

Whilst the Albanian campaign has thus been begun, a truce will be observed in the direction of Salonika. Only a small number of Bulgarian troops will be left behind in the trenches and strongly organised defences to guard against a possible Anglo–French attack. This explains why the Greek Germanophile Press announced prematurely, some days ago, that an important body of Austrian troops was near Scutari, which was being desperately defended by the Montenegrins, and that the fall of the town was imminent. Immediately after the fall of Scutari the Austrians were to join the Bulgarians and march upon Valona.

This report, which I found to be utterly false, was spread purposely in Greece by German agents, but it shows, nevertheless, what are the aims of the Austro–Bulgarians at present.

When the above false news was printed in Athens the Austrian army was still being held in check by the Montenegrins in the Sanjak of Novibazar, and had been repulsed in successive attacks at Vucido and Batcova Bora, as I learned from persons who had been with the Serbian army, and had just returned from Albania. In fact, at Batcova Bora the Austrians, after being repulsed in a murderous engagement, lost a certain number of prisoners, whilst the Montenegrins also captured a considerable amount of war supplies. A rapid advance of the enemy is, moreover, impossible, as the Serbians in the neighbourhood have been refurnished with food and supplies, and are again in a position to engage the enemy with advantage.

Meanwhile, the Italian Government has, from feelings of humanity, taken charge of the Austrian prisoners held by the Serbians, and fed and clothed them. About 30,000 have been sent to the island of Sardinia, or are on their way thither. Among them are 600 officers. They are mostly sheltered in healthy spots, away from the towns, in the province of Cagliari, the commune of San Vito and Montenerba. Many of them were in a deplorable state of health, and without the timely assistance of Italy they might have perished.

About 500 Montenegrin refugees have also arrived at Naples. They report, however, that their army, if furnished with supplies by the Allies, will continue to fight the Austrians with success, and if assisted further by such a large contingent of Serbians as may readily be revictualled and put in a fighting condition there is no immediate danger of the Austrians forcing their passage to Scutari. As to the Bulgarian advance, it was already announced some days ago that after serious engagements west of Ochrida, the Bulgarian troops had occupied the district of Elbasan, in the direction of Central Albania, and about half-way between Ochrida and the Adriatic. The Serbians were not numerous enough to oppose a long resistance, their main army, moreover, being further north. But since then the Bulgarians, who are now also up against serious difficulties in the mountains, have made no further progress.

The Italian troops have not as yet come into contact with any Austrians, and the rebel Albanians have failed to put in an appearance. Quite the contrary has happened, and it is now confirmed that Essad Pasha has definitely thrown in his lot with the Allies, and, as Commander and Pasha of Tirana, has declared war on Austria and Bulgaria. Being acknowledged by the Allies as the only man who has any authority over the natives in Albania, his act will have an important bearing on the forthcoming Albanian campaign.

2 June 1916

ITALY'S CAMPAIGN

Fight for Trentino Passes, *Milan, Thursday*

By A. Beaumont

The Trentino battle continues uninterrupted along the entire front of 50 kilometres, but the main Austrian effort is still concentrated on the narrow gorge between Val Posina and Val Astico. It is at Pria Fora that the action has become a real struggle of giants. Out of the eighteen divisions which the Austrians have thrown against the Trentino front, more than half seem to be trying to force their passage through this valley, of which Pria Fora and Monte Cengio are, as it were, the lofty gateposts, the former being 1,653 metres and the latter 1,351 metres high. The Austrians, after capturing Pria Fora at a terrific cost of men, were driven from it, and the summit was reoccupied by the Italians, who again abandoned it as too easy a target for the Austrian artillery, but they hold fast the northern slopes.

The Austrians lost no time in bringing forward their artillery and establishing batteries on the heights captured by them along the Posina Valley, but the Italian artillery has met the challenge, and is answering shot for shot from the line still held by them from Monte Forni Alti to Summano. The attacks on the positions south of Posina, which began on 28 May, have thus lasted three days, without enabling the Austrians to obtain any decisive advantage. Of six divisions held in reserve, more than one-half had already been called upon at the end of the first fortnight. The enemy's policy is evidently to throw the largest possible mass of infantry against the smallest point, and force a passage at any cost. This explains the violent action in the Posina Valley, the principle being that if the centre is broken through the right and left wings will have to yield automatically. But this strategic principle, so dear to the Austrian mind, has failed, as the Italian left wing from Coni Zugna to Pasubio is standing as firm as a stone wall, and the Austrians have been unable to make progress against the Italian resistance on the tableland of Asiago.

At the moment of writing the Italians still hold the outlet of Val d'Assa, which is celebrated for heroic deeds. It was here that in August 1509, the Austrian Emperor Maximilian tried to invade the territory of the Venetian Republic with a large army, which had crossed the Vezzana and was approaching the tableland of Sette Comuni. The invaders were met by a handful of mountaineers, who obstinately defended the pass and compelled the Austrian army to retire. Thus, it is not the first time that the Austrians have attempted to invade the plains of Italy through the gates of the Trentino, and the shortest road always seems to be that between Trentino and Vicenza. The Italian troops today, however, are rivalling in valour their heroic ancestors, and the brigades of Sicily, with those of Taro and Catanzaro, have repeated the exploits of their predecessors. Monte Mosciagh, Monte Zebio, and Monte Zingarella have seen Sicilian troops vie in courage with those of Central and Northern Italy, and have received special mention for valour in the daily official bulletins.

An officer from Lucca, who has been with a battery in the line between Monte Pasubio and Coni Zugna, gives a graphic description day by day of the intrepid courage of the Italian gunners. He writes on 17 May: Since the night of 14 May we have been the object of a violent attack, which had been expected for some time. The bombardment from guns of every calibre continues uninterruptedly for the last forty-eight hours, and is splendidly answered by our artillery. We are facing the storm with calm courage and magnificent obstinacy. The Austrian bull will here, as elsewhere, smash his horns. My batteries are answering with a hail of steel.

19 May – We have now repulsed with admirable spirit nine successive attacks of the enemy, and are getting ready to repel fresh attacks without hesitation. Reinforcements are coming. We are hoping to make a counter-charge which will help us to push forward our lines. We have inflicted heavy losses on the enemy, and captured prisoners. Our losses are ridiculously small. We shall resist to our last drop of blood. We here hold our ground, and no Austrians shall pass – not one of those dogs.

20 May – The battle continues pretty stiff. We are holding out, standing firm. Enthusiasm and familiarity with danger have given us nerves and constitutions of iron. For six days no time to eat or sleep. We are under constant fire; but no fatigue is able to overcome our resistance. We shall not yield; my group has made it a question of honour. Our four magnificent batteries, despite the advanced positions, although bombarded with explosive shells and asphyxiating

gas, pour forth their shells every instant on the Austrian batteries and silence them. If it comes to the worst we shall also take our rifles. Since yesterday two detachments of infantry, volunteers of death, have reinforced our command. What splendid fellows! Like heroes of the Middle Ages, with their helmets of steel and their shining breastplates, they fight like devils, and the Austrians, not we, will have to yield.

24 May – The fray continues incessant, ferocious, without truce. We had tonight to abandon our new pit of command. It is the third time we have changed. We waited to be relieved, then each of us dug out a hole to sleep in for two or three hours, the only respite we have during the battle. Sleeping is only a figure of speech; the tumult of the guns and the crash of the shells continues, and the telephone is always calling, and our batteries are always firing. They fired in all these days 1,000 shots per gun. We sometimes have to stop firing too fast, because the guns get too hot. As a result the Austrian fury has had to relent, checked by our obstinate defence, impotent to break through the rigid line of trenches, guns, and men, but what days of horror.

This is a picture drawn in a few rapid lines of what every Italian battery is accomplishing on the summits of Coni Zugna, Mezzana, Pasubio, Forni Alti, Alba Cogolo and Campiglia. The Italian artillery and infantry officers and men fighting on these lofty summits, at elevations of 4,000ft and 6,000ft, with often no way of retreat open to them excepting an abrupt ravine or yawning precipice, are fully worthy of those who defend the trenches at Verdun. North-east of Asiago and Callio fighting continues chiefly between Alpine troops, and the Austrian successes here are of small importance.

3 November 1916

ROUMANIA

'Pivot of the War', *Rome, Wednesday Night*

By Dr E. J. Dillon

In the deliberate judgment of the few who possess accurate knowledge of the driving forces of the war and a keen feeing for the politico-military necessities of the moment, Roumania is become the pivot of the European campaign. Circumstance, not choice has made it so. Tested by accepted standards, by comparison of belligerents' resources, or even by the purely military consequences of recent events, this statement is undoubtedly paradoxical. For we have been repeatedly assured that so long as Roumania's armies are intact the loss of her territory can be logically proved to be of little moment to the Allies, and even to be positively disadvantageous to the enemy. But to reason on these lines in Roumania's case today would be misleading and dangerous. I venture to emphasise this view because it is based upon varied and carefully sifted data, and is therefore well worthy of the attention of those upon whom prompt and energetic action depends. Events are certain to bear it out, in whatever direction they may point. The tidings from Bucharest still have a cheering ring, and the magnificent stand of the Roumanian forces at the Predeal front and the counter-offensive there are hailed with joy by the Allied Press. And rightly. For, won in the face of deterrent obstacles, they encourage the hope of further great achievements.

But the obvious facts should prevent us from describing the Roumanian campaign as already virtually decided against the enemy. The well-informed *Giornale d'Italia* holds that Hindenburg's plan has so completely failed that Hindenburg himself must now recognise it, because an invasion of Roumania over the Carpathian passes or across the Danube is become impossible. In reality this consummation is ardently desired, eagerly striven for, and in some quarters confidently anticipated. But it is not yet attained. Hindenburg's forces will certainly find the passage of the Transylvanian Alps, especially now that Russian contingents have arrived, a much tougher task than was the defeat of the half-armed Russians in the Masurian swamps; and the Roumanian armies are resolutely pressing this difference home. Moreover, if the German commander fails to reach the Roumanian plain before the winter fully sets in, his enterprise in that direction will have fallen through. As for the other alternative, the crossing of the Danube, with Bucharest for its objective, it is in some respects a more arduous and dangerous undertaking than the forcing of the mountain passes. These elements of the problem explain the unshaken faith professed by Entente critics in the discomfiture of our adversaries. What strikes me, however, more forcibly than even those considerations is the enormous power of attraction which the invasion of Roumania has for Hindenburg and the Kaiser.

It is no exaggeration to affirm that for them it connotes a definite victory over all the Allied nations, and everything else which that would involve. We may laugh this notion to scorn, but we cannot gainsay that it is the conviction of the Germans, and supplies them with an astonishing driving power of which, at this stage of the campaign, they were deemed incapable. However difficult the invasion of Roumania seems, and is, Hindenburg may deem it well worthwhile to attempt it repeatedly at a seemingly prohibitive cost, and for this eventuality it behoves the Allied nations to be prepared. Unwonted promptitude and thoroughness on their part are essential to success. Russia having discerned this, is now doing her part, and during the past few days has been despatching troops which the enemy hoped would never come. It would be contrary to public interest to disclose the number, but it may be permissible to say that it represents a very liberal contribution to the undertaking. Italy's effort is already known. In short, all the Allied Governments are strenuously exerting themselves to belie the popular proverb that prevention is better than cure. And this is as it should be. For to frustrate Hindenburg's scheme no efforts can be too strenuous, no sacrifices too costly, because, as already stated, the bearings of the Roumanian campaign are become so far-reaching and varied that they can no longer be gauged by the standards of strategy, nor by those political criteria still in vogue which were hitherto looked upon as infallible.

The sooner, therefore, we readjust our system of valuation to the changed conditions, and take a true view of the interplay of psychology, national politics, and strategy, and of the limits which each sets to the others, the better for the common cause.

6 November 1916

KING OF MONTENEGRO

At the British Front, *British Headquarters, France, Thursday*

By Perceval Gibbon

The population of these busy roads – riders, drivers, and trudgers – is used to the sight of strange uniforms, from the horizon-blue and gold braid of the French to the grey-green and constellation of Orders of visiting Russians; but even men who would scarcely turn their heads for the peacock-splendour of a Haitian field-marshal stopped to gaze yesterday when the King of Montenegro and his suite went up towards the front. For the King wore his native costume, and added to it the enhancement of his own venerable and impressive presence. Old now, his tiny kingdom overrun by his big and gluttonous neighbour.

Nicholas, of the Black Mountain, preserves still that fine loftiness of demeanour which was his in the days when he administered justice in person before his palace in Cettinje. The title 'majesty' is something more than a courtly convention when applied to him; the habit of power and Royal precedence is in his every gesture and tone; and the tall old warrior-chieftain, grizzled, with his eagle-beak and still black eyes, wearing the costume which his mountaineers have made glorious as a uniform, is not a figure that could pass unremarked anywhere.

His visit to the front lasted only three days; it was upon the last of them – having upon the first two visited a hospital and the Staff of one of the armies – that he motored up to the Somme battle front. It was a windy, chill day, clear and rainless; at two points along our front the enemy was shelling steadily, with no particular object in view that anyone could discover; and the King, with a set of staff-maps to make things clear, showed a keen and soldierly interest in the shape and possibilities of this long and spacious river-battle. There was one village upon his route where there are yet children; they range up as one passes and ask – one can hardly call it begging – for pennies. 'Gimme penny, please – one penny, please.' One little girl help out her hand as the King and his suite went by and piped her request to one of the English officers. The King stopped. 'What was she saying?' he inquired. The officer laughed and explained, and would have walked on, but not the King. 'No, bring her here,' he commanded. She was brought.

It is part of the business in life of good kings to live up to the story-books, and Nicholas of Montenegro was equal to the demands upon him. He produced a Louis – not a *billet de banque* such as one pays mere bills with, but the real thing, the authentic gold. *'Tenez, mon enfant!'* He smiled and gave it to her.

The King was greatly impressed by what he saw of the great organisation of power – gun-power, man-power, and money-power – which is the sign and visible token of Britain's impulse to victory – the unbelievable guns, the spate of munitions which flows towards the batteries, the vast accumulation of magnificent manhood. The time at his disposal was short, but to all with whom he came into contact he expressed his wonder and his admiration of the great effort which is still growing upon the Somme. This morning, before leaving, his Majesty utilised his last moments in the war zone in a manner which those who know him best describe as entirely characteristic of him. He inquired for the church. There was one near by, and thither the old King went, to offer up prayers for the success of the British arms.

ITALY'S VICTORY ON THE CARSO
Nearly 9,000 Prisoners, *Milan, Sunday*

By A. Beaumont

The three days' battle on the Carso, begun on the first day of November and concluded on 3 November, was the greatest victory achieved by Italian arms since the taking of Gorizia. The number of prisoners captured in those three days amounts to close on 9,000 officers and men, including the staff officers of an Austro–Hungarian brigade, as already mentioned in Friday's bulletin, and large quantities of munitions, eleven guns, and numerous machine-guns. Comparative figures published here concerning the prisoners taken at the Russian, French, and Italian fronts show that since 1 August this year the Russians have taken 137,000, the French and English 51,000, and the Italians 43,000 prisoners. These approximate figures, covering the same period, are proof that the Italian army all by itself is doing its full share in working towards the final victory of the Allied cause.

King Victor Emmanuel witnessed the action from the very beginning – during a great part of the time from the observatory close to the enemy's lines – and from time to time he received visits from the Duke of Aosta, commander of the Carso army, who informed him of the victorious progress. The new line now occupied by the Italian army at Veliki Hribach, at Faiti, and on Hill 319, as far as Castagnavizza, forms a sharp salient into the Austrian line, endangering the enemy's position to the north and south. It also represents the destruction of formidable Austrian defences extending for a distance of nearly 12 miles, and at its most advanced point a depth of over 1¾ miles. No small share in this success is due to the shelling of Nabresina station, which was entirely destroyed some days before the attack, and which so far smashed the enemy's lines of communications as to make it impossible to send reserves over that line by train.

The behaviour of the Italian troops during the attack was magnificent, and numerous incidents are recorded of splendid individual bravery. The rapidity of the attack was responsible at many points for the capture of such a large number of prisoners. The Austrians were surrounded before they were aware of it. An Italian detachment had already got beyond Veliki and Yolkovniak and occupied Faiti Hrib, whilst another detachment had moved up from the opposite direction and taken Dos Faiti. Behind them they observed, almost hidden in a hollow in the midst of a clump of trees, a certain number of sheds and barracks, from which a big network of telephone and telegraph wires issued. Closing round it, the Italians soon made the discovery that it was the headquarters of a brigade command. A combined surprise attack from two sides compelled the staff officers, with their commander, a brigade colonel who had temporarily taken the place of Brigadier-General Saenkl, who was wounded, to surrender. The colonel at first made a show of offering resistance, seizing his revolver and pointing it at his assailants. His officers did the same, but they were twice ordered to drop their weapons and surrender, which they finally did, seeing that all escape was impossible. General Saenkl, who had been wounded earlier in the action, had been taken away to hospital, and thus escaped capture. The colonel who replaced him had not even time to destroy his documents, and he looked sadly at his maps as they were being taken up and folded by his captors.

Luigi Barzini writes from the Carso that the first important point, Veliki Hribach, was, in fact, taken in less than fifty minutes. The Austrian retreat behind their abandoned lines was executed amid great confusion. The Italian field-guns, hurriedly rushed forward, poured a murderous fire into the retreating masses. The chief concern of the Austrians was to save their batteries, and these could be seen as they were hurried along the roads. The Italian guns immediately made them their target, and at one point there disappeared as if by magic, under the concentrated fire of a number of Italian guns, an entire Austrian battery that was galloping away in full retreat. At another point, for a considerable time an Austrian battery was pursued by a detachment of Italian infantry, which, 'au pas de charge', was trying to overtake it on the road.

As Guelfo Civenini wires to the *Corriere della Sera*, during the first two days the chase after guns was the main preoccupation of the Italian troopers. Nothing else was thought of, not even the crowds of prisoners taken. These were summarily sent behind the lines, with only a few men as escort. Every ditch and cavern was searched. A Bersaglieri is seen at Pecinka returning, and holding his hand over a fresh wound. He is shouting and making signs to his comrades. 'There it is,' he says, pointing to a hill, 'we have captured it up there; it's a whole battery of six guns.' He is asked about his wound, but refuses to talk of it. The wound is nothing; the great thing uppermost in his mind is that the battery is captured. A few steps further on he staggers, and, poor fellow, is about to fall, exhausted by the loss of blood, when he is taken on a stretcher by helpers. Perhaps he expired before he reached the Red Cross tent, but on the way he still had time to shout to some comrades that guns were captured. Another soldier, with one leg gone, is sitting on a barrel, waiting for someone to help him along. But he has nothing to say about his lost leg. All he repeats is, 'What a fine day; a great day!'

20 November 1916

A VISIT TO THE ROUMANIAN FRONT

Enemy's Brutalities, *Bucharest, 14 November*

By M. H. Donohoe

During the last week I have had an opportunity of visiting the Roumanian front-line trenches on the Moldavian and Southern Transylvanian fronts. Two days were passed in the neighbourhood of the Vulcan Pass and Targu Jiu fronts, where the enemy a fortnight ago sustained a temporary defeat.

North of Targu Jiu the 11th Bavarian Division was practically annihilated by the Roumanians. It had been sent specially from Kovel, on the Russian front, with the Kaiser's telegraphed benediction. It had been selected for 'strafing' the Roumanian people and army for their temerity in setting themselves against the Imperial will and fighting for the realisation of the ideal of a greater Roumania. Much equipment was abandoned when the Bavarians fled towards the frontier broken and panic-stricken. German military paraphernalia is still littered on the battlefield. Motor-cars, machine-guns, field-pieces fell trophies to the Roumanians.

The German general, in the haste of his retirement, lost his pickelhaube, with a gilt-spiked top. Judging by the number found on the battlefield, a blank recommendation for the Iron Cross seems to form an essential part of the field kit of every German regimental commander. The humane treatment by the Roumanians of their wounded enemy is in marked contrast to the savage cruelty exhibited by the Hungarians when some Roumanians fell into their hands. In one hospital I saw two Roumanians, portions of whose tongues had been amputated by their Hungarian captors. These maltreated soldiers were captured by a patrol, and because they refused to give information of essential importance to the enemy the tips of their tongues were hacked off with sword-bayonets. They then set at liberty the victims, who are recovering from their terrible injuries, though they have lost the power of speech and it is feared they may be dumb for life.

The Roumanian is a splendid soldier. In the difficult passes of the Carpathians they have held back a powerful and well-organised enemy. They have defended their fatherland and at the same time fought the battle of our common cause with a tenacity and heroism unequalled perhaps in the annals of history. Here is an edifying spectacle of a little nation, undaunted by the odds, exhibiting all the abnegations and resolution of the ancestral Romans unhesitatingly, shedding its blood that its sons might be saved from the humiliation of passing beneath the Prussian yoke.

Life at the Roumanian front is much as it is elsewhere along the hundreds of miles of the vast European battlefield. Roumanian Tommies generally have a trench mascot. In one sector it was a white kitten which one day had wandered across the shell-swept zone into the shelter of a trench seemingly from nowhere. In another sector it was a blackbird, which the soldiers taught to whistle Roumanian airs.

On both fronts I saw and spoke with many prisoners, wounded and unwounded. Unwounded Austrians, Saxons, Bavarians, and Prussians were among the earlier contingent of prisoners, especially Bavarians, callow, underfed youths of nineteen, lacking stamina, who had been rushed to the Roumanian front to fill the depleted ranks after but a few weeks of training. They expressed their satisfaction that they were still alive and faced the prospect of captivity with smiling equanimity, since it meant the absence of rationless days and the certainty of snug shelter from the bitter cold of the Carpathian Alps with a generally inclement sky for a canopy.

The prisoners more recently captured were Prussians – sturdy fellows, possessing a considerable but diminished quantity of national arrogance. They are for the most part frank as soldiers are who have fought and been vanquished. One Prussian of expansive girth and a face like a ripe apple said he had been told that the Roumanians were an untrained rabble who were sure to run when the Germans appeared and shouted 'Hoch!' but by that time personal contact with the previously despised enemy had inspired respect for the Roumanian soldier.

From chats with the prisoners I found it was the Roumanian bayonet which Bavarian and Prussian alike dreaded most. The Roumanian 'Hura' uttered by a charging line of infantry invariably produced a disquieting and oft-times a demoralising effect among the Boche troops. In the base hospital I came across a Prussian who had been fighting since the war began. He had been on all the European fronts. Unbaring his arm, he showed a scar from a British bullet received at Ypres. Now he had come from the Russian front, and was laid low by Roumanian shrapnel in an attack through the Vulcan Pass. He was a philosophic chap, keen to seek any bright side lurking amidst all the dark horrors of war. He said laughingly that the amount of metal of one kind or another which he had carried in his body would be worth melting down.

Wounded Austrian officers were inclined to cordiality, being convinced that the war could not last much longer and that the sooner it was over and the whole world going about its legitimate business the better for humanity. This view visibly shocked a wounded German officer in the ward who was within hearing. With an effort which must have caused him a good deal of physical pain he raised himself on his elbow and in sharp, staccato tones, as if rapping out an order, said, 'Peace will only come when our Kaiser wills it.' Then he collapsed, and a sympathetic nurse, who, when suffering is to be assuaged, does not discriminate between wounded friend and wounded foe, hastened to soothe the feelings of the ruffled Prussian and readjust the head bandage which his violent emotion had sent awry.

21 November 1916

FRENCH ENTRY INTO CAPTURED CITY
Scenes of Rejoicing, Monastir, Sunday (Noon)

By G. Ward Price

The Allies are in Monastir at last – here in the heart of the town. Down the streets, which are black vistas of closed iron shutters, come French cavalry, which were the first to enter. They are now maintaining a strict patrol. Their horses' necks are hung with wreaths of flowers, for the inhabitants, after peeping timidly out from behind their barred windows for a while, have at length ventured out, and are offering posies and garlands to the French and Russian soldiers, who come constantly marching in. Even to me, though unworthy, these signs of welcome have been proffered, for I have had the fortune to be the first Englishman to arrive in the town, just 2¼ hours after the first French troops entered.

It was at 8.15 this morning that the last battalion of Germans marched out of the northern end of Monastir, and were seen by French scouts pouring along the Prilep road. A quarter of an hour later the final battery left to protect the rear of the retreating army, limbered up and made off at a fast trot through the streets. French cavalry and mounted scouts were close upon its heels as it went. At 9 a.m. the first French company of infantry marched in past the still burning barracks that the enemy had set afire during the night. A Russian battalion was with them. The two columns, in fact, came abreast along the road.

And so Monastir became Serbian again, for, though French and Russian troops have had the privilege of first arriving there, they themselves are anxious to admit that it was chiefly the tireless advance of the Serbs among the mountains in the loop of the Cerna River, supported as they have been, of course, by the co-operation of the French infantry and French artillery, that has forced the Bulgars and Germans to evacuate Monastir.

'It is thanks to the Serbs that we have won the town,' said a French colonel, who was one of the first to get in. The whole of the centre of the town is being reserved as quarters for the Serbians to dispose of as they require, should a triumphal entry of the Serbian army into their redeemed city be afterwards arranged, and when the inhabitants of Monastir sent a deputation just now to the headquarters, which have been temporarily established, to ask if they might hoist the French flag, they were told no, but that they might hoist the Serbian flag.

After a whole year of captivity Monastir became free again, and that on the very anniversary of the day when the Serbs first won it four years ago from the Turks. By its liberation the Allies in the Balkans have won their first victory of mark, for Monastir is more than one of the most considerable towns in Serbia; it is a symbol. What Delhi is to India Monastir is to Macedonia. She is the queen city, a recognised token of dominion. Ever since, on Tuesday night, the Bulgars and Germans crept away from the Kenali lines there has been a feeling of victory in the air, and those tall, white minarets that have shone so long down on this hard-fought plain of Monastir have drawn nearer. But still there seemed much to do. The enemy's new line of defence on the Bistrica had been prepared for over a month past, and was a regular line of double trenches with wire in front. The Italians on the left were fighting among the snow, trying to advance in order to turn the defences of the Bistrica. The French next on their right before Kanina village had only one narrow road open to attack along and that was commanded by machine-guns. The Russians were vigorously opposed as they tried to follow up the enemy retirement from Kenali, though they forced the Viro River breast-high and along the next French sector the Germans and Bulgars seemed determined to give no more ground. In the loop of the Cerna a prisoner certainly told the French that Negotin was to be evacuated today, but up at Tepavtsi, where I was with the French artillery yesterday, the Germans were holding on firmly to their rearguard positions.

It was the Serbian capture yesterday of the three peaks to the left of the famous Hill 1,212 and beyond it that finally obliged the enemy to fall back from Monastir by threatening his line of retreat up the Prilep road. Up that road he is retiring now, and at the moment of writing (noon) the Bulgar rearguard forms a firing-line of two and a half miles out from Monastir towards Prilep, while the Russians and French are already pressing on to drive the retiring enemy back as far as possible.

30 December 1916

WOMAN SOLDIER

Fought in Serbia, *Salonika, 12 December*

By Frederick Calvert

In a clean and comfortable bed, amidst comfortable and quiet surroundings, lies a comely, motherly-looking little lady. Though her short-cropped hair is grey, her unfurrowed face is young and fresh, with a peachy bloom in the rounded cheeks that tells of perfect health. But her bed is in the nurses' ward of Military Hospital Camp, No. 41, and the little lady is a patient – the only patient of her sex in a camp that has accommodation for 1,600 sick or wounded Serbian men. A few days ago a Royal aide-de-camp came to her bed-side, and, on behalf of the Prince Regent of Serbia, pinned to her breast, with much ceremonial, the gold and silver Cross of Kara-George – a rare badge that is only given for conspicuous bravery on the field of battle. Her honest dark-brown eyes sparkle with pride as she pulls it out from under her pillow and holds the handsome trinket up to the light for our inspection. To do this she uses her left hand. Her right hand and arm are strapped in bandages. Bandages, she tells us, also protect her right side and right leg, the whole of that side of her body from the shoulder to the knee was lately a mass of torn flesh and shattered bone – the work of a Bulgarian hand-bomb that chanced upon her as she was helping the Serbs to clear out an enemy trench, but now it is healing as satisfactorily as any surgeon could wish.

Miss Flora Sands – that is the little lady's name – is a Scotswoman. Working in Serbia as a hospital nurse since early in the present world-war, her sympathy was so keenly aroused by the sufferings and heroism of the people that, when hospital units were broken up during the great retreat of October–November, 1915, she solicited, and obtained, permission to enlist as a private in the rear-guard that protected the withdrawal of the retreating army. Before that army reaped the Adriatic shore she had deserved and won promotion, and become Sergeant Sands. She stood high in the regard of both officers and men of the crack regiment to which she still belongs. With it she proceeded to Corfu, enjoyed the pleasant months of rest and recuperation provided for the exhausted army in that sunny isle, came on with it to Salonika, and went up with it to the sector allotted to the Serbian Army on the Macedonian front. There she went through the whole of the arduous and successful offensive campaign that began on 12 September.

For more than three months Miss Sands lived in an atmosphere of bursting shells and whistling bullets, through many a hand-to-hand encounter she passed scatheless, clambering up in the intervals each of those towering heights from which the Serbs drove the Bulgaro–Germans, steadily fighting their way northward from Gornitchevo and Kajmakchalan to the mountain that is known as Hill 1,212. There, however, luck deserted her. It was in the decisive assault on the highest crest of that position that Miss Sands's active career was temporarily cut short. How this happened let her relate in her own words: 'We had been crouching and shivering in our little shallow pits, for hours, waiting impatiently for the order to break cover and attack. At 7 a.m. the order came. It was snowing and snow lay on the ground. I was out of my pit in half a second, and running as fast as my legs could move. I am always the first to leave cover. It is my duty as a petty-officer. But, unfortunately, I am not so nimble as most of my men, so it happens that I am generally among the last to reach an enemy trench. Well, I had nearly reached the brink of the Bulgarian trench in which our men were already at grips with the defenders. I was one of a small group of laggards – perhaps half a dozen – when a well-aimed grenade fell in our midst. A couple of men besides myself were in the radius of its explosion and fell wounded, but I seem to have got most of the scatter. Yes, the shock was awful. Yet I don't think I lost consciousness for more than a minute, and I was not left long untended. A young officer of my battalion, standing behind a rock close by, had seen me drop. He crawled up towards me on all fours over the snow, and, seizing my hands, pulled me over its smooth surface to the shelter of the rock. The torture of being dragged by the hand of my broken arm was acute, yet it was not very much greater than that I had already been suffering. It had to be borne and the strain was soon over. Wonderfully deft and tender are Serbian soldiers in dressing wounds on the field. A couple of them, men of my own company, did me up in the quickest time imaginable, and I was soon lying on a stretcher on my way to the nearest field hospital.'

Miss Sands's wounds will take some time to heal completely. There are some twenty-five of them, and one or two splinters have yet to be extracted. But the surgeons tell her she may rely upon recovering the use of her injured limbs. Her spirits, her appetite, and general health are, wonderful to say, unimpaired, and she yields to none of her fellow-patients in hospital in impatience to return to the fight. As I took my leave Miss Sands begged me to procure for her a volume of Kipling's verses, preferably one containing the couplets entitled 'If'. 'That,' she said, 'is the finest poem that was ever written, and I do so want to read it once more.'

The whole Serbian Army mourns the loss of Voyno Popovitch, familiarly known as Voyvode 'Vouk', or 'the Wolf', commander of the corps of Volunteer Irregulars, or Comitadjis, which has played such an active and glorious part in the five campaigns that Serbia has waged since the autumn of 1914. Only thirty-two years of age was Voyrode 'Vouk'. But, though young in years, he was a veteran in warfare – his experience reaching back to 1905 in a long series of unofficial hostilities, now with Turkish troops, now with Bulgarian comitadjis, a master of guerilla tactics, and one of those iron disciplinarians who know how to inspire their followers with love, as well as with fear and respect. Discipline amongst the comitadjis was formerly of the slackest kind. As stern in its observance as he required his men to be, he established and maintained such a rigid code that his corps are today 'irregulars' no longer but in name. Their drill and discipline are unsurpassed in any branch of the regular army. The use of hand grenades was unknown to the Serbs before the Austrian invasion of 1914. It was Popovitch who introduced them amongst his comitadjis when they crossed the Drina and attacked the Austrians on Austrian ground. Their great utility was quickly recognised. The hand-bomb has become the most popular weapon in the Serbian armoury, and its lavish use by the Serbian infantry, every man of whom, become expert, claims the privilege of carrying one or two grenades into action, is one of the remarkable minor features of the present campaign.

It was in one of the desperate encounters that have just taken place around Grunista, while rallying his men against an overwhelming onset of the enemy, that this gallant warrior met his death. Though already wounded in the arm, with the wound yet unbandaged, he threw himself into the wavering line of Serbs, and restored their courage by his example. But he was mortally hit by a Bulgarian sniper firing from behind a rock. His last words were: 'Dead or alive, do not leave me to the Bulgars.' His dying wish, I am glad to say, was faithfully obeyed, and Voyrode 'Vouk' was buried with all due honours by the victorious Serbs.

3 January 1918

FIERCE BATTLE FOR JERUSALEM
Turks' Great Defeat, *Jerusalem, Monday*

By W. T. Massey

Since Boxing Day General Allenby's army has followed up one brilliantly fought battle by a series of engagements which have brought into the control of the British Palestine army the whole watershed between the Mediterranean and the Jordan as far north as Bireh, and we have a splendid line across a high pass which was the scene of many conflicts in ancient times. Our troops are well north of this line, for yesterday we occupied Beitin, the Bethel of the Scriptures, and the beautiful water supply between Bireh and Ramallah has been secured. This rapid advance in a most difficult country is due to the overwhelming defeat of the Turkish attempt to retake Jerusalem on 27 December, when, after resisting desperate attacks for nearly twelve hours, the British delivered a masterly counter-stroke, and rolled up the enemy's right, causing the Turks, who sustained tremendous losses, to yield almost impregnable positions and fall back along the Nablus road, leaving in our firm possession points of great strategical importance.

London Territorials, Welshmen, Home Counties, dismounted Yeomanry, and Irish troops showed the highest courage, and their dashing work will adorn the pages of our military history, but their efforts would not have been so fully successful if not backed by perfect Staff work. There was no semblance of a hitch at any part of the wide battle front, although the army was confronted by a colossal task. The problem of transport was rendered terribly difficult by unfavourable weather. The Turks are now so far away from Jerusalem that when the Greek Orthodox service of thanksgiving was held in the church of the Holy Sepulchre yesterday, not a sound of the guns reached the Holy City, and it was only when one went out a considerable distance on the Nablus road that one could see our artillery driving back the enemy rearguards.

The Turks seem to have read aright the lesson of their heavy defeat, and appear to be retiring northwards. The enemy used two corps in making the attempt to retake Jerusalem. His attack was made by the 3rd Turkish Corps, including a new division from the Caucasus, from the north along the Nablus road, the 20th Turkish Corps making a demonstration from the east and fighting very hard for some vital positions. Prisoners state that one Turkish battalion commander told his men there were no English troops on their front; he had been watching for days, and assured the battalion that no English were there, and they could go straight into Jerusalem, where they could get food. It would be the last chance of retaking the city, and if it failed they would have to go back. These Turks were given strict orders not to mutilate the wounded.

The enemy's first objective was Tel-el-Ful, a high, conical-shaped hill, just east of the Nablus road, a commanding height dominating our lines east and west for a considerable distance. During daylight on Boxing Day the Turks showed no movement, but just before midnight a post north of Ful was driven in, and at 1.20 a.m. the first attack on Ful was made. At the same time an advance was begun against Beit Hannina, about a mile west of the road. This line was defended by London Territorials, who added to their grand record during the campaign by meeting attack after attack with magnificent steadiness, standing like rocks against most furious onslaughts, and never once yielding an inch of ground. Two companies defending Hannina were attacked four times by storming troops, each attack being stronger than the last. The fourth was delivered by 500 picked Turks, but was entirely beaten back after prolonged hand-to-hand fighting. The enemy's dead show many bayonet wounds, and the hillside is strewn with Turks killed by machine-gun fire.

There were eight attacks on Tel-el-Ful. These likewise were made with great weight and determination. The strongest of them all, delivered with a reinforced line, was made at dawn, supported by heavy artillery fire. All were defeated with great loss to the enemy. At daylight one of our positions had (?) [sic] dead Turks in front.

Between seven o'clock and noon the enemy organised for a last big effort, and about half-past twelve the Turks tried to assault the whole of the Londoners' line except the Nobi Samwill height, crowned by the mosque, ruined by enemy gun-fire. This final attack was pressed right up to our positions, the Londoners and Turks getting to deadly grips, and the enemy fighting with the bravery of desperation. He proved no match for the London Territorial, who, after raking the advancing waves with machine-guns, cleared his breastworks at a bound, met the foe with the bayonet, and forced him back, and then, with a well-supported counter-attack, made the enemy cry 'enough'.

That was the last attempt of the Turks to get to Jerusalem, and in the fighting on subsequent days we see how much their morale has been affected by the terrible losses they sustained in the series of attacks, which lasted more than twenty-four hours, on the north and east.

Before describing how the Welsh and Home Counties troops smashed up the advance of the Turkish 20th Corps east of Jerusalem, I will tell how the British commander, swiftly realising how deeply committed the Turks were to the attack on Jerusalem, put in Irish and dismounted Yeomanry against the enemy's right, and caused the Turks to divert their new Caucasian division from the Jerusalem attack to try to save their right flank. But the flanking movement was carried out with such dash that we actually made much more ground than we could possibly hope for if the British had been acting on the offensive. Those who have seen the terrain marvel at the dismounted Yeomanry's and Irishmen's achievement. They moved from Bethhoron, where there has been much fighting, north-eastwards. The Yeomen attacked at Tires. At the time it was not strongly held, but just as they secured it a Turkish storming battalion was advancing to it. The enemy thus forestalled the counter-attack, but the Yeomanry rushed at them and counted seventy Turks killed by the bayonet alone. The hill near by was so steep that it took two hours to get supplies up to the top. Another hillside was so precipitous that the only way the troops could get up the terraced slopes was by men standing on each other's shoulders.

This hillside was so nearly perpendicular that the Turks on top could not fire on the climbers till they were at close quarters.

While the Irish and the Yeomen were advancing, the men in reserve were making roads for the guns, which had to be hauled by hand, and when the Yeomen captured Beit Ania they had the whole brigade of guns just behind the front line, though it was sometimes necessary for a whole company of infantry to haul the ropes attached to one gun, which at moments was literally dangling in the air. The Zeitun Ridge, taken by the Irish, was a tremendous obstacle to scale. It was a great feat, but to fight and defeat a stubborn foe on the top was to achieve the impossible. The Irish captured seven machine-guns on this ridge. At one place the Yeomen got to an absolutely unclimbable kill. Several men made the attempt, but found it impossible, and had to make a long detour.

On the 28th the Londoners attacked Er Ram Hill, the Ramah of Benjamin, three miles north of Tel-el-Ful, and found the Turks' morale so shaken by the previous day's defeat that they soon retired, leaving thirty-six prisoners and two machine-guns, and after one sharp fight with the rearguard, we made considerable progress and occupied Bireh next day. The Yeomen having captured Beitania took Ramallah about the same time as the Londoners entered Bireh. Ramallah is a picturesque town, with a population of 5,000, with nice buildings and several big churches. To show how completely the enemy was taken by surprise by the rapidity of the Yeomen's and Irish advance, we found nine of the enemy standing guard over the springs, entirely unaware of their force's retreat. The Irish captured a few German prisoners, who were amazed at finding British troops against them, having been told they would only have to fight Indians and the 'scum of Egypt'.

Welsh and Home Counties troops also took a glorious part in beating off the attack on Jerusalem. They had taken Zamby and White Hill, north of the Jericho road, and held White Hill against three counter-attacks. On the 27th the Turks attacked all day, and White Hill became a No Man's Land. Zamby was held, and the fighting was at bombing distance. At dusk the enemy tried to take White Hill, but the Welshmen charged with the bayonet, and killed over 100 Turks. Further south a post at the village of Obeid was attacked by 700 of the enemy, and was surrounded, and the Turks fired 400 shells into the monastery, but the Middlesex men, who garrisoned the post, held out, and next morning the Turks hurried away, heavily fired upon by infantry who had occupied the high ground near by. The post's casualties were trifling.

It was important to take from the enemy Ras-es-Suffa, which looks down the Jericho road. Its loss denies him a view all ways on the south. The approaches are very difficult; there is a narrow front, and the sides of the hill are steep; but the Welshmen and Herefords rushed the place in darkness, and secured it with slight loss. The enemy had to make a considerable retirement to the east.

In these operations since Boxing Day it is estimated that the Turks have lost at least a thousand killed. Up to the 29th over 700 dead had been counted. More than 600 prisoners, including about fifty officers, were brought in. The importance of the victory is the protection of Jerusalem, secured by a very strong line of positions. The British have gained seven miles of ground, and the Jaffa–Jerusalem road is well out of the enemy's reach. We have got unlimited water. The behaviour of our troops was beyond praise. The physical difficulties of the country and the trials of wet and cold winds had no effect on their spirits. They all feel that they have got the Turks beaten. As an instance of the enormous labour entailed in supplying the troops over tracks made slippery with mud, I may mention that all supplies and material for the Irish and Yeomen during their break-up of the Turkish right had to be drawn from the railhead, first in motor-lorries as far as the road ran, then by wheeled transport to a point where no wheels could travel, and afterwards by camel transport, till the tracks got too bad for the camels, when donkeys carried the loads. Finally, men took them where donkeys could not obtain a foothold. Victory was purchased at the cost of much exertion, but every soldier agrees it was worth even a greater price.

18 January 1918

SERBIA'S MARTYRDOM
Austro–Bulgarian Savagery

A terrible indictment of the Austrian and Bulgarian forces in occupation of Serbia is contained in a memorandum issued for publication by the Serbian Legation. This document has been presented to the International Socialist bureau at Stockholm by the Serbian Parliamentary deputy, Mr T Katslerorvitch, and the general secretary of the Labour party, Mr Dushan Popovitch, both of whom have been eye-witnesses for two years of the iniquities they record.

From the appended extracts it will be seen that the Austrians and Bulgars have little to learn from their German masters. Large numbers of the unfortunate population have been massacred, many thousands have been deported and interned, and the remainder are leading a miserable and precarious existence under a veritable reign of terror. An urgent appeal is made for help if this remnant is to be saved from starvation.

The first act of the authorities in occupation consisted in interning in Austria and Hungary, for no reason and out of no political or military necessity, more than 150,000 persons belonging to the civil population. Serbia was thus stripped of her last reserves of labour, and countless families lost their last resources. Hundreds of thousands of children, women, and old men were in this fashion condemned to die of starvation. Everything indispensable to production, all working material, was requisitioned. Serbia's most important factories no longer exist; the machinery has been taken down and transported to the other side of the frontier. The peasants were deprived of their last carts, their horses, and their oxen. Almost all the products of the country, including even metal utensils indispensable in every household, have been seized, the forests have been felled, and the whole of the harvest has been commandeered. The plight of the population will be truly terrible this winter and next spring if they are left without assistance. The last grain of their crops is now being exported. Swift and extensive help is necessary, both in money and in food.

To the foregoing is added political slavery. In the villages the gendarmes possess unlimited powers and are absolute masters. Police espionage, denunciations, chicanery of every kind, theft, often murder, are the methods employed. In Belgrade a lieutenant named Widmann has power of life and death over the inhabitants. He can at his own discretion cause an inhabitant to be arrested, flogged, and interned. Arrests of perfectly innocent citizens, and their condemnation to imprisonment and even to death, are among the most ordinary occurrences. This year, for instance, the schoolmaster Glislaitch and thirty-five peasants of the village Ramatja and the district of Gruza were shot or hanged, and 250 men and women put in prison, because some quite unusable weapons and a few old shotguns had been found in the village. Nothing is more frequent than individual sentences of death pronounced by the courts (or even by the gendarmes), and carried out on the spot. In numerous cases perfectly innocent hostages were murdered. In many places, men have been hanged.

A whole book would be necessary to depict the plight and the conditions of life of the 150,000 interned civilians. The fact of being interned in Austria–Hungary or in Bulgaria is in reality equivalent to being indirectly sentenced to death. About 30 per cent of these unfortunate people have already died. Those who are left lead a wretched existence, a prey to atrocious sufferings, and to ill-usage baffling description.

In the numerous concentration camps, which contain on an average several thousand interned persons, the occurrence of ten, twenty, and thirty deaths a day is the rule but there are some, especially in Hungary, where the death-rate is from 200 to 300 persons a day. There are concentration camps where one-half of the inmates have died. And this is not a case of an epidemic which has claimed countless victims. They die there of cold and hunger. Last year a certain number of peasants from the district of Taza, who had been sentenced to internment, hoped to escape by hiding and failed to respond to the first summons of the authorities. All these poor people were summarily shot. Their houses were burnt, their property destroyed, and their families interned.

Conditions under the Bulgarian occupation are even worse. The Serbs in this region are condemned to a veritable state of slavery. Such as the Bulgars did not succeed in murdering in Serbia itself have been transported in great numbers to Asia Minor. And here it is not a question of punishment inflicted upon individuals, but of a system determined by a definite policy. The revolt which took place last March was planned and undertaken by Serbian soldiers and comitadjes, who had succeeded in eluding the authorities, assisted in all probability by Bulgarian deserters and disaffected Austro–Hungarians. Yet it was the innocent population which was held responsible. When the unfortunate people tried to exonerate themselves by declaring that it was physically impossible for them to resist the insurgents, they received the most callously cynical replies, such as: 'It was your duty to oppose all their demands, and, if necessary, to let yourselves be killed. As you would not be killed by them, we are going to do it for you ourselves.'

About 20,000 Serbs were executed under this pretext, and not more than 3,000 among them had really taken part in the revolt. Thousands of women and children were interned, and thrown into prison; thirty-six villages in the neighbourhood of Leskovso were razed to the ground, and numerous families were rendered homeless.

4 February 1918

PALESTINE WAR
Sir E. Allenby's Despatch

Vicissitudes in war are proverbial; so long as our armies are in the field we are not defeated; the fortune of war may turn, especially in favour of a new wooer. The first news of Allenby's triumph were synchronous with the Italian disaster. The fall of Jerusalem came to balance Cambrai, and the soldier-like despatch, describing the matchless courage and endurance of our army in Palestine, should hearten us to encounter the colossal German attack which is now being threatened in France. The bare facts are already familiar. How Allenby took over the command from Sir A. Murray after the 'breakdown' at Gaza. How he swiftly reorganised the army, prepared its transport and communications for an offensive à outrance. How the Germans sent Von Falkenhayn, their ex-Commander-in-Chief, the great leader who planned and directed the downfall of Russia in 1915, to oppose the British general.

Allenby took command early in July. By the end of October he was ready to move. In the meanwhile the Turks had reinforced their army, and had had leisure to prepare a most formidable chain of fortifications from the sea to the wilderness east of Judea. Gaza converted into a modern fortress constituted the sea-bastion of their line. The Turkish left held Beersheba as a detached bastion dominating the track by which a direct advance against Jerusalem might be attempted. Vast stores of munitions, every engine of contemporary war, and heavy artillery partly manned by Austro–German gunners, were at Falkenhayn's disposal.

By skilful use of his cavalry Allenby rushed the Turkish garrison of Beersheba, and followed up the stroke by infantry attacks which perplexed the foe and pinned Turkish divisions to their posts while he developed his great attack east of Gaza. The Navy and Air Service co-operated most skilfully, both to paralyse the defence of the fortress and to interrupt its communications by rail and road with the north. The advance east of the place turned its flank, so the Turks were compelled to abandon their stronghold, and a general retreat from the first line of fortifications ensued. The intention of the Turkish Commander-in-Chief was to fall back from one strong position to another, thus rendering the British advance wearisome, tardy, and costly beyond proportion with the results. Everything promised well for this plan, owing to the extreme difficulty of bringing along our guns and heavy material in a country which was almost devoid of roads, and to a great extent waterless. But the enemy reckoned without the invincible determination with which Allenby has been able to inspire his soldiers.

Disregarding thirst, hunger, fatigue, and sleeplessness, cold by night and heat by day, our divisions – Londoners, Scottish, Welsh, and Australians – pressed relentlessly on the track of the beaten enemy. While retreating he was kept on the move. Whenever he halted to make a stand he was fiercely attacked before he had time to organise his defence. This pursuit was only possible owing to the consummate skill with which Allenby, a former Inspector of Cavalry, utilised his horsemen. The rapidity with which he followed up his offensive by a cavalry pursuit, and even by many cavalry attacks upon artillery and infantry in position, utterly disconcerted the Turks, and prevented them from forming a new line of battle across Palestine. The final stand was made on the heights which surround Jerusalem.

The part of the despatch which describes the final defeat of the enemy and the capture of the sacred city itself is comprehensible to everyone, and is a model of modest, clear, historical narrative. Once again English Yeomanry and Australian horsemen vied with one another in close co-operation, with the staunch infantry of the Army. In spite of a stubborn defence the Turks were hurled from their vantage points, and were forced to surrender Jerusalem. Since this climax to the campaign our troops have steadily pushed the Turks further from the city, and have in turn formed a strong chain of posts extending from Jaffa, on the coast, to where the majestic mountains of Judea abruptly descend 4,000ft into the gloomy valley of the River Jordan.

Before this campaign was launched the army of Palestine had not been fortunate. At the first battle of Gaza it had met with a most discouraging 'setback'. The enemy was greatly superior in numbers, had had ample time to prepare his defence, and has been famous throughout history for the tenacity with which he clings to his fortresses. The Turkish triumphs at Plevna in 1877, at Chatalja in 1912, and in Gallipoli in 1915 prove the fact. More important still, his strategy was directed by a Commander-in-Chief of proved and consummate ability – the German Field-Marshal von Falkenhayn. Nevertheless, he has been completely defeated. The fact is a most encouraging proof that no fortified lines are impregnable to British troops when well directed. The victory was got by the timely, accurate and loyal co-operation of all arms, their leaders and staff, and by avoiding the mistakes in staff work and troop-leading which have led to disaster before.

Very notable has been the triumph of the cavalry arm. It may be open to question in a democratic State whether newspapers can or cannot profitably criticise the military policy of the rulers of the nation when it is at war. Something is gained, and something is lost.

The balance depends on the skill and good faith of the critics; but if the crude suggestions of some writers had been adopted the cavalry which won Palestine for us would be disbanded. Cavalry is an arm of exceptional opportunity. It is the hardest to lead, the slowest to train, and the most difficult to keep up, but its skilful use at the right moment has turned the scale in countless battles and wars. This conclusion holds good just as much today as on the fields of Rosbach and Waterloo.

7 November 1918

FIGHTING IN PALESTINE
A Trying Campaign

A supplement to last night's *London Gazette* contains a long despatch from General Sir Edmund Allenby, describing the operations of the Army in Palestine, from the capture of Jerusalem in December 1917, to the middle of September last. The despatch is dated 18 September, the day before the opening of the brilliant campaign in which General Allenby annihilated three Turkish armies, overran the whole of Syria, and reduced the last centre of enemy resistance – an accumulation of triumphs which finally brought about Turkey's unconditional surrender. The present despatch deals with less exhilarating events. It is mainly a record of minor operations directed in the first place to securing the Army's possession of the territory previously won, and subsequently to harassing the enemy and preparing the way for the larger operations to follow. In the second half of the period the demands of the Western Front imposed a heavy drain on the forces, British divisions being withdrawn and replaced by Indian troops, and during the process of reorganisation a policy of active defence was rendered necessary.

The operations which ended in the fall of Jerusalem had resulted in the enemy's army being broken into two separate parts. One part, consisting of five divisions, had retired northwards, and had come to a halt in the hills overlooking the plain north of Jaffa and Ramleh. The other part had retired in an easterly direction towards Jerusalem. Here the remains of six divisions had been concentrated. In order to provide more effectively for the security of Jerusalem and Jaffa, it was essential that the line should be advanced. At Jaffa this operation was successfully carried out by the 21st Corps. By increasing the distance between the enemy and Jaffa from three to eight miles it rendered Jaffa and its harbour secure, and gained elbow-room for the troops covering Ludd and Ramleh and the main Jaffa–Jerusalem road.

At Jerusalem the carrying forward of the line was entrusted to the 20th Corps, but before the advance had begun it became apparent that the enemy was preparing an attack with the object of recovering Jerusalem. On the night of 26–27 December the attack was launched with great determination bestride the Jerusalem–Nablus road. The outposts of the 60th Division on the ridge north of Beit Hanninah repelled four determined attacks, but the heaviest fighting took place to the east of the Jerusalem–Nablus road. Repeated attacks were made against Tel el Ful, a conspicuous hill from which Jerusalem and the intervening ground can be overlooked. The attacks were made by picked bodies of troops, and were pressed with great determination. At only one point did the enemy succeed in reaching the main line of defence. He was driven out at once by the local reserves. In all these attacks he lost heavily. In the meantime the enemy had delivered attacks against various points held by the 53rd Division east of Jerusalem. On the extreme right, at Kh. Deir Ibn Obeid, a company of Middlesex troops was surrounded by 700 Turks, supported by mountain artillery. Although without artillery support, it offered a most gallant resistance, holding out till relief came on the morning of the 28th. None of the other attacks on this division's front was any more successful. A final attack of unexpected strength on the 60th Division front north of Jerusalem was also defeated.

At once a British counter-attack was launched, and by the evening of 30 December the 20th Corps advanced on a front of 12 miles to a depth varying from six miles on the right to three miles on the left. This advance had to overcome, not only a determined and obstinate resistance, but great natural difficulties as well, which had to be overcome before guns could be brought up to support the infantry. The Turkish attempt to recapture Jerusalem had thus ended in crushing defeat, and at the end of three days' fighting the enemy found himself seven miles farther from the city than when his attack started. He had employed fresh troops, who had not participated in the recent retreat of his army from Beersheba and Gaza, and had escaped its demoralising effects. The determination and gallantry with which the attack was carried out only served to increase his losses.

Before a further advance could be made it was necessary to drive the enemy across the Jordan to render the British right flank secure, and the observations directed to this end, and those which followed with the object of clearing the Jordan Valley of the enemy, were undertaken in February and March. They were carried through against strong opposition and over country offering the greatest obstacles to the movement of troops. The despatch recalls that a battery of field artillery took thirty-six hours to cover a distance, as the crow flies, of eight miles. The nature of the difficulties which had to be overcome is sufficiently indicated in the following passage: 'The descent of the slopes leading down to the Wadis el Nimr and El Jib and the ascent on the far side presented great difficulties. The downward slopes were exceptionally steep, almost precipitous in places. It was impossible for companies and platoons to move on a wide front. The slopes were swept by machine-gun and rifle fire, and the bottom of the wadis by enfilade fire. The ascent on the far side was steeply terraced. Men had alternatively to hoist and pull each other up, under fire, and finally to expel the enemy from the summits in hand-to-hand fighting.'

The Jordan Valley having been sufficiently cleared of the enemy to enable operations to be carried out against the Turkish line of communication to the Hedjaz, in conjunction with the Arab forces under Sherif Feisal, General Allenby decided to carry out a raid on Amman, where the Hedjaz railway crosses a viaduct and passes through a tunnel. The operations, which started during the night of 21–22 March, were hampered considerably by rain, which rendered the tracks in the hills slippery and the movement of horses, and especially of camels, slow and difficult. The delay thus caused enabled the enemy to bring up reinforcements. Before Amman could be attacked in strength some 4,000 Turks, supported by fifteen guns, were in position, covering the viaduct and tunnel, while another 2,000 were moving on Es Salt from the north. To have driven the enemy from his position without adequate artillery support would have entailed very heavy losses, and a withdrawal was ordered, which was carried out without serious interruption. Although it had not been possible to effect any permanent demolitions, five miles of railway line, including several large culverts, and the points and crossings at Alanda Station, were destroyed to the south of Amman; while to the north of the town a two-arch bridge was blown up. Considerable losses were inflicted on the enemy, and in addition fifty-three officers and over 900 other ranks were taken prisoner, including several Germans.

After the troops employed in the raid had been withdrawn to the left bank of the Jordan, the enemy reoccupied the Shunet Nimrin position, which he held with some 5,000 rifles. General Allenby determined to seize the first opportunity to cut off and destroy this force, and, if successful, to hold Es Salt till the Arabs could advance and relieve his troops. On 30 April the 60th Division captured the advanced works of the Shunet Nimrin position, but were unable to make further progress in face of the stubborn resistance offered by the enemy. The mounted troops, moving northwards, rode round the right of the Shunet Nimrin position and captured Es Salt, leaving an Australian brigade to watch the left flank. On 1 May this brigade was attacked by the 3rd Turkish Cavalry Division and a part of the 24th Division. The enemy succeeded in penetrating between the left of the brigade and the detachment on the bank of the Jordan. The brigade was driven back through the foothills to the Wadi El Abyad. During its retirement through the hills nine guns and part of its transport had to be abandoned, being unable to traverse the intricate ground.

On 2 May the mounted troops in Es Salt were attacked by two Turkish battalions which had arrived from Amman accompanied by heavy guns, as well as by cavalry from the north, and troops from Jiar Ed Damich. These attacks were driven off, but the force intended to attack Shunet Nimrin from the north-east had to be weakened and was checked at El Howeij, five miles south of Es Salt. The 60th Division was also unable to make any substantial progress, in spite of determined efforts. Further Turkish reinforcements were known to be on their way. 'It was evident that the Shunet Nimrin position could not be captured without losses which I was not in a position to afford. In these circumstances I ordered the mounted troops to withdraw from Es Salt. Their retirement was accomplished successfully. The enemy, who followed up closely, was held off without difficulty. By the evening of 4 May all the troops had recrossed the Jordan.'

The despatch of troops to France in April and the reorganisation of the force prevented further offensive operations for the time being. The 52nd and 74th Divisions, nine Yeomanry regiments, five and a half siege batteries, ten British battalions, and five machine-gun companies were withdrawn, and in May the force was further reduced by twelve battalions. These units were replaced within the next few weeks by Indian troops. During the summer a number of successful raids were carried out. The enemy, too, made an attack in July on both banks of the Jordan, which failed ignominiously, and caused him heavy losses.

General Allenby concludes: 'In driving back the enemy my troops suffered considerable hardships. The rugged country in which the majority of the fighting took place not only favoured the defence, but demanded great physical exertion on the part of the attackers. In the early months of the year their task was often rendered more difficult by the cold and heavy rains, which added greatly to their discomfort. They responded to every call made on them, and proved their superiority over the enemy on every occasion.'

Tribute is paid to the excellent work of the Royal Air Force and of the transport services, who had great difficulties to overcome in the rainy season. General Allenby acknowledges his indebtedness to General Sir Francis Wingate, High Commissioner for Egypt, for his cordial assistance, and to Rear-Admiral T. Jackson, Commanding the Naval Forces in Egyptian waters.

Chapter 7

The War in the Air

15 August 1914

AIRCRAFT IN WAR
Reconnaissance Work

The decisive influence of reconnaissance by aircraft has already made itself felt during these opening stages of the war. Within a week of the outbreak of hostilities the French General Staff possessed definite and accurate information regarding the exact position of every single army corps massed along the German western frontier and occupying Belgium. The points of concentration of the vast German army are known, and the necessary measures have been taken by the Allies. All this is due to the wonderful success of the French and Belgian aviation service, which has not only dispelled – so far as the General Staffs are concerned – the fog of war, to a great extent, rendering a surprise attack en masse impossible, but has proved itself unquestionably superior to the German aircraft.

Apart from the general effect exerted upon the conduct of hostilities by aircraft – an effect which cannot yet be precisely estimated, although its influence is already perceptible – several specific instances of the useful employment of aeroplanes have been reported. Thus on Thursday during the German advance upon Diest three German aeroplanes are reported to have been brought down by Belgian artillery. The report, though lacking official confirmation, bears the stamp of probability. Events have proved that rifle fire is largely ineffective against aeroplanes, which, travelling swiftly, offer a very difficult target; the planes may be struck repeatedly by bullets, but, unless hit in a vital spot, such as the engine or the propeller, an aeroplane, even though riddled with shot, could continue its journey with its efficiency scarcely impaired.

With shell-fire the case is different; a fragment of a shell striking an aeroplane would, in the majority of cases, inflict irreparable damage and bring it down to earth. On the other hand, an aeroplane travelling at a great height and moving at 60 miles an hour or more forms a most elusive target, and it is only when the necessity for detailed observation causes the pilot to fly low that the ordinary artillery, incapable of high angle fire, has a reasonable chance of bringing an aeroplane down.

During the past few days German aeroplanes have been repeatedly sighted flying over the Belgian lines, and even so far afield as Brussels; but in every case these were flying at so great an altitude – from 5,000ft to 6,000ft – as to render effective observation impossible. Experience has shown that an aeroplane pilot can only make accurate observations of the movements and positions of troops from a height not exceeding 4,000ft, at which altitude it is within range both of rifle and shell.

The official statement that a French aeroplane reconnoitring over German territory in the Lorraine region was pursued by two German machines, but succeeded in escaping, and returned safely to the French lines, is interesting in that it proves that the light, fast French aeroplanes can without difficulty elude the more ponderous and slower German machines.

The bombardment of the fortress of Vesoul and the town of Lure by a German aeroplane 'flying a French flag' confirms the opinion generally held by experts that the small bombs which alone can be carried on an aeroplane are incapable of doing serious damage. In each case the railway station formed the target, and was repeatedly struck, but the damage done was only slight and easily repaired. That the machine in question was flying a French flag is obviously a misapprehension. No aeroplane carries a flag, but the French machines bear on the underside of each wing a large Tricolor formed of concentric circles, in order that they may be identified and not fired upon by their own troops. A German aeroplane similarly disguised would undoubtedly be liable to be fired upon, on returning, by the Germans.

Hitherto the famous German Zeppelin airships do not appear to have been employed to any useful purpose, although one vessel, based either upon the Cologne or Metz stations, is stated to have taken part in the initial bombardment of Liège. Their advent upon the scene will undoubtedly introduce a new element in the war, and is eagerly awaited by the French aviators, who are confident of their ability to destroy them.

11 February 1915

ALLIES' AIR RAID ON DÜSSELDORF
War Stores Destroyed, *Rotterdam, Wednesday*

News reaches me of a very successful air raid by the Allies over Düsseldorf, resulting in the destruction by bombs and fire of a large quantity of war materials. The story illustrates both the failure of the Germans to preserve secrecy as to the whereabouts of their materials and the daring and skilfulness of the French aviators.

Having learned by experience that the Allies' aviators, though failures at the art of killing non-combatants, are experts in finding and damaging lawful targets, the Germans became very nervous as to the safety of their war stores in the very important arsenal at Düsseldorf. Accordingly they erected a number of wooden buildings a considerable distance from the arsenal and giving no outward indication in position or construction of their real purpose. To these buildings they removed secretly from the arsenal great quantities of war material, including ammunition, motor engines, tyres, and petrol. But shortly afterwards the secret was discovered.

The sequel was a visit by aviators, who ignored the arsenal and concentrated their attention on the timber buildings. Several bombs were dropped, and the buildings and their valuable contents destroyed by fire.

This event, the news of which comes to me from a reliable source, is probably one reason for the recrudescence of the advice from German official quarters to the public not to talk in public about the war. The Mayor of Cologne has issued one such warning. It tells the people that so long as their interest in and discussions on the war and war news are confined to their own homes and in circles where everybody can be trusted, it is well; but, he adds: 'To talk about these things openly can bring a great shadow on the Fatherland. It is only for a single thoughtless word to be spoken about new formations of troops or the direction of transports, or to mention the names of high authorities in connection with the troops, for such things to reach the ears of the enemy and bring great difficulties and danger to the Fatherland.' The proclamation then proceeds to warn people not to discuss these things in railway trains or cafés, or anywhere where there are unknown people present, but to keep silent on all military matters.

31 January 1916

ZEPPELIN RAIDS ON THE FRENCH CAPITAL
Bombs on Paris, *Paris, Sunday Night*

About a dozen bombs were dropped by a Zeppelin last night, killing twenty-five persons, the majority being women and children, and all of the labouring classes, and wounding twenty-seven others.

On the alarm being given thirty aeroplanes rose, five of which found the Zeppelin out, but only one was able to attack. The Zeppelin was then driven off, but unfortunately, as far as is known, unscathed.

It was about 10 p.m. that we heard the fire-men motoring through the streets sounding the military tattoo, the pre-arranged signal announcing Zeppelins. We had not heard the signal for ten months, since 21 March last. A Zeppelin had been signalled at 9.20 p.m. at La Ferté Milon, on the Ourcq, a few miles south-east of the trenches near Soissons and some 40 miles due north-east of Paris. Thus the

Zeppelins were following the Marne valley, straight for a neighbourhood of Paris which is one of the most populous and poorest, whereas last year the Zeppelins passed over the chief residential district.

Last night was still and fine, but very misty. Thus the best atmospheric conditions prevailed for a Zeppelin raid. The same conditions continue and we are quite prepared for another raid tonight.

In common with all Paris I went out to look for the Zeppelin, but it remained invisible to me. Few stars could be seen in the hazy sky. French aeroplanes carrying lights dashed across the sky now and then, but even the searchlights, which were constantly playing, were dimly seen. I saw an aviator this morning who told me it was not surprising that I had vainly looked for the Zeppelin. The latter remained constantly at a height of about 12,000ft above the thick mist lying over Paris.

The Zeppelin was actually seen only by five aviators. One of those was a plucky young pilot, whose name we do not know, and who alone was able to attack the pirate airship. It seems to have been he alone who single-handed drove the Zeppelin away. Shots were exchanged between the Zeppelin and the aeroplane in what must have been one of the most weird encounters, even in this war, at a height of 12,000ft in the dense darkness over fog-shrouded Paris.

No sooner was the alarm given last night than, of course, all Paris flocked into the streets, which had been completely darkened. Crowds gathered in the pitch-black Place de la Concorde, the Place de l'Etoile, the Place de l'Opéra, and especially on the Montmartre heights, whence the best view was expected, but none was obtained owing to the mist.

In the working district, where nine houses were more or less demolished, involving the death of or injury to nearly sixty poor workers, the alarm during the few minutes of the bombardment was naturally considerable. Beyond that Paris is absolutely unmoved.

The only feelings are pity for the victims and ever-increasing anger against the Boches, and Paris feels not only anger, but contempt. Last night's raid, one more characteristic piece of combined German savagery and childish frightfulness, obviously meant the celebration of the Kaiser's birthday, 27 January. Presumably the raid was planned for Thursday night, but was put off for two days owing to the atmospheric conditions.

The bombardment lasted only a few minutes but this sufficed for the infernal machines to do considerable damage. One bomb burst through a tunnel, and the train which had left the station a moment before had a lucky escape. Several workmen's dwellings were shattered. One still preserved its frontage, but when one entered the courtyard all the back part seemed to be in ruins. The bomb literally sliced off all the back of the house, leaving the façade. Here casualties were severe.

In another workmen's dwelling-house one family had a wonderful escape. Though living on the top floor, they are safe and sound, whereas the family on the ground floor were killed. One old man, picked out of the wreckage and thought to be dead, suddenly came to though still confused in his mind, and said to a fireman: 'Hullo! Are you the pompier? I thought you might be the Boche.' Then he saluted the captain of the brigade.

A policeman was just dressing to go on night duty when he was killed.

President Poincaré, the moment the alarm sounded, motored out to the scene of the bombardment, with the Home Secretary, the Military Governor of Paris, and other officials. M. Poincaré visited all the ruined houses, spending the great part of the night on the scene of the disaster. Just after one o'clock the fire brigade motors passed through the streets, sounding a second bugle-call to signal that the raid was over.

3 January 1918

FINE AIR FEATS

War Correspondents' Headquarters, France, Wednesday

Over the snow-bound battle-ground of France, high in the icy sky, beardless boys of Britain have again been proving that they belong to the breed of the unafraid. Christmas week and the New Year have been made glorious by acts of pure courage, outshining the fairest deeds of the lion hearts of the classics; for three miles, high over the frozen snowdrifts, battles have been fought singlehanded, more beautiful because of the perfect heroism displayed there than any to be read of in ancient heroics.

Take the story of just one youngster of twenty-two as an example. This lad but for the war would still be in school. Today to his credit is a list of over thirty enemy planes which he has engaged in mortal combat amongst the outposts of cloudland, and sent hurtling to the ground wrecked and splintered. Three of these were accounted for in one day at the very end of the Old Year. Flying at 17,000ft this boy engaged a two-seater at fairly close range. Both his guns he brought to bear on the enemy, who, attempting to get off, went into a right-hand spiral dive. Immediately both right wings broke off, and in two parts the wreckage fell behind our lines. Before ten minutes passed he engaged another similar machine, which, after a short burst from the deadly machine-guns, burst into flames, and went down like a misdirected rocket, crashing well within our territory.

The young Englishman stayed aloft, still at about three miles, when, a quarter of an hour later, he spied a river of white anti-aircraft bursts a few thousand yards away. These bursts were from our guns, so the young airman went to see what the trouble was. Our guns kept up their firing until the boy was within easy range of the target – an enemy two-seater – then he took over the job from the artillerymen on the ground. He fired a short burst to force the German to dive, which the German did, but with the Englishman on his tail. At a height of 9,000ft the latter turned on a stream of bullets from a distance of a hundred yards, and the fleeing plane burst into flames. From the first it had been doomed. So skilfully had the British fighter handled his craft that his adversary never had the chance to fire a shot, and like a fireball it sizzled out of the sky, leaving within our lines only a black splotch on the ground where he fell and melted the snow and the charred skeletons of plane and men who had manned it.

Rising to a great height again, the steel-nerved British lad attacked his fourth plane that day, or rather within the hour, but this one, after at first catching fire, was extinguished immediately, and dived away rapidly to the east. Not having any more petrol aboard, the victor went home. I have heard of a very curious incident, of which the same pilot was the hero. During Christmas week a German plane surrendered to him at a height of at least three miles. It came about this wise: Leaving the ground shortly before noon, looking for trouble, he found it coming from the east, at about 17,000ft. He gave chase, and caught up with the German plane which careered and whirred away to the south.

Securing a good firing position he gave the enemy a burst with both guns. The German's engine stopped, and water poured from the radiator as the plane dived steeply away, and always to the south.

Then came the surrender. The observer raised his right arm and waved it frantically, and the English boy ceased firing, at the same time striving to head the enemy plane off and force him to turn westward, so as to land him behind the British lines. But the staff work between the German observer and his pilot did not seem of the best, for the pilot continued his dive southward, whereupon the captor was forced to fire another burst into the machine at very close range. At once it made a sickening lunge earthward, and crashed to bits in the British lines. The false surrender – the first I have heard of in the sky – proved a costly game.

Immediately following this scrimmage, this rival of Bishop and Ball bore down upon a German two-seater, climbing as he charged. For twenty minutes he climbed and manœuvred for a good position, then he opened fire. He says himself that the enemy 'fought extraordinarily well', showing the gallantry that is part and parcel of the stuff of which every hero is made; and diving and spinning, charging and firing, the duellists dropped until they were only 9,000ft over the snow-crusted ground. Here the English airman pumped short bursts with both guns into his enemy, and both the latter's right-hand wings dropped off, the wreckage falling inside our lines. Two more planes a few minutes later were taken on by this tireless wonder, but these planes, working together admirably, and firing from both front and rear guns, succeeded in getting off eastward, and home.

Now all this industry took place in the forenoon. After returning to his mess and lunching like any good workman, the lad went forth into the skies again in search of adventure. His first prey was spotted shortly after he got off the ground. This plane he drove down to 6,000ft, and sent crashing to the ground. Next he fired twenty shots into an enemy aeroplane, sending it down absolutely out of control – diving, stalling, rolling, turning upside down, and spinning before stalling again, and repeating the fearsome repertoire. It took the stricken plane five minutes to reach the ground, where it landed upon a train well inside our country.

This gallant boy is not the only one out here who has done great things these past few days. I could tell of many more whose grit is adding lustre to the British shield, but their deeds are so like the deeds of this lad that to tell of them would sound like mere repetition.

I hear that German air officers are complaining of the difficulty they are now experiencing in getting first-class fighting machines. Prisoners say only a small percentage of the newer and improved varieties is to be found in the various flying units. Certainly there is reason to believe that inside Germany they are rushing aeroplane construction to the limit, and it may be that to some extent hasty construction and faulty materials are now beginning to have a physical effect on the Western Front. In the fighting described above it will be remarked that in several cases the wings of enemy machines dropped off after they began to spin downwards. Perhaps things are not so wonderfully rosy in Kaiserland as German statesmen try to make the world believe.

23 April 1918

RICHTHOFEN KILLED ON THE BRITISH FRONT
Famous Airman's Fate, *War Correspondents' Headquarters, France, Monday*

By Philip Gibbs

In our Royal Air Service yesterday great interest was aroused by news that Von Richthofen, the most famous German air fighter after the death of Immelmann, had been killed and brought down in our lines. It was only the day before yesterday that a German official communiqué announced that Rittmeister von Richthofen, commanding their 'trusty 11th Pursuit Squadron', had achieved his seventy-ninth and eightieth victory in air combats. It will be a great blow to the morale of the German air pilots when they learn that he has at last been destroyed by us.

How it happened is not yet quite clear, and there are various theories as to the way in which he was brought down, because there was a general fight over our lines, with many machines engaged on both sides, and in such cases it is difficult to get exact evidence. Richthofen went about with a 'circus', as it is called, of about twenty-seven to thirty fighting scouts, and each of his pilots was renowned for daring achievements. This circus never served on the ordinary routine work of reconnoitring and signalling and spotting for the artillery, but had a roving commission up and down the lines, and their pilots were out for blood all the time. This swarm of raiders appeared yesterday over our lines near the Somme

Valley, and gave chase to some of our planes. Two of these were suddenly attacked by four or more fighters, and then the raiders swooped off and the battle passed into another air space northward.

Something like fifty machines were engaged in what the flying men call a dog fight, that is when every aeroplane up for miles around joins in the tourney. There was a general mêlée in the air, pairs of machines closely engaging each other, manœuvring for position, and trying to get in a burst of machine-gun bullets. I hear that some machines on both sides were disabled.

The fighting swept over a wide area of sky, so that no single observer could see its details, but as far as Richthofen is concerned it is certain that he was seen flying low, not more than 150ft above the ground, just before his machine crashed in full view of the enemy. Immediately they started shelling fiercely, no doubt with the intention of destroying its wreckage. It was only when they examined the papers of the dead man that he was known to be the German champion who has killed so many of our gallant fellows in fair fight, but with a most determined and ruthlesss desire to increase the number of his victims. He was a young man of about thirty, slight of build, with fair hair and a clean-shaven face. It is said out here that he had an English mother, and that he was educated at Oxford, but I do not know whether this is true. He was shot through the side close to the heart.

According to the custom of our Air Service and of that chivalry which exists between the flying men on each side, Freiherr von Richthofen was buried today with full military honours, and his funeral was attended by many of our flight commanders, officers, and men, who paid their respects to a brave enemy, for whose skill and daring they had profound admiration, though he was a deadly menace near our lines.

On Sunday night the German communiqué stated: 'Captain Baron von Richthofen, at the head of the trusty chasing echelon, gained his seventy-ninth and eightieth serial victories.' Whether that referred to the number of the Allied airmen he himself had brought down or those for whom his squadron was responsible is somewhat doubtful, but his name will always be coupled with those of Immelmann and Boelcke as one of the trio of the enemy's most successful fighting aviators. By our men he was recognised as a sporting opponent, though the principle on which he fought was not theirs. The British Flying Corps or RNAS man is ever willing – sometimes too willing – to take on any odds, but with all his skill and daring Richthofen was always ready to break off an encounter and make for home if the odds proved too great or the conditions too adverse: his principle was to fight only when the opportunity presented itself of doing the maximum damage without encountering overwhelming opposition. His earlier work was done under Boelcke, after whose death he succeeded to the command of the famous 'flying circus' which has always been used by the Germans on that part of the front to which they attach the greatest importance, or where our squadrons have asserted the most pronounced ascendancy.

Last September it was reported that he had received two bullet wounds in the head in a fight with a British airman over the German lines, but in the following month his marriage was announced to Fraulein von Minkwitz, the heiress of the Duke of Saxe-Coburg's Master of Horse, and he was appointed equerry-airman to the Kaiser. It was then said that he was to devote himself for the future to the training of fighting squadrons, but early last month Reuters' correspondent with the French army reported that Richthofen had reappeared on the Western Front in command of a powerful squadron of fighting machines, and during the earlier stages of the enemy's push for Amiens it was in action in the vain endeavour to neutralise the fine work of the Royal Flying Corps. Two or three weeks ago the Kaiser bestowed on him the Order of the Red Eagle, with Crown and Swords.

In a book he recently published, extracts from which were given in *Cassell's Magazine*, he described some of his encounters. Of his principal opponents he wrote 'The British airman is a dashing fellow. I hardly ever encountered an Englishman who refused battle.'

Speaking of his first fight he said 'In a few seconds the dance would begin … The Englishman nearest to me was travelling in a large machine painted in dark colours. I did not reflect very long, but took my aim and shot. He also fired, and, so did I, and both of us missed our aim. A struggle began. Apparently he was no beginner, for he knew exactly that his last hour had arrived at the moment when I got at the back of him. At that time I had not yet the conviction "He must fail!" which I have now on such occasions, but, on the contrary, I was curious to see whether he would fall.

'My Englishman twisted and turned, going criss-cross. I was animated by a single thought: "The man in front of me must come down, whatever happens." At last a favourable moment arrived. My opponent had apparently lost sight of me. Instead of twisting and turning he flies straight across. In a fraction of a second I aim at his back with my excellent machine. I give a short series of shots with my machine-gun. I had gone so close that I was afraid I might dash into the Englishman.

'Suddenly I nearly yelled with joy, for the propeller of the enemy machine had now stopped turning. Hooray! I had shot his engine to pieces. The enemy was compelled to land, for it was impossible for him to reach his own lines. The observer died at once, and the pilot while being transported to the nearest dressing-station. I honoured the fallen enemy by placing a stone on his beautiful grave.

'During my whole life,' he went on, 'I have not found a happier hunting-ground than in the course of the Somme battle. In the morning, as soon as I had got up, the first Englishman arrived, and the last disappeared only long after sunset. Boelcke once said that this was the El Dorado of the flying men.

'It was a beautiful time. Every time we went up we had a fight. Frequently we fought real battles in the air. There were then from forty to sixty English machines, but unfortunately the Germans were often in the minority. With them quality was more important than quantity. Still, the Englishman is a smart fellow. That we most allow … They absolutely challenged us to battle, and never refused fighting.'

Captain Ball he looked upon as his most formidable foe, and expressed his opinion that when Captain Ball was lost the English would give up the attempt to catch him. 'I should regret it,' he added, 'for in that case I should miss many nice opportunities to make myself beloved by them.' The British did not give up the attempt, and Richthofen had another 'nice opportunity', but it was his last.

Chapter 8

The Western Front 1916–17

3 January 1916

BLUEJACKETS IN THE TRENCHES

New Year's Eve Visit, *British Headquarters, New Year's Day*

By Philip Gibbs

There was more than half a gale blowing yesterday on the eve of the New Year, and today, as I write, the wind is howling with a savage violence across the rainswept fields, so that the first day of a fateful year has had a stormy birth, and there is no peace on earth. As I went down a road near the lines I saw, 1,000 yards or so away, from concealed positions, the flash of gun upon gun.

There were no New Year's Eve rejoicings among those rows of miners' cottages on the edge of the battlefield. Half those little red-brick houses were blown to pieces, and when here and there through a cracked window-pane I saw a woman's white face peering out upon me as I passed I felt as though I had seen a ghost-face in some black pit of hell. From a shell-hole in a high wall I looked across the field of battle, where many of our best have died. The Tower Bridge of Loos stood grim and gaunt above the sterile fields. Through the rain and the mist loomed the long, black ridge of Notre Dame de Lorette, where many poor bodies lie in the rotting leaves. The ruins of Huisnes and Hulluch were jagged against the sky-line. And here, on New Year's Eve, I saw no sign of human life and heard no sound of it, but stared at the broad desolation and listened to the enormous clangour of great guns. They were our guns. I heard a single shell come answering back to all that rush of shells from our hidden batteries.

At the street corner in the war zone I met the naval men. They had first come out of the trenches away there in the dead fields, and they were high-strung with the thrill of all they had seen and done. It was good to see those men picked from thirty ships or more of the Grand Fleet, and representing all ratings in the Royal Navy – petty officers, seamen, stokers, and his Majesty's 'Jollies'.

They were dressed in khaki uniforms hurriedly fitted on from the stores of the Union Jack Club, and with their ships' ribbons on their caps, but they were not disguised. Those clean-shaven men of all types and sizes were as unmistakably bluejacket in this soldiers' kit as though they stood in their own togs on a British battleship.

They had a quarrel with me, which made us good friends at once, after my apology. When the first batch of bluejackets came to the trenches I gave the reason as a correction of the idea prevailing in the Fleet that Tommy was having a softer time than Jack.

'Sir,' said a petty officer in a very grave and simple way, 'you have done the Fleet an injustice. Far from envying the men in the trenches, we have always acknowledged their marvellous courage to endure so much suffering and hardship. Now we have seen for ourselves, and we are still more astounded at the cheerfulness and high spirits of the soldiers. We wouldn't change with them.'

It was a great adventure for these men of the Grand Fleet that night in the trenches when they stood guarding this section of the Western Front side by side with the soldiers. It was not a quiet night. Quite unaware that the British Navy was paying a visit to the trenches, the Germans began to whizz-bang the parapets, knocking out one poor Tommy just as the bluejackets arrived. Then they attacked with a bombing party. But it was an ill-advised idea.

The British gunners were glad to show Jack that landsmen could do a little shooting, and, as one of the seamen told me, 'The Germans were put on their heads, sir – fairly done in.'

Then the bluejackets did their little bit, feeling that they had come to work. They discovered the bomb store, and opened such a Brock's benefit that the enemy must have been shocked with surprise. One young Marine was bomb-slinging for four hours, and grinned at the prodigious memory as though he had had the time of his life. Another professed to me that he preferred rifle-grenades, which he fired off all night until the dawn.

'I don't mind saying,' said a petty officer who has fought in several naval actions during the war and is a man of mark, 'that I had a fine fright when I was doing duty on the fire-ship. I suppose I've got to look through a periscope, he said. "Not you," said the sergeant. "At night you put your head over the parapet." So over the parapet I put my head. And presently I saw something moving between the limes. My rifle began to shake. Germans! Moving, sure enough, over the open ground, I fixed bayonet and prepared for an attack … But I'm blessed if it wasn't a swarm of rats!'

The soldiers were glad to show Jack the way about the trenches, and some of them played up a little audaciously, as, for instance, when a young fellow sat on the top of the parapet at dawn.

'Come up and have a look, Jack,' he said to one of the bluejackets.

'Not in these trousers, old mate!' said that young man.

'All as cool as cucumbers,' said a petty officer, 'and take the discomforts of trench life as cheerily as any men could. It's marvellous. Good luck to them in the New Year!'

I should have liked to have had those splendid seamen with me today when I paid another New Year's visit. They would have seen, as I saw, some of the finest fighting men in the British Army enjoying a New Year's jollification with a spirit which has lost nothing of its keen edge because they have seen and suffered all that is worst in war, except defeat. They were the heroes of Loos – or some of them – Camerons and Seaforths, Argyll and Sutherland Highlanders, Gordons and King's Own Scottish Borderers, who, with the London men, were first on Hill 70 and away to the Cité St Auguste. There were young men there from the Scottish Universities and from Highland farms, sitting shoulder to shoulder in a jolly comradeship which burst into song between every mouthful of the feast. On the platform above the banqueting board a piper was playing when I came in, and this hall in France was filled with the wild strains of it.

'Ah, they're gran', the pipes,' said one of the Camerons. 'When I've been that tired on the march I could ha'e laid doon an' dee'd, the skirl o' the pipes has sent me on again.' The piper made way for a kiltie at the piano, and for Highlanders who sang old songs full of melancholy, which seemed to make the hearts of his comrades grow glad, as when they helped him with 'The Bonnie Banks of Loch Lomond'. But the roof nearly flew off the hall to 'The Song of the Cameron Men', and the walls were greatly strained when the regimental marching song broke at every verse into wild Highland shouts and the war-cry which was heard at Loos of 'Camerons, forward!' 'Forward, Camerons!'

Out in the rain-slushed street I met the colonel of a battalion of Argylls and Sutherlands with several of his officers, a tall, thin officer with a long stride. He beckoned to me and said, 'I'm going the rounds of the billets to wish the men good luck in the New Year. It's a strain on the constitution, as I have to drink their health each time!'

He bore the strain gallantly, and there was something very noble and chivalrous and sweet in the way he spoke to all his men, gathered together in various rooms in old Flemish houses, round plum-pudding from home, or feasts provided by the Army cooks.

To each group of men he made the same kind of speech, thanking them from his heart for all their courage.

'You were thanked by three generals,' he said, 'after your attack at Loos, and you upheld the old reputation of the regiment. I'm proud of you. And afterwards in November, when you had the devil of a time in the trenches you stuck it splendidly, and came out with high spirits. I wish you all a happy New Year, and whatever the future may bring, I know I can count on you.'

In many billets, and in many halls, the feast of New Year's Day was kept like this in good comradeship by men who have faced death together, and, who in the year that is coming will fight again with a gallant spirit which is quite unconquerable, whatever the odds may be.

2 March 1916

BATTLE OF VERDUN
The Curtain Falls

Yesterday afternoon the German and French Headquarters issued bulletins which were singularly in agreement. Although the opposing troops lie within a few yards of one another on the blood-stained hillsides north of Verdun, yet forty-eight hours had elapsed without a renewal of the general conflict. The battle as such is over. It lasted a week, and having cost the lives of an unknown but appallingly large total of soldiers, it must be classed with the numerous sanguinary drawn battles of this obstinate war. Drawn it may be called, because the Germans, in spite of having gained a few miles of ground at an important point of the entrenched line, have absolutely failed to capture the fortress, or to drive the French from the hills which surround it. Verdun is still to be taken, so that neither the moral nor the material result has been achieved. It was not in order to carry their trenches three and a half miles forward on a front of less than a score of miles that the German Chief of the Staff sacrificed two entire army corps.

Although the Germans' great effort has been foiled and heavy loss has been inflicted on their army, yet it would be rash to assume that the aggressive attitude is at an end. Fresh attacks may, and probably will, be made if fresh opportunities occur. These opportunities arise when a surprise can be effected by various artifices. The German Main Headquarters, from its central position at Mézières, near Sedan on the Meuse, are particularly skilful in attracting the Allied forces and reserves to points which are of secondary importance, or which are not threatened at all; while if they secretly mass the legions intended for a decisive attack close to their objective. Thus they achieved the fatal victory on the River Dunajec over the Russians last May, and their strategy has been on similar lines elsewhere. The Allies have a numerical superiority in France, but that superiority in numbers certainly does not justify the concentration of vast forces on the shores of the Eastern Mediterranean without an objective and without hope of shooting a single German soldier whatever betides.

The first battle of Verdun will have driven home some tactical truths, and even at this distance it is apparent that no position where the surface of the ground is irregular can be so strongly entrenched but that determined infantry, backed by an adequate artillery, and led by a capable staff, can storm it, at a price. The question of whether the position is worth the price will always vary with the circumstances and general situation. It is also plain that there has been too much loose talk about the absolute impregnability of the Allied lines. Instead of this attitude of mind, our military brains should perpetually be anticipating the enemy by thinking out and foreseeing his future moves. Above all, the utmost economy and efficiency of administration and staff work is called for, as well as the simplest and most effective methods of troop-leading in the field, if we aspire to attack successfully.

Much has been heard about blasting the way with high explosive, the necessity for guns, ammunition, and so forth. All these requirements are essential, but the best conceivable Staff arrangements are no less necessary, and also one other indispensable arm. Where our attacks failed, it has been not only because our infantry was unskilfully handled, but also because there was nothing like enough of it, even with the most judicious dispositions, to win an important victory. We must have plenty of infantry in reserve for our next offensive. Incidentally, they will also be very handy if the enemy perseveres in his attacking policy.

BRITISH FRONT

Holding the Enemy, *British General Headquarters, Monday*
By Philip Gibbs

While the French are fighting at Verdun, in a battle upon which the Germans seem to have staked all their chances of final victory or final defeat, the situation along the British front is normal and unexciting. The impatience which frets us all seems to suggest that now is the acceptable hour for a great British offensive to deliver a smashing blow at the enemy on this part of the line while his big battalions are so heavily engaged to the east of the Meuse. Amateur critics are probably discouraged because of the dry brevity of our official communiqués, which indicate a complete lull in our lines after the series of minor attacks which seemed to threaten a general action on the salient.

The truth is that we are waiting and watching for any sign that the enemy intends to take the offensive elsewhere than at Verdun, when all attention is directed to that point; and that meanwhile we are holding great German forces which cannot be thinned because of our strength. By this means – that is to say, by standing on guard in Flanders and on the Somme, we are helping our Allies more effectively than if our troops were being used on the actual battlefield of Verdun. The presence of our Third Army, which took over last summer a big stretch of ground formerly held by the French, has enabled them to concentrate greater strength in men and guns round the fortress city which is now attacked, and they know that our troops along the Somme relieve them largely of any anxiety in this region should the enemy be tempted to try another and shorter way to Amiens and Paris.

It is improbable that the German Headquarters Staff has dared to dislodge many units, if any, from the positions which we confront. The series of minor attacks which they hazarded against us during recent weeks were sufficient to prove that we were more formidable than ever in men and munitions. Whatever the failure or success at Verdun – and we know that their losses will be staggering to the national morale of Germany – they must still keep a big army opposed to us, or lose the ground most essential to their safety and pride. How long it will remain a big army depends upon the battle in which they are sacrificing their youth with an utter disregard of human life flung into the furnace fires. If that is a vain sacrifice they will be unable to maintain their strength along the whole length of their battle line, and then we have our chance for the one great blow which should end the war.

In the meantime we are thinning them down by a daily wastage, which must reach dreadful figures. Our artillery has been active at certain parts of the line during recent days, and especially in the direction of the Ypres–Comines Canal. It was here (as I reported) that on 15 February the enemy exploded five mines and took some of our trenches by a surprise attack. Since then they have paid dearly for this venture. Day after day our artillery, heavy and light, has bombarded them here so intensely that all their attempts to consolidate the position have cost them a heavy toll in life, and their working parties have been continually swept by our fire. In an official despatch these incidents seem trivial. But they mean casualty lists to the enemy which mount up day by day into a big total.

We never give the enemy a day's peace. Even during the snowstorms here our guns fired through the thick veil of the whirling flakes at registered positions, and knew that by the law of averages they had added to the sum of death. The gunners do their work methodically and with a grim sense of humour. Yesterday to a party of visitors in the trenches a gunner officer gave the advice not to go forward to the front line just then. 'We are going to tickle up the Germans a little,' he explained, 'and they're sure to answer back.'

The 'tickling up' process consisted of several rounds from the field batteries, and some salvoes of trench mortars, followed by the 'heavies'. It was an infernal tumult, which ceased as suddenly as it began, and left a dead silence in which one could hear the drip of melting snow from the sandbags on the parapets. Then the Germans 'answered back', and their shells came howling over the trenches, in which men crouched low, hoping that this flying death might dodge them again.

'Oh, would they?' said the gunner officer. 'Well, we'll teach 'em!'

Our heavies fired a double round again, and it was more than a retort courteous. The German trenches were badly 'crumped', and the enemy did not ask for more. Our observing officer watched the work of the batteries with a critical eye. One of the shells was a 'dud' – that is to say, it did not explode, but just buried itself in the soft earth. 'Ah, you son of a gun!' said he. 'So you're a conscientious objector, are you?'

It was a joke which caused great laughter. It is surprising how good any little jest like that seems at a time when high explosives are about. But when the artillery is at work it is not so amusing to the infantry upon whom the enemy 'answers back'. Many of them would prefer the policy of 'live and let live', when there is no attack in hand. But that policy is not adopted, and although the official communiqué says 'Nothing to report', the noise of gun-fire rolls along the line and the carnage goes on. There is only one thing certain – that it cannot go on for ever.

At Verdun the Germans are hastening the end.

3 July 1916

THE BRITISH OFFENSIVE

All Saturday and yesterday London and the Empire thrilled to the news of a great British attack. Long expected and ardently desired, the movement on the Western Front has begun at last, and the opening stages of the fight have been so prosperous for the Allied arms that we may reasonably have high hopes for the issue. 'The day is going well for England and France' – so ran the words of the correspondents at Headquarters on Saturday, and the message stirred our spirits like a clarion. From the Somme northwards to Gommecourt, on a front of some 22 miles, following an artillery preparation of extreme intensity which lasted an hour and a half, British and French troops leaped from their trenches and fell with irresistible force on the German lines. After a few hours desperate work, they had made notable captures. Serre had fallen, south-east of Hebuterne; Beaumont-Hamel was closely attacked. On the right of the British advance success was still more clearly marked. Montauban, north-east of Bray, was captured and held, despite a violent counter-attack from the Germans; La Boiselle was in our hands; Mametz and Contalmaison were being fought for, and Mametz was won, after a struggle. Round Fricourt the battle raged with conspicuous fury; the village was gradually surrounded by our men, and captured after an obstinate resistance. A large number of prisoners had fallen into our hands – at least 3,500 – and the German total losses in killed and wounded had on Sunday reached a high figure. Nor were the French less victorious in their southern sector. Just north of the Somme they had established themselves in Hardecourt and Curlu; while on the south of the river they had possession of Dompierre, Becquincourt, Bussu, and Fay. We may summarise the results so far by saying that along the front exposed to the Allied attack – from below the valley of the River Ancre up to the Gommecourt salient – we have penetrated to the depth of between two and three miles, and that, though savage fighting has gone on for the last forty hours, we are holding our conquests and warding off the attacks of German reinforcements.

More important than the acquisition of territory is the fact that British and French together have taken 8,500 prisoners, from which one may argue as to the German total loss. Perhaps the most promising feature of the affair is the steadiness of the advance. It is not a brilliant and ephemeral dash; still less is it what the enemy calls 'a through drive'. It is a well-organised invasion of the opposing lines, carried out in a methodical manner, each section of the attacking troops playing its part in the magnificent exactness of the whole.

Many points in this deliberately planned offensive are well worth study. It was clearly a surprise for the Germans, for it fell upon them from an unexpected quarter. The region where the lately extended British line meets the French has not been the scene of many fights for several months past, and it was looked upon as a relatively peaceful zone. Round Albert, which, with Bray, is the most important town in the neighbourhood, the country, quite unlike the flat and marshy character of Flanders, consists of rolling downs and densely-wooded chalk hills, suggesting in a fashion Surrey and Sussex. The places referred to in the communiqués are for the most part quite unpretentious villages, though some of the more important have been turned into defensive positions. Doubtless, it was part of the strategy of the Allies to lull the enemy into a false sense of security and to accustom him mainly to attacks in the more northern sector, where Ypres and Neuve Chapelle and Loos have acquired so sinister a notoriety. But though we have gained a brilliant success so far, we must not imagine that our further advance will be rapid. The Germans are immensely strong on the Western Front, and we know that if they have depleted their effectives elsewhere they have not taken any troops away from the line which confronts the British. Doubtless, they will despatch with all speed whatever they can spare from the north to the region now threatened by the Allies, and many desperate combats will be waged before we can securely consolidate the positions recently gained. We may be sure, however, that Sir Douglas Haig will not give them many opportunities for readjusting their defences. If our troops have advanced near Albert, they will also keep the Germans busy in Flanders. Every day they are being disturbed and perplexed by an almost continuous bombardment and by incessant raids. Lille, we observe, has recently been the object of an air attack, and there are signs that activity will be shown in many other quarters than the one which is now engrossing our interest. But it is a welcome feature that our artillery and heavy guns should have proved so fully adequate to their task The Germans will speedily discover to their cost how ample is the munitionment which we have amassed all along the line behind our gallant and well-equipped Army in France.

So good has been the overture that we may expect the main body of the work equally to flatter our hopes. Apart, however, from the details of this brilliant episode, what is the outstanding feature of the campaign? We may answer the question in different ways. We may point to the fact that Germany is now compelled to do what her Higher Command has always tried to avoid. She is forced to fight on two fronts simultaneously, or, to be more accurate, on more than two. We speak regretfully of the mistakes which the Allies have made in the conduct of the war, and if we desire to point the moral, we emphasise especially the attempt on the Dardanelles and the unfortunate expedition to reach Bagdad in Mesopotamia. But how do these compare with the two gigantic blunders of the enemy? At all events, Gallipoli and Kut-el-Amara stand outside the main area of warfare. The fruitless attack on Verdun and the foiled Austrian offensive in the Trentino are closely connected with the paramount interests of the Central Powers. Whatever may be the ultimate issue round Verdun – and we notice that once more our valiant Allies have regained the much-disputed Thiaumont work – the loss of life and the loss of time have been equally fatal to Berlin. As to the Austrian enterprise, whether or not it was sanctioned by Falkenhayn, it has been a ruinous error, which has entailed the gravest consequences for the Teutonic cause, and has practically resulted in the loss of the Bukovina. Looking at these events from our own point of view, we derive the comfortable assurance that the strategy of the Allies is now closely co-ordinated, and that the scheme of war is proceeding with clockwork regularity. The Austrian effort between the Val Sugana and Ligurina led to the splendid onset of Brussiloff on the Eastern front. That, in its turn, enabled General Cadorna to drive back the Austrians in the Trentino. And the Italian success paved the way for an outburst of British activity, which, indeed, was to be expected in order to relieve the pressure on Verdun. Thus we have profited by the mistakes of the enemy, and checkmated his ambitious schemes, by a more perfect co-operation of our conjoint forces. We must look with stern composure for bitter losses in the campaign which has just begun. But our heroes will not have died in vain if their self-sacrifice ensures our final victory.

FIRST PHASES OF THE BATTLE

Terrific Artillery, *British Headquarters, Saturday*

By Philip Gibbs

The great attack which was launched today against the German lines on a 20-mile front began satisfactorily. It is not yet a victory, for victory comes at the end of a battle, and this is only a beginning. But our troops, fighting with very splendid valour, have swept across the enemy's front trenches along a great part of the line of attack, and have captured villages and strongholds which the Germans have long held against us. They are fighting their way forward, not easily, but doggedly. Many hundreds of the enemy are prisoners in our hands. His dead lie thick in the track of our regiments.

And so, after the first day of battle, we may say with thankfulness: All goes well. It is a good day for England and France. It is a day of promise in this war, in which the blood of brave men is poured out upon the sodden fields of Europe.

For nearly a week now we have been bombarding the enemy's lines from the Yser to the Somme. Those of us who have watched this bombardment knew the meaning of it. We knew that it was in preparation for this attack. All those raids of the week which I have recorded from day to day were but leading to a greater raid when not hundreds of men but hundreds of thousands would leave their trenches and go forward in a great assault. We had to keep the secret, to close our lips tight, to write vague words lest the enemy should get a hint too soon, and the strain was great upon us and the suspense an ordeal to the nerves, because as the hours went by they drew nearer to the time when great waves of our men, those splendid young men who have gone marching along the roads of France, would be sent into the open, out of the ditches where they got cover from the German fire. This secret was foreshadowed by many signs. Travelling along the roads we saw new guns arriving – heavy guns and field-guns, week after week. We were massing a great weight of metal.

Passing then, men raised their eyebrows and smiled grimly … A tide of them flowed in from the ports of France – new men of new divisions? They passed to some part of the front, disappeared for a while, were met again in fields and billets, looking harder, having stories to tell of trench life and raids.

The Army was growing. There was a mass of men here in France, and some day they would be ready, trained enough, hard enough, to strike a big blow. A week or two ago the whisper passed 'We're going to attack.' But no more than that, except behind closed doors of the mess-room. Somehow by the look on men's faces, by their silences and thoughtfulness, one could guess that something was to happen. There was a thrill in the air, a thrill from the pulse of men who know the meaning of attack. Would it be in June or July? ... The fields of France were very beautiful this June. There were roses in the gardens of old French châteaux. Poppies put a flame of colour in the fields, close up to the trenches, and there were long stretches of gold across the countryside. A pity that all this should be spoilt by the pest of war.

So some of us thought, but not many soldiers. After the misery of a wet winter and the expectations of the spring they were keen to get out of the trenches again. All their training led up to that. The spirit of the men was for an assault across the open, and they were confident in the new power of our guns. The guns spoke one morning last week with a louder voice than has yet been heard upon the front, and as they crashed out we knew that it was the signal for the new attack. Their fire increased in intensity, covering raids at many points of the line, until at last all things were ready for the biggest raid.

The scene of the battlefields at night was of terrible beauty. I motored out to it from a town behind the lines, where through their darkened windows French citizens watched the illumination of the sky, throbbing and flashing to distant shell-fire. Behind the lines the villages were asleep, without the twinkle of a lamp in any window. The shadowy forms of sentries paced up and down outside the stone archways of old French houses.

Here and there on the roads a lantern waved to and fro, and its rays gleamed upon the long bayonet and steel casque of a French Territorial, and upon the bronzed face of an English soldier, who came forward to stare closely at a piece of paper which allowed a man to go into the fires of hell up there. It was an English voice that gave the first challenge, and then called out 'Good night!' with a strange and unofficial friendliness as a greeting to men who were going towards the guns.

The fields on the edge of the battle of guns were very peaceful. A faint breeze stirred the tall wheat, above which there floated a milky light transfusing the darkness. The poppy fields still glowed redly, and there was a glint of gold from long stretches of mustard flower. Beyond, the woods stood black against the sky above little hollows where British soldiers were encamped.

There by the light of candles which gave a rose-colour to the painted canvas boys were writing letters home before lying down to sleep. Some horsemen were moving down a valley road. Further off a long column of black lorries passed. It was the food of the guns going forward.

A mile or two more, a challenge or two more, and then a halt by the roadside. It was a road which led straight into the central fires of one great battlefield in a battle line of 80 miles or more. A small corner of the front, yet in itself a broad and far-stretching panorama of our gunfire on this night of bombardment.

I stood with a few officers in the centre of a crescent sweeping round from Auchonvilliers, Thiépunt, La Boisselle, and Fricourt, to Bray, at the southern end of the curve. Here, in two beetroot fields on high ground, we stood watching one of the greatest artillery battles in which British gunners have been engaged. Up to that night the greatest.

The night sky, very calm and moist, with low-lying clouds not stirred by the wind, was rent with incessant flashes of light as shells of every calibre burst and scattered. Out of the black ridges and woods in front of us came explosions of white fire, as though the earth had opened and let loose its inner heat.

They came up with a burst of intense brilliance, which spread along a hundred yards of ground, and then vanished abruptly behind the black curtain of the night. It was the work of high explosives and heavy trench mortars falling in the German lines. Over Thiépunt and La Boisselle there were rapid flashes of bursting shrapnel shells, and these points of flame stabbed the sky along the whole battle front.

From the German lines rockets were rising continually. They rose high, and their star-shells remained suspended for half a minute with an intense brightness. While the light lasted it cut out the black outline of the trees and broken roofs, and revealed heavy white smoke-clouds rolling over the enemy's positions.

They were mostly white lights, but at one place red rockets went up. They were signals of distress, perhaps, from German infantry calling to their guns. It was in the zone of these red signals, over towards Ovillers, that our fire for a time was most fierce, so that sheets of flame waved to and fro as though fanned by a furious wind. All the time along the German line red lights ran up and down like red dancing devils. I cannot tell what they were, unless they were some other kind of signalling, or the bursting of rifle-grenades. Sometimes for thirty seconds or so the firing ceased, and darkness, very black and velvety, blotted out everything, and restored the world to peace. Then suddenly, at one point or another, the earth seemed to open to furnace fires. Down by Bray, southwards, there was one of these violent shocks of light, and then a moment later another, by Auchonvilliers to the north. And once again the infernal fires began, flashing, flickering, running along a ridge with a swift tongue of flame, tossing burning feathers above rosy smoke-clouds, concentrating into one bonfire of bursting shells over Fricourt and Thiepval upon which our batteries always concentrated.

There was one curious phenomenon. It was the silence of all the artillery. By some atmospheric condition of moisture or wind (though the night was calm), or by the configuration of the ground, which made pockets into which the sound fell, there was no great uproar, such as I have heard scores of times in smaller bombardments than this.

It was all muffled. Even our own batteries did not crash out with any startling thunder, though I could hear the rush of big shells, like great birds in flight. Now and then there was a series of loud strokes, an urgent knocking at the doors of night. And now and again there was a dull, heavy thunder-clap, followed by a long rumble, which made me think that mines were being blown further up the line. But for the most part it was curiously quiet and low-toned, and somehow this muffled artillery gave one a greater sense of awfulness and of deadly work.

Along all this stretch of the battle front there was no sign of men. It was all inhuman, the work of impersonal powers, and man himself was in hiding from these great forces of destruction. So I thought, peering through the darkness, over the beetroot and the wheat.

But a little later I heard the steady tramp of many feet and the thud of horses' hoofs walking slowly, and the grinding of wheels in the ruts. Shadow forms came up out of the dark tunnel below the trees, the black figures of mounted officers, followed by a battalion marching with their transport. I could not see the faces of the men, but by the shape of their forms could see that they wore their steel helmets and their fighting kit. They were heavily laden with their packs, but they were marching at a smart, swinging pace, and as they came along were singing cheerily. They were singing some music-hall tune, with a lilt in it, as they marched towards the light of all the shells up there in the places of death. Some of them were blowing mouth-organs and others were whistling. I watched them pass – all these tall boys of a North Country regiment, and something of their spirit seemed to come out of the dark mass of their moving bodies and thrill the air. They were going up to those places without faltering, without a backward look – and singing! Dear, splendid men.

I saw other men on the march and some of them were whistling the 'Marseillaise', though they were English soldiers. Others were gossiping quietly as they walked, and once the light of bursting shells played all down the line of their faces – hard, clean-shaven, bronzed English faces, with the eyes of youth there staring up at the battle fires and unafraid.

A young officer walking at the head of his platoon called out a cheery goodnight to me. It was a greeting in the darkness from one of those gallant boys who lead their men out of the trenches without much thought of self in that moment of sacrifice.

In the camps the lights were out and the tents were dark. The soldiers who had been writing letters home had sent their love and gone to sleep. But the shell-fire never ceased all night.

A Staff officer had whispered a secret to us at midnight in a little room, when the door was shut and the window closed. Even then they were words which could be only whispered, and to men of trust.

'The attack will be made this morning at 7.30.'

So all had gone well, and there was to be no hitch. The preliminary bombardments had done their work with the enemy's wire and earthworks. All the organisation for the attack had been done, and the men were ready in their assembly trenches waiting for the words which would hold all their fate. There was a silence in the room where a dozen officers heard the words – men who were to be lookers-on and who would not have to leave a trench up there on the battlefields when the little hand of a wrist watch said, 'It is now.' The great and solemn meaning of next day's dawn made the air seem oppressive, and our hearts beat jumpily for just a moment. There would be no sleep for all those men crowded in the narrow trenches on the north of the Somme. God give them courage in the morning …

The dawn came with a great beauty. There was a pale blue sky flecked with white wisps of cloud. But it was cold, and over all the fields there was a floating mist which rose up from the moist earth and lay heavily upon the ridge, so that the horizon was obscured. As soon as light came there was activity in the place where I was behind the lines. A body of French engineers, all blue from casque to puttee, and laden with their field packs, marched along with a steady tramp, their grave, grim faces turned towards the front. British Staff officers came motoring swiftly by, and despatch riders mounted their motor-cycles and scurried away through the market carts of French peasants to the open roads. French sentries and French soldiers in reserve raised their hand to the salute as our officers passed. Such men among them guessed that it was England's day, and that the British Army was out for attack. It was the spirit of France saluting their comrades in arms when the oldest 'poilu' there raised a wrinkled hand to his helmet and said to an English soldier, *'Bonne chance, mon carmarade!'*

Along the roads towards the battlefields there was no movement of troops. For a few miles there were quiet fields, where cattle grazed, and where the wheat grew green and tall in the white mist. The larks were singing high in the first glinting sunshine of the day above the haze. And another kind of bird came soaring overhead. It was one of our monoplanes, which flew steadily towards the lines, a herald of the battle. In distant hollows there were masses of limber and artillery horses hobbled in lines.

The battle line came into view, the long sweep of country stretching southwards to the Somme. Above the lines beyond Bray, looking towards the German trenches, was a great cluster of kite balloons. They were poised very high, held steady by the air pockets on their ropes, and their baskets where the artillery observers sit, among the rays of the sun. I counted seventeen of them, the largest group that has ever been seen along our front; but I could see no enemy balloons opposite them. It seemed that we had more eyes than they, but today they have been staring out of the veil of the mist.

We went further forward to the guns, and stood on the same high fields where we had watched the night bombardment. The panorama of battle was spread around us, and the noise of battle swept about us in great tornadoes. I have said that in the night one was startled by the curious quietude of the guns, by that queer muffled effect of so great an artillery. But now on the morning of battle this phenomenon, which I do not understand, no longer existed. There was one continual roar of guns which beat the air with great waves and shocks of sound, prodigious and overwhelming.

The full power of our artillery was let loose at about six o'clock this morning. Nothing like it has even been seen or heard upon our front before, and all the preliminary bombardment, great as it was, seemed insignificant to this. I do not know how many batteries we have along this battle-line, or upon the section of the line which I could see but the guns seemed crowded in vast numbers of every calibre, and the concentration of their fire was terrific in its intensity. For a time I could see nothing through the low-lying mist and heavy smoke-clouds which mingled with the mist, and stood like a blind man, only listening. It was a wonderful thing which came to my ears. Shells were rushing through the air as though all the trains in the world were driving at express speed through endless tunnels, in which they met each other with frightful collisions. Some of these shells, fired from batteries not far from where I stood, ripped the sky with a high, tearing note. Other shells whistled with that strange, gobbling, sibilant cry which makes one's bowels turn cold. Through the mist and the smoke there came sharp, loud, insistent knocks, as separate batteries fired salvoes, and great clangorous strokes, as if iron doors banged suddenly, and the tattoo of the light field-guns playing the drums of Death.

The mist was shifting and dissolving. The tall tower of Albert Cathedral appeared suddenly through the veil, and the sun shone full for a few seconds on the golden Virgin and the Babe, which she held head downwards above all this tumult as a peace-offering to men. The broken roofs of the town gleamed white, and the two tall chimneys to the left stood black and sharp against the pale blue of the sky, into which dirty smoke drifted above the whiter clouds. I could see now as well as hear. I could see our shells falling upon the German lines by Thiepval and La Boisselle and further by Mametz, and southwards over Fricourt. High explosives were tossing up great vomits of black smoke and earth all along the ridges. Shrapnel was pouring upon these places, and leaving curly white clouds, which clung to the ground.

Below there was the flash of many batteries, like Morse code signals by stabs of flame. The enemy was being blasted by a hurricane of fire. I found it in my heart to pity the poor devils who were there, and yet was filled by a strange and awful exultation, because this was the work of our guns, and because it was England's day.

Over my head came a flight of six aeroplanes, led by a single monoplane, which steered steadily towards the enemy. The sky was deeply blue above them, and when the sun caught their wings they were as beautiful and delicate as butterflies. But they were carrying death with them, and were out to bomb the enemy's batteries and to drop their explosives into masses of men behind the German lines. Further away a German plane was up. Our anti-aircraft guns were searching for him with their shells, which dotted the sky with snowballs.

Every five minutes or so a single gun fired a round. It spoke with a voice I knew, the deep, gruff voice of old 'Grandmother', one of our 15 inches, which carries a shell large enough to smash a cathedral with one enormous burst. I could follow the journey of the shell by listening to its rush through space. Seconds later there was the distant thud of its explosion.

Troops were moving forward to the attack from behind the lines. It was nearly 7.30. All the officers about me kept glancing at their wrist-watches. We did not speak much then, but stared silently at the smoke and mist which floated and banked along our lines. There, hidden, were our men. They, too, would be looking at their wrist-watches.

The minutes were passing very quickly – as quickly as men's lives pass when they look back upon the years. An officer near me turned away, and there was a look of sharp pain in his eyes. We were only lookers-on. The strong men, our friends, the splendid Youth that we have passed on the roads in France, were about to do this job. Good luck go with them! Men were muttering such wishes in their hearts.

It was 7.30. Our watches told us this, but nothing else. The guns had lifted and were firing beyond the enemy's first lines, but there was no sudden hush for the moment of attack. The barrage by our guns seemed as great as the first bombardment. For ten minutes or so before this time a new sound had come into the general thunder of artillery.

It was like the 'rafale' of the French soixante-quinze, very rapid, with distinct and separate strokes, but louder than the noise of field-guns. They were our trench mortars at work along the whole length of the line before me.

It was 7.30. The moment for the attack had come. Clouds of smoke had been liberated to form a screen for the infantry, and hid the whole line. The only men I could see were those in reserve, winding along a road by some trees which led to the attacking points. They had their backs turned, as they marched very slowly and steadily forward.

I could not tell who they were on the road a day or two before. But, whoever they were, English, Irish, or Welsh, I watched them until most had disappeared from sight behind a clump of trees. In a little while they would be fighting, and would need all their courage.

At a minute after 7.30 there came through the rolling smoke-clouds a rushing sound. It was the noise of rifle fire and machine-guns. The men were out of their trenches, and the attack had begun. The enemy was barraging our lines.

The country chosen for our main attack today stretches from the Somme for some 20 miles northwards. The French were to operate on our immediate right. It is very different country from Flanders, with its swamps and flats, and from the Loos battlefields, with their dreary plain pimpled by slack. It is a sweet and pleasant country, with wooded hills and little valleys along the river beds of the Ancre and the Somme, and fertile meadowlands and stretches of woodland, where soldiers and guns may get good cover. 'A clean country,' said one of our generals, when he first went to it from the northern war zone. It seemed very queer to go there first, after a knowledge of war in the Ypres salient, where there is seldom view of the enemy's lines from any rising ground – except Kemmel Hill and Observatory Ridge – and where certainly one cannot walk on the skyline in full view of German earthworks 2,000 yards away.

But at Hebuterne, which the French captured after desperate fighting, and at Auchonvilliers (opposite Beaumont), and on the high ground by the ruined city of Albert, looking over to Fricourt and Mametz, and further south on the Somme, looking towards the little German stronghold at Curlu, beyond the marshes, one could see very clearly and with a strange, unreal sense of safety. I saw a German sentry pacing the village street of Curlu. Occasionally one could stare through one's glasses at German working parties just beyond sniping range round

Beaumont and Fricourt, and to the left of Fricourt the Crucifix between its seven trees seemed very near as one looked at it in the German lines. Below this Calvary was the Tambour and the Bois Français, where not a week passed without a mine being blown on one side or the other, so that the ground was a great upheaval of mingling mine-craters and tumbled earth, which but half-covered the dead bodies of men.

It was difficult ground in front of us. The enemy was strong in his defences. In the clumps of wood and beside the ruined villages he had many machine-guns and trench mortars, and each ruined house in each village was part of a fortified stronghold difficult to capture by direct assault. It was here, however, and with good hopes of success that our men attacked today, working westwards across the Ancre and northwards up from the Somme.

At the end of this day's fighting it is still too soon to give a clear narrative of the battle. Behind the veil of smoke which hides our men there were many different actions taking place, and the messages that come back at the peril of men's lives, and by the great gallantry of our signallers and runners, give but glimpses of the progress of our men and of their hard fighting.

I have seen the wounded who have come out of the battle, and the prisoners brought down in batches, but even they can give only confused accounts of fighting within their own experience.

At first, it is certain, there was not much difficulty in taking the enemy's first line trenches along the greater part of the country attacked. Our bombardment had done great damage, and had smashed down the enemy's wire and flattened his parapets. When our men left their assembly trenches and swept forward, cheering, they encountered no great resistance from German soldiers who had been in hiding in their dug-outs under our storm of shells. Many of these dug-outs were blown in and filled with dead, but out of others which had not been flung to pieces by high explosives crept dazed and deafened men who held their hands up and bowed their heads. Some of them in one part of the line came out of their shelters as soon as our guns lifted, and met our soldiers half-way, with signs of surrender. They were collected and sent back under guard, while the attacking columns passed on to the second and third lines in the network of trenches, and then if they could get through them to the fortified ruins behind.

But the fortunes of war vary in different places, as I know from the advance of troops, including the South Staffords, the Manchesters, and the Gordons. In crossing the first line of trench the South Staffordshire men had a comparatively easy time, with hardly any casualties, gathering up Germans who surrendered easily. The enemy's artillery fire did not touch them seriously, and both they and the Manchesters had very great luck.

But the Gordons fared differently. These keen fighting men rushed forward with great enthusiasm until they reached one end of the village of Mametz, and then quite suddenly they were faced by rapid machine-gun fire and a storm of bombs. The Germans held a trench called Danzig Avenue on the ridge where Mametz stands, and defended it with desperate courage. The Gordons flung themselves upon this position, and had some difficulty in clearing it of the enemy. At the end of the day Mametz remained in our hands.

It was these fortified villages which gave our men greatest trouble, for the German troops defended them with real courage, and worked their machine-guns from hidden emplacements with skill and determination. Fricourt is, I believe, still holding out, though our men have forced their way to both sides of it, so that it is partly surrounded. Montauban, to the north-east of Metz, was captured early in the day, and we also gained the strong point at Serre, until the Germans made a somewhat heavy counter-attack and succeeded in driving out some of our troops.

Beaumont-Hamel was not definitely in our hands at the end of the day, but here again our men are fighting both sides of it. The woods and village of Thiepval, which I had watched under terrific shell-fire in our preliminary bombardments, was one point of our first attack, and our troops swept from one end of the village to the other, and out beyond to a new objective. They were too quick to get on, it seems, for a considerable number of Germans remained in the dug-outs, and when the British soldiers went past them they came out of their hiding-places and became a fighting force again.

Further north our infantry attacked both sides of the Gommecourt salient with the greatest possible valour.

That is my latest knowledge, writing at midnight on the first day of July, which leaves our men beyond the German front lines in many places, and penetrating to the country behind like arrow-heads between the enemy's strong-holds.

In the afternoon I saw the first batch of prisoners brought in. In parties of fifty to a hundred they came down, guarded by men of the Border Regiment, through the little French hamlets close behind the fronting lines, where peasants stood in their doorways watching these first-fruits of victory. They were damaged fruit, some of these poor wretches, wounded and nerve-shaken in the great bombardment. Most of them belonged to the 109th and 110th Regiments of the 14th Reserve Corps, and they seemed to be a mixed lot of Prussians and Bavarians. On the whole, they were tall, strong fellows, and there were striking faces among them, of men higher than the peasant type, and thoughtful. But they were very haggard and worn and dirty.

Over the barbed wire which had been stretched across a farmyard, in the shadow of an old French church, I spoke to some of them. To one man, especially, who considered all my questions with a kind of patient sadness. He told me that most of his comrades and himself had been without food and water for several days, as our intense fire made it impossible to get supplies up the communication trenches. About the bombardment he raised his hands and eyes a moment – eyes full of a remembered horror – and said, '*Es war schrecklich*' – it was horrible. Most of the officers had remained in the second line, but the others had been killed, he thought. His own brother had been killed, and in Baden, his mother and sisters would weep when they heard. But he was glad to be a prisoner out of the war at last, which would last much longer.

A new column of prisoners was being brought down, and suddenly the man turned and uttered an exclamation, with a look of surprise and awe. '*Ach, da ist ein Hauptmann!*' He recognised an officer among these new prisoners, and it seemed clearly a surprising thing to him that one of the great caste should be in this plight, should suffer as he had suffered. Some of his fellow-prisoners lay on the ground all bloody and bandaged. One of them seemed about to die. But the English soldiers gave them water, and one of our officers emptied his cigarette-case and gave them all he had to smoke.

Other men were coming back from the fields of fire, glad also to be back behind the line. They were our wounded, who came very quickly after the first attack to the casualty clearing stations – close to the lines, but beyond the reach of shell-fire. Many of them were lightly wounded in the hands and feet, and sometimes fifty or more were on one lorry, which bad taken up ammunition and was now bringing back the casualties. They were wonderful men. So wonderful in their gaiety and courage that one's heart melted at the sight of them. They were all grinning as though they had come from a 'jolly' in which they had been bumped a little. There was a look of pride in their eyes as they came driving down like wounded knights from a tourney. They had gone through the job with honour, and had come out with their lives, and the world was good and beautiful again, in this warm sun, in these snug French villages, where peasant men and women waved hands to them, and in these fields of scarlet and gold and green.

The men who were going up to the battle grinned back at those who were coming out. One could not see the faces of the lying-down cases, only the soles of their boots as they passed; but the laughing men on the courier – some of them stripped to the waist and bandaged roughly – seemed to rob war of some of its horror, and the spirit of our British soldiers shows very bright along the roads of France, so that the very sun seems to get some of its gold from these men's hearts.

Tonight the guns are at work again, and the sky is flushed as the shells burst, over there where our men are fighting.

18 August 1916

SOLDIERS' STOICISM
Undecorated Heroism

The public probably realise now a good deal more than they did before the present Allied offensive north of the Somme as to the terribly far-reaching character of the destruction wrought by the kind of fighting that is waged on the Western Front. The wars of the past have been child's play by comparison with this kind of fighting.

I was talking one morning with a newly landed RAMC officer, who had carried on his work of tending and dressing wounded men for several hours after being badly mauled himself by shrapnel splinters. His point of view was different, of course, from that of the fighting man, but not less interesting and valuable, I thought.

In a war like this, you know (he said), one comes across all sorts of bravery quite outside killing and being killed. Perhaps the public hardly realises yet what a lot there is in soldiers' lives, outside fighting. I sometimes think the actual fighting is among the least of the strains placed upon the soldier.

The recent fighting has been on such an epic scale; such a huge and devastating business. What's the word I saw in the papers this morning? 'Grandiose.' Yes, that's it. Our chaps remain just as human as ever, in their rough kindliness one to another, and, don't forget, in the different ills and disabilities to which humans are subject.

Fighting makes plenty of demands for two o'clock-in-the-morning courage, of course; but so do other things in this life at the front, I assure you. And, whereas the public hears something about the fighting heroism, it knows very little about the other kinds. Oh, well, they are all fighting courage, of a kind, of course.

What I mean is this: toothache, neuralgia, dyspepsia, colic, stomach cramps, sick headaches, sore throats, whitlows, and homely little things of that sort are not washed out by terrific bombardments and epoch-making advances. Not a bit of it. The world's greatest philosophers have often admitted that neither their philosophy nor anyone else's was proof against a stomach-ache or the torments of an exposed nerve in a hollow tooth.

Well, I'd like the public to bear in mind what is known to every medical officer in the Army, that in every single unit on the front there are officers and men who are 'sticking it', hour after hour, and day after day, with never an interval of rest or comfort, or anything to ease them, when if they were at home, no matter how urgent or important their business, they would be in bed, or, at least, receiving such ease and comfort, such relief from pain, as medical attention can provide in civil life.

I'd like everyone who is doing his bit at home, every man and every woman, to remember this. These brave fellows of ours, they won't go sick, you know, during an offensive. It's as much as one can do to get some of them out of the fighting line, even when they are quite badly wounded; and as for the wounds of sickness – sometimes much more exhausting and trying to bear – well, they just set their teeth, and say nothing about these.

In the last week, I assure you, I have been quite glad to see men coming my way with wounds, so that I could get them the rest and medical attention they needed; soldiers, from colonels to privates, who, to my certain knowledge, must have been suffering horribly for days, and in some cases for weeks, without the slightest kind of alleviation of any sort, whilst keeping a stiff upper lip; men with acute internal troubles, racking neuralgia, or violently painful things like whitlows, living on biscuits and bully beef, in shell-pounded, sun-baked chalk ditches for a week or so on end, half blind for lack of sleep.

The very last man I dressed, a slight wound in the left hand. 'You might fix this up as soon as you can, will you, doc,' he said, cheerily, to explain why he did not want to wait his turn. 'I must get back to my platoon as quick as I can. We've got a little raid on this evening.' A moment later he was vomiting. Well, I won't bother you with detail, but his case was perfectly clear.

In ordinary life he'd have been in bed, and probably operated on, weeks before. I knew beyond any possibility of doubt the sort of torment he must have been suffering for weeks, and the exact reasons why he looked such a scarecrow.

I fixed him. I was his senior in rank, and when he tried to get away I placed him under arrest; begad, I did.

At the clearing station later on I found out from his company commander, who was wounded, that though everyone could see he was pretty ill, this lieutenant had never said one word about his condition, or allowed anyone else to talk about it. He had just gone on with his job, day and night ... 'About the best officer I've got, too,' said his company commander. 'Couldn't eat himself, but he never missed seeing the last handful of his platoon's rations properly dished out. Oh, he mothered 'em well.'

To a medical man some of these cases are wonderful. We know precisely what they mean. It's the kind of heroism that doesn't win decorations; but it's the real article all right, I can assure you; and this New Army of ours is full of it. I'd like the people at home to understand something about it. It should make it easier for them to stick their bit without bothering too much about missed holidays and things.

This medical officer had nothing to say about the quiet heroism of many of his comrades of the RAMC. One has to look elsewhere for appreciations of that very real bravery.

30 October 1916

SOMME FIGHTING

The Tenacious Mud, *British Headquarters, France, Saturday*
By Perceval Gibbon

There is no rest for the 15th Bavarians. Today, again, for the sixth time since Monday, they have to fight for that string of shell-craters, whose lips crumbling together make some sort of a line, which is what remains of Hazy Trench. As I have related previously, this is a position opposite our lines west of Les Bœufs – lines already considerably straightened and simplified as a result of the last week's fighting – and five times already they have been bombed and bayoneted and rough-and-tumbled out of it, and five times they have come desperately back. Dewdrop Trench, a little to the north of Hazy, is also attacked, and already news has leaked back through the shell curtain that British troops have gained a footing in its northern end after a frightful struggle with that tenacious German ally, the mud of these fields. There was a trench between us and Dewdrop – Rainy was the name of it on the trench map – but that troubles us no longer. A constellation of machine-guns lived there, and they, too, are troublesome no longer. Rainy Trench, throughout its 180 yards of length, has ceased to exist – it and its wasps' nests have been gouged out of the ground by a week of cannonading.

Men wounded in this week of white-hot fighting in the blasted fields between Les Bœufs and Le Transloy speak chiefly of the mud. They are to be found in the casualty clearing station behind the battle. The great tents lead one into the other – long, shadowy halls where the wounded lie to each side. Such tents I have seen a hundred times in Russia, but never such wounded. The Russian wounded man has always the childlike side of him most developed when he brings his hurt back to be nursed. Then it was: 'Well, where have you got it?' 'In the leg, sir – and, God help me, it hurts a lot.' But here, 'Got a puncture, sir. Machine-gun bullet while we was goin' over the top … Yes, sir, a rest was all I wanted … No, it don't hurt nothin' to speak of!'

One of them showed a face on which the invalid's beard had grown like stiff fur, and the white teeth spilled through it. The nose of a shrapnel had taken him upon the forward curve of his steel helmet, denting it and contusing his head, glancing thence and breaking his right arm. His tale was triumphant. 'Yes, Zenith Trench, sir – that was the name. We got in all right. And them Germans had just got their mail. We found it there. Letters, they 'ad, an' parcels. No, I don't know what was in the letters; somebody took charge o' them all right. But the parcels – there was bread, an' sossidge, and little bottles, that long' – he spanned five inches with a graphic, splay-fingered hand – 'of rum.' The grin again; grins from neighbouring patients; the shadows of the big marquee aglint with grins. 'Good rum it was too, sir,' he added sincerely. Most of them spoke of the mud which is the last ally to join Germany, the awful mud which is 'the fourth element of war', as some square-head truly remarked.

A child who lay between two hairy men-of-war told me about that. He looked like a pretty girl, with the high roses on his thin cheeks and his tumbled hair and his blankets drawn to his chin. He thrust them back to rise on his elbow and show himself a bonny boy of nineteen. 'I was up to my waist when we started to go across,' he said. 'I'd never have got out at all, but two chaps gave me a hand and just hauled me out of the mud. And then my rifle was clogged and wouldn't fire. I didn't get five yards.' 'Whereabouts were you hit?' I asked him. He smiled. Mark that, he smiled! 'Neck, right arm, back, and both legs,' he replied, still smiling. He hesitated. 'I've only been out six weeks,' he added, like one who makes excuses.

Then there was the mighty man, with an accent as English as roast beef, who had, besides a bullet in the chest, a bayonet through his left upper arm. That was at the gun pits, when they fought man to man in front of Hazy Trench, and, man to man, covered the ground with dead Germans and took the pits. It is from those pits – as we have developed them – that we are today attacking Hazy. 'Big beggar he was,' he reminisced. 'I seen him afterwards, where he was lying on the ground. Red 'air 'e 'ad, too.' 'Bayoneted you, did he? What did you do to him?' 'Clouted 'im over the 'ead with the butt, sir. That done 'im proper. Reg'lar frightened me, it did – the way 'e went down on 'is back!' The ward grinned. Each man there knew that feeling, probably – the fear, seeing your man go down, down, that you have hurt him. That is the way they were taught to feel when they fought honest fighters, and the habit sticks.

31 October 1916

SCENE AT VERDUN

'A Vast Cemetery', *Verdun, 27 October*

By E. Ashmead-Bartlett

I have just returned from a visit to the site of the great French triumph of 24 October. That is to say, I have been able to cross to the right bank of the Meuse and to see, at close range, all the historic ground round Fleury, Thiaumont, and Douaumont which has just been won back to France. The four forts of Thiaumont, Douaumont, Vaux, and Souaville form an armed square in front of Verdun. Thiaumont and Douaumont are on the same ridge and form one side of the square; Vaux and Souaville the other. Now, before you can say you command Verdun it is necessary to take the whole of this fortified square, which the Germans never did. They captured Douaumont, Vaux, and Thiaumont, but they never arrived within striking distance of Souaville; whilst beyond Thiaumont they were held up by the French positions on the Côte de Froide Terre, which also forms part of the Thiaumont–Douaumont ridge. Thus, when the Kaiser boasted that Douaumont was the key to Verdun and Verdun the heart of France, he was not only very ignorant of the topography of the country in his front, but even more ignorant of the character of the French people. The heart of France lies in no entrenched position. It moves with the French troops wherever they may be sent, and is seen in whatever work they are asked to undertake.

It may be asked what tactical advantage the French have gained by the recapture of these positions, quite apart from the sentimental interest attaching to them, when it was obvious that the German offensive had been definitely broken since the beginning of the Battle of the Somme. The answer is very simple. As long as the Germans held three sides of this armed square they not only held the most dominating heights round the town, but their line formed a powerful salient close to Verdun. It was necessary to give Verdun air, as one general explained the situation to me, and make the French line comfortable and secure for the winter. Now, instead of having the German lines close to what remains of the city, and overlooking all the French positions, it has been pushed back three kilometres in the centre, and the French are once more in possession of all the dominating observation posts. Neither must it be forgotten that in the process some fifteen or twenty thousand Huns – to judge from the number of prisoners – must have been placed hors de combat. Vaux still remains in the enemy's hands, but he holds it only on sufferance. The fort, or rather its ruins, are surrounded on three sides, and it can be taken at any moment the French Higher Command think favourable for the enterprise.

A great deal of mystery attaches to the capture of Douaumont, for the French entered the work almost without firing a shot. It would seem as if the Germans, although anticipating an attack, were taken completely by surprise when the advance was made. An Army Order has been found warning the commanders of positions that the French would almost certainly attack on the 25th. There is no doubt now that the attack was materially assisted by the prevailing conditions of rain and heavy mist, and the French infantry were right on top of the enemy lines in places before the Germans discovered their presence. At some points they merely exclaimed, '*Mais c'est les Français,*' and surrendered without attempting to defend themselves. At other points they had already thrown away their arms, and came out to meet the advancing waves with hands up and the customary cries of 'Kamerad'. Some of the French battalions actually reached their objective without suffering a single casualty. Actually in the whole day's fighting the French losses were under half the number of prisoners. The attack was most carefully planned and successfully carried out. The assaulting divisions were only brought up the day before, and one of them at least had never been at Verdun. It is sometimes wise to attack fixed positions with fresh troops, and not with those who have been in the trenches opposite to them for a long time. The ground in front and the obstacles to be encountered assume an importance they do not warrant, and the men say to one another, 'It is impossible to attack there,' or 'That part of the line is too strong.'

A very mixed pack was found holding the German lines. Amongst the prisoners taken are elements from no fewer than nineteen different regiments and thirty-one battalions. It would seem as if the divisions are echeloned back with one regiment in the front trenches, a second in reserve, and a third in rest billets. Over 5,000 prisoners were taken in all, including 108 officers and 500 NCOs. Amongst the officers are no fewer than ten battalion commanders, unwounded, including three of the 7th Prussian Guards Division. Two days before the attack sixty-three men, including three officers, deserted to the French lines. This fact is most significant, because when officers desert an army must be in a most serious state of demoralisation. It shows the change that has come over the German army, its personnel and morale, after two years of war. The idea of a Prussian officer deserting in 1914 or 1915 would have been laughed at. In fact, the German army, both on the Somme front and before Verdun, gives you the impression of slowly rotting away. Chunks of it disintegrate from the main body under the smallest pressure. Up to the present the counter-attacks launched against the quarries of Haudromont and Douaumont have excited derision and even sorrow for the victims in the French ranks more than anything else. Four attempts were made on the 26th, but all broke down under the French barrage-fire, without ever reaching their objective. The Crown Prince seems to have no large force in hand which he can immediately hurl against captured positions, neither has he a sufficient concentration of artillery adequately to support such attacks, which only add to his losses. Nevertheless the Germans are almost certain to collect what reserves they can and make a last fling for Douaumont before winter stops the operations. It will be an excellent thing for the Allies if they do. Douaumont attracts the Huns as a candle does moths, and they invariably get their wings singed. Room can still be found for a few thousand more German corpses round Douaumont, and every Hun under the soil brings the end just a little nearer.

On the Sunday preceding the attack the French 400-millimetre guns managed to land three successive shells on Fort Douaumont in identically the same spot. These penetrated into the interior of the fort and caused a big fire that was seen and noted at the time by the French. It was hoped then that great damage had been done. Now some months ago, another French shell set fire to the fort and caused a terrible explosion of ammunition and grenades collected there, which resulted, according to the prisoners, in a death-toll of not less than 1,000 of the garrison. Since that date the fort has been a nightmare to the troops holding it, and when it again caught fire on Sunday nothing could induce the men to remain. Amongst those captured was an artillery officer who, not knowing the attack was in progress, had come up to the fort to examine how much damage had been caused by the fire. This seems to point, as well as do many other incidents in the fight, to a state of demoralisation not only in the ranks, but also in the higher command.

I do not wish to create the impression that the French have had a complete walk-over and are now comfortably settled in the new positions. This is far from the truth. Although winning the ground was easy, holding it is quite another matter. It must be remembered that the German trenches have been completely knocked to pieces by the French bombardment and that when the assaulting waves reach their objective they find nothing but thick mud and shell-holes full of water. In these the men have to pass night and day whilst new trenches are being dug under a murderous shell-fire, for the enemy knows the range to an inch. When I add that the weather is bitterly cold and the men are soaked through by rain, mist, and mud, and that it is impossible to get up food except in small quantities by night, some idea can be formed of what the French infantry are enduring without a murmur.

For five days and nights the assaulting divisions have held their conquest under these conditions. It seems incredible that the men can stand the cold, but the French infantry are perhaps the toughest in the world. Yesterday, for instance, the Germans were bombarding the front practically the whole day, and they had brought up a 16in gun with which to pound Douaumont once again. Their *feu de barrage* goes wildly all over the place when it roams away from the beaten track. One general described it to me as '*le feu d'une femme soule*' ('the fire of a drunken woman'). But whether it is or not it is most unpleasant. It is remarkable how these forts have justified their existence. In spite of the stupendous bombardments to which it has been subjected during the last nine months by the heavy artillery of both armies, the interior underground works of Douaumont have been very little damaged, and can still be utilised for the shelter of the garrison. You see on a hill a mass of churned-up earth, rubbish, and smashed concrete, without shape. Each of the hills round Verdun has one of these heaps, with a name, if you look at the map. But when you climb to the summit you find a narrow passage leading underground and the galleries intact and as sound as ever. You can remain in these completely sheltered from the fire of the guns.

The throwing back of the German lines enables you to visit for the first time since the battle of Verdun commenced last February acres of ground which has long remained No Man's Land, and which remains littered with all the debris of a long series of terrible fights. There are thousands of rifles and half-buried corpses sticking out of the mud, broken machine-guns, debris of every description, and thousands and thousands of exploded and un-exploded shells. Corpses are in all stages of decay, some reduced to skeletons, others with some flesh still remaining, and grinning horridly, as if they were pleased to see the line again. As new trenches are cut in the valley of Fleury the bodies come out of the ground or form part of the walls. There has been no time to clear up the mess, and the scene presents perhaps the most awful spectacle of the horrors of war I have ever seen. Both sides are fighting over a vast cemetery, where every shell throws up to the surface what remains of an old victim of an Emperor's ambition and perhaps buries a fresh one in the open tomb. Of the village and station of Fleury nothing remains whatsoever. You cannot tell until you are actually on the spot that any dwellings ever stood there. It is impossible to read the topography of the country from the map, because so many former landmarks have been pounded into the bosom of mother earth.

A general in command of one of the attacking divisions said to me: 'In former days before the war I was stationed at Verdun, and knew the ground well. I came back a few days ago to prepare for this attack, and I could not recognise my surroundings.' In every German account of the early assaults the soldiers speak of the horror of facing the French artillery and how it was impossible to live under such a tornado of shells. You can now follow the successive stages of the gradual retirement of the French guns before the enormous wave of men poured against Douaumont and Vaux by the Crown Prince. Each spot where the French 75s made their desperate stands is clearly marked. You can see the remains of what once were guns before they were smashed to bits by heavy shells. The gunners simply died round their pieces, firing until the guns were finished or they themselves were killed. The remains of the guns are surrounded by countless thousands of copper shell-cases piled in great green heaps, for the rain and the atmosphere have turned them this colour. There must be hundreds and thousands of pounds' worth of this precious metal that has been lying within a few yards of the German lines for months without their being able to collect any of it. Now it will all be brought in, sent back to be remoulded, and will serve France again. Those were the days when the Germans' guns had the upper hand, but now all is changed.

The superiority of the French artillery places the Germans before Verdun in a hopeless position. The slightest sign of an infantry attack is signalled back to the batteries before the first of the enemy has time to clear the trenches. Then those 75s speak with a fury that is awful in its majesty and power. Until you have seen and heard a *feu de barrage* from French 75s you have no idea of what artillery can attain to in these days. Imagine what infantry have to face. The gunners can get off twenty rounds a minute, which means that every battery of four guns is hurling eighty shells every sixty seconds along the enemy's front. No wonder the German infantry is cowed and demoralised.

I wonder what the Emperor and the Crown Prince would think if they could see their beloved subjects in captivity. The French soldier is the upper dog so completely now that he can afford to be benevolent. He behaves as if he were anxious to restore lost sheep to the fold of humanity, rather than to be avenged for past wrongs. Kind treatment and white bread work wonders. A few sausages slowly drawn towards the French lines on the end of long strings would, I believe, cause the desertion of the greater number of the troops before Verdun, but for the trenches and barbed wire, which makes it so difficult for them to get away without being seen. If we were fighting an open war in open country, I really believe the German army would disintegrate altogether. The clothes of the latest captives are in a terrible state – filthy rags held together with mud, and totally unsuited for the wintry weather we are experiencing. The prisoners declare that shirts are no longer served out to them, and that they only get linen trousers as there is no more cotton or wool. The youth of the captives is also very marked.

13 November 1916

A NIGHT VISIT TO FORT DOUAUMONT

Thrilling Experience, *Verdun, 8 November*

By E. Ashmead-Bartlett

Ever since the great victory of 24 October I have been doing my utmost to get into Fort Douaumont, and to see for myself what that historic fort – which the Kaiser called the key to France – was really like. I returned once to Verdun for this purpose, but then only succeeded in getting as far as the ruins of Fleury, further progress being rendered impossible by the enemy's incessant *feu de barrage*, which at that time completely cut off the fort during the day from the French lines behind. Two days ago I received an intimation from the General Staff that they had no objection to my making an effort to get through to Douaumont, but warning me that the task would be neither pleasant nor easy. I have now just returned, having successfully accomplished the object of my curiosity with two companions and a French officer, and have no hesitation in saying that the experience was one of the most trying and difficult I have ever undertaken, and that I never wish to see Douaumont again until 'the war drum throbs no longer and the battle flags are furled'.

It must not be supposed that the Germans are quietly acquiescing in the recapture by the French of all the ground they won after six months' fighting. Far from it. They know they cannot retake the positions, and therefore they have become 'of no military importance', but, on the other hand, to show their rage and spite, they bombard them and the lines of communication behind incessantly night and day, so as to render the occupation as difficult as possible by preventing supplies and ammunition from being sent up during the day. In fact, all this work has to be done at night under an incessant *feu de barrage*. It is only possible to approach the fort at night, and so I was told I must be ready to start at midnight, so as to have time to get in and get out again before dawn, otherwise I would remain a prisoner in Douaumont until the following night. That evening I dined with the famous General Mangin, who accompanied Marchand to Fashoda, at his headquarters. General Mangin conducted the great attack which retook Douaumont on 24 October, and he was wearing for the first time the Grand Star of the Legion of Honour, which President Poincaré had conferred on him the previous day in recognition of his great services. The General is one of the hardest fighters in the French army, and has been wounded no fewer than five times in the course of the war. He is a short, dark, strongly built man, and his features strike you as being more Italian than French.

It was a beautiful moonlight night when I set out for Verdun. At the gate the sentry complained that the Germans had just sent a shell close to his post, and advised us to move on quickly. A minute later there is the whistle of a shell, a crash, and the sound of falling masonry. Another bit of the ruins has been brought to earth. It is now ten o'clock, and we stop for two hours at the Archbishop's Palace. It was formerly the Archbishop's Palace until sequestered by the State. Two rooms are still intact. They are ornate and gaudy and decorated with gold and crimson hangings. In the centre of the largest is a fine statue of a lady in a very light costume for the time of year. She looks singularly out of place amidst the surrounding ruins, the crumpling cathedral, and the fine old college with its superb cloisters. In fact, these two ornate rooms with their gilded furniture and crimson hangings and the lady in marble are about the only things left intact in Verdun. Why they have survived I cannot tell, but perhaps the Crown Prince had heard of her and wished to add so fair a form to his collection. The ruins of Verdun are singularly beautiful by moonlight. You could stop and gaze on the wondrous scene for hours were you not constantly brought back to realities by the screeching of shells and the crashing of masonry, as Europe's Housebreakers continue their favourite job. We have two hours to spare before starting, so I decide to sleep in the motor until the fateful moment arrives. It is in a courtyard surrounded by ruins. Close by is a substantial arch, which has only been damaged. The chauffeur suggests we move the car under it as a measure of precaution. This we do, and then a shell crashes somewhere in the courtyard, but we feel comfortably safe and soon fall asleep. It only seems a minute later when I am

aroused and told it is time to start. My companions join me, and we motor
through the ruined streets to the foot of the hills where the first line of forts
stand. Here we abandon the car, and start to climb to the top. It has been raining
for days, and the mud is as thick as a wheat field and as heavy as glue. I have not
gone more than a few yards when my feet slide from under me, and I roll into the
slush, emerging covered with yellow slime from head to foot. I curse, but the
officer with us remarks: 'That does not matter, as in half an hour we shall all be
in the same state. You are merely anticipating our fate.'

From the crest of the first line of defence we look down on the ruins of the
fortress. What a superb sight! The moon lights up the ruins, shining on a thousand
shapeless forms of what were once houses, churches, colleges, shops, and military
barracks. The shell-fire is incessant. The projectiles come screeching from afar
and burst in fire over the town. But the work goes on just the same. If motor
lorries are damaged they are dragged aside and others take their place. If men are
killed they are buried by the roadside and others take theirs. The same thing goes
on month after month, and will continue to go on until the enemy cries 'Enough!'
That cry will never be heard from the French nation. With grim determination
the French people and their Allies are slowly choking the German Empire to
death. The French artillery is replying to the German fire. It seems monstrous
that you cannot have a respite even at right. When do gunners sleep? Never, it
would appear, when you are on a modern battlefield. The shell-fire night and day
is incessant. No wonder the munition makers can hardly keep pace with the
demand. The battlefield of Verdun has a different atmosphere from any other I
was ever on. Its horrors are also greater. But, withal, there is a feeling of intense
satisfaction. You recognise the completion of a great masterpiece. You feel, as
you so seldom have the chance of feeling in this war, that something vital and
decisive has been accomplished, and that the work can never be undone. You
stand on the ground where the last supreme effort of the Huns was broken. It
was here that the turning-point of the war was reached. It was here, and as was
only fitting, that the French nation fought out the issue alone with their lifetime
enemy, and thus gave time to the Allies to prepare for the great retribution which
is now slowly moving on towards its inevitable end. It was at Verdun that the
French people found themselves again, and emerged from the clouds which have
hung over them for forty-five years. We stop and gaze for some time on this
wonderful scene. The night is so bright, lit up by a full moon and thousands of
stars. Suddenly one star of peculiar brightness steers a course at amassing speed
amidst its companions. It is a strange phenomenon we have never seen before.
Then someone suggests it is a giant French aeroplane brilliantly illuminated with
electric light sweeping homewards from the German lines.

But now it is time to pass on if we are to enter Douaumont and get out again
before dawn. It takes, so our guide reminds us, at least three hours' walking even
under the most favourable conditions. We now enter the 'boyau' to make our
way to the foot of the Côte de Froide Terre, the last position held desperately by
the French for six months on that long, dreary corpse-sown ridge, which rises
gradually to Thiaumont, and then on to Douaumont itself. The mud in the

'boyau' is frightful. It comes up to your knees, and crawls down to your ankles through the tops of your boots. You slip and slide and fall and curse as kilometre after kilometre is passed. The French officers, in their blue uniforms, are soon khaki-coloured like ourselves. After an hour and a half's walking we climb to Froide Terre. This is a solid concrete shelter that has remained intact under the incessant bombardment. We enter it for here we must find a new guide, who can take us the remainder of the way. Inside the scene resembles the foc'sle of a ship in the days when merchant sailors were little better than slaves. There is a wooden table, and ranged round it are wooden bunks. The atmosphere is fœtid. Each bunk contains a form rolled in a blanket. All are trying to snatch a few hours' sleep before the game of war is renewed at dawn. The officer on duty is seated on a bench by the telephone. He is surprised at the entry of strangers, and still more so when he learns we propose to go on to Douaumont. He points out the difficulties and dangers of the enterprise, and then, having done what he considers his duty, he offers his aid on hearing we are authorised to make the attempt. A guide is what we require, and he gives orders for a man who knows the direction – there is no road – to be aroused. It seems cruel to take anyone on such a trip. Then he asks if everyone has a helmet and a gas mask. At this point I discover I have left mine at home, as usual, so he kindly lends me another. Then we emerge from the warmth into the cold night air again, having discarded everything and every garment that was not absolutely essential. We stand shivering outside, and contemplate the next stage in our dreary journey.

The sight is not encouraging. The shell-fire is incessant, and you hear the screech of the missile and watch the bursts as the Huns put up an incessant barrage in front of Douaumont right across the track we must take. The bright moon has disappeared behind dark clouds which are rolling up from the southwest. Behind us the French guns continue to thunder away. Our guide shouts 'en avant', and plunges forward into the mud. There is still the remains of a track, and on this boards have been placed. We try to walk on these, but in the darkness it is difficult. I hear a groan from one of my companions, and on looking back see him trying to pick himself out of the slime. Suddenly the track ends, and we strike across country, entering a moon crater of shell-holes full of water, which, with the moonlight shining on them, resemble a vast number of small ponds, separated by tiny banks of mud. Over these mud tracks we try to progress, but the task is almost impossible. You fall at every step, even with the aid of a stick. I can only relate my own experiences, but everyone else's were the same. I stumble and fall and recover, only to fall again. I am now simply a moving portion of the mud which surrounds me. The guide makes no better weather than I. He stops suddenly and says 'Take care you don't fall into the shell-holes; they have 6ft of water in them, and if you fall in you may never come out.' This is an obvious truism. If you do slide into one of those glittering moonlit holes it is doubtful if you ever would emerge. To avoid such a catastrophe you must proceed most of the way on all fours. Your arms are just as good as legs in such an emergency. Now we enter the shell zone, or, in other words, the last 2,000 yards which separate you from Douaumont. The Huns bombard this furiously with 6in shells which come from all directions and burst at the most unexpected places at the most unexpected moments. The countryside is alive with them. You hear an appalling screech coming through the darkness. Instinctively everyone falls flat in the mud. The monster then bursts with the sound of the final crash of a brass band. You do not look up; you lie with your face buried in the mud waiting for the humming birds – the fragments of shell which fly round like bees humming for the particular flower on which they long to alight. You wonder on which part of your anatomy they will descend. You thank God when the last bit has alighted with a thud in the earth beside you. You don't bother about the chunks of mud thrown up by the explosion. They can and do hit you anywhere you like. It is almost a pleasure when one has struck you and you realise it is not encasing a fragment of steel. Then you push on another few yards until you hear the next aerial motor-bus coming your way. At first you are horribly frightened, but then you are grateful for being alive. It seems incredible that any of the party can be alive.

Now the moon goes in, for the clouds have come over us, and it starts to pour with rain. We are soon soaked through, but hardly notice the annoyance and discomfort. We crawl on, sweating profusely in spite of the cold. Excitement keeps you very warm on a cold night. Suddenly there looms up before us a dark mound. There are figures round it, and we make for it. It is a Poste de Commandment, that is to say, a kind of concrete shelter that existed before the war, and which has not been destroyed. The Huns are now redoubling their fire, and we rush down the narrow entrance to this post, using the excuse that we want to get out of the rain. Inside are sleeping figures rolled in grey blankets, lying on the muddy floor. The place seems a palace of luxury and comfort. The officers on duty welcome us, and undertake to provide another guide, for ours says he doesn't know the way any further, and if he does he has a perfect right to cut such an acquaintance. A very small and active soldier is aroused from his slumbers. He regards us with a mingled look of curiosity and annoyance, and small blame to him. He will surely cut his annual subscription to the local paper when he returns from the war. We are about to proceed when the local officer says: 'Do not attempt to go yet. This is the worst time to pass. The Boches are firing their hardest now.' This seems both sound and true, for the ground which separates us from the dark outlines of Douaumont is lit up with bursting shells. 'Rest here for an hour.' Never were words more gratefully received. I lie down on the floor in the mud, with the rain trickling down on me, and soon I fall asleep. I remember thinking, 'If only that captain with us had any regard for our feelings he would say: "You can't go any further."' But this captain has suffered so much already that he is determined to make the three of us suffer fully for our sense of curiosity.

I have no sooner gone to sleep it seems than I am aroused again. One of my companions says, 'Wake up. It is quieter now, and we have the chance of getting through.' I curse him and go outside. 'Quieter now.' The words are ironical, for the shells seem to be bursting thicker than ever, and an icy cold rain is pouring down in torrents. Our guide proceeds. We follow as best we can. This guide is horribly active, and we would soon lose him altogether had not the captain ordered him to go slower. 'How far to Douaumont,' I ask. 'Fifteen hundred metres,' is the reply. A chorus of groans from the darkness shows that everyone of the party feels the same as I do. We curse the day we were born, and our folly at not being neutrals. The procession is now like the moving figures in a local shooting gallery. The shell-fire is incessant, and the projectiles burst around every thirty seconds, or maybe ten seconds. You no longer fall; that is quite unnecessary, because every time you hear a shell coming the entire party drop automatically, and lie as quiet as the corpses which surround them. One of our number falls too far in his anxiety to escape a fragment of Von Essen's preferred stock, and rolls over into a shell-hole fall of water. Awful oaths arise from its muddy depths.

It takes a full hour to move 1,100 yards when another black spot emerges out of the darkness. Someone says, 'Is this Douaumont?' Oh, no,' says the guide, 'there are 500 yards more, much more severe than this.' It is, in fact, another little local shelter used as a 'Place de Secours'. We pass down the passage which leads to it. There are recumbent forms on every side. Groans arise from the darkness. Here are the fruits of the night's bombardment waiting until the stretcher bearers can carry them back. Inside, the surgeons are working. They suggest we should stop for a while until the Huns have cessed their *feu de barrage*. When does it stop we ask. One officer says, 'In half an hour.' Another says, 'Not until 6 a.m.' A third says, 'It does not matter when you go. They fire all day and all night.' This seems to be the nearest approach to the truth. The groans of the wounded are so unpleasant to listen to that we decide to proceed. Then I notice that all the party are drinking from flasks. Out we go into the darkness again. The guide says, 'You must move quickly here, for this is the worst bit of all, where they concentrate their fire.' Move quickly! The wicked irony of those words. Move quickly on such a ground and under such conditions! It is on this last 500 yards that the heaviest guns of both sides have been concentrated. The ground is torn to pieces, and the shell-holes are three times the size, and contain 8ft of water, some of them much more, but I like to average a night's troubles. If you fall into one you will be drowned unless someone can pull you out, and if you cling to the narrow ridges between them a fragment of shell will probably hit you. On and upwards we crawl scared to death. The guide moves too fast. He is small and light, and does not sink into the mud as much as the heavier members of the party. Instead of striking the mild bombardment which we were promised we next ran into the very worst of the Hun barrage. Instead of single shells every ten minutes there are salvoes bursting round us. It is really getting too hot altogether, even for our guide. There is a huge crater with only 2ft or 3ft water at the bottom. He flings himself into this and yells to the rest of us to do the same. In we go, and remain with our faces buried in the mud, not daring even to look up for a second. The shells burst all round, and the fragments continue their horrid humming. We share this crater with the dead. All through the night I have been putting my hands on to nasty cold lumps or bones or fragments of uniform. At first I had no idea what they were in the darkness, but now the moon emerging from behind a cloud, I discover I am lying alongside fragments of the Crown Prince's legions. A decaying German, eaten away by time, is on one side of me; some bits of another are on the other. The smell is like the interior of a newly opened vault. It is disgusting.

The shell-fire does not stop for a moment. In fact, it rather augments. Suddenly there are cries from the darkness, and three figures emerge from the gloom. Two of them are endeavouring to support the third. The third is groaning horribly, and the two say, '*Est ce que c'est le poste de secours?*' We can only reply 'No,' and point vaguely to the darkness behind. The three stumble on their way. Suddenly our guide has had enough, and no wonder, for the shell-fire becomes worse and worse. He yells out, '*En avant; il faut arriver au fort.*' The only lump of battered earth looming up ahead certainly seems the only chance of salvation. He jumps up, and, considering the difficulties, proceeds with amazing speed. We are in the real barrage now around the remains of what was once the fosse of the fort. I find I can travel almost as quickly as he can. There are now cursed Roman candles which the enemy are throwing around the fort. They seem to make you the most conspicuous figure in the world, and you forget all about Hughes and Wilson. After a Roman candle come a dozen shells. Suddenly my guide disappears. He has arrived at the sea of mud which forms the 'fosse', and has jumped in. I roll in after him. We cross the fosse and reach the escarpment, which is merely a bank pitted with a frightful attack of smallpox, which has left holes 12ft deep. We hug the bank like trout, crawling along it so as to allow the shells to burst on the further side. We hear shouts which seem a long way off, but we do not take any notice of them. We imagine our companions are close at our heels. I shout out to the guide 'Stop!' But, without lessening his pace, or even looking back, he replies, '*On ne peut pas arrêter ici.*' He has reason on his side, for the shells are tumbling into the fosse with appalling detonations. 'How much further?' I shout. '*Cent mètres*' comes out of the gloom. I follow him, stumbling and crawling and creeping through the mud. Suddenly he disappears into a tiny dark hole, which I would not have even noticed. I don't know what it is or where it leads to, but it is a hole, and to me a hole at such a moment offers more attractive possibilities than a blameless life. So I follow. I rather dive into it. The narrow passage opens up, and I find myself in a concreted cellar with shivering figures standing round. I am in Douaumont.

It was five o'clock in the morning when I followed the guides into the narrow hole which is the entrance to Douaumont. I passed down a narrow passage which shortly opened into a wide and high gallery with a stone roof. It was packed with shivering Chasseurs, who form the garrison. These men had just been aroused from their slumbers, and were waiting the signal to leave the fort to go back for supplies and ammunition, &c. They were greatly surprised to see a stranger suddenly pop into their warren out of the darkness of the night. I waited a few minutes to recover breath, and then discovered that my companions, whom I had imagined were close on my heels, had not yet made their appearance. I asked the guides what had become of them, but they did not know, so it seemed we must have lost touch in the darkness. We waited about ten minutes, and then, as there was still no sign, we went back to the entrance and looked out into the ruins of the fosse. No one was in sight. We shouted, and then a voice was heard from somewhere in the gloom calling for the entrance. The shell-fire was still intense. We shouted back, giving the direction, and a minute or two later we saw dark figures apparently attempting to climb up the escarpment of the fort instead of going along the bottom of the fosse. One of the guides yelled down to them to keep down, and we saw all three figures stumbling and rolling down the bank and falling into the thick mud at the bottom. A minute later all three safely reached the entrance and came inside thoroughly exhausted. In truth we presented a woebegone spectacle. All of us were simply a mass of mud from head to foot, our clothes, our faces, boots, and hands being caked with it. The party then explained what had happened to them. In the darkness they had been unable to keep the pace set by the guides, and had been left behind. After falling hundreds of times into shell-holes they became so exhausted that they had to wait in a shell-hole under a heavy fire, expecting every moment would be their last. The captain, who is a big man, sank so deeply into the mud that they could only pull him out with difficulty. After a rest they reached the edge of the fosse without recognising the fort, which is, in fact, a shapeless mud heap. One of the party then took a false step and fell 8ft into the fosse beneath. He thought his last hour had come, but, fortunately, the mud was so soft and deep that he suffered no injury. Not knowing where they were or where was the entrance, they decided to climb up the bank in front, which would have brought them on top of the fort in full view of the enemy at dawn, when fortunately they heard our shouts and reached the entrance safely.

Being once more collected together we pass down the gallery, which is quite uninjured, and descend a long flight of steps to the low galleries where the commandant is installed with his staff in a square concreted room. He was just up when we arrived, and welcomed us warmly. To our surprise the interior of the fort is lit with electricity, for the Germans had left the motor in perfect working order. It was very pleasant finding ourselves in a comfortable, concreted, electric-lighted room after five hours' trudging through the mud, exposed to an incessant shell-fire, which had somewhat shattered the morale of the party. Someone suggested that a drink would be very agreeable. Here we made a curious discovery. We had set out with enough whisky to last for two days, in case we should be shut up in the fort, but on arriving at our destination every drop of it was gone. But never mind. It had undoubtedly helped us through the journey. In fact, I think a little was drunk in every shell-hole in which we stopped. The commandant in charge of Douaumont looks about thirty years of age. He says: 'You have only a short time to stop if you wish to get out again this morning. The enemy's barrage will not be so intense, and you will have a comparatively quiet hour in which to get back to Thiaumont. Come, I will show you round the fort.'

We follow. The fort of Douaumont is the largest and most important of the Verdun defences. A thousand men can, in fact, live comfortably in its capacious interior. It is a two-storeyed structure; that is to say, there is an upper level of galleries and a lower. Above the concrete is 30ft of earth, or rather there was 30ft of earth, but now the exterior has been churned into a troubled ocean of shell waves, and in some spots the earth is deeper and in others much less. The counterscarp galleries have been destroyed, except in two places, where machine-guns can still sweep what remains of the fosse immediately in front of those undestroyed counterscarp galleries. The only entrance is the small hole I have already described in the rear. The fort has two 75mm guns mounted in a revolving steel turret, and also two 130mm guns similarly mounted. The material damage to these turrets has been small, but the guns are out of action through the breakdown of the machinery and the smashing of the guns themselves at the muzzle. Although you can hardly recognise Douaumont as a fort from the outside, the interior has suffered extremely little damage, even after eight months of incessant shelling from the guns of both friend and foe. The lower galleries and the chambers which radiate from them are entirely intact, but the upper have been pierced in one place by the fire of the French 400mm guns, which have cut off all communication between the east and west of the fort on the upper level. It is said that it was the entry of three successive 400mm shells which did the damage, and caused the Germans to abandon the position before the attack on 24 October.

The old fort has, in the eyes of the French, more than justified its existence, and has withstood a terrible hammering in a truly marvellous manner. There are wells, but at the present time the water is undrinkable, and all the water for the garrison has to be brought up by hand and stored in the tanks, which were found intact. The commandant showed us every detail of his interior organisation. The Germans have certainly been good tenants, and had no time to work any destruction before they abandoned the position. Every gallery and chamber has its use denoted on white sign-boards, which still bear their German lettering. The first steps taken by the French were to provision the fort and to collect a sufficient water supply to enable the garrison to hold out for several days should their communications be cut by the enemy's barrage fire. This has been no light task, because every biscuit and every litre of water and of petrol for the engine has had to be brought up by hand over the ground I have already attempted to describe. But each day the carrying parties bring back a double supply of food and water, so that now reserve supplies have been accumulated. The life of the garrison is no bed of roses. The underground galleries are damp and cold, and there is no means of warming them, for no fuel was found in the fort, and it has been impossible to bring any up. Both officers and men live on biscuits or bread and canned meat, as it is impossible to do any cooking for a similar reason. The barracks for the garrison consist of long vaulted chambers radiating from the galleries, and containing double rows of wooden bunks. Inside you see hundreds of warriors off duty rolled in their blankets asleep.

Especially interesting was the spot in the upper galleries where the 400mm shells had entered. Dawn was breaking, and the pale light was shining through this arch cut out of the solid concrete by these heavy shells. Sentries stood guarding the aperture, which is rapidly being put in a state of repair. You look out and beyond on to a sea of huge shell craters. There are no luxuries or comforts of any sort for the garrison, for it has only been possible to carry up the bare necessities of life and a reserve supply of ammunition. I made my way through all these long galleries, damp, cold, and filthy, and studied the heroic defenders. They are great fellows, these Chasseurs. They are cold, and caked with mud, and weary from the incessant labour of carrying up supplies, but ever determined and indomitable. They have got back the fort and will never give it up. The French officer is supremely efficient. He understands his job and revels in his work. This young commandant had every detail at his finger-tips. He knows to the last biscuit and tin of meat exactly what supplies he has in the fort and how he could daily augment his reserves. Every step necessary for the defence of the fort is being taken by him. His machine-guns cover every avenue of possible approach. As he completes new embrasures for his machine-guns the German gunners endeavour to smash them up. All day and all night this work of putting Douaumont in fighting trim again goes on. It will soon be just as good as it ever was, but for its battered exterior, which must remain as it is until the end of the war.

By the time we have completed our inspection of the interior the commandant remarks: 'You ought to leave at once if you wish to get down before the barrage commences again.' We have to go, but the prospect of going outside again when you feel so safe after the night's adventures is not a pleasant one. Endeavouring to show a detachment we are far from feeling, we say good-bye and make our way to the narrow exit. It is now broad daylight. A stream of men are working their way amidst the shell-holes to the fort. They are laden and can hardly walk or even crawl in the heavy mud. Some are carrying a dozen water bottles, others biscuits, others sacks of bread, others petrol; everything in fact necessary to keep the fort and its garrison going for another day. One man reaches the door and collapses from sheer fatigue, dropping his burden with a crash. His officer helps him up, remarking, '*Allez, reposez vous un peu.*' The man drags his weary feet down the gallery and disappears. It is terrible hard work, this carrying supplies to Douaumont. These figures stumbling, rolling, and picking themselves up again amidst the countless miniature lakes make a curious picture. They hardly resemble human beings, so caked are they with mud. They look like mud balls animated with life, but with no control over their limbs. Do not imagine that the shelling has stopped. Far from it, but it is not so heavy as when we entered, and now we can see our way a little. Even as we clear the narrow entrance a succession of three big shells burst within a few yards, throwing the mud in all directions.

We do not linger in that horrid ditch, but climb the counterscarp as quickly as possible and pass on down the slope towards Thiaumont. It being daylight you are able to see the exact nature of the ground over which we passed in the darkness. The marvel is that we ever succeeded in getting into the fort at all without falling into the innumerable shell-holes which contain 6ft to 8ft of water. Some of these pools look clean and fresh, others are covered with a dark slime, and yet others are bright yellow, caused by the explosions. In some of these holes bodies are protruding above the water; in others fragments of humanity are floating. Others contain broken rifles, bits of uniform, fragments of shells, and the countless debris of the battlefield. We find we have passed over an open cemetery. You cannot move a yard without treading on or jumping over what was once a man or a portion of one. Every square foot of this ghastly wilderness is sown with human bones. Over this ground infantry have fought for months. The majority of the corpses are German, as you can tell by the fragments of uniform and equipment. God knows how many thousands must lie in this waste. There has been no effort to bury the dead, or if there has the bodies have been thrown to the surface again by the incessant shell-fire. The smell is revolting. Our clothes carry the odour away from Verdun, and you cannot get rid of it, because all through the night, unknown to ourselves at the time, we have been crawling over this cemetery. On our way down we pass the endless swarm of blue, sweating, cursing, toiling human ants, who are carrying up supplies to the fort. Some get there, some are killed, and many wounded, but the stream never stops. A delicious sense of relief comes over you as you get farther and farther down the slope of this ghastly ridge, the bloodiest and most vile in the whole world. How you pity the poor devils who have to make their way up. Further on you find a battalion of Territorials endeavouring to make a road amidst the mud. The task is almost beyond human powers, and all they can do is to throw shell-holes into one another. We have yet further trials to face. The hour of comparative respite is soon over, and we are chased by the enemy's shells right back into the town of Verdun. But we have been into Douaumont, and you feel that is an achievement. Someone asks if we want to visit another fort. This bad joke does not go down and we enter our motor-cars 'fed up' with forts, mud, and shells.

16 November 1916

BRITISH VICTORY ON THE ANCRE
'Biggest Since Thiepval', *British Headquarters, France, Tuesday*

By Perceval Gibbon

The moment has not even yet arrived when it is possible to enumerate the whole of our gains in Monday's great battle, 'the biggest since Thiepval', as one of our generals, whose command bore a part in it, has declared. For our gains in ground are enlarging themselves while I write; the 2,000 or so prisoners of last night have already grown to some 5,000, and the glorious total of Douaumont is in sight. And the machine-guns which we failed to discover in the fight, dotted like poisonous weeds among the fields, have come to light in the long galleries of the wonderful 'tunnel' at St Pierre Divion.

What was lacking in the first accounts, as they came up in the stress of those hours while our men were yet digging in on their new-won lines, and while there were yet caches and pockets of undetected Germans in little isolated trenches about the countryside behind them, was the tale of the clean-cut and scientific co-ordination of the means of war which made a victory on this scale possible. The moment of the assault, when the barrage lifted and pounced forward, and the eager infantry-waves flowed over the parapets, came only at the close of long stages of detailed and scientific preparation by flying men, staffs and intelligence officers.

In that section of the field which lay south of the Ancre, for example, our victory reveals how complete was our previous observation of the enemy's dispositions, strength, and communications. His one practicable road for supplies and reliefs was peppered with shrapnel by day and night; his bridges across the Ancre were shelled continually; his machine-gun positions were located and treated to doses of intense fire. And the day of the attack happened to be that on which the 38th Division was being relieved by Ludendorff's new-laid 223rd, so that both divisions were caught on the ground and held there by our barrage to swell the number of dead and prisoners. We even knew that among the regiments against us was the 93rd (of the 38th Division), whose Colonel-in-Chief, the Duke of Albany (Duke of Saxe-Coburg-Gotha), is now in the Somme battle area, waiting to inspect it when it is relieved.

The gunfire against the machine-gun positions was so effective that those which were not destroyed were removed from the front, and our casualties were therefore very light. Taking, again, the sector south of the Ancre as an instance, fully two-thirds of the wounded walked up to the casualty clearing stations, and the actual figure of our losses is small. The men who come up wounded out of the fight are in themselves a barometer of our success. When, as now, our fighting has been victorious, when the matter has gone profitably and triumphantly, they come up in muddy bands of limping, hilarious Tommies, each with his cigarette glued to his lower lip, helping each other along, grinning at passers-by, hailing passing prisoners joyously.

I saw today a wounded British soldier helping a wounded German prisoner into the clearing station. Both had 'got it in the foot', both wore one boot and a bandage, both limped painfully. The Briton had a hand under the Teuton's arm, and was encouraging him in the lingua franca of all the world. 'No walkee much further,' he said. 'Soon there now. Compree, Fritz?' 'Ja,' groaned Fritz. He 'compree'd'.

St Pierre Divion, from the nature of its fortifications, and its position as outflanking a variety of positions on the northern bank of the river, was an important objective in itself. Of the pleasant, tree-shaded village that stood above the river there remained, of course, no trace; villages melt like snowflakes in these battle-heats. Between it and our lines there was a maze of new and old trenches, some strongly held, some deserted, half-full of a treacly ooze of the local mud, in which the late occupier had thoughtfully bedded a cocoon of barbed wire. It was in the advance upon St Pierre Divion that there occurred the most strenuous of the fighting which took place to the south of the river.

Here there entered into the battle, ahead of the infantry, a tank. If ever one of these mechanisms falls into the hands of the Germans I suppose it will be possible to describe the apparatus; but that seems unlikely. The tank is very thoroughly qualified to take care of itself. This one lurched and curtseyed into action with the characteristic gait of the beast, that undulating belly-crawl which to me always suggests a vast wounded reptile, some 'lame dragon of the prime'. Upon the lip of a shell-hole it halted and remained, and the Germans, taking it for stuck and helpless, swarmed out to meet it with rifles and hand-grenades. A hand-grenade bursting against a tank makes a pretty firework, and upon all accounts it is a pity that those inside the apparatus cannot see it. Probably they never know when it happens.

Upon this occasion, at any rate, they merely hung where they were and fought his Majesty's ship 'Landcrab' – or whatever her name was – for two lively hours, during which the tank showed to the Germans only its toad-complexioned carapace of inviolate steel and the spit of its guns. And then – when they were due – up came our infantry, and the fight was over. St Pierre Divion was already known to us as the site of that remarkable underground labyrinth which our intelligence officers have christened 'The Tunnel'. The village stands – or stood, when it was yet a village – upon a shelf of upland above the little brook Ancre; and below it the ground broke towards the stream.

A perpendicular bank of clay, some 20ft high, showed towards the water-meadows on the riverside, and into this the industrious Germans had burrowed wonderfully. His trenches were on the lip of the bank, and under them he had burrowed a vast refuge whose plan resembles, roughly, a capital T. The stem of the T is a gallery 300 yards long, full 8ft high, and 4ft wide, neatly timbered in, traversed in methodical zigzags in order to increase its proportions without adding to its length from end to end, and electric lit. One arm of the T; the other has yet to be explored.

From the main galleries there branch minor passages, leading to the chambers where beds and bunks are fitted, and where an enormous deposit of various stores has been discovered. Some of these chambers aim so close to luxury that the walls are even papered. Along the main galleries are innumerable shelves, crowded with stores and provisions, and hooks with bundles hanging from them. The labyrinth is connected with the trenches above by broad flights of steps. The whole is so deep that it is not only proof to the impact of the largest shell, but the very barrage is inaudible from its chambers.

Hither, when the squall of shell-fire burst over the trenches, the garrison could be hurried below, to sit under a roof of 20ft of earth, like deep-buried corpses; then, when the barrage had jumped and the attack was coming forward, they could be resurrected and hustled up the broad stairways to man their parapets. And here, when the Intelligence Officers came to explore, was the chief treasure. The electric light system had been disconnected when our exploring party arrived; the search and examination had to be carried out with torches.

There was need for care, for it was not yet sure that the place was clean of Germans. They searched the length of the stem of the T, marking its many exits to the river-bank, where men driven back from the water's edge could duck into holes in the bank like water-gnats, to emerge still whole and dangerous a couple of hundred yards away.

A noisome smell pervaded the place that was not at first to be accounted for. It proved to be from the quantities of Kriegsbrod – the war-bread which the Germans make out of potato and flour and other matters.

Perhaps all Kriegsbrod does not smell like that which is issued from the field-bakeries on the Ancre. An odour sickly and suggestive of staleness – something like the inside of an old four-wheeled cab, but with an undertone of decay – it is the kind of food which a starving man would be inclined to try first on a dog. The electric pocket-torches of the explorers flashed here and there, till at length they found what they had been looking for. Here, 20ft deep and scores of yards in, was the stuff – the gallery was a mine of machine-guns. They had been driven from their squatting-places in the open by the threat of our shells, and carried hither for safety. It is probable that the plan was to bring them up at the critical moment, and flow back the attack with them, but our barrage prevented that.

Near the door by which they entered the explorers found a packet of twenty rifle cartridges furnished with explosive bullets. This helps out the story of a captured German machine-gunner, who was found in possession of this devilish pattern of ammunition. He had been ordered, he said, to arm his cartridge-belts with one explosive round to every twenty rounds of common cartridge. They were designed to be fired at aeroplanes, but naturally, in the event of an infantry attack the belts would be run through the guns just the same. Twenty-nine officers and 1,300 men were made prisoners in and around the positions of St Pierre Divion alone. It is curious to note that all the officers have their packs, containing their kits, and all the men have their greatcoats; there is not one that was not ready to be transported to the cages.

The officers, of course, do not go to the cages; and these were lodged for the night in a village behind the lines. Accommodation was scarce, and they found that there were too many of them in the room in which they were put. A couple of them, who had swallowed the camel of surrender, so strained at the gnat of their temporary rough lodging that they complained loudly to the urbane British staff officer who called round to see that they were made as comfortable as possible under the circumstances. He heard them politely. 'I'm sorry you don't like your quarters,' he answered them, pleasantly. 'If only you'd let me know you were coming, I'd have made better arrangements.'

Fifteen hundred yards of progress took our men to a German rear-line of trenches. Here, according to precedent, they would have crouched in the trench, toiling in desperate haste to turn it round and get a parapet erected while the enemy shelled them with fervour.

But nothing of the kind happened: there was no shelling and no counter-attack, and instead of crouching and sweating the men were strolling about in the open, smoking German cigars from a store of full boxes which some of them had picked up on their way through. 'They are now consolidating in comparative comfort,' was the official statement. The cigars, no doubt, were a chief part of the comfort.

North of the river the troops entrusted with the attack to the Beaucourt road (running from Beaumont Hamel to Beaucourt-sur-Ancre) thrust forthwith so directly and swiftly to the goal that 'pockets' of neglected and unstaffed Germans remained intact in their rear. These have had to be attended to today. Their advance carried the attackers to the outskirts of Beaucourt, where the Germans were in force, with the 2nd Guard Reserve among the formations of the garrison. The ground rises to Beaucourt, and the slope, which is a gentle one, was against the attack. Therefore throughout yesterday the fighting continued, with fresh attacks through the night, and this morning we took the village and carried our line well round it.

At this moment, while I write, I have but to stop tapping the typewriter to hear the great drum-music of the guns that are pounding at the enemy beyond the village. For nothing has ceased; the momentum of victory is not arrested; and the men who took Beaucourt are still shoving on. The 'pockets' made a curious situation. They varied in quality from the desperate and brave men who came suddenly out of the earth when our men had passed – to seize their legitimate advantage of ambush and open fire on them from behind – to the poor, limp creatures, dazed and unmanned by shelling, who came timidly up from their broken ditches and followed along with their hands above their heads.

A man of ours, shell-shocked and partly buried, came to during the night sufficiently to extract himself, and endeavour to get back to his own lines. Going cautiously among the shell-holes, he found a trench, and hailed it, and was answered in German. Nobody fired on him, however, and he strolled on. Eventually he passed the night in a crater, and was rescued in the morning by a sergeant-major of his own battalion. I was able to find a wounded German who had been in one of the 'pockets' by Beaumont Hamel. A Rhinelander, this man, little and moderately plump, and spectacled, he was wounded in the face and in the arm. He told me, in grievous tones, that he had been an engine-driver on a light railway at home till five months ago, and had always been exempted from military service on account of the nature of his occupation. 'But now everybody must serve,' he said. His trench had been near Beaumont Hamel, and the attack had gone past it. Presently, there appeared British soldiers, from nowhere, running towards the trench. Up on the right, out of his view, there had been fighting; but then men in khaki came running along 'the top' above the trench, slamming bombs into it. One exploded near him and gave him his wounds.

Whereupon, like a sensible German, he hoisted his hands, and all the men to right and left of him whom he could see did likewise; and were rewarded by being gathered in, slapped on the back, furnished with cigarettes and first-aid bandages, and helped back to the calm mechanism of the clearing station, with its instant medicine of rest and food and fine humanity to the beaten and captured enemy. Beside this man was an 'Unteroffizier' of the 2nd Guard Reserve, also wounded by a grenade, who had been in the force that invaded Belgium and marched through to France, where he had been ever since. Six feet in his bare, sore feet, thirty-six years of age – a fine human brute! Around him were rags of men, drooping and whining; he sat in his place rigid as a guardsman on parade, lifting to his questioner a heavy, hatchet face where blunt brutality, cruelty, and vileness stood as plain as though they were painted on a signboard. Lest my own impressions should mislead me I asked a companion to look at him. He did so, and came back to me. 'Helps one to understand what happened in Belgium,' was his comment.

I asked each of them whether he had been well treated. In each case the answer was an enthusiastic affirmative. A swarthy, lean face looking over the edge of a blanket grinned in my direction and asked when the war would end. The others pricked up their ears. One cannot throw down gauntlets to wounded prisoners so I answered that I did not know. The swarthy man grinned again.

'Well, it's finished for us, anyhow,' he said. 'We're going to learn now to love the English.'

At one point another tank came into action and bedded herself down in the massive and reposeful way which tanks have, behind a scrap of trench where 400 'pocketed' Germans were huddled, cuddling their courage back to life. But they abandoned the attempt when the warship 'Clodhopper' – or some such name – backed her mainyard and hove to alongside of them; and they were duly gathered in.

To the south of Beaumont Hamel there is a deep cutting leading to a quarry, which has the name, from its shape, of the 'Ravinen Y', or 'Y Ravine'. Here 700 Germans waited through the night and half of today for someone to come and fetch them and lead them home. Their time came about noon, when the whole 700 of them were added to the swelling figure of fine physical types whom we are nourishing to replenish Germany's manpower at the end of the war, when our own poor, starved, and fever-stricken men come home from Wittenberg and the like prison-camps in Germany.

And still they come, in hundreds, marshalled along the roads by Lancers, in little gangs following a leisurely infantryman, in lamentable wagon-loads, with bound-up heads and slung arms. And Tommy slaps them on the back or helps them along, cheery always, with never a memory for their long, foul fighting. And it is assuredly worth a few thousand Germans nursed back to strength and viciousness, to keep the British soldier what he is – the finest human being in the world.

29 November 1916

GERMAN VIEWS OF THE SOMME BATTLES
'The Blood-Bath', *British Headquarters, France, Sunday*
By Philip Gibbs

Before the ending of the first phase of the Battle of the Somme – the second phase begins, I imagine, with our great advance on 15 September from the Pozières–

Longueval–Guillemont line – the German troops had invented a terrible name to describe this great ordeal; it was 'The Blood-Bath of the Somme'. The news could not be hidden from the people of Germany, who had already been chilled with horror by the losses at Verdun, nor from the soldiers of reserve regiments quartered in French and Belgian towns like Valenciennes, St Quentin, Cambrai, Lille, Bruges, and as far back as Brussels, waiting to go to the front, nor from the civil populations of those towns held for two years by their enemy – these blonde young men who lived in their houses, marched down their streets, and made love to their women. The news was brought down from the Somme front by Red Cross trains, arriving in endless succession, and packed with maimed and mangled men. German military policemen formed cordons round the railway stations, pushed back civilians who came to stare with sombre eyes at these blanketed bundles of living flesh, but when the ambulances rumbled through the streets towards the hospitals – long processions of them, with the soles of men's boots turned up over the stretchers on which they lay quiet and stiff – the tale was told though no word was spoken.

The tale of defeat, of great losses, of grave and increasing anxiety, was told clearly enough – as I have read in captured letters – by the faces of German officers who went about in these towns behind the lines with gloomy looks, and whose tempers, never of the sweetest, became irritable and unbearable, so that the soldiers hated them for all this cursing and bullying. A certain battalion commander has a nervous breakdown because he has to meet his colonel in the morning. 'He is dying with fear and anxiety,' writes one of his comrades. Other men, not battalion commanders, are even more afraid of their superior officers, upon whom this bad news from the Somme has an evil effect. The bad news was spread by divisions taken out of the line and sent back to rest. The men reported that their battalions had been cut to pieces. Some of their regiment had lost three-quarters of their strength. They described the frightful effect of the British artillery – the smashed trenches, the shell-craters, the great horror.

It is not good for the morale of men who are first going up there to take their turn. The man who was afraid of his colonel 'sits all day long writing home with the picture of his wife and children before his eyes'. He is afraid of other things. Bavarian soldiers quarrelled with Prussians, accused them (unjustly) of shirking the Somme battlefields and leaving the Bavarians to go to the blood-bath.

All the Bavarian troops are being sent to the Somme (this much is certain, you can see no Prussians there) and this in spite of the losses the 1st Bavarian Corps suffered recently at Verdun! And how we did suffer! … It appears that we are in for another turn, at least the 5th Bavarian Division. Everybody has been talking about it for a long time. To the devil with it! Every Bavarian regiment is being sent into it, and it's a swindle.

It was in no cheerful mood that men went away to the Somme battlefields. Those battalions of grey-clad men entrained without any of the old enthusiasm with which they had gone to earlier battles. Their gloom was noticed by the officers. 'Sing, you sheep's head, sing!' they shouted. They were compelled to sing, by order. A man of the 18th Reserve Division wrote: 'We had to go out

again: we were to learn to sing. The greater part did not join in, and the song
went feebly. Then we had to march round in a circle and sing, and that went no
better. After that we had an hour off, and on the way back to billets we were to
sing "Deutschland über Alles", but this broke down completely. One never hears
songs of the Fatherland any more.'

They were silent, grave-eyed men who marched through the streets of French
and Belgian towns to be entrained for the Somme front, for they had forebodings
of the fate before them. Yet none of their forebodings were equal in intensity of
fear to the frightful reality into which they were flung. The journey to the Somme
front on the German side was a way of terror, ugliness, and death. Not all the
imagination of morbid minds searching obscenely for foulness and blood in the
great deep pits of human agony could surpass these scenes along the way to the
German lines round Courcelette and Flers, Gueudecourt, Morval, and Les
Bœufs. Many times, long before a German battalion had arrived near the
trenches, it was but a collection of nerve-broken men bemoaning losses already
suffered far behind the lines and filled with hideous apprehension. For British
long-range guns were hurling high-explosives into distant villages, barraging
cross-roads, reaching out to railheads and ammunition dumps, while British
airmen were on bombing flights over railway stations and rest-billets, and high
roads down which the German troops came marching at Cambrai, Bapaume, in
the valley between Irles and Warlencourt, at Ligny-Thilloy, Busigny, and many
other places on the lines of route.

German soldiers arriving at Cambrai by train found themselves under the fire
of a single aeroplane which flew very low and dropped bombs. They exploded
with heavy crashes, and one bomb hit the first carriage behind the engine, killing
and wounding several men. A second bomb hit the station buildings, and there
was a great clatter of broken glass, the rending of wood and the fall of bricks. All
lights went out, and the German soldiers groped about in the darkness amidst the
splinters of glass and the fallen bricks, searching for the wounded by the sound of
their groans. It was but one scene along the way to that blood-bath, through
which they had to wade to the trenches of the Somme.

Flights of British aeroplanes circled over the villages on the way. At Grevilliers,
in August, eleven 112-16 bombs fell in the market square so that the centre of the
village collapsed in a state of ruin, burying soldiers billeted there. Every day the
British airmen paid these visits, meeting the Germans far up the roads on their
way to the Somme, and swooping over them like a flying Death. Even on the
march in open country the German soldiers tramping silently along – not singing
in spite of orders – were bombed and shot at by these British aviators, who flew
down very low, pouring out streams of machine-gun bullets. The Germans lost
their nerve at such times, and scattered into the ditches, falling over each other,
struck and cursed by their 'unteroffizieren', and leaving their dead and wounded
in the roadway. As the roads went nearer to the battlefields they were choked
with the traffic of war, with artillery and transport wagons and horse ambulances,
and always thousands of grey men marching up to the lines, or back from them,
exhausted and broken after many days in the fires of hell up there.

Officers sat on their horses by the roadside directing all traffic with the usual swearing and cursing, and rode alongside the transport wagons and the troops, urging them forward at a quicker pace because of stern orders received from headquarters demanding quicker movement. The reserves, it seemed, were desperately wanted up in the lines. The English were attacking again. God alone knew what was happening. Regiments had lost their way. Wounded were pouring back. Officers had gone mad … Into the midst of all this turmoil shells fell – shells from long-range guns. Transport wagons were blown to bits. The bodies and fragments of artillery horses lay all over the roads. Men lay dead or bleeding under the debris of gun-wheels and broken bricks. Above all the noise of this confusion and death in the night the hard, stern voices of German officers rang out, and German discipline prevailed and men marched on to greater perils.

They were in the shell zone now and sometimes a regiment on the march was tracked all along the way by British gunfire directed from aeroplanes and captive balloons. It was the fate of a captured officer I met who had detrained at Bapaume for the trenches at Contalmaison. At Bapaume his battalion was hit by fragments of 12in shells. Nearer to the line they came under the fire of 8in and 6in shells. Four-point-sevens found them somewhere by Bazentin. At Contalmaison they marched into a barrage, and here the officer was taken prisoner. Of his battalion there were few men left. It was so with the 3rd Jaeger Battalion, ordered up hurriedly to make a counter-attack near Flers. They suffered so heavily on the way to the trenches that no attack could be made. The stretcher-bearers had all the work to do.

The way up to the trenches became more tragic as every kilometre was passed, until the stench of corruption was wafted on the wind, so that men were sickened and tried not to breathe, and marched hurriedly to get on the lee side of its foulness. They walked now through places which bad once been villages, but were sinister ruins where death lay in wait for German soldiers. One of them wrote: 'It seems queer to me that whole villages close to the front look as flattened as a child's toy run over by a steam roller. Not one stone remains on another. The streets are one line of shell-holes. Add to that the thunder of the guns, and you will see with what feelings we come into the line – into trenches where for months shells of all calibre have rained … Flers is a scrap-heap.'

They had reached the Bath of Blood at last, above that river of the Somme which as long as the history of this war lasts will be coloured in the imagination of men by the crimson flow of life spilt on these battlefields, though it runs silver-bright between the high rushes on its banks. In the fire-trenches and support trenches and communication trenches up by Thiepval, Martinpuich, and Courcelette, by Flers and Gueudecourt and Morval, even farther back by Grandcourt and Le Sars, British shell-fire came in great storms, ploughing up the earth, burying living men, unburying dead men, searching for German flesh and blood, many days before the British infantry leapt from their own trenches and began the second phase, or, if you like to reckon differently, the third phase, of their advance, on 15 September.

Again and again men lost their way up to the lines. The reliefs could only be made at night, lest they should be discovered by British airmen and British gunners, and even if these German soldiers had trench-maps the guidance was but little good when many trenches had been smashed in, and only shell-craters could be found. They stumbled through the darkness and into these pits, sometimes waist-high in water. The British flares shot up with a vivid white light, and the men crouched low and still between the rockets, and then crawled on again. Shells burst over them, and there was the chatter of English machine-guns. A letter written by one of these Germans says: 'In the front line of Flers the men were only occupying shell-holes. Behind there was the intense smell of putrefaction, which filled the trench – almost unbearably. The corpses lie either quite insufficiently covered with earth on the edge of the trench or quite close under the bottom of the trench, so that the earth lets the stench through. In some places bodies lie quite uncovered in a trench recess, and no one seems to trouble about them. One sees horrible pictures – here an arm, here a foot, here a head, sticking out of the earth. And these are all German soldiers – heroes! Not far from us at the entrance to a dug-out nine men were buried, of whom three were dead. All along the trench men kept on getting buried. What had been a perfect trench a few hours before was in parts completely blown in … The men are getting weaker. It is impossible to hold out any longer. Losses can no longer be reckoned accurately. Without a doubt many of our people are killed.'

That is only one out of thousands of such gruesome pictures, true as the death they described, which have gone to German homes during the battles of the Somme. These German soldiers are grand letter-writers, and men sitting in wet ditches – in 'fox-holes', as they call their dug-outs – 'up to my waist in mud', as one of them described, scribbled pitiful things, which they hoped might reach their people at home, as a voice from the dead. For they had had little hope of escape from the 'blood-bath'. 'When you get this I shall be a corpse,' wrote one of them, and one finds the same foreboding in many of these documents. Even the lucky ones, who could get some cover from the incessant bombardment by English guns, began to lose their nerve after a day or two. They were always in fear of British infantry, sweeping upon them suddenly behind the 'Trommelfeuer', rushing their dug-outs with bombs and bayonets. Sentries became 'jumpy', and signalled attacks when there were no attacks. The gas-alarm was sounded constantly by the clang of a bell in the trench, and men put on their heavy gas-masks and sat in them until they were nearly stifled.

Here is a little picture of life in a German dug-out near the British lines, written by a man now dead.

The telephone bell rings. 'Are you there? Yes, here's Nau's battalion.' 'Good. That is all.' Then that ceases, and now the wire is in again, perhaps for the twenty-fifth or thirtieth time. Thus the night is interrupted, and now they come, alarm messages, one after the other, each more terrifying than the other, of enormous losses through the bombs and shells of the enemy, of huge masses of troops advancing upon us, of all possible possibilities, such as a train broken down, and tortured by the terrors that the day can invent. Our nerves quiver. We clench our teeth. None of us can forget the horrors of the night.

Heavy rain fell, and the dug-outs became wet and filthy.

Our sleeping-places were full of water. We had to try to bail out the trenches with cooking dishes. I lay down in the water with G----. We were to have worked on dug-outs, but not a soul could do any more. Only a few sections got coffee. Mine got nothing at all. I was frozen in every limb, poured the water out of my boots, and lay down again.

The German generals and their staffs could not be quite indifferent to all this welter of human suffering among their troops, in spite of the cold scientific spirit with which they regard the problem of war. The agony of the individual soldier would not trouble them. There is no war without agony. But the psychology of masses of men had to be considered, because it affects the efficiency of the machine. As I shall show, the German General Staff on the Western Front were becoming seriously alarmed by the declining morale of their infantry under the increasing strain of the British attacks, and adopted stern measures to cure it. But they could not hope to cure the heaps of German dead who were lying on the battlefields, nor the maimed men who were being carried back to the dressing stations, nor to bring back the prisoners taken in droves by the French and British troops. Before the attack on the Flers line, the capture of Thiepval, and the German debacle at Beaumont Hamel the enemy's command was already filled with a grave anxiety at the enormous losses of its fighting strength, was compelled to adopt new expedients for increasing the number of its divisions. It was forced to withdraw troops badly needed on other fronts, and, as I shall point out, the successive shocks of the British offensive reached as far as Germany itself, so that the whole of its recruiting system had to be revised to fill up the gaps torn out of the German ranks.

21 September 1917

THE BATTLE OF MENIN ROAD

Fight for the Wood, *War Correspondents' Headquarters, France, Thursday Evening*

By Philip Gibbs

Our troops attacked this morning before six o'clock on a wide front north and south of the Ypres–Menin road, and have gained important ground all along the line. It is ground from which during the past six weeks there has been that heroic and desperate fighting which I have described as best I could in my daily messages, giving even at the best only a vague idea of the difficulties encountered by those men of ours who made great sacrifices in great endeavours. It is the ground which in the centre rises up through the sinister woodlands of Glencorse Copse and Inverness Wood to the high ground of Polygon Wood and the spurs of the Passchendaele Ridge, which form the enemy's great defensive barrier to the east of the Ypres salient. Until that highland was taken progress was difficult for our troops on the left across the Steenebeke as the enemy's guns could still hold commanding positions. The ground over which our men have swept this morning was assaulted again and again by troops who ignored their losses and attacked with a most desperate and glorious courage, yet failed to hold what they gained for a time, because their final goal was attained with weakened forces after most fierce and bloody fighting. The Empire knows who those men were – the old English county regiments, who never fought more gallantly; the Scots, who only let go of their forward positions under overwhelming pressure and annihilating fire; the Irish divisions, who suffered the most supreme ordeal and earned new and undying honour by the way they endured the fire of many guns for many days.

As long as history lasts, the name of these woods, from which most of the trees have been swept, and of these bogs and marshes which lie about them, will be linked with the memory of those brave battalions who fought through them again and again. They are not less to be honoured than those who with the same courage, just as splendid, fought through them again, over the same tracks, past the same death-traps, and achieved success. By different methods, by learning from what the first men had suffered, this last attack has not as yet been high in cost, and we hold what the enemy had used all his strength and cunning to prevent us getting. He used great cunning and poured up great reserves of men and guns to smash our assaulting lines. For the first time on 31 July we came up against his new and fully prepared system or defence, and discovered the power of it. Abandoning the old trench system which we could knock to pieces with artillery, he made his forward positions without any definite line, and built a great number of concrete blockhouses, so arranged in depth that they defended each other by enfilade fire, and so strong that nothing but a direct hit from one of our heavier shells would damage it. And a direct hit is very difficult on a small mark like one of those concrete houses, holding about ten to twenty men at minimum, and fifty to sixty in their largest. These little garrisons were mostly machine-gunners and picked men specially trained for outpost work, and they could inflict great damage on an advancing battalion, so that the forward lines passing through and beyond them would be spent and weak. Then behind in reserve lay the German 'Stoss-truppen', specially trained also for counter-attacks, which were launched in strong striking forces against our advanced lines after all their struggle and loss.

Those blockhouses proved formidable things – hard nuts to crack, as the soldiers said who came up against them. There are scores of them whose names will be remembered through a lifetime by men of many battalions, and they cost the lives of many brave men. Beck House and Borry Farm belong to Irish history. Wurst Farm and Winnipeg, Bremen Redoubt and Gallipoli, Iberian and Delva Farm, are strongholds round which many desperate little battles, led by young subalterns or sergeants, have taken place on the last day of July and on many days since. English and Scots have taken turns in attacking and defending such places as Fitzclarence Farm, Northampton Farm, and Black Watch Corner in the dreadful region of Inverness Copse and Glencorse Wood. Today the hard nut of the concrete blockhouse has been cracked by a new method of attack and by a new assault, planned with great forethought, and achieved so far with high success.

I should like to give the full details of the preparations which have made this success possible and the methods by which some at least of the terrors of the blockhouse have been laid low, but it cannot yet be done, and it is enough now that good results have been attained. One thing was against us as usual last night. After several fine days the weather turned bad again, and last night many men must have looked up at the sky, groaned, and said, 'Just our luck.' At half-past ten it began to rain heavily, and all through the night there was a steady drizzle. It was awful to think of that ground about the woodlands, already full of water-holes and bogs, becoming more and more of a quagmire as the time drew near when our men have to rise from the mud and follow the barrage across that ground. All through the night our heavy guns were slogging, and through the dark wet mist there was the blurred light of their flashes. Before the dawn a high wind was raging at 30 miles an hour across Flanders, and heavy water-logged clouds were only 400ft above the earth. How could our airmen see? When the attack began they could not see, even when they flew as low as 200ft. They could see nothing but smoke, which clung low to the battlefields, and they could only guess the whereabouts of German batteries. Later, when some progress had been made at most points of the attacking line, the sky cleared a little, blue spaces showed through the black storm-clouds, and there were gleams of sun striking aslant the mists.

This sky on the salient was a strange vision, and I have seen nothing like it since the war began. It was filled with little black specks like midges, but each midge was a British aeroplane flying over the enemy's lines. The enemy tried to clear the air of them, and his anti-aircraft guns were firing wildly, so that all about them were puffs of black shrapnel. Behind, closely clustered, were our kite balloons, like snow-clouds where they were caught by the light, staring down over the battle, and in wide semi-circles about the salient our heavy guns were firing ceaselessly with dull, enormous hammer strokes, followed by the shrill cry of travelling shells making the barrage before our men, and having blockhouses for their targets and building walls of flying steel between the enemy and our attacking troops. In the near distance were the strafed woods of old battle grounds like the Wytschaete Ridge and Messines, with their naked gallows-trees all blurred in the mist.

Our men had lain out all night in the rain before the attack at something before six. They were wet through to the skin, but it is curious that some of them whom I saw today were surprised to hear it had been raining hard. They had other things to think about. But some of them did not think at all. Tired out in mind and body under the big nervous strain which is there, though they may be unconscious of it, they slept. 'I was awakened by a friend just before we went over,' said one of them. The anxiety of the officers was intense for the hours to pass before the enemy should get a hint of the movement. It seemed that in one part of the line he did guess that something was in the wind and in the mist. This was on the line facing Glencorse Wood. An hour or two before the attack he put over a heavy barrage, but most of it missed the heads of the battalions. There were some casualties, but the men stood firm, never budging, and making no sound. They all thought that some of their comrades must have been badly caught, but, as far as I can find, it did not do great damage.

All along the line the experience of the fighting was broadly the same. Apart from local details and difficulties, the ground was not quite so bad as had been expected, though bad enough, being greasy and boggy after the rain, but not impassable. The shell-holes were waterlogged, and they were dangerously deep for badly wounded men who might fall in, but for the others there was generally a way round over ground which would hold, and our assaulting waves who led the advance were lightly clad, and could go at a fair pace after the barrage. 'I saw wounded men fall in the shell-holes,' said one lad today, 'and God knows how they got out again, unless the stretcher-bearers came up quick, as most of them did; but as for me I had lain in a shell-hole all night up to the waist in mud, and I was careful to keep out of them.' The barrage ahead of them was terrific – the most appalling fence of shells that has ever been placed before advancing troops in this war. All our men describe it as wonderful. 'Beautiful' is the word they use, because they know what it means in safety to them.

In the direction of Polygon Wood the plan of attack seems to have worked like clockwork. The assaulting troops moved forward behind the barrage stage by stage, through Westhoek and Nontieboschen, and across the Hannebeke stream on their left, with hardly a check, in spite of the German blockhouses scattered over this country. In those blockhouses the small garrisons of picked troops had been demoralised, as any human beings would be, by the enormous shell-fire which had been flung around them. Some, but not all, it seems, of the blockhouses had been smashed, and in those still standing the German machine-gunners got their weapons to work with a burst or two of fire, but then, seeing our troops upon them, were seized with fear, and made signs of surrender. At nine o'clock this morning the good news came back that our men were right through Glencorse Wood. Later messages showed that our troops were fighting their way into Polygon Wood. They swept over the strong points at Black Watch Corner, Northampton Farm, and Carlisle Farm. There was stiff fighting round a blockhouse called Anzac Corner, east of the Hannebeke stream, and it was necessary to organise two flank attacks and work round it before the enemy machine-gun fire could be silenced by bombs. In another case near here the enemy came out of a blockhouse ready to attack, but when they saw our men swarming up, they lost heart and held up their hands. It is difficult to know how many prisoners were taken here in these woods and strong points. The men's estimates vary enormously, some speaking of scores and others of hundreds.

All this time the enemy's artillery reply was not exceptionally heavy, and, though it was prompt to come after the first SOS signals went up from his lines, it was erratic and varied very much in the success of our counter-battery work, which all through the night and for days past has been smothering his guns. South of the attack in Glencorse Copse and Polygon Wood the assault in Inverness Copse and

Shrewsbury Forest, across the boglands round the Dumbarton Lakes, went with equal success. It was the vilest ground, low-lying and flooded, and strewn with broken trees and choked with undergrowth, but the troops here kept up a good pace, and flung themselves upon the blockhouses which stood in their way. At an early hour our men were reported to be on a ridge south-east of Inverness Copse and going strong towards Veldhoek. The enemy's barrage came down too late, and one officer, who was wounded by a shell-splinter, led his men, 160 of them, to their first position with only nine casualties.

Most of our losses today were from machine-gun fire out of the blockhouses, and that varied very much at different parts of the line. There was some trouble at Hot Pappotje Farm in this way, where a party of German machine-gunners put up a desperate resistance, shutting themselves in behind steel doors before they were routed out by a bombing fight. Southward from a strong point called Groenberg, or 'Green Bug' Farm, to Opaque Wood by the Ypres–Comines Canal, the attack was successful, though the enemy still holds out up to the time I write in Hessian Wood, where he is defending himself in a group of blockhouses.

I have dealt so far with the centre of the attack, and I know very little as to the fighting on the north, except that we have swept past a whole system of blockhouses, like Beck House and Borry Farm, running up through Gallipoli, Kansas Cross, and Wurst Farm, across the Langemarck–Zonnebeke road. All through the morning our lightly wounded men came filtering down to the safer places in the Ypres salient and then to the quiet fields behind, and they were in grand spirits in spite of the mud which caked them and the smart of their wounds. Some of them were brought down on the trolley trains, which go almost as far as the battle-line, and some in open buses, and some by German prisoners, but there were many Germans among the wounded – some of them with very ghastly wounds, and these took their place with ours and mingled with them in the dressing stations, and were given the same treatment. Our wounded told some strange tales of their experiences, but there was no moan among them, whatever they had suffered.

One man described to me how he saw a German officer run out of a dug-out which had been a blockhouse blown in at each end by our heavy shell-fire and made for another one which still stood intact. With some of his comrades, our man chased him, and there was a great fight in the second blockhouse before the survivors surrendered, among them the officer who gave to my friend a big china pipe and a case full of cigars as souvenirs. He was killed afterwards by one of his own men, who sniped him as he was walking back to our lines. In another strong point there was a great and terrible fight. The Prussian garrison refused to surrender, and a party of ours fought them until they were destroyed. 'It was more lively than Wytschaete,' said a man who was in this fight. 'It was less tamelike, and the Fritzes put up a better show.' They fought hard here and there round Prince's House and Jarrocks Farm and Pioneer House, not far from Hollebeke Château.

The prisoners I saw today were shaken men. Most of them were young fellows of twenty-one, belonging to the 1916 class, and there were none of the youngest boys among them. But they were white-faced and haggard, and looked like men who had passed through a great terror, which indeed was their fate. They belonged mostly to the 207th Prussian Division, and had suffered before the battle from our great shell-fire, which had caused many casualties among their reliefs and ration parties. Many other prisoners belonged to the 121st Division. I can only give this glimpse or two of the crowded scenes and the many details of today's battle. Tomorrow, there will be time perhaps to write more, giving a deeper insight into this day of good success, which is cheering after so much desperate fighting – over the same fields, although never to so far a goal.

28 September 1917

AMERICAN ARMY IN FRANCE
Visit to a Camp

By Laurence Jerrold

The 'American Expeditionary Forces in France' are not yet at the front, although they are burning to be there, but they are not far from the front. I have just spent a few days with them watching them get to business. They are getting to business with real American energy and go-aheadness, and with the warm help, gratefully received, of French and British instructors who have had three years of war already and know what it is. The first American troops landed in France in June. I saw them land, and when I recollected that the other day I was amazed at what I saw. The American troops in their billets, their camps, their training-grounds, their rifle and gun practice grounds near the front, are already absolutely at home. The French villagers have adopted now a broken Franco–American language – sister tongue, though different, to the now classic Anglo–French spoken for three years from Calais downwards. The American troops have made themselves at home, have settled all their arrangements with business-like finality, and are out to do their job thoroughly. Their bases near the front seemed to me already definitely organised. They are settled in villages, where they disturb the villagers by aggressive sanitation. They have abolished all dunghills, to the old farmers' amazement and alarm. They have purified the water, cleaned up streets, cottages, and farmyards. The villagers, at first terrified by these wild measures, are now reconciled, and every little village grocery sells American matches, American tobacco, American groceries, sterilised milk, 'canned goods', American mustard, and everything American except American whisky. For at the messes, where I was received with open arms as an ally of today and for ever – no American officer makes any doubt about that – cold American purified water and French coffee with American sterilised milk are the only drinks. Villages of France have become American, and American café au lait, coloured cars, and motor-bikes with side-cars tear all over the country, driven by university boys turned 'chauffeurs'.

Our new Allies are learning from us both – from us old Allies, English and French. I first saw a French division in horizon blue teach the new American army, in khaki and wearing British trench helmets, what a modern battle is like. It was a moving sight. It was poignant really, when one heard that the French division had just come back from Verdun and was enacting over again in play what it had just done in terrible and glorious earnest. The American Staff stood on a knoll watching, with the French Staff explaining. On the edge of the hill to the left of the Staff the new American army watched. Further to the left the French troops came on. Every 'poilu' among them had just come from the real thing. He grinned as he played at war this time, and one felt how he must enjoy playing at it now. But he played very well and earnestly. The whole thing was done as one has before watched it being done under less reassuring circumstances for oneself. The lines advanced in open formation, then stopped for the barrage fire to be pushed forward. Flares were sent up to signal to the artillery. There was another step forward under barrage fire, another (sham) barrage fire, more flares and rockets, the horizon-blue line crept cautiously round to take the first trenches, the machine-gun parties came up. One more barrage fire and more signals, then the Boche trenches below us were taken. It was all exactly as it would have been in real war. The French colonel of artillery, straight from action, explained it to the American generals, General S—— and General D—— (who has just won the French Military Cross at Verdun). The American troops understood and appreciated keenly. Who would not? These play-actors in the hollow at our feet had just come from the real tragedy, and had fought and won, but had paid the price of victory. The American soldier (officers told me) understands the manœuvre well. The officers find that their men are quick at grasping individual field work, i.e., make admirable non-commissioned officers with initiative, enterprise, and intelligence. French officers, many of whom speak English perfectly, while several American officers I met speak very good French, give enthusiastic and intelligent assistance. French and Americans are not much alike in method or by temperament, I heard a French officer describing a battle with perfect technical accuracy, but also with dramatic expressiveness and with the literary sense. An American officer immediately translated the French into American, and it was American – short, sharp, almost crackling with crisp Americanisms. It was the same battle described, but the difference in the descriptions was delightful to note. Differences are nothing. The French are keen to teach, the Americans, if possible, keener still to learn, and each understands the other thoroughly to a common end.

British instructors and American pupils understand each other equally well. I never was more amused, pleased, cheered, and bucked up than by watching British sergeant-instructors training American officer-cadets. Imagine a typical British sergeant, with three years of war behind him and with seven or more years of British military training before that, spending every ounce of his energy, every particle of his keenness, and every word of his vocabulary teaching young

Americans what they will have to do in a few months' time, and the young Americans using every muscle of their body, all their alertness, and all their keenness, too, to make themselves ready for the fight that all are yearning to be in. Parties of American officer-cadets (including young Lieutenant ----) dug line upon line of sham trenches, killed dummy Boches on the way, dashed through four lines of trenches, dug themselves in at the last, and began instant rapid fire at more Boche targets. 'Advance!' said the sergeant. A second later 'Go!' and the young chaps leapt out. 'Kill 'em sweet and clean! Clean killing is what we want!' shouted the sergeant. The young Americans were at the dummies, and each dug his dummy with a wild 'Yah!' or college yell or scream. 'Go on!' roared the sergeant; 'there are more Boches beyond. Clean killing is what we want.' And the Americans charged at several more lines of dummies before they leapt into the front trench and began firing. This sort of exercise they do something like twenty times a day, from 8 a.m. to 4 p.m., but it is not always the same exercise. After one minute's breathing, British sergeants take them into a communication trench which has to be cleaned out. The sergeant shows them how, bayonet in hand, to peer round dug-outs and trenches. 'Now Fritz is there with a sausage! Fritz is no dud, he knows you may be coming. Get round him this way.' The American gets round and digs the dummy with a wild yell. How to creep through communication trenches, the different ways of bayoneting right and left, how not to show the point of the bayonet, how not to be caught by wily Fritz, the British sergeant explains with the same marvellous activity and verve. Then, again, the sergeant explains that monotony is a fatal thing in training.

All over the countryside in these splendid sweeping valleys and green woods, the American army is training with furious zest. To drive or walk in woods and fields is almost as dangerous as visiting front-line trenches. In every field, round every knoll, the American army is blazing away with rifles, guns, and machine-guns. Machine-gun parties with plenty of ammunition tear up and down a valley and from different points sweep the same poor old hill with rapid fire. There is very little left of the trees on the crest. Further on as one walks round the corner the officer signals hastily because we are almost in the line of the butts, against which American marksmen are shooting away. Good shots in the American army wear the word 'Marksman' in silver letters on their tunic, and one saw an astonishing number of these insignia worn. The countryside all round is ringing with gunfire, rifle fire, and the rattle of machine-guns. In another field a machine-gun party is doing a little 'resting'; that is, the boys are having a mule race in which they must pick up their hats on the way. Half a dozen of them fall off over and over again on hard ground, but they seem harder than the ground, and go on yelling with laughter all the time. There is nothing the matter with the 'morale' of the American Expeditionary Forces in France.

4 December 1917

AMERICANS IN ACTION

Engineers' Experiences, *War Correspondents' Headquarters, France, Sunday*

By Philip Gibbs

I had not time to tell yesterday of my meeting by chance a number of American railwaymen and engineers who had been engaged in construction work near Gouzeaucourt, and running up trains laden with supplies for our troops in the neighbourhood of Villers-Pluich and Villers-Guislain. I saw these men yesterday morning after they had been surrounded by the enemy for hours, and had then, with great cunning made their escape to our lines. They are a splendid body of men, hard and keen and good-humoured, who made a joke of their thrilling danger, which was not at an end, as the enemy was putting over heavy shells at odd moments, and one burst with an enormous explosion only 100 yards or so away from them when I stood among them.

'I guess I had a near call,' said one of them from St Louis, Missouri, and he told me how, when he was standing by his train, which had a full load of rations for the English troops, he was suddenly startled by shells bursting round his engine and saw the enemy approaching over the ridge by Villers-Guislain. 'One of your Tommies was standing near by,' said the American, 'and he bent down and picked up a bit of shrapnel and said, "Blowed if it ain't hot," and then he looked up again and said, "I'm blessed if old Fritz hasn't gone and broken through." Just as he said that a shell burst close, and the poor lad was killed, not an arm's length away from me. I guessed it was time to quit, and so I ran hard and found the enemy all round. So I took to hiding in a shell-hole and lay there until this morning.'

Four of his comrades in the engine crew had the same experience, and one was wounded in the thigh, but they all had the luck to escape. Another American engineman was first startled by a German aeroplane, which came straight down the track near Villers-Pluich, flying very low and firing a machine-gun. 'I hadn't a steel hat handy,' said this man, 'so I picked up a petrol tin and put that on my head, and thought it might be better than nothing. Then I saw Germans, and thought to myself "This is a queer kind of fix for a fellow from America laying rails behind the English lines," so I crouched down behind the engine and hoped the Germans wouldn't see me. I guess they didn't, or I shouldn't be here.'

Another American came up with a grin on his face. 'I'm from Tennessee,' he said, and he was a tall, lean, swarthy fellow, as like a Mexican cowboy as any fellow of that kind I have seen on the films. 'What happened to you?' I asked, and he told me that all sorts of things had happened to him since six o'clock the previous morning, but he hadn't time to tell the yarn, except that after his escape from the Germans, who were all round him, he got through and borrowed a Tommy's gun and fought all day with our infantry, and liked it. 'It's not the first time I've held a gun in my hand,' he said. 'I was in the Spanish–American War and other places. I guess I knocked out a few Boches for you.'

One of the American railway teams had their track blown up ahead of them by forward patrols of Germans, and these also tell me that they thought it time to quit, and quitted. But afterwards they formed part of some patrols who volunteered for service with our infantry, and so saw some very hard fighting with our Guards at Gouzeaucourt. Among them was a number of New York men. All these Americans showed a high and splendid spirit, and our men are loud in praise of them. 'It was the doggonest experience I have ever had,' said one of them, 'and a mighty close call anyway.' They had some casualties among them, but by good luck only a few.

7 December 1917

SECRET RETIREMENT

Surprise to the Enemy, *War Correspondents' Headquarters, France, Thursday*

By Philip Gibbs

The Commander-in-Chief has announced this afternoon in his official communiqué the news of our withdrawal from part of the ground captured in our advance on 20 November, in order to avoid holding the sharp salient made by Bourlon Wood and our line running down east and west of it. This operation has been very secretly done, and carried out with the greatest courage and discipline by our troops after the plan was decided. It was not an easy or safe thing to do, and its success depended on the enemy's complete ignorance of our intention and the valour of the rearguards holding on to their positions to the last possible moment, ready to fight hard until the main bodies of troops had withdrawn to our present line of defence. Any premature discovery might have led to immediate pressure of the enemy against our forward posts, and considerable danger to those falling back behind them. So far from this happening, the enemy was thoroughly deceived as to our intentions, and long after the withdrawal had been effected on our left yesterday morning he put down a heavy bombardment on the abandoned trenches near Mœuvres, and afterwards launched a strong infantry attack on those positions, watched at a distance by our troops, who chuckled at this furious advance upon mythical defenders. It seemed a huge joke to our men, whose sense of humour was sharpened by their sense of safety.

The withdrawal began the night before last. It was very cold and still over the battlefields, with a hard frost on the ground and a bright moon shining over its whiteness. But mist floated about the fields, and our men moved silently like shadows in it, and if the enemy saw any movement he did not suspect anything more than a relief. It was in the Bourlon Wood area that, as yesterday morning drew on, he first suspected a strange emptiness. He sent his patrols forward, and as they crept into the wood and south of Bourlon village they must have seen pretty quickly signs of our having packed up and gone. We left nothing behind, and destroyed the dug-outs and works which the enemy had built and we had occupied during the fortnight's adventure. At midday yesterday small bodies of Germans were seen advancing very cautiously over the rising ground south of Bourlon village, and half an hour later groups of them approached the ruins of the sugar factory, which had once been their balloon shed, near the Cambrai road. They hesitated here, did not seem to like the look of things, crept round and about, and then, spurring their courage, went inside. Later, after the news had been taken back or signalled back, strong forces of the enemy came forward, showing themselves on the sky-line and advancing in open order down the slope.

At one o'clock our artillery, which had been very quiet, waiting for their targets, opened fire, and swept this ground with shrapnel, so that all these standing figures fell, some of them killed or wounded, and all of them taking to earth. Our bombardment was maintained; but all through the day up to seven o'clock in the evening groups and scattered bodies of German troops were seen working southwards to get in touch with our new line of defence, which they could not locate. A little while after dusk yesterday about 400 of them were seen on the south side of the Cambrai road, and at nine o'clock our men saw another 300 on the south-east of Bourlon Wood. I hear that two prisoners were captured by our men from these forward patrols, and they said that three battalions of their regiment were all advancing in order to maintain pressure on our rearguards and get in contact, if possible, with our main line. All through the day hostile aeroplanes flew over our lines, trying to observe our new positions, but they could not have discovered what they wanted for long after our abandonment of Bourlon Wood and other positions around it the enemy heavily shelled these places. During the afternoon considerable bodies of men seemed to be assembling in the centre of our line for an assault in mass, but our guns dealt with them and shattered them where they were, under the cover of a sunken road.

This morning the enemy still seemed bewildered as to our exact positions and intentions. On our right wing yesterday there was violent fighting again around La Vacquerie, but the enemy's new thrust in that direction was repulsed after much killing of his men, and we pressed him back from some of the ground he had gained in the earlier fighting.

The events between 20 November and our strategical withdrawal from Bourlon Wood to our present line form one of the most thrilling and extraordinary episodes of this war. It began when Sir Julian Byng's audacious and cunning plan of attack, without a preliminary bombardment and with large numbers of tanks, stupefied the enemy with surprise and opened a wide breach in the Hindenburg line, through which our infantry and cavalry passed out into the open country round Cambrai and did amazing things which have not yet all been told, as, for instance, the story of German prisoners that some of our troopers actually rode into Cambrai itself on that first night of victory. Ten thousand prisoners were taken by us, and it is conceived that but for certain elements of bad luck Cambrai might have been ours, though it was not within our expectations. The enemy was quick in hurling up guns and reinforcements and developed violent counter-attacks. In all these he lost prodigiously in men, and the number of his casualties must have been extravagantly high, even according to the accounts given by his own prisoners. After all this fighting and one day of vicissitudes, during which the enemy had the luck to get through a weak place in our advanced lines and to overrun some of the country we had gained, we have withdrawn to strong positions on ground seized from the enemy in a cheap and easy way. Here we remain secure, with good observation and strong lines behind us.

18 December 1917

SNOW-CLAD FRONT

'A White Truce', *War Correspondents' Headquarters, France, Monday*

By Philip Gibbs

Last night snow began to fall over the British Armies in France, and this morning all the countryside is deep in snow. It has been blown across the roads in deep drifts by a wind with a wail in it, and lies piled against the banks in beautiful whiteness. The old villages of France where British soldiers are billeted are pictured as in a fairy-book with their thatched roofs like the tops of sugarcakes, and their old beams and shutters tipped with ermine. The white mantle lies over all the fields unspotted with any smudge of black except where crowds of crows are gathered about the haystacks. The woods are wonderful with all the tracery of their branches and twigs outlined in white, and all their undergrowth heavy with big bunches of snowflakes overhanging like the petals of chrysanthemums. The peace of the white, cold world seems to have come over the fields of war, where all the ugliness of human strife, all the slaughter of beauty, all this smashing of decent things, all the death of youth is covered up by this veil of snow, upon which for a little while the sun is shining – a pale cold sun – so that there is a glamour of light and shimmer of crystals over the landscape. And the great hush, the queer stillness that comes after a snowfall has fallen upon the war zone. The very guns seem silent for once, as though sleeping under the white counterpane that hides their ugly snouts. For a few hours this morning anyhow there was a white truce because the aeroplanes could see nothing in the scudding clouds of snowflakes, and could not spot for the batteries.

'Any news?' was the usual morning question at headquarters, and over the wires presently came the answer, 'Nothing of special interest to report.' There had been a quiet night on the front, except for the howl of the wind. Some of us set out this morning for Arras, where the modern prison is a rag of ruin, and did not get there because of the snow. There must have been many officers and men who set out on a journey today or last night, and did not get to the end of it because of the snow. My journey ended in a drift blown to 3ft deep across the road, with a chauffeur who said, 'Well, that's done it!' and a car which struggled with a brave panting heart to get out of this soft obstruction, and skidded the bank every time. So that meant a long walk back to a snowed-up house remote from all the war because of this barrier of whiteness which closes it in. For an hour or two there is an illusion that the snowstorm has stopped the war, like a spirit of peace, in a white shroud, which has spread its wings over the world and over the slaughter fields. It is only an illusion, and in a little while this snow will melt into rivers of mud, as it did last year, and in the mud there may be fighting again.

'It makes Christmas seem nearer than ever,' said an officer this morning. 'The world is like a Christmas card.' For the first time one is beginning to think of Christmas, though it is only a week away; and somehow this snow and this cessation of fierce fighting makes it seem more reasonable. The small shops in the French villages behind the lines – some of them are built of wood, between streets of ruined houses, left behind in the wake of war – are exhibiting trinkets and painted cards and toys, and Christmas dainties, as though nothing had happened in the last few years to lower the morale of Santa Claus. And fellows who have had fighting a day or two ago, who still wear the steel hats with which they fought at Masnières and Marcoing, and up by Bourlon Wood, stare in at these windows and wonder what they will buy their best girl or for the kids at home. I came upon a group of them the other day in a biggish town through which the French and English pass on their way along the roads of war. There was a Jock with the scarlet hackle of the Black Watch in his bonnet, and an English soldier who, by his way of speech, came from my town, which is no mean city, and three French Poilus, who were with a Zouave in his baggy red breeches. 'There ain't much choice in Christmas gifts in this blinking town,' said the English soldier, 'but a bit of that lace might please the missus. It's like the stuff the old geezer used to make on Kemmel Hill. What do you think, Jock?' 'Ay,' said the Scot, 'it's a bonny wee thing, but they'll ask you a fearful price, man.' ''Ang the expense,' said the London man. 'After all, there is a war on, Jock, and don't you forget it.' 'Forget it,' said the Scot, 'they keep reminding me of it.'

Such conversations are taking place now round many queer little shops behind the lines, and men just relieved from the line are looking forward to Christmas and the New Year with just as much of the old sentiment as though the spirit of peace had not been blown to blazes by high explosives. In the EFC canteens and those of the YMCA farsighted men are already laying in stores of supplies for company messes before the rush comes, and the mess sergeants are going a-marketing with new light of enthusiasm in their eyes, which has inspired hope in the breasts of the old ladies who sit among the pigs and poultry. That is where the luck is – behind the lines. Up in the trenches the prospect of Christmas is not warming to men who are standing to with their feet in newly fallen snow, and whose hands are numb as they hold their rifles and gaze over the parapet in No Man's Land, where the snow is drifting into the shell-holes and furring the barbed wire, and where the wind comes howling like big shells in flight. The only comfort is the thought that if Fritz has any dirty work on hand when the thaw comes, he will get stuck in the mud with his guns and his men.

Chapter 9

War Miscellany

14 August 1914

BRITTANY IN WARTIME
'Vive Les Anglais'

By An English Lady

The doors of the glorious cathedral of Dol were wide open. Its fine spaces were quite deserted. Out of the dim shadows came the organ strains of a sonata by Schubert. In the rich cornfields, laden this year with an exceptionally fine crop, the apple trees afforded a strange sight for English eyes. Vast spaces of purple vetch and pink clover, growing together, made a combination of colour that the most daring of our neo-impressionists would despair to emulate. The peace of God seemed to be on this beautiful land of Brittany.

Later, as we sat at the little café, a spectacled curate of the Established Church translated laboriously from a French newspaper the news of the Austrian advance on Servia. He talked in pulpit tones, and his words went beyond his listening companion and reached our table. They were the first hint of war in this peaceful land. Our next stopping-place was a garrison town. Hussars and artillerymen, a kaleidoscope of blue and red and silver, occupied the town. The air was filled with murmurs of war between France and Germany. And the one question on the lips of all men and women alike was 'Will England help?' The sturdy, hard-bitten, pious-pious, whose lack of uniformity in the matter of beards and moustaches is something of a shock to the orderly English mind, discussed it among themselves, and gave the only possible answer. The officers, sitting at the tables in the little café of our hotel, debated the subject, and could only come to one conclusion.

Yet there was one day – a day of doubt – when we waited with anxious hearts, knowing all the time, however, that England could not desert this noble people in its hour of peril. What splendid men these cavalry officers were – elegant, yet not dandified – in spite of wrist watch and monocle – extraordinary distinction of manner and bearing, graceful, charming – but, above all, men. Then came the great transformation – and in one instant the shadow of war overspread the land. We had gone to the railway station to ask about the trains to our next stopping-place, Morlaix. The station was closed, the train service, too, had been suspended, and was to be used only for the transport of troops and stores – a woman outside the station was weeping because she could not reach the next town to say goodbye to her son.

The night that mobilisation was proclaimed we went to the principal café of the town. From the Hotel de Ville, hard by, came the strains of the 'Marseillaise', and the vast crowds outside took up the wonderful melody. People in the café echoed it, and we shouted with them 'Vive la France'; they cheered and cheered again. A moment later the band struck up 'God Save the King'. Immediately the group of French officers who had been seated during the 'Marseillaise' sprang to their feet and stood at the salute until the notes had died away. The applause from the crowd was almost frantic. We made our way into the street, and the people noted the unusually tall fair man with me; the cry went up, 'Vive les Anglais', in a moment it became a roar of welcome, and of trust, and of hope, and confidence.

We made our way back to the hotel, followed by a cheering crowd, half of whom it seemed had been shaking our hands vigorously, the other half uttering cries that would have brought a sense of pride to the most phlegmatic Englishman. There was exhilaration, but no 'mafficking', either that night or during the next three days. Nor was there any sign of depression – only a sense of quiet and grim determination. For two days a constant stream of peasants came into the town leading their horses – the peasant with one horse which meant more than half his means of livelihood, the horse that fetched and carried and drew his plough – the more prosperous farmer with two horses, perhaps three. All were wanted for the great war machine and were delivered uncomplainingly on the altar of the country's needs. For two days it was an incessant coming and going of dapper remount officers and of veterinary surgeons, standing the accepted animals. A race meeting was to have been held on Sunday; it was cancelled. And the next day we saw the string of horses led through the town in charge of the soldiery. A huge open-air fête and ball, too, was to have been held that night. There was no dance. The floor was torn up, and in the morning 500 horses were picketed in the space. What a wonderful exodus had begun!

The men departed on their stern duty with smiling faces, the women repressed their tears. But at night, in the darkness … There was a farm near by, and the farmer and his three sons had gone. In the dusk I knocked, but no answer came. There was a sound from the cow-house. I entered. The farmer's wife was milking the one cow. Her head lay against the animal. Her whole body limp. She went mechanically on with her task. And as she spoke her voice was terrible to hear. She did not weep, but her sobs came pitifully through these staccato phrases, the disjointed words. She had given her husband and three sons to France. She could not weep.

The new exodus was complete. Not only had the middle-aged men gone to the front, but there seemed an amazing dearth of young women – only old women and children and quite old men were left. The effects became apparent very quickly. First the hotel-keeper had to collect stores in small quantities, the buying of a score of eggs meant application at a dozen farmhouses, the delicious little breakfast rolls were no longer to be had; the man who made them had gone to the war. In place of the fresh Brittany butter we were offered a substitute so rank and nasty that we deposited it gently outside our rooms. Three days after the declaration of war we were eating, or trying to eat, musty bread made from obviously mildewed flour, and even that threatened to be unobtainable on the morrow. Still there was no grumbling. The priests, in their cassocks and shovel hats, drove off to the war to take their place in the ranks like all the citizens of France.

One day we got a newspaper, a half-sheet of coarse, yellowish paper, but it told of the Belgians' glorious defence at Liège. But there was no demonstration outside the Hotel de Ville. There was nobody left to demonstrate. My friend, the tall, fair Englishman, offered the 'rag' to a group of five officers at the table opposite. Instantly they were on their feet and at the salute. When we left they saluted again. To be English was to be honoured, and it was impossible not to feel a thrill of pride in the universal evidence of faith in and gratitude to the British people, once more France's companion in arms.

When we reluctantly made up our minds to leave we went to the bank. The gates were being shut, but we told our errand. We were English. We were welcomed inside; they changed English banknotes, and paid 25 francs for each pound. And the air of courtesy and goodwill with which this unusual act of kindness was performed was indescribable.

Now to get to St Malo, 40 kilometres away. With great difficulty we found a pair-horsed brake, and the journey began. Two French flags and a Union Jack, the latter discovered with difficulty, decorated the carriage, which made a sort of triumphal progress through this pleasant land. Pathetic beyond words was the sight of the wonderful landscape. Some of the fine crops had been cut, and much that was stacked was mildewing because there was no one to gather it in. Here and there an old woman was bending in the fields, cutting the corn. It almost brought tears to one's eyes to watch the feeble efforts. One of the party said it was like watching an old man trying to cut down an oak tree with a pair of nail scissors. They said that elderly men from Paris and other large towns would come and cut the crops in answer to the beautiful appeal made by the Minister of Agriculture calling for volunteers to do this work, so that the splendid peasants of France who had gone to the front might know that the fruits of their labour had not been wasted.

As the old brake rumbled through the villages all those who were left came to their doorways and shouted 'Vive les Anglais', and clapped their hands and wished us God-speed. It was an enchanted journey with this frank and open evidence of affection and trust. We were a fiercely proud party as we bumped over the uneven road and strove like good Britishers to hide our emotion.

15 August 1914

ENGLISH TOURISTS IN GERMANY
Sir John Hare's Experiences

By Sir John Hare

I left London on 22 July, before anyone – at any rate, at home – was talking of war. When we reached Cologne all the people there were charming; three weeks later we returned to that city practically prisoners.

At Homburg, at first, we found things just as usual. There were not many English visitors, but many were expected.

As the days passed, some uneasiness was caused by the political outlook, but when we expressed a desire to leave for London influential people advised us on no account to do so, as the railway lines were occupied by troops.

Immediately after the mobilisation, so we were told, the Government would place a train at our disposal. With that assurance we had to be content.

What first created anxiety in our minds was an order that all Russians should be collected together at the Hotel Augusta, outside which sentries were posted.

In that hotel were a few English people, including Miss Clark, a Scottish friend of hers Miss Bing, and Lord Egerton of Tatton. These were ordered to go to the Hotel Victoria, at the doors of which sentries were also posted, ingress and egress being barred.

During this time the attitude of the inhabitants was not really hostile. Beyond once or twice having fists shaken in our faces nothing happened. The party with whom I was so intimately to be associated were fortunate in having an influential and distinguished friend.

We heard a rumour on the Tuesday that all the English were to leave Homburg on the following afternoon. That evening Colonel Calley, late of the 1st Life Guards, dined with us at Richard's Hotel. 'We shall meet tomorrow,' he said, when we parted. We did not meet. I now fear that he is confined in a German fortress.

At eleven o'clock at night our friend sent a special message, imploring us to be at the railway station at five in the morning.

When we reached the station in the grey of the dawn we found that those who had been interned in the Hotel Victoria were not there. That unfortunate party included, amongst others, I believe, Miss Clark, Lady Violet Greville, Mr Leveson-Gower, and Lord Joicey, who, I am glad to hear, has since returned to England.

Mr Crawford, the clergyman of the English Church, his wife, and son joined our party. Mr and Mrs Crawford were allowed to leave, but their son was detained, the official reason given being that he was of military age. There was another reason which I cannot give. I may add here that later Mr and Mrs Crawford could not be found by us when we re-assembled to leave Cologne. Like Colonel Calley, they had disappeared.

Our friend aided us greatly in our railway journey, but we were ordered not to show our faces at the windows of the carriages or the guarded waiting-rooms in which we were placed. We were also warned not to talk more English than was necessary.

But let me say that the officers and men of the German army treated us with the greatest courtesy. The officials of the train by which we finally neared Cologne were of a different stamp. When we were four miles from that city, but within the radius of its fortress, they turned us out of the train on to a platform. There we remained, men and women, till eleven o'clock next morning. We were unable to lie down on the platform, and were forbidden to enter the waiting-rooms.

Finally, when we reached the city, we found that the Governor had issued an order that no Englishman was to be allowed to leave. From the moment of our arrival till the time we did depart was one long period of tension.

We learned that a steamer was, on the following morning, to take those who had permits to Rotterdam. Even with the aid of the American Consul, it was almost impossible, by speech or letter, to get our requests for permits laid before the Governor. That we succeeded in achieving our object must to a large extent be attributed to the indefatigable energy and influence of Lord William Cecil. Indeed, my chief desire in writing this, is that I may, on behalf of myself and the whole of the thirty-five English fugitives of our party, acknowledge the large debt of gratitude that we owe to Lord and Lady William Cecil, who were the shepherd and shepherdess of our little flock.

When we had obtained our permits, Lord William Cecil, at very considerable risk to himself, went round, at midnight, to every hotel in which members of our party were living – and even routed people out of their beds – so that he might make known the time of the departure of the boat. Lady William Cecil, by her cheerfulness and courage, set an example to all the women of our party, who, without exception, behaved with the utmost courage, patience, and endurance.

We left our hotel in the grey of the morning, feeling like a set of criminals. At the boat – where we missed Mr and Mrs Crawford – we were refused permission to leave, notwithstanding that our permits were signed by the Governor, passed by the police, and endorsed by the Dutch Consul. We were told that we could not go on board, because no authority had arrived from the police. For some minutes we suffered agonising doubt and dread.

At last the necessary permission was received by telephone from the police, and I need hardly say with what relief we saw, soon after, the spires of Cologne grow dim.

Even then our troubles were not ended. Passenger vessels were not running from Rotterdam to Flushing. Through the intervention of Sir George Armytage, who was also of our party, we were, however, able to make the voyage on a cattle-boat, and for the second night the unfortunate ladies of our party – they had to remain on deck – were practically without shelter.

And so, guarded by the battleships of England, we reached home in safety, thankful to God for his mercies, our happiness being only clouded by the knowledge that so many of our countrymen and women were left behind to the tender mercies of our enemies.

23 November 1914

THE PRESENT STATE OF GERMANY
Plans and Resources

By An American

Of course, it is hopeless to expect to find accurate information in the Press of any country in a great war such as the struggle in which the European Powers are now engaged. If you stay in one country for any length of time, you are certain to lose your proper sense of perspective, because you will naturally be reading purely one-sided reports, which cannot be checked in any way by seeing for yourself what relation they have to the true facts in the country to which they refer. When I left England for Germany I expected to find that country, and more especially Berlin, a city of the dead. I expected to find the whole German nation in mourning, and the population depressed by the repeated failure of the army to obtain decisive successes over the Allies after the tremendous sacrifices which have been made.

On my arrival in Berlin I found my preconceived ideas immediately falsified. I have known Berlin for many years, and yet I could notice very little change in the life of the capital. The hotels and restaurants are open, and are doing a very big business. So also are the theatres and operas. The most marked difference was the vast number of troops one saw in the streets. I made most careful inquiries and found there were 70,000 men of the Landwehr, all in the younger thirties, who had recently been called up to the colours. As far as I could discover, none of these men had yet been in action. Never before have I seen so many soldiers in Berlin. To me as an American the Germans were extremely civil.

Every facility was given me to carry on the investigations I most desired to make, and both the military and Foreign Office officials treated me with a frankness which was truly remarkable. From the first I realised the danger of only hearing one point of view. I therefore have taken the greatest pains to check every statement made to me by comparing it with the views held by all classes of the population, from the man in the street to the small government employee, the upper classes in society, and the middle classes. I have also talked with a great number of American Consuls and others whose business has compelled them to remain in Germany during the war. The opinions which I now set forth represent my considered opinions after careful study of all the subjects with which I deal.

First of all, let me deal with the attitude of the German people as opposed to the Prussian military clique, of which we read so much in the English papers. It would be a great mistake for the English nation to deceive themselves on this subject. I have seen the intense patriotism of the English people and of the French. I have realised most forcibly their unbending determination to carry this war through to a successful conclusion, and not to make peace until they have obtained those terms which they believe necessary to secure lasting peace in Europe in the future. Let me say at once that the patriotism and determination of the Germans is not one whit behind that of the Allies.

At no time have the Emperor and the Crown Prince been more popular than at the present. At no time has the personal ascendancy or influence of the Emperor been greater. Even the extreme Socialists have joined hands with the Prussian Junker to see the war through. Those who expect to see a sudden outburst of Socialism which will force the Government to make peace are living in a fool's paradise. In just such a one were the Germans living when they believed the outbreak of war would be the signal for an insurrection in Ireland. Amongst the various German tribes the war is equally popular. There is no chance of the Bavarians, Saxons, or Wurtemburgers breaking away from Prussia. All intend to stand or fall together.

The German people are firmly convinced that this war has been forced upon them. They produce diplomatic correspondence to show that France had an arrangement with Belgium for the passage of her troops through that country. They entirely overlook the fact that this understanding was contingent on the violation of the neutrality of Belgian soil by the German army. They point to the fact that the English Fleet was ready for hostilities and fully mobilised prior to the declaration of war. As proof of their own innocence they point to the shortage of certain essential commodities at the present time owing to their trade routes being closed. They maintain that had they known war was certain they would have laid by ample supplies of these particular articles, with which I shall deal later. By this process of reasoning they manage to deceive themselves even if they do not deceive anyone else.

It is impossible to realise the extent of their hatred against England. This blind obsession has caused them to forget their former anger against France and Russia. They act and talk about England just like a spoilt child behaves over something it desires above all else, yet cannot get. Nevertheless, to be just, nothing could have been more generous than the tributes of the German Press on the day the death of Lord Roberts was announced. This hatred of England is extended to Japan, whom the Germans hate even more than they detest the English. The loss of Kiao-chau has affected them far more than any other event in the war. Because they know that whatever happens they can never hope to regain this, their only possession in the Far East, which was the Emperor's peculiar conception, handiwork, and pride. He loves to pose before Orientals, and now England and Japan have shown him up, which he will never forgive.

I myself am firmly convinced that the German people intend to fight to the finish, and that nothing will induce them to give in until they run short of certain essentials which I shall name later. I will quote you the remark of an old Countess whom I know. On my visiting her she said: 'Of my three sons whom you formerly know, two are dead, and the other is wounded. I have only one regret, and that is that I have not three more to fight for the Fatherland.'

There is one fact which must strike any impartial observer of Germany during the present crisis, and that is the inexhaustible supply of men which she seems to possess. The authorities themselves are surprised at the vast number of volunteers who have come forward, which has exceeded all their previous expectations. These are men who, from some slight ailment, have been able to escape the conscription or who have been excused for other reasons. I was shown the various strengths of the army at different times during the campaign.

At the present moment the Germans have sixty-eight corps fully mobilised, each of an average strength, of 43,000 men of all arms. This, you will see, makes nearly 3,000,000 of men fully mobilised in the field. I have read in England that there were twenty-nine active corps under arms and twenty-nine of the Reserve. The military authorities have, however, created ten fresh corps out of the surplus of the Landwehr and from the vast numbers of volunteers who have come forward. They claim they have applications from no fewer than 2,000,000 volunteers, but this, I think, is an exaggeration, and also great numbers of them are probably not fit to take the field at all, but they can be employed in guarding the lines of communication and on other light work. They claim that they have ample reserves to fill up the gaps in the ranks of these sixty-eight corps for a long time to come from the volunteers and from the class of 1915 who are now training at the depots.

To my certain knowledge, very large numbers of the Landsturm have not yet been called up, and comparatively few of this class have been sent to the front, although, as a fair number were sent to Belgium, they may have been locally absorbed in the firing line. The 70,000 men of the Landwehr I saw in Berlin were excellent troops, keen, and anxious to fight. Of course, I could not find out which was their destination, the East or the West. There is, in fact, a continuous movement of troops in Germany, both from East to West and from West to East.

I tried to find out the reasons for this, but the only explanation I got from the authorities was a strange one. They told me they were continually changing the units from one front to another, as they found the journey in the train rested the men and removed them for a time from the firing line. Also they found it an excellent practice to give the troops a change of scene, as they became stale if kept in one place for too long. Of the distribution of the German armies, I could obtain but little accurate information except this. They have roughly one million and a quarter men along the Eastern Front, from East Prussia to Cracow.

Now let me deal briefly with the subject of the German losses. These have been immense, but according to the statements made to me they have been greatly exaggerated in the Allied Press. I was shown all the available figures up to the time I left Berlin, and I was able to check them myself. They then totalled almost exactly 950,000 men killed, wounded, and missing. Their losses on the Western Front have been vastly greater than those on the Eastern. This number of nearly a million, of course, includes a very large number of slightly wounded men, who have either rejoined the colours or are being kept on light duty until their recovery is complete. It is a great mistake to suppose that the Germans are so downhearted as has been represented by this tremendous loss of life. The people are so bitterly against the English that all other ideas appertaining to humanity and suffering seem to be temporarily driven out of their heads.

Responsible German opinion on the war up to date is extremely interesting to study. The educated Germans, who really know what has happened, readily admit that their original plans of campaign have hopelessly miscarried. They are extremely disappointed at the failure of their armies to occupy Paris. They feel that this would have given them a great moral victory, if not a final one. They attributed their failure to occupy the capital to Von Kluck's decision to march on the Marne. Von Kluck's explanation is that he was afraid of being outflanked and surrounded if he entered Paris with the French armies still undefeated on his right flank.

The Germans are again bitterly disappointed at the failure of their armies to seize the coast and occupy Calais. Nevertheless, I was amazed to find that even the military authorities had far from abandoned hope, and were very confident that this, their later goal, would be reached some time in December. There is one fact which both the German military and civil mind seems incapable of grasping. This is the futility of throwing away lives in continual offensive movements long after all real hope of their ultimate success has vanished. In this lies the great hope of the Allies. The German armies are slowly, but none the less surely, exhausting themselves in a series of minor offensive movements long after the only pre-arranged grand offensive conceived before the war has failed.

I could discover few traces of great anxiety amongst either the officials or civilian classes over the Russian advance in East Prussia and through Poland. The Germans do not underrate the prowess or skill or numbers of the Russians, but they are firmly convinced they can easily hold back the enemy, even although he may pass their frontier at points. They maintain that the Russians have too many natural obstacles to overcome, that they cannot concentrate a sufficiently large army to overcome their fortresses and defensive line, and that the Germans, aided by their strategic railways, will be able to make up for shortage of numbers by increased mobility. They expect easily to hold the Russians along or in advance of the line Dantzig–Thorn–Posen–Breslau, covered by the Rivers Vistula and Varta.

The ground along this front is favourable for defence, and has been fully prepared. They say that the battles in Poland have been greatly exaggerated, and that they only fought a delaying action, which caused them but small loss. The military authorities also maintain that even if this line is forced and their field armies are obliged to retreat, they will be able to guard Berlin by holding the line of the Oder, which is immensely strong, as the positions on the left bank command those on the right.

Although the Germans claim that they still mean to continue their offensive in France and Belgium, I am inclined to think this is really a bluff to cover the construction of two great defensive lines in Belgium. Those who believe that at any moment the Germans may abandon their conquest and fall back to the Rhine are likely to be wrong. They will hold on to Belgium at all costs. It is the *sine qua non* of their whole policy, now they realise the great campaign against the French has failed. They mean, in fact, to keep Belgium, or, rather, all the east of that country, as their final asset with which to negotiate for peace. They know, if they abandon Belgium, that when it comes to talking over a settlement, they have absolutely nothing to offer the Allies by way of exchange.

To meet all emergencies, in case they are obliged to abandon their present positions, they are constructing two great lines of defence. The outer one stretches from Antwerp, west of Brussels, to the French frontier at Maubeuge, which is the salient of the angle. The other is the line of the Somme and the Meuse, and the mountainous region of the Ardennes. They are confident that the Allies will never be strong enough to drive them from the latter position, even if they are obliged to abandon their present line, and the one stretching from Antwerp to Maubeuge. But, mind you, they are only preparing these two positions for unforeseen emergencies. They have not abandoned hope of gaining decisive successes in France and Western Flanders. They told me, as proof of the preconceived hostility of England towards Germany, that they have recently captured English maps of Germany which are far better and more detailed than any they possess themselves.

Generally speaking, the German military party hold their Austrian ally somewhat cheaply. There are some who even go so far as to declare that they could get on better without Austria's help. I have recently had reports from Vienna which do not seem to show that the war has yet made much impression on the Austrian capital. The life continues in much the same manner as in London and Berlin. The Germans stoutly declare that the reports of the Austrian defeats and losses in Galicia have been grossly exaggerated. They maintain that the Austrians are like a racehorse which in a race suddenly falls off, but comes again with its second wind. The Austrian army, they maintain, is still full of fight, and has entirely recovered from its recent reverses and retirements.

The Germans rely on the constant intervention of the Austrians on the Russian flank in any attempt to invade Germany through Poland, and also of the resistance of Cracow, which will guard the road to Breslau for a long time to come. I have noticed that all German plans for a defensive campaign against Russia are based on their own powers of resistance alone, and do not include any aid which Austria may be able to lend. The Germans still hope great things from the powerful Austrian armies, but they are building no castles in the air which may crumble away if these hopes are not realised.

In my opinion, Germany has very large supplies of men to keep the war going for an indefinite period. I do not believe there will be any collapse in her credit or finances during the duration of the struggle. Her recent war loan was subscribed four times over, in spite of contradictory statements which have appeared from time to time in the Press. If we hope to get any true perspective on the probable duration of the struggle we must turn to her material resources and examine how they stand. Of this subject I have made a most careful study, and will give you a summary of my considered opinions.

There is absolutely no shortage of food supplies in the country. Both of wheat and rye and meat there is plenty. Germany in normal times provides 78 per cent of her own foodstuffs. But she also exports, and as the export of food has been stopped by law she has no difficulty in feeding her entire population. The crop this year was one of the best on record. Where Germany will fail is in those articles essential to war which require raw material which she cannot produce herself. I have seen great hopes placed on the failure of her supply of petrol. These hopes are ill-founded. The officials assure me there is still enough petrol in the country to last for another year and a half. My own personal investigations bear out this statement.

On the other hand, everyone admits that there is a terrible scarcity of rubber. This cannot be obtained, and there were no large supplies in the country when war was declared. There are hardly any private cars now running in Berlin. Unless owners laid in a stock of tyres previous to the war they cannot now obtain them. The sale of rubber has been absolutely prohibited in any shape or form. Even India-rubber balls such as children play with are no longer obtainable.

More serious still is the shortage of copper, which is essential for the manufacture of shells and ammunition. The Germans are very alarmed at their failure to obtain any further supplies of this all-precious material. They simply do not know which way to turn for it.

I have every reason to believe that the supply of gunpowder is causing the General Staff the gravest anxiety. They lack saltpetre and the nitrates necessary for its manufacture. They carefully avoid giving direct answers to all questions on this subject and prefer to turn them away with some feeble excuse. When asked why they are using old ammunition they state, 'We wish to get rid of it.' I do not mean to imply that there are not still immense reserves of ammunition in the country, but from my inquiries I am convinced that even on a scale vastly below the present they will be unable to carry on the war for this reason alone after next June. I am sure that the most vital considerations of this struggle are Germany's lack of copper and gunpowder or the essentials necessary to make the various explosives now in use.

I have talked with many Germans over the question of the inactivity of their fleet. I have pointed out that there is not a single case in the history of naval warfare where a fleet which had allowed itself to be blockaded has ever emerged safely or with credit from the struggle. I am convinced that the Germans will do anything rather than seriously risk their fleet in a general action. They regard its safety and retention intact as being essential to any peace negotiations with the Allies. They would rather lose large stretches of land than risk the total destruction of this weapon peculiarly forged for use against England. I consider it extremely improbable that the Germans will come out and really fight at sea. They may attempt short excursions and raids, but will never risk having their lines of communication cut.

In their inner hearts the German official classes realise quite well that there can only be one result to the present struggle in Europe. They know, in fact, that they are beaten. They realise that the odds against them are too great. They are fighting now to obtain the best terms possible. They are determined to fight to the bitter end rather than yield, and they are equally determined to hold on to Belgium and to preserve their fleet, as they are the only two weapons left with which they can obtain favourable terms. They hope by prolonging the war to exhaust the patience and endurance of the Allies. They hope to offer such a strenuous resistance on both frontiers that, rather than continue the war, the Allies will meet them half-way.

I have spoken with many who frankly admit they expect to lose Alsace and part of Lorraine. On their eastern frontier they expect to lose part of East Prussia, so that Russia can straighten out her frontier. They expect Austria to lose Galicia for a like reason. All they hope is to preserve the unity of Germany and to save what remains of the empire. The official classes, society, in fact, all those who know, keep up a smiling face. At heart they are in despair, because they know that, however long they continue their resistance, before a year is out the lack of certain essentials in the destruction of mankind will bring them up against a stone wall, in which there is no exit except by the acknowledgment of their defeat.

26 November 1914

ARRIVAL OF THE SANTA CLAUS SHIP
Reception at Devonport, *Devonport, Wednesday Night*

In all the history of the comity of nations there has been no such event as the despatch of the ship loaded with gifts from the children of America for those little ones whose fathers are now in the battle line. Fitting was it that its reception at Devonport this afternoon should have unique honours worthy of so notable an occasion. All the distinction that the Government and both Services could accord was manifested in an official welcome by Earl Beauchamp, Lord President of the Council, and by naval and military guards of honour.

Only the weather was unkind. Grey fog robbed the arrival of much of the significant pageantry that would have marked the incoming, and at the actual berthing rain was falling. Many rumours were afloat as to the time that the *Jason*, an auxiliary of the navy of the United States, might be expected. For the last six days she had been in wireless touch with Poldhu, the Eiffel Tower, and some of the German war stations, and last night it was confidently affirmed that noon today would see her in the Hamoaze.

As a matter of fact she slipped quietly into Cawsand Bay at eight o'clock this morning, and in the fog there was not the escort of torpedo-boats that had been expected. Flag Captain Back, on behalf of Admiral Sir George Egerton, Commander-in-Chief, and Mr Carter, who, on behalf of Lord Beauchamp, has made the local arrangements, paid an early visit to the ship on an Admiralty launch. As far as the limited number of privileged spectators who were able to go over the ship were concerned, the real interest began at No. 1 berth of the Prince of Wales basin, immediately below the Royal Naval Barracks.

Surely in all the wildest imaginations no one ever conceived a vessel so unlike the pre-conceived idea of what a Santa Claus ship could be, for she is the latest word in the construction of a naval coaling ship, and can fill up two cruisers or battleships with coal in a day. Ranged along her very long decks are ten pairs of cranes. Their heavy iron supports suggest nothing so much as the supports for a mighty bridge as yet unfinished, and it was also not inaptly that a spectator compared her to a floating wharf.

No one, indeed, at first could believe that this was the ship at all, but imagined it to be something connected with urgent naval construction. Very slowly she was brought round by an immensely strong steel hawser. Then it was seen that she was not displaying the flag bearing the Star of Bethlehem, and the single word 'Inasmuch', that it had been stated she would fly. But this was due to the perfectly correct naval etiquette of the occasion, which demands that a ship entering the dockyard of another Power shall only display her own flag or ensign. Hence it was simply under the Stars and Stripes that she came in.

Hardly had she made fast before Admiral Egerton, accompanied by his flag captain and secretary, went on board and greeted cordially Commander Courtney, of the United States Navy. The gallant officer is already known to many in the Royal Navy, as he was on Admiral Seymour's staff in the troubles in Pekin. All the officers of the *Jason*, it may be said here, belong to the American Navy. On board, too, were Mr John Callan O'Loughlin, on behalf of the American Government, and Mr Stopley. Almost immediately there came on board the brilliant procession which expressed the official significance of the whole reception. Earl Beauchamp himself was followed by Major-General A. Penton, the fortress commander, and several of the principal military officers now stationed at Devonport. The Mayor, Mr King Baker, the Town Clerk, Mr J. H. Ellis, and several members of the Corporation gave civic recognition to the proceedings, and Major Astor, MP for the borough, was also present.

Lord Beauchamp at once proceeded up the gangway, and together with all the officers stood at the salute while the band played 'The Star-Spangled Banner'. There were then no further formalities. Commander Courtney conducted all to the ward room, showing the general plan of the ship and explaining something of the cargo that she conveys as a demonstration of the sympathy of youthful America in the sorrows that the war is causing in so many families. One and another told the full tale of the gracious enterprise that has established a new sense of united purpose among the States. It originated in the columns of the *Chicago Record Herald*, but no fewer than 200 papers up and down the vast continent took up and commended the idea. As a result, something like 8,000 tons of cigarettes were poured in, taxing the resources of Chicago to such an extent that the army authorities were first asked to allow 100 soldiers to assist in the work of sorting and classifying them, and later a further request for a like number of sailors had to be made.

To come down to yet more striking figures, there were something like 5,000,000 separate articles. Among them are vast cases filled with caps for boys and Tam o'shanters for girls. There are frocks and coats, blouses, stockings, under-garments, boots, and the various items of wear; indeed, Mr O'Loughlin calculates that quite 80 per cent of the contributions are of useful character, but the lighter side has not been overlooked. Toys there are in good supply, and as for the dolls, Mr O'Loughlin could only say that they have given to hundreds of lonely women a new interest in life to dress them for the little children of the war.

There is a fair amount of clothing for women and some for men. The great aim has been as regards the distribution to make an equitable apportionment, so as to prevent any one of the countries to be benefited from receiving too much or too little of any one class of gifts. Some food there is also, notably in the form of flour and apples, these latter being the special offering of the kindly growers of Spokane, Washington, but there is not a State that has not shared in the generous offering to the war-stricken Old World, not a child who has not had a new and practical interest given to it by the collaboration of little friends or playmates, even if for any reason it could not make a contribution actually of its own.

The American Government, in its rigidly correct attitude of neutrality, rightly insisted that all the belligerents should share fairly in the children's tribute of love; hence, as soon as the share allotted to Great Britain is discharged the *Jason* will go to Marseilles, or possibly Bordeaux, with the presents for the little French and Belgian folk. The gifts for Austria and Germany are to be landed at Genoa. As the *Jason* could not be detached long enough from her special service to convey the gifts for Russia those will be taken by way of Archangel in a merchant ship.

Thus has come to Europe an olive-branch of love from the boys and girls of America, a sweet message of goodwill in this Christmas, when the cannons' roar is drowning the gentler music we have associated with the season. Though peace still may be far off, 'a little child shall lead them to think of the friendship and kindness of the great American nation towards all the sad hearts of Europe, to take courage and to be of good hope'.

14 December 1914

GERMAN OFFICER IN A PACKING CASE
Attempted Escape, *Gravesend, Sunday*

Lieutenant Otto Koehn, of the German army, was a prisoner of war in England. By an ingenious device he almost succeeded in getting unobserved aboard a steamer at Tilbury about to sail for Holland. His scheme failed at the eleventh hour, and he is once more in safe custody.

Koehn, according to his own story, had tired of being a prisoner of war, and desired to reach Germany to take his place in the fighting line. He voluntarily imprisoned himself in a large case artfully secured from the exterior, but capable of being opened from inside.

Provided with food, a blanket, and an air-cushion, and curled up in his case, the man travelled from Dorchester to the deck of the steam ferry *Katherine*, in the Thames, at Tilbury. The captain of the *Katherine*, which at the time was acting as tender to the SS *Batavia V*, witnessed the discovery of Koehn, and told me the story this afternoon at his home at Gravesend.

It is necessary, in order to place the facts in their proper sequence, to begin at Dorchester. There a number of Germans have been interned, and arrangements were completed for certain of them who were incapacitated by age or ill health from military service to be sent home.

On Friday night a party of these prisoners arrived in London from Dorchester, and were sent off from Fenchurch-street station to Tilbury. With them was a considerable quantity of luggage, which, on reaching Tilbury Railway Station, was placed upon trolleys and wheeled down to the pontoon.

One piece of luggage was a wooden packing-case, about 8ft 6in square – the ordinary kind of case in which matches are imported from Sweden. It was weighty, and the porters had some difficulty in getting it from the trolley to the luggage shoot. The captain of the *Katherine*, Mr James Jewiss, himself told me the story. 'The train arrived from Fenchurch-street on Friday night, and at 1.25 yesterday morning I took the tender up to the pontoon, and the prisoners came on board. A case came down the shoot – I believe it turned over in the descent – and when it was on deck the other luggage was piled on top of it.

'Two Dutch sailors came off the *Batavia* boat, which had steamed down from Custom House Quay, and was to leave for Rotterdam. They gave a hand with the luggage, and when all the trunks and bags had been removed they tackled the case, and decided to "roll" it. It was turned over and over five or six times, and then slid a further distance of about the same length to the rails of the tender, ready to go on to the *Batavia*. The "rolling" had broken a piece off the case, and a boy named Stiles, employed on the tender, exclaimed, "There's a man in the box!" The Dutch sailors then looked up to me on the bridge, and pointing to the damaged case said, "Man in box!"

'I went down to the deck. The side of the case was opened, and a man crawled out. He was about 6ft in height, a powerful-looking chap, but he appeared to be dazed and dizzy. He rubbed his head, and it was obvious that he had had a bad knocking about while being tumbled over down the shoot and across and along the deck.

'I asked him, "How long have you been in there?" and he shook his head, indicating that he did not understand English. I repeated the question, and eventually he said, "About thirteen hours."

'"How did you get in?" I asked.

'"Got in myself," he replied, and when I asked who had helped him he answered, "No one."'

There were two fasteners on the case, Captain Jewiss explained, and the lid had opened at the side opposite to them. The case had been tumbled over so that the lid was at the side when it opened. In stencil were the words, 'Non-poisonous safety matches', and a diamond with the letter 'D' in it.

'When the man crawled out,' Captain Jewiss added, 'he stood up with some difficulty. He had no hat, and wore a lounge suit. I pressed him as to where he came from and how he could get out unaided, and he said he came from Dorchester, and could release himself without assistance.'

This was the captain's story. From other sources I learnt that Koehn admitted to the local emigration officer that he had been in the United States, and sailed for Southampton in the *Potsdam* just before the war started. He was made a prisoner of war at Southampton, and later was taken to Dorchester, where he secreted himself in the case amongst the baggage of the interned Germans who were being sent home.

Koehn was brought to the Kent shore and lodged in Gravesend Police Station.

No one believed his story that he received no assistance in making his escape. The case was provisioned for the journey, which would have ended across the Channel but for the rough and ready transit from the pontoon to and from the tender. Three of a dozen bananas had been consumed, and there were a tube of meat extract, and two bottles of water in the box, also a blanket and an air cushion. It is stated that the cushion was pumped full of oxygen.

At two sides of the case were arm rests made of leather. One of them was broken, and that appears to have been Koehn's undoing. It is assumed that the bump on deck at the end of the shoot had the effect of tearing away the arm rest, or sling, and in the subsequent bumps across the deck of the *Katherine* the man's head was so badly injured that he almost lost consciousness. So long as he could hang on to his slings he had been able, although curled up, to control his position.

RETURN TO DORCHESTER
Dorchester, Sunday Night

Otto Koehn was brought back to the Dorchester concentration camp this evening. He is said to be an officer of the German mercantile marines.

It is believed that he succeeded in getting away last Friday, when a party of about fifty old men, who were to be released, were marched to the station and conveyed to Tilbury, where they were to take steamer for Rotterdam. The box in which the man was hidden must have formed part of the prisoners' luggage. They were made to do their own fatigue work and practically to handle their own luggage, so the plot, in which a number of the men must have been concerned, was really simple.

20 January 1915

IN THE HANDS OF THE GERMANS
Experiences of an English Doctor

One of the most interesting narrations which has yet been made in this country, in regard to the experiences of British officers who have had the misfortune to be captured and interned in German camps or fortresses, was given yesterday to the *Daily Telegraph* by Mr L. J. Austin, FRCS, Surgeon-Registrar of the London Hospital. Mr Austin, who only recently returned to London, after having been well-nigh five months in the hands of the Germans, has the distinction – enviable or unenviable – of having been one of the first British officers to be taken prisoner by the German army.

The tale he tells is a remarkable one in many ways. Under the pretext of being suspected as a spy, he was subjected to sundry cross-examinations and trials, the issue of which really meant life or death to him; but finally he was able to prove that he was a bona-fide surgeon, and no spy, and henceforth he was treated as prisoner of war, and interned at various places along with other captured officers, British, French, Belgian, and Russian.

While, as will be seen, Mr Austin makes no direct charge of positive ill-treatment or cruelty against his captors, his story abounds in illuminating details concerning the petty annoyances and irritations – indignities, even – to which he and his fellow-prisoners were subjected. He was no personal eye-witness of the treatment accorded to our captured soldiers in the camps or prisons to which they were relegated; but the one piece of second-hand evidence which reached him is ominous, and – if all the details could be published, which they cannot – almost revolting in certain of its features. But let Mr Austin tell his own story. 'I left England,' he said, 'on 16 August of last year as a member of Sir Frederick Treves's first Belgian unit of the British Red Cross Society. Finding nothing to do in Brussels, to which we first went, Mr Elliott (also of the London Hospital) and myself were lent to the Belgian Red Cross, and on the evening of the following day, the 17th, we went off by motor-car to Namur, on the understanding that we were required for hospital work in that district. On the morning of 18 August we set out for Havelange, where we encountered the pickets of the German army, but were allowed to proceed towards one of the châteaux, Saint Fontaine by name, in which a Belgian hospital was to be installed. The Belgian who accompanied us was a Count, and the owner of the château I have just mentioned.

'But as we moved from this château to another near by we ran right into the head of the German army advancing on Namur. Our car was stopped and searched for arms, and we ourselves were put into a little hut of a post-office, where our papers were examined. Thence we were taken later in German staff cars to the commander-in-chief of this German army. There were four of us – Mr Elliott and myself, the Count, and the chauffeur. Singling me out from the group, he said in English, "You are obviously a spy," and straightway he looked about him for a tree. At this point, however, an officer who spoke excellent English intervened, and we were taken back and solemnly tried by court-martial.

'Before my examination I was addressed in these words: "I wish you clearly to understand that you are on your trial for espionage, the penalty for which you doubtless know." I was then stripped naked, my clothes were searched for secret pockets, and I was cross-examined for about an hour and a half. For about one-half of that time I was questioned as to how I had managed to get where my captors had found me; and for the next three-quarters of an hour I was interrogated as to the strength and position of the British Army and Fleet – matters on which, of course, I was absolutely ignorant.

'At the close of this examination the English-speaking officer said to us, "Gentlemen, you have been incredibly foolish to come anywhere near the German army. I do not know what will become of you. Clearly, having seen our army, you cannot return; but you will be treated as gentlemen." That night we spent in the post-office, and were allowed to purchase what food we desired.

'Next day I was examined by Prince Heinrich XXXIII of Reuss, but unfortunately the officers who had interrogated us on the preceding day had gone on with our papers, and consequently we had no documents to support our story. Prince Heinrich told us frankly he was under the impression that we were British officers in disguise, acting under cover of the Red Cross; and when we protested we were doctors, he replied that it would be necessary for us to prove that we were medical men.

'That night also we spent in the little post-office, but at five o'clock on the following morning we were taken out at the point of the bayonet and thrust into a motor-lorry. In that vehicle we travelled against the advancing stream of the German army, first to Malmedy and subsequently to Bouvigny. Through the booking-office window at the latter place little girls, with red crosses on their arms, made grimaces at us, indicating that hanging would inevitably be our fate. Here, too, we were joined by four or five Belgians who had fallen into the hands of the enemy.

'At Bouvigny all of us were transferred to horse-boxes that had but recently been vacated, and we were taken to Ulflingen, whence we were marched across country for some four miles through German troops. Then we entrained once more, and after passing the night at Gerolstein, we set out on the following morning under heavy guard for Cologne. At Cologne we were marched through the streets amid crowds that became extremely violent, and obviously wished to lynch us. At times, indeed, we had to cut into side streets, while mounted police held off the menacing crowd. After covering some two or three miles in this fashion we reached a prison, which is ordinarily used for deserters from the navy.

'There I was thrown into an ordinary cell, and underwent fifteen days' solitary confinement. The only book I was permitted was a German–English grammar, and the only work given us to do was the menial work of the cell. The food was indifferent. For breakfast, at 5.30 a.m., we had a sort of coffee substitute; for dinner we had vegetable soups, in which, occasionally, a square inch of meat floated; and for supper we were given a sort of "skilly". In addition we had a loaf of bread each day. The nights, I ought to say, were rendered hideous by the swarms of bugs that infested us.

'During my stay in this prison I underwent no fewer than three trials. First of all I was examined by a major on the staff of the Commandant of Cologne. Next day I was subjected to a professional examination – really for my life, inasmuch as I was called upon to prove whether I was a doctor or not. Through an interpreter who translated the questions put by medical officers on the Cologne military staff, I was first invited to tell all I knew about pneumonia; and in the second place a spot on my body was touched, and I was asked to name the organs that would be injured "if a bayonet were thrust straight in there". Mr Elliott, on his part was interrogated about typhoid, and about the details of a particular operation. In the third place I was still further examined by three or four other officers, who, I was told, constituted the court of inquiry, until whose judgment was delivered I should have to remain in prison.

'On the sixth day of my solitary confinement I was allowed to purchase tobacco, but I was never allowed to supplement my dietary. Repeated requests for English books were unavailing. It was on the sixth day, also, that I was first allowed to converse with Mr Elliott, and we were told that although we were still under a certain amount of suspicion we were about to be transferred to Torgau, where, with other officers, we should be treated as prisoners of war.'

From this point Mr Austin's narrative covers the wider field of the German treatment accorded to captured British officers, and to that extent accordingly the drift of the story becomes more interesting. Continuing, Mr Austin said: 'At Magdeburg, on the way to Torgau, I met seven officers of the Royal Army Medical Corps, and we made the rest of the journey together. Arriving at Torgau at four in the morning we had ourselves to carry our baggage up to the fort, and as the medical officers had got some of their field panniers with them, the bringing up of the baggage was an extremely exhausting business. At Torgau there were interned about 200 British officers and 800 French. Our own officers had practically all been captured at Mons and Le Cateau, and in the course of the retreat that followed; while the French officers had belonged almost entirely to the garrison of Maubeuge.

'Although at Torgau some very insulting letters were written to them by the local military authorities, the British officers were comparatively happy. The exercise ground was adequate; there was a football field; the French officers set up one or two tennis courts; and it was possible to obtain a bath every day. The German attendant who looked after the bath remarked that if the British officers went on taking a bath every day, as they were doing, none of them would survive the winter!

'The British officers were here under the command of Colonel Gordon, of the Gordon Highlanders, and subsequently of Colonel Jackson, of the Hampshires. The officers usually paraded at eleven o'clock each day, when the orders from the German authorities were read out. These orders related to such matters as the prohibition of alcohol, the impossibility of obtaining chocolate, the necessity of saluting German officers, whatever their rank, the regulations as to correspondence, and so forth.

'For the first three or four weeks of our stay at Torgau we were not permitted to communicate with home in any way. One day, however, it was suggested by the commandant of the fort that it would be a tasteful thing for the officers to contribute to the German Red Cross Society, whereupon the brilliant idea occurred to one of our number that the contributions might be made by means of cheques which would require to be cleared in London. Accordingly, the cheques were drawn on an Amsterdam bank, and covering messages were written on the backs of them, asking the clearance of the cheques to be notified to the relatives of the officers concerned. It was such a message, written on a cheque, that conveyed to my relatives the first intimation that I was alive. But the name of the place from which we dated our cheques was carefully cut off. Shortly afterwards the British officers were allowed to communicate with their relatives at home, but the amount of correspondence was limited to one letter or two postcards per week.

'Whilst at Torgau the wounded British officers were placed under the care of their British medical comrades, and the German medical authorities carried out only spasmodic inspections. At Torgau, I ought to mention, there were no fewer than thirty-five British medical officers interned. Most of them had been captured by the enemy whilst they remained behind to tend the wounded on the retreat. Continual protests were made by these medical officers at Torgau against the position in which they were placed, but no satisfaction was obtained.

'Whilst we stayed at Torgau we played an unlimited amount of bridge. There was no difficulty in getting English books – indeed, an officers' library was formed – and for a short time, by means which I need not mention, we even managed to get a few English newspapers through.

'On 26 November we were told we were to be transferred to Burg, and for Burg accordingly we set out in two parties. A story has been circulated to the effect that we were taken thither in open cattle-trucks in the snow. That is not true. Our four hours' journey was made in third-class carriages. On our arrival at Burg we were rather mocked by the inhabitants as we marched to our new prison, because the people had been told we were a fresh lot of officers captured at Dixmude.

'Our new quarters consisted of mobilisation and artillery wagon sheds. When we got there the order was given to the Irish Roman Catholics of the party to fall out. They did so, and they were taken to a special room, where they did not mix with the officers of other nationalities – the remainder of the officers sharing rooms with the Russian officers whom they found already in the place. The Irishmen were taken before German officers, and were asked whether they would serve against his Majesty George V. These advances were, of course, indignantly rejected. In what we used to call the "rebel" room were some fifteen officers, and in so far, for instance, as they were not required to mix with other nationalities they enjoyed some minor privileges.

'Precisely the same game did the Germans endeavour to play with the Russian officers from the Caucasus who happened to be Mohammedans. These were asked if they would take part in a holy war against Russia. In this case also the sinister suggestion of the Germans was rejected contemptuously.

'The Russian officers, by the way, had been informed before our arrival that the Englishmen were savages, that they would break the windows to obtain fresh air, that they would beat the Russians with sticks, and that they were personally dirty. The very same sort of thing was said to us about the Russian officers. Most of the rooms at Burg contained ten British and ten Russian officers.

'For a short time at Burg we were allowed white bread, but subsequently we had to live on "kriegsbrod". The exercise-yard was bad, the sanitary arrangements were indifferent, and we were allowed only one bath a week; but on the other hand the canteen arrangements were good, and for the first time since we had entered Germany we were able to obtain a cup of genuine coffee.

'All officers above the rank of captain have been receiving 100 marks per month from the German Government, while junior ranks received 60 marks monthly. About half of this money has been immediately taken back to pay for food, and the rest has served for pocket-money. All the medical officers received 100 marks per month.

'On 6 December the British officers learned with regret that they were about to be split up into small parties. One-fifth, including Colonel Gordon and Colonel Jackson, remained at Burg, one-fifth went to Halle, and the remaining members of the original party were transferred to three prisons in the Magdeburg district – the citadel, "Waggon-house No. 9", and the Kavalier Schornhurst. Personally I was at Waggon-house No. 9, along with some sixty other British officers, sixty French officers, eighty Russians, and about 200 Belgians.

'As you know, the Germans claim by last accounts to have captured 8,850 officers and 577,000 men. Speaking roughly, the prisoners are officially said to be thus comprised: 280,000 Russian, 200,000 French, 20,000 British, and 70,000 Belgian. About a month ago the number of British officers who were prisoners was put at 416.

'But to continue. When we settled at Waggon-house No. 9 we experienced a change for the worse. The exercise-yard was small, the sanitary arrangements were poor, and the rooms were badly ventilated. There was always a struggle between the "fresh-air" party and the "fug" party; and the British officers, I need not say, were always on the side of fresh air.

'The canteen here was worse supplied than anything we had hitherto encountered. Soon after our arrival we were told we must yield up all the money we had, and thenceforward the officers' pocket-money was paid in little metal discs of copper or brass, each representing 1d in value. Senior officers still continued to receive their 100 marks a month, but the medical officers were suddenly reduced to the lower figure of 60 marks, so that after paying for our messing we were left with 5d a day for extras. I understand that the idea of paying us in metal discs instead of in coin was to prevent any bribing of sentries.

'One day we were informed that we were moving to yet another camp. So we packed up everything, and paraded in the courtyard at five o'clock next morning. Then the British officers were marched into a shed, and were informed that it was necessary for us to give up all our personal effects and valuables. This action was keenly resented; but the officers were put upon their word of honour that they had no gold, no rings, no watches, no cigarette cases, above the value of fifteen marks apiece.

'These valuables were given up and sealed in packets, and the word of honour of a German officer was given that the packets would remain sealed until the end of the war, when the property would be returned to the owners. We know for a fact, however, that these packets were opened shortly afterwards, the money removed, and German paper substituted. In the face of protests from the officers, wedding rings were returned, but other rings have not been given back. The officers have been given a list showing the articles that are in charge of the German authorities.

'The medical officers protested vigorously against this whole business, pointing out that they were not prisoners of war, and absolutely refusing to give their word of honour on any question at all. They were then searched. I do not pretend that the search was rigorous, but our packets and our baggage were examined by a non-commissioned officer. Among the officers of all nationalities this affair gave rise to the very keenest dissatisfaction, because under The Hague Convention it is recognised that officers who are prisoners of war are allowed to retain their personal valuables.

'A few days after this search somebody was indiscreet enough to change some money, and on the following morning, at eight o'clock, the rooms were suddenly locked, sentries were posted over them, every officer in the building was searched by police experts, and valuables discovered were taken away. Apart from this continual searching, the chief irritation of this prison life is the utter lack (owing to the prevailing congestion) of any place of rest or quiet.

'I think all the prisoners agreed that wherever the English came there the restrictions and petty annoyances were at their worst.

'Looking back upon the whole thing, from beginning to end, one cannot exactly say that one has been actually bullied, but certain indignities and certain small punishments meted out to officers for various things have caused irritation. Several officers at Magdeburg, for instance, were placed in cells by the German authorities – one because he did not salute a German officer, and another because he was what they regarded as insubordinate while being searched. This last-mentioned officer was awarded five days in the cells.

'Just before I left, too, terrible trouble was brewing on account of some officers having played Rugby with a loaf of bread. I have learned since that they each got eight days in the cells.

'In none of the camps I knew did any British officer die, and only a few deaths occurred in the larger number of French officers.

'While we were at Magdeburg the soldiers of various nationalities were allotted to us as servants – about three to every thirty officers. Finding that the British officers were rather short of servants, the authorities brought in a few extra men from one of the concentration camps somewhere near Berlin.

'A British soldier whom I have in my mind at the moment, and whose name I have, told me he had been in a camp with thousands of French and Russian soldiers, but with only 100 British comrades. He had never had any clothes issued to him since his capture in the retreat; he had never had a proper bath, and the facilities for washing clothes were very bad.

'He was covered with vermin from head to foot when he came to us, and he said that this was the condition of all his fellow-prisoners. At first, he said, the food was deficient in quantity, but latterly that lack had been remedied. Finally he said that the British "Tommies" were put to do all the filthiest work of the camp. Observe, I have not seen any of the men's camps; that is the only piece of information.

'On Friday, 8 January, the ten British medical officers who were in Waggon-house No. 9 were summoned to the commandant's office. A large document was produced and Mr Elliott's name and my own were read from it. So we stood aside. The commandant then asked, "Are any of you gentlemen married?" One man held up his hand, and he was at once told, "You can go home." Next the commandant said, "There are two more to go home, and the matter must be decided by lot." Seven matches of varying lengths were then placed between his fingers, and the two officers who drew the two shortest matches went home.

'The five of us left at midday on Sunday, 10 January, in taxi-cabs of our own providing, each under a guard. In this way we travelled through Germany to Rheine, where we spent the night huddled together in a guardhouse. Early next morning we proceeded to Bentheim, on the Dutch frontier, and awaited the arrival of the officer on duty, who was immensely surprised to see us, and informed us he had no instructions regarding us. Thereupon the sergeant, who had brought us, produced his orders which, it turned out, were in the form of a telephone message written on a slip of paper. At this, the officer decided we must wait until he had communicated with Magdeburg.

'So we sat down and awaited the departure of the next train for Holland, due to leave some three and a half hours later. Meantime, the soldiers who had escorted us had returned to the interior, and their places had been taken by men of the Landsturm. As the Dutch train eventually drew up and there was still no sign of the officer returning, one of the party observed to our guard, "The officer said we were to leave by the 2.30 train." "He certainly did," replied the soldier.

'Accordingly, with some anxiety as to whether, after all, our departure would be delayed, we took our places in the train and journeyed to the nearest station within Dutch territory, Ozendaal.

'In the refreshment-room there we celebrated our release in the first drink we had had for many days without having a bayonet within two inches of our necks. Remember, all the time we were in captivity we could not move without guards, and, besides, there were great watchdogs around the barbed-wire entanglements that enclosed us.

'When we reached Flushing there was fresh difficulty in store for us. The Dutch authorities arrested us because we had no papers, and the officer in charge obviously suspected that we might be British officers who had escaped from internment at Groningen. Eventually, however, word came through from

Ozendaal that five British "sanitat" officers had crossed the frontier by a particular train, and so the way was clear for our return to Folkestone.

'In conclusion,' said Mr Austin, 'I regret extremely I have no information about officers wounded or missing after 12 October, as no officer coming from the front subsequent to that date joined our party. Let me say this also: It is useless to attempt to send out chocolates, tobacco, cakes, or sweets to officers, because these things are confiscated. By the way, I forgot to mention that a fortnight before I left the officers were forbidden to smoke. This was the last blow to them, and it was stated by the German authorities that this measure was taken by way of reprisal for the treatment of German officers in France.

'I have found, by the way, that insured parcels reach their destination more safely than those which are not insured. But it is no use sending out articles of mufti to British officers. They are not delivered, presumably on the ground that they might be used to facilitate escape. Undoubtedly, the percentage of parcels delivered has been disappointingly small. Again, if officers write home requesting that money be forwarded to them, the money ought not to be sent by any sort of private messenger. The best method is to get one's own bank to arrange the transmission of money through the Dutch banks to a German bank. I myself have found that the Mitteldeutschen Privat-Bank transmits money with promptitude and care.

'The money is credited to the officers, and, although they are not allowed to handle it, they can draw on it for the purchase of clothes, extra food, and so on, by means of such "chits" as one uses on board ship. Before I came home all the money I had taken out with me was returned to me.

'Undoubtedly, in the early stages of the war, officers captured by common soldiers were stripped of everything they had. I have also heard allegations as to loss of valuables during the stay of wounded officers in German hospitals; but in these camps of which I have spoken an accurate account was kept of the things surrendered. Personally, I think these valuables will be returned at the end of the war, though financial pressure may offer great temptations in the other direction.'

2 February 1915

ARRIVAL OF THE *DAILY TELEGRAPH* RELIEF SHIP
American Gifts for Stricken Belgium, *Rotterdam, Monday*

After a very rough voyage across the Atlantic the British steamer *Lynorta*, laden with gifts from America for the stricken people of Belgium, arrived at Rotterdam last night, and is now in the Park harbour discharging her cargo.

'Everything, from a peanut to a silk hat,' was the phrase in which one of the officers of the ship described to me the nature of her freight. Included in it are 10,000 barrels of flour, value £11,250. These were bought by the American branch of the *Daily Telegraph* Shilling Fund, and constitute the second consignment of flour sent to Belgium from this source. One of a score of ships of mercy which are carrying the American people's bounty for the relief of innocent victims of the war, the *Lynorta* has on board, in addition to the *Daily Telegraph* readers' present, the special contribution of the State of Virginia, bringing the total value of her cargo up to £60,000.

There are no fewer than 90,000 packages of foodstuffs and 770 packages of clothing – a golden argosy of charity.

This morning the work of discharging the cargo into barges, for transit to Belgium, was commenced. It is a task which will take at least four days to complete, and is only a preliminary stage, for, after the barges have gone up the river to Antwerp, their contents have to be divided for distribution throughout the towns and villages of the desolated and starving country. For this mission responsibility rests with the American Commission of Relief for Belgium, which chartered the *Lynorta*, owned by Johnston, Sproule, and Company, of Liverpool, and also defrayed the cost of the transport of goods to the coast, and of the journey by sea.

It is no fault of the officers and crew of the *Lynorta* that her arrival here was delayed by nearly a week. They did all they could to expedite her passage. From the captain to the cabin boy, every member of the crew was inspired by the knowledge that he was assisting in the cause of humanity. All worked their hardest, sharing the feeling in the heart of the *Lynorta*'s commander, Captain Willis Waring, of Liverpool, who said that, in the course of a long life at sea, he had never undertaken so noble a mission of charity, or one which he more keenly appreciated.

But wind and weather were against a quick passage. When the *Lynorta* left Norfolk (Virginia) three weeks ago, amidst the cheers of the people on land and salutations from the sirens of every vessel in port, the weather was perfect, a typical southern day of calm and sunshine.

On the way out she was not detained, because she flew from her foremast the flag of the American Relief Commission, a long streamer with the words 'Belgian Relief Ship'. But, though this was a passport through the patrolling lines, and ensured pilotage through the mines of the North Sea, it was no guarantee against Atlantic storms. Apart, however, from a little delay no harm was done to ship, crew, or cargo.

The *Lynorta* called at Falmouth last Tuesday, and then went to Brixham to take in bunkers before coming on here to her destination.

2 September 1915

GERMAN WOMEN IN LONDON
Berlin Lie Campaign

Last night the Press Bureau issued the following statement: 'The Attention of the Home Secretary has been called to an article in the *National Zeitung* professing to be based on a statement in the New York *Staats-Zeitung,* which, in its turn, professes to be based on information from London, and which makes a series of untrue statements about the condition and treatment of German women and children in London. This article states, for example, that these women and children are exposed to the fury of the mob whenever they venture out of doors; that they are compelled to beg in the streets; that the hatred of the English towards them pursues them even to bloodshed; that they wander about the streets of London all day and ask for charity; that the German Hospital is the only place in London where they can receive free medical treatment; that they have been prevented from buying food, &c. The author even goes to such lengths as to state: "When the mob has a chance, it chases them like a wild animal, and the police do not interfere until, in each individual case, they receive orders to do so from their superior officers, but then it is, as a rule, too late. One must have seen a London mob to believe what it is capable of; it has consideration neither for women nor infants."

'The falsity of these disgraceful statements is patent to any candid observer of the actual conditions, but it may be well to state briefly what the actual conditions are. Every German woman who desires to return to Germany is given facilities for doing so, together with her children. Arrangements are made for assisting those who have not the means to make the journey, but who none the less wish to go. Nevertheless, thousands of women of German birth have made most urgent application to the British Government to be allowed to stay, and while the general policy is one of repatriation, exceptions have been granted in suitable cases.

'The allegation that German women and children are exposed to mob violence, and are not given all necessary protection by the police, is wholly untrue. Had any such instance occurred it must have been known to the authorities, and inquiry at Scotland Yard shows that no report of any such instance has ever been received, and no complaint relating to it has ever been made by anybody.

'After the destruction by the Germans of the lives of many women and children in the *Lusitania,* there was, for a short time, some rioting in certain of the poorer parts of London, and the destruction of property of some German shopkeepers. Such conduct was instantly suppressed and the wrong-doers were punished. Even at that time no instance is known of any ill-treatment of any German woman or child. Even when popular indignation was deeply stirred by the dropping of bombs upon harmless civilians in poor quarters of certain towns, and by the destruction of the lives of British women and children thereby, there has been no disposition to take personal revenge on German women and children who happened to be in the neighbourhood.

'The statements with regard to the destitution of these people are equally false. No doubt, many of them have found their incomes reduced owing to their husbands' internment; this is a consequence which is regretted, but unavoidable. But it is untrue that they have fallen into destitution. A German woman who is in want has exactly the same claim upon the local guardians of the poor, and receives from them the same measure of relief as an English woman in similar circumstances.

'No instance is known to the police of German women begging in the streets. It is untrue to say that the German Hospital is the only place where they can receive medical treatment; they have the same access, on the same terms, to all hospitals as the British population themselves.

'The whole of the article is written without any regard to the truth, and is evidently an unscrupulous attempt to influence public opinion in neutral and hostile countries against Great Britain.'

4 November 1915

GERMAN INTRIGUES IN PERSIA
Difficult Problems

By Perceval Landon

At least it cannot be said that the increasing gravity of the internal situation in Persia is complicated by the difficulties that sometimes make Oriental policy a sealed book to the plain Englishman. The facts are as clear as the day. Anarchy reigns throughout the country. Advantage has been taken by Germany of the position to attract by her usual methods of sympathy and the assistance of a large number of men who are nominally the subjects of the Shah, and a certain amount of brigandage and murder has resulted.

But it would be a mistake to suppose that because Prussia has found a willingness on the part of Persians to accept gold when thrust into their hands that therefore she has, or is even likely to have, the same ability to guide the policy of Persia as a whole that her distribution of money to Bulgarians enabled her to acquire in that luckless country. First of all; there is no 'Persia as a whole'. A year or two ago she was described to me with ugly vigour and a touch of art by a dweller on her frontiers as a decayed sheep of which the leg came off in your hand when you wished to drag the corpse from the road. So that what German diplomacy – or, for that matter, any diplomacy – can achieve remains effective in a merely local sense. There is only one thing that can be said to be a link between every part of the kingdom – almost every part, for the English, fortunate or not, will always have stout friends among the Bakhtiari, the Persian Kurds, the Arabs of the Karun, and many of the southern tribes – is neither race nor religion. It is an earnest determination to be on the winning side. Even King Ferdinand of Bulgaria cannot surpass them in this plain ambition.

Therefore, to estimate the actual difficulties ahead of us, we have to remember that every man distrusts every other man in Persia, that there are no leaders and, that there is no Government in any sense of the word. It is opportunism run wild.

For example, the news of the arrival at Baghdad of our Indian Expeditionary Force would probably send Southern Persians fluttering in undignified haste to make terms while yet there is time with the strange Englishmen, who neither assassinate nor bribe, and who are therefore of less importance just now. On the other hand, German reports of the successful corruption of the Bulgarian King, and the defection of Greece from what appeared to be a plain path of obligation, have their influence, and the individual Persian is apt in these uncertain circumstances to take the cash, let the credit go and shout with the crowd which seems likely to be the biggest. The whole situation is a little tinged with ignominy; it is to be remembered that no one had much cause to expect anything else: We are ourselves largely to blame. Our gift of constitutional government to Persia completed the wreck of a once great people. Twenty years ago Iranic highways were as safe as those of Worcestershire. The personal responsibility of the keepers of the chappar-khanehs, or posting stations, was not a question of discussion before a judge or of questions asked in the Mejliss. If murder or robbery took place on a road there was a man hanged for it. It was always the right man, too, for reasons that may be imagined.

Now the German action fails, because once more the East is misunderstood in Berlin. Were there a man in Persia today in the position which our friend the Zill-es-Sultan occupied twenty years ago in the southern provinces some kind of concerted action might have been arranged, though in that case it would scarcely be of a kind to please the Teutons. Without a man of that kind – and Persia has not a man of that kind within her borders – bribery becomes merely an expensive hobby. There is no man to take command in Persia, and whatever the action of the quasi-Arabian tribes that have seemed to respond best to the shower of gold, no one knows better than Herr Wassmuss, the German agent in Southern Persia, that an occasional successful assassination of an official attached to the Allies is no guarantee that the well-subsidised tribe to which the assassin belongs will move a finger in aid of Turkey if Baghdad fails. In short, 'the leg comes off in the hand'.

For these and other reasons the chaos which reigns in Persia can be used by neither side for its own advantage. The somewhat childish suggestion has been made that an armed force might possibly make its way from the terminus of the Baghdad Railway at Ras-el-ain, through Baghdad, the Bakhtiari or Kashgai hills, the Kerman deserts, and the Mekran, to India. To those who know these districts the absurdity of transporting across them even a single brigade of infantry in this manner is apparent. The desiccated Mekran, through which 2,200 years ago Alexander forced his way, is a very different country now from what it was then, and the alternative routes are still less practicable, as even Sven Hedin will confess. From a military point of view the successful corruption of certain persons in Persia and sporadic local emeutes cannot affect the position in any way. From a point of view, however, which is of much importance to us, it will be understood that, we must at all costs retain our full authority in the only part of the Middle East for which we have asserted any exclusive responsibilities – the Persian Gulf and its immediate vicinity.

The matter is not one which will cause us much trouble, but it must be considered in all its bearings, and the probable action of German agents in such places as Linga, Debai, Bandar, Abbas, and Maskat, outside the gulf, nipped at once. The presence of Russian troops in the north will, for the reasons that have been stated, only have a steadying effect locally. Persia is so utterly disorganised that nothing has much influence beyond the limits of a province, the walls of a city on a main road. A strong man might still set the place in order, though it would be a hard matter; and we have no time now in which to wait for the compelling character that Asia throws up once in a hundred years. Whether we still continue in military occupation of Bushire, or whether we shall have afterwards to re-occupy the place, is a matter that may make some difference in the time required to clear up our region of influence. But the deciding factor in all this viscous trouble is that, while the West demands to be governed by law, the East prefers to be governed by a man.

3 January 1916

CARRIER PIGEONS
Warning to the Public

The Press Bureau issues the following announcement: 'Attention is called to the fact that a large number of carrier or homing pigeons are being utilised for naval and military purposes, and that recently many of these birds have been shot at and killed or wounded when homing to their lofts. The public are earnestly requested to exercise the greatest care to avoid repetition of such unfortunate incidents and are warned that persons convicted of wilfully shooting such birds are liable to prosecution. Persons who are unable to distinguish with certainty carrier or homing pigeons on the wing from wood pigeons, doves or the like should refrain from firing at any birds of these species.

'Any person who finds any carrier or homing pigeon dead or incapable of flying from wounds, injuries, or exhaustion is earnestly requested immediately to take the bird to the nearest military authorities, or to the police, or if unable to secure the bird he should immediately give information to one or other of those authorities. Information regarding the shooting of such birds should be given to the same authorities.'

10 January 1916

GERMANY AND SHAKESPEARE
His 'Second Home'

Another party of British subjects, from Ruhleben and other parts of Germany, landed at Tilbury on Saturday night. They spoke in bitter terms of the German people. 'Gott Strafe England' was placarded everywhere in Germany, and the hatred of the British subject was carried to intolerable limits.

There were two or three women with the party, one being a teacher, who was on her way to friends at Norwood. She had seen a great deal of German life during the war, and she expressed the opinion that starvation was not going to beat the Germans. They know how to economise, and did not mind a change of diet. Everywhere one could see the placard 'Gott Strafe England', and they had gone so far as to publish a prologue to Shakespeare's *Much Ado About Nothing* to point out that Shakespeare had lost his home through England having sacrificed her honour, and he had come to his second home – Germany. 'Very little war news is given to the people,' she said. 'They are told everything that is bright, and whenever an article of a despondent character appears in the English Press it is reproduced in bold type.

'It horrified me when the war broke out to see the "solid walls" of men march through the streets to the front. No nation, I thought, could stand up against such terrible hordes. However, time has proved that I was mistaken. Their best men have gone. There are hundreds of maimed soldiers in the town where I came from. What do the women think of the war? Well, you know, a German woman is always brought up at the feet of a man; in other words, she is under his thumb, and so they grin and bear the horrible war.

'The general public in Germany do not know the Kaiser is very ill,' she added. 'Some considerable time ago he had a severe cold, and the news was published, but on this occasion nothing has been allowed to sift through.'

1 July 1916

CONSCIENTIOUS OBJECTOR
Mr Bernard Shaw's Evidence

Private Clarence Henry Norman, formerly member of the No-Conscription Fellowship, and now belonging to the Grenadier Guards, was court-martialled at Chelsea Barracks yesterday on a charge of disobeying the lawful command of a staff sergeant to parade at 9.15 a.m. It was a district court-martial, the members being Major du Plat Taylor (president), Captain the Hon. L. Gary, and Lieutenant Lord Erskine.

Mr R. C. Hawkin, who represented Norman, took objection to the jurisdiction of the Court in view of the Prime Minister's statement that courts-martial on conscientious objectors would be referred to the scrutiny of the War Office.

Norman gave evidence in proof of the statement that he was a conscientious objector, and said he had never been before a tribunal. He had studied the law under the Military Service Act, and had several reasons for not appearing before a tribunal.

Mr George Bernard Shaw said he had known the accused for about nine years, and had met him frequently, and had had special professional relations with him. Norman's opinions were pronounced, and witness unquestionably regarded him as a conscientious objector. He employed him to take shorthand notes of his public addresses, and, with regard to addresses of a religious character which he (Mr Shaw) had delivered at the City Temple, accused made the very unusual application to be permitted to read a transcript of his notes to a circle of his friends, interested like himself in religious questions. He and Norman got into correspondence, and witness found that he had strong religious views. Norman attacked him with regard to certain views which he had expressed.

'I was a strong advocate of compulsory service,' said Mr Shaw, in relating how Norman attacked him strongly. 'I have no doubt whatever that in every sense he is a conscientious objector. He is unshakable on the question of passivism. Knowing that he was under suspicion as a shirker, I conceived it my duty to the Court and to him to come here.'

Mr A. R. Orage, editor of the *New Age*, to which accused had contributed articles, said he believed him to be a genuine objector.

Captain Hewitt, Assistant Provost-Marshal, called evidence to prove that Norman was fined by a magistrate and handed over to the military.

Mr Hawkin contended that the law had so changed that he could claim that accused was still a civilian, and not subject to the Court's jurisdiction.

The President: 'Do you contend that any man now called up is no longer a soldier if he is a conscientious objector?' – 'No; it depends on the individual.'

'Or that any man taken under the Act who says he is an objector automatically becomes a civilian?' – 'No; I say that he becomes a man in a sort of purgatory. He may be a soldier or a civilian.'

The point was overruled, whereupon Norman refused to plead in order to maintain his protest that he was a civilian.

This was taken as a plea of not guilty.

Mr Hawkin submitted that accused had already been punished, as there was only one offence – a conscientious offence.

Norman, interposing, told the Court that he had been in close detention, had had no mattress to sleep on, and had not been allowed to write any letters.

Captain Hewitt objected.

Mr Hawkin said he was going to call evidence that accused had suffered privations that were simply astounding.

Accused said he had been punished under the Detention Barracks regulations. While suffering punishment for refusing orders, he refused orders again.

Mr Hawkin declared that the punishment had been serious, substantial, and violent, and there had only been one offence.

Staff Sergeant Andrew said that on 12 June, at Wandsworth Detention Barracks, he ordered Norman to parade in marching order at 9.15. At that time accused was dressed, and said, 'I still refuse.'

Corporal Whittington said, when given the order, prisoner replied, 'I shall not be there.' Witness did not hear him called a coward or a swine.

Accused, giving evidence, said he was not fit to obey the order, as he was suffering from the atrocious treatment of the last week. On two occasions he had been put in a strait-jacket for over twenty hours, and he was in hospital for seven days. He then declined to attend parade, and was put on bread and water diet, and went on a hunger, thirst, and sleep strike for forty-eight hours. He was forcibly fed on two occasions, being laid on the bed in a strait-jacket. Food was pumped up his nose on the first occasion for fifteen minutes, and he was afterwards kept in a strait-jacket, and the commandant was abusive and insulting. The next day he declined food, and he was fed for twenty minutes through a tube in the mouth. It occasioned him the utmost agony.

He contended that the treatment accorded him was unnecessary, because he would have taken food if administered in the ordinary way. It was done as a punishment. The commandant called him a swine, a beast, and a coward, though he had never said a discourteous word to anyone. He was put in a strait-jacket fifteen minutes after he had entered the place, and it was deliberately done to break his health.

Captain Hewitt: 'Have you anyone to support your evidence? They are serious allegations.'

Accused: 'So serious that the commandant has been removed by the War Office.'

'Do I understand that you take credit for that?' – 'I take no credit for it. What I give you are facts. When I was in hospital I was given fifty-six marks for good conduct, but the commandant struck them off and falsified my record. I intend to make it a matter of civil action, and shall assert my civil rights when I can at the earliest opportunity.'

Mr Hawkin asked the Court to discharge the accused.

Captain Hewitt said the accused was at present serving a sentence for refusing a lawful command. He was convicted by district court-martial at Caterham for disobeying a lawful command, and sentence of two years was passed, but that had been commuted to 112 days.

The sentence will be promulgated in due course.

18 November 1916

GERMANY'S NEW EFFORTS

'Transferring' Food Supplies, *Rotterdam, Friday*

By Leonard Spray

From the frontier I learn that all ordinary goods and parcel traffic on the German railways has been suspended for three days. The reason given is 'on account of the exceptional transport of foodstuffs and war material'. This item of news, not perhaps very illuminating in itself, must be taken in connection with Hindenburg's letter to the Imperial Chancellor, emphasising the necessity of the better feeding of labourers engaged in the war industries. This letter, written as long ago as September, is only just published. Its public divulging at this moment is undoubtedly associated with the vast scheme of internal organisation now being worked out. Not the least important feature of this plan is the taking of measures for obtaining increased supplies of food for the workers, not only in munition factories, but in all coal, iron, and other industrial districts. Where are these additional supplies to be obtained? The answer is from the larders of those classes of the population not now engaged in manual labour.

Direct compulsion in this matter has not been proposed – that is to say, publicly – but it will certainly be exerted indirectly, in conjunction with the new general civilian conscription. By stricter regulations, by further rationing, by limitations in certain districts, sedentary Peter is to be robbed to pay manual Paul. Every private interest in Germany is to be sacrificed, during the coming winter, to the cause of increased production of munitions, and munition workers are to have a first call on food supplies, especially containing fat in any form. Already raids are being made on country districts, and immense quantities of confiscated foodstuffs transferred to the industrial centres. Only nominally is von Batocki still 'Food Dictator'. Even he is subject to another dictatorship, the real and absolute one of the War Office and General Groner, as head of the new interior organisation. To the latter's previous office of Chief of Field Railway Service has just been appointed Colonel von Oldershausen, a Saxon army officer. The whole nation, for feeding purposes, is to be regarded as an army, and those whose work requires it will now get higher rations at the expense of the others.

It is now clear that the forced labour of the populations in the occupied territories is part of the German Government's new scheme for increasing during winter their output of war materials for next year's campaign. They are applying their 'general civilian conscription' not merely to their own subjects, but to the unhappy people groaning under their yoke in the invaded countries. It is for this that the manhood of Belgium is being dragged away to slavery in Germany – not, as we have been told in that specious lie, to find employment for the workless, but to compel them to aid their enemies directly or indirectly in the conduct of the war.

Far from listening to the noble appeal of Cardinal Mercier, in the name of all the bishops of Belgium, the Germans are effecting deportations on a greater and even more wicked scale. Belgium's army of 65,000 men railway workers is being raided. These men have consistently refused in their own country to do any work on the lines used by their enemies for military purposes. Now revenge is being taken on them. Daily large numbers of railway workers are deported to Germany, where it will be a case of obeying orders or starving. Many of them will choose the latter alternative.

20 November 1916

GERMAN PLANS FOR FORCED LABOUR
Drastic Measures, *Rotterdam, Sunday*

By Leonard Spray

Germany has again become a land of mystery. Her frontiers are closed to all but very few privileged travellers. Her life is shrouded under a veil of censorship thicker than any yet drawn. In consequence of the reduced railway service, the newspapers are arriving tardily, and, when received, prove more than ever dumb oracles. But sufficient glimpses are still afforded to indicate that revolutionary changes in the whole social and economic life of the Empire are in preparation, and to some extent have already been effected. No one can yet say all that is or will be embodied in the great scheme of 'civilian conscription', 'patriotic auxiliary service', or by whatever other title it may eventually be christened. But its purport, if not its scope, is plain. The German Government is reorganising the country, with a view to meeting the challenge of its enemies to a gigantic contest of men and material next spring. More soldiers, more guns, more shells – to meet that demand imposed by the ever-growing resources of the Allies. Every individual and every social interest of every individual in Germany, is to be sacrificed. 'Better an end with terrors than terrors without end.' That is the German people's new battle-cry. In other words, a supreme effort is being prepared to end the war next year, regardless of whether that end be national triumph or national suicide.

The problem in course of attempted solution divides itself into three heads: the provision of more men for the Army, increased output of munitions, and greater supplies of food, particularly fat, for those engaged in war industries, and especially, of course, in the manufacture of guns and shells. The last-named is by no means the least important. Something terrifically drastic has already been achieved, though its exact nature is unknown as yet outside Germany, if not outside the districts directly concerned. It appears, however, that that matter has been taken in hand by none other than Hindenburg. The idol of the German people is now their absolute master, the real god of war, whose every word must be obeyed. In his recently published letter demanding better feeding of munition workers, there was more even than could be read between the lines. That communication, written a long time ago, was a warning to the politicians and administrators concerned with the distribution of foodstuffs. Apparently it had no effect. At any rate, Hindenburg took affairs into his own hands so far as the feeding of munition workers is concerned. He swept aside Herr Batocki, the so-called Food Dictator, and all his minions. Exactly what he did is still a secret. But this much is known, that enormously increased supplies of certain classes of foodstuffs are now available in the war industrial districts, that they are likely to be maintained, and that those responsible for provisioning the remaining population have been told that they must do the best they can with what does and will remain. Hindenburg has decreed, and his decrees will be put into operation, that every man and woman not engaged directly in war industries requiring physical exertion will get in future only enough food to keep him. Equally drastic measures are expected in regard to clothing. The purchase of certain classes of articles is already limited by law, and infinitely extended restrictions are expected.

The main reason for this measure, as indeed most others for the limitation of the use of everything except the strict necessities of life, is not, as hitherto, the conservation of supplies. It is rather for the saving of labour. The sole object of that is, in its turn, an increase of manpower for the Army. Another step in this direction, already partly taken, is the limitation of railway traffic. Here, again, the War Office, or, more truly, Hindenburg, has said the first and final word – in the new phase first and final are synonymous terms. He has demanded the cancellation of the exemption of all railway servants from military service. A certain number must, of course, remain, but probably very few. It is merely a matter of freeing the railway workers of military age by methods of substitution. Great numbers of others are to be freed by much simpler means, namely, making their ordinary duties unnecessary. To this end the train services everywhere are to be reduced. All facilities for what may be called superfluous travelling will be swept away, and it is rumoured that it is proposed to make it compulsory on everyone wishing to travel to obtain permission in advance and show good cause for this request.

As to the form civilian conscription will take nothing is yet certain. It is probable that absolute compulsion, in name at least, will not exist, except as a last resource. In the first place everybody at present idle, or doing work not scheduled as of national importance, will be required to seek some – or as his case may be – different occupation. If he does not do so, or cannot find a position in a scheduled employment, he will be 'called up' by the authorities and have to do just what he is told by them. Of course, this is in effect forced labour – absolute as far as those now idle are concerned, and practically so for those not engaged either in war industries proper or in services necessary to the national existence. At all events every man within certain, comprehensive age limits will be required to justify by labour his membership of the nation engaged, as the people are now told every day, in a 'struggle for its existence'.

With regard to women it is consistently stated that force will not be exerted. A flashing light is thrown on this by the Berlin correspondent of the *Nieuwe Rotterdamsche Courant* who writes: 'Possibly for the present it will not come to practical obligation for women. But it is certain that a tremendous increase in the manufacture of munitions is approaching. Probably it will be possible to find volunteers for all the new factories, but certainly the Government will not hesitate to take a measure of force in regard to women if voluntary labour proves insufficient. How long will it be sufficient? The demands of the army are for ammunition, still more ammunition. Germany must compete with the powers of production of almost the whole world. If the creation of new factories continues at the present tempo – and there is no single doubt as to that – a day will come when women will be forced to go to shell factories.'

Elsewhere in this interesting letter the correspondent asks: 'Has the last round been rung in? It looks as if the final spurt were beginning. The war has now lasted long enough. Germany does two things to make an end to it. In the first place she gives it to be understood that she is ready to make peace – peace which gives good guarantees against future wars. At the same time she collects her uttermost forces for unparalleled exertions if this should be necessary, namely, the beginning of the last spurt. The new lesson of this war seems to be approaching. The world must now see what it really means – the exertion of the whole force of the nation. General conscription and what was formerly reckoned as belonging to it are now going to appear modest. All special compromises for the benefit of individuals will cease. All the forces of the country are to be concentrated to the uttermost to bring the struggle to a good end.'

This is the road on which we are now launched. A strong wind is blowing in high spheres. Mars governs the hour – who and what Mars in Germany, everybody can guess for himself. No measure which appears desirable to the war god is too strong for him. He no longer concerns himself with political effect. What he does, reactionary, revolutionary, anarchical, tyrannical, it is all the same to him. There must be munitions, and that comes in the first place. Bad food distribution in the Western industrial districts became in the long run a danger to manufacture. What headaches and difficulties this connection had caused the civil government! Mars came, saw, and conquered. He had no time to wait until gentlemen around a green table had found a solution. He simply decreed that for munition labourers in the first place there must be food, and said to the others, 'You may deliberate as much as you like, but you have to make both ends meet with what is left.' From the military point of view, therefore, the affair was finished. Civilian conscription will undoubtedly come, and is only one of the radical measures which are to give Germany an unknown force. It is clear, then, in any case it must come to a final spurt. The only thing with which a reckoning is held is the limits of possibility, and these, too, are being continually widened.

25 November 1916

HUNGARY AND THE LATE EMPEROR
Bitter Attack, *Milan, Friday*

By A. Beaumont

The Italian Press continues, with justifiable severity, to comment upon the character, person, and reign of Francis Joseph, and expects little better from his successor. All the arbitrary acts of the early part of Francis Joseph's reign, when Italy was fighting for her independence, are recalled with bitter memories. The defunct Emperor seldom reprieved a political prisoner, and never pardoned an Italian. Capital punishment and executions for political crimes survived longer in Austria under his reign than in any other country in the world, and Italians in the unredeemed provinces were among the chief sufferers up to the last. But that bitter memories are also preserved of his reign by his other subjects, and, curiously enough, by a large mass of Hungarians, is brought home to me today by a communication I have received via Switzerland. The document is a violent protest against the venal, servile, and hypocritical funeral eulogiums printed in the Austrian Press. It is signed by the name of a very prominent Hungarian, which I am asked to keep secret; he speaks for the members of the Independence party in the Hungarian Chamber. I believe I may say that all members of that party heartily subscribe to this manifesto on the part of one of their leaders, and I herewith transmit it textually as it reaches me.

There was hardly ever a King living such a long life who has caused so much misfortune, and was so unfortunate himself, as King Francis Joseph. Now he is dead all the papers praise him, not only in Austria and Germany, but even in Hungary, which really has no reason whatever to keep this Sovereign in grateful remembrance. However, none of these praises and glorifications in the Hungarian papers are sincere, even their own writers do not feel what they are expressing by the dead letters of their articles. They are paid for this work, and more than ever they have to write now in the way ordered by the owners of their papers and by our so-called Constitutional Government. If the world could know what the Hungarian nation feels at the death of King Francis Joseph, what it feels reading these untrue eulogies in its own country's papers, I am sure the world would think and judge very differently of us.

No power in this world is able to efface the hatred, deeply rooted in every Hungarian heart against this Sovereign. Since his accession to the Throne up to the last moments of his long reign, he has never made a stroke of the pen, has never uttered a word, has never done a deed voluntarily and sincerely in favour of and for Hungary's weal and prosperity. God knows this is so. He hated the Hungarian nation, and the Hungarian nation hated him. Unfortunately his hatred ruined Hungary, whilst the Hungarian nation's hatred did no harm to him.

The many thousands of young Hungarian lives lost on the battlefields of '48 and '49, the thirteen generals shot by his order on 6 October 1849, in Arad stained his hands with innocent blood, and he died with these bloodstained hands. At the price of this blood he deprived Hungary of its ancient Constitution and legal rights; he broke his own and his ancestors' oaths, who had acknowledged Hungary's legitimate claims to this Constitution and these legal rights, and when he set ablaze the present abominable war he was deserted and betrayed by all those whom he had trusted, favoured, and overwhelmed with privileges and power all his life. The nation which he hated to the utmost all his life, which he deprived of all its dues, and led to the brink of complete decay – this nation, deserted by all its friends and protectors outside of the Monarchy, was so chivalrous as to save its greatest enemy. It saved him and saved his throne, without expecting any special reward, but trusting to get back what was robbed from it.

But the chivalrous Hungarian nation was deceived once more. It did not get back anything, and it will not get back anything after this either. The faint flash of hope, the weak faith in justice and gratefulness, have gone now, and hatred, deeper and fiercer than ever, fills every Hungarian heart. The nation's hatred did not do any harm to King Francis Joseph; no, it could not do so. But Providence has taken up the judge's part; Providence has constantly struck this unfortunate Sovereign without mercy, as he deserved, and his sudden death is sure to be the supreme punishment inflicted on him by this never-failing judge. That it was a visitation of Providence will soon appear.

The above document, representing the opinion of a large number of Hungarians, is curious in many respects. It is, as it were, the last agonised cry of those Hungarians who still adhere to the ideals of independence of their leaders of 1848, heard over the tomb of the defunct Monarch. It does not, of course, represent the opinion of courtiers like Count Tisza, nor probably altogether those of Count Apponyi and the members of the Hungarian Liberal party, and certainly not those of Count Julius Andrassy, except insomuch as these two last leaders represent opposition to Austria. Andrassy, however, we know, has by his ostensible hatred for Austria led his party toward some sort of union – annexation or federation – between Hungary and Austria, encouraged and supported by Pan-Germanist friends in Berlin, which accounts for the frequent journeys of Andrassy to the German military headquarters and visits to the Kaiser. How large a part of the Hungarian nation really retains the hatred against the memory of Francis Joseph, as alleged in the above article, it is difficult to ascertain. Certain it is that the Independence party in Hungary has made no secret among the people of its allegations against Count Tisza and against Francis Joseph of being really responsible for the European war and for all the sacrifices it entailed upon Hungary, and it is due to its propaganda that in some Austrian towns, in the course of riots and demonstrations, there were cries in the past of 'Down with Austria! Down with Francis Joseph!' Only one thing can be really inferred, and that is that an element of discontent still exists in Hungary, and that the death of the old Emperor has revived its animosity against the Hapsburgs and its antagonism to the continuation of the war.

2 March 1917

NEW GERMAN PLOT
Overtures to Mexico

Telegrams received yesterday from New York announce that the papers there publish the interesting revelation that the German Foreign Secretary, Herr Zimmermann, on 19 January instructed the German Minister at Mexico City, Von Eckhardt, to endeavour to get Mexico to declare war against the United States, and try to lure Japan from the Entente to join in an attack on the United States, Germany promising financial support to Mexico. The full text of Herr Zimmermann's instructions to Von Eckhardt, dated Berlin, 19 January, is given as follows: On 1 February we intend to begin unrestricted warfare. In spite of this it is our endeavour to keep the United States neutral. If this attempt is not successful we propose an alliance with Mexico on the following basis 'That we shall make war together, and together make peace. We shall give general financial support, and it is understood that Mexico is to reconquer her lost territory in New Mexico, Texas, and Arizona.'

Details are left to you for settlement.

You are instructed to inform the President of Mexico, or myself, in greatest confidence, as soon as it is certain there will be an outbreak of war with the United States, and suggest that the President of Mexico, on his own initiative, should communicate with Japan, suggesting adherence at once to this plan, and, at the same time, offer to mediate between Germany and Japan.

Please call the attention of the President of Mexico to the fact that the employment of ruthless submarine warfare now promises to compel England to make peace in a few months. – (Signed) Zimmermann.

The documents, it is added, have been in the hands of the United States Government since the break in the relations with Germany.

EXCITEMENT IN AMERICA
New York, Thursday

There is only one thing discussed in the United States today – Germany's overtures to Mexico to join with her and Japan in an alliance against the United States, which are disclosed with the full authentication of official documents. Through Count Bernstorff at Washington, the German Foreign Secretary, Herr Zimmermann, on 19 January, two weeks before the new 'barred zone' was proclaimed, approached Carranza with the proposal of an alliance, holding out the alluring inducement of financial aid and a chance to reconquer Texas, Arizona, and New Mexico.

No event since the outbreak of the war and the sinking of the *Lusitania* has excited such tense interest in America, and the universal remark one hears today is: 'Washington acted none too soon in severing relations with Germany, and in sending home the Ambassador who was her instrument in an effort to raise up enemies against the United States.' The effect of the publication of this remarkable document upon public opinion here will be very prompt, and the demands upon Congress to aid in defending American interests will be vastly strengthened. At the time of cabling public opinion, except for a general tone of exasperation, has not crystallised very clearly, and the pacifists, many of whom are also patriotic at heart, are in a quandary. It is known that the document was in the possession of President Wilson at the very time when Herr Bethmann-Hollweg was declaring that the United States had placed an interpretation on the submarine declaration 'never intended by Germany', and that Germany had promoted and honoured friendly relations with the United States 'as an heirloom from Frederick the Great'. In itself, if there were no other reply, the Note is considered a sufficient answer to the German Chancellor's plaint that the United States 'brusquely broke off relations' without giving authentic reasons for its action.

The document supplies the missing link to many separate chains of circumstances which until now seemed to lead to no definite point. It sheds a new light upon the frequently reported, but indefinable, movements of the Mexican Government to couple its situation with friction between the United States and Japan. It adds another chapter to the celebrated report of M. Jules Cambon, French Ambassador at Berlin before the war, of Germany's worldwide plans for stirring up strife on every continent where they might aid her in the struggle for world-domination which she dreamed was close at hand. It adds the climax to the operations of Count Bernstorff and the German Embassy in this country which have been marked by passport frauds, dynamite plots, and intrigues, the full extent of which have never been published. It gives new credence to the persistent reports of submarine bases on Mexican territory in the Gulf of Mexico. It takes cognisance of the fact, long recognised by the American army chiefs, that if Japan ever undertook to invade the United States it probably would be through Mexico over the border and into the Mississippi Valley, so as to split the country in two. It recalls that Bernstorff, when his passports were handed to him, was very reluctant to return to Germany, but expressed preference for an asylum in Cuba. It affords a new explanation to the repeated arrests on the border of men charged by the American Military authorities with being German intelligence agents. Last of all, it seems to show a connection with General Carranza's recent proposal to neutrals that exports of food and munitions to the Entente Allies be cut off.

29 October 1917

THE BRITISH FIGHTING MAN

Today Parliament will be asked to pass a Vote of Thanks to the fighting men of the Empire. That is the Order of the Day – thanks and praise to all, men and women alike, who have upheld and are upholding, at home and abroad, by sea and land, with willing, loyal, and self-sacrificing service the honour and freedom of the race. It is a noble and a swelling theme, and they to whom falls the privilege of putting it in words would want a hundred tongues, a hundred mouths, and a hundred voices, and the eloquence of all the ages to pay an adequate tribute. We will not attempt to anticipate the eulogies which will be pronounced today. Our purpose is rather to dwell upon what is, perhaps, the most inspiring feature of all the tremendous effort which the British Empire has made in this war. That is the dogged courage of the British soldier and – a virtue no less priceless – his unquenchable cheerfulness of spirit. We do not forget the debt that is owing to all the rest – to our sailors, to our generals, to our organisers, to our nurses, to all who will receive their meed of well-won praise. But as we look back upon these three years of war and suffering, the figure on whom the pure, ennobling light of transfiguration shines most radiantly is that of the plain fighting man. Gazing upon him, the distinctions of rank are no longer seen. We discern only the fighting man in khaki, soiled and stained, the captains of companies, the gallant boys – those countless second lieutenants – who have played their last game so finely; the sergeants, the privates; the British soldiers of the firing-line who have borne the heaviest brunt of war, and on whose staying-power the issue of victory or defeat has, in the last resort, all the time depended. Our statesmen have made many mistakes; our strategists have been often at fault. But when has the fighting man failed either one or the other? His superb courage has been at once the rock of our resistance and the spring of our attack. Whatever else may have gone wrong – this never. Of no single British operation can it be said that it failed because the heart of the British regimental officer quailed before the desperate nature of the enterprise, or because the British soldier would not follow where his officers led.

That valour is nothing new in the history of the British Army the British Empire is ours to testify, and if today we lavish our gratitude upon the fighting men of our own generation, it is not that we are unmindful of what the soldiers who fought under the same flag dared and endured in the campaigns of the past. One of the few imaginative military monuments in St Paul's Cathedral is that to the officers and men of the Coldstream Guards who fell in the South African War. It depicts the shadowy figures of the men of the old regiment looking down from the skies upon a dying soldier who is soon to join their number. They wear the uniforms of Marlborough's day and of Wellington's, and of the Crimean War; but the idea that the artist contrives to convey is that the proud tradition of the regiment has been carried on through the years without a break, and that the old spirit endures. What must they think now, after three years of this war – the heroes of the old fighting regiments of the Line, the men who won the deathless nicknames which their descendants have so nobly upheld? The world may have become more civilised, but war in many respects has become more horrible and devilish. The British soldier of today has been wonderfully fed and clothed; he has escaped many of the unspeakable horrors that were daily endured in winter fighting by the ragged, starved, and frozen victors of the Peninsula and the

Crimea. The soldier who is wounded in France that morning may find himself tonight safe in a London hospital. This is the brighter side of the comparison. But, after all, the darker side predominates, when we consider the accumulated horror of being shelled for hours together with high explosives, the tornado of death which fills the air, the scale of destruction by which the soldier is compassed, the diabolical, lurking menace of the gas attack, the lurid terror of liquid fire, and, to crown all the unutterable slime and quake of the morasses of mud which too often form the fighting terrain in Flanders. Yet, through it all, the British soldier comes smiling and cheerful, loathing it as dirty, senseless work and eager for it all to end, yet determined that it shall not end without victory, and that this war and his sufferings – or, as he would put it, the sufferings of his fellows – shall win a lasting peace. Success does not make him boastful; reverses do not depress or dispirit him. He does not talk or sing of glory or of patriotism. But he does glorious deeds, and the best proof of true patriotism is a cheerful readiness to give all for duty. The British soldier, and in that word, of course, we include every fighting man of the Empire, wherever his home, is as indomitable, as patient, and as chivalrous a man-at-arms as the world has ever seen.

What an answer the British soldier has given to those who counted so confidently on the degeneracy of the British race! And what a marvellous evenness there has been in the emphasis of that answer throughout these desperate years! It was first given by the Regular Army, the original British Expeditionary Force, those superb divisions which were the vanguard of the Armies of today, the spearhead which thrust so gallantly and which cut so clean. Is there any other Army in the world of its size which could have done what those immortal seven divisions did during the first three months when the enemy came within an ace of bringing off their great coup in the West? Britons can never be sufficiently grateful to the regiments of the old Regular Army, which were thrust into the furnace time after time, with scarcely a breathing-space for recovery and filling up the gaps, for they were all we had, and there were no others ready to take their places. It is just three years ago to the very day when the issue of the first Battle of Ypres was decided, and the hard-pressed remnants of the original British divisions, reinforced by the Indian contingent and a few English Territorial regiments, beat off the fierce German thrust at Calais. That was one of the crucial moments of the war, and it was the Army, which may truly be said to have perished where it stood in its last great fight against overwhelming odds. But by that time their successors were pressing forward to take up the tale. The Territorials, Kitchener's Army, the New Armies, the Conscript Armies – many and various are the names which have had their passing vogue, and some are already almost forgotten. What should most excite our pride is not that we have raised an Army of so many millions, but that the civilian and conscript armies of today are imbued through and through with the fighting spirit of the old Regular Army. Such differences as exist are much more obvious to the keen eye of the professional soldier than to the enemy who has to withstand them in the field. To him it is the same Army; to him it is the same British soldier. The men who fought at Neuve Chapelle, at Loos, in Gallipoli, in Mesopotamia, in Salonika, and on the Somme, and those who are now slowly clearing the Germans off the last ridges near Ypres, are of the same true brotherhood with the men who fought at Mons, at the Marne, and on the Aisne, and who held the Germans at bay at Gheluvelt and in the blood-drenched salient. Shame on us if we allow any hardships that may fall upon us this coming winter to cause us to forget for an instant what we owe to them! Parliament today will pass them a Vote of Thanks with emotion and with acclamation; but let Parliament itself, before it turns again to its ordinary duties, listen and catch the sound of

> The song of courage, heart and will,
> And gladness in a fight,
> Of men who face a hopeless kill
> With sparking and delight.
> The bells and bells of song that ring
> Round banners of a cause or king
> From armies bleeding white.

Nothing will be said today by even the most eloquent tongue which can express one-half of the unbounded admiration and unstinted love which we all feel in our hearts for the devotion, courage, and endurance of the British soldier.

3 January 1918

WOMAN'S PART IN THE WAR

Among the many messages of greeting and sympathy interchanged at the coming of the New Year, there are none so moving, none so significant of the vast social changes brought into being through the awful travail of the war, as the telegrams which have passed between the Women's Committee of the American Council of National Defence and Queen Mary, as reported in our columns yesterday. The Committee, 'representing every loyal woman in America', have made use of the occasion to send, through her Majesty, a tribute of admiration and a firm pledge of co-operation to their British sisters. None, they say, will manifest their loyalty more thoroughly in word and deed than the women of the United States, now that their country has joined hands with the European Allies in 'this last and greatest of all crusades'. They have had before their eyes, during the period of American neutrality, 'the fortitude, the unfaltering purpose, and unflagging effort of the women of the United Kingdom to further the cause', and they are proud now to be associated with them. In some branches of our war activity, as many workers know, not a few American women have long been taking part, and showing in it the characteristic energy, as adaptable as untiring, of their people. But practically the huge reservoir of working power, ability, and morale

represented by the womanhood of the United States was as untapped, until the
entry of that country into the war, as the strength of its manhood. When the
whole power of the nation is fully engaged in the winning of the war, we may be
very sure that the women's contribution will be as remarkable and decisive in its
way as that of the men. For however the honours of pioneership may be disputed
in other fields, the United States has unquestionably led the world in the
emancipation of women. Their active participation in professional and business
life, and to a great extent in political life, is already almost a tradition in America.
A raising of status which has come about with us as it were at a bound has been
with them the outcome of steady progress, and the fruits of it in wartime should
be the more abundant. In the medical profession alone – which has so great and
so honourable a part to play in the conflict of nations – there must be a far greater
proportion of women engaged than in any other country; and we, with our own
record of great military hospitals managed with supreme success by women
exclusively – such as the Endell-street establishment organised two years ago –
and of women's medical units in the field, can understand what that means. The
co-operation of British and American women in this and all the other tasks laid
on them by the time is full of promise for the future of the two peoples. 'The
horrors of war,' writes Queen Mary, in her reply to the American Committee's
greeting, 'have taught us to know one another better, and have strengthened the
ties of kinship and mutual sympathy by uniting the women of the English-
speaking races heart and soul in the struggle for liberty and civilisation.' In
praying for 'God's richest blessing on our efforts,' her Majesty will have touched
directly that sense of dedication to a sacred cause which has been the deeper
inspiration of the American entry into the war.

Warm as is the sympathy, and sincere as is the respect, expressed in the
Committee's message for the part played by British womanhood in these terrible
years, it can scarcely be realised by anyone not living in the midst of the country's
and the Empire's war activity what that part has been and is. The varieties of
effort are so many and so different, often so much below the surface of things;
they are all so seldom brought into the light of publicity as compared with the
work of the Armies and the Fleets. Not many, even among ourselves, have a full
knowledge of the scope of women's medical and nursing work, the most
prominent of all. Not all of us know the noble and wonderful history of the
various women's hospital units in the Western war, in the East, in Russia, and,
above all, in Serbia. How many have heard the story of the little cellar in Pervyse,
where two English girls, three years ago, established and carried on unaided an
advanced dressing-station for the Belgian Army under the fire of the enemy's
guns, living – we believe to this day – the indescribable life of the soldier under
bombardment? If we turn to the work under the Munitions Department we find
a record, largely unknown to the public, of what can only be called marvels of
organisation and management carried out by women of directive talent, in
addition to that immense body of skilled women's labour, non-existent three
years ago, without which we should have been long ago a defeated people. A
Minister may tell us of the 700,000 women doing munition work, and of the

exacting nature of their innumerable employments; we may read of the overwhelming responsibility of 'welfare work' undertaken by women in looking after this great host throughout the country; but we can never realise these things without seeing them. There is the management by women of the canteens and 'huts' for the Armies, a wonderful and invaluable war-service; there is the organisation, largely performed by women, of musical and theatrical entertainment for the big camps. There is the labour of women on the land, not the least remarkable chapter in the history of our war organisation; 'not a case of lilac sun-bonnets', as Mr Prothero has remarked, but 'hard work – fatiguing, monotonous, back-aching, dirty work, in all sorts of weather'. There is the invaluable work done by women with experience of horses in connection with the Army Remount Depots. There is the heavy and responsible work of the still growing Women's Police Service, whose patrols are now doing a much-needed task throughout the country. There is the work of women as Army motor drivers; there is the work of the women Army cooks; there are the many unadvertised but indispensable labours of the Women's Auxiliary Army Corps. There is the women's task of collecting literature for the soldiers and sailors. There is the invaluable work of the Hospital Supply Depots. In merely naming all these we have by no means completed the tale of the direct contribution of British womanhood to the cause of their country; but enough has been said to indicate to American women, who have so eloquently honoured the achievement of their British sisters in the message to Queen Mary, that those words of praise are even better justified perhaps than many of them had realised.

Chapter 10

The Eastern Front and Revolution in Russia 1917–18

8 September 1917

CHAOS AND SHAME

Results of CWSD Folly, *Petrograd, Tuesday Evening*

Riga is in flames, say refugees. The principal Gothic buildings in the old town on the hill are burning, roofs are crashing down into the quaint narrow streets, fires are blazing by the river and down towards the sea. The Russian troops, after blowing up the bridge across the Dvina, retired slowly, contesting every inch, and now they are moving slowly up along the coast. The refugees declare that there was no panic among troops defending the city. The soldiers marched with set faces in firm, unbroken ranks. And at the last they played their true part, and hundreds fell doing their duty with honour.

But it was not against Riga itself that the Germans concentrated their heaviest blow. Through the breach opened at Ikskul they pushed their heavy artillery and picked infantry with a rapidity and force recalling Mackensen's 'phalanx' in Galicia. They are winding their way northward, scattering before them a deadly fire, and the Russians, whose morale is uneven and whose condition is enfeebled by long months of inaction, fell back before them. I say particularly that their morale was uneven, for while some of the regiments are fighting magnificently with the old stubbornness for which the Russian army was once renowned, the co-ordination of impulse and will is incomplete, and again and again a regiment only half healed of its prolonged moral paralysis, breaks down at the critical moment, exposes its neighbours, and decides the action in the enemy's favour. According to the last official report, the retreat, which up to Valdenrode was orderly in parts, at that point developed into a blind stampede for safety, and the Germans again effected in the Russian lines a breach nine miles wide.

The task of the commanders under such conditions is almost superhuman, but the very greatness of the calamity provokes a desperate effort, and measures are being taken to check the German inrush. It is useless to speculate on the possibilities and probabilities. What is happening in Russia now is a catastrophe. There are no words to describe the strange tumult of feeling here, the despair, the burning sense of shame, the bitter recrimination, the gathering wrath, and with all that an incomprehensible apathy, a childish babbling in abstractions, a morbid insensibility to danger and disgrace. There is a fever abroad in Petrograd, a vague delirium that distorts all perspective. Outwardly the city is quiet, but there is a welter of conflicting emotion that makes it impossible to put the finger on one fact and say, 'This is characteristic; this is dominant.' Every intelligent man and woman one meets is sunk in gloom; overwhelmed with shame. And yet one picks up the papers and finds the organ of the CWSD saying Yes, yes, it is a great disaster. We must take arms against Wilhelm's hordes. We must save the country and the revolution. But, workers and soldiers, be on your guard. This is the time when dark forces will work. Watch, and suppress every attempt at a counter-revolution.

And M. Chernoff's organ, apart from a short warning against panic, and an appeal from the committee of the Social Revolutionary party to organise for defence, has no reference to the Riga disaster. On the contrary, it makes querulous complaints against the repressive measures of the Government. It also publishes a long and laboured article on the Stockholm conference.

Not only the CWSD is dreading a counter-revolution. The Government is following up the clues of an alleged reactionary plot, and has placed the Grand Dukes Michael Alexandrovitch and Paul Alexandrovitch under arrest. And, on the other hand, there is the extraordinary spectacle of the results of the municipal elections, with the Bolsheviks, or Leninites, second on the list with 88,000 votes, while the Social Revolutionaries are first with 120,000, and the Cadets third with 2,000. It sounds too incredible, did not one know the ignorance and credulity of the masses, that at a time like this the Bolsheviks, who nearly wrecked Petrograd six weeks ago, should secure 88,000 votes in the city. An old woman who was proudly carrying to the ballot-box an envelope with the list of Bolshevik candidates, wept when she was told that those men were responsible for the shooting in the streets of Petrograd.

Today in the crowd at a street corner I saw a man violently reproaching a knot of soldiers. A decent-looking soldier listened sullenly to the reproaches, admitted their truth, and then said in justification, 'But where's the Government? What's the Government doing?' And again and again I have heard soldiers saying: 'We are dark and ignorant, and the educated people have always deceived us.' It is painful to see these humble folk, unprepared, untrained, and yet assured month after month that they are one and all competent to solve complete social and international problems. No wonder their instincts are confused; no wonder that in such a crisis so many of them are apathetic to all appeals save that of hunger. For among the crowds there is more talk of the food scarcity than of the German menace. Existence is being reduced to its gaunt elements in Russia. There is a strange confused ranging and rallying of rival forces. Night and day one watches and waits to see what the issue will be.

12 September 1917

THE STRUGGLE FOR RUSSIA
Korniloff and Kerenski

Thin, tense, and with a touch of the false brilliancy that constant illness often bestows, clean-shaven Kerenski faces the small, tough, and bearded Korniloff. The prize is Russia. The challenge glove has been dropped and taken up; and before the first blow is delivered it may be worthwhile to sketch out in such bald and all-too-incomplete outline as is now possible the nature of the struggle and its protagonists. For us, though in a far lesser degree, the issue of the contest is as interesting, if not as vital, as it is to Russia herself, the Andromeda for whom this latest duel between Perseus and the Dragon is being fought. At this distance, and from the scanty materials that we have at hand, it is hard for Englishmen to see clearly which is the Dragon and which is Perseus. It is a grim thought that in this crisis of all crises in her chequered life Andromeda herself can make up her mind no better than we.

The present political chaos in Russia has been reached with rapidity and with clearly defined steps. A year ago the traditional autocracy of Russia seemed as well able as ever to defy the storm of criticism that it had so long weathered in safety. The mask of the Emperor, borrowed for the purpose as he slept by his own wife, was worn by a small coterie of reactionaries, no one of whom felt secure except the most sinister of all the personalities of the age, Rasputin, the Court favourite, the apostle of a half-mesmeric and altogether foul creed, the dispenser in the last resort of the full Imperial power. Against this stronghold of privilege popular agitation and public protest alike broke itself in vain, and German cunning readily utilised the abnormal situation thus created, and Stürmer was fast guiding Russia into an ignominious and faithless agreement with her enemy when in November Miliukoff denounced him in the famous 'Herr Geheimrat' speech, and Stürmer fell. But there was little improvement. In the last days of 1916 one or two of the Grand Dukes took upon themselves to remove the prime cause of Russia's trouble, Rasputin. There was a momentary reaction of absolutism, but the door had been forced, and all parties, both within the frontiers of Russia and without, waited for the catastrophe of the spring of 1917.

Immediately after the dethronement of the Tsar, Kerenski rose into prominence. His first action was to defeat the milder measures proposed by the leaders of the revolution, Miliukoff, Lvoff, and Gutchkoff, and to insist on the extinction of the Monarchy. Next he compelled Prince Lvoff to admit him to the Ministry, first as Minister of Justice and afterwards as Minister for War. His activity was ceaseless, and the authority he wielded through half a dozen Socialist organisations could not be countered by the Constitutional Democrats. In the end he was called forward to deal with the trouble that his own party had created and became Prime Minister in July last. At once his attitude changed, and he boldly set himself to counteract the chaos that either a misreading or the natural consequences of his Socialism had created in the army. He is a strong and fearless man in spite of his weak health, but the forces that he had himself armed wavered in their allegiance when self-sacrifice was demanded; and the call of patriotism sounded but faintly in ears that he had himself deafened with the 'International'. All that a man could do he did. In the teeth of the growling opposition of his own people he restored the death penalty for military offences. Wisely or not, he at least dismissed his commanders fearlessly, and by his personal presence did all that he could to stop the rot that had set in along the Russian front. But he was throughout in a false position, and the i's of his desperation were dotted when, but a few days ago, he publicly implored his own new Generalissimo, Korniloff, to hold his tongue about the hopeless case of the Russian army unless drastic and anti-Socialistic changes were instantly made. Korniloff persisted. At the Moscow Conference he bluntly warned Russia that Riga must fall unless he were given an entirely free hand to reorganise the military defence of the country. Riga would have fallen anyhow, but its fall afforded the sturdy General the opportunity he sought, and he at once took it. Kerenski paid him a hasty visit to his headquarters in a hopeless endeavour to stave off the evil day, and returned on the morrow to Petrograd to issue the challenge with which the whole world is ringing today.

His opponent, Korniloff is a hard nut. All through his life he has steadily fought his way to the front against odds that would have daunted another man, and he will certainly not lose his head now. In the present war he has risen by sheer capacity to the almost autocratic position he now holds, and in the contest between himself and Kerenski he has the great personal advantage of excellent health.

But he has much more than that. He has a clearly defined programme – which includes the elevation to the throne of Russia of the head of the family of Dolgorouki, a far more ancient house than that of Romanoff – a military reputation which no other Russian general, except Brussiloff, can rival, and the enthusiastic support of the Cossacks. He calls to the Russians to defend their country, and he makes his call at the right moment. If the German is to be kept away from Petrograd the Russian army must put its house in order. Korniloff's reputation, should he succeed in obtaining his dictatorship, will inevitably be reinforced by success in this matter, as it seems clear that the Germans have no intention of pushing through to the Russian capital this autumn. Above everything, Korniloff makes an appeal which all can understand. Strength is the only god before which the Russian countryman bows down, and the widespread knowledge of an almost certain famine of next year is paving the way for the use of absolute power where nothing but absolute power can save the land.

On his side, Kerenski possesses practically all the political organisation in Russia that is still effective; he has as an asset of doubtful value the unwillingness of men once routed to reform themselves, even under the spur of military necessity: he has a burning conviction that the subordination of the civil power to the military is a step back to the bad old days at the very moment when freedom seemed most assured; and he has personal magnetism. Upon this chaotic aggregation of men and minds which goes by the name of Russia these two will bring their influence to bear, and the result of those influences will be carefully and most anxiously watched by all the world.

21 September 1917

RUSSIAN CRISIS

Disquieting Signs, *Petrograd, Wednesday*

I am perfectly convinced that Russia will, in the long run, surmount her difficulties, and that stability and continuity of authority will be secured. The prospects for the immediate future are, however, not encouraging. The Bolsheviks or Leninites are again very active.

As I have already reported, the Soviet has summoned what is known as a democratic conference for next Monday. This is a conference of all the bodies who accepted the resolution proposed by Cheidze at the Moscow Conference; that is to say, it will be a Social caucus. The Bolsheviks are now making every effort to capture this conference and make it serve as the instrument of their own purposes. The more moderate Socialists assert that the caucus will reaffirm the principle of a Coalition Government, and will sit for only four or five days. The Bolsheviks, on the contrary, aim at making of the assembly a kind of Parliament which will elect a Socialist Ministry, seize all the power, and then remain in session as a legislative body.

The Bolsheviks alone are not strong enough numerically to carry through such a policy, but they are encouraged by the ambiguous attitude of the Social Revolutionaries led by M. Chernoff. M. Chernoff, since he left the Government, has been carrying on a curious agitation. Immediately after his resignation he placarded the whole town with a proclamation to peasants and soldiers, assuring them that, though no longer Minister, he would work harder than ever in their interests. He has inundated his organ, the *Dyelo Naroda*, with articles full of insinuations and open charges against M. Kerenski – charges which the Premier, in *Volia Naroda*, the organ of the pro-war minority of the Social Revolutionary party, has practically stigmatised as lies. M. Chernoff, moreover, has been very active in the Soviet, and the idea of the democratic conference is directly attributed to his suggestion. It may be that the exposures of the *Volia Naroda* will provoke a schism in the Social Revolutionary party, but in the meantime the Central Committee and its following are entirely in the hands of M. Chernoff.

However that may be, with or without the connivance of the Social Revolutionaries, the Bolsheviks are working hard to secure a victory. The very fact that the Government in its efforts to suppress the Korniloff movement was compelled to fall back on the Left for support stimulated the Bolshevik agitation.

The various committees formed to combat the counter-revolution show no disposition to disband, the workmen have not been disarmed, and the adoption of a Bolshevik resolution by the Petrograd Soviet has led to the resignation of the more moderate executive, including M. Cheidze and Tseretelli.

From other towns come reports that Bolshevik tendencies are dominant, and that the revolutionary committees are seizing power. The Moscow Soviet has passed a resolution even more radically Bolshevik than that passed by the Petrograd Soviet. It demands not only the establishment of a Socialist Government, but the publication of the secret treaties, immediate declaration of peace, immediate transfer of all lands to the peasantry, and the attribution of legislative functions to the democratic conference in Kharkoff, and in several other towns the local Soviets have seized administrative power. In Tiflis the Government Commissaries for the Caucasus have been ousted by a Socialist Committee. All these facts indicate that the moment of decisive conflict cannot long be postponed.

Strange news comes from Finland. It is reported that the Finnish parties are holding secret consultations, and that, using as a pretext the proclamation of a Republic in Russia, they are prepared to reassert their claim for independence. This movement is obviously not wholly unconnected with the demand of the Moscow Soviet that all nationalities, and particularly Finland and the Ukraine, should be given complete liberty to decide their own fate. The Government is preparing its own measures. It intends forming a Coalition Government this week, so as to face the Democratic Conference with the accomplished fact. It is carefully watching Finland, and altogether it is thoroughly aware of the possibilities of the situation.

29 September 1917

RUSSIAN CRISIS

Depression and Distrust, *Petrograd, Wednesday*

There are moments when one would prefer to be silent about what is happening in Russia. It is possible, perhaps, to cultivate an attitude of cool detachment, to observe events from a purely historical standpoint, to calculate that the calamities of today are a particularly stern form of discipline, and that Russia will be stronger in the end for what she is suffering today. Without some such outlook in the more vitalising form of active faith in the future, it would be impossible to endure the stress of the present. At times the atmosphere is suffocating, the stress is almost intolerable. Russian patriots of every shade of opinion are subjected to an almost unrelieved moral torture, and none living here, unless he has a heart of stone, can fail to share their suffering. The bright hopes of the revolution are darkened, the collective energy of the people is paralysed, the whole life of the nation is entangled in a network of almost insoluble contradictions, patience and hope are exhausted by a series of fruitless compromises between warring forces. If these forces were only positive instead of being negative, if they only displayed real energy and real organising power, then the crisis might be short, sharp, and decisive, but it is protracted by an extraordinary lassitude, born of the long war and the oppression of the old regime. This lassitude was concealed for a time by the excitement of the revolution, but the freshening impulses of the revolution were frittered away in words and too soon paralysed by bitter party strife. And now the general weariness is expressing itself in a profound moral reaction. I lived through the reaction that followed the last revolution, in 1906, and again I see the familiar signs – the chase after pleasure, the reckless gambling, the steady decline of interest in politics, the sudden demand for 'penny dreadfuls' of the Nat Pinkerton type. The other evening, in a workmen's quarter, I saw a ball going on next to a house where a Bolshevik meeting was being held, and, generally speaking, in the workmen's quarters dances are more popular now than political meetings. At the same time, the difficulties of living in the towns, the steady rise in prices, the shortage of food, the impossibility of getting any satisfactory share of material goods in exchange for money, have increased the general discontent and established a general attitude of profound disillusionment.

The Korniloff affair has intensified mutual distrust and completed the work of destruction. The Government is shadowy and unreal, and what personality it had has disappeared before the menace of the Democratic Conference. Whatever power there is is again concentrated in the hands of the Soviets, and, as always happens when the Soviets secure a monopoly of power, the influence of the Bolsheviks has increased enormously. M. Kerenski has returned from headquarters, but his prestige has declined, and he is not actively supported either by the Right or by the Left. M. Terestchenko, the last representative of the bourgeoisie in the Government, has handed in his resignation. Lenin has emerged from his concealment, and has been elected by the Bolsheviks as their representative at the Democratic Conference. This conference will meet tomorrow or the day after. The Bolsheviks hope to capture it, and by its means to establish a purely Socialist Ministry, but, so far as can be judged, the feeling of the great majority of the delegates is in favour of a real coalition of all parties. There is much talk of General Verhovsky, the new War Minister, as the coming man, but the non-Socialist papers criticise his policy as commander of the Moscow military district, and are not at all hopeful as to the results of the application of this policy to the army as a whole.

So we live from day to day amidst rumours and phantoms and a general depression that at times has the quality of a nightmare.

29 October 1917

SITUATION IN RUSSIA
Baltic Fleet's Revival, *Petrograd, Tuesday*

The Germans have begun a new, interesting, and not wholly intelligible manœuvre. Moon Island forms a bridge between Oesal and the mainland. So long as Russian ships remained in Moon Sound access to the mainland was barred, but with the retirement of Admiral Bakhirev's squadron northward there was nothing to prevent the Germans from attempting to bring troops across the narrow strip of water to the farther shore. They made an attempt without delay, and with the help of their fleet succeeded in landing two companies on the Werder Peninsula, just opposite the southern tip of Moon and 38 miles north of Pernau.

By the last report a farther landing was being attempted in Matsal Bay, to the north of Werder. Russian resistance was apparently insufficiently organised at Werder, and it may be that the chief preparations to repel a landing were made at the more important points of Pernau and Hapsal, while the intervening coastline was thinly guarded. Whether the new German manœuvres succeed or fail depends entirely on the resisting power of the Russian army. It ought not to be difficult to crush the landing force before it attains serious dimensions, and, indeed, it still remains doubtful whether the Germans can devote any very large force to an operation of this kind. It is significant that while landing their troops in the north the Germans slightly withdrew their line above Riga. The object of this move is two-fold; first, to economise troops in order to increase the reserve for a possible transfer northward; second, to draw the Russians on and hamper a deployment of their forces to meet the threatened thrust in the rear.

General Dukhonin, the acting Commander-in-Chief, who is now in Petrograd, does not consider the danger to the capital pressing so long as the Baltic fleet retains its effectiveness. The revival in the spirit of the Baltic fleet is astonishing. Bolshevik crews express an eagerness to defend their country to the last breath, and ask that their officers should be returned to them. The Central Committee of the fleet, which until recently was constantly at loggerheads with the chief of the naval staff, is now working in complete accord with the naval authorities, and is doing its utmost to organise the defence. The *Grazdanin*, formerly *Paul I*, was well known as a Bolshevik ship, and yet when the call came to fight it did its duty bravely with the other ships in Bakhirev's squadron. If the army could rise to the occasion in the same way as the fleet is doing there could be no question of any serious German success.

10 November 1917

SOVIET CONFERENCE
A Dramatic Coup, *Petrograd, Thursday*

The revolution has advanced another stage, perhaps the most definite one of all. The history of the last thirty-six hours is peculiarly tangled. As far as is at present ascertainable, the honours lie with the Military Revolutionary Committee, now exactly a week old. On Tuesday night the Petrograd Soviet held a meeting, when the political situation was discussed in the light of M. Kerenski's threats a few hours earlier at the Democratic Council. The Bolshevik leaders were still hesitating over the wisdom of a demonstration. The minority parties apparently took it for granted that an armed demonstration was improbable.

At three o'clock on Wednesday morning unanimity was reached as the result of a series of reports from the garrison units expressing their readiness to accept orders from the Military Revolutionary Committee. It was decided to strike. The Provisional Government was forthwith declared non-existent. At 4.30 the first detachments left the Soviet headquarters and descended upon the Government Bank in accordance with a plan produced by the Military Revolutionaries. The whole success of the Bolshevik coup turns upon this plan of campaign. The promoters are naturally unwilling to divulge its details yet, but gossip at Smolny Institute, their headquarters, declares that its authors were three hitherto unheard-of youths, and dwells lovingly on the completeness of the details.

Petrograd awoke and went about its normal business, and only towards midday realised, except in the centre, that the old Government had been painlessly replaced. Some hundreds of young men, members of the Officers' Training Corps, and women and soldiers, formed the sole defence of the Provisional Government. These encircled and garrisoned the Winter Palace, and were themselves surrounded by garrison troops. The cruiser *Aurora* arrived from Kronstadt, and took up a position in the Neva opposite the Winter Palace. In the afternoon the cruiser fired a blank shot as a warning to the Palace inmates. This started a slight panic, and a party of sailors, landing for a pourparler, were fired on, one being killed and one wounded. This apparently was the most serious case of bloodshed on Wednesday.

In the afternoon the Nevsky was cleared of traffic, and machine-guns and quick fires were placed at the principal crossings throughout the city. Perfect quiet was maintained.

I have been spending the night at the Smolny Institute. The great building, formerly a school for the girls of the Russian aristocracy, still preserves its slightly convent like effects inside, forming an odd background to the crowds of soldiers filling it. The All-Russian Conference of Soviets was timed to open here at noon, but delay after delay was imposed on the patient and steadily increasing crowd of delegates packing the large hall. In the afternoon various sectional meetings were held, the Bolsheviks being addressed by Lenin and Zinovieff. Apparently the secret of Lenin's successful disguise lies in the fact that he has shaved off his beard. At 9 p.m. a final postponement of one hour was announced. At 10.45 the Conference at last opened.

The proceedings, which lasted till 5.30 a.m., were threefold. At first there were the usual wranglings about procedure. Then came the adoption of the programme of the new Soviet Government. Finally, occasional bulletins were read from the Military Revolutionary Committee reporting progress. These last invariably recorded success for the Bolshevik operations. The entire Provisional Government, excepting M. Kerenski, was stated to be under arrest, principally at the fortress of Peter and Paul, where a curious irony makes them fellow inmates of the ex-Ministers who provoked the March revolution. Comnmissaries had been appointed by the Military Revolutionary Committee at all important stations exhorting the soldiers moving on Petrograd not to obey the Provisional Government's orders. The entire garrison was now supporting the Soviet. M. Kerenski had disappeared. At 5 a.m. he had left Petrograd. At 10 a.m. he had exhorted a great meeting of soldiers at Gatchina to come to the rescue of the Provisional Government. The soldiers, principally Cossacks, communicated with the Soviet, and refused. M. Kerenski was now, apparently, at the front, seeking an army willing to march on the capital.

The programme adopted by the Conference declares that the Provisional Government is suppressed, and that the Conference has sovereign power. On the immediate fronts democratic peace terms are to be formulated, and if offered and refused by Germany the war is to continue. Privately owned land is to become the property of the peasants' committees for redistribution by them. Working men are to control the factories. The Soviets are to tackle the food problem. The soldiers at the front are exhorted to stay in the trenches until further notice and to keep cool.

The discussion showed that the Bolsheviks were completely masters of the Conference. The Mensheviks, Internationalists, Jewish Bundists, and a section of the Social Revolutionaries in turn denounced the Bolshevik usurpation and refused their co-operation, but these sections formed a small minority of the Conference. We had been told that the Councils of Peasants' Delegates and the army organisations were opposed to the Conference, but the Bolsheviks produced a long array of peasants and soldiers, every one of whom declared in one-minute speeches that the peasants and soldiers generally were imbued with Bolshevik enthusiasm. In spite of the protests of the Mensheviks, &c., an enormous majority of those present completely accepted the Bolshevik Government.

It should be noted that the moderate leaders, M. Cheidze and M. Tseretelli, were absent, both being in the Caucasus recuperating from overwork. M. Chernoff, a doubtful quantity, the leader of a fluctuating section of the Social Revolutionary Party and the Council of Peasants' Delegates, was also absent. Just now, to be absent is to be forgotten.

Today the new Government probably will be elected. It is said that the Bolsheviks will have no Premier, the members of the Cabinet taking turns to preside. Perfect order prevails in Petrograd. The Conference was particularly anxious to avoid all bloodshed. At two o'clock this morning the Winter Palace was entered at the bayonet-point. The defending troops surrendered, having practically no ammunition, but they killed six and wounded many of the attackers. The defending party sustained no losses. Only then the CWSD learned that twenty-four hours earlier M. Kishkin, by this time in gaol, had been appointed Dictator.

18 January 1918

KING OF ROUMANIA
Order for Arrest and Removal to Petrograd

It is announced from Petrograd that the Bolshevik Commissaries are to take the sensational step of having the King of Roumania arrested and taken to the Russian capital. The message, which is of Wednesday's date, is as follows: 'The evening papers announce that the People's Commissaries have ordered the arrest of the King of Roumania, and his removal to Petrograd.' – Reuters.

The pretext is obviously the friction which has arisen between the Roumanians and the Russian forces on the south-western front, and which led Lenin to send an ultimatum to the Roumanian Government demanding the release of the troops and others arrested, punishment for those responsible, and guarantees against a repetition of the occurrence. It was also the cause assigned for the arrest of the Roumanian Minister, whose release at the request of the Allies is regarded as a diplomatic triumph for the Leninite Government, as it has thus succeeded in obtaining recognition from the Entente Powers.

It should be recalled, however, that it was recently reported that the Bolsheviks were trying to provoke a Socialist revolution in Roumania.

TROTSKY'S TRIUMPH
Object of Arrest Gained, *Petrograd, Tuesday*

An incident almost without parallel in the history of diplomatic relations has just been taking place here. Trotsky lately has been seriously annoyed at the behaviour of the Roumanian Government. Bolshevik Commissaries have been shot recently by the Roumanians, who are taking no pains to conceal their hostility towards Lenin's Government. Some days ago an Austrian officer was arrested by the Roumanians, who threatened to shoot him as a spy. The officer pleaded the armistice, and the case was taken up at Brest by Count Czernin, who apparently invited Trotsky to take joint action with Austria against recalcitrant Roumania. Trotsky thereupon ordered the arrest of the Roumanian Minister in Petrograd, and the members of the Legation. This extraordinary infraction of diplomatic practice and international law was carried into effect late on Sunday night, when the whole body of Roumanian official representatives were taken to the fortress of SS Peter and Paul. On Monday morning the Ambassadors and Ministers representing nineteen Powers met at the United States Embassy and decided upon common action. In the afternoon the nineteen diplomatists visited Lenin at Smolny, and made a formal protest. The Italian Ambassador was especially indignant. Seizing the opportunity, he informed Lenin that on Saturday soldiers raided the cellars of the Italian Embassy, but the wine was saved, as it happened, by the arrival of the Red Guards. Lenin urbanely asked: 'But why didn't you ring me up? I'd have had the fellows shot at once.'

Finally, Lenin explained that the arrest of the Roumanian Minister was a deliberate protest against the shooting of the Bolsheviks. The object of the arrest was certainly gained, as Europe had undoubtedly been impressed by this action, and the Minister would be released the same night. It is argued that the visit of the nineteen Ambassadors renders it impossible to continue to refuse official recognition to the Smolny Government.

The same evening a detachment of the Red Guards, a nucleus of the future volunteer army, started for the front. Lenin arrived after a long delay, due to the nineteen diplomats, and gave the departing volunteers, whose destination is uncertain, his blessing. For over an hour we waited in a huge garage, the size of which may be estimated by the fact that some forty armoured cars took up a very slight proportion of its space. The Bolshevik soldiers discussed their possible front, sang revolutionary songs, and danced. Suddenly Lenin arrived. Few have ever seen him so good-humoured as he was last night. He was obviously so pleased with the afternoon's events that he had no fight left in him. His speech was platitudinous. The effect of his oratory was spoilt by his twinkling eyes. Yet it is important to note one thing, typical of the man. Notwithstanding the prompting of the chairman, Lenin refrained from referring to the nineteen diplomats. He had scored one of his greatest triumphs that day, yet he thought it not worth mentioning for the sake of raising an extra cheer. And that is how Lenin spent New Year's Day.

30 January 1918

CIVIL WAR IN RUSSIA

Complete Anarchy, *Petrograd, Saturday*

It becomes daily more difficult to give a connected account of this wild dance of actors which is called Russia. The country is involved in a chaos of civil war, irregular and undisciplined, with a perpetual alternation of easy victories and easy defeats, with panics and betrayals, and half-hearted fraternising and drunken riots and plots, and denunciations and looting, and murder and continual wanton destruction of property, and an almost complete paralysis of the political and economic functions of the State. Lenin glories in civil war. 'Yes,' he cried in his speech at the Soviet Congress, 'we are physical force men. We stand for violence against all exploiters, and we are not abashed by the cries of those who weep and shudder in the presence of a great struggle. We are the first Government in the world that openly declares that it is carrying on civil war, and we pledge ourselves to carry on this war to a finish.'

The air is full of conflicting rumours of brilliant victories and crushing defeats of various parties. It very often proves that the victory was practically bloodless, simply because the other side ran away, and the seizure of a town or a district by one party is followed by its recovery in a day or two by the opponents. And very frequently fierce and bloody battles are reported from places where there has been no battle at all. Again and again, for instance, we have heard of great battles between Bolsheviks and Ukrainians at Bokhmach Junction, near Kieff. It is true that considerable forces on both sides have collected there, but there has not been a serious battle yet. Neither side shows great inclination to begin, and the soldiers live peaceably together.

The Bolsheviks are particularly determined to carry on civil war against the Kieff Rada and General Kaledin. Their grievance against the Kieff Rada is twofold. First, the Rada does not recognise the Bolshevik Government, and has disarmed and disbanded the Bolshevik troops in Southern Russia, and concluded a military alliance with Roumania and General Kaledin. And secondly, the Ukrainians, by negotiating independently with the Central Powers, have seriously complicated Trotsky's policy. A split between Austria and Germany would give Trotsky a trump card in the negotiations. But the south-western front facing Austria is in Ukrainian hands. If Ukrainia makes a separate peace with the Central Powers, this will primarily affect Austria. The Austro–Russian front ceases to exist, and then Austria, having secured peace for herself, no longer has any direct interest in opposing the excessive German pretensions in northern Russia, which now protract and complicate the negotiations. This explains the present acute indignation of the Bolsheviks against the Ukrainians, and their determination to overthrow the Kieff Rada.

They are acting both by military force and political stratagem. In Kharkoff they have set up a rival Bolshevik Ukrainian Government, and are trying to agitate among the Ukrainian soldiers. A recent attempt to provoke a rising in Kieff was frustrated by the disarmament of the local Red Guard by the Ukrainian Government. From the north and east Bolshevik forces from time to time make more or less successful raids into Ukrainian territory, and Bolshevik troops from the Roumanian and south-western front indulge in frequent skirmishes with the Rada's troops within Ukrainia.

Matters are further complicated by the struggle between the Roumanian and Russian troops. The Roumanians are now waging a regular battle with the 9th Siberian Division near Galatz. Kharkoff, however, is the real centre of the Bolshevik military operations. Here a staff under Antonoff sits in a railway carriage, and, directing its forces against the Ukraine on one side and the Don on the other, tries to cut communication between the two autonomous territories. The forces at Antonoff's disposal consist of sailors, soldiers, Red Guards, and German and Austrian prisoners. A certain success was achieved against the Ukraine in the capture of Poltava Ekaterinoslav, and Alexandrovsk, but the Ukraine has recovered Ekaterinoslav and Alexandrovsk. In Kharkoff itself there are five authorities which apparently enjoy equal power – Antonoff's staff, the local Bolshevik committee, the Soviet Rada, a nondescript military revolutionary committee, and the Commissary of the Provisional Government.

In the Crimea the Tartars and Bolsheviks wage war with varying success. Kertch is reported to be in the hands of the Bolsheviks, and for that reason communication by the Indo–European telegraph between Odessa and Tiflis is interrupted. As to the Don the position is not wholly clear. General Kaledin has given strict orders to the Cossacks not to cross the frontiers of their own territory. Apparently the Bolsheviks have seized part of the mining area near Taganrog. The position of the South-Eastern Federation is complicated by the irruption of bands of Bolshevik soldiers from the Caucasian front, by continual raids of the mountain tribes on Vladikavkaz and Grozny, by a Bolshevik agitation in Rostoff, and by internal political dissensions. On the other hand, the formation by General Alexeieff of a strong disciplined force of patriotic officers and soldiers is proceeding apace, under the shelter of Cossack hospitality. The Bolsheviks are pressing hard on General Duloff's Orenburg Cossacks, and the wavering issues are complicated by the ambiguous attitude of the local Tartar troops. The Polish legions, in revenge for the arrest of the staff of the volunteer Polish army at Minsk, have seized the junction of Orsha, and the neighbouring stations between Moglieff and Petrograd.

Further, the Bolsheviks, whose recognition of the self-determination of nationalities is dependent on their recognition of Bolshevik authority, are fomenting a social revolution in Finland. During last week the Socialist Red Guard, supplied with arms by the local Russian garrison and Petrograd, has committed acts of violence in Viborg, Helsingfors, Tammerfors, and other towns, assisted in many cases by Russian soldiers and sailors. The Finnish Socialist party has formed a military revolutionary committee to watch the situation and direct the action of the Red Guard, and at the fitting moment to wrest power from the 'bourgeoise' majority in the Diet. The 'bourgeoise' parties demand the evacuation of the Russian troops from Finland. The Socialists oppose this, on the ground that the troops are needed for 'defence against Imperialist Germany'.

And while all over Russia civil war is hopelessly raging, Petrograd at last, after repeated warnings, has come face to face with starvation. The supplies of corn are almost exhausted. Flour has to be brought to the bakeries secretly, lest it be seized by the angry crowds, and in some parts of the town riots have begun in the bread queues. A procession of women went to the Smolny Institute to beg in vain for bread. The Food Committee proposes to establish two-day intervals in which no bread ration at all shall be issued. The epidemic of hunger typhus is spreading. Yet with all this Lenin glories in civil war, and says, 'The real terror has yet to come.'

18 February 1918

'PEACE' FIASCO
Armistice at an End

Under the agreement signed at Brest-Litovsk the armistice between Russia and the Centrals extended originally from 17 December to 14 January. It was, however, prolonged by mutual consent, and was terminable by seven days' notice on either side. Reuters correspondent at Amsterdam, writing on Saturday, says: 'According to a Berlin telegram, the Imperial Government states in an official communication that the Petrograd Government by its conduct has in fact denounced the armistice, and that this denunciation is to be regarded as having occurred on 10 February.

'Conformably therewith,' the communication proceeds, 'the German Government must, after the lapse of the seven days' notice of termination provided for under the treaty, reserve a free hand in every direction.'

In this connection the German Staff's official communiqué of yesterday afternoon has the following significant sentence 'Great Russian Front – The armistice expires at noon on 18 February.'

According to a message forwarded yesterday by the Admiralty, per Wireless Press, Trotsky has sent the following wireless to the 'Government of the German Empire, Berlin': Today, 17 February, we received a message by direct wire from Brest Litovsk from General Samoliu that General Hoffmann declared on 18 February that from 18 February at midday the state of war will be resumed between Germany and Russia. The Russian Republic supposes that the telegram received by us was not issued by those persons by whom it was signed, and we consider that it has a provocative character, for even if the cessation of the armistice on the part of Germany is to be assumed, a notice of seven days must be given, according to the conditions of the armistice, and not merely two days. We request an explanation of this misunderstanding, and ask that it may be sent by radio. Please give a receipt.

This means that from today the Centrals' war with Russia, i.e. the Bolsheviks, is resumed. The German and Austrian technical and economic commissions have already left Petrograd. Their departure was preceded by a Berlin semi-official Note complaining bitterly that the 'work of the German Commission is meeting with constantly increasing difficulties', and stating that the Russian Government had abrogated the decision to exchange military and civilian prisoners of war.

According to the *Berliner Tageblatt*, the conference at the Kaiser's Headquarters resulted in a decision to resume hostilities against northern Russia. It is thought likely that the enemy may occupy the whole of the province of Esthonia. The Germans, as a pretext, are already spreading repeats of the ill-treatment by the Bolsheviks of the German baron landowners of the district, and are asserting that these people are demanding the immediate occupation of the country by the

German army. Reuters' Amsterdam correspondent telegraphs: The German public is now apparently being prepared for action by the Central Powers against the Bolsheviks. The *Norddeutsche Allgemeine Zeitung* in an article telegraphed on Saturday from Berlin vehemently denounces the proceedings of the Bolsheviks in Finland, Esthonia, and Livonia, and adds that it learns that the Finnish plenipotentiaries now in Berlin have already taken steps to win the support of the German Government on behalf of Finland. The article farther points out that, simultaneously with the order for demobilisation, the Russian Government ordered the formation of a 'Red Army'.

Reports, all of which originate in enemy quarters, and must therefore be regarded with suspicion, concerning the Central Powers' relations with Roumania, are conflicting. One telegram says that the armistice has been extended for a few days. The *Lokalanzeiger* asserts that 'peace with Roumania is now only a matter of days'. A Reuters telegram from Amsterdam, dated Saturday, states: 'The *Handelsblad* learns from Vienna that the Roumanian Government intends to enter into negotiations with the Central Powers provided the latter give a previous assurance that they will not assail the sovereignty of Roumania and will leave the solution of the dynastic question to the Roumanians themselves. Roumania, it is declared, will then declare her readiness to cede the Dobrudja to Bulgaria, provided the Central Powers grant Roumania their benevolent support in the Bessarabian question. The Averescu Cabinet has not yet been formed, but it is stated, the *Handelsblad* adds, that the first point in its programme is peace by agreement with the Central Powers.'

The cession of the Cholm region to the Ukraine continues to cause great turmoil, both in Poland and among the Poles in Austria–Hungary. The *Lokalanzeiger* admits that great excitement is prevalent in Warsaw: Rumours of organised demonstrations of students and workmen are in circulation, and mounted and unmounted military detachments are patrolling the streets. Count Rostorowski, Director of Political Affairs has resigned. The newspapers appeared with black borders in consequence of the treaty with the Ukraine. All the Cracow papers publish the appeal of a committee formed of all Polish parties in favour of a one-day's general strike on 18 February as a protest against the severance of the Cholm region. In Lemberg a general strike on Monday was resolved on, suspending work in all departments, institutions, schools, workshops, &c.

According to the Vienna *Fremdenblatt*, the deputy, M. Glombinski, the former leader of the Polish Club, has returned all his Orders and decorations to the Austrian Government.

The probability of continued warfare in the Ukraine between the 'Reds' and the Reds causes great perturbation in Germany and Austria, where the half-starving populations are looking with greedy eyes for the promised supplies of food from the new 'Republic'.

20 February 1918

TROTSKY'S PANIC
Complete Surrender

With a precipitancy wholly out of keeping with their high-sounding protestations, Trotsky and his accomplices in Russia's ruin have hauled down their flag in face of the recommencement of hostilities by the Germans. The armistice terminated on Monday, and at noon on the same day German troops crossed the Dvina, without resistance, and marched towards and occupied Dvinsk. At the same time the enemy moved from Kovei into Ukrainia. In less than twenty-four hours the Bolsheviks had surrendered. At 4.15 yesterday afternoon the Admiralty forwarded, per Wireless Press, the following declaration, signed by Lenin and Trotsky, which had been intercepted from the wireless stations of the Russian Government: To the Government of the German Empire, Berlin.

The Council of the People's Commissaries protests against the fact that the German Government has directed its troops against the Russian Councils' Republic, which has declared the war as at an end, and which is demobilising its army on all fronts. The Workmen's and Peasants' Government of Russia could not anticipate such a step, because, neither directly nor indirectly, has any one of the parties which concluded the armistice given the seven days' notice required in accordance with the treaty of 15 December for terminating it.

The Council of the People's Commissaries in the present circumstances regards itself as forced to formally declare its willingness to sign a peace upon the conditions which have been dictated by the delegations of the Quadruple Alliance at Brest Litovsk. The Council of the People's Commissaries further declares that a detailed reply will be given without delay to the conditions of peace as proposed by the German Government.

Shortly afterwards the Admiralty furnished the subjoined further intercepted wireless from the Bolshevik Government:

To Count Czernin, Vienna.
The German Government has renewed hostilities against Russia, even without seven days' notice, and I have the honour to ask you whether you consider the Austro–Hungarian Government also as being in a state of war with Russia? If not, do you consider the Austro–Hungarian Government—.

The conclusion of the message is missing. In the meantime, the German forces continue to advance. The official communiqué issued at Berlin yesterday afternoon states: Eastern Theatre – Yesterday evening German troops entered Dvinsk. They met with little resistance. The majority of the enemy have fled. The Russians were not successful in blowing up the Dvina Bridge, for which preparations had been made. On both sides of Luzk our divisions are on the march. Luzk was occupied without any fighting.

The Berlin official report of last night states: From Riga as far as south of Luzk the German armies are advancing towards the east.

Dvinsk is about 320 miles south-west of Petrograd, with which it is connected by a direct railway. Luzk is 230 miles west of Kieff. Whether Trotsky's panic-stricken *volte face* will cause the Germans to pause for the time being is doubtful.

The plain truth is that the Russian army, having been utterly destroyed by Lenin and Trotsky, the invaders have practically nothing to fear in the way of opposition for the present. The following message sent out to Russian Headquarters and to all fronts by Krylenko, the Bolshevik Commander-in-Chief, has been received by the Admiralty per Wireless Press: The Council of the People's Commissaries has offered to the Germans to sign peace immediately. I order that in all cases where Germans are encountered missed, pourparlers with the German soldiers should be organised and a proposal to refrain from fighting should be made to them. If the Germans refuse, then you must offer to them every possible resistance.

According to the *Frankfurter Zeitung*, Germany and Austria have made an agreement according to which Germany will take military action in the Great Russian frontier districts, while Austrian duty will conduct all the necessary military operations in Ukrainia.

It is a sinister coincidence that a German paper should have discovered that Trotsky is of German birth. Reuters' correspondent at Amsterdam wires: The Essen *Allgemeine Zeitung* professes to have made the discovery that Trotsky was born at Wipperfuerth, near Remscheid, in the Rhine Province, and that his real name is Bronstein. The journal also adds that Trotsky studied at the University of Bonn, which town he is alleged to have left hurriedly, having been detected in the act of thieving. Later, the journal adds, he married a rich girl, who came to a sudden end.

Telegraphing under date 17 February, Reuters' Petrograd correspondent states: It having come to the knowledge of the British Chargé d'Affaires here that the position taken up by the British Government towards the Ukraine had given rise to some misunderstanding, he has issued a statement declaring that neither the Ukraine nor any other integral portion of the Russian Empire had been recognised by Great Britain as an independent State. Consequently, the delegates of the Ukraine Rada at the Brest-Litovsk peace negotiations exercised Powers. Such action on their part was absolutely inadmissible as far as the British Government was concerned.

Large numbers of telegrams, delayed by the interruption of the wires in Finland, were received yesterday from Petrograd, bearing dates as far back as 8 February. These belated messages throw very little light on the general situation.

Lurid accounts are given of more or less furious fighting between the Bolshevik partisans and their opponents at, among other places, Odessa, Simferopol, Rogatcheff, near Minsk, in North and South Finland, in the Don region, in the Aland Islands, &c. All these reports are evidently coloured according to the side from which they emanate, and the claims advanced are therefore open to suspicion, if not absolutely worthless. But they show that civil war is spreading with appalling rapidity, and, combined with famine and disease, threatens to involve the once great Empire in the most terrible catastrophe known to history.

A 'Red Navy' is to be formed by the Bolsheviks. An instance of the present insecurity in Petrograd is shown by the fact that at midnight on 14 February a sleigh in which the Italian Ambassador was being driven was stopped in the centre of the town by a motor-car which blocked its advance. Three armed men, on the pretext of a search for arms, robbed the Ambassador of his fur coat, pocket book, and valuables.

It is stated that some of the imprisoned ex-Ministers of the Provisional Government have been released, including MM. Kartacheff, Konavaloff, and Kishkin. An attempt to murder M. Rodzianko, formerly president of the Duma, was made recently at Novo Cherkassk, in south Russia. While returning home he was stopped by a group of officers, who ordered him to follow them. Several shots were fired at him on his refusal to do so, and both he and his coachman were slightly wounded.

General Nazaroff is reported to have succeeded General Kaledin as Hetman of the Cossacks. Kaledin is said to have committed suicide. Reuters' Petrograd correspondent wired on Sunday: The Official Telegraph Agency reports that General Kaledin has committed suicide after a sitting of the Coalition Government which has been endeavouring to direct the affairs of the Don region. After a series of long debates the Government eventually decided to resign its authority in favour of the Soviet. On this decision being come to Kaledin went into another room and shot himself, the bullet entering his heart. General Nazaroff, who has assumed the vacant command, has given orders for the mobilisation of the population, both Cossack and non-Cossack, for the fight against troops of the Soviets.

General Ivanoff, formerly Commander-in-Chief on the south-west front, has died or been killed under mysterious circumstances at Kieff. A Reuters Petrograd telegram, dated 15 February, says that his body has been identified in the anatomical theatre in Kieff. According to one version he was killed during a sortie from Petchersky Monastery, but another message says his death was accidental.

LIFE AT MOSCOW

A City of Refuge, *Moscow, 13 February*

Moscow has become for many a city of refuge. The Bolshevik regime is rather milder here: the menace of starvation is not so imminent; there is a little more space, a little more freedom; there is some shelter and comfort in the multitude. Here are many ruined land-owners who have escaped from their plundered and pillaged estates; here are officers in hundreds, driven from the front by the soldiers; here are former Government employees who have drifted hither from Petrograd in search of work, and a very miscellaneous throng of men and women who have found the results of the slow labour of years crumble away in their hands, who have lost occupations, who have now no use for their talents, their painfully acquired knowledge, and who cling here to the faint shadow of intellectual life that seems still to afford some outward justification of their hopeless existence. The bourgeois well-to-do middle class has been hard hit by Bolshevik rule, but the greatest sufferers are the intelligentsia, whom the crude Bolshevik classification ranks with the bourgeoisie as the enemies of the proletariat.

I walk down the street and listen to the cries of the news-vendors. I hear a strange accent, and turning see a young officer, without shoulder straps or any marks of distinction, shamefacedly offering for sale a cheap evening paper. There are scores of such officers now selling papers in the streets of Moscow. The voice that again and again led a company to the attack now, with a note of bitter defiance, cries *Ruskkia Viedomosti* or *Epocha*, vainly competing with the shrill calls of the agile and impudent newsboys. There are women, too, among the news-vendors – girl students, office girls, teachers. Some officers are employed in guarding houses against robbers, others unload trucks on the railway; a few others, more fortunate, have found employment as cabmen, and others still are crossing-sweepers. Once prosperous writers and journalists are now almost penniless owing to the stoppage of many newspapers and magazines, and the almost complete cessation of the publishing business. Well-to-do families, whose money is invested in now valueless securities or deposited in inaccessible bank accounts, are selling their heirlooms to secure the wherewithal to support life. A family driven by peasants from its estate is crowded together in one room in a state of semi-starvation, and was recently joined by the eldest son, an officer who barely escaped with his life from the front.

All this suffering would be a minor evil if the prosperity of the working-classes were secured, but the factories are gradually closing down, unemployment is steadily increasing, and the attempts of the Bolshevik Soviet and committees to prevent unemployment by the payment of huge subsidies in wages to workmen who do not and cannot work for want of raw material simply aggravate the financial crisis. There are people with money, of course – the tradesmen who charge exorbitant prices for goods, the profiteers who get boots, cloth, and butter by all kinds of crooked devices and sell them at fabulous prices, the highwaymen, who take their nightly toll in the dark lanes of Moscow, and the bagmen. The bagmen are a specific product of this troubled time. They are soldiers, or men in soldiers' uniform, who travel about on the railways free of charge, buy flour where it is cheap, and sell it in the cities at a profit of 500 roubles a sack, in cool defiance of the regulations of the corn and flour monopoly. I know of a case where a man who began as a bagman carrying three sacks at a time later developed into a truckman – that is, a man who brings in a whole truckload of flour – and last week he offered to bring in a whole trainload, his immense profits having put him in a position to evade the inconvenient regulations.

Never have bribery and corruption attained such dimensions as now, and there are all kinds of fantastic ways of making money. In one government not far from Moscow some enterprising businessmen have formed a company for the recovery of goods plundered by the peasants from estates. They secured from the Revolutionary Committee a paper authorising them to confiscate from the peasants goods constituting national wealth. Then they hired eleven soldiers at 50 roubles a day, and these soldiers, armed with the committee's authorisation, go from village to village, flog the peasants, and extort from them the plundered goods, which are ultimately restored to the original owners with a deduction of 10 per cent commission. This business is highly profitable.

Moscow is a city of refuge, but for how long? Even here life is continually haunted by vague and monstrous fears. Is there any security or hope here in Russia? 'Whither shall I flee from the wrath and the terror?' is the cry of the helpless and distracted. This anarchy is perhaps less destructive of human life, but to the spirit it is far more crushing, more paralysing, than war, for war has its rhythm, its calculable orders, its conditions and laws, but this anarchy is war that has broken all bounds and gone mad; it is the brutal essence of war which has escaped control, has thrown off all the draperies of political theory and flaunts its nakedness mockingly in unshamed fratricide, in senseless suicide. Refuge there is none. The process of destruction must work itself out. This strange anarchy is sweeping from end to end of Russia.

The Ukraine is a broken reed, the Siberian Government was overthrown as soon as it was formed; Turkestan is a prey to formless anarchy; the Tartar Government in the Crimea is maintaining a desperate struggle against Bolshevik sailors and Red Guards; the contending forces in Bessarabia are swallowed up by a Roumanian invasion which now threatens Odessa. The Don territory is threatened from north, south, and west, though Alexieff's army, rapidly growing and well-disciplined, effectively repels the attacks of many times more numerous irregular Bolshevik troops. But its position is endangered by the spread of Bolshevik infection among the Cossacks.

It is true that while Bolshevism is spreading in the south, a reaction against Bolshevism is growing in the northern centres, but for the present it is impossible to fix any term to Bolshevik rule, impossible to forecast what power will replace it. The course of events must necessarily lead to the restoration of strong Government, but how and in what form no one can say. Apart from the Don no active organised centre of opposition is visible.

Chapter 11

The Western Front 1918 and Victory for the Allies

7 January 1918

AMERICA AND THE WAR

What is Being Done?

By Herman Whitaker

Mr Herman Whitaker is the author of several successful novels and a contributor to all the leading American magazines. Born in Huddersfield in 1867, he served for three years in the British Army, after which he went to Canada and then to America. He has travelled much in Mexico, and in 1914 acted as war correspondent with General Villa's force in Central Mexico.

How are your people taking the war? This question has been put to me repeatedly. I might answer, somewhat paradoxically, that they are taking it very seriously and very lightly. They are taking it lightly because, as yet, our feeling lacks the intensity which is born only out of suffering and sacrifice. Our blood offering has still to be laid on the altars of our patriotism, and until it is paid, till we have in our own flesh and blood the threat of war, we shall not awaken to the real spirit. We are, on the other hand, taking it seriously, in that we are shoving our preparations with the dynamic energy characteristic of our people. During the last two years there was not wanting, of course, a large minority among us that chafed in bitter anger against our inaction. We had begun to doubt whether any saving grace were left in us; to wonder if the charge were really about to be proved that Americans thought only in dollars. But under the clearer vision of 'hind sight', we now perceive the difficulties under which President Wilson and his advisers laboured. Even the bitterest of his enemies now gives President Wilson credit for his clever handling of an almost impossible situation. The way in which overpowering evidence was massed against the Hun was only to be equalled by the astute manner in which it was given forth, little by little, never more than was sufficient to keep alive the flaming indignation excited in all Americans by German intrigues in Mexico.

Since war was declared that spirit, thus fostered, has crystallised in action. Our war loans, as you know, were tremendously over-subscribed. Other hundreds of millions of dollars flowed into the coffers of the Red Cross. A mercantile shipbuilding programme is in course that calls for the delivery in the near future of 2,000 vessels of large tonnage and high speed. One hundred and fifty destroyers are to be added to our flotilla in the next six months, and if I am to judge of future results by those I witnessed during a recent three-week cruise on an American destroyer, their addition will put the finishing touch on submarine war. We have just tried out our 'Liberty' engine, specially designed for our war planes. It flew a heavily loaded plane for 1,200 miles at high speed without stopping – good enough! Better! 20,000 of these planes are included in our war plans and the aviators are already in our training camps. We drew ten millions of men in our first draft. A million of them, the cream of our young manhood, are already in our camps. Thousands have already crossed, or are in transit to France. It is no exaggeration to say that half a million will be ready for the spring offensive.

On their part our civilian population is equally active. We have no lack of foodstuffs for our own use, but realising the necessity of saving for our Allies, the entire American nation has set itself to save and scrimp to swell the exports. In all our towns electric signs flash out the warning against the night skies, 'Food will win the war.' Housewives' associations have sprung up all over the land to supervise and stimulate food conservation. From recipes supplied by the Government, our women have preserved immense quantities of fruits without the use of sugar, also vegetables and perishable foods, thus releasing a corresponding bulk of keepable foods for export.

This accomplishment of ours has not, of course, been unattended by a fair batting average of mistakes. Wrong men have been put in high places, and with that curious obstinacy which, in the present juncture, forms rather a desirable asset in President Wilson's character, he has kept some of them there after their demerits were clearly perceived. Our mercantile programme was held up for some time by an unseemly squabble. Congress talked when it ought to have been working. The Senate did the same. We had to expect a certain percentage of bungling from inexperience and – we were not disappointed. Yet all this having been conceded, the bitterest enemy of President Wilson's administration will have to acknowledge that results are large and fine. Better progress could not be expected than has been made in the limited time.

In passing lately from San Francisco to New York, I secured a close-up view of that continental preparation. Before leaving California I saw the drafts go into our camps. In Chicago they were entraining as I passed. Officers packed the trains on the five days' journey across the continent. On every siding we passed long military trains. In the towns and villages the high school boys were drilling with real guns. Women were already to be seen in some of the towns taking in new industrial duties. Washington, where I stayed some days, was aflame with martial spirit. New York buzzed.

It was an inspiring sight, this of a nation rising in arms to support a great world cause, and its full significance was attained when the vessel on which I had engaged passage to Europe turned out to be a military transport. Here, again, President Wilson and his advisers had scored, disproving at the same time another of the Hun's bad guesses. He said, first, that the American nation would never stand for conscription: next, that even if it did, years would be required to shape and drill our raw levies: third, that we could never get them across the Atlantic; fourth, that we could not keep them supplied if we did. Recognising that the crux of our military problem lay in the transportation of our troops across, our war college started at once the flow of troops out of New York. It is not advisable to speak in numbers. But the Hun can take no comfort out of the thought that the convoy with which I came was one unit of a never-ending stream that will not cease its full flow until he himself is beaten back beyond his bounds. We can, whenever necessary, send 40,000 or 50,000 men at once. Once across, their training can be finished to advantage in France. Lastly – answering the final bad guess – one ship can carry supplies for a force that ten ships could not ferry over the ocean.

I should like to say a word concerning the morale of our troops. Four hundred American doctors, and as many engineers, came over on my ship. Among them were men who had relinquished large and lucrative practices to take a lieutenant's pay. The engineers were drawn from the great trunk lines of our country. The casual manner in which they spoke of their sacrifices rendered them still more impressive, and this fine temper was equally evident among the enlisted men. The more powerfully because of its quiet, the remark of one private soldier revealed the spirit of all: 'The Germans are all wrong. We are going to put them right.'

So far our people have looked on with admiration, but still have looked on while you English and French and your Allies bore the first great shock of war and prolonged following strain. We feel that it is now up to us to take as much of that burden as is possible upon our shoulders. I want to answer, in conclusion, one doubt that I have heard expressed. 'Can a Republic like yours stand the punishment you are bound to get? Will your people stick?' The history of our Civil War furnishes the answer. For four long years we fought the forces of 'Secession' and won. We'll stick! Very sagaciously, Mr Wilson took advantage of the first enthusiasm to provide funds to carry on the war for, at least, two years. He is thus in position to proceed without noticing popular fluctuations. But if he were not – if I know anything of the American temper – our people are prepared to use the last unit of our tremendous man-power, to give the last dollar of our enormous wealth to crush the German. Moreover, if I know anything of President Wilson's character and disposition, he will stand by his plighted word to make no peace with a Hohenzollern.

14 January 1918

REIGN OF TERROR IN BELGIUM
Continued Executions

Although Germany has been in occupation of Belgium for over three years, the blood-lust of the enemy continues. So far from introducing a humaner rule over that unhappy people, the sword, the gibbet, and the prison are still the main factors in their Government. There seems to be little civil administration of the population, and military rule remains supreme.

News has reached this country lately from Belgian official sources reporting fifty-eight more executions in that unhappy country. This brings to 170 the number of Belgians killed since January, 1917, for some patriotic 'crime' under the rule of General von Falkenhausen, who succeeded von Bissing. Among them we know the names of at least ten women, three girls of from fourteen to sixteen, and several boys under twenty. They are supposed to be guilty of spying, but in many cases the arrest, condemnation, and execution have taken place within three or four days, so that no serious inquiry could have been made.

Under the rule of von Bissing, who rendered himself responsible for the murder of Miss Cavill, about a hundred executions took place in one year (1915–16), according to an official German statement, von Falkenhausen, surnamed 'the tiger', thinking very likely that his predecessor had been too clement, increased this number threefold. He ceased to publish the official lists of the murdered men, in order that the names of the martyrs of Belgium should not be worshipped by their compatriots, and had them buried inside the prisons where they were executed, so that their tombs should not be covered with flowers by their friends. Most of these victims of German terrorism were subjected, before their execution, to most cruel torture, in order to force them to denounce their 'accomplices'.

The two daughters of Mr Groneret, a shopkeeper of Liège, were forced to witness the death of their father and mother. Then they were promised that their lives should be spared if they consented to speak. The eldest, aged twenty, refused courageously, and was killed beside her parents. Pressure was then put on the younger, a girl of fourteen, but she remained firm in spite of all the efforts of her tormentors, and suffered the same fate.

In a group of twenty prisoners shot recently at Ghent was a young girl of sixteen, whose only crime had been to carry letters over the frontier. She begged for her life until the last moment, and was shot kneeling. Before his execution a well-known sportsman of Ghent, van Rentegen, was dragged through the streets of the town attached by a long chain and subjected to the insults of the soldiers, who pelted him with mud and spat on him.

Here is an extract of a letter to his wife written a few hours before his death by a young Fleming, aged twenty-six, father of a family, one of the latest victims of German terrorism: 'My hour has come. I have received the last Sacraments. I am going to give my life gladly for God and country. For the last time I kiss your dear picture and those of my beloved children. Goodbye, my poor, dear wife; goodbye, my little innocent children. My love for you will not die with me. From Heaven I will watch over you and pray for you.'

The German public is well aware of these wholesale executions. The *Kölnische Zeitung* complained recently (10 December) that the number of Belgian spies who were granted their lives was far too large, and that the Belgians were not worthy of Germany's generous mercy.

16 April 1918

FIERCE CONFLICT FOR NEUVE EGLISE

Hand-to-Hand Fighting, *War Correspondents' Headquarters, France, Monday*

By Philip Gibbs

During the past three days the enemy's main effort in Flanders has been to capture Bailleul and its railway and old Kemmel Hill, from which one can look over to the Wytschaete Ridge from a commanding height. For this purpose the enemy has thrown in all the weight he could gather for these attacks north of Merville, hurrying up fresh divisions all through the fighting to replace his shattered and exhausted troops, and concentrating a large amount of heavy and field artillery. Up to last night our troops in this area between Merris and Wytschaete had engaged some fifteen divisions, only one of which had been previously in action in the Somme battlefields, with battalions of special storm troops and part of an Alpine Corps, who had orders to take Bailleul at all costs. They have not taken Bailleul nor the railway south of it, and our outnumbered men, some of whom had been fighting for many days and nights without sleep and always under fire, have repulsed the enemy again and again and inflicted frightful losses on him.

The enemy's objective was Kemmel, on the first day of this fighting, that is 10 April, and his officers are amazed at the resistance made by British soldiers so weak in numbers against their tremendous forces. Their dead lie piled up below the railway embankment near Bailleul, living waves of Germans being mown down by our machine-gunners, who had great targets for their shooting, and although once yesterday our flank was momentarily threatened south of this city, now filled with the fire of monstrous shells, the line was fully re-established last night by counter-attacks, and thirty Germans were made prisoners, with machine-guns.

In order to surround Bailleul two heavy attacks were made, on the west towards Meteren, and on the east at Neuve Eglise. Near Meteren the enemy failed utterly, and suffered immense losses. There has been fierce fighting round a place called Steam Mill, near Meteren, the enemy having been ordered to capture the Meteren road and the high ground beyond, at whatever sacrifice. They made the sacrifice, but did not get the ground. Neuve Eglise is now theirs, and last night our troops, who had held it through the day, through three days and nights of intense strife, withdrew, unknown to the enemy, to a line a slight way back from the village, in order to avoid staying in a target for unceasing shell-fire. It is now the enemy soldiers who this morning are in the ruins under a great bombardment.

This battle at Neuve Eglise has been filled with grim episodes, for the village has changed hands several times, and each side has fought most fiercely and with any kind of weapon, small bodies of men attacking and counter-attacking among the broken walls and bits of houses, and under the stump of the church tower, at dawn and in the darkness, with rifles and bayonets and bombs. The attack on this place was really begun further back, when the enemy struck up through Plug Street on 10 April and drove forward every day since towards this goal of Neuve Eglise. All the time he was faced and resisted by troops from Wiltshire, Cheshire, Staffordshire, and Lancashire, while other Lancashire troops, along with Northumberland and Worcestershire men and others, were holding up the line of the Lys and fighting rearguard actions round Croix-du-Bac as I have told before. A body of Wilts, Cheshire, and Staffs men held the east of Plug Street Wood when the attack burst upon them, and kept their lines intact for two days and nights, though the enemy had pierced behind them and west of the wood, against other troops fighting back under overwhelming pressure towards Neuve Eglise.

The situation became serious when the enemy broke into Plug Street village and made a nest of machine-guns there which could not be routed out by fierce Lancashire counter-attacks. Some of our own machine-gunners on the west of the wood acted as infantry and charged the enemy outposts, and when the Germans thrust forward again to a hamlet called Romorin and a huddle of houses called Les Trois Pipes they were pioneers of the South Wales Borderers, not trained for fighting, who attacked them most gallantly. But the enemy poured up to this place, and there was severe fighting there for hours.

Meanwhile, on the night of 11 April the men holding Plug Street Wood were ordered to abandon this dangerous position, in which they were nearly surrounded, and fall back to a line in front of Neuve Eglise and La Nieppe. They did this in face of the enemy, and the last men in the wood were two subalterns, who were entirely surrounded by Germans. They gathered some bombs together, made their way down an old trench in the darkness – there was the glare of fire through Plug Street Wood; where in old days I used to visit friends on summer days when snipers' bullets came whisking off the leaves – and by the light of this they made their way, and at last made a flash through the enemy lines and so escaped. Some other officers were not so lucky. On the way back to the line outside Neuve Eglise a colonel with a machine-gun section led his men against a body of the enemy in possession of a ruin called La Grande Munque and killed a number of them before getting back wounded with a little party of his surviving men. Later, or about this time, the enemy broke through to the neighbourhood of an old estaminet called Kort Pyp (the Short Pipe), and round here a body of our infantry fought almost to the last man in a desperate action. Another party of the same regiment suffered heavily in an heroic action to check the enemy south of Neuve Eglise, towards which they were pressing in great strength.

The night before last our line fell back from near La Crèche and swung round in the loop south of Neuve Eglise towards Ravelsberg Farm. It was then that Neuve Eglise itself became a place of hellish battle. The enemy broke through into its ruined streets, and small parties of Wiltshires, Worcesters, and others sprang upon them and killed them or were killed, and fought desperately in back yards and over broken walls and in shell-pierced houses wherever they could find Germans or hear the tattoo of machine-guns. Several times the enemy was cleared out of most of the town and our men held the hollow square containing most of the streets, and defended it as a kind of fortress, though with dwindling numbers, under a heavy fire of shells and trench mortars and machine-guns. The enemy was savage in his attacks against these men, and from behind the German commanding officers sent up fresh troops with stern orders to have done with the business and destroy our men, whom they vastly outnumbered. But they could not take Neuve Eglise by direct assault, and last night our troops made a counter-attack at Crucifix Corner, won ground, and brought back five machine-guns and left there many German dead. It was an astounding feat of grim courage. But Neuve Eglise was given up by us for the reasons I have stated. The enemy, unable to get it by infantry assault, shelled it fiercely by the fire of many guns and made it a death-trap, as now it is for them. Without yielding to direct assault, our men obeyed orders and stumbled out of the cursed place silently and unknown to their enemy and took up a line further back.

Southwards the situation is much the same as when I last wrote. The enemy has not made any progress of importance beyond Merville and along the Lys Canal above St Venant, where our men have been holding the line against repeated attacks. On Sunday they were attacked four times, but each time the enemy was swept by our machine-gun fire. For a while they got into a hamlet called Cornet Malo, and fixed machine-guns in its cottages, but Scotsmen drove them out by rifle fire and bombing. They came on again last night, and made another breach in the village, but were again routed out, while another struggle went on about some brickfields near by.

For the moment, therefore, the enemy is checked in his ambitious plans, and the heroism of our soldiers has foiled all his main efforts, broken, for the time being at least, his drive towards the coast, and shattered many of his proud divisions, many times more in number than our forces in this northern battle zone. Fortunately, many of our most tired men have been relieved, fresher troops are facing the enemy, and the front line is now strongly supported. So one may breathe with relief after the anxiety of three days ago, when things were at their worst. From prisoners and other sources the proud plans, enormous hopes, and detailed preparations for this mighty assault upon us with the great strength of the German army are becoming known to us. Before the Battle of Armentières the greatest secrecy was kept, no letters were allowed to be sent, and no leave was given to any German officer or man, and no information of any kind was given to the officers until they reached the line a few hours before the battle began, after forced marches from the detraining point. The order then came, 'The Sixth German Army on 9 April is breaking through the English position, and will advance on Hazebrouck.' It was stated that the 2nd battalion of the 156th Infantry Regiment would follow the 32nd Division and march on Fleurbaix. Later an order came saying that the division was held up at Fleurbaix, and the 156th Infantry Regiment would swing to the left and go to Bac St Maur.

It was when they were crossing the Lys that their casualties were heaviest, and the infantry was cut up by our artillery fire. The enemy brought up great numbers of field-guns, many of which were not allowed to register before the battle. Many shells fell short and killed German infantry. They were especially strong in trench mortars brought up in baskets, and it is said that only one mortar in each group was allowed to register before the action. Their greatest trouble was in getting their transport forward over the sticky mud in the old No Man's Land, and no doubt thousands of men are now working furiously to make roads and lay tramlines. The German officers seem to have been inspired with a fanatical faith in victory, with which they tried to animate their men. Major-General Hofer, commanding a brigade of the Ersatz Reserve, who is a one-armed man, led over the first wave, brandishing a stick before his astonished soldiers, who had never seen one of their high officers going over the top. The night before the attack their losses were heavy under the concentrated fire of our guns on their assembly places, and the first waves had to climb over wreckage and dead bodies on their way of advance. This first exaltation must have flickered out, I think, for since the beginning of the attack the German losses have been ghastly and their gains have not been as great as their hopes.

30 April 1918

GREAT DEFEAT FOR GERMAN ARMY

Fruitless Attacks, *War Correspondents' Headquarters, France, Monday*

By Philip Gibbs

There was violent and widespread gunfire all last night from the enemy's batteries from the Belgian front down through Flanders to districts about Bethune, and this morning the German bombardment was intensified to heights of fury all round Ypres and upon our lines near Voormezeele and Vierstraat and against the French front west of Kemmel Hill to the country south of Dranoutre, where the British troops join them again. Then began at about six o'clock this morning that attack which was the inevitable plan of General Sixt von Armin after the capture of Kemmel Hill, that is, an attempt in strong force to gain the chain of hillocks running westwards below Ypres and Poperinghe and known to all of us as familiar landmarks – the Scherpenberg, Mont Rouge, and Mont Noir. These hills, forming the central keep, as it were, in our defensive lines south of Ypres, are held by the French, and are of great tactical importance at the present moment, so that the enemy covets them and is ready to sacrifice thousands of men to get them.

In order to turn them, if the frontal attacks failed against the French, German storm-troops – they are now called 'Grosskampf' or 'great offensive' troops – were to break the British lines on the French left between Locre and Voormezeele, and on the French right near Merris and Meteren. It obviously was the intention of the German High Command this morning, judging from their direction of assault.

So far they have failed utterly. They have failed up to this afternoon to break or bend the British wings on the French centre, and they have failed to capture the hills, or any one of them, defended by the French divisions. They have attacked again and again since this morning's dawn, heavy forces of German infantry being sent forward after their first waves against the Scherpenberg and Voormezeele, which lies to the east of Dickebusch Lake, but these men have been slaughtered by the French and British fire, and have made no important progress at any point.

For a time the situation seemed critical at one or two sectors, and it was reported that Germans had been seen storming the slopes of Mout Rouge and Mont Noir, but one of our airmen flew over those hills at 200ft above their crests and could see no German infantry near them. Round about Voormezeele North Country and other English battalions had to sustain the determined and furious efforts of Alpine and Bavarian troops to drive through them by weight of numbers after hours of intense bombardment, but our men held their ground, and inflicted severe punishment upon the enemy. All through the day the German losses have been heavy, under field-gun and machine-gun fire, and our batteries alongside the French soixante-quinzes swept down the enemy's advancing waves, and his assemblies in support, at short range. There is no doubt that the French guarding the three hills have fought with extreme valour and skill. For a brief period the Germans were apparently able to draw near and take some ground near Locre, but an immediate counter-attack was organised by the French General, and the line of French troops swung forward and swept the enemy back.

Further attacks by the Germans north of Ypres and on the Belgian front were repulsed easily, and again the enemy lost many men. The battle continues, but the first phase of it has been decided in our favour, and it has been another day of sacrifice for the German regiments, who one by one as they come up fresh to reinforce their battle-line, lose a high percentage of their strength in this continuing slaughter. The German High Command still has many divisions untouched, but their turn will come, and if, as today, they are spent without great gain, the enemy's plans of decisive victory will be thwarted for ever. There is a limit even to German man-power, and, surely to God, their people will tire of making these fields of France and Flanders the graveyard of their youth. This frenzy must pass from them, and from our stricken world, when the truth comes home to them at last:

War Correspondents' Headquarters, France, Monday (Later)

It becomes clearer every hour that the enemy has suffered a disastrous defeat today. Attack after attack has been smashed up by our artillery and infantry, and he has not made a foot of ground on the British front. The Border Regiment this morning repulsed four heavy assaults on the Kommel–La Clytte road, where there was extremely hard fighting, and destroyed the enemy each time.

One of the enemy's main thrusts was between Scherpenberg and Mont Rouge, where they made a wedge for a time and captured the cross-roads, and it was here that a gallant French counter-attack swept them back. We had no more than a post or two in Voormezeele this morning, and the enemy was there in greater strength and sent his storm-troops through this place, but was never able to advance against the fire of our English battalions. His losses began yesterday when his troops were seen massing on the road between Zillebeke and Ypres in a dense fog, through which he attempted to make a surprise attack. This was observed by our low-flying planes, and his assembly was shattered by our gunfire.

After fierce shelling all night, so tremendous along the whole northern front that the countryside was shaken by its tumult, German troops again assembled in the early morning mist, but were caught once more in our bombardment. At three o'clock a tremendous barrage was flung down by the German gunners from Ypres to Bailleul, and later they began the battle by launching the first attack between Zillebeke Lake and Meteren. South of Ypres they crossed the Yser Canal by Lock Eight, near Voormezeele, which was their direction of attack against us, while they tried to drive up past Locre against the French on the three hills.

Our successful defence has made the day most bloody for many German regiments.

25 September 1918

GERMANS AND POISON GAS

A Cynical Lie, Paris, Tuesday

The most monstrous monument even of German hypocrisy is the German Government's reply to the Geneva Red Cross on the subject of the use of asphyxiating gas in warfare. The reply is a tissue of lies. To begin with, the French inventor, Turpin, who is accused by the Germans of having invented poisonous gases, never dealt with the latter at all, and all his researches were concerned solely with explosives; secondly, it is well known that the Germans employed gases months before we had ever made any or thought of any, and that the German Staff published a deliberate lie stating that we were using gas. This statement was a matter of the utmost astonishment to the Allies' Staffs, who did not even know what gas meant. Six weeks later the Germans began the use of poisonous gas at Ypres, and then we understood the purpose of their previous lying statement; but there is more evidence still of their long preparation for the use of gas as a weapon, which, of course, is absolutely forbidden by The Hague Convention. A well-known French chemist has an intimate Dutch friend who is a distinguished professor at Leyden and a staunch friend of the Allies. This Dutch professor, towards the end of 1914, wrote to the French chemist stating that the Germans were making active experiments with poisonous gases in Belgium, near the Dutch frontier. The French chemist at once reported the matter to the War Office, which refused to believe him. Everyone whom he saw scouted the idea as a mere fable. The chemist, however, worked at the subject on his own in order to discover what gases the Germans might be using. While he was experimenting, and while the military authorities were so deriding his information, the Germans suddenly began the use of poisonous gases, with, as everyone knows, terrible effects.

At that moment neither in France nor in England had the question of gas as a weapon even been considered. It was, indeed, months after the Germans began the use of gas that Commissions were appointed in England and France to commence the study of the question, and more months again elapsed before we had prepared any gas at all. Finally, when we did start using gas, all we had were tear bombs, with which we tried to reply to much more dangerous gases sent over by the Germans.

The German reply to the Geneva Red Cross is thus the most cynical lie even the German Government has ever been guilty of. It is satisfactory, by the way, to learn from those who know that for a considerable time past the enemy is being paid back in his own coin, and that though late in this field of scientific barbarism we now have gases that are worse than any German gases.

4 October 1918

HEROIC DEEDS OF OUR DIVISIONS

The Canal Exploit, *War Correspondents' Headquarters, France, Thursday*

By Philip Gibbs

By our attack this morning across the St Quentin–Scheldt Canal south of Cambrai, where our men have taken many prisoners and broken into the country about Le Catelet, we have succeeded in driving the enemy still farther away from his main defensive lines, and if we have luck we may force him into a retreat to Le Cateau, and, by cutting his line of communications across the road which goes that way compel him to abandon Cambrai. Owing to our constant pressure north and south of the battle front he is already in wide retreat from his La Bassée salient. God forbid that we should give ourselves up at this time of day, after frightful disappointments through many years of effort, to rosy and optimistic dreams not based on reality or truth, but this at least we may say – we are on the eve of amazing possibilities, and perhaps there may be open to us a supreme chance of bringing this war to decisive issues.

It will not be our fault if we miss this chance. Does the world even now understand what these troops of ours have done and are still doing? I think not, for even we who are among them out here, who follow their battles, and go through the battlefields, can hardly realise the heights of endurance which these men have achieved. It is now October, and the soldiers who are advancing today belong to the same divisions as those who fought in the beginning of our offensive battles when the tide turned in August, and every day since then, or almost every day, have fought forward through trench systems and village fortresses against the desperate resistance of the German troops until they have 30 miles of liberated land behind them from Albert to Le Catelet, and every mile of it is strewn with relics of their frightful strife. They have lost many comrades on the way – this wake of war is scattered over with little white crosses – and new drafts have come out to fill up the gaps, but the spirit of the old divisions goes on, and the new boys mingle with veterans not much older than themselves and carry on the tradition.

They are just working men of England and the Colonies, farmers and factory hands, clerks and office boys, and the lads who were at school four years ago, and in their steel helmets and their khaki, with dust and mud on them, they are all reduced to a dead level of humanity and discipline, and one sees no difference between them. One young Tommy trudging along the road is the type of all British Tommies; one lean Australian stands for all of Australia; one Canadian for all Canada. But in all this mass of men there has been revealed anew in recent weeks a high and wonderful average of courage and devotion to some ideal that burns inwards and does not flame in their eyes or their speech, and day after day they fight and trudge on through fields of fire, and whether death may or may not await them, whether they have a few hours sleep or no sleep, whether their bones ache with fatigue or the bodies are weak with their burden of toil, they keep going until they reach the breaking point which is in human nature. Knowing the frightful hours ahead of them, they go towards the enemy's guns. Knowing the full cost of victory, they go and claim it. There are cowards among them, no doubt, and they are all afraid – because there is nothing funny in shell-fire – but they kill their cowardice by some magic they have, and many who are most afraid do the most heroic things.

Not only the men, but the young officers and their headquarters staff, do not spare themselves to the last spark of vitality, and a tribute is due to those brigade, divisional, corps, and army staffs who have been toiling for victory, and what comfort and help they can give their men. In the old days of trench warfare they lived in châteaux of France, behind the lines, and were targets of satire because of their comfort. There is precious little comfort for them now, and corps flags and divisional flags fly over holes in the ground, amidst old trenches and old ruins, and generals and their officers are very far forward with hostile fire digging pits about them, while in German dug-outs abandoned by the enemy they direct battles within sight of them, and snatch a few hours sleep in some narrow bunk between oozy walls, if they have the luck to sleep. Every other day now they have to shift their lodgings in the earth to some spot farther forward, and yesterday, for instance, I met a general washing outside his dug-out like a private soldier who only a week or so before I had met in a dark cave 15 miles back, which is a long way for men to fight when every yard of it is under fire.

So the whole army is animated by a single purpose of grim endeavour to make haste to victory, so that the world may get back to its sane life and men to their women and babies, after these years of exile and agony.

I have already written an account of the astounding feat of our 46th Midland Division, who on Sunday last flung themselves across the Scheldt Canal at Bellenglise and captured 4,200 prisoners, great numbers of guns, and over a thousand machine-guns. But further details that come from those Leicesters, Staffords and Sherwood Foresters increase the marvel of the achievement, which will rank in history as one of the most heroic achievements of the war. These men were not romantic fellows like Greek heroes. They are boot-makers from Leicester and lace-makers from Nottingham and potters from Arnold Bennett's 'Five Towns', where life is rather drab and its colour monotone. I met them five years ago near Armentières, and afterwards at 'Funky Villas', as they called Fonquevillers, near Hébuterne, and the Robin Hoods or the Sherwood Foresters in their steel hats and their muddy khaki would have frightened Friar Tuck if he had met them on a summer's day all under the greenwood tree of that orchard in Hébuterne, where every day the birds of death came howling. The look of them was as little heroic as that of any muddy men who trudge along the duckboards leading to hell fire. But the spirit of England's old heroic soul was in them, and on this last Sunday of battle they went headlong into the gates of death, and what they did would be incredible if we did not know its truth.

Between them and the enemy's main defences in the Hindenburg line was the wide water of the Scheldt Canal, and on the other side a long tunnel, where the Germans could be safe from all our shell-fire, and then come up to meet our men with their machine-guns. A frightful place to assault by frontal attack. The boot-makers and lace-makers, and the potters and the factory hands of the English Midlands practised for their passage of the canal. One of their brigadiers, a VC – he was the Elizabethan touch of character – borrowed all the lifebelts of a leave boat, and, putting one on himself, went down to the Somme and led his men in, wading and swimming the river, which is cold these days. And he taught them how to keep their rifles dry and their heads above water. It was with these lifebelts on and with scaling ladders and hand bridges and hawsers that the Midland men went forward to the canal in a thick fog last Sunday morning, and made their crossing. Shells burst about them, machine-gun bullets whipped the water and the banks, but, some swimming and some wading, and some hauling themselves across on ropes which they had fixed by throwing lead lines across, and then by the first men over pulling the ropes to the other side, they gained the German banks at Bellenglise, and, forming up in line, went ahead to the Lehaucourt and Magny La Fosse. On both sides of the valley where the Germans had their guns the gunners were firing, and hard fighting ensued before the guns could be captured.

Some of our tanks were the first to advance upon these gun positions, and came under direct fire at close range before the Midland men closed in. Large numbers of Germans were in hiding in the great tunnel by the canal. A thousand of them were down there and would not come out, hoping to fight again when our waves had passed and then to blow up mines below our troops. One of our sappers, advancing almost alone, and cutting down two Germans who tried to kill him as he crossed the bridge, broke the leads of the mines and saved the lives of many of his comrades. One of the captured German howitzers was placed at the mouth of the tunnel and fired down it. It made a noise as though mines had been blown and the bowels of the earth were rent, and before its echoes died away the Germans came rushing out of their tunnel in mad panic and were captured by the Midland men above, who by this day's work – it was all over by ten o'clock that morning – had seized the key of the Hindenburg line above St Quentin.

The German withdrawal from the neighbourhood of La Bassée was preceded by a heavy bombardment as final salute from his guns, which have ravaged this mining country for four years, and then his troops stole away on a wide front, leaving only a few machine-gun crew here and there. Our men, among whom were Lancashire, Scottish and Irish units, followed up as soon as the withdrawal was noticed, and went into empty trenches around the Aubers Ridge, and through old ruins such as those of Wingles, Salome and Illies, into which our guns had poured shells year after year, and whose towers they have seen, as I have seen them, from trenches about Hulluch and the Hohenzollern Redoubt. There are no towers there now, for the enemy destroyed them before he left by fire and explosives. In the Cité St Auguste, the mining village north-east of Lens into which some Gordons went on the first day of the battle of Loos, in the September of 1915, and never came back again, there were yesterday some rearguards of machine-gunners, and fighting took place there before our men routed them out. Elsewhere there was scarcely a shot fired and the enemy went away rapidly to his new line of defence. It may possibly run behind the Haute Deule Canal, at Pont-à-Vendin, to the outskirts of Lille, or, rather, to the edge of these formidable defences round Lille which make that town a strong fortress.

The abandonment of the Cité St Auguste means that Lens itself has been delivered into our hands, with its neighbouring coalfields, for which English and Canadian troops have fought some long and fierce battles, and our men are going through its ruins today. The report comes to me that one of our cavalry patrols has met a German patrol on the road south-west of Fournes, which is east of Illies, but I am unable to confirm that by certain knowledge. In any case, however, our men are far forward from their old line of yesterday, and from ruined villages like Salome they are staring at the chimneys and roofs of Lille, which seems near, though perhaps a river of blood away if we tried to take it now. Meanwhile, farther south, in the real storm centre of our present fighting, Cambrai still remains in German hands, within the close girdle of the British line. North of the city the Canadians have not attacked this morning, and are holding their gains against that mass of men which the German High Command have concentrated here in order to safeguard their line between Cambrai and Douai, which would be of deadly consequence if broken through. South of the city our English and Scottish troops are in the suburbs and streets close to Faubourg St Sepulchre and the Faubourg de Paris, and drew closer last night by the capture of a redoubt near that last-named avenue, from which there comes a continual patter of machine-gun bullets. The enemy has organised a strong machine-gun defence of Cambrai, under some commander who knows his job, and has posted his gunners on the roofs of Cambrai, with a clear field of fire over the glacis below them where our troops have to move in the open. There do not seem to be many troops, apart from those machine-gunners, in Cambrai. After disgraceful orgies of looting, in which officers joined with their men, the city was put out of bounds to all German troops except the garrison of defence. Several new fires were started yesterday and are burning today, their flames burning red among the houses, and there are also big fires in neighbouring villages, like Niergnies and Cauroy.

The chief fighting this morning was a good deal south of Cambrai, round Le Catelet and Joncourt, where English and Australians made an attack shortly after six today. Here the enemy had a strong defensive line, which is part of the Beaurevoir–Masnières line, broken farther north, and in front of it there are a number of villages, all strongly fortified for machine-gun defence, and able to bring enfilade fire to bear from one another. Very terrible positions to attack, and not easy to hold. One village called Sequehart has been the scene of fierce fighting for two days or more by our men of the 32nd and 46th Divisions. Twice they have captured its garrison of twenty men, and now once again it has been taken. The troops fighting here have advanced successfully and have taken nearly 2,000 prisoners beyond Levergies, and north of them Australians have gone forward south of Le Catelet and Gouy towards the Beaurevoir line, having hard fighting round the village of Wiancourt. On the left of the Australians English troops have captured Le Catelet and Gouy, which by an error had been claimed by some papers as already in our hands. Three thousand prisoners at least have been brought back today, and if we break the Beaurevoir line there is not much to hold our men back from Le Cateau, where the 'Old Contemptibles' fought on their way down from Mons in the first days of the war. On the right of the line above St Quentin the French army was moving today at ten o'clock, but I know nothing of their part in the battle.

It is wonderful weather, with sunshine like liquid gold in the fields and a sky of unclouded blue. Even the ruins of the battlefields have a spell of beauty in this light, and I noticed yesterday how their broken walls were dazzling white and all the rubbish heaps of timber and bricks and twisted iron were touched with a hint of glamour.

ALLIES' PRISONERS
254,012 in Eleven Weeks

An addition to the French official communiqué of Wednesday night, received yesterday, gives the following summary of the captures by the Allied armies in France and Belgium during the period from 15 July, when Marshal Foch finally defeated the German rush on Paris, to 30 September:

From 1 to 30 September:
2,844 officers
120,192 men
1,600 guns
More than 10,000 machine-guns

Totals from 15 July to 30 September:
5,518 officers
248,494 men
3,669 guns
Over 23,000 machine-guns
Several hundred mine throwers

Of the above the British captures in August and September amounted to:
Prisoners, 123,618
Guns, 1,400
The Americans have taken about 24,000 and the Belgians at least 10,000.

Adding to the captures on the Western Front the 69,500 Turks taken in Palestine up to the present, the 22,000 (so far as is known) captured in Macedonia, and some thousands taken in Italy, this brings the grand total since the middle of July to at least 350,000 officers and men.

21 October 1918

BRITISH IN SOFIA
Visit by Aeroplane, *Sofia, 11 October*
By G. Ward Price

I arrived here this morning by the first British aeroplane to land here since the capitulation, the start having been delayed by bad weather. Leaving behind Lake Doiran and that grim cluster of steep heights on which British troops, aided by French and Greeks, engage all the available reserves of the Bulgar army, while the French and Serbs farther west pushed on and cut their communications in the rear, we flew straight up the course of the Strume. Across a neck of corrugated, chocolate covered landscape below us gleamed out at last the buildings of Sofia, conspicuous in its widespread plain. Even from 11,000ft there was no mistaking the great stone hangars of the German aerodrome, large as a cathedral and elaborate with folding doors and partitions. A throng of brown-clad Bulgar mechanics, with a dozen of their flying officers, watched the landing of three British aeroplanes with curiosity, while two or three Germans, who must be the last of those who used to strut about this ground the lords of all they surveyed, walked disdainfully away.

Introductions are made easier by the assured way in which most foreigners are taught to announce their own style and title, and there follows a moment of constraint which an English officer characteristically bridges by offering a cigarette. The Bulgars seem, if anything, the more at ease than the representatives of their conquerors, and in a few moments we were in their mess talking freely in French while waiting for the car to take us to the American Legation.

'We are glad the war is over, and we realise that we have been fighting against our true friends and our own interests.' That is the substance of the Bulgarian officers' views. 'We are ready to receive willingly and in friendship British, French and Americans.' For the Germans they professed disgust and ill-feeling. 'Especially lately the Germans have treated us abominably.'

The people in the streets looked at the English uniform with apparent indifference, but officers who reached here by car tell me that in the villages on the way the peasants were anxious to shake hands when they heard that the strangers were British, and showed a distinctly hostile attitude when they were addressed in German. So far everything shows all signs of going smoothly, expeditiously and well. The French and ourselves have a small staff of officers here who are in touch with the Bulgarian civil and military authorities. They are quite satisfied with the attitude of the Bulgarians and the Bulgars have expressed appreciation of the way in which the officers who are in charge of matters have treated them.

I have just seen the first of four British officer prisoners of war who have reached Sofia. They say that their treatment at Philippopolis internment camp was not bad, as they were left almost entirely to themselves. Three of these four tried, however, to escape, and after reaching the seashore opposite Thasos Island were recaptured, after which the attitude of the Bulgar authorities was harsh towards them. Their physical condition looks poor, though not serious in any way.

I have already had talks with several Bulgarians, though none of official standing. They realise that they have no right to look for much, but two or three have told me that they consider the question of the Dobrudja as the most serious one affecting them. One thing is certain, and that is that the Bulgar envy and fierce ambition for territory that is or was before the war under the Serbian or Greek Government is not dead, though it may be scotched. It must not be imagined that the Bulgars, because they have confessed themselves beaten, have changed their political skin. Our armies have done great things, indeed, in the Balkans; it remains to be seen if our diplomacy will come equally well through the tremendous task that lies ahead of it in finding a settlement to the age-old questions.

2 November 1918

FIERCE BATTLE FOR VALENCIENNES

Canadian Advance, *War Correspondents' Headquarters, France, Friday*

By Philip Gibbs

Valenciennes was apparently closed in by the Canadian troops this morning, after heavy fighting, and the enemy will probably have to abandon it within a few hours. It seems almost certain that it will be ours tonight or tomorrow morning; when all the thousands of civilians living there and waiting with desperate anxiety for our entry will be rescued from these days of terror. For during recent days they must have passed through terrible emotions, crowded down in their cellars, listening to the noise of gunfire, and to the tattoo of machine-guns served by German soldiers in rooms above them. This morning, after many days like this, a tumult of gunfire, louder than anything they had ever heard, opened north and south of them, and the battle came close to their streets. When I went up among the Canadians today the sound of this shell-fire was terrific, and the Canadian officers tell me that their troops attacked today under support of a more powerful concentration of guns than they have ever had on so narrow a front since they have been in France.

Valenciennes itself is not being touched by our fire, under strict orders; but the ground over which the Canadians had to advance this morning was smothered in high explosives. They had in front of them the high ground called Mont Houy, from which they had fallen back two or three days ago under German counter-attacks, and this was still strongly held by machine-gun posts. There were also a number of farms, farmsteads, and cottages, like La Targette and the Chemin Vert, to the left of the village of Aulnoy, just below Valenciennes railway, in which the enemy had organised defences. Over these places our barrage fire rolled as a devastating tide, wiping them off the map of France, and at the same time our guns fired a number of smoke shells, which made a dense white fog, obliterating all view of our advancing troops, and putting the Germans in a haze so thick that they could not see three paces about them. Their machine-gunners could not find their human targets, and were helpless. The German infantry of the 6th Division were as baffled as if blankets had been flung about their heads. One German officer, taken prisoner this morning, with many others, said that his position was so hopeless in this fog that he told his company there was nothing to do but surrender, and led them forward as the Canadians advanced to hand them over. At a small place called La Vessie, at the southern edge of Valenciennes, there was a German field-gun in action, firing at close range through this mist, but the Canadians closed round it and captured it.

The enemy's guns had put down a fierce line of fire before the attack started, or soon afterwards, but their batteries were quickly silenced by the power of our artillery, and after that the Canadians were only faced by machine-gun fire from positions in ruined buildings and in embanked ditches, where Germans held out to the last. The Canadian casualties were not heavy, I am told by their own officers, and they were perfectly successful in reaching their objectives along the railway, which is the southern boundary of Valenciennes.

While that attack was taking place another brigade of Canadians on the west side of the city where the canal forms the boundary line, were pushing outposts across, and establishing themselves on the inner bank. So they held Valenciennes in a tight grip, as Cambrai was held on the last day in German hands, and the enemy must get out. At midday today he made one last effort to check us, and a counter-attack was delivered from the village of Saultain, on the eastern side, but orders were given for the artillery to deal with this, and I have no doubt that it was shattered. The Germans have already lost many men on this southern side of the city, and the Canadians were surprised at the number of German dead lying about the Rhonelle River after the fighting of recent days.

For the survivors it is a hopeless business, for they know now that they are not only beaten in the field, but in the world. 'We have been betrayed,' said one of the German officers today, 'and that is why we have lost the war.' He had a list of betrayals, beginning with Italy and going on to Roumania and then to Bulgaria, and now, worst of all from his point of view, Austria. They acknowledge that with Austria out of the war they will find it impossible to fight on alone except in a losing fight to save their pride, so humiliation and despair have entered their souls where once arrogance had a dwelling-place and a sense of victory over all the world.

So it is today around Valenciennes, where all the neighbouring country is beautiful in the light of a golden All Souls' Day, with a blue sky over the coloured woods through which the uproar of gun-fire comes, and where in villages very close to the fighting-line women and children liberated from German rule are walking with bouquets of autumn flowers to put on the altars of their churches in memory of the dead to whom they owe their rescue.

Further north, across the French frontier, towards the town of Audenarde, in Belgium, there is another battle in progress, which began yesterday and is continuing today, with Belgian, French, American, and British troops attacking side by side. It is a battle among Flemish villages and farmsteads, where peasants are still living, helplessly entangled in the nets of horror, with German machine-gunners firing from their windows, and Allied troops trampling into their courtyards with naked bayonets, and the killing of men in their bed-rooms and cellars. Into villages from which the enemy has been lately driven poison-gas comes from shell-fire, which is not very loud, but makes a little hiss as each shell bursts and liberates its fumes. We have stopped all use of gas because of these civilians, but the Germans are using it every day, and in the Flemish villages many babies are dead and dying, and our ambulances are carrying away women and girls gasping for breath and blinded by this foul weapon of war. Our men give these village people gas-masks, taken from German prisoners now safe behind the lines, and teach them how to use them, but it is of no avail, because it needs long training and discipline to keep on gas-masks for any length of time.

Last night, in front of our lines near Audenarde, where Scots and Welsh Fusiliers were approaching Elseghem, and south of them Lancashire Fusiliers and Durhams were close up to the Scheldt Canal at Meersche, the enemy set fire to many houses and farms, and all the sky was lit up by the red glare, so that the German soldiers might see the movements of our men. It added to the terror of the night to women who stood with their children clinging to them, watching this scene of war which had engulfed them. Our advance during these last two days has been steady and successful, and today the enemy is retreating in front of our Scottish Rifles and King's Own Scottish Borderers, and other troops south of Audenarde. With the French to the north of us American troops are fighting, and have done very gallant work through these villages and woods. They have had a hard time, for the artillery in support of them have been unable to fire as effectively as usual owing to the anxiety of our gunners to avoid shelling civilians, so the Americans have had to advance against machine-gun fire with rifles and bayonets. They were fighting hard yesterday in a wood called the Spitalbosch, where the enemy was strongly defended behind tree-trunk barricades and wired enclosures, and machine-guns hidden in branches and holes dug beneath the roots of trees. It is like the fighting American troops have had in the Argonne, and very difficult and perilous. But these men have gone forward with fine courage, and have routed the enemy out from many of his lairs in this woodland, and by their good service have helped the progress of the French on their left. All this movement striking for Audenarde and the country north of it breaks through the German line south of Ghent, and will lead surely enough to the liberation of that Belgian city, which is yearning for the luck of Bruges.

Meanwhile our soldiers, like their French and American comrades, and all the world, believe that the war is reaching its end, and that the last battle will soon be fought, and they wait with splendid hope for the news that peace is theirs, with the victory for which they have struggled and suffered so long.

4 November 1918

ITALIAN VICTORY
Caporetto Redeemed, Milan, Friday Night
By A. Beaumont

The victorious advance of the Allied Armies beyond the Piave is evidently even of far greater magnitude than the reports so far published indicate. Doubtless, however, ere many hours have passed, more sweeping defeats will be chronicled, and we shall hear of the lightning and forcible ejection of the enemy's vampire host from Italy's hallowed soil. The redemption of Caporetto is now an accomplished fact, and its valiant avengers, with the full traditional courage of Rome's most renowned legions of old, are determined that the despicable and despotic enemy shall pay the full penalty in blood for his knavish, treacherous, barbaric acts of cruelty and rapine. Rino Alessi, in his despatch in today's *Secolo* from the war zone, states that the advancing Allied Armies are steadily realising the fruits of their masterful plans of manœuvre. The Italian armies, with the other Allied Forces, leave historic regions of defence, advancing with rapid strides, redeeming in twenty-four hours hundreds of square kilometres of ground. The number of the districts and towns liberated are no longer reckoned. Yesterday morning at dawn, Alessi relates, he traversed the ruins of Conegliano and the streets of Vittoria, thronged with an exulting population. When trying to reach the columns of the advancing troops on the march towards the Fadalto Pass the news was transmitted to him like wildfire that the enemy's front had utterly collapsed before the prolonged and serious attacks of the Fourth Army, also between the Brenta and the Piave.

The moving arc is assuming such colossal and extensive proportions that history will recall the battle, not as of one river, but of all the rivers and majestic mountain chains that form the natural structure of the Venetian province. The hour is at hand when the armies of Generals Giardino, Graziani, and Caviglia will unite on the only rocky highway between the Trentino and the Friuli. The enemy's forces now consist of but two chaotic masses – one desperately endeavouring to reach the high valleys of the northern mountainous region, and the other beating its precipitous retreat towards the east, driven beyond the River Livenza by the joint armies of Lord Cavan and the Duke of Aosta. The Austro–Hungarian defeat has been transformed into such a hopeless state of chaos that henceforth it may be finally considered as irreparable. The knell of the Dual Monarchy at last is vibrating far and wide. Neither the Livenza nor Tagliamento represent the goal of Italy's march onward. All the gates that gave access to the ancient frontier, and the waterways that for three years have witnessed scenes of bloodshed, are now being thrown wide open for the retreating foe.

In the plains various combats are taking place between the Livenza and the Tagliamento. The enemy's rearguards, frequently supported by numerous machine-guns in inhabited centres and along the roads, vainly try to impede the Italian advance, while in numerous parts Italian and British advanced patrols hurriedly ford the rivers, thence dashing onwards. The enemy, judging from his actual operations, is doubtless preparing for the systematic evacuation of Pordenone and all the region comprised between the Livenza and the Tagliamento. The populations, swelled by Italian prisoners numbering 60,000, flock in the invaded territory to meet the advancing Italian divisions, with tears of joy. The prisoners have been employed in military defence work, and many have been allowed to die of hunger and fatigue. It is evident from what they say that the enemy is also preparing a hurried flight from Udine. Trains are leaving, overflowing with all sorts of material, towards Pontebba and Gorizia. Frenzied scenes of gladness are witnessed in towns and villages alike, also in farms, on the part of the liberated inhabitants.

Italian and British troops on entering are greeted with wild enthusiasm. Liberated inhabitants of all creeds and classes rush madly forward in great foaming waves of humanity to welcome the valiant infantry, who for six days have been incessantly marching onward gaily singing patriotic airs. Windows and balconies are aglow with the tricolours which during the tragic period of the enemy's occupation had been religiously concealed from view, while during this painful period of hellish existence these poor people, villagers, peasants, and mountaineers, heroically and unflinchingly bore the burden of extreme suffering, of famine, and the like, ever cherishing fervently the unshakable belief in their final redemption. Stirring scenes of welcome are recorded. Eye-witnesses are almost moved to bow in reverence to such sturdy and staunch folk, who in token of recognition warmly kiss their redeeming soldiers' hands and even kneel down in the mud to do homage to the regimental banners, throwing the few autumn roses left in their devastated garden homes at the motors as they go whizzing past on the way to the new front.

7 November 1918

HEROIC FEAT OF A BRITISH AIRMAN
Fight with Fifty Machines, *War Correspondents' Headquarters, France, Wednesday*

By Philip Gibbs

The blow inflicted upon the enemy by our victory of 4 November south of Valenciennes, at Landrecies, and Le Quesnoy was so heavy and vital that the German battalions which had escaped capture and were in the reserve lines have been forced to retreat from the Forest of Mormal and on a wide front east of it. Our troops are following them closely, and behind them once again that vast machine which is a modern army with its engineering services, its material needed for roads and rails and bridges, its food for men and guns, is on the move, so that the fighting men shall not be out of touch with their supplies. No mortal can imagine what this means in tides of traffic and in human energy unless he has seen the mechanism of war. It means the surging forward of lorry columns and transport wagons far back for scores of miles from the new front line, for when one link of the chain is extended all the chain has to be dragged ahead, and it is a chain made by hundreds of thousands of men with all the material of their labour. It means that big guns have to get on the move, crawling up narrow roads on monstrous caterpillar engines. It means that tanks have to find new hiding-places. It means that all our roads are strait channels down which battalions on the march are crowded to one side, mud-splashed and jammed by endless columns of field batteries, by motor-buses, and motor lorries swaying perilously along the highly cambered tracks on the edge of greasy ditches, by staffs, and the transport of corps and divisional headquarters shifting their lodgings from one village to another, by pontoon bridges on heavy wagons, by aerodromes packed up for removal, by field kitchens, ammunition columns, and an army of road menders, who follow up the fighting men. All that happens when our troops advance a mile or two day by day, and it is happening now, when we are getting faster forward, so that these scenes of war are filled with stupendous movement.

The first day of our last battle was wonderfully fine, with an utterly blue sky and a golden autumn light shining on every russet leaf. But at night there was a wild gale, which tore down the branches of trees and flung down telegraph poles, with their tangle of wires broken by the Germans on their retreat. Yesterday it rained steadily, and was foully dismal in a wet blanket of fog above roads so sticky in mud that there was a great slithering and wallowing of horse and motor transport, slowing down the progress. That was bad for us, but imagination fails to conceive what it must be on the German side of the lines, where the retreating army looks back over its shoulders at the menace in pursuit, and where every block of traffic means the terror of death or capture, because our flying men are out and our guns are pounding the roads, and our troops are marching on. Our flying men, who are harrying the enemy's retreat, have beaten all their records lately in air combats, and their most famous day, when they destroyed something like seventy hostile aeroplanes, has already been recorded. But one exploit is now the talk of our Army, and it seems to me as wonderful as anything that has been done by these knights errant of the air. It happened over the Forest of Mormal, now in our hands since yesterday, and there, over those dense woods, with a queer kind of Eiffel Tower in the centre of them, flew a major of one of our flying squadrons, searching for the whereabouts of our troops, and for any German fighting plane which he might challenge to a duel. He saw a two-seater flying at 21,000ft to escape our archies and any other trouble, and our major climbed up to it in a wide spiral, and then, from below, fired at it. The German pilot and observer fell, their machine breaking in the air, and one man dropping in the parachute.

Immediately a Fokker biplane came into view, and the major heard the whistling of bullets through his plane, and then felt a hammer-stroke on his left thigh. He was hit, and for the moment stunned. His aeroplane began to spin out of control, but the major became conscious of his danger, and instinctively touched his levers and got his grip again on the engine. Then he saw that he was surrounded by fifteen Fokkers, crowding about him for the death-shot. His defence was by attack, and by a marvellous manœuvre he got his shots in first, and three enemies fell. But machine-guns were chattering about him and bullets were singing past his wires. Another hammer-blow struck him, this time shattering his left thigh-bone. He fainted clean away, and his machine dived helplessly. But once again the spirit of the man awakened to the instinct of self-preservation and anger against those who were out to kill him. He handled his machine again, mastered it, and looked out for Germans. Twelve to fifteen scouts were in his sky-space, taking up the hunt for him. He flew at one, and saw that his burst of fire set it alight, so that it became a falling flame. At the same time bullets were about him like wasps, and one of them smashed his left elbow, and his arm dropped and hung loose and useless.

He was a one-handed man now to steer and shoot against a new swarm of enemies that came like midges. He dived steeply to escape them, but eight more scouts chased him down. He could not avoid them, so he fought them. He fought them by manœuvring for position with every 'stunt' known to airmen with a little morning wildness in their hearts. But this was cold, deadly skill. It was watched by ground observers, who held their breath at the sight of that one British aeroplane banking, nose-diving, looping with a flock of Germans about him. For ten or twelve minutes he juggled with his aeroplane to get his target among the vultures. He hit two and put them out of action, and then they had enough, and he landed successfully. But when his machine came to rest he did not jump out. He sat all crumpled up, with his head drooping, and it was on a stretcher that he went away. He is now in hospital gravely wounded, and every man out here who knows how he fought between fifty and sixty hostile aircraft, and destroyed four and drove down six, hopes with all his heart that this air knight of ours will get well of his wounds. It is no wonder that German soldiers have a constant fear of our airmen. They make no disguise of it, and in every village we take every cottage with a cellar is marked 'Flieger Schutz' or 'Flieger Deckung', that is, shelter from aircraft, showing how they are afraid of all this raiding and bombing by our Royal Air Force, which has no mercy on them. They are afraid, though they are not cowards.

There was nothing of the coward about that German garrison of Le Quesnoy, which would not surrender all day, though New Zealanders had completely surrounded them, and by astounding valour had stormed their outer ramparts. One's mind goes back to that siege, to the deputation sent by the New Zealanders, promising to give them honourable treatment as prisoners, and to the silence which was a refusal by those thousand Germans who would not yield until the New Zealanders broke through their last defences. That episode of our battle on 4 November has a mediæval touch because of that old walled town and the breaching of its bastions and the challenge from its ramparts. In other places like Catillon, where our 1st Division fought at the chapel, and the embankment outside Ghissignies, where our 37th Division was engaged, and at Jolimets, outside the Forest of Mormal, and along the Sambre Canal, crossed by English County troops, Surreys and Kents, Lancashires and Cheshires, and Essex men, with Gordons and Welshmen and Irish, many battalions weakened by heavy losses and by the knowledge of defeat now that their country stands alone, fought manfully and stubbornly. They have always been great soldiers, and not all of them have lost their quality, though they fight in the last ditch of despair. It is fair and true to say that. On the other hand, their defence was 'patchy', and while some men put up a fierce struggle, others yielded easily without much show of fighting. In the advance on Landrecies – it was a dense white mist of early morning, so that the tanks had to steer by compass when they broke through the quick-set hedges and searched out machine-gun nests ahead of the infantry – there were some German machine-gun teams in well-camouflaged positions who did not fire a shot. Three hundred Germans defended Landrecies bridge and made a demonstration of defence, but gave in when they saw the rafts and canoes with British soldiers crossing the canal further south. Some men were found hiding without firing in rifle pits, behind hedges, and were ready to surrender. From one village near the Forest of Mormal fifty Germans came out of cellars, where they had been in hiding with the inhabitants, and gave themselves up. Other Germans were in hiding in trees, and had to be brought down by a whiff of case-shot.

There is one tragedy in this phase of war which all our soldiers find distressing. It is the presence of those civilians in the villages and farmsteads through which our men have to fight their way. Yesterday I went into the village of Neuville, near Landrecies, which we captured a few days ago, and saw women and children standing about among our field batteries and transport. That very morning they had been only just behind our fighting-line, and their cottage walls were pierced with recent shell-holes and scarred with bullet-marks. Their courage is astounding, and after crouching in their cellars – poor protection from shell-fire – they came up to greet the entry of our men with wild enthusiasm. Every day some of them are killed, and their peril has not passed when our men have freed them. The enemy is utterly ruthless of these people, and is flinging large quantities of gas-shells into villages which he knows are crowded with civilian inhabitants. Round about Courtrai there has been this tragedy in an appalling way. Directly the enemy starts shelling villages, the women go down into the cellars with their children, and the shell-gas filters down to them, with its deadly poison. The hospitals of Courtrai are crowded with dying mothers and babies. A lady there – Madame Van de Venne, whose house was the headquarters of General Sixte von Armin, commanding the forces against us in Flanders, and from which she was turned out at intervals because her rooms were wanted by the Kaiser, Ludendorff, Hindenburg, and von Deimling – told me that whole families of Flemish people have been killed by this gas-shelling. Out of one family of nine, eight had died when I went to Courtrai, and the scenes in the hospital with these women and children gasping their life away, and all burnt about their faces and bodies by corrosive fumes, are almost unbearable to the nursing sisters there. It is a widespread horror, and one prays for the end of all this devilish thing which has put its spell upon mankind.

12 November 1918

ARMISTICE SIGNED
Hostilities Cease

After lasting nearly four years and four months the Great European War, carefully organised and provoked by Germany, virtually came to an end yesterday by the signature of an armistice. This event was notified to the British public by the subjoined official communiqué issued from the Press Bureau at 10.20 yesterday morning The Prime Minister makes the following announcement:

The armistice was signed at 5 a.m. this morning, and hostilities are to cease on all fronts at 11 a.m. today.

This was followed at 10.50 a.m. by the issue of the following:

Admiralty, per Wireless Press.
News transmitted through the wireless stations of the French Government:
    Marshal Foch to Commanders-In-Chief:
    Hostilities will cease on the whole front as from 11 November at eleven o'clock (French time).
    The Allied troops will not, until a further order, go beyond the line reached ion that date and at that hour.
    (Signed) Marshal Foch

Admiralty, per Wireless Press.
News transmitted through the wireless stations of the French Government:
    German Plenipotentiaries to German High Command.
    To be communicated to all the authorities interested. Radio 3,084 and G.Q. 2, 11 November, 386 received.
    Armistice was signed at five o'clock in the morning (French time). It comes into force at eleven o'clock in the morning (French time).
    Delay for evacuation prolonged by twenty-four hours for the left bank of the Rhine, besides the five days; therefore, thirty-one days in all.
    Modifications of the text compared with that brought by Helldorf will be transmitted by radio.
    (Signed) Erzberger

At 2.05 p.m. the following American official communiqué was published:
France, Monday morning:

In accordance with the terms of the armistice, hostilities on the fronts of the American armies were suspended at eleven o'clock this morning.

KAISER'S FLIGHT TO HOLLAND
Scene at the Frontier, *Amsterdam, Sunday Night*

A frontier correspondent informs me that the ex-Kaiser's party arrived at the frontier this morning in eight automobiles. The party included the Crown Prince, Field-Marshal Hindenburg, and also, it is reported, the King of Wurtemburg. The guards at the frontier refused to allow the party to pass into Holland, and after some argument the Royal exiles and party beat a retreat along the route by which they had come.

Several hours later they appeared, this time coming by train. Again the frontier guards refused to allow them to pass, and at the time the message left Eysden they were still retained there, pending instructions from The Hague.

It is reported that the motor-cars conveying the party were fired on during the journey in Belgium.

Another message says there is a question of the Kaiser being interned, as he endeavoured to cross the frontier in military uniform and wearing his sword.

Eysden, Sunday (10.17 a.m.)

Last night a German general arrived at Eysden in a motor-car on a secret mission. Later it leaked out that he had come to notify the Dutch authorities of the imminent arrival of the ex-Kaiser. A number of Dutch officers were immediately despatched from The Hague to Eysden, and this morning a Royal train steamed into the station shortly before eight o'clock, in which were a number of officers of high rank and members of the Emperor's suite. But the Kaiser himself was not in the train, and it became known that he had previously arrived in a motor-car via Mouland. He had decided not to travel by train, because during the journey several shots had been fired at the carriage windows. The Kaiser therefore alighted at an early stage and got into a car which, shortly before the train steamed in, drove up to the station platform.

The Kaiser alighted and went on to the platform. He looked haggard and broken down, and though he maintained a stern countenance to all beholders, his nerves seemed to be not far from the breaking-point. He paced up and down the platform with slow steps until the train steamed in, and then joined officers, and spoke to them in turn. After a short interval the Emperor entered the train, which steamed away in the direction of Maestricht.

LONDON WELCOMES THE GLAD TIDINGS
Great Scenes of Joy

London has heard no such paean of exultant joy as that which, just on the stroke of eleven upon the grey November morning, thrilled the hearts of the whole population. The effect was magical and indescribable. A minute or so before the amazing outburst there was nothing in the aspect of the streets or the demeanour of the citizens to suggest that anything unusual was astir. Under leaden, threatening skies people were going about their business in the ordinary way, just as though nothing in the least unusual was happening or likely to happen.

Then, all of a sudden, came the sounds of gunfire, and, as the maroons, transformed from portents of danger into signals for rejoicing, thundered out their message of peace, there went up from end to end of the metropolis such tumultuous cheering as no mere words could even faintly describe. The thrill of it will live in the memory alike of the oldest and youngest of us. So, too, will the unforgettable scenes that followed.

As though at a pre-arranged signal, the whole population, as it seemed, rushed headlong out of houses and shops and factories and places of business, and burst simultaneously into a wild clamour of cheering which drowned the booming of the maroons. And, as though by magic, London from north to south and east to west blossomed into a vivid gala-dress of flags and bunting. The flags fluttered out from windows and balconies and roofs, and from the waving hands of the teeming multitudes that swarmed into the streets in an outburst of delirious, irrepressible joy. And as time went on the cheering throngs grew in density, until it was manifest that all London had, as it were, 'downed tools' and was making unofficial holiday.

With incredible rapidity the main arteries of traffic became hopelessly congested, and for a long time the buses and taxis – from the tops of which excited occupants stood up to wave flags and cheer frantically – found it hard to make any headway. 'Tommies' in their thousands were literally swept off their feet by the throngs which, carried away by enthusiasm, were determined to make them the particular objects of their thanksgiving and rejoicing.

But, of all the day's impressive scenes of heartfelt jubilation none, perhaps, was more unforgettable, more thrilling, both as a spontaneous manifestation of joy and for the sentiment underlying it, than that witnessed in front of Buckingham Palace at the moment when, in response to the tumultuous cheers of the surging crowds – cheers that seemed ever to grow in volume and intensity – the King and Queen came out on to the balcony overlooking the forecourt to be acclaimed with full-throated fervour by countless thousands of their loyal and loving subjects. That was a moment never to be effaced from the memories of man, woman, or child that took part in the glorious tributes of affection and thanksgiving.

Later in the afternoon, when their Majesties, accompanied by Princess Mary, drove in an open carriage into the City, they were the recipients again of such tokens of deep-seated love and loyalty as in all probability have never before marked the triumphal progress of any King and his consort through the streets of their Empire's capital.

At one o'clock yesterday Big Ben, the massive bell in the Clock Tower of the Houses of Parliament, struck the hour for the first time since the commencement of the war.

KING AND QUEEN AT THE PALACE
Address from Balcony

News of the signature of the armistice was communicated immediately to the King at Buckingham Palace, and was received with feelings of deep thankfulness. In the course of the morning Viscount Milner, the Army Council, the General Staff, the First Lord of the Admiralty, the Naval Staff, and Lord Weir and the staff of the Air Board, waited upon his Majesty, who held an informal reception, and received congratulations on the cessation of hostilities and the prospect of peace.

In response to the ovation by the enormous crowds which all day long gathered about Buckingham Palace, the King and Queen twice came out on the balcony. On the first occasion, obtaining a moment of comparative silence, his Majesty, addressing the people, said: 'With you I rejoice and thank God for victories which the Allied arms have won, and have brought hostilities to an end and peace within sight.'

By noon the great open space before Buckingham Palace and far up the Mall was packed densely with a crowd, eagerly anxious to manifest their loyalty and thanksgiving. Not a few in it could recall how they had stood there in August 1914, when there was still a hope that war might be averted, and had promised themselves to be there again when victory was won. Great lorries were filled with girl munition workers, who had left their ordinary headgear at the works and had knotted the ribbon of the Allies into their hair, or had devised coifs from small flags, that were curiously becoming to their happy faces. Taxi-cabs were drawn up, and women as well as men clambered up on the top to wave flags from the end of walking-sticks or umbrellas. Men had climbed up the pedestal of the statue of Queen Victoria, and some American sailors found a place beneath the arms of the great figure that symbolises maternal love, while others even more daring secured a perilous vantage along the very wings of the representation of Peace.

For the ceremony of the changing of the guard officers in uniform and the women of various branches of the national services were allowed into the Palace forecourt, but presently it was found necessary to close the gates, and deny further applicants. The people gave expression to their feelings in a volley of cheering.

It was a tense, eager half an hour before the King and Queen, with Princess Mary and the Duke of Connaught, came out on to the balcony, hung with crimson and gold. The crowd wanted the supreme moment to arrive, and meantime you caught the familiarly affectionate phrases, not too courtly of diction, but infinitely more expressive as to the spirit which the London crowd expresses:

'How our King is one with us,
First among his peers.'

As their Majesties appeared they were met by such a roar of cheering as London has never heard before. It was obvious how radiantly proud and happy were the King and Queen. Her Majesty was carrying a silken Union Jack, such as one as those below were waving. Then followed a crash of sounds – the band played the National Anthems of the Allies, the grand old hymns, 'O God Our Help in Ages Past', 'Now Thank We All Our God', followed by 'Land of Hope and Glory'.

Sometimes the crowd joined in for a line or two; sometimes it cheered, and no one will ever give a very connected account of that quarter of an hour into which so much pent-up enthusiasm was crowded. Then, in the clear, resonant tones which the King knows so well how to use, the few words from his Majesty given above were caught by those who were nearest to the rails.

The guard and the band had been fairly imprisoned. Still the crowd and the enthusiasm increased, and when the Royal family had withdrawn there was no sign that the people were satisfied. Cheering, singing and shouting continued without intermission, and so matters went on until, just after one o'clock, when their Majesties, with various other members of the Royal family, appeared again on the balcony. They had once more a most fervent reception, and there was a repetition of the scenes that marked Britain's entry into war.